Bernhard Eduard Fernow

BY THE SAME AUTHOR

Liberty Hyde Bailey, A Story of American Plant Sciences

"Noble Fellow": William Starling Sullivant

American Botany, 1873–1892: Decades of Transition

John Torrey: A Story of North American Botany

John Merle Coulter: Missionary in Science

BERNHARD EDUARD FERNOW

Bernhard Eduard Fernow

A Story of North American Forestry

BY ANDREW DENNY RODGERS III

FOREST HISTORY SOCIETY
DURHAM, NORTH CAROLINA
1991

London: Geoffrey Cumberlege, Oxford University Press
Reprinted 1991, Forest History Society by arrangement with
Princeton University Press

Rodgers, Andrew Denny, 1900–1981
Bernhard, Eduard Fernow, a story of North American forestry.
Princeton, Princeton University Press, 1951.

1. Fernow, Bernhard Eduard, 1851–1923. 2. Forests and forestry—North America. [2. North America—Forestry—Hist.]

SD129.F4R6 634.9097 Agr 51-517

ISBN 0-89030-047-X

Printed in the United States of America
Forest History Society
Durham, North Carolina

To the memory of

CLIFTON DURAND HOWE

CONTENTS

FOREWORD

I first became more familiar with Bernhard Fernow at about the midpoint of my career with the Forest Service. I was deputy regional forester in Atlanta and gave a speech at the Cradle of Forestry, near Asheville, North Carolina, where much of forestry's early history was filled by Schenck and Pinchot. All of that history in one place piqued my interest and in my reading I came to realize that Fernow's contribution to forestry in the United States was quite significant as well, though not very well known.

Later in my career, as chief of the Forest Service, I was invited to give a lecture in Canada to commemorate the 75th anniversary of the Faculty of Forestry at the University of Toronto. It was a formal, academic occasion. I worked on the lecture closely with Len Carey and came to realize that Fernow had made an even larger, yet still under-recognized, contribution to forestry in North America. This book makes the extent of that contribution abundantly clear.

Very simply, Bernhard Eduard Fernow was instrumental in establishing forestry on this continent during the latter decades of the nineteenth century, both in the United States and Canada. Forestry was still largely unknown in North America, and Fernow arrived in the early infancy of a growing public interest in it. Serving first as an ardent advocate for forestry and later as a professional forester and forestry educator, Fernow built support for forestry and helped firmly establish it as a profession. His career in North America reads as a chronology of major advances in forestry and forestry education.

In 1882 the first American Forestry Congress met in Cincinnati, Ohio. Fernow was the only professional forester to attend and served as the secretary of the Congress. At the invitation of the Canadians present, the Congress reconvened in Montreal later in the year. During the Congress, Fernow met many people with whom he later worked in Canada. Years later he wrote that it was this American Forestry Congress that launched the real forestry movement of North America.

In 1885 Fernow was instrumental in drafting a law that created the huge Adirondack Forest Reserve in New York State and made that state the first in the United States to undertake public forest administration.

In 1886 Fernow became the first professionally trained forester to head the Division of Forestry in the U.S. Department of Agriculture (an early predecessor to the Forest Service). By the time he left twelve years later, Fernow had built a strong technical program and published many reports on forest conditions and the importance of forests. These provided a strong foundation for the subsequent successes of Fernow's successor, who was Gifford Pinchot. Fernow recruited Pinchot and was one of his mentors. Pinchot became the first chief of the Forest Service when it was established from the Division of Forestry in 1905.

In 1896 while Fernow was still in charge of the Division of Forestry, he drafted a bill for the New York legislature to establish a forestry school at Cornell University. The forestry school was established in 1898; it was the first collegiate-level institution in the United States to offer a four-year forestry degree. Fernow was employed as its director.

Fernow's career was not without controversy, a fact some of us today can take comfort in amid our own forestry controversies. The Cornell forestry school's resources included a 30,000-acre forest in the Adirondacks, which Fernow managed as a demonstration forest and to teach forestry in the field. Fernow used the selection system in his management, but then he began clearcutting some of the native northern hardwood stands to plant spruce—which was a valuable species at the time.

This clearcutting enraged some wealthy New Yorkers who had summer residences nearby. These people raised such a protest that the governor vetoed the appropriations for Fernow's school in 1903, thereby halting professional forestry education at Cornell for many years and putting Fernow out of a job.

However, the Cornell School of Forestry at its last registration was said to be larger than any French or German forestry school—a good indicator of Fernow's abilities. He remained active in education, and when the University of Toronto established the first Canadian faculty of forestry in 1907 Fernow was selected as dean. He retired as dean emeritus in 1919.

What is most notable about this part of Fernow's career, though, is his larger influence on the establishment of other programs of forestry or forestry education in North America. During his twelve years with the Division of Forestry, five years at Cornell, and twelve years at Toronto, he assembled and trained many of the foresters who went on to head other forestry schools or who otherwise made substantial contributions to forestry in North America.

Fernow's influence on the development of North American forestry and forestry education was so broad in scope and of such an extent that it is not possible to summarize it briefly without leaving something out. Fernow occupied a unique position in North American forestry and forestry education, in that he carried to this continent the traditions and the forestry principles that had evolved over two- or three-hundred years of German thought and experience. Fernow adapted those forestry principles to the conditions he found in North America. He taught them to others and rooted them firmly in our institutions. He nurtured these forestry institutions so those principles of forestry could be developed further and applied throughout North America.

R. MAX PETERSON

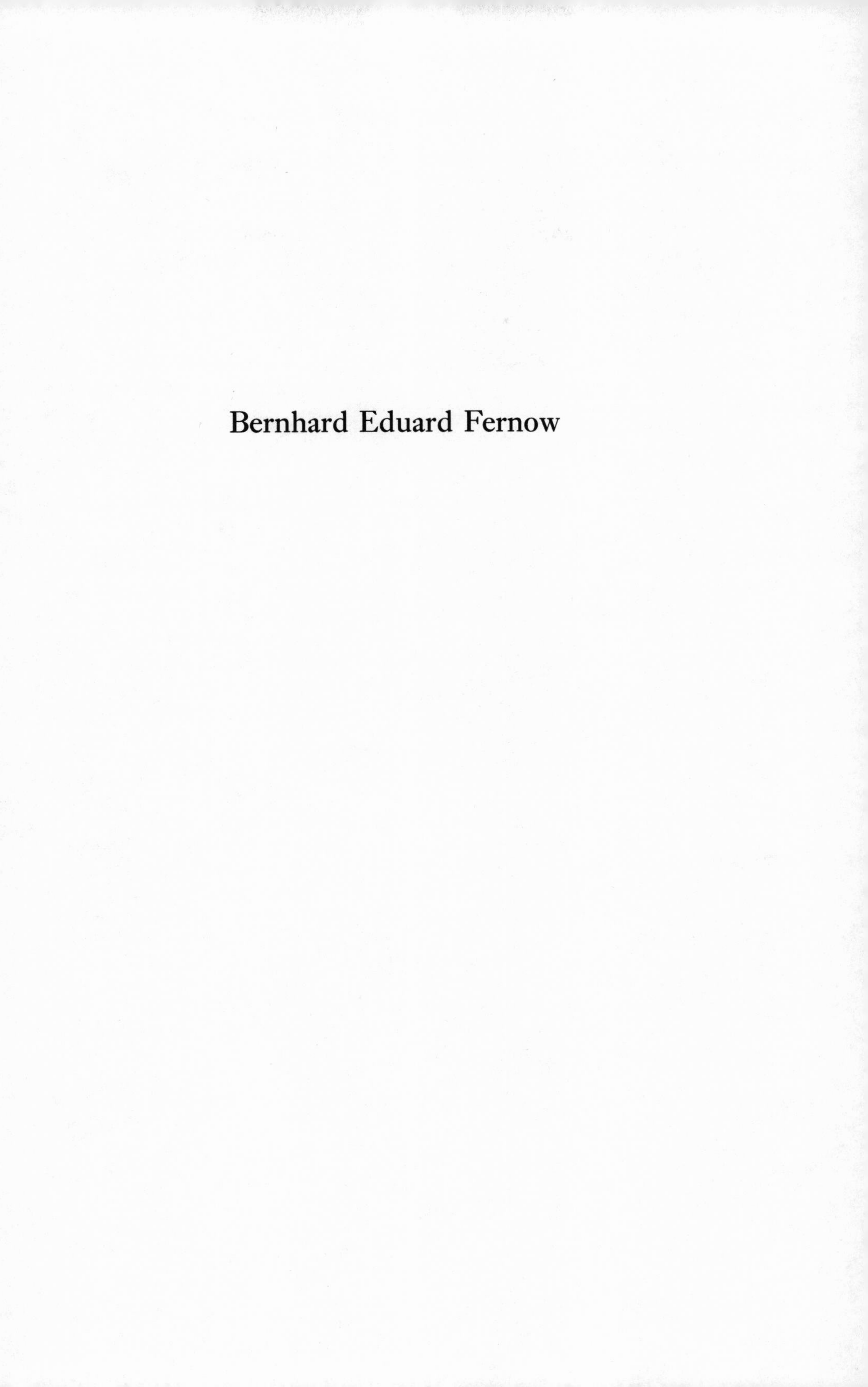

Bernhard Eduard Fernow

CHAPTER I

The Beginnings of Forestry in North America

Centennial celebrations, world expositions, and fairs have contributed significantly to the growth of American civilization. They have portrayed the development of the nation's economic life. Cultivation of the arts has been aided. Especially has this been true of those industries and arts connected with the land and the land's products. In this book we must confine ourselves to one such industry or art, forestry, a subject having to do with the rational treatment of forests for useful purposes. Forestry made its first strong start in America when Bernhard Eduard Fernow, the subject of this book, visited the Philadelphia Centennial Exposition of 1876.

From the earliest exploration of the North American continent, pilgrims and pioneers had seen a forest growth so enormous and expansive that for several centuries it was assumed that the continent's forest resources were inexhaustible. The forest provided shelter and warmth. The axe hewed the logs and the cabin was built. From the forest was built the cabin's furnishings. When the forest was cleared, a fertile field on which to raise garden and farm crops was provided. Through the period of settlement man had relied on the forest from the building of his cabin to the fencing of his field. indeed, from the cradle to the coffin.

In the early years of North American colonization botanists merely descriptively classified trees as plants, in genera and species. The forest as a conceptual whole was little regarded. The first scholars of plants in America were observers of exterior structures, analysts of external differences and affinities. Only incidentally were inquiries directed toward interior structures and processes, the physiology and biology of development. The botanist, therefore, saw the trees first. Only as he became a student of geography and plant distribution did he begin to consider the mass organizations of plant life, including the woods and forests. The development of evolutionary concepts and the plant society concepts indicated by physiological and paleobotanic research widened the orbit of botany and increased its significance as a science.

In America the need of a special economic science to deal with forest problems was foreseen many years before professionally trained foresters began their work on this continent. Forestry, or forest science as it is known in Europe, examined and treated everything relating to forests—forest formation, cultivation, preservation, valuation, and especially the production and utilization of forest products as a crop. Whereas the botanist studied all vegetation, the forester, as his name implies, focussed his attention on management and conservation of the forest resource. At this point, we cannot engage in a discussion of what constitutes a forest, nor the exact spheres of the botanist or forester, but with the forester emerged an enlarged concept of the forest, its work and functions. With the expansion and intensification of forest study and research, botanists and foresters have joined hands. Whenever and wherever the forest has become regarded as something to be protected and preserved as a supply of wood materials for future and present generations, as an aid to and a part of agriculture, as a protection against soil depletion, as a means of conserving moisture and water supply, and as a source of pleasure in the beauty of the landscape, in a few words, when forestry has been regarded as something necessary to maintain civilization and life on this planet, educational forms and professional practice have been originated and forestry has asserted itself as a matter of far-reaching economic importance.

What brought forestry into prominence on the North American continent? Opinions may differ on this point, but it can scarcely be denied that a forestry movement, whose principal weapon was education of the public in what forestry meant and what its practice might accomplish, preceded establishment of a profession of forestry. Among this movement's small but able leadership, Bernhard Eduard Fernow early assumed an unique prestige in both spheres of influence—as propagandizer and professionally schooled forester. It will be shown that centennial expositions, a featured vehicle of early forestry propaganda, were in large part responsible for bringing to this continent two of the first professionally trained foresters who visited our shores. Fernow arrived to visit the Philadelphia Centennial Exposition of 1876, and remained in America. The other forester returned to Germany, but only after he had thrust the strength of his influence behind the incipient forestry movement developing in the United States. Richard von Steuben, a chief forester of the Prussian forest service and one of several descendants of the famous Prussian general, Baron von Steuben, who in 1781 had collected troops in Virginia and helped the Army of the American Revolution to secure the defeat of Cornwallis at Yorktown, visited this country to attend the centennial celebration commemorating that decisive victory. Oberförster von Steuben conferred with Secretary of the Interior Carl Schurz about forest conservation and the need to institute governmental forestry practice in the United States; and he also addressed a formal communication to the first American Forestry Congress, held in Cincinnati, which exerted considerable influence on the delegates.

An interesting study could be prepared which would trace the influence of forestry development of such historic events as the Philadelphia Centennial, the World's Industrial and Cotton Centennial Exposition held at New Orleans in 1885, the World's Columbian Exposition held at Chicago in 1893, the Cotton States and International Exposition held at Atlanta in 1895, the Pan-American Exposition of 1901 held at Buffalo, and of course the Louisiana Purchase Exposition of 1904 at St. Louis. The picture of the forest situation which Fernow found presented at the Philadelphia Centennial shows that such expositions early assumed the important educational function of presenting to the public facts concerning the status of the forest resource, the dangers of forest exploitation and destruction without adequate and intelligent provision for replacement. These expositions made clear the importance of forestry as a discipline by which the people may systematically utilize, expand, and improve the productive efficiency of their natural forests and may establish and manage new forests whenever and wherever it is found advantageous to do so.

In the history of North American forestry there have been two principal currents of development: public forestry, fostered by the state and federal governments, and private forestry practiced by the farmer or private owner of forest land. In the United States, as government land ownership west of the areas possessed or claimed by the states was enlarged, the government found itself possessed of millions of acres susceptible of agricultural development, millions of acres which might be "homesteaded" as part of a mighty effort to encourage migration and settlement westward. Once the great lumbering regions of the eastern states were shorn of accessible timbers, or the imminence of exhaustion threatened, it took little effort on the part of the government to encourage industrial interests to move westward. The opening of rich mining and other western industrial resources sent huge caravans west through the forests and across the prairies. Railroads followed, taking advantage of trails and stream-and-river paths cutting westward toward the Pacific. Settlers penetrated into every region where a livelihood and fortune were promising. The government granted large areas to the railroads adjacent to their rights-of-way. Land grants were made to the states. Forest conservation was hardly considered, but fortunately some legislation restricted timber cutting in a few particulars which we will presently discuss. Almost no restrictions or regulations were aimed toward realizing continuous forest production, except for the small tree-planting requirement which conditioned a right to a legal title of a homestead. Agricultural settlement, a nation of small homes, indeed an attractive and democratic concept, dominated the government's early public lands policy. In classifying public lands, two principal categories controlled. Lands were regarded either as mineral or as agricultural lands. A concept of lands chiefly valuable for forest production was not recognized, owing first to the exaggerated notion that the nation's forest wealth was inexhaustible, and second to the fact that foresters and forestry were tardy in arriving on the American scene. What was to be done with the millions of acres of government-owned forest land, much of it situated in remote and inaccessible mountain areas and stretching within a vast scientifically unexplored region from the Great Lakes to the Gulf of Mexico and west to the Pacific coast? Little accurate information concerning the forest resources of these huge areas was known. Most of the available knowledge was contained in a report by William H. Brewer, *Woodlands and Forest Systems of the United States*, prepared for the United States Census of 1870. Brewer was a botanist and agriculturist, who, before becoming a professor of agriculture at Yale University, had reconnoitered Pacific coastal regions as an assistant in the botanical department of Josiah D. Whitney's geological survey of California.

Forestry in the United States was born of a need in the 1870's. Intelligent voices—Reverend Frederick Starr, Jr., J. William Dawson, and others—years earlier had sounded sensible warnings against forest destruction and the need of constructive action toward forest restoration. But their pleas had fallen on deaf ears. The sight of forest plenty blinded real insight into the necessities. Even though the forest wealth of Maine, New York, Pennsylvania, Michigan, Wisconsin, Minnesota, and other states and territories was being lumbered at a rate that clearly could not last, the apostle of abundance could always direct the attention of the well-meaning alarmist to the inexhaustible supplies to be found in the west. Not much heed was paid to the fact that the western forest wealth was largely in mountainous regions protected by natural barriers. Not much attention was given the fact that spreading agricultural settlement would clear in time many valuable forest areas.

Perhaps the first great American to contemplate the realities of the inevitable future problem of forest supplies and the existence of forests was William Penn. As early as 1681-1682 there was enacted in the Pennsylvania colony an ordinance which required one acre of timber land to be reserved for every five acres cleared.[1] More than a century, however, elapsed before another organized action within another forward-looking commonwealth took place. Toward the end of the eighteenth century the Society for Promotion of Agriculture in New York State was formed, and in 1795 a committee of the Society reported on the best-known means to preserve and increase timber growth in that state. Regions of early settlement naturally were among the first to become aroused. Forest destruction continued unchecked and unabated

[1] Only a brief account of early forestry legislation is attempted here. For more details see Richard H. D. Boerker, *Behold Our Green Mansions*, University of North Carolina Press, Chapel Hill, 1945, pp. 178-179. See also B. E. Fernow, "Development of a Forest Policy" in *Report upon the Forestry Investigations of the U.S. Department of Agriculture 1877-1898*, Government Printing Office, Washington, 1899, pp. 166ff. Also, John Ise, *The United States Forest Policy*, Yale Univ. Press, New Haven, 1920, Chapter I ff.

with the advance of civilization, and the New England states soon sensed the need of some constructive action which would not only preserve but restore if necessary their forest wealth. In 1837 Massachusetts, alarmed at the extent of reported forest depletion within its borders, ordered a forest survey to be made. Where wagon roads or trails, where canals or waterways, later where railroads were constructed, wherever civilization and agricultural development moved into the interior, the forests were cleared. Swamps were drained, cabins, schools, and churches were built, towns and cities emerged, industries arose, and wood and forest uses increased. In many instances, to further the nation's internal improvement, state governments lent aid by grants of land, much of it the more valuable because of its rich forest growth. In some New England and Atlantic coast states, town or community forests supplied wood necessities. Some industries such as brick and iron manufacturing concerns owned and maintained forests, and in their maintenance elements of forestry practice doubtless were involved. No one of these employed professionally trained foresters. If management existed, it was essentially private forest management. The great forestry challenge lay in public forestry. What were the governments going to do about the depleting forest resource?

The federal government was created as a government of delegated powers. Only as much authority as had been granted in the constitution by the states was vested in the central government. With the acquisition of huge territorial lands in the west, the federal government became the largest forest owner of the western hemisphere. What of the forest wealth within the states? The states from the beginning were vigilant and jealous of their sovereign rights; and strong constructive forest policies commensurate with needs within either sphere, state or federal, were to require years of educational effort. Neither knowing what was owned or how it should be maintained, the great mass of our population believed the delusion of unlimited forest abundance. The early emphasis was not on the need to protect and conserve natural resources for future generations but to encourage each generation to use and develop the riches available. So much was available that there seemed no need of restoration. There were some prophets who warned against eventual doom and disaster, but their prophecies seemed so unreal and untimely that they were regarded as cranks. In such an atmosphere, forestry could not thrive.

Although forestry as we know it today was still unthought of, the first far-reaching favorable forestry legislation grew out of a need for adequate military defence. From the years of the Revolution to the War of 1812, the American navy became widely known for the quality of its vessels and for its victories in armed conflict. The importance of a strong navy was recognized, therefore, as pivotal in assuring the new nation's future safety.[2]

To equip the navy required timber-built vessels of the greatest strength and durability possible. For national defence, congress, as early as the last years of the eighteenth century, had appropriated $200,000 for "the purchase of growing or other timber, or of lands on which timber [was] growing, suitable for the navy, and for its preservation for future uses." Congress wanted to secure a supply of live oak timber, considered to be especially valuable for shipbuilding. Two small islands containing about two thousand acres and located off the Georgia coast were purchased under an act of 1799. Some years thereafter, the secretary of the navy was directed to explore lands which would produce live oak and red cedar and to select suitable tracts necessary to furnish the navy with a sufficient supply of such timbers. Nineteen thousand acres on Commissioners, Cypress, and Six islands, in Louisiana, were reserved under an act of March 1, 1817, and in 1828 by still another appropriation lands on Santa Rosa Sound were purchased. Directory and punitive legislation ensued, aimed at realizing the ends of timber cultivation, preservation, and protection of these lands. These were the first publicly owned forest reservations in United States history and during the first decades of the century some 244,000 acres of forest land in Alabama, Florida, Louisiana, and Mississippi were reserved.[3] In the process of their acquisition the exportation from Florida of live oak timber was investigated. Indeed, access to this timber supply may have been a basic reason for acquiring Florida from Spain. In any event, during the first three decades of the nineteenth century congress enabled the president to provide an adequate timber supply in the south for the navy's needs by withholding from sale lands on which a sufficient amount of timber might be cultivated and by penalizing the cutting of timber there by other agencies than the navy. The entire intention evinced a forestry project and, when brought before the Supreme Court of the United States for review, was construed as an authorization to protect all public timber lands from trespass and theft. It seems to have made no difference where the land was located and under what conditions it was owned.

Forestry legislation had an uphill climb, especially in the national government. Year after year some proposed legislation having to do with

[2] See Jenks Cameron, *The Development of Governmental Forest Control in the United States*, Studies in Administration, Institute for Government Research, Johns Hopkins Press, Baltimore, 1928; Edward A. Bowers, "The Present Condition of the Forests on the Public Lands," American Economic Association, Pub. VI, 3, May 1891, pp. 58-59; B. E. Fernow, *A Brief History of Forestry*, University Press, Toronto, 1911; John Ise, *op. cit.*

[3] See references in footnote 1 of this chapter.

public timber land was introduced in congress, only to be defeated.[4] For a number of decades the United States government was forced chiefly to rely on the old law which provided for the construction of a wooden navy to protect its timber throughout the arid western regions where none of the naval timber which the law contemplated was found.

In 1872 the first true forestry bill was introduced in congress and defeated by only seven votes. Had this become law, ten per cent of the public lands patented to an individual or group would have been required to be left in, or planted to, timber.

Timber legislation slumbered until 1878 when an act was passed which permitted bona fide residents of the Rocky Mountain states and territories within mineral districts to fell and remove trees for building and other domestic purposes. It is important that cutting was restricted to trees on *mineral* lands. Purchase and sale legislation was embodied in the historic "Timber and Stone Land Act," which permitted the acquisition at $2.50 per acre—no person or association allowed to enter more than 160 acres—of government owned timber lands unfit for cultivation in the Pacific coast states and Nevada. These laws, however, worked inequalities and gave rise to vicious abuses. It was certainly unjust to require a resident of Colorado, before cutting timber, to sink a shaft or employ a chemist to ascertain that his lands in fact were mineral lands, when the same requirement was not made of the timber cutter who resided in Arizona! The residents of Colorado preferred to steal timber in a multitude of instances. The government employed special protective agents, agents of the Land Department; and when a willful trespass was committed and discovered the lumber was seized and sold or payment of stumpage was demanded. The expenses and the amounts recovered were widely disproportionate to the losses. Although entrants on the Pacific coast and Nevada lands were required to give affidavits that the lands were entered for their own use, and although no individual or group was permitted to enter more than 160 acres, the restrictions proved of small consequence. Large corporations entered the land and required their laborers to make entries and convey over to the corporation their lands at $2.50 per acre. Under this law, according to Edward Bowers, it was discovered that the "finest body of timber existing in the United States [was] rapidly being absorbed by corporations." Furthermore, foreign and domestic capital were acquiring large areas of vastly more worth than their cost. The lumber from one large tree was worth the cost of many acres.

What might have resulted, had a concept of "lands chiefly valuable for forests" been clearly and exclusively written into the public lands

[4] See B. E. Fernow, "Forestry Legislation," *Proc. Am. For. Ass.* XII, Feb. 5, 1897, pp. 41-68; *Forestry Investigations of the U.S.D.A., 1877-1898*, pp. 194-202; concerning the "Free Timber and Timber and Stone Acts," see John Ise, *op. cit.*, pp. 55-60, 62-118. Ise says that Nevada was the only state to which both acts applied.

classification at this time, can scarcely be conjectured. Actually, excluding the procedure applicable to the Pacific coast states and territories and Nevada, the only recourse of one desiring to acquire title to lands valuable for timber as well as agriculture was to comply with the homestead or preemption laws. Unless lumbering or mining or some other special form of industrial pursuit was his primary intention, agriculture in the great preponderance of instances dominated his purposes. If his land was forested he either cleared or sold a large portion of his timber. If his land was not forested, he planted only those acres required by law, and often these requirements were circumvented or the land was abandoned as he moved on to another more fertile tract before the planting requirements were complied with. Time would reveal that of many millions of acres patented, only a very small fraction would be patented to the entry-man. Even at the law's inception forest growing was secondary or incidental to the main intention, agriculture. The comparatively small number of acres sold by the United States government in the western states as mineral lands proved astonishingly small when viewed over a perspective of many years.[5] Neither nominally nor actually were the laws of this period written in full anticipation or knowledge of the huge developmental task before the nation.

On April 5, 1877, Secretary Schurz threw the weight of his energetic support to the recommendations of General James A. Williamson, Commissioner of the General Land Office, who earnestly sought strong enforcement of the laws dealing with the public lands and their administration. He pursued most urgently those laws aimed at preventing or punishing timber thefts and depredations. These men did not hesitate to place a strong faith in what legislation might accomplish, notwithstanding the exasperating difficulties of this tremendous task. At least, under enforceable regulations and rules of their department, a maximum of orderly industrial expansion with a minimum of wastage in the care, custody, and sale of timber and timber lands could be achieved. At the same time, posterity's interests could be safeguarded under intelligent provisions enacted with a view to protecting the forest's "natural renewal" and encouraging "careful preservation of the young timber." A policy of growing timber on "lands unfit for agriculture" was endorsed. President Rutherford B. Hayes incorporated the recommendations in his first annual message to congress. Indeed, conforming legislation was submitted to congress; but the reform of securing so comprehensive a forestry administration under the department of the

[5] See A. C. Shaw, "The Perversion of Mineral Land Laws," *Forestry and Irrigation* XII, 10, Oct. 1906, pp. 449ff. John Ise, *op. cit.*, pp. 71-72, points out that by the "Timber and Stone Act" sales were restricted to *surveyed* lands "chiefly valuable for timber but unfit for cultivation" which had "not been offered at public sale." Furthermore, under the "Free Timber Act" timber on mineral lands could be cut for building, agricultural, mining, or other domestic purposes. The practical effect was that timber lands of all kinds were made use of, both for cutting and sale purposes. See Chapter II of this book.

interior was too sweeping. The proposal was shelved almost immediately. Nevertheless, a cornerstone in the history of forest conservation had been laid, and the course of a struggle to last many years had been mapped.[6]

This reform movement, it is to be noticed, began in the Department of the Interior with an advocacy that "all timber lands still belonging to the United States should be withdrawn from the operation of the preemption or homestead laws." These were not the only federal legislative enactments which, more than enormously reducing the public land domain, served neither the best interests of forest preservation nor brought to the government a proper financial return based on the actual or potential value of the disposed lands. Under the Indemnity Act of 1874, for instance, railroads, where their grants conflicted with bona fide settlers' claims, were permitted to select in lieu thereof other lands; and often choice, valuable tracts covered with commercially good forests or possessed of rich mineral resources were substituted for lands far less in value. Furthermore, timbermen and industrial concerns made use of the Desert Land Act of 1877 to enter lands with no intention of perfecting title or placing a permanent cultivator on the land, take from the tract whatever timber was of value, and go on to newer areas. The net result was more often exploitation of the land and its resources than agricultural extension and improvement. Nor did reducing the homesteader's residence requirement from five years to six months, at which time instead of acquiring a free title he might buy the land at $1.25 an acre, help the situation much. Public land titles were still acquired in large amounts by corporate interests. We need not set forth in detail every enactment which became the object of later legislative reform.

Dr. Fernow, we will show, in federal forestry administration directed his principal efforts to secure adoption of a forest reservation policy, which, applying to the remaining public lands, contemplated wise use of the forests under management and the setting apart of agricultural areas for settlement and homesteading. But by the time he emerged into forestry leadership, the government already had granted large areas to canal, turnpike, wagon-road, and other industrial concerns of a quasi-public nature, and enormous land grants had been made to individual states. To illustrate, under the Swamp Land Act of 1850 millions and millions of acres, much of it in rich forest growth, were turned over to the states to be drained and reclaimed, but without provision for forest preservation or replacement where timbered areas were cleared. Grants for education and for internal improvements,

[6] See Jeannie S. Peyton, "Forestry Movement in the Seventies in the Interior Department, under Schurz," *Journal of Forestry* XVIII, 4, April 1920, p. 391; John Ise, *op. cit.*, pp. 43-45, 45-55. Concerning the "timber culture acts," see *Forestry Investigations U.S.D.A.*, *op. cit.*, pp. 200-202, also "Forestry Legislation," *op. cit.*

grants to establish in each state agricultural colleges the scrip of which was sometimes sold in large blocks to private interests, grants for military bounties, for public sale, and for many forms of public land disposal further reduced the nation's public land area; and it is possible that some of these regions could better have been kept in forests. Fernow, however, was to see enough work left with the remaining forest public lands, and to try to secure legislation for their preservation and conservation, combining with this efforts to secure changes in the timber culture laws, another matter quite properly within the forestry ambit.

The timber culture acts, usually described as part of the homestead laws, encouraged the growing of timber on the western prairies by granting government lands to the successful planter of forests on one-quarter of his entry; that is, a person who planted 40 acres of timber trees on government land became entitled to a patent for 160 acres at the expiration of ten years. In 1874 the act was amended to permit the family head or person of over twenty-one years of age to obtain a patent within eight years by planting trees on one-sixteenth of the homestead acreage. Although this provision was repealed in 1878, the lasting act which amended the act of 1873 reduced the required tree-planted acreage to ten acres of every quarter section (and in the same proportion for small quantities) and exacted closer planting—2,700 trees per acre, five acres to be broken the first year and five acres the second year, and plantings were required during the third and fourth years. By another amendment, it was permitted to plant seeds and nuts instead of trees. If grasshoppers destroyed the trees, the time limit within which to perfect the title was extended. This arrangement, which was designed to stimulate the planting of ten-acre groves upon the treeless plains, was to endure until the year 1891. Under its provisions large numbers of entries were made and held until they could be sold and converted into homestead or preemption. Surviving lashes of scorn and bitterness in congress and reaping much popular contempt for the law's inadequacy and lack of proper enforcement, the law remained on the federal statute books until its repeal by an act of March 3, 1891, and brought into being an improved forestry system.

Under the laws large areas of excellent pine lands in Minnesota and elsewhere were patented. Many of the same industrial frauds arose. Lumber companies, employing hundreds of wood choppers, had each of them take up 160 acre tracts, represented as homesteads, secured the lands, stripped them of their timber, abandoned them, and soon "over great areas once located for homes one [could] pass . . . without finding an occupant, the dead trees and barren stumps or an occasional cabin alone attesting the former occupancy of man." Schurz had urged that "no large areas be entirely stripped of their timber" so as to preclude nature's renewing the economically valuable forest cover. Nevertheless, vast areas of barren and waste lands resulted. Land frauds and timber thievery increased. Public discontent became aggravated. The government, despite urgent warnings of its public commissioners, Secretary Schurz, President Hayes, and others, continued to be a heavy financial loser.

On January 28, 1878, Senator Plumb of Kansas introduced a bill "said to have been the work of Schurz and Williamson [which] was in fact a thoroughgoing forestry measure. It provided for the withdrawal of all timbered lands from settlement, and for their administration and protection by a forester and a corps of assistants, who were empowered to sell timber as needed under careful cutting restrictions that would preclude destructive denudation. It provided also for the sale of agricultural lands in the timbered areas reserved, at a price that would cover timber as well as land. . . ."[7] Other provisions as to fire prevention and penalties for trespass made it by far the most advanced forestry legislation introduced in congress and "a landmark in the history of our forestry movement since it [was] distinguished as being . . . the initial effort on the part of the Interior Department to secure a forest administration. . . ."[8] Requested by congress to give their views on the matters involved, Schurz and Williamson reported themselves strongly in favor of the bill, but the measure failed to be reported out of committee, and it met an unmerited death. The more amazing was the fact that the "Mineral Land Act" and "Timber and Stone Land Act," both of which Schurz and Williamson vigorously opposed and both of which were denounced by President Hayes as vicious, were passed by congress within a week. Thus forestry, which might have become a reality in America as early as 1878, had to storm through nearly two more decades of conflict to be established on this continent. A new leader had to come forward, a strong friend of Carl Schurz—Bernhard Eduard Fernow.

Fernow came from Germany to the United States in 1876 to attend the Philadelphia Centennial celebration which commemorated the one hundredth anniversary of United States independence. This celebration gave attention to exhibiting the earth's products; a collection of woods, principally assembled by botanists L. F. Ward, G. R. Vasey, Edward Palmer, J. G. Lemmon, A. H. Curtiss, and John Wolfe, representing materials from the western and southern states, and containing collections of cones, fruits, and seeds, was a noted feature of the exposition. Fernow must have examined the statistical exhibits, which represented by color tints the distribution of American forest areas, the comparative value of farm lands, the distribution of cereal and textile crops, and the areas of fruit culture. He probably also examined the statistics bearing on industrial education, with engraved pictures of college buildings.

[7] Jenks Cameron, *op. cit.*, p. 202. [8] Jeannie S. Peyton, *op. cit.*

In this year Franklin B. Hough of New York State had been selected by the commissioner of the United States department of agriculture to inquire statistically into forest conditions of the United States. At the Centennial Exposition there were available to the young forester from Germany much interesting data concerning the forest resources and other wealth of the American continent. Eminent botanists, including such scientific leaders as William James Beal and Thomas Jonathan Burrill, had searched the forests of their states and supplied wood specimens for the natural resources exhibit.

The Philadelphia Centennial was the reason for Fernow's visit to America. At least, he told this to his family and to his friends. As a matter of fact, there was a much deeper reason than merely satisfying a forester's zeal for knowledge. Young Bernhard had fallen desperately in love with an American girl, Olivia Reynolds of Brooklyn, New York, who had lived in Germany to keep house for her brother John while he attended the University of Göttingen. Fernow and John Reynolds had become acquainted. Calling one day on "Jack," Fernow had met Olivia. From that time forward he had called often. They all played skaat together. Whoever lost at the game had to learn so many lines of poetry. Olivia lost so often and learned her lines of German poetry so well that Bernhard and she entered into a pact; she was to teach him English and he was to teach her German.

Bernhard Eduard Fernow, born in Inowrazlaw, province of Posen, Prussia, January 7, 1851, had received his early education in the gymnasium at Bromberg. His family were German aristocrats, his grandfather Graf Karl Frederick Leopold von Ferno being the owner of a large estate in East Prussia. Bernhard's father, the eldest son, was named Eduard Ernst Leopold. He was married three times and by each marriage had children: Berthold (1839),[9] Marie (1843), Anna (1844), Hans (1845), Paul (1847), Hermann (1849), Bernhard (1851), Clara (1853), Sophia (1857), Eduard (1860), Frederick Wolfgang (1864), Helena (1865), and Frederick Leopold (1866). Young Bernhard was a child of his father's second marriage. Despite the considerable wealth of his family, with so many children it became necessary for each son to stake out his own future. Bernhard's uncle Frederick Edmund, the younger brother of Bernhard's father, had children by adoption and none of the blood. He wanted to provide that in the event of his death a blood member of the family would take charge of the family estate which had fallen to his care. Bernhard's father had relinquished his right as eldest son to the estate's care to take up the profession of law. Bernhard's uncle interested himself in the nephew who showed a pronounced interest in agriculture and forestry.

[9] See life of Berthold Fernow in *Dictionary of American Biography* VI, Scribner's, New York, p. 337.

As a youth Bernhard had spent days on his uncle's estate, where he learned farming, and attention was given to breeding and raising livestock, especially horses for the German army. But Bernhard's imagination centered on the forests and forest growth.

To be educated for the responsibility of caring for his uncle's estate, young Bernhard had to acquire a knowledge of both law and forestry, since a large, well-managed forest constituted part of the estate. Uncle Frederick Edmund decided to make Bernhard his heir. Family tradition relates that the uncle promised Bernhard he would become his heir if he would equip himself to oversee and manage the estate.

In 1869, at the age of nineteen and just out of the gymnasium at Bromberg, Bernhard took up the study of forestry. He did not enter the forest school immediately. He entered the forest service; that is, he became a candidate for a position. He subscribed to the oath of allegiance and "became to all intents and purposes a member of the forest department." One year was spent in the woods under the direction of a district officer, where he was, as he later said, "put through the ropes" doing various "pieces of work." He then passed his examination and went to the famous forest academy at Muenden in the western part of Prussia, in the province of Hanover. He spent about two and one-half years at the forest academy. For a while he studied under the great Heyer. "There was a forest connected with the school," Fernow explained.[10] "I don't recall the area of that forest; probably it was somewhere like ten or fifteen thousand acres; several districts together; there were probably 25,000 acres accessible. I mean several forests right at the door.

"The methods of forestry pursued in these forests were [various]. They had a clear cutting system. . . . Besides the clear cutting system, there [were] systems known as the selection and shelterwood systems. The slow removal [of mature or overmature or other trees] system is the selection system. . . . There is a system called the shelterwood system. That is a rapid removal system. The trees raised on this forest at Muenden were to a very large extent hardwoods and also pine and spruce. . . ."

Fernow's forestry education was interrupted by the Franco-Prussian War, during the course of which he spent one year with the army in France, serving as a Lieutenant. Returning from the war, he spent a year studying law at the University of Königsberg. He had studied the principles of law at the university, and returning to the forest academy at Muenden, he applied his legal knowledge in a practice course.

10 *People of the State of New York vs. Brooklyn Cooperage Company*, 147 N.Y. Appellate Division 267, affirmed by the Court of Appeals in 205NY531, Clerk's Office, Albany, New York, pp. 349 (1393) and 364 (1452). Here Fernow was establishing his qualifications as a forester.

"It was not four years and a half," observed Fernow, "from the time I entered the forest work in 1869 until I got my license to practice forestry and become a forester. You start right after you leave school. I have counted out that year in the Franco-German war. Really seven years was my employment and immediate relationship to the department but one year was spent in France. [After the school work] I went immediately into the forest work. First, in what they called Silesia, then in Brandenburg, then in Eastern Prussia; three places. The character of those forests was absolutely different from the one at Muenden. In Silesia it was hardwoods with conifers mixed. It was a hilly country, not as mountainous as at Muenden. Most of the Muenden surroundings would be classed with the western type of the Adirondacks. The difference in altitude between the highest and lowest point at Muenden approximately . . . I should say is 600 or 800 feet. It is not a rolling country. I call it mountainous. In east Prussia the land was flat. In Brandenburg it was all kinds; the northern forest type was represented in eastern Prussia. They disposed of the tops of the trees in these forests; they cut them and sold them as cordwood. . . . The tops that were smaller than cordwood . . . could be sold too. . . .We cut very little brush, because the market was very limited. We sold the best we got for cordwood and left the brush. We left the brush in the forest. We protected the forest from fires by forest rangers and by having proper morals in the neighborhood. . . ."

Fernow by nature was an austere Prussian. He enjoyed forestry and he was a patriotic German. His brother Berthold had emigrated to America, but this fact alone probably would not have been sufficient to persuade the youthful forester to leave Germany, a country where there was real forestry to be practiced, to go to America where no forestry at all was practiced.

"I am a fatalist, or rather a believer in chance and accidents shaping to a large extent our lives," said Fernow.[11] "While I would admit that there is much truth in the old Latin proverb: 'Everybody is the architect of his own fortune,' my own experience has been that small accidents have much to do with the progress not only of the individual, but of whole peoples—much more than historians are apt to admit. Big events may be traced back to absurd beginnings, small means may work great wonders.

"It was an accident that an American girl located with her family in a little town in Germany where I was studying forestry; it was an accident that I became acquainted with her, and in part at least an accident that I became engaged to her—all of which accidents conspired to bring

[11] "The Birth of a Forest Policy," lecture given at Syracuse University in 1916; also given at Mont Alto Academy, Pennsylvania.

me over to the United States for a visit which extended to over thirty years. . . ."

Near Wartburg Castle, Germany, close to Landgrafen Loch, Eisenach, in a forest magnificence, Bernhard and Olivia became engaged to be married. Olivia went to visit the Fernow family, but was icily received. The family had educated Bernhard and his future was assured. To go to America with Olivia meant the collapse of all their dreams and ambitions for the future of the brilliant young Bernhard Eduard, a namesake of his father and a favorite of his uncle. The household cook said, "She isn't black, she isn't black." Olivia left Germany with her brother in 1876. Bernhard followed her to America the same year. They did not marry immediately. Not until June 20, 1879, did Dr. Henry Ward Beecher, the celebrated pastor of Plymouth Congregational Church of Brooklyn, unite the two courageous lovers in accordance with the laws of the State of New York. Samuel W. Grierson and John Reynolds appeared as the witnesses on the marriage certificate. Olivia Reynolds Fernow many years later wrote, "If anyone should ask me who was the originator of the forestry movement in this country, I should modestly reply, 'It was I.' If a certain young girl had not gone to Germany in the year 1872 and fallen in love with a certain young forestry student, who knows but that the movement might have been delayed for a decade or more? Said young girl imported the young Forstkandidat soon to become the first forester of the United States at a time when the very words forester and forestry were [generally] unknown in this country and [in some dictionaries] not to be found. . . ." In announcing to her friends her engagement to a forester she was asked, "What is a forester? A Robin Hood who takes from the rich to give to the poor?" The words "forestry" and "forester" were in American dictionaries but the concepts had not been given familiar currency. Fernow himself found the Robin Hood concept widely prevalent. Certainly it was true that forestry as a profession had not begun to be established in the United States or Canada. Mrs. Fernow related, "My husband, a trained German forester . . . found no business opening, for forestry was as yet unknown in this country. . . ." But Rossiter W. Raymond, a pioneer in the organization of the mining and metallurgical industry in America, was Mrs. Fernow's "good friend." He aided them.

On December 14, 1877, Bernhard Fernow declared his intention to become a citizen of the United States in the County Court of Kings, New York State. A second copy was made out on October 30, 1882. The affiant as to the applicant's character and his residence, which was given as 80 Willom Street, Brooklyn, New York, and as to his occupation which was recited as "Engineer," was Thomas Reynolds, the father of Olivia. The oath to support the constitution and renounce allegiance to all other powers was taken in due course, and by December

14, 1883, the proceedings were completed. Fernow had become a naturalized American citizen in the minimum possible time.

For a while Fernow was a scribe in a New York law office. Insistently he sought to establish himself as a consulting forest engineer. But where should he look for business? The mining profession had need of some consulting work. Rossiter Worthington Raymond gave some of his professional time in this capacity. It is interesting to realize that, in part, out of the mining industry originated in America the practice of the consulting forest engineer.

In May 1871 a few gentlemen had met at Wilkes-Barre, Pennsylvania, and organized the American Institute of Mining Engineers. Perhaps the first professional utterances made formally to urge conserving the nation's natural resources were expressed "in the appointment, at the first session of the institute, held in Wilkes-Barre, Pennsylvania, in 1871, of a committee of eminent mining engineers 'To consider and report on the waste in coal mining. . . .'

"Earliest of those who preached and impressed in America the lessons of forest conservation was Dr. J. T. Rothrock of Pennsylvania, who lectured on forestry in the Michaux Lecture Course given at the University of Pennsylvania in 1877. . . ."[12] Rothrock was a botanist, a student of Asa Gray, and an explorer of note in southwestern United States. He never claimed to be a professionally trained forester, although while a student of De Bary in Strasburg, Germany, he had observed forestry methods as practiced in Europe. Returning to America, he became interested in developing medical botany at the University of Pennsylvania and did much to shift the American emphasis of botanical study from taxonomy to the physiological and anatomical study of plant life. As years passed in his work in Pennsylvania he became more and more interested in forestry and was selected by the American Philosophical Society of Philadelphia to present each year for a period which lasted almost two decades, 1877-1894, the historic Michaux lectures, significant in both the forestry and conservational history of the United States. Especially fundamental were these lectures to the practically unknown venture of forestry education, either in a public or private sense.

The Michauxs, father and son,[13] were among the first of the great botanical explorers of North America, men who viewed botany not as a fad or pastime but as a profession. In part their trips to America were made to study social and economic conditions, but more, to examine and learn our forest trees, especially our oaks, with a view to the possible

[12] Henry S. Drinker, *On Making Public Opinion Effective*, p. 38, an address given at the dedication of the Forestry Building of Cornell University, May 15, 1914.

[13] Gilbert Chinard, "The American Philosophical Society and the Early History of Forestry in America," *Proc. Am. Phil. Soc.* 89, 2, 1945, pp. 444-488.

introduction and use of some by their native land, France. In their writings were incorporated many of the earliest taxonomic concepts regarding our forest species. Only a superficial acquaintance with the botanical literature of North America is required to comprehend the vast contribution of these two men in helping to systematize descriptively the plant life of eastern United States. While their prominence and fame have survived more in the literature of botanical taxonomy and geographical exploration, one writer has recently brought to notice that recognition is long past due to François André Michaux for his well reasoned presentation of the need in America of forest conservation and forest management. Michaux observed that, unlike Europe, neither the federal nor state governments were reserving forest lands to safeguard the nation's future economy. Writings of a few other Europeans, perhaps of a few Americans, warned of the perils of unrestrained forest exploitation, but these pleas had received little serious notice and no widespread active response. Not many persons, even today, remember the Michauxs except as authors of great classics in botany—André Michaux for his *Flora Boreali-Americana* (1803), and François André Michaux for his three-volume work on *The North American Sylva* (1819), descriptive of the forest trees of the United States, Canada, and Nova Scotia. Thomas Nuttall in 1849 prepared another *North American Sylva* which, adding forest trees not described by Michaux and those discovered in the Rocky Mountains, Oregon territory, California, and various parts of the United States, formed the basis for a combined authoritative treatise of enduring value. These, and other outstanding botanical classics of the period, were regarded by Bernhard Eduard Fernow as fundamental in the development of the forestry movement in America.

Other points of remembrance, however, are necessary to evaluate their worth to American forestry and conservation. Of outstanding significance were François André Michaux's contributions toward silvicultural advancement in America. André Michaux had established two nurseries, one at Bergen, New York, and the other at Charleston, South Carolina. The scientific bents of both father and son combined in fortunate fashion a blend of botanical, horticultural, and forestry interests, and found expression in both descriptive and experimental study. At different intervals of the last years of the eighteenth century, father and son together journeyed through American forests. This exploratory zeal continued so the younger Michaux alone widely enlarged the boundaries of their examinations during early years of the next century. François André Michaux's enthusiasm was so heightened that this, combined with his gratitude to Americans, especially the American Philosophical Society for hospitality and aid accorded him and his father, plus his awareness of the lesson from his native land that abundantly resourceful nations can experience serious distress from deforestation and depletion of timber supplies, prompted him to include in his will a provision which bequeathed $12,000 to the American Philosophical Society and $8,000 to the Society of Arts and Agriculture of Massachusetts[14] for "the extension and progress of agriculture and more especially of sylviculture" in the United States. When the American Philosophical Society's trust fund became available, the amount, because of exchange rates, had been diminished to $6,000; nevertheless, the Society, honoring Michaux's scientific service, resolved that there should be "a grove of Oaks in the Fairmount Park [of Philadelphia] forever to bear the name of 'Michaux Grove' in which, if practicable, [should] grow two oaks of every kind that [would] endure the climate."

Moreover, the Society, on May 4, 1877, appropriated $200 to defray the expenses of a course of lectures on silviculture. These lectures, named after the creator of the trust fund, were delivered by Dr. Rothrock in Horticultural Hall in Fairmount Park, and for many years proceeds from the fund were used to foster forestry education and further the program of propagating and planting trees in Fairmount Park. Of course an intention to beautify the park was evident, but the lecture syllabi show that silvicultural advancement was paramount. Rothrock confessed he had to prepare his lectures in popular style to sustain interest. He said with a smile that he had to have some ears in the audience besides his own. Some lectures were illustrated by lantern slides. As a botanist, he had learned the forest regions of North America, the "fungal foes" of the farmer and the forest, the localities of the big trees of the world, the significance of plants to man. Although later the lectures became much concerned with Pennsylvania forestry, at first they dealt mainly with forest botany and "agitated," to use Rothrock's word, the cause of forestry. As Rothrock gave more and more of his energies to the forestry movement, he concentrated on the great rich state of Pennsylvania and its forest conditions. The splendid situation in Pennsylvania forestry today owes its origin to the work in forestry performed by Joseph Trimble Rothrock, and he is honored with the title of "father of Pennsylvania's forestry."[15] We shall see that he was more than this.

[14] This fund was used for the botanical garden at Harvard, the Arnold Arboretum, and the publication of forestry pamphlets. The Massachusetts Society had also offered prizes for successful forest planting since 1804. See *Forestry Investigations of the U.S.D.A., 1877-1898, op. cit.*, p. 166. Also Gilbert Chinard's discussion, "The American Forest as Seen by Foreign Travelers," concerning the Michauxs, pp. 467-470. Michaux, the younger's, legacy was signed "André François Michaux." His scientific publications usually are signed and referred to as by "François André Michaux," and sometimes "F. Andrew Michaux."

[15] See "Michaux Free Lecture Course," *Forest Leaves*, Feb. 1899, p. 21; Joseph S. Illick, "Fifty Years Ago," *Forest Leaves* XXI, 1, Feb. 1927, p. 9; Jenks Cameron, *op. cit.*, p. 121. For more detailed information on Michaux and Rothrock see *Noble Fellow, John Merle Coulter, John Torrey,* and *American Botany 1873-1892* by A. D. Rodgers, Princeton University Press.

In 1878 Fernow became a life associate of the American Institute of Mining Engineers. In this field he discovered an electrical process for removing the tin coating from iron "tin cans," and he turned this discovery into a business venture. Years later he acknowledged that he had done "work in [his] factory in Brooklyn [on] an electric process for de-tinning, using therein a common salt bath. Unfortunately," he explained on February 18, 1909, "the patent has run out. It was in 1878 that I worked the process and there was probably nothing in it for me. It succumbed at the time due to the constant panic in the iron market. I can say that the process was perfectly good as far as the removal of tin from the iron shape was concerned. . . ." The venture was not financially successful. Fernow turned to teaching German by private lessons. It has been said, "He was one of the first to use the 'natural method' in teaching a foreign language and while his success as a teacher was excellent, it did not prove lucrative. He then accepted a position as assistant bookkeeper for a hardware firm."[16]

Fernow was residing at 374 Pacific Street in Brooklyn when he was made an associate member of the American Institute of Mining Engineers. The Institute enjoyed a total membership of 673 persons, including 6 honorary members, 104 associate members, and 52 foreign members.[17] Fernow was proud of the sudden rise of the Institute to a place of influence in American industrial life. "In 1872," he later observed, "that profession was somewhat [unrecognized]. Mining engineers were as little recognized as foresters." He characterized the Institute as "a lively infant [which] has grown lustily and steadily, all because of having an attentive nurse in its Secretary," Rossiter W. Raymond, who served from 1884 to 1911.

In 1864 Raymond[18] had formed a partnership with Dr. Justus Adelberg, a consulting mining engineer of New York. At one time Adelberg had been mining and metallurgical engineer for John Charles Frémont. Three years later Raymond began editing the *American Journal of Mining* and later, from 1874 to 1890, served as joint editor with Richard P. Rothwell of the *Engineering and Mining Journal*. In 1868 he had been appointed United States Commissioner of Mines and Mining and in this position he had served until 1876, making long trips to the far West to compile the valuable and voluminous annual reports, *Statistics of Mines and Mining in the States and Territories West of the Rocky Mountains*. John Ise, in his study of *The United States Forest Policy*, points out the fact that in 1870 Raymond began to write "in forcible terms of the wanton destruction of timber in the mining districts." Ray-

[16] R. C. Bryant, "Bernhard Eduard Fernow," *Yale Forest School News* XXI, 1933, p. 3.

[17] *Trans. Am. Inst. Mining Eng.* VIII, pp. xii. 131.

[18] *D.A.B.* XV, pp. 414-415; Newell Dwight Hillis, "In Memory of Rossiter W. Raymond," *Brooklyn Daily Eagle*, Jan. 6, 1919.

mond was one of the first federal officials to warn of the necessity of protecting the western public land forests from spoliation and waste, and others soon took up the appeal of this authority on mining and mining geology. In 1875 he became consulting engineer for Cooper, Hewitt and Company, owners of iron works in New Jersey. Dr. Newell Dwight Hillis has said that Raymond's reports on western mineral resources were accounted so informative and interesting that when the reports were republished by a commercial publishing house they earned quite a popular reputation. So valuable were the reports and so astute was Raymond's knowledge of mining that state legislatures and even the Supreme Court of the United States called him into consultation. His advice was eagerly sought from Pennsylvania and West Virginia to Montana and California. Evidently as a friend of the court, he advised on economic policies. Many of Raymond's opinions were "practically adopted by the Supreme Court, and enunciated in the decisions. . . . As the years went on, these 'legal opinions' of Dr. Raymond were used in the Transvaal and became a part of the laws of South Africa. . . ." In addition to shaping a sound working program for American mining, he made a great contribution to forestry in the United States. Of course, his contribution was made through Fernow.

In the course of his many trips to the far West, Raymond became acquainted with the conditions and the extent of the nation's vast western public timber domain. For years he travelled incessantly over what is now Colorado, Utah, New Mexico, Nevada, Arizona, Idaho, Montana, and California. Raymond probably first acquainted Fernow with factual data about the forest areas where real forestry knowledge might be applied. Considerably older than Fernow, he was an ardent religionist; even though a layman, he was so devout that at one time he was offered the Plymouth Church pulpit, which for many years was occupied by the eminent divines, Henry Ward Beecher and Newell Dwight Hillis. In the course of Fernow's entire career he had no closer friend than Raymond. He referred to Raymond's wife, Sarah Mellen Dwight, as "Aunt Sally." Raymond sent Fernow literature, including books on theology and science, such as Le Conte's study of evolution and religion. It is significant that Fernow early gained the friendship of a man such as Raymond, an author and editor of wide prominence, a student of law and later a lawyer, a past officer of the United States Army, an authority on Old Testament literature, an engineer who was granted honorary degrees by at least three American educational institutions, a member of many American and foreign scientific societies, and a moving force in the management of Cooper Union, one of the country's most important centers of learning. For many years Raymond lectured at Cooper Union and directed the Saturday Evening Free Popular Lectures on Science, which formed the basis for a vast lecture system in the public schools of Brooklyn and New York. In 1879 he procured for Fernow a position with Cooper, Hewitt and Company.

Abram Stevens Hewitt, whose help was also encouraging to Fernow, was a nationally known man of affairs. He was a prominent iron manufacturer, a partner of Edward Cooper, who was the son of Peter Cooper, the founder of Cooper Union. Hewitt was the first chairman of the board of Cooper Union, and at his death he and his wife, Sarah Amelia, daughter of Peter Cooper, endowed the institution. Devoted to education, he served as a trustee of Columbia University, as chairman of the board of Barnard College, as an original trustee and member of the executive committee and first chairman of the board of the Carnegie Institution. In 1876 Hewitt was chairman of the Democratic Party's national committee. A reformist in politics, he served for many years as a United States congressman and later as mayor of New York City. Such a man could be of great importance to Fernow and to forestry.

In 1876 and 1890 Hewitt officiated as president of the American Institute of Mining Engineers. Raymond had held that office from 1872-1875. Both were founders of the Institute and both remained strong influences. Both aided Fernow's later appointment as chief of the forestry division in the United States Department of Agriculture and as director of America's first professional forestry school, The New York State College of Forestry at Cornell University.[19]

Fernow entered upon the study of American forestry conditions in earnest. In 1878 he attended the twenty-second meeting of the American Institute of Mining Engineers "with a view to interesting the Institute in [his] subject, forestry. [He] ventured to discuss the advantages of red charcoal over black charcoal from the standpoint of fuel saving for blast furnace use. As [he] had then only an indifferent command of the English language the reading of the carefully prepared article was all [he] was capable of, and fortunately not much discussion arose."[20] In the sixth volume of the Institute's *Proceedings*,[21] Fernow's article was published as "The economy effected by use of red charcoal." In the following year[22] another article by Fernow appeared, "Remarks on the production of charcoal."

The central office of Cooper, Hewitt and Company was 17 Burling Slip in New York City. The company's iron works were located at Trenton, New Jersey; Hewitt, New Jersey; Oxford, New Jersey; and Riegelsville, Pennsylvania. A large glue factory was part of the holdings. Near Slatington and Slatedale in eastern-central Pennsylvania, where the beautiful Blue Mountain range is bisected by the Lehigh River in its slow winding course to the Delaware River and the Atlan-

[19] *D.A.B.* VIII, pp. 604-605.

[20] A manuscript of B. E. Fernow, never published.

[21] pp. 196-206.

[22] Vol. VII, pp. 157-158.

tic Ocean, the company maintained its Lehigh Furnace. Here also it kept a 15,000 acre forest tract to supply wood materials for the manufacture of charcoal. Materials were transported over a rugged country highway and shipped by canal and railroad to the East. The year of his marriage, 1879, Fernow was employed by the company to manage its furnace. Today the furnace building and the dwelling where Fernow worked and lived, built of Blue Mountain stone with a mortar of clay and lime, still stand. The remnants of a storage building for mined iron, the site of the blacksmith shop, and other evidences of a small milling community life, are clearly discernible. Raymond said, "But you are not going to take 'Livy' to that pig stye." But Mrs. Fernow wanted to go. The young husband went to the region of the courteous Pennsylvania Dutch folk before she did. When she arrived there "the German forester . . . [had] cleaned and papered the house with his own hands, and made it into a comfortable and dearly loved home. Oh, what good times we had," Mrs. Fernow exulted.[23] "I can't begin to tell you the joys of those six happy years, how I learned surveying and my husband housework; and how we both learned the charcoal business, driving around to the 'meilers,' for the charcoal was all made outdoors and how we found we had to institute a country store [located within one part of their home] for the benefit of the wood choppers." To the simple region folk Fernow was regarded as a gentleman, an aristocrat, and she as "stuck up." A maid that she employed regarded her as "too proud to fetch her own food from the kitchen but who rang a bell and expected to be waited on." Such attitudes, however, were changed when one day the townspeople saw her, aided only by her servant, tremulously driving a wagon and two decrepit mules to a railroad car some miles distant to load flour and meat and other provisions for their small company store. Fernow, when told of this bit of daring, professed to be shocked and exacted a promise that she never do it again—then, inconsistently, he began to boast of his wife's accomplishment.

"It was all as beautiful and satisfying," wrote Mrs. Fernow, "as any author ever portrayed, but the rapid advent of three children [Rossiter and Gordon, boy and girl twins, and Edward] made us see that their future demanded more in the way of worldly wealth than could be furnished by a salary of $60 a month out of which we had to support a horse. . . ." Their "happy idyll" had to come to an end. Bernhard and Olivia Fernow struggled against returning to "the prose of city life and the agony of job hunting." Rossiter Raymond and Hewitt sought to aid them.

Fernow undoubtedly won the complete confidence and admiration

[23] From a letter in rough draft, addressed to Walter Mulford and sent by him to Ralph Bryant. Other data were collected by the author during a visit to Slatington and the furnace location.

of Raymond and Hewitt. When a slate quarry project was proffered, Hewitt offered to lend Fernow three thousand dollars to enable him to remain where he was, and earn an additional sum of money. They authorized Fernow to construct a sawmill at his own expense and, under an agreement, to have free water power for a year. Should the company decide at some future time to become the owners of it, the mill was to be worked on shares. Early in 1882 Raymond requested Fernow to prepare a map of the company's Lehigh Mountain property, near Lehigh Gap, Pennsylvania, to trace the roads and distances to nearby towns, to describe the property under timber and that used or suited to farming. Fernow arranged to go before the county grand jury in the autumn of 1882 to secure repairs of a bridge and dam which, when high water from Trout Creek threatened, endangered the house and furnace. There were numerous matters which strongly pointed to a complete satisfaction with Fernow's services, but he was dissatisfied with his position. As early as 1881, however, Fernow and Raymond were discussing the period as one of waiting, one which drew on Fernow's resources of philosophical contentment. Raymond approved Fernow's expressed preference for "a quiet home, and a slow advancement." In a New Year's letter of 1883, Raymond said, "Realizing the justice of your observation that the greatest hardship of your present position is the circumstance that it neither offers a prospect of improvement nor permits you to learn what might lead to an improved position, I have been casting about to see what could be done in the way you suggested, of giving you some chance at some other works to gain a knowledge that would be useful. . . ." At length it was arranged that Fernow was to spend part of his time at the company's Pequest Furnace at Oxford, New Jersey, with a view to taking charge eventually of the Ringwood Furnace when the latter was blown in again. Raymond wished to send Fernow to the Durham works at Riegelsville, Pennsylvania, but he regarded the Pequest Furnace as a better place. Fernow commended the Oxford venture but decided to return to New York. He stayed on the Lehigh Furnace forest property until 1883, and although he left Slatedale, he remained in charge of the forest property until 1887.

In the remote "sylvan seclusion" of Pennsylvania forest life Fernow enjoyed a unique opportunity to study eastern American forest conditions. In Pennsylvania, forest reproduction and management were closely studied. He studiously observed the coppice-deciduous trees sprouting from the stumps and the broadleaved trees sending forth shoots varying according to species. He noticed that the old stumps tended to die out. A tendency toward forest deterioration in composition and density seemed manifest. The white oaks and hickories were being crowded out by the chestnuts, a superior sprouter. He saw that the only solution was to aid the forest by adding fresh blood, by encouraging new reproduction from seed.

Fernow began to write about forestry in the regions with which he was becoming familiar and in those regions concerning which he read and studied. His article on "Forest Protection" (1881) was written from direct experience. His article, "Signification of the Forests for the Country, by B. E. Fernow, late member of the Prussian Forest Department," was more general and inclusive. For many years in his writings Fernow referred to concepts formed during his years at Slatedale. For example, in 1879 Fernow became a subscriber to the American cause which held that the nation's natural resources should be conserved. As late as 1916 he placed the origins of the conservation movement within these years, saying, "Conservation ideas a few years ago apparently suddenly became popular, but I can assure you it had taken more than a quarter century of arduous pounding to prepare the public's mind for these ideas, and it has been the persistent work of the forestry reformers which has given the initiative for reforms on broader lines." In other words, the conservation movement emerged from forestry, not forestry from the larger-gauged movement which included all the various types of natural resources.

The article on "Forest Protection" was written as a letter addressed to John Birkinbine, editor of the *Journal of the United States Association of Charcoal Iron Workers,*[24] which had been organized in 1879. Birkinbine, as editor and publisher of the flourishing *Journal,* "sounded," Fernow said, "even in the seventies the note of conservation on economic grounds." Fernow always regarded him as "one of the staunchest, sanest, oldest, and most faithful friends [of] the forestry movement in the United States."[25] Birkinbine was born in Philadelphia in 1844. He studied at the Polytechnic College of Pennsylvania. His father, chief engineer for Philadelphia water supply, was assisted by John, who years later emulated his father and became chairman of the state's water supply commission. In this capacity he contributed notably to forestry advancement, relating the vast subject of forest influences to his official work. An engineer by profession, he was president of the American Institute of Mining Engineers from 1891-1893. He especially acquired prominence in promoting the growth of the Franklin Institute of Philadelphia and the Pennsylvania Forestry Association, serving both for many years as president and the latter as editor of its official publication, *Forest Leaves.*[26] At the August 1882 meeting of the American Institute of Mining Engineers, he read a paper, "Charcoal as a Fuel for Metallurgical Processes,"[27] in the course of which he said,

[24] Vols. I and II, April 1880 to Dec. 1881, August 1881, No. 4, pp. 223-226.
[25] *Forestry Quarterly* XIII, 2, June 1915, p. 296.
[26] *Journal of the Franklin Institute* CLXV, April 1908.
[27] *Trans. Am. Inst. Mining Eng.* XI, May 1882-Feb. 1883, pp. 78-88.

.... An industry dependent upon charcoal as fuel must, to be permanent, maintain large forest areas, thus benefiting the surrounding country; and much of the growing timber, being suitable for other purposes than charcoal making, will be so used whenever the compensation is greater. Anomalous as it may at first appear, the probabilities are that, in the near future, the large consumers of charcoal will be among the most enthusiastic patrons of forest cultivation and preservation.

Fernow early cried out against unintelligent propaganda, even though it was issued in the name of forestry. In his letter to Birkinbine on "Forest Protection," he said, "The vague newspapers' cry of the wanton destruction of our forests is liable rather to create a bugbear and a run for new offices among politicians than to produce any serious measures toward the arrest of the menacing calamity." Fernow appealed to the charcoal iron workers to "create an influence that will tend to bring about sound policy in regard to our timber supply." He believed the charcoal iron workers had the "least to fear from the approaching danger of dearth." They might have to pay higher prices, "but they [would] not lose their supply as long as the country is traversed everywhere by stony mountain walls, which are not fit for anything but coppice-grown" forests. Forests naturally would be assigned to the poorer soils, he argued, since forests do not need a chemically good soil. It was proper to take "only those trees or parts of trees" which could not find any other use, "namely, the branches and above all the coppice growth. The latter I presume," he said, "will be sufficient to furnish all the wood necessary for charring to supply the present number of charcoal furnaces."

Fernow referred generally to the "science or art of forestry." He pleaded for an emphasis on "forest management" rather than "forest culture," which Dr. Franklin B. Hough stressed as a present need. Undoubtedly this was one of the first times the phrase "forest management" had been used in American literature, and probably the first time by a professionally trained forester writing in America of American conditions. In 1874, aside from his other forestry advocacies soon to be described more fully, Dr. Hough had prepared a report on forestry for the committee on public lands of the federal Congress. A few years thereafter Hough's official *Reports on Forestry* began to appear, and in these volumes forest management as practiced in Europe was sketched, the materials for the elaboration culled in most part from European literature. Fernow's estimate of these reports and their influence was later revealed in his *Report upon the Forestry Investigations of the U.S.D.A., 1877-1898* (*op. cit.*, p. 6). "Dr. Hough," wrote Fernow, "produced three voluminous reports, transmitted to and published by Congress in separate volumes in 1877, 1880, and 1882, and comprising in all 1,586 pages of information on a wide range of subjects. The appropriations being extremely limited, special original research was excluded, and Dr. Hough being acquainted with the subject as an interested layman and not as a professional forester, these reports, while valuable compilations of existing facts from various sources, naturally did not contain any original matter, except such suggestions as Dr. Hough could make with regard to the duties of the Government with reference to the forestry interests of the country and especially of the public domain."

Fernow, therefore, told the members of the Charcoal Iron Workers Association they could present "to the public the advantages of a well regulated management of their own timber resources [and create the] influence which, in Germany, has been so successfully exerted by the government on the private land owners." In the "promotion of [that] branch of economic science . . . badly neglected in this country . . . the principal efforts of charcoal users will have to be directed towards a proper management of the coppice in order to prevent its exhaustion. Even in this," he said, "nature requires very little help if I may judge from the woods under my care, where the soil and stocks seem productive beyond measure, and have withstood all sorts of abuses. What we have to look for, then, is means of preventing such destructive causes as lie entirely outside of the science of forestry." Two evils should be legislated against—forest fires and domestic animal grazing. Fernow believed that some advances had been made against the first "enemy" which had been "discussed to satiety." But there was need of more regulation of grazing rights and privileges.

Fernow in Germany had studied the wild life of the forest. Years later he admitted, "I have in years gone by carried my gun and cast my line occasionally, and taken pleasure in it. Indeed my profession as a forester in my native country where I studied and practiced it includes both, in the theoretical teaching and in the practice, the art of sportsmanship hunting and of conservative fishing, and I can assure you, there is a high standard of sportsmanlike behavior kept up by the foresters. . . ." Wild-life management was to become in America a very important phase of forest management. Even more important, however, the phases of domestic animal management, especially grazing, have occupied a place of economic interest. Fernow wrote on this subject at his first opportunity. "There is nothing more aggravating than to see your promising young coppice stunted, nay, often destroyed by the cattle that run at large."

Fernow complained that no one seemed "to look for the reasons of the destruction of our forests." Although lumbering was in a golden age in some parts of the country, lumbering operations were wasteful. Farmers cut down their woods before they yielded a good crop. Cattle were feeding on the young sprouts. Americans in general were squandering the treasures of their soil. "Forestry, after all," said Fernow, "is as little a matter of pleasure as mining or any other enterprise. . . . Forest-growing is not an undertaking for a day, or even a decade; though, from a well-managed forest, near a good market, returns may be derived in a man's lifetime. A cultivated forest requires at least 70 or 80 years to be a profitable investment. . . . I write all this," said Fernow, "to persuade you that the time has not yet arrived when the profit from forest-growing will induce private capital, at least in the East, to arrest the devastation of our timber lands. The protection, therefore, of this factor of national wealth must be, at present, mainly expected from a sound, protective legislation. . . ." The nation's interest, the rights of present and future generations warranted "the adoption of restrictive measures in the disposal of woodlands," even though private rights in instances might be violated. These were doctrines that issued from the quiet solitude and meditation in which Fernow indulged at Lehigh Furnace, Pennsylvania.

On December 30, 1881, Fernow also sent Birkinbine for his *Journal*[28] a letter on "The Yield of Wood and When to Cut It." He argued for the establishment of standards for wood chopping operations and he discussed the basic relation of forestry to agriculture, particularly with regard to the important factor of soils.

Fernow early subscribed to the view that in forestry the basic question was whether a tract of land was best suited to agriculture or to forest cultivation. To determine what lands were appropriate for farming, both physical and chemical elements were controlling. For forest purposes, the physical properties most often were decisive. Fernow was living in a mountainous region. He saw vast problems of utilizing barren and waste lands and also lands so situated physically that farming was impractical. Sound forestry, according to Fernow, studied first the physical environment and its most appropriate use.

Fernow believed that forestry was, like agriculture, an art and a potential science. Moreover, forestry could be made a national policy. In his article, "Signification of the Forests for the Country"[29] he began by saying, "The wealth and power of a nation is not so much a consequence of the gifts, which nature has bestowed upon her soil, as of the prudent and systematic utilization and the intelligent concurrence of skill and labor in the economical management of these gifts. . . . The means of this country seem equally distributed in the mineral resources and in the agricultural capacities of the soil. In the development of the former, the necessity of a systematic management has at last forced itself upon the private individual as well as the government. . . . The mightiest of the agents, which contribute at once to the prosperity and wealth of the

[28] III, 1, 19, published in 1882.
[29] Probably written in 1878, unpublished.

nation [are] the forests. . . . Even though wood might be replaced as fuel by coal, peat, etc., it must be remembered, that the forest gives us our building timber, the masts for our ships, and indirectly exercises an influence on climate and cultivation of the soil, which is by no means of small moment in a nation's financial balance sheet. . . . Without wood, mankind would be without civilization, [since] almost all mechanical arts would necessarily have to be thrown aside and with them all our physical culture, the mother of our spiritual life and advancement. . . . It seems that for regulating the climate the woods are the only means which is generally open to human application. . . . The distribution of woodlands and the ratio between these and the plough-land and meadows are the main agents of climatical differences." The effects of forests like the effects of large sheets of water on air movements, on temperature and humidity, on evaporation and fog, the effects of forests on the control of stream courses, as mechanical barriers to torrents and floods, to land inundation and avalanches, to hot blasts of wind in summer and cold blasts in winter, the effects of forests on soil temperature both for forest growing and as windbreaks for agricultural pursuits, the effects of forests on breathing beings by "absorbing carbonic acid and exhaling the oxygen necessary for respiration"—these and other influences attested to the forest's value and necessity to man. In the exact ascertainment of the scope and nature of these indirect beneficial influences on the life of man and the earth lay phases of a potential forestal science. The direct benefits of forests were observable in fences, telegraph poles, fuel, furniture, housing—all the wood uses. The indirect benefits of reforestation yet remained to be investigated. History attested plentifully to the disastrous consequences of deforestation. Now what would reforestation accomplish? This was body, sinew, nerve, and impulse to Fernow's love of forestry. But it is interesting to observe that Fernow began with an analysis of conditions as they were. He saw that the forest needs were forest management for those regions where forests were, and forest planting for those unused regions unfitted or unsuited to agriculture where forests might be made to grow. He began to warn not against lumbering but against deforestation and its evil consequences. He began to argue for forest management to realize maximum timber production and a future growth for future generations. Conservation was the essence of Fernow's appeal.

The American Nurserymen's Association found that the total forest area of the United States was 380,000,000 acres. Forty thousand acres annually were being taken for railroad tie supply; six hundred thousand acres for fuel; fifty thousand acres for charcoal furnaces. Lumber consumption annually required three million acres. "Add to this," said Fernow, "the incalculable amount of forest destroyed by fires, either intentionally or carelessly and even allowing for a reasonable percentage of forest to renew itself, the grand total of 380,000,000 acres will be exhausted in less than 100 years." Something had to be done!

Fernow examined the chart of the United States Census of 1870. Forestry matters of the census were principally compiled by William Henry Brewer, whom Torrey and Gray had established as professor of agriculture at Yale University. Working with Samuel William Johnson, one of the first great founders of a scientific agriculture in North America, Brewer realized the close partnership of forestry and agriculture; in fact, in 1878 he was teaching a course in forestry at Yale University as part of its pioneering work in agricultural education.

Brewer's taxonomic analysis in the 1870 census of American forest and woodland systems and their distribution over the continent constituted perhaps the first source of forest information of which Fernow availed himself after arriving in the United States. Using Fernow's own words, he studied the "distribution of woodlands and the ratio between these and the plough-lands and meadows." He noticed particularly those sections of the country where, although the woodlands were "rapidly diminishing," there yet remained "large forests of excellent timber almost untouched by the axe." New York and Pennsylvania were representative. Wood manufactures, including the shipbuilding industry, in New England more than other regions, were taking large timbers, but woodland areas were not decreasing proportionately. He said, "In many places the large trees fit for sawing are cut, without clearing the land of the smaller growth, leaving it still woodland and as such the census-takers, upon whose report we have to rely in this matter, have noted it." From Virginia to Florida woodland areas had "probably not much diminished of late years, only the trees suitable for sawing and hewing [were] decreasing under the heavy drafts made by commerce." The census revealed that the region from Ohio to Iowa and Minnesota, including northern Michigan and Wisconsin, was furnishing more sawed lumber than any other part of the country. Fernow studied the statistical information available and concluded that Michigan and Wisconsin then were "producing upwards of 1/4 of the whole yield of the country" in sawed lumber, and "a fearful tale of destruction" was being written. To the southwest, "from Kentucky and Mississippi to Alabama and Texas," the diminution of woodland areas was not serious. "Only, as elsewhere, in places most available for commerce the better timber trees are disappearing," especially on the western borders. The prospect of "a broad treeless plain from 6 to 15 degrees wide" separating the East and West, and the possibilities of tree-growth "artificially planted and cared for" immediately had aroused his imagination. Fernow said, "It is possible to cross the continent from the Pacific coast to the Gulf of Mexico without passing through a forest, five miles in extent or large enough to be noticed on the map in the census atlas." True, such "oases" or "forest islands" as the Black Hills were to be found, and to the west of the "treeless belt" were the great parks, the Colorado forest, and the great forests of California. Not cutting but fire was regarded as the first enemy of these. "Where one tree is cut for use," wrote Fernow, "ten perhaps are killed by fires. . . ." Fernow believed that in the West forest supplies were "diminishing rapidly, vastly faster than a legitimate use" demanded. His knowledge, however, at this time was based on book learning and verbal reports, not on actual observation and exploration such as formed the basis of Charles Sprague Sargent's investigations.

Sargent was aided by Sereno Watson, George Engelmann, and others for purposes of the 1880 census. Sargent's "Report on the Forests of North America, exclusive of Mexico," published in 1884 as a part of the census of 1880, was scientifically produced. Already established as an authority on North American forest trees and their distribution, Sargent went west with the purposes of the census investigations foremost in mind. In Cambridge, Massachusetts, was the leading center of botanical investigation, the Gray Herbarium. Asa Gray, America's leading botanist, and Sargent were close co-workers. Gray supported Sargent in the plans for the work. Sereno Watson, Gray's dependable associate, went into Montana and the far Northwest to make census investigations. George Engelmann and Charles Christopher Parry joined Sargent in his far western botanical explorations.[30] The tradition inaugurated by Brewer was carried on by Sargent, who prepared a map showing the relative average density of existing forests. Many of his conclusions were later found to be in error, but for many years his report was the most authoritative source of forest knowledge. Sargent also collected wood specimens of American trees. On December 25, 1881, Gray wrote to Sir Joseph Dalton Hooker of the famous Kew Gardens of England, Sargent "seems to have made a mark in his Census forestry work. . . ." Sargent's "Report on the Forests of North America,"[31] which included analysis of 412 species, brought him instantaneous acclaim. For a while Sargent served as a professor of horticulture at Harvard University and directed the university Botanical Garden. This work led to the "noble foundation for an arboretum," which was made possible about a decade earlier by a bequest of James Arnold to Harvard University. Under Sargent, its first director, the Arnold Arboretum flourished in an expanded program of arboriculture which included planning and constructing a park system for the city of Boston.[32]

[30] Fuller accounts of Brewer and Sargent are given in A. D. Rodgers, *John Torrey and American Botany 1873-1892*, Princeton University Press.

[31] See *Report of the Chief of the Forestry Division of the U.S.D.A. for 1886*, p. 192, Washington, 1887; also *Forestry Investigations of the U.S.D.A. 1877-1898*, p. 381.

[32] "The First Fifty Years of the Arnold Arboretum," *Journal of the Arnold Arboretum* III, 1922, pp. 127-171.

The progressive spirit of Sargent was shown in the census investigations in two especial particulars. First, he attempted to determine the cause of forest fires which during the 1860's and 1870's had ravaged vast areas in Wyoming, Michigan, Wisconsin, all the northwestern states, New Jersey, northeastern Pennsylvania, and New York.[33] As early as 1867 Wisconsin had appointed a commission of inquiry to investigate and report on forest destruction. Individual citizens and the governments became interested in eliminating causes and finding ways to control forest fires. Requisite action sufficient to cope with the problem, however, was very tardy. In 1887 Edward A. Bowers carefully estimated the annual fire loss on publicly owned timber lands, and irrespective of incidental damage to soil, young growth, et cetera, arrived at a figure of $8,000,000. Subsequent canvasses failed to produce effective measures to solve the problem. Second, by tabulating special data and results of mechanical timber tests, Sargent widened knowledge of the practical utilization of certain forest species. Sargent and Sharples deserved more credit than they received for indicating this new and necessary direction in American timber study. Both Sargent and Brewer were militant conservationists. Both had planned programs of timber utilization and warned of the dangers of exhaustion of timber supplies. The 1870 census analyzed the amount of timber being sawed according to states, and the need of conservative action was plain.

A fallacy of Sargent's census investigations lay in the fact that no timber trees of a diameter of less than twelve inches were counted. The factors of second growth and growth accumulation were not included.[34] It was observed in 1903 by the National Wholesale Lumber Dealers' Association that, "If for instance the conclusions of the census of 1880 had been valid, the entire stock of White Pine in the United States would have been out of existence in 1890." Nevertheless, Sargent's statistical accounts did awaken many persons. He called attention to the fact that New England white pine would become increasingly valuable because of the rapidly diminishing and depleted pine forests there and in New York and Pennsylvania. It was said that Michigan, Wisconsin, and Minnesota, the great pine states, could "show only a few scattered remnants of the noble forest to which they owe their greatest prosperity. . . ." Sargent went so far as to say that no unexplored pine areas remained. Except the narrow redwood belt of the California coast, furthermore, there was to be found no area which could yield a substitute in quantity.[35] Though the facts proved exaggerated, the census in-

33 "Brief Account of the Development of the Forestry Movement in the United States," *Forestry Bulletin* 1 (May 1884), pp. 5-6; R. H. D. Boerker, *op. cit.*, pp. 147-149.

34 *Forestry and Irrigation* IX, 4, April 1903, p. 203.

35 See William Little, "Alarming Destruction of American Forests," *Proc. Am. For. Ass'n* (1885), pp. 26-35, at p. 27. See also, Sargent's paper, "Forest Fires," *Rpt. St. Bd. of Agric. of Mass.* (1882), p. 277, which published in part what Little quoted him as saying.

vestigations of Brewer and Sargent awakened the American public to the dangers of forest destruction. Intelligent students like Fernow examined the conclusions of Brewer and learned that large areas of the continent were treeless, sparsely wooded, or being denuded and destroyed. The public press began to discuss the relationship of forests to the welfare of the nation.

Unhappily the discussion turned on the point as to whether or not the facts as revealed were correct. Were the continent's forests inexhaustible, or would exhaustion really take place? How long would the forests last? Here and there a voice pleaded the cause of reforestation. The antidote seemed to be the planting of young trees. Statisticians pointed out that although ten million acres of forest lands were being destroyed annually, not more than ten thousand acres were being planted in trees. When Sargent's report was published, the alarmists who believed Sargent's predictions were dubbed with the epithet, "denudatics." The sponsors of the original forestry movement took up a fight against forest destruction. Their program loomed as a threat to the lumber and wood-using industries. It remained for a professionally trained forester, Bernhard Eduard Fernow, to clear the atmosphere for intelligent handling of the problem. No man, however, could perform the task alone. There were ardent patriots who for years had fought for the interests of forest cultivation and preservation. Some had been inspired by the example and methods of Europe, but most could be classified as "tree planters." They failed to grasp the basic problem, and their discussions became absorbed in determining what tree species to plant. Most of them had the analyst's concepts of the taxonomic botanist and horticulturist. The synthetic concept of the forest and forest planting which Fernow advanced was slow to be accepted. As early as 1878 when Fernow discussed the American forest resources according to regions, he treated the woodlands in terms of areas and aggregate value. Were forest areas decreasing? What was happening to the larger and better trees? Fernow was an enemy of waste and an advocate of a constructive forestry program which embraced two fundamental concepts, forest planting and forest management. He was the first advocate of large-scale scientific forest management in North America.

CHAPTER II

The Organization of Forestry in the United States and Canada

IN AUGUST 1873 at Portland, Maine, the American Association for the Advancement of Science took an aggressive stand in favor of the introduction of forestry practice in the United States.[1] At this meeting, Dr. Hough read a paper, "The Duty of Governments in the Preservation of Forests," and in response thereto a resolution was passed which provided for the appointment of a committee to memorialize congress and the state legislatures "on the importance of promoting the cultivation of timber and the preservation of forests," and to recommend legislation. A committee of notables in American natural science comprised its membership: Asa Gray, Josiah D. Whitney, John Strong Newberry, Lewis H. Morgan, Colonel Charles Whittlesey, Eugene Woldemar Hilgard, and William H. Brewer. It is interesting to observe that four members, Gray, Newberry, Hilgard, and Brewer, were botanists. Other members were leaders in geology, mining, and agriculture. None of these had established a reputation in forestry. George B. Emerson, another committee member, in 1846 had prepared and published a *Report on the Trees and Shrubs of Massachusetts*. It was a regional book, valuable as a manual and for its special knowledge, and it rivalled a few books of wider compass such as R. U. Piper's *Trees of America*. One member, Franklin Benjamin Hough, was outstanding for his knowledge of forest conditions in the United States. But even he was at that time best known as a doctor of medicine, a student of botany, geology, and mineralogy, and as a historian of St. Lawrence, Franklin, Jefferson, and Lewis counties in New York State.

The medical profession contributed outstanding professional men to botany and agriculture. Usually they have furthered physiological analysis. Hough, however, was more preeminent as a statistician than as a doctor of medicine. Hough's published works eventually included historical, statistical, scientific, and constitutional subjects. He was a prolific writer and investigator, before his death the list of his writings

[1] Sources for the period 1873-1881, especially 1876-1878, are primarily Fernow's own writings; also see *Report upon the Forestry Investigations of the United States Department of Agriculture 1877-1898*, Government Printing Office, Washington, 1899; an original of the memorial to the state governments found among Fernow's papers; the *Proc. Am. For. Cong.* of the Cincinnati and Montreal meetings of 1882; the yearly reports of the Commissioner of Agriculture, especially for 1878, pp. 27-32; Jenks Cameron, *Development of Governmental Forest Control in the United States*, Johns Hopkins Press, Baltimore, 1928; Romeyn B. Hough, "The Incipiency of the Forestry Movement," *American Forestry* XIX, 1913, p. 547; Filibert Roth, *Journal of Forestry* XVI, 2, Feb. 1918, p. 145, and *Forest Leaves* III, 2, June 1890, p. 22.

amounting to seventy-eight titles. Except for his more important writings on forestry and his meteorological observations of wide range, Hough's work was principally confined to New York State.

Because Hough was a New Yorker and because of his knowledge of the Adirondack wilderness, he had been chosen in 1872 to serve on a commission created to establish a New York State Forest Preserve. Seven commissioners were appointed, Verplanck Colvin one, and Horatio Seymour served as the chairman. Their official report, made in 1873, was prepared by Hough and greatly increased his prominence as a student of New York State forests. "Most unfortunately this report was pigeonholed by the Legislature but it was not forgotten and ten years later helped to bring about the definite action that was taken in 1885. . . . It is well to remember that Doctor Hough stood for a plan that recognized the place of the lumberman in forest management and that provided for what in more recent years has been called 'perpetuation of the forest through wise use.' In this attitude he was opposed by Mr. Colvin, who held that a great state park was the right solution."[2]

On February 6, 1874, Hough and Emerson, with the authority of the Association's committee, transmitted to President Ulysses S. Grant a memorial which asked for the creation of a commission of forestry to be appointed by the president and senate. The report to the congress was on the general subject of the amount and distribution of woodlands, the rate of consumption and waste, the measures to be adopted to provide against future needs in the preservation and planting of timber, the importation and exportation of lumber and other forest property, and the more elusive subject of forest influences on climate, rainfall, temperature "and other atmospheric conditions upon which agricultural success depends." The third and concluding bracket of the memorial was especially significant and forward looking. It sought "a full statement of the methods practiced in Europe in relation to the planting and management of forests, and an account of the special schools of forestry that have been established in foreign countries."

In 1874, at Lowville, Hough delivered a course of lectures, including within his forestry compass topics such as: tree growth and the physiology of timber, distribution of forest species and qualities, chemical properties and special products, forestry in Europe and schools of forestry, planting and management, irrigation, climate in its relation to forestry, timbers in commerce and their supply and demand, destroy-

[2] Ralph Sheldon Hosmer in *Bulletin to the Schools* XXVI, 7, March 1940, p. 230, The University of the State of New York. Immediately following material concerning Hough is based on *Forestry Investigations U.S.D.A., 1877-1898, op. cit.*, pp. 6, 37-39 (the memorial to the President and Congress and the joint resolution of House and Senate), and an important study by Edna L. Jacobsen, "Franklin B. Hough, a Pioneer in Scientific Forestry in America," *New York History* XV, 3 (July 1934), pp. 311-325, at 317-321, founded on Hough's autobiography, diaries, notebooks, memoranda, reports, etc., at the manuscript and history section of the New York State Library, Albany.

ing agencies and preservative processes, ages of timber and time of cutting, transportation, forest restoration and protection afforded by woodlands, investments and profits, and duties to the present. December 3, 1874, he also addressed a letter to James Little of Montreal, Canada, a wealthy lumberman with rare foresight who was interested in forest conservation. "Within the last few years," Hough told Little, "I have had occasion to give much attention to the subject of Timber Supply, and I have noticed in the course of my readings, reference to some articles by yourself upon the supply of timber in Canada. I have seen only extracts from your communications. Would you favor me with any pamphlet or other articles you may have published, or that may be within your reach upon this subject. I spent last winter in Washington, in presenting this subject to Congress on behalf of the American Association for the Advancement of Science, and procured a favorable notice from Committees, etc. . . ."

Within the month Little had sent the requested articles and Hough thanked him by a letter of December 21st. "My attention was called to the subject" of forestry, Hough explained, "in its relation to Climate, rainfall, etc. and from its connection with Census statistics with which I have had much to do in an official way. Believing the dangers from exhaustion of supplies to be *real* and *imminent* I have applied myself most carefully for a long time to the study of methods adopted in Europe as a remedy for the evil that must come. I think it quite probable," he informed, "that I shall be able to deliver the lectures noticed in the enclosed circular in several of our agricultural colleges." He inquired of any ship-timber reservations in "L[ower] C[anada]" and sent a copy of "the first and only report of our 'Adirondack Park.' The second Commission has expired," he said, "and nothing but this done." His letter set forth the problem confronting New York with reference to its Adirondack forests: "The fact is, the land is nearly all in private hands already. The State would be forced to buy, and this the people would not approve, as some of them say it is to accommodate certain sporting gentlemen who want a hunting ground. Our Commission was united in resisting overtures from owners who having cut off the timber wanted to sell worthless land which must soon revert and be forfeited for taxes. The land is *good for nothing* except to grow wood, and all the valuable timber is either cut off or is in the hands of men who will do this and cannot be prevented."

Progress toward forest conservation in New York went little beyond the filing of reports by the state commissions. Extension of the park concept prevailed for years over utilization and reforestation recommendations. In 1883 the original recommendation of the commissioners was enacted into law forbidding further sale of state-owned northern wilderness lands in Clinton, Essex, Franklin, Fulton, Hamilton, Herkimer, Lewis, Saratoga, St. Lawrence, and Warren counties. The full program recommended was thus realized only in part, and would be reshaped by Fernow in 1885. During the 1870's some results had been achieved. A good topographic survey of the Adirondacks had been sent to the state senate, and the commissions' reports had brought forestry into real notice.

Hough's work established a foundation of forestry also within the federal government. In 1874, after delivering a lecture on forestry at Albany before the New York State Agricultural Society, he had gone to Washington and with Emerson held a conference at the Smithsonian Institution with Joseph Henry, Commissioner Watts and botanist George Vasey of the United States Department of Agriculture, and several congressmen. These men agreed that a federal statute should be enacted creating a commission of forestry similar to the commissions of mining and of fisheries. To the memorial of the American Association for the Advancement of Science, prepared by Hough and Emerson as a subcommittee of the main committee, was added a recommendation to this effect. In February, President Grant, with a special message, approvingly sent the memorial to congress where the matter was referred to committees on public lands in both the House and Senate, and ultimately a bill was favorably reported back, introduced by Congressman Mark H. Dunnell of Minnesota, Hough's "loyal spokesman." No action on this was taken by the forty-third congress, and so Hough continued writing and lecturing upon the subject of forestry, delivering, it is said, a series of lectures at the Lowell Institute of Harvard in 1874-1875 and later at the Peabody Institute in Baltimore. Already, in 1874, his Albany lecture before the New York State Agricultural Society had stimulated the aggressive interest of President Andrew Dixon White of Cornell University in the subject, so much so he had informed Hough that he had "urged the establishment in connection with our Botanical Garden, of an Arboretum, which we have already begun."

In January 1876, when the forty-fourth congress met, Representative Dunnell again introduced a bill, similar to one which had failed in 1874 and the object of which was to secure the appointment of a commission of inquiry into forest destruction and measures necessary for timber preservation. This again was referred to the committee on public lands. But, in August 1876, on motion of Mr. Dunnell, the substance of the bill was added as an amendment or rider to the general or annual appropriation bill for the year ending June 30, 1877, which provided for the expenses of the legislative, judicial, and executive branches of the government. August 15, 1876, therefore, became an important day in the forestry history of the United States, and within fifteen more days the appointment was made since the Commissioner of Agriculture was directed to "appoint a man of approved attainments and practically well acquainted with the methods of statistical inquiry . . . with the view of ascertaining the annual amount of consumption, importation, and exportation of timber and other forest products; the probable supply for future wants, the means best adapted to the preservation and renewal of forests, the influence of forests on climate, and the measures that have been successfully applied in foreign countries or that may be deemed applicable in this country for the preservation and restoration or planting of forests, and to report upon the same to the Commissioner of Agriculture, to be by him in a separate report transmitted to Congress." Later, when writing of this, Fernow commented, "Curiously and significantly enough this clause and the appropriation of $2,000 for the purpose appears as a part of the provisions for the distribution of seeds."

Accordingly, in his report of November 1, 1876, the year of the centennial celebration at Philadelphia which brought Fernow to America, Commissioner of Agriculture Frederick Watts announced that pursuant to the direction of congress he had commissioned Franklin B. Hough for the forestry work at a compensation of $2,000 per year allowed the department from the sum appropriated for the purchase of seeds. Just how conversant Commissioner Watts was with real problems of forestry may be inferred from his comment in the same report: "The Department grounds are yearly becoming more and more a source of deep interest to students in forestry, a subject that is justly attracting the attention of practical as well as scientific men. Comparisons can here be made in regard to the rapidity of growth of the various species, and their adaptability to various purposes and uses."

Hough immediately began to collect statistical data concerning United States forest regions. Corresponding with the commanding officers of distant army posts, he obtained much valuable data concerning the forests of the western states and territories. In 1877 a new commissioner of agriculture, William G. Le Duc, addressed a general communication to the chief of engineers of the United States government asking for information concerning the present extent of the forest area, the lines of natural drainage, elevations and rainfall, timber characteristics, growth conditions and rate of decrease whether by fire or the agency of man, and whether tree planting had been resorted to, and if so, whether "shoots or transplanting" had been the principal methods used. In the fall of 1878 Hough visited the British provinces of Canada and made use of their official forest reports. He learned much and did much to educate agricultural circles to the real needs in forestry. He saw much to be learned from European experience, especially in the management of forests and the application of scientific research methods to ascertain forest laws and principles which might be applied productively on the American continent. He held a wide vision for forestry in America and was familiar with much of the world literature on the subject. There were then about twenty forestry journals published in various parts of the world. There were more than twenty forestry schools in Europe. It was arranged that Hough should visit Europe, but the preparation of his ponderous exhaustive *Reports on Forestry* (the first published in 1877-1878, the second in 1878-1880, and each more than six hundred pages long) commanded most of his time, since he was afforded very little assistance. Because of these reports he was awarded a diploma by the Vienna International Congress of 1882. In 1881 another commissioner of agriculture, George B. Loring of Massachusetts, announced in his first report that forestry was to be segregated as a distinct division in the federal department of agriculture. Moreover, in 1877 and 1878 the senate was petitioned by the American Nurseryman's Association to examine the condition of European forests and forestry. On November 13, 1877, Senator Paddock introduced into the forty-fifth congress a bill directing two commissioners and a secretary to inspect the European forests and "report on forestry and tree planting" and the influence of forests on climate, rainfall, and water supply.[3] The failure of these sensible actions disappointed Fernow much, and he said so in unqualified terms. On reorganization of the department of agriculture in 1881, Hough was sent to Europe; but the motive behind this, Hough believed, was to shelve him and his work. What he learned in Europe formed an important part of his third *Report on Forestry*, published in 1882.

Meanwhile much had happened in forestry in various states. Fernow later summarized the movement, saying:

> In [1876] two forestry associations were formed; one for the State of Minnesota, at St. Paul, and a national one organized by Dr. Warder at Philadelphia [actually at Atlantic City], which latter failed to thrive or secure membership. . . . A few years before several States had appointed committees or commissioners, notably the State of Wisconsin [1867], to investigate and report on the subject. Legislation to encourage, by bounties or tax releases, tree planting was inaugurated in many States from Maine to California as well as by the federal government. These laws, mainly applicable to the prairie States, remained, however, without much result. In 1872, to stimulate enthusiasm for tree planting the first Arbor Day was instituted at the instance of Governor [J. Sterling] Morton of Nebraska. I am not sure but this otherwise interesting and beautiful idea has had a retarding influence on practical forestry by misleading people into thinking that tree planting was the main issue instead of a conservative management of existing forests.[4]

Indeed, states as far west as California, during these decades, had enacted laws to safeguard forests against fires. California, as early as

[3] Materials of this paragraph have been taken from reports of the commissioner of agriculture; for 1876, pp. 8-13; for 1878, pp. 27-29, 515ff.; for 1881, pp. 5-16; Jenks Cameron, *op. cit.*, pp. 188-191, note 26, and other cited authorities.

[4] Fernow, "Birth of a Forest Policy," *op. cit.*

1864, forbade timber to be cut on state lands, but rendered the legislation practically of no use by excepting from its provisions timber cut for lumber, firewood, tanning, agriculture, or mining purposes. During these decades states from Maine to the Middle West and West enacted laws providing procedures for reports on forests, forest policy, and forestry. Minnesota, as early as 1867, allotted funds to its state agricultural society to enable it to give premiums for the best five acres of cultivated timber or for the best continuous half mile of live fence hedge. Enactment of state timber culture laws soon followed and spread west and east, one of the last states to pass such a law during these decades being Massachusetts in 1878.

The most important of these laws to encourage tree planting, either by exempting lands from taxation or by giving bounties, originated in 1868 in the prairie states where tree planting was most needed—Iowa, Kansas, and Wisconsin. The following year tree planting became more extensive. New York and Nebraska passed encouraging laws, and in New York a highway tax abatement was permitted to persons who planted trees along public roads. The Maine board of agriculture appointed a commission to report on a forest policy for the state. This action led to legislation in 1872 which exempted from taxation lands planted to trees. In 1870 Missouri initiated legislation, and in 1871 Minnesota joined the ranks of states which encouraged tree planting enterprise. Some laws were amended and changed; others were repealed and new laws enacted. Within a few years that most barren of states, Nevada, sought by legislation to promote the spread of tree planting within its borders. In 1874 Illinois joined the movement. By 1877 Dakota, Washington Territory, and Wyoming had passed acts to encourage tree planting. In the same year the Connecticut[5] legislature enacted a tree planting law and sent to Europe a commissioner, B. G. Northrop,[6] to report on forestry. In 1878 Rhode Island enacted a tree planting encouragement statute. Massachusetts had taken a lead in 1837 by ordering a forest survey of the state's timberland; and on May 25, 1882, this state's celebrated Public Parks Act was passed. In 1881 New Hampshire began to inquire into the condition of its forest resources. Vermont followed. Among the southern states Florida in 1879 placed on its statute books an act to regulate the burning of wood. By 1882 tree planting laws among the states were found both east and west, among both states and territories. Crossing the international boundary, the movement extended

[5] Connecticut had enacted a tree-planting law in 1875, but the 1877 law was regarded by Fernow as much more important. This paragraph gives those laws which Fernow considered important. Doubtless there were others of minor importance; Iowa, for example, had several statutes.

[6] See the writings of Birdsey Grant Northrop, "The Schools of Forestry and Industrial Schools of Europe" (1878), "Tree Planting and the Schools of Forestry in Europe" (1879), and "Forests and Floods" (1885).

into Canada. The climax was reached in Colorado where, when in 1876 the state was admitted to the Union, a provision to preserve the new state's timberland was written into the constitution in its Article XVIII.[7]

Arbor Days were allied to the forestry movement; in 1874 the Iowa Horticultural Society sponsored the celebration, but officially the observance was not designated by the superintendent of public instruction until 1887. In 1875 Kansas and Tennessee followed the examples of Nebraska and Iowa and observed or established an Arbor Day. Still other states followed: in 1876 Minnesota and Michigan; in 1881-1882 Ohio; in 1883 West Virginia; in 1884 New Jersey, Maryland, Indiana, and Dakota; in 1885 Colorado, Vermont, and New Hampshire; in 1886 Massachusetts, Connecticut, Rhode Island, Florida, Kentucky, Missouri, and California; in 1887 Maine, Pennsylvania, Alabama, Illinois, Idaho, Montana, and Nevada; in 1887-1888 New York; in 1888 Wyoming; in 1889 Wisconsin, Texas, and Oregon; and within a few years other states and territories were added, among them Arizona, New Mexico, Utah, Georgia, Louisiana, Oklahoma, Mississippi, North Carolina, and Virginia.[8]

Although Fernow urged each state to adopt the celebration of Arbor Day and the federal government to make it a national observance, he did not wish to see this practice regarded as a forestry fundamental. He wished no confusion to exist between forest management and forest reproduction.

In 1876 there was introduced in congress a bill to create genuine national forests adjacent to navigable streams and their sources. During the period prior to the American Forestry Congress of 1882, only one other year, 1872, can claim possible superiority to 1876 as a year of forestry advancement. During 1872 the national government set aside an area of 3,600 square miles as a national park, known today as Yellowstone National Park.

Naturally no forestry movement within the states could gather momentum without having a resounding effect in the halls of congress. During the embryonic period, 1868-1871, about a dozen tree planting bills were introduced in congress. More appeared in 1872. The public timberlands and their problems, however, overshadowed these.

The historic twin acts of June 3, 1878, the "Mineral Land" act, applicable to the Rocky Mountain States and Territories and the Dakotas, and the "Timber and Stone" act, applicable in the Pacific regions and

[7] See B. E. Fernow, *A Brief History of Forestry in Europe, the U.S., and Other Countries*, Univ. Press Toronto; *Forestry Quarterly*, 1911, pp. 472, 475, 481ff.; "Brief Account of the Development of the Forestry Movement in the United States," *Forestry Bulletin*, May 1884, pp. 5-6; "Outstanding Events of Importance in Forestry in America," *Forest Leaves* III, 11, 1885, p. 151; R. H. D. Boerker, *op. cit.*, pp. 179-180; John Ise, *op. cit.*, pp. 27-28, 33-34, 37, 96-97.

[8] See "Arbor Day Observance in the United States," *Report of the Chief of the Division of Forestry for 1892*, U.S.D.A., p. 316.

Nevada, had been preceded by some protective and policing measures. Nevertheless, under the new laws neither waste, destruction, thievery, nor fires were being brought under control. Enormous amounts of timber continued to be reported stolen. Remedial compromises and legal process both failed of their principal objective to replenish the government coffers for its material losses. Indeed, the losses mounted to many millions and the replenishment amounted to only a few hundred thousand dollars. The employment of protective agents proved ineffectual. So spacious was the public timberland area, so unsympathetic and at times hostile were local residents to the laws and the regulations of the Department of the Interior, that the results were for the most part negligible. Difficult land title problems thwarted much law enforcement. Whole alternate sections of railway land grants remained unsurveyed, often making it almost impossible to determine whether cutting by a railroad was on its own land or that of the government. Often the prosecution of a timber depredator turned on an uncertain question of land ownership. Certain curative legislation was enacted whereby the site of a depredation could be purchased by a trespasser, but its application was limited to trespasses committed prior to March 1, 1879. Other legislation permitted railroads to cut timber on public lands for construction purposes and even in one instance for repairs. The government, of course, was encouraging western settlement and industry. Administrative problems increased in complexity every year. In 1879 Secretary Schurz and others began to call attention in the strongest terms to the fact that only about twenty-five agents were employed to protect a forest area of about 70,000,000 acres! It has already been pointed out that very valuable timberlands were being sold at far less than their worth. Furthermore, of millions of acres entered under the homestead laws only a small percentage of the entries were carried to patent by the entry-man. To avert a national scandal in the administration of the public lands a new organizational structure under new laws was needed. All the circumstances argued for the establishment of a strong national forest policy. The opportunity for reform had arrived.[9] The hope of reform lay foremost in establishing a federal forestry administration but also needed were state educational programs.[10]

In 1867 Thomas Jonathan Burrill, a botanist, accompanied Major John Wesley Powell on one of his famed explorations of the Colorado

[9] See B. E. Fernow, "Brief Account of the Development of the Forestry Movement in the United States," *op. cit.*, pp. 5-6; also Fernow's *History of Forestry*. In 1877 the land office had a change of policy toward its practice of allowing compromise settlements of claims instead of legal prosecutions for thefts. See also Edward Bowers, "The Present Condition of Forests on the Public Lands"; Jenks Cameron, *op. cit.*, pp. 105-116, 174-217; Treadwell Cleveland, "Forest Law in the United States," *The Forester* VI, 7, July 1900, pp. 153ff.

[10] See "Condition of Forestry Interests in the States," *Annual Report of the Division of Forestry for 1887*, U.S.D.A., G.P.O., Washington, 1888, pp. 97ff.

River and the Rocky Mountain areas and had an opportunity to view the vast treeless prairies between Illinois and the Colorado Rockies. He returned to the Illinois Industrial University (now the University of Illinois), was appointed to its first faculty as professor of natural history, and determined to study forest planting experimentally on the university campus. He wanted to substantiate his theory that with proper treatment of the soil, trees could be grown on the prairies and plains.

Fernow accounted the first report (1872) made by this university's experiment station as a significant event in forestry development in the United States.

It is interesting to go to the University of Illinois today and on the campus examine the experimental forest plot planted by Burrill. Interested from the standpoint of agriculture, Burrill planted saplings and during the balance of his life observed a small forest emerge.[11] He was interested in improving crop production and yields, but the work on which his fame as a plant scientist rests was his original recognition of pear and apple twig blight as of bacterial origin. This discovery laid the basis for bacterial plant pathology in America.[12]

Pathology was taught to Fernow in Germany as a part of a course in Forest Protection. Diseased conditions and life histories of disease-producing agents[13] were being described. The work was more observational than experimental. When Fernow arrived in America he found only the rudiments of plant pathology started. Botanical study in plant diseases was primarily mycological and principally confined to horticultural and agricultural species. Except in descriptive studies, forest species were almost entirely excluded. Like Asa Gray in botany and Sargent in horticulture, Fernow wanted to stimulate pathological investigations in forestry, but because of the magnitude of other more immediate tasks he had to be content with applying what little knowledge of the subject he had brought from Europe. Robert Hartig has been called the "father of forest pathology." Not until 1878 was he taken from the Forest Academy at Eberswalde, where he had served as a lecturer on botany and zoology, to the chair of botany in the Royal For-

[11] See William Trelease, *Botanical Gazette* LXII, 1916, p. 153; Charles F. Hottes, "Personal Recollections of Thomas J. Burrill," *Illinois Alumni News*, Feb. 1940, pp. 6-7.

[12] See A. D. Rodgers, *Liberty Hyde Bailey*, Princeton University Press, 1949. The author will also consider the subject further in a biography of Erwin Frink Smith, now in preparation.

[13] In 1876 congress authorized the organization of the United States Entomological Commission. This commission consisted of C. V. Riley, A. S. Packard, and Cyrus Thomas. A volume on *Forest Insects*, prepared by Packard, was issued. Entomologists in the United States and Canada early related their work to the forest. Especially important were studies made by Leland O. Howard, Harry B. Weiss, and William Saunders. See also Herbert Osborn, *Fragments of Entomological History*, published by the author, Columbus, Ohio, 1937.

estry Experiment Station at Munich, where he remained the rest of his life.[14] We will see that several, if not all, of the first American forest pathologists studied in Europe.

For many years the forest species were studied taxonomically. A *Catalogue of the Forest Trees of the United States which usually attain a height of 16 feet or more,* with notes and brief descriptions of the more important species, was compiled and published in 1876 by George Vasey, botanist of the United States Department of Agriculture. Without foresters, systematic studies by other than botanists were not to be expected. The works of the Michauxs on our sylva were designed primarily as botanical studies. Authorities on various forest genera and species, such as George Engelmann on the pines, oaks, and junipers, or Michael Schuck Bebb on the willows, were numerous; but in every case the approach was from the botanical standpoint, rather than the standpoint of forestry.

Certain trees were known to have economic values to the lumber and wood-using industries. The railroads, particularly in the West, were early to experiment in tree plantings for their own use. Railroad ties were soon found to consume a vast amount of timber. In 1870 the Kansas Pacific railroad initiated some experimental plantings. During the period from 1872-1875 the Burlington, Northern Pacific, and Santa Fe Railroads each established nurseries for the growing of tie timber. These plantings, and a few others by some less important railroads, initiated "railroad forestry" and not the least valuable of the results were experimental proofs as to the adaptability of various tree species to differing soils and climates, and some learning as to nursery practice on the prairies, demonstrations of land values, and ways to ornament and beautify localities.[15]

Probably the first American educational institution to give lectures in forestry was Yale, perhaps as early as 1873, under William Henry Brewer. Brewer's course was listed in the 1878 catalogue of the Sheffield Scientific School in New Haven, but the details of the course and the number of students were not given. In the 1870's, at Iowa Agricultural [State] College at Ames, a department of horticulture and forestry was placed on a "scientific and professional basis," and to this chair, following Charles Edwin Bessey and Henry H. McAfee, went Joseph Lancaster Budd who, in a letter to Hough in 1878 praised Hough's first *Report on Forestry* as "the only valuable and original work on this vitally important subject." At that time Budd was regarded as a pro-

[14] See Herbert Hice Whetzel, *An Outline of the History of Phytopathology,* W. B. Saunders Co., Philadelphia, 1918, pp. 73-75.

[15] See Fernow's "Brief Account of the Development . . . etc.," *op. cit.*, p. 6. A paper on this subject was read at the American Forestry Congress at Montreal. Franklin B. Hough was an authority on railroad forestry. See also John Ise's brief discussion of "Tree Planting by the Railroads," *The United States Forest Policy, op. cit.*, pp. 37-38.

fessor of forestry although his principal work was in horticulture. In 1874 Albert Nelson Prentiss conducted classes in forestry at Cornell, and two years later a similar course was recommended at Massachusetts Agricultural (State) College. The course at Massachusetts may have started informally in 1874, for in that year an experimental planting of larches and Scotch and Austrian pines was made on a barren hillside, but the records of this course are incomplete.[16]

The first course that Fernow recognized as true forestry was given by Volney Morgan Spalding at the University of Michigan.[17] At the first American Forestry Congress, held in 1882 at Cincinnati, it was announced in the *Cincinnati Enquirer* that Spalding, the accredited representative of "Ann Arbor University," had organized a special class of fifty students in forestry.[18]

A national school of forestry was sponsored by General Christopher Columbus Andrews. A New Englander by birth and a graduate of Harvard Law School, Andrews had grown restive in the practice of law and gone to Fort Leavenworth, Kansas, where his fellow townsman, President Pierce, had given him an appointment in the federal Treasury Department. He remained only a short while and again went west, this time sailing up the Mississippi in the *Lady Franklin* to St. Paul and then by stage coach to Crow Wing and, later, St. Cloud. While in Minnesota, Andrews became a well-known writer and a lawyer of prominence. Although a Douglas Democrat before the Civil War, he attended the Republican convention which nominated Grant for the presidency. In 1869 President Grant appointed Andrews Ambassador to Sweden, and there he studied the Swedish methods of forest culture. His report to the United States government on European forestry was one of the most valuable documents on forestry to reach American shores in the early years of the forestry movement. From the pine forest of Minnesota, one of the most magnificent and valuable stands of pine

[16] See B. E. Fernow, "Conditions of Forestry Interests in the States," *op. cit.*, pp. 97-147; H. H. Chapman, "Early Forestry at Yale," *Journal of Forestry*, 42, 446, 1944; *ibid.*, August 1944, p. 600; Ernst A. Bessey, "The Teaching of Botany Sixty-five Years Ago," *Iowa State Coll. Jour. of Sci.* IX, 2 and 3, 1935, pp. 13-19; Earle D. Ross, *A History of Iowa State College*, Iowa State College Press, Ames, 1942; see also L. H. Pammell, "Joseph Lancaster Budd," *Prominent Men I Have Met*, Ames, 1926, pp. 9-14.

[17] Dr. H. H. Bartlett of the Department of Botany at Michigan has informed the present author, "This formal course [in Forestry] was continued only four years. It was offered in a new 'School of Economics' and was planned to be taken quite independently of Botany. The background was economic and philosophical but the 'School of Economics' did not prosper and since the only students who cared about forestry and conservation proved to be, after all, the botanists, who could be perfectly well indoctrinated in their courses in botany, the formal instruction in Forestry ceased. It started auspiciously but was premature. The tradition that something more had to be done about Forestry at Michigan was kept very much alive, and Spalding's course was the beginning that grew into the present School of Forestry and Conservation."

[18] See Fernow's *Report of the Division of Forestry for 1887*. These reports are found in the annual reports of the U.S.D.A.

timber on the North American continent, General Andrews in 1889 voiced a strong plea for rational forest management.[19] In 1880 he spoke before the St. Paul Chamber of Commerce, advocating establishment of a school of forestry on 300 sections of public land in the vicinity of St. Paul. He argued that if the national government can grant lands to endow state colleges of agriculture (as it had done under the Morrill Act of 1862), why could it not endow a school of forestry? The state school lands and private lands of the railroads were selling their timber at $30 per acre; but the national government was getting only $1.50 or $2.00 an acre, when it was not giving the land away. On March 2, 1880, Andrews procured the introduction of a bill in congress to create a school of forestry. The chamber of commerce of St. Paul memorialized congress to pass the bill. General Andrews even procured an endorsement of the measure at the American Forestry Congress held at Cincinnati.[20] Despite the General's argument that there were thirty schools of forestry in Europe and not one in the United States or Canada, the bill in congress failed to pass on the ground that the nation was not yet ready for a school of forestry. President Eliot and Charles Sprague Sargent of Harvard University opposed its enactment. Doubtless they believed that when the Arnold Arboretum, scarcely a decade old, was fully functioning, a school of forestry might be established there.

Fernow seems to have sympathized with this view. In his *Forestry Bulletin*, May 1884, he said, "The Arnold Arboretum under Prof. C. S. Sargent, may readily serve as experimental grounds for a forestry school when the time comes." Immediately after the Forestry Congress had adjourned, Fernow wrote, "We believe that it would have been better to try to extend the plan adopted at Ann Arbor, Michigan University, where Prof. Spalding has gathered a class of some thirty of the pupils, to whom he gives lectures in a popular style with the intent mainly of interesting his hearers in the question and making them acquainted with the principles of forestry." This must have represented the opinion of the committee on which Fernow served with Andrews, Adolpf Leué, Spalding, and R. B. Warder. Nevertheless Andrews' proposals enjoyed the support of Dr. John Axton Warder, the leading figure of the early forestry movement in America.

In 1880 the American Association for the Advancement of Science had carried out its original plan to memorialize the legislatures of the several states. The memorial urged the state legislatures to give attention to the need of future forest supplies. It stated that "consumption and waste of the Forests of the country much exceed their restoration

[19] "Forestry in Minnesota," *Forest Leaves* II, 7, Nov. 1889, p. 105.

[20] Andrews *Recollections 1829-1922*, edited by his daughter Miss Alice Andrews (who also supplied some information directly to the present author), published by Arthur H. Clark Co., Glendale, Calif., 1928. See also *D.A.B.* I, pp. 284-5; and *Cincinnati Enquirer*, April 26, 1882.

by natural growth"; it encouraged "more economical use, and the proper maintenance of our Timber Supply." Plantations along highways should be encouraged and protected in addition to model plantations "established and maintained by a State Government under the care of persons specially trained to the profession of Forestry. Their location should be chosen with a view of affording convenient opportunity to those who might wish to learn approved methods of management, by the study of a work worthy of imitation." Educational institutions should be encouraged to introduce courses in "practical sylviculture." Stations at the colleges might be established "under State patronage, for experiments and observations in cultivation and acclimatization." These should include plantations of the various species of forest trees adapted to the soil and climate. The "appointment of a Commission of Forestry under State authority (analogous to the Commission of Fisheries in many of the States)" was recommended. In other respects, the memorial was similar to the memorial which sought congress to authorize the creation of an office of national commissioner of forestry. The memorial to the states underwent a much more difficult struggle before it was presented to the legislatures than the memorial to congress. In 1874 and in 1878 the association's committee was compelled to report only that progress had been made. But in 1880 the final document was submitted and circulated. Strangely enough, the active interest of the American Association for the Advancement of Science in forest policies ceased at this time. Not until 1889 when Fernow addressed the association's Section I on the "Need of a Forest Administration for the United States"[21] was its aid again summoned to the forestry cause.

The "father of American forestry," many might argue, was John Axton Warder, a doctor of medicine who had risen in the ranks of horticulture and agriculture and become interested in scientific forestry. Warder was the founder of the first organized effort in the cause of forestry in America, the American Forestry Association. He was born of Quaker parentage in Philadelphia, where as a youth he made the acquaintance of such celebrated naturalists as John James Audubon, André François Michaux, and Thomas Nuttall. His family moved to a farm near Springfield, Ohio, before the boy went to medical school. On this farm he acquired an intimate knowledge of agriculture and fruit-growing. After graduating from Jefferson Medical College, young Dr. Warder took up a medical practice at Cincinnati. But about the middle of the century he moved to part of the old Harrison homestead near North Bend. During the 1850's, Warder edited the *Western Horticultural Review, Horticultural Review*, and *Botanical Magazine* and was active in the Cincinnati Natural History Society. His interests em-

[21] *Proc. A.A.A.S.* XXXVII; in pamphlet form, Salem Pub. and Printing Co., 1889, p. 366.

braced medical science, astronomy, meteorology, and the study of plant life. His fame, however, was acquired in fruit culture; he became an officer many times and president once of the American Pomological Society. He held offices in a number of influential associations and was the recipient of many honors. His articles in the *American Journal of Horticulture* won for him a national reputation. In 1871 he began serving six years as a member of the Ohio State Board of Agriculture. He wrote several books, including *Hedges and Evergreens; A Complete Manual for the Cultivation, Pruning and Management of All Plants Suitable for American Hedging*, and *American Pomology*, on apple culture. The great honor of his life came in his appointment as one of the commissioners to the International Exhibition in Vienna. Rossiter Raymond was another of the commissioners. Warder had always been interested in forestry, but it was the type of amateur forestry fostered by practical farmers. In Europe Dr. Warder came in contact with the actualities of professional forestry. He wrote for the United States government the first volume of the *Report of the Commissioners*, treating principally the subject of forests and forestry.[22] Published in 1876, the volume set forth clearly and correctly, Fernow said, the methods employed in the forests and forestry of Germany.

At Chicago on September 10, 1875, Dr. Warder, Henry H. McAfee of Iowa, and a group of about three dozen members formed the American Forestry Association. It was Dr. Warder's organization, and he became its first and only president. McAfee, author of "Forest-Tree Culture," published by *Patron's Helper*, December 7, 1876, became the vice-president. No constitution was adopted, but a committee on correspondence and statistics headed by T. J. Allan of Nebraska and composed of thirty-five members, was formed. At the Philadelphia Centennial of 1876 Dr. Warder's American Forestry Association strengthened itself by absorbing another small organization, the American Forestry Council. The latter was an outgrowth of the memorial of the American Association for the Advancement of Science to the federal and state governments asking protection for forest resources. On September 7-8, 1876, at Sea Grove, Cape May Point, New Jersey, the council had met to find only three members in attendance. Discussions of the need for forestry in America at the Farmers' Clubs of the American Institute had convinced a few believers, particularly George May Powell, that forestry in America was important. The three attendants of the council hurriedly invited their friends to the sessions, regardless of their qualifications or interest. Only about twenty persons responded. These ad-

[22] *D.A.B.* XIX, pp. 444-445; also *Proc. Twenty-seventh Session Am. Pomological Soc.*, Sept. 12-13, 1901; Otto Juettner, *Daniel Drake and His Followers*, Harvey Pub. Co., Cincinnati, 1909. Warder is remembered in botany for having been the first to name the timber catalpa (*Catalpa Speciosa*) of the Mississippi Valley states and to distinguish it botanically from the related tree of the Gulf states.

dressed a communication to Dr. Warder's American Forestry Association meeting in the Judges' Pavilion upon the grounds of the Centennial Exhibition at Philadelphia, September 15, and suggested that the two organizations consolidate. Committees of each were appointed to merge the two organizations. Furthermore, a committee within the American Forestry Association was appointed to draft and report on a constitution and by-laws. Dr. Hough read his paper, "The Duty of Governments in the Preservation of Forests." In 1876, the rider to the annual appropriation for the Department of Agriculture was obtained which, as has been explained, placed Dr. Hough in the Department as a special agent in forest investigations. Had Dr. Warder's organization done no more than help to bring about the creation of the special agency in the Department of Agriculture, it would have more than justified its existence. But at the 1876 centennial the American Association for the Advancement of Science accomplished more. Thomas Meehan, the distinguished American horticulturist, presented his view that tree culture and tree planting should be carried out primarily by private enterprise and not by the government. Furthermore, Burnet Landreth, chief of the Bureau of Agriculture of the Centennial Exposition, described his memorable experimental tree plantings begun in Virginia in 1871 and designed to cover seven thousand acres. So noteworthy did a plantation of 300 or more acres become that Fernow in an official report of 1886 mentioned it as a leading example of forest planting and management in the United States. Young Landreth evidently was associated with his father, David Landreth, in at least part of this work which was located in Lancaster County, Virginia. White pine, chestnut, catalpa, and other species were included. Before the early American Forestry Association, plantations, some of them experimental, in black locust, black walnut, cottonwood, persimmon, larch, and sumac as a possible material for tanning preparation, were described.[23]

Another contribution of Warder's association was made at its January 1880 meeting at Washington, D.C., when a memorial was adopted which recommended to congress that a commission be appointed to obtain information on the subject of forestry in Europe. On July 1, 1881, Dr. George B. Loring, formerly of the state board of agriculture of Massachusetts, was appointed United States commissioner of agriculture. Dr. Hough then was sent to Europe to collect the desired information and to observe forestry methods there.

Loring took back into office three men who had been previously dismissed. One was apparently hostile to Hough and while Hough was in Europe turned Loring's mind against him. "I was received coldly, and

[23] See the account of the Association's meetings in *Proc. Am. For. Cong.*, Cincinnati and Montreal meetings of 1882, *op. cit.*, p. 36. Also "Report of the Chief of the Division of Forestry," *Report of the Commissioner of Agriculture for 1886, op. cit.*, p. 171.

treated in a most insolent manner," wrote Hough later. "For the next two years nearly we had no communication worth mentioning upon any subject, although I was in daily attendance at the department. I received no instructions. I made a report of my journey [through the chief clerk] —but this still lies in manuscript [December 28, 1884]. My third report was withheld from Congress until he was compelled to send it in, by the events in Cincinnati. . . ."[24]

The "events in Cincinnati" were the proceedings of the first American Forestry Congress, an organization at its start entirely distinct from Warder's American Forestry Association. This congress, Fernow believed, launched the real forestry movement of North America. Although the American Forestry Association retained Warder as president, McAfee as secretary, and Hough became its treasurer at its Washington meeting, Warder's association did not survive beyond 1882.

A month and a half before the American Forestry Congress assembled at Cincinnati, the organizers of the congress invited members of the American Forestry Association to participate in the deliberations. Dr. Warder became a leading figure of the congress. The initiators of the congress did not plan to unite at Cincinnati the congress and Warder's association. Evidently it was believed that forestry interests in America could support two organizations. Although many of the members of Warder's association participated in the ceremonies and discussions at Cincinnati, not until the American Forestry Congress had met and it was realized that the congress had been a failure did a real movement take foot to unite all forestry organizations. During the year 1882 another American Forestry Congress gathered at Montreal. Unification of all organized forestry was a dominant force at the Montreal congress, and in response the merger was effected.

Even after this the American Forestry Association met on June 29, 1882, at Rochester, New York. The meeting took place the day before the annual meeting of the American Nurserymen's Association. Warder's forestry association was reorganized, a constitution was adopted, and George B. Loring was named president. It remained for Fernow, Hough, and William Little of Montreal to persuade Warder that there should not be two antagonistic forestry organizations in America. On September 14, 1882, Warder informed the members of his association to remit their annual dues to Dr. Charles Mohr of Mobile, Alabama. Mohr at that time was treasurer of the American Forestry Congress.

[24] Hough's third report was published in 1882, although evidently 1880-1881 were also considered in the volume. Miss Jacobsen, *op. cit.*, devoting several paragraphs to discussing these reports, says that the second report in a revised form included statistics of 1879. The third report was planned to contain Hough's practical program for scientific forest management, and, published only as a House miscellaneous document (38, 47 Cong., 1 sess.) with no separates for distribution, encountered more opposition. He prepared four articles for a fourth report which evidently formed a basis for the report published when Nathaniel H. Egleston was in charge of the forestry division.

Hough, Warder, Little, and Fernow each knew what real forestry practice involved. Fernow regarded Hough's first report on forestry as "open to criticism," and he was not alone in this belief. C. S. Sargent or W. H. Brewer(?), in the *Nation* of January 1879, also criticized the work. Despite its faults, Fernow believed that the report was "by far the best and most useful publication of its kind on Forestry in this country."

In 1876, at Montreal, James Little, father of William, had published a valuable study of "The Timber Supply Question of Canada and the United States." Warder's forestry knowledge requires no further explanation. If when the two forestry organizations were merged he remained "obdurate," as he is said to have done, he did so mainly on the basis that his organization was first in point of time. Fernow later described Warder as the "Nestor of forestry in this Country [who had] no small share in educating his fellow citizens to the needs of forestry in the Ohio Valley."

The American Forestry Congress which met at Cincinnati in April 1882 founded a permanent forestry organization which endures to the present time; and equally as important, it started the organization of the forestry movement internationally. This was the first of three important meetings held in North America that year. But Fernow said to John Birkinbine, "How weak the Cincinnati organization was, may be inferred from the fact that none of the officers then elected were present. The president [George B. Loring] arrived on the second day and did not stay over for the final session. . . . Yet the Cincinnati meeting has, indirectly at least, done good in giving the impetus to the formation of several local associations. . . ."[25]

Early in 1882 Fernow had been working diligently at Slatington, managing the forest property of Cooper, Hewitt and Company. His forestry activities occupied most of his time. He also studied the English language. On March 13 Raymond wrote him, "I shall forward to you in a day or two Hough's Forestry Rept. franked to me in your care." He read them carefully but learned that the "two voluminous publications,

[25] B. E. Fernow, "The National Forestry Congress," *Journal of U.S. Assn. of Charcoal Iron Workers* III, 3, 1882, pp. 126-132, at p. 233; see also "Appendix. Report of Committee appointed to attend the American Forestry Congress at Cincinnati, Ohio," *Report of the Fruit Growers' Association of Ontario*, for the year 1882, printed by order of the Legislative Assembly, Toronto, 1883, pp. 145-165, wherein were listed 85 papers, abstracts of several addresses, including the communication from Royal Chief Forester Richard Von Steuben of the German Empire, and accounts of the proceedings of the Forestry Congress April 25-28, each prepared by William Saunders, D. W. Beadle, and William Brown, delegates from the province of Ontario. See the same volume, "General Report on Forestry," pp. 181-283, for the text of many of the more important addresses presented at the 1882 American Forestry Congress meetings at Cincinnati and Montreal. D. W. Beadle was secretary of the Ontario Fruit Growers' Association.

had not made much impression." His account of the congress began thus:

> But, in 1881 one of those accidents, which move the world, occurred to advance at least the popular interest in forestry. It is a curious fact that a historic event of highest national importance furnished a basis for the popular movement on behalf of forestry.
>
> The centennial celebration of the surrender [of Cornwallis] at Yorktown, which practically ended the war of the Rebellion—brought as guests of the nation seven descendants of the Great German General Baron von Steuben, the man who had done so much to bring the continental army to efficiency. Among these seven was an official of the Prussian Forest Department—an Oberförster, not the *chief* forester, as the newspapers had it, but *a* chief forester of whom there are several hundred.
>
> This forester found the same difficulty that I had experienced, in explaining what he represented. In Cincinnati, in the office of Judge Warren Higley . . . Oberförster von Steuben explained in the presence of several gentlemen what forestry meant and pointed out the need of it in the United States. . . .[26]

Speaking of the occasion in another historical address, Fernow explained that he had no doubt that Baron von Steuben answered the questions, "What is a forester and what is forestry?" by saying that forests could "be used in several ways. You can either exploit them or you can manage them."

> Exploiting means to take all the cream, all the useful material you can find, and leave the rest to perdition. That is exactly what has been done on this continent ever since the first settlers came. For forest destruction is the beginning of civilization.
>
> In a forest country it is necessary first in order to have farm lands to remove or destroy the timber. Therefore, there is no fault to be found with those who have been exploiting the forests, who have burned them in order to get rid of them, and to get the land for food production.
>
> The forester, then, probably will have told his questioner that it is possible to take any forest and treat it in such a way that it will reproduce a wood crop. In other words, forestry is nothing different from agriculture except in the crop which it grows. Forestry uses the soil for the purpose of getting a wood crop.
>
> And the gentleman very likely pointed out what a valuable material wood is, how from the cradle to the coffin we are surrounded by it. He may have shown the enormous quantity used, and dilated on the fact that in spite of the substitution of iron and steel, stone and cement, every year the use of wood per capita was increasing, and is increasing even to the present day.
>
> In other words, he would have explained what forestry is, namely the application of scientific methods in the production and reproduction of wood crops.[27]

26 "The Birth of a Forest Policy," *op. cit.*

27 Address by Fernow to the Canadian Forestry Association, Victoria, British Columbia, Sept. 4-6, 1912, and presented in the report of the 14th annual meeting, Feb. 3, 1913.

The *Cincinnati Commercial* on April 26, 1882, described the importance of Richard von Steuben's visit. It published his letter congratulating the American Forestry Congress on its enterprise, extending well-wishes, and saying that during his stay in the United States he had discussed the rapidly growing necessity to introduce a regulated government of the forests to prevent future calamity. Von Steuben had been pleased especially that Secretary of the Interior Carl Schurz had honored him by consulting him on forestry. In the opinion of the *Cincinnati Commercial* the reading of the letter[28] from von Steuben was a highlight of the congress's proceedings. It was even more important than Fernow's paper on the "Development of a Forest Policy in Germany," which he read before Section A (devoted to the "Uses of Forests").

The *Cincinnati Enquirer* commented, "To Judge Warren Higley belongs the honor of suggesting the Forestry Congress. During a ride with the von Steubens he became so interested in their conversation, about what is done in Germany to protect and cultivate the forests that it occurred to him that something similar might be done in this country."

On at least two later occasions Fernow insisted that the motive which instigated the congress savored at first of politics by providing a method to boom the candidacy of one seeking to become mayor of Cincinnati. It is evidently true that in December 1881 Alderman J. M. Ray, at the request of an unknown person interested in forestry, "laid before the Board of Aldermen a communication asking that body to take some action with reference to the holding of such a Congress in Cincinnati. . . ." A committee which failed to accomplish anything was appointed. Again several months later the matter came before the board. Independently John Simpkinson, Colonel W. L. De Beck, and a group including Judge Higley formed an organization. They, in turn, enlisted the aid of Dr. John A. Warder. Invitations were sent to dignitaries of national and state prominence—President Arthur, members of the cabinet, senators, congressmen, governors and mayors. On April 19 the *Enquirer* editorially announced the approach of the congress, informing its readers that such notables as Dr. Warder, B. G. Northrup,[29] Franklin B. Hough, C. V. Riley, and Robert Douglas would be present.

Sunday, April 23, the paper announced that "the Committee having charge of the great National Forestry Congress have about completed their laborious task, and only await for the huge doors of the grand Music Hall to open at ten o'clock" the following Tuesday. President Simpkinson went to Washington in the interest of the congress. At the general executive committee meeting held April 23, Judge Warren

[28] A paper by Baron Richard von Steuben on "Advantages Resulting from the Preservation of Forests" was presented at a general session of the congress.

[29] Sometimes spelled Northrop.

Higley presided in his place. Thirty thousand tickets were distributed from Maine to California and from Canada to Florida. A ceremonial spade of steel and silver, decorated with mottos and description in gold lettering and with its handle embellished with ribbons and a buckeye, was prepared.[30] The grandstand of Eden Park was decked out with flags and bunting and a portrait of George Washington in anticipation of the tree planting ceremony on Arbor Day, inaugurated that year in Ohio. The planting of forest groves to honor presidents, authors, pioneers, statesmen, and special memorials, enlivened the plans. The Music Hall was decorated with national flags alternating with a white flag which bore the congress's insignia, a green oak leaf and acorn. Huge signs saying "Welcome Foresters" were hung out. Fernow described the congress as "a grand affair of five days' duration, the city in bunting, with orators at the street corners and in lecture halls; and on Thursday many school children marched with music to Eden Park to plant memorial trees—the first arbor day in schools." Although Fernow clung to his view that the congress originated from "small municipal politics," he said, "It must be admitted that the enterprise . . . was really furthered by genuinely patriotic citizens."

Some facts corroborate an imputation of political motivation behind the congress. The real organization, however, was sincere in its enthusiasm for forestry and sponsored the congress for this reason alone. April 25, at the grand opening of the congress, an audience of only 250 persons "scattered among the 4,500 seats in the Music Hall" was greeted by the surprising news "that but for the dishonorable conduct of the chairman of the Finance Committee of the Ohio House [of Representatives] who locked up the bill providing for an appropriation to pay the expenses of the Forestry Congress, and prevented its being brought before the house, the committee would not have been obliged to call upon the citizens of Cincinnati for contributions. . . ." That the congress became a municipal occasion was further shown by the announcement that the $3,000 expenses of the congress would be met by the citizens of Cincinnati and not by the delegates. Furthermore, at the evening meeting of April 26, in the absence of Mayor Means, General E. F. Noyes introduced General Durbin Ward who welcomed with great pleasure to the "Queen City of the West the Knights of Forestry. . . . In our Garden of Eden, our Eden Park," he said, "on Thursday we hope

[30] The ceremonial spade was "of steel, thickly coated with silver. On its face is etched in bold medieval, but distinct, lettering: 'From churlish wreck and wrong, our Prayer; for bloom and beauty everywhere'. . . . On the back, inclosed in a wreath of oak branches, appears the inscription: 'The service and the loyalty we owe the earth, by doing, pays us back.' An adaptation of a thought from Shakespeare. The lettering and decoration appear in dead gold on a burnished silver background. Up the handle is carved, 'Forestry Congress, Cincinnati, Ohio, April 25 to 29, 1882.' The handle, where not covered with the ribbon, is decorated with the buckeye." W. H. Venable wrote a "Forestry Song" and dedicated it to the congress.

to initiate a movement in miniature of the great scheme of replanting our denuded hills and valleys by planting groves of trees for each of our Presidents, and to the memory of . . . many poets, orators, and statesmen." Any convention in which Dr. Warder took part might well have been expected to stress scientific, ornamental, and practical features. In addition to his active interest in agricultural societies, he had long given attention to matters of sanitation and hygiene. Most appropriately, as a background for a forestry congress, however, he had been a landscape gardener of some prominence, had helped to landscape the beautiful Spring Grove Cemetery, and suggested and designed a park system for Cincinnati.

President Harrison had discovered the catalpa growing wild at Vincennes, Indiana. The grove in Harrison's honor, therefore, was catalpas. To honor Washington they planted the southern oak; Jackson and Polk were honored with hickories; Pierce with sugar maple; Hayes with white elm; and Lincoln and Garfield with red oak. Other species may have honored other presidents. Less significant tree planting ceremonies than the Arbor Day exercises took place at Garfield Park on the second day, April 26, and on the afternoon of the fourth day at Washington Park. Each ceremony was accompanied by addresses from important officials.

Wednesday morning, April 26, Ohio's governor Charles Foster addressed the Forestry Congress in general session, and among the notables present were General Cassius M. Clay, son of Henry Clay of Kentucky and a speaker at other occasions, and George W. Minier of Minier, Illinois, who later presented a paper to the congress on "Timbers in Illinois."

Two thousand persons attended the evening session on April 26, when the "somber looks of so many botanists, entomologists, and professors of agricultural science [were] relieved by the more graceful and handsome members of the Ladies Commission." This elaborate Forestry Congress did much to curry popular favor for the forestry movement, especially in Ohio. But from the standpoint of real forestry progress it accomplished little.

Fernow represented Birkinbine's *Journal of United States Association of Charcoal Iron Workers* and reported to it on the meetings.[31] On April 27 Rossiter Raymond wrote to Fernow and asked that a private report on the meetings be furnished him. Fernow was impressed by the dearth of woodlot owners, lumber operators, and owners of extensive forest tracts. Perhaps to him the most valuable contribution of the congress lay in being introduced to responsible leaders who had succeeded in securing "a promising and healthy start . . . for this new seedling in the national nursery of culture"—Dr. Warder, who presided

[31] III, 3, 1882, pp. 126-132.

over Section B of the congress devoted to the reading of papers on "Conservation and Practical Forestry"; Dr. William Saunders, who presided over Section C, devoted to the general subject of "Beneficial and Injurious Influences of Forestry"; Nathaniel H. Egleston, who was presiding officer of Section D, on "Forestry Education"; and surely Fernow became acquainted with Dr. Hough, who was presiding officer, and William Little, secretary of Section A, before the members of which Fernow read his paper, "Historical Sketches of the Development of the Forest Policy in Germany."

Although it seems that Fernow attained little prominence as the congress's only delegate who was also a professionally educated forester, the fact that immediately after the Montreal congress began he sprang into the limelight indicates that during and immediately following the Cincinnati congress he began to enjoy a wide circle of acquaintances among the delegates. William Saunders, D. W. Beadle, and William Brown, all from Ontario, were delegates; Little and A. T. Drummond were leaders of the constituency from Quebec. Professor Beadle, from St. Catharines, Ontario, on behalf of the Canadian delegates, may have invited the congress to hold its next meetings that year in the Dominion at Montreal. On the day after "Arbor Day," April 27, Beadle urged: "It has been a serious problem with us how to interest the general public in the subject of forestry, so as to secure the preservation of what yet remains and the replanting of places that have been needlessly denuded of trees. But you have taught us a lesson we shall strive to learn to our profit. Yesterday will not soon be forgotten by us. You have brought out your Senators, legislators, Governors, lawyers, clergymen, merchants and artizans, your wealth and beauty, to celebrate the planting of trees and lend their influence to the promotion of your Association. We thank you also that you propose to hold your next meeting within our Dominion. . . . I know that the residents of Montreal will exert themselves. . . ."

Nathaniel H. Egleston had wanted the next meeting to go to Niagara Falls, New York, to permit the congress to share in the movement to create an International Park there. Dr. Hough informed them that New York authorities were cooperating with Canadian authorities with a view to purchasing the shore lands of the two governments. But that year the American Association for the Advancement of Science and the Society for the Promotion of Agricultural Science were meeting in Montreal, August 21-22, 1882. An executive committee was appointed to choose the next meeting place, and the choice of Montreal was approved by the congress on the fifth day of the sessions. William Little, appointed a vice-president for the Quebec district, immediately became the dominant figure of the proposed Montreal congress. When he returned to his home in Montreal, one of his first actions was to enlist the help of the Dominion government at Ottawa, authorities of which referred him to H. G. Joly whose interest in forestry was known by virtue of his articles in Canadian newspapers. On the first day of the Montreal congress, August 21, William Little would present with his compliments to the "Honorable H. G. Joly" a copy of *The Elements of Forestry* written by Franklin Benjamin Hough and published that year by Robert Clarke and Company of Cincinnati, a book which Ralph Sheldon Hosmer has said, "stands as one of the first modern books on forestry in the English language."[32] Joly would become a presiding officer of the Montreal congress.

While in Cincinnati Dr. Hough ended his week at the forestry congress sessions by a visit with Robert Clarke at his home in Glendale. On Saturday morning, April 29, the day of and evidently before the congress's final ceremonies at Lincoln Park, Fernow, Little, Verplanck Colvin, George Vasey, and others of the delegates, under the guidance of Dr. J. A. Warder and Adolph Leué, were driven about and shown many points of local interest around Cincinnati. Hough was in the party for at least part of the journey. He had taken a leading role in the deliberations of the congress. On April 21, at Washington, he had finished his paper to be offered at the congress at Cincinnati, and on the next day asked Commissioner of Agriculture Loring if he should go to Cincinnati, where he was scheduled to give the address. To his amazement the commissioner replied he should go at his own expense. Hough learned that Dr. Loring had told Benjamin Silliman that Hough had "brought home [from Europe] a few German books that [he] could not read and that that was all that [his] journey amounted to."[33] Hough left Washington by train and at Cumberland, Maryland, "took a palace and sleeping car for the rest of the way." Arriving on Monday morning, April 24, he was "introduced to a great number of persons, all of whom," he observed, "appeared much pleased to meet me. In fact it appears that I am much better known and appreciated here than at Washington." The next morning he and Loring were named on the committee on permanent organization, and he "carried [his] points every time." On April 27 Hough read his paper "Forestry of the Future." Fernow commented:

> We do not see but what national, state or local government here might, with perfect consistency, repurchase waste lands unfit for agricultural purposes with a view to [re]forestation; as in Germany, where several million dollars appear in the national appropriation bill for this purpose. The policy is of quite recent date. . . . [While] impetus to action will come mainly through private interest, we believe that in this one question the national government, as owner of large tracts of woodlands, is called to precede with good example in the management of the same.

[32] "Franklin B. Hough, Pioneer in Forestry," *op. cit.*, p. 263.
[33] Extracts from Hough's diary, State Dept. of Education archives, Albany, N.Y.

Fernow was especially pleased with the enthusiasm of the members of the congress and with the fact that Hough agreed to publish *The American Journal of Forestry*, a publication devoted to the interests of forest tree planting, the formation and care of woodlands, and ornamental planting. While this *Journal* lasted only one year and its publication did not begin until after the Montreal congress, it interpreted the valuable year 1882-1883. Hough's membership in the American Philosophical Society, indeed his memberships in thirty-eight historical, statistical, and scientific organizations, added prestige to his leadership, which was assumed naturally because he was the first chief of the forestry division of the U.S. Department of Agriculture.

Fifteen states were represented at the congress. Some were accredited delegates of the state authorities, notably, Nathaniel H. Egleston from Massachusetts, who in 1883 was to succeed Hough as chief of the forestry division. Fully eighty-seven papers, perhaps many more than this number, were presented, a few read only by titles, and of them Fernow said, "Among the papers were some most valuable monographs, results of long research and thorough study, that will be of lasting value to the literature of forestry. The work of the botanists excelled, especially in treatises upon a single species or the distribution of a genus or description of the forest flora of certain sections."

Mohr's treatise on "Southern Pine," A. T. Drummond's study of the "Distribution of Canadian Trees," F. L. Harvey's "Arboreal Flora of Arkansas," Dr. George Vasey's "Distribution of Conifers in the United States," and William Saunders' study of "Forest Insects" were especially praiseworthy. From one state, Michigan, came three important papers: "Forests of Michigan" by V. M. Spalding, "Useful Trees of Michigan" by W. J. Beal, and "Roadside Planting for Utility" by Charles W. Garfield. Among several papers submitted by Dr. Warder was one, prepared with D. L. and Joseph F. James, on "Woody Plants of Ohio." From Texas was T. V. Munson's paper on the trees of that state. J. G. Knapp of Limona, Florida, presented a paper on "Profitable Trees for Florida." Among papers from the far west was Dr. Robert E. C. Stearns's on "Forest Tree-Culture in California." The papers from eastern states were proportionately not so numerous, although John S. Hicks' consideration of "Culture of the Locust on Long Island" was presented. Papers from the central western states showed where forestry work was most active. Robert Douglas of Waukegan, Illinois, discussed "Planting by Railroads"; former governor R. W. Furnas of Brownville, "Sylva and Plantations of Nebraska"; James T. Allan[34] of Omaha, "Cheap Hardy Trees for the Prairies"; and J. L. Budd of Ames, "Iowa's Work in Tree Planting." In other sections of the nation,

[34] Frequently this name appears as "T. J. Allan" and occasionally is spelled as "Allen."

small forest plantations on lands unfit for agriculture were thriving. To learn what trees to plant and how to plant them, and to be informed of financial returns from planted areas, enthused the delegates from the beginning of the congress. Nearly every aspect of forestry development to that time was discussed. Fernow advocated the establishment of forest stations to "gather the statistical data and institute experiments necessary to establish the elements upon which a science of forestry, adapted to the conditions and needs of this country, may be built," especially inducing farmers and owners to observe locally the conditions of woodlot growth. The results should be coordinated at a central station. But of the congress's proceedings, he confessed, "The real science of forestry, questions pertaining to the management of forests, effects of particular measures to be adopted in the management, proper methods of propagation, suitable times of rotation for divers species and conditions, et cetera, did not find much consideration."

On the economic side, two papers or addresses were especially interesting—the account by the first arrival at the congress, William Little, who told how he and his father, James Little, had struggled alone to protect the Canadian white pine supply. The Littles were wealthy lumbermen, among the first to export square pine and oak timber to the United States and Great Britain. For many years they supplied timber to Canadian contractors to provide wood for the British navy. The other paper of special economic significance was "Forest and Waters Supply" by Verplanck Colvin, superintendent of the Adirondack Mountain survey. At this congress Hough succeeded in procuring endorsement of a resolution which favored setting aside by legislative action a great forest preserve of state lands in the Adirondacks "to preserve such forests as are valuable conservatories of moisture and important as reserves of timber." There was also presented a paper on "Forest Reserves at the Head Waters of the Ohio."

The absence of two important figures in forestry was noticeable. Neither Secretary Schurz nor Charles Sprague Sargent was present. Schurz's interest in the forests was mainly protective. He waged a relentless war against timber thieves and depredators. Forestry legislation was to him a means of protection, regulation, and conservation.[35]

Fernow and Schurz could not have disagreed on the desirability of laying foundations for a United States forest policy modelled after appropriate time-tested features of European forest policies. Fernow, however, aware of his on-the-site unfamiliarity with American forest regions, aware that he lacked acquaintance with the government's forest problems in undisposed areas of the public domain, had not presumed

[35] C. M. Fuess, *Carl Schurz, Reformer*, Dodd, Mead & Co., New York, 1932, pp. 267-268. In 1882 H. M. Teller of Colorado became Secretary of the Interior. In 1885, under the administration of Grover Cleveland, L. Q. C. Lamar was to be the secretary. In 1888 Secretary Vilas was to occupy the office, and in 1889-1893 John W. Noble.

in his address to the Cincinnati congress to outline a forest policy for the United States. Rather, he had presented a sketch of the historical development of the forest policy in Germany, a subject with which he had some scholarly acquaintance. Trusting that among the delegates his paper might stimulate a "desire to study more closely the history of this branch of economic sciences in other countries, and that this great republic," he said, "may so avoid the mistakes and profit by the successful methods of the countries of the old world," he had chosen an audience of "patriots" interested "in the preservation of America's forests," and his announced purpose was: "that the most distant descendant of the Pilgrim father may never lack the shade of the spreading oak to see with prophetic vision still greater prosperity in the future than was beheld by his forefather."[36]

This address, descriptive of the history and management features of the German forest policy, was important for its explanation of the evolution of state-owned and privately-owned forests in Germany, as distinguished from and in addition to the communally-owned forests of Charlemagne's time. The nature and some of the procedures of management of state-owned forests were described, and the matter of government regulation of privately-owned forests was said to have practically ceased except in those instances where the interests of public safety required supervision. Quite obviously, this address anticipated Fernow's later preparation of books on the economics and history of forestry in Europe and other countries of the world.

Charles Sprague Sargent was not present at the American Forestry Congress, although at the Cincinnati congress he was appointed a member of a committee to memorialize state legislatures to create forestry commissions. In 1882 Sargent was invited by Spencer Baird of the Smithsonian Institution to prepare his great *Silva of North America*. During these years Sargent was still busily engaged completing a number of tasks incident to his "Report on the Forests of North America" for the United States census. Among these was his participation in the Northern Transcontinental Survey in the course of which glaciers were found. From this discovery emerged a strong movement which later culminated in the setting apart of Glacier National Park. During the years 1882-1883 Sargent was very active in stirring up favor for establishing national parks in the western mountain forest regions. The American Forestry Congress learned of his work from several sources.

At the Cincinnati congress, John Robinson, author of some important botanical treatises, a former student at Harvard, and later prominent in botanical and forestry contributions of the Essex Institute, the

[36] *The American Journal of Forestry, op. cit.*, pp. 193 and 254; also see an account of Fernow's address in the *Cincinnati Enquirer*, Thursday, April 27, 1882.

Massachusetts State Horticultural Society, and State Board of Agriculture, supplied a paper on the work of the Arnold Arboretum. At the opening session on the morning of April 26, Nathaniel H. Egleston from Williamstown, Massachusetts, concluded his address to the Cincinnati congress by describing Sargent's "garden of acclimation, where already [were] gathered thousands of trees from all parts of our own country and from the other side of the Atlantic, with a view to the practical study of their growth, and their adaptation to different soils and climates. By its publication the Arboretum," continued Egleston, "has diffused throughout the country much valuable information in regard to tree culture, and influenced the legislation in several of our States upon this important subject. . . . Specimens of the various woods of the country have been gathered and a great deal of information in regard to their habits of growth and value for different purposes. Maps have been constructed showing the amount of timber that has been cut off, and the amount now standing in each State and Territory. Maps have also been constructed which indicate at once to the eye the extent of forest destruction by fires."

At the Montreal congress, Dr. John A. Warder, in a paper on "Tree Planting for Railroads," described a plan whereby Robert Douglas & Sons, "the largest and most successful raisers of forest-tree seedlings in the United States," agreed to establish western forest plantations of catalpa, ailanthus, and other species. Warder alluded to a contract with an individual, similar to one used by railroad companies, by which from a 560 acre tract 60 acres were to be allocated as an experimental ground where were to be "tested trees of several varieties, to be selected by Professor Sargent. . . ." It was believed that this plantation would "soon lead to the formation of others, both by the railroad companies and by individuals, or corporations chartered to plant and own timber lands in the prairie States."

The Cincinnati congress, more than gathering together a knowledge of forestry at work in the United States, established an organization and an organized movement. A "novel feature" of the congress was that the entire continent was divided into districts, and for each district a vice-president of the association was elected. Two districts were created from the provinces of Canada.

The Canadian government was host to the American Forestry Congress which met at Montreal.[37] While this lacked the festive Arbor Day and memorial tree planting ceremonies of the Cincinnati congress, Fernow complimented the Montreal congress as "a dignified, well-

[37] *Journal of U. S. Ass'n of Charcoal Iron Workers* III, 4 (1882), pp. 223-226; *Proc. Am. For. Cong. for 1882, op. cit.*; *Report of the Fruit Growers' Ass'n of Ontario for 1882, op. cit.*, pp. 165-283; *Montreal Herald*, August 21-26, 1882; *Forestry Bulletin* 1, *op. cit.*; extracts from Hough's diary, *op. cit.* Fernow's accounts of the congress are found in the first two citations.

attended, representative meeting." Canadians thus far knew little of organized forestry. That the Dominion and provincial governments responded cordially to the presence of the forestry congress in Canada was soon shown by the number of official representatives who attended the sessions. The Honourable Mr. Joly,[38] in his opening address, told that some ten years before "Mr. Levesque Daillebout was instrumental in starting a Forestry Association in [Quebec], one of the laws incumbent on its members being that they were bound to plant a certain number of trees every year. But unfortunately this association did not live very long." Later in the congress Joly told of seeing in the newspapers "that the western railways have started the culture of trees on their own account; the St. Paul, Minneapolis and Manitoba Railway is reported," he said, "as having appointed a superintendent of tree culture, who has just contracted for three hundred thousand trees, and most of the roads west of the Mississippi and Missouri rivers have also begun to raise trees, in order to insure a supply of ties, and for other purposes." Both to preserve the North American heritage of existing timber resources and to provide new forests by tree culture (considerable experimental knowledge of which he had accumulated and published), Joly held out hope for the future of Canadian forests. "Having no School of Forestry in Canada," he told one of his audiences, "we must educate ourselves; we have got books written on the subject by eminent and practical men, and we have got, always before our eyes, the great book of Nature."

The subject of Joly's opening address was "The Study of Forestry as an Important Contribution to Practical Education." His emergence to the front ranks of the American forestry movement's leadership was immediate, and before the Montreal congress was concluded he was to be chosen first vice-president of the American Forestry Congress. His paper "Forest Tree Culture" was to be one of the most important presented at Montreal. Principally he had experimented with black walnut, oak, elm, maple, ash, tamarack, Russian pine, fir, and poplar. "In selecting forest trees for planting," he urged, "the first consideration ought to be the nature of the soil where they are to be planted; if the soil is not favourable to one kind of tree, do not waste your time in planting it there; you will find another tree that will suit the soil. After paying all due deference to soil and climate, you must be guided in your selection of a particular kind of tree: 1st. By the value of the timber. 2nd. The greater or lesser ease and certainty with which the tree can be grown. 3rd. The rate of growth."

Commissioner of Agriculture Loring did not arrive for the opening session of the congress. On the evening of the second day he delivered

[38] See Alain Joly de Lotbinière, "Sir Henri Joly de Lotbinière . . . ," *Forest and Outdoors,* March 1940, p. 83.

his presidential address at Queen's Hall. He was continued in the office of president, and the second vice-presidency went to Dr. Warder. The dividing of offices between Canadian and United States citizens was carried out also in the position of secretary: William Little became corresponding secretary and Dr. Hough recording secretary. Joseph S. Fay of Massachusetts continued as treasurer.

Charles Mohr, Alabama botanist, and Hough arrived at Montreal on August 17 and immediately communicated with William Little and Stewart Thayne, an Ottawa resident who was to read to the congress a paper on the "Forest Economy of Canada." Asked to prepare an address to be given at one of the first sessions, Hough, on Sunday, August 20, went to the home of James Little, and, while consulting with Dr. Warder and William Little, Fernow, Mohr, and Thayne called. Together they discussed the next day's business and the proposed merger of the congress and Warder's forestry association. The American Forestry Association, at its June meeting at Rochester, had appointed a committee, consisting of D. W. Beadle of Ontario, Norman J. Colman of Missouri, and E. Moody of New York, for the purpose. It remained, therefore, only for the congress "to negotiate the union," and so, after the preliminary arrangements were completed, Hough, at the opening session of the congress on the afternoon of August 21, moved that Mohr, Fernow, and William Saunders be appointed to effect the merger. The *Montreal Herald* reported that Dr. Warder then announced that his association had come prepared to cooperate with the congress and, in the interest of American forestry, to submit to whatever its committee recommended. Immediately thereafter the congress adjourned its general session until the next day when the meeting was to be composed in sections.

More than "one hundred gentlemen" had gathered at the opening session to hear Dr. Hough announce that section officers of the Cincinnati congress would be continued, and that Joly would serve as temporary president. Joly's nomination was enthusiastically ratified by the delegates, and in him Fernow was to find a staunch supporter of scientific forestry. For centuries the Joly family had owned a beautiful well-wooded estate or seigniory on the St. Lawrence River west of Quebec city. A dominant figure in governmental matters in Quebec province—for a while its prime minister—his appointment later as lieutenant governor of British Columbia, and his years of service in the Dominion parliament, greatly helped to advance the cause of forestry in Canada. Fernow often journeyed to Quebec and sailed up the St. Lawrence to visit this distinguished Canadian statesman at his beautiful chateau situated on high palisades overlooking the river.

Montreal welcomed the great "three Congresses," the American Forestry Congress, the Society for the Promotion of Agricultural Science, and the American Association for the Advancement of Science. In elaborately appointed quarters, a suite of rooms arranged for by William Little designated "Forestry Chambers" and located at 132 St. James Street, the congress held its section meetings and daily sessions. The meeting was honored by the presence of a number of official representatives of the Canadian provinces and the British Crown. Said Fernow:

> The Americans present were "shaded out" by a body of influential and well-to-do Canadians, representing the lumber interest, the statesmen, and the promoters of public welfare. . . . [We] should be mistaken if our Canadian friends do not in a short time eclipse their cousins over the line in the cultivation of this field of political economy.
>
> In its literary aspects the meeting carried with it the stamp which was impressed on it by the interests of the western treeless prairie states. Tree planting and arboriculture was the theme of most of the papers offered. The questions how to preserve and how to manage extant forest resources were hardly touched upon. The majority of the 61 papers [64 papers were entered for reading] may be characterized as laborious attempts to gather information without any critical discernment of what was important, what unimportant, what was required for the present, what may be left for the future to decide.

Sections were presided over by Warder, Hough, and William Saunders, who were all notably interested in tree planting. Fernow's implied criticism of a dominant tree planting and arboricultural interest characterizing the Montreal congress had been true also, though to a lesser extent, of the Cincinnati congress. On this account, perhaps, or for some other reason, Horace William Shaler Cleveland's paper read before Warder's Section B and entitled "The Culture and Management of our Native Forests, for Development as Timber or Ornamental Wood," received a somewhat belated recognition. The Ontario Fruit Growers' Association reported the full text of the address in its recital of the proceedings of the Cincinnati and Montreal meetings. Not, however, until 1884 did Fernow place an estimate on Cleveland's paper, possibly because he did not hear it read at Cincinnati. In his first *Forestry Bulletin* Fernow approved its contents as a "most able paper." Cleveland, a noted landscape gardener and author, born in Massachusetts, residing then in Chicago and later in Minneapolis, had confined himself to "the special features of forest growth which need to be regarded in the effort to develop and improve a native wood, wherever it may be. The planting and culture of an artificial forest is quite another affair," he said, "and I have made no allusion to it because my special object has been, if possible, to urge the fact, and arouse attention to it, that we still have vast resources of latent wealth on every side, susceptible of development by proper management, which we are everywhere suffering to run to waste. The work of planting and rearing artificial forests cannot indeed be urged too strongly, and there is no danger of its being overdone. . . ." He called for the inauguration of "an experimental or illustrative forest as a means of exciting public interest. . . . Let any State or city," he urged, "select a tract of woodland at some easily accessible point, and put it under a proper course of management, as an experimental forest. . . . A portion of it should be suffered to remain in its original unimproved condition. Another part should be improved as 'open park,' for the best development of individual trees in their fullest natural capacity of dignity and grace, and a third portion should be devoted to the production of timber by the process of thinning, pruning and proper culture. The progress of development could then be seen and watched from year to year in all its stages, and the demonstration thus afforded would touch the interest of every owner of a wood lot." While Fernow, like Cleveland, favored primarily the proper care and management of already available forest resources, he also strongly advocated the creation of artificial forests and the establishment of experimental tracts to study the adaptability and growth of economically valuable forest species.

Perhaps the first example of forest planting (as distinguished from tree planting) in the United States was that made by Robert Douglas of Waukegan, Illinois, for the Kansas City, Fort Scott & Gulf Railroad. One hundred and sixteen miles south of Kansas City, in the vicinity of Farlington, Kansas, he planted a several hundred acre plantation of catalpas and other species near the station of that railroad. In 1886 Orange Judd, editor of the *Prairie Farmer* and a leading promoter of agricultural science, traveled "hundreds of miles" to examine this forest plantation. The seedling trees on broken prairie soil were cared for until they were four feet or more high. Then they were sold for thirty dollars per acre, "each acre containing an average of about 2,500 trees —only 1¼ cents per tree!"

The 640 acre tract required a manager, but the impressive new fact was that "the trees take care of themselves." Orange Judd beheld on the tract one and one-half million trees, mostly catalpas, in vigorous growth varying from three to eight years old and from five to twenty-five feet high. In 1850 Robert Douglas, who prepared the ground and furnished and planted the trees, had read Andrew Jackson Downing's "Landscape Gardening and Ornamental Trees" and been impressed with the prophecy that trees on the North American continent would have to be planted for timber. Going west the year before, Douglas noticed that "after passing through a forest belt about three miles in width on the western shore of Lake Michigan, all the timber [he] traveled through in the next two thousand miles, if placed together, would fall far short of making another three miles belt. Consequently [he] came to the conclusion that the time had already come when they should be planted."[39] Douglas's papers before nurserymen's and forestry assemblages carried authority, and he had read abundantly from European literature. In the June 25, 1887, issue of Judd's *Prairie Farmer,* Douglas published an extensive article on "American Forestry."

At the Cincinnati congress Robert Douglas discussed railroad forest planting and the "Flora of the Black Hills"; Thomas Douglas, "Colorado Hardy Conifers in Cultivation"; and at the Montreal congress Robert Douglas presented papers on "Timber Trees of the Black Hills" and "Three Motion Plan of Planting." At the Montreal congress, Dr. Hough described an "Experimental Plantation of the Eucalyptus near Rome." Dr. Warder brought the subject of tree plantations closer home by describing in a paper, "Larchmere, a Plantation on Drifting Sands" situated on the shore of Lake Michigan, near Waukegan, Illinois, Douglas's home. This paper, along with an article by Warder entitled "Larch-Wood: a plan for tree-planting on the open prairies of Iowa and elsewhere," were among the first treatises published by Hough in his new *American Journal of Forestry.* What could be done on quarter sections or farms of an extent of 160 acres or more in planting groves, shelter-belts, windbreaks, and hedge-rows was illustrated by the work of Jesse W. Fell in northern Iowa and at Normal, Illinois.

Dr. Warder appears to have presented more papers than any other individual. Before the Cincinnati congress he had discussed "Grouping in Forestry," "Mixed Plantations," "Nurse Plants in Forests," "Cheap Trees as a Shelter for Better Kinds," and "Evils of Woods Pasture." His paper on "Measures of Locust Trees," as well as two of his three studies offered to the Montreal congress on "Black Locust Growths" and "Classification of Oaks," were in the spheres of economic and scientific forestry. The Cincinnati congress had merely adjourned to meet that year again in Montreal. Some studies, therefore, were continuations of former ones.

For instance, Dr. George Vasey's Montreal paper, "The Coniferous Trees of the United States and Canada," extended his Cincinnati disquisition, "Distribution of Conifers in the United States." Southern forests were the subject matter of two papers by Charles Mohr: "The Southern Pine," given at Cincinnati, and "The Distribution of Hardwood Trees in the Gulf Region of the Southern States," presented at Montreal. The region bounded on the east by the Chattahoochee river and on the west by the upper Trinity and lower Brazos rivers was considered in this discourse.

Special attention to the regional distribution and industrial uses of

[39] See *The Prairie Farmer,* June 25, 1887, pp. 407, 409; *Report of the Division of Forestry for 1885,* pp. 200-201, and *Report . . . for 1886,* p. 171 for Fernow's comments. See also *Garden and Forest,* Feb. 25, 1891, pp. 93ff.

economically valuable forest species, moreover, was continued at Montreal. Much thought was given to the white pine and spruce, much to poplar, ash, Russian mulberry, European larch, and other species. Dr. J. Beaufort Hurlbert of Ottawa considered those "Forest Trees Most Suitable for Streets, Lawns and Groves" and the "Climatological Range and Geographical Distribution of Forests, and the Climates Favourable to Them." Sereno Watson of the Gray Herbarium of Harvard University, who had spent some months in the far northwest investigating forest areas for the United States census, had supplied the Cincinnati congress with a paper on "The Poplars and Cottonwoods."

With much attention focused on foreign varieties introducible to northern latitudes, the cultivation of the black walnut, chestnut, and trees, shrubs, and vines suitable for domestic and ornamental purposes, did not go neglected. Professor William Brown of the Ontario agricultural college at Guelph submitted an important paper on "Tree and Shrub Introductions at the Ontario Experimental Farm." While studying comparative growth rates of oak, pine, spruce, and other species, Joly had interested himself in introducible tree varieties, and his demonstration that the black walnut could be grown in Quebec as far north as the St. Lawrence River valley added weight to the argument of Thomas Beall's paper that the black walnut's "cultivation under proper management" in Ontario "may reasonably be regarded as the most remunerative employment in connection with the cultivation of the soil."

Nor were the regions limited to eastern and northern United States and Canada. Prairie tree planting in the west for various purposes was the subject of several papers. In a paper, "Remarks on the Canadian Cultivation of the Catalpa Speciosa," by Robert Burnet, an experimental planting of catalpas in 1880 at Pictou, Nova Scotia, was described at the Montreal congress. Both Hough and Warder discussed tree planting by and for railroads, and the experimental plantations of the Northern Pacific Railroad in Minnesota and Dakota, those of the Union Pacific under the supervision of J. T. Allen, and others—for instance, a contracted plantation of the Iron Mountain Railroad to be set out in western catalpa near Charleston, Missouri—were among those mentioned.

Perhaps the most picturesque region of small forest plantations was on Cape Cod, Massachusetts. There, generations before, to quote the language of N. H. Egleston, when "the Pilgrims sighted Provincetown, and coasted along Cape Cod . . . that great arm of land, as well as Nantucket and other islands on the south, was covered with a stately forest growth." But the forests were "recklessly cut" and the "land became a desert waste of sand. So barren was much of the region made that the dwellers there have, in many cases, carried soil from the main land over leagues of intervening water in order to secure a proper return of crops from their seed-sowing. But now," said Egleston, "in these later years, these barren stretches of sand are being reclaimed. All along that exposed coast, from the point of the Cape to Martha's Vineyard, may be seen plantations of forest trees, many of which have attained a growth sufficient to furnish marketable timber, while many others, more recently planted, are making effective wind breaks for the ordinary crops of the farm, thereby increasing the value of the land for tillage purposes." At the Cincinnati congress James S. Fay of Boston, Massachusetts, gave a paper on "Experiments in Planting on Cape Cod," and at the Montreal congress Joseph Storey Fay of Woods Hole described "Experiments in Tree Planting on Cape Cod." Oak, hickory, and pine had supplied timber for ships, fuel, and other purposes. As elsewhere, for years the sheep industry impeded forest growing. Fires and a blight affecting planted native pitch pine added to the difficulties. But plantations were finally achieved.

In 1885, at the Boston meeting of the American Forestry Congress, the members would not only visit Fay's tree plantation at Woods Hole but also hear his paper, "Some Practical Hints on Tree-raising." William C. Strong would discuss "Sea-coast Planting: Its Importance, Practicability, and Methods." Strong was another Massachusetts man and his paper, and that of the Connecticut educator Birdsey Grant Northrop on "Reclamation of Waste Lands," would illustrate two directions in the forestry of New England regions. Fay's pine forest at Falmouth or Woods Hole was regarded as of real importance. More than twenty years earlier, on worn pasture land, Scotch pine had been planted from seed. A plantation of 150 to 200 acres with many thousand native and imported plants, it had by then native pitch-pine, some white pine, Austrian, Scotch, and Corsican pine, Norway spruce, and European larch; and, while Scotch pine had proved to be the best grower, the Norway spruce, Scotch birch, and English oak also had done well.[40] Boston and its environs, a strong center of botanical and horticultural interest, also advanced an aggressive interest in forestry.

By 1886, on the improved but once worn, excessively pastured, somewhat rocky and hilly New England farm at Jamaica Plain, Massachusetts, on which his Arnold Arboretum had been laid out and planned, Charles Sprague Sargent had begun to plant trees on a large scale and in permanent groupings. Sargent's task was to create a scientific garden, public in nature yet administered as a private institution, where the growth of all trees, shrubs, and herbaceous plants, indigenous and exotic, and capable of growing in the climate, could be tested and studied. It

[40] See Commissioner Loring's address, *Report of the American Forestry Congress for 1885, op. cit.*, p. 55; also Fay's paper, "Experiments in Tree Planting on Cape Cod," *Report of the Fruit Growers' Ass'n of Ontario for 1882, op. cit.*, p. 232.

is said[41] that the work began when a former president of Massachusetts agricultural college sent to Sargent the first seeds to reach America of the now familiar tree lilac and climbing hydrangea. By 1886-1887 the work had expanded so astonishingly that within this one year alone 70,000 trees and shrubs were planted at the arboretum. Seeds of trees from northern China, Japan, and other regions were imported. The proximity of the Bussey Institution and Harvard's school of agriculture and horticulture provided adequate greenhouse facilities. Sargent's beautiful estate, "Holm Lea," at Brookline was among the famous private gardens of the United States. While his claims to greatness were more as an arboriculturist than forester, it may be noticed that he had spent three years in European travel and probably had made a considerable acquaintance with forestry work on the continent.

Tree planting and arboriculture were the dominant but not the only themes of the Montreal congress. From the Atlantic to Pacific coasts, small forest plantations existed, some of these hopeful nuclei for more extensive tracts like the Farlington plantations in Kansas and Landreth plantations in Virginia. Plantations were reported from California and the western prairies. These, like natural forests, required protection; and so the foremost menace, forest fires, shared, if in fact did not supersede other phases, in the attention of the congress. Joseph S. Fay's paper on "Forest Fires" was one of the most important presented, and other actions of the congress placed this subject in the foreground. But tree planting was acquiring, over and above its practical and financial aspects, an academic significance. The experimental plantations of Burrill at the University of Illinois, of the University of Nebraska even before Bessey went there, and elsewhere, were preparing groundwork for a more exact science.

In 1886, when writing of "Forest Planting and Management in the United States," Fernow would enumerate many of these plantations as affording "a hopeful prospect in respect to the creation of new forests." However he would say as to management in the natural forests of America, "This hopeful prospect does not exist in regard to the remaining natural forests. With the exception of more carefully conducted lumber operations in Maine, where there is less recklessness than formerly in the destruction of young growth, and beyond the rarely enforced rules in regard to cutting on Government lands . . . no attempts at management, so far as known . . . have been made; or if any have been made, they are so isolated and primitive as hardly to deserve mention or the name of management."[42]

By this time William Little, at the Boston congress of 1885, would

[41] "Charles Sprague Sargent," *Journal of Forestry* XXV, 1927, pp. 513-514.

[42] "Report of the Chief of the Division of Forestry," *Report of the Commissioner of Agriculture of U. S. D. A. for 1886*, pp. 171-172; also *Report of the Commissioner of Agriculture for 1882*, p. 690.

have raised another plea against the "alarming destruction" of North American forests; and in defense of his claims would have cited as to United States forests the paper read by Sargent in 1882 before the Massachusetts State Board of Agriculture and as to Canadian forests a report prepared about 1875 by Henri G. Joly for the government as a member of the Dominion council of agriculture. White pine and spruce, both for Canada and the United States, were more and more shown to be the major future needs. Joly, in his opening address at the American Forestry Congress at Montreal in 1882, singled out for special recognition the fifteen years of effort of the venerable lumberman, James Little, who so courageously had waged a lonely battle for the preservation of Canada's pine forests. By a formal resolution, furthermore, the Montreal congress gave to Little the honorary appellation of "Nestor in American forestry." Little's forestry plea was validated by dependable estimates and statistics of the forest resources. "While my efforts have been mainly directed toward the protection from destruction of the forests of white pine," James Little wrote to the Cincinnati congress of 1882, "it has been painful to me to witness that our other commercial woods, such as walnut and oak and ash, are nearly all gone, and our pine, spruce, birch and tamarack are following so fast that we will soon have nothing left of commercial value."

The warnings voiced by James Little and his plea for forestry practice were carried forward by his son, William, by Joly, William Saunders, and others. By 1890, at meetings of the American Forestry Association, Director William Saunders of the Dominion Experimental Farms would be describing the forestry work being pursued at the farms particularly with reference to forestation of the western plains of Canada. Joly would be informing the meeting of forestry experiments at twenty-five points along the Canadian Pacific Railway, including Moose Jaw, Swift Current, Gull Lake, Crane Lake, Maple Creek, Medicine Hat, Bowell, and Langdon. He would make it plain to his audience that the plan of granting lands to encourage tree planting had worked no better in Canada than in the United States. Tree planting on the prairies of Canada, Joly correctly maintained, was important, the subject having attained considerable scientific stature.

From his very first years of participating in the forestry movement, the position of Fernow was uncompromisingly in favor of raising up a true science, as well as the art, of forestry. At the conclusion of the American Forestry Congress meeting at Montreal, he wrote to Birkinbine: "Of the real science of forestry, there was no glimpse, unless you allow the writer to mention his own effort to lay down and explain those scientific principles which underlie forest growth, and the resulting general rules for forest management."

In this paper, styled "Conditions of Forest Growth,"[43] Fernow admitted he had "only incompletely and in a general way pointed out some of the more important conditions which underlie the growth of our forests. I have done so," he explained, "without any attempt to exhaust the theme in any particular, but have merely endeavoured to draw your attention to the fact, that the whole science of forestry is built, or in the case of this continent, is to be built, upon a very complicated system of elementary knowledge, which can only be gathered by local observations based on a correct understanding of the physical forces at work."

Neither attempting to discuss the "many minor and local influences" nor to trace "step by step the deductions possible from these for a correct management of forests," he had considered the major, or "principal and determining," factors of forest growth, each in relation to the requirements of various forest species. Drawing on his knowledge of scientific agriculture, experimental soil science, meteorology, plant physiology, and other branches of learning as well as his experience as a forester in the forests of Germany and America, he coordinated and yet distinguished the work in agriculture from that of forestry. "The object of forestry," he maintained, "is a financial effect, which is represented by the highest rent from the soil through the cultivation of the same for timber growth," and differentiating the fitness of lands for agriculture from those for forests he summed up "the influence of the soil on forest growth by stating that its chemical [or mineral] composition is only of minor importance, almost all soils furnishing sufficient inorganic bases of the description which is needed by forest growth; . . . its main influence consists in its physical properties, represented by its depth, looseness and, depending on these, the capacity of absorbing and retaining moisture, which properties may be increased or even compensated for by a sufficient layer of humus."

That Fernow sought to make his discussion more practical than academic was indicated throughout. Reaching the "question of climatic influence on tree-growth," he argued that this "becomes of practical interest, when the possibility for existence and prosperity of a tree species under certain climatic conditions is to be ascertained for the purpose of introducing new species, and it becomes necessary to determine whether the thriving of a species depends on the mean yearly, the mean summer or winter temperature, or on the extremes of temperature. The solution of this question is as yet possible only on grounds of observation in regard to the natural distribution of trees, or else must in each individual case be ascertained by experiment."

With regard to conditions of soil, air, climate, and their intermin-

[43] *The American Journal of Forestry*, 1882-1883, *op. cit.*, pp. 68ff; *Report of the Fruit Growers' Association of Ontario for 1882, op. cit.*, pp. 214-223.

gled factors such as temperature, atmospheric carbon, moisture and evaporation, humidity, and so forth, it was not possible, except over "an extended period of time and by careful forestry," to make substantial changes. But when "the relation of the forest trees toward light and shade" was elaborated, Fernow found a condition which the forester "is able to create and control, on the understanding of which a successful management of his plantation must be based throughout. In fact," he pointed out, "we may say that the most important criterion in forestal operations" is here formed. "The conditions created by the existence or absence of the proper amount of light, we should characterize as the principal one for the consideration of any manager of forests. We do not mean here to discuss the physiological influence of light on vegetation in general, which shows itself in the decomposition of the carbonic acid of the air, thus furnishing the means of assimilation of the carbon which is necessary for the growth of the plant, its colouring, the ripening of the seed, etc.; but the necessity of providing in the forest a proper amount of light and shade according to the wants of different species in their different ages."

Twice in the course of his address Fernow referred to the work in this connection of his former teacher, Dr. G. Heyer, then professor of forestry at the forest academy of Munich, Germany. America's first professionally schooled forester confessed he was "as yet not sufficiently conversant with the requirements . . . of the species, which form the forests of North America, to be able to attempt the establishment of a scale, denoting the relative capacity of the species to sustain shade or their comparative demand for light." But the results of European experimental knowledge could point the way for experimental research in America. At the Cincinnati congress Professor William Brown had submitted a paper on "Forest and Rainfall in Ontario," which pleaded "the necessity of independent experimental action" in America. He had disclaimed the trustworthiness of European conclusions "because physical conditions [here] are just the extreme, so to speak, of those averaging in the eastern hemisphere." He outlined some of the physical conditions of Ontario with a view to showing "their intimate connection with tree surface," and projected six questions with suggested solutions. When the paper was published in the *Report of the Fruit Growers' Association of Ontario for 1882* (pp. 181-183), one of the first pleas for "a system of forest management" of the province's vast natural forest resources was made. Moreover, such a plea for governmentally sponsored programs of forest tree planting, supplemented by a popular interest and action, as presented by A. T. Drummond in his paper, "Forestry in Canada," must have gone far toward stimulating both an economic and scientific interest in forestry as it was then understood in Canada and the United States.

Fernow's intention was to promote forestry practice among members of the American Forestry Congress. His expressed aim was to point out the "primary essential" of knowing "the natural conditions of forest growth." To this end he offered twelve definitions, rules of management and care—nothing new or original, he admitted, but known facts of the natural sciences so arranged as to "contribute to the understanding of the conditions of plant-growth, that these [might] easily be applied to the study of forest-reproduction." These rules were:

1. The principal effort of the forester must be to preserve and increase the "soil bonity" as defined . . . since upon it depends the productivity of the forest.

2. The measures to be adopted for this purpose are not much to be sought in direct operations on the soil, but mainly in certain considerations in the selection of species, methods of management, terms of rotation, interlucation, methods of reproduction, and in the general care of the forests.

3. Only such species should form the predominant part of the forest as are able to preserve the "soil bonity." These are the shade-enduring and the evergreen.

4. Where an increase of depth, looseness and humidity is especially needed, it is essential that such species should be cultivated as, through a plentiful fall of leaves, favour formation of humus, and by the density of their crowns keep out the two enemies of humification: sun and wind.

5. If for a length of time one species alone is to be cultivated, it must be one with a dense foliage. Light foliaged ones can only be allowed where Nature has provided in some other way for the conservation of the "soil bonity," because these not only furnish too little material for humification, but impede the latter by giving sun and wind access to the soil, thus drying it up and impoverishing it.

6. Mixed forests afford greater security against damages by wind, fire, frost, snow, diseases, besides yielding a larger amount of wood. In these the predominant species must be one of the shade-loving or enduring, densely-foliaged, which protect the soil. The light-needing, thinly foliaged species are only to be mixed in by single individuals, and not in groups, and must be quicker growing or have an advantage in age or height.

7. Two or more shade-enduring kinds can only be mixed, if they are equally quick growing.

8. In growths which in later years become less dense any underbrush is favourable as protection against sun and wind; the cultivation of such artificially may be advisable from financial considerations, though it may not be justified.

9. The distance of the plants in new plantations ought not to be more than three to four feet, as only thus a sufficient covering of the soil can be effected. Besides the yield of wood per acre stands in direct proportion to the density of growth, i.e. the number of plants per acre.

10. Of all the methods of management, the timber forest with natural reproduction from seed trees is best calculated to maintain the vigour of the soil, for shade-enduring species, if the cutting is done with necessary prudence, so that the soil is exposed as little as possible. Next to this method comes absolute clearing, with immediate artificial reseeding or replanting. This is almost the only method advisable for light-foliaged trees.

11. Short terms of rotation remove the protection oftener from the soil;

long ones carry the danger of soil impoverishment, owing to the natural thinning out of most species in later stages of growth.

12. For interlucation the principal rule is never to deprive any portion of the soil of the protecting cover of the crowns; it is best to confine the thinning out to the overshadowed, dying trees.

Fernow restated the substance and main conclusions of this address in another paper presented that year to the United States Association of Charcoal Iron Workers. There he ventured again his belief that forest owners, to improve their tree growth and supply and to secure more careful and economic utilization of raw material, would have to apply principles of European, especially German and French, scientific forestry. He was ready to confess that "many important questions of forestry [were] still in the field of controversy. . . . Forestry, though practiced abroad for centuries," he explained, "is by no means an abstract fully developed science, but depending largely on the development of natural sciences has, like those, only of late, taken a more progressive start. Its progress is, besides, so much slower than that of any other science, because the answers to many of its questions and experiments are given only in decades and centuries."

During these decades American plant scientific research, with regard to both the wild and the cultivated floras, was undergoing transition. The necessary and fundamental taxonomic study still confronting scientists on this continent retarded progress in applied science. Experimental morphology and developmental physiology were only beginning to cross the scientific threshold of America from Europe. Moreover, what exact experimental knowledge had been accumulated in America consisted largely of results from trial and error methods. Principles of scientific agriculture were still few. Principles of forest study were woefully lacking, and Fernow plainly saw this need. He knew what forest experiment stations and schools might accomplish. But were American scientists adequately prepared to conduct and maintain forest stations and schools effectively? Could small beginnings in these directions be made now, secure against ultimate failure due to lack of properly trained personnel? To Fernow, forest schools and experiment stations were goals which should be achieved in time. In 1882, in the United States, even the agricultural experiment stations were yet few in number; and, while agricultural colleges on the federal land-grant basis were working to advance a scientific agriculture, forests were studied only as incidents to agriculture. Fernow realized that individual scientists interested in forests and forest preservation could study the American forests and their composition. He would delay a complete program of forestry research until several years later, when as chief of the division of forestry of the United States Department of Agriculture he would include this in a series of lectures on forestry education and submit official reports to the commissioner of agriculture. When the Cincinnati and Montreal meetings of the American Forestry Congress took place, he was equipped with the knowledge he later presented in more elaborate form. He astutely chose, however, first to describe the evolution of a forest policy of one of the leading nations of the world and second to discuss the immediate need, the bases on which the growth of scientific forestry in America might be predicated.

In a sense, Fernow's paper brought the classroom of a German forest school to "Forestry Chambers" of the American Forestry Congress at Montreal. Begin, he said, with a factual study of forest growth and its variable conditions, regionally and locally, in America. Deduce principles from the exact study of interacting elemental and environmental factors involved in forest growth—soil, climate, light, water, temperature, all the physical phenomena at work in relation to each and all forest species. By organizing the principles already known in a system of elementary knowledge, the basis on which research might proceed was supplied. Fernow's paper, "Conditions of Forest Growth," was in reality a condensed textual treatise, elaborating "those scientific principles which underlie forest growth, and the resulting general rules for forest management. . . . When we speak of a forest in connection with the science of Forestry," said Fernow, "we do not mean a mere collection of trees, a wood, or park, a plantation, but an aggregate of trees or woodlands which are intended and so set aside for the production of timber or lumber." In other words, the forest reservation or preserve was of the essence of forestry.

St. Paul, Minnesota, was chosen at Montreal for the next meeting, partly because the American Association for the Advancement of Science and the Society for the Promotion of Agricultural Science were planning to hold their meetings in August 1883 in the adjoining city of Minneapolis. The St. Paul congress was to be fairly convincing proof that tree-planting as a movement had seized the imagination of almost the entire United States. Fernow heartily believed in this movement as a practical way of inaugurating full-scale forestry and its inevitable corollary, the conservation of natural resources. The prairies and plains were not the only regions in need of forest planting. In travels and at his home in Slatington he had seen that there were vast waste areas in the mountainous regions. In his article, "Planting in Waste Places,"[44] written at Slatington, he said:

Most of the methods recommended and described in American papers for planting forests presuppose that the ground to be planted is arable, or at least workable with the spade. This may be all right for the Prairie States, yet there are probably on every farm in the mountainous regions more waste places than anywhere else, that will never pay to get the stones out—that

[44] *American Journal of Forestry*, Jan. 1883, pp. 153-155.

won't grow any grass of value, and that defy all cultivation. There are others which are too wet, and, on account of their nature, drainage for agricultural uses is impossible or unprofitable; others, again, which on their dry shifting sand will not bear any crop.

These are the very places to which, in time, the forest in every well settled country will be more or less confined, the better portions being needed for farming purposes; and fortunately enough, not only can such places be made to bear forests, but, being so used, they are improved, and often, after some time, gain in value, even for agricultural crops.

At the 1883 congress held at St. Paul to honor western planting, which centered in Minnesota and neighboring states, Fernow presented a paper on the "Management of Burned Forests, and the Effect of Forest Fires on the Soil and Forest Growth." The control of forest fires by requirements of removing brush and other fire hazards and by prohibiting brush burning near fir trees during certain months, the control of injuries by cattle and the roaming at large on public woodlands by cattle, sheep, or swine, the prevention of trespass, and restricting the cutting of pine, spruce, hemlock, or hardwood to diameters at the stump of less than fourteen inches, the encouragement of timber planting, highway and farm boundary planting, government management of public forest lands, and the reservation of lands more suited to timber forests than agriculture, the organization of sufficient law enforcement officers and patrols to discover and guard against fires, and numerous other subjects were considered at the Montreal congress, especially with reference to their special application to Canadian conditions.

On the second day of the Montreal congress, following the report of a committee appointed at Cincinnati on forest fires, another committee, composed of Canadians and Americans—six in number and evidently gradually enlarged to ten, Mohr, Hough, Fernow, Joly, Little, Sargent, J. K. Ward, P. White, E. D. Baker, and Honorable Mr. Bryson—was appointed to draw "respectful representations on the subject [of better precautions against forest fires which] would receive due attention from the Governments of the United States and Canada." On the third day the report was presented and adopted. Soon thereafter a resolution was enacted authorizing the executive committee to appoint referees to prepare papers on (1) legislation with regard to forest fires, (2) prevention and control of forest fires, (3) distribution of the white pine, (4) technology of the white pine, and (5) forest management of the white pine. Fernow's report of the meeting added one other subject: (6) management of burned forests, and effect upon the soil and forest growth. Featured recommendations of the forest fire precaution memorial were the creation of a protective force superintended and financed by the government and also the reservation of pine and spruce lands unfit for settlement. The division of timberlands into districts and the taxation of parties owning or leasing timberlands to defray the cost of maintaining protective forces were included. Since for many years the Canadian government clung to the park concept for reserved lands, the recommendation to reserve for lumbering purposes all pine and spruce lands unfit for settlement was especially noteworthy.

H. G. Joly and William Little, the leading Canadian members of the Montreal congress, were immensely pleased with the work, particularly with Fernow's contribution. William Saunders of London, Ontario, Canada's leader in the study of entomology, was also profoundly impressed. William Little arranged for the printing of a large edition of two numbers of the *Montreal Herald*, in which sixteen pages were devoted exclusively to the congress's proceedings. Two evening meetings of the congress took place in Queen's Hall, which was decorated with potted plants, the flags of the nations, the congress's shield, and the legend "Woodman, Spare That Tree." Fernow procured a copy of the folio edition of the *Herald* and on September 1, 1882, sent it to Abram S. Hewitt, saying ". . . I take the liberty of sending a copy of the Montreal Herald containing a paper I read before the American Forestry Congress, which besides receiving high praise from the N.Y. Tribune, has been deemed by the Canadian Government worthy of reprinting for distribution."

"Conditions of Forest Growth" was not the only valuable contribution made by Fernow to the American Forestry Congress at Montreal. On the second day of the congress Fernow introduced the resolution to have the chairman appoint five members to revise the constitution "so as to adapt it to the wants of the Congress." Fernow, Hough, Warder, Little, and Mohr were appointed. On the night of August 22 the committee worked until three o'clock in the morning, and on the next day Fernow presented the committee's report.[45] Fernow, as chairman, had succeeded in writing into the constitution of the first permanent forestry organization of America a progressive policy for the future of forestry on this continent.

There were other important papers presented at the congress. William Saunders' "Growth of Poplar Trees for the Manufacture of Paper and Charcoal" exemplified how small waste areas, unsuitable for agriculture, could profitably be utilized in forests. Saunders' study of insects which attack roots, trunks, and leaves of forest trees and C. V. Riley's discourse on "Injurious Insects" took a segment of entomology and applied it to the forest. At Montreal, Byron D. Halsted, who enduringly contributed to plant physiology and pathology, gave an able paper on "Fungi Injurious to Forest Trees." The Michigan horticulturist, T. T. Lyon, discussed "Forests in Connection with Water as Aids

[45] "Draft of a New Constitution for the American Forestry Congress," *Am. Jour. For.*, Sept. 1882-Oct. 1883, Dec. 1882, pp. 115-116.

to Climatic Amelioration." Even the subject in which William Henry Brewer took so much interest, forests in relation to hygiene, was discussed by a member of the medical profession, Dr. Henry Howard, under the title "Forestry from a Hygienic Standpoint." Of this paper Fernow said:

> . . . an amusing incident happened, which although remaining without any deleterious effect on the movement, might have proved a setback but for the tact of a Canadian gentleman, the best beloved and strongest advocate of forestry . . . Seigneur, Sir Henri Joly de Lotbinière.
>
> The then U.S. Commissioner of Agriculture [George B. Loring] was the chairman of the meeting. An old gentleman, a local physician, had been invited to deliver a paper and he had hauled out from the beginning of the universe, developing in great detail, the theories of evolution, and demonstrating that all things are matter and under the law of matter. He had arrived at a summing up sentence: "and so a goldmine is matter, a sheep is matter, a forest is matter, and for that matter man is matter," when down came the gavel of the chairman and up got the chairman with great aplomb, calling the gentleman to order. "I will not allow any one at any meeting over which I preside to utter such heterodox ideas," and therewith left the hall to the consternation of the large assemblage and the innocent speaker.
>
> Sir Henri immediately slipped into the chair, explained that there must have been something misunderstood, and asked the speaker to continue. . . . The Congress proceeded without a hitch.[46]

Early in 1883 William Little, the corresponding secretary, was obliged to go to Europe. He resigned his office and Fernow was appointed to the position. Immediately he began preparing a circular to arouse interest in the St. Paul meetings. Although the association had begun with a large membership, the number, said Fernow,

> dwindled to a small number of faithful ones and was without funds. . . . Endless struggle to keep alive, always on the brink of bankruptcy but undaunted, we held our annual meetings, often with not more than a dozen participants. But the newspapers were good to us and we kept them supplied with trumpet blasts before the meetings, and glowing accounts of what was achieved during the meetings. I learned then the power of the press and the names and methods to conjure with. The gospel spread! At that time it turned out that our friends were our greatest enemies, owing to the extravagant statements in which they indulged regarding the rapid approach of a desert condition of the whole country and to their vociferous cry of "Woodman, spare that tree," which led the lumber journals to coin a new word for us: "denudatics," a term intended to be vituperative, but which we bore as a badge of honor.[47]

Small wonder that it was decided that the third congress, at St. Paul,[48] should be devoted to informing the public about the real meaning of tree planting and the forestry movement; that the fourth congress, at

[46] "The Birth of a Forest Policy," *op. cit.*

[47] "The Birth of a Forest Policy," *op. cit.*

[48] After the St. Paul Congress, Joly, Saunders, and Beadle went to Winnipeg and organized the Manitoba Forestry and Horticultural Society. In 1882 Quebec citizens also organized a forestry association.

Saratoga, should be held in New York State to spread forestry "gospel" and encourage the state to create a forest preserve of its immense Adirondack lands; that the fifth congress, at Boston, should be held in New England to enlist popular interest there; that the sixth congress, at Denver, should carry the same to the great Rocky Mountain states, from where the agitation might spread to the entire forest domain of the West. Indeed, the seventh congress, at Cleveland, would adjourn and reconvene in Atlanta, Georgia, to unite with the Southern Forestry Congress and make forestry in the United States a national enterprise. Forestry found that its first great task was to educate the public to its worth. Its progress had been no less slow in Canada than in the United States.

Immediately after the American Forestry Congress at Montreal was held, the provinces enacted legislation that placed Canada among the governments that recognized the advantages of forestry. At the St. Paul congress H. G. Joly, representing the committee on forest protection created at the Cincinnati congress to deal with the matter of forest fires and cattle depredations, reported that Ontario, in addition to its fire prevention act, had passed a law to encourage forest tree planting. Quebec province, following the recommendations of the Montreal congress, passed legislation which classified public lands as either land fit for cultivation or lands to be used to grow pine and spruce and to be reserved for lumbering purposes. Quebec province also had amended its forest fire protection law and adopted the suggestion of the Montreal congress's committee to appoint superintendents to guard against fires.[49] Nova Scotia had enacted similar legislation and designated an Arbor Day. The Canadian provinces had older legislation which systematized the disposal of Crown Lands and provided for land surveys. With industrial growth the provinces sought by law to regulate milling, culling, mining, and other strictly industrial activities. This book cannot serve as a complete compendium of all forestry legislation in Canada, but it can show the influence which forestry enterprise had upon legislation in Canada and the United States.

An illustration is afforded from the forest history of Ontario. Before the middle of the century, when Sir J. William Dawson had warned of the peril to the forests from fires, the province had investigated forest protection "from unnecessary destruction." In 1854 legislation aimed at preventing careless fire setting when lands were cleared failed,

[49] "During the sittings of the Legislature the Committee on Agriculture devotes some attention to the question of forestry. The Commissioner of the Department of Crown Lands, Woods and Forests is answerable for the management of the Government forests, and has the power to regulate the disposing of timber limits, the manner of lumbering and rafting etc." Joly was elected president of the Quebec association and each member was pledged to sow or plant twenty-five trees every year. *Forestry Bulletin* 2, Sept. 1884, p. 3.

although it was recognized that "important modifications of the system of management of public lands and forests were imperatively required." Indeed, it is said that as early as 1863 "a committee advised against the opening of pine lands for settlement, and in the following year further inquiry was instituted 'into the causes of the rapid destruction of pine,' and into the expediency of reserving timber areas for forestry purposes." With the growth of the lumber industry and the spread of devastating fires, the province during the next quarter of a century came to realize that "preoccupation with the larger political issues of the period" was an error, and the "pressing forest and land settlement problems" should no longer be set aside. Accordingly in 1878 the first forest protection legislation in Ontario was passed. "The bill entitled 'An Act to Preserve the Forests from Destruction by Fire,' " Minister of Lands and Forests N. O. Hipel has written,[50] "provided among other things for the establishment of fire districts in which, during the summer months, the use of fire was restricted. Officials of the Department were responsible for the enforcement of this Act, but it was not until 1886 that the first system of fire ranging was instituted. Under the plan proposed, licensees were invited to cooperate with the Government in protecting their limits on a cost sharing basis. The system was extended, and in 1897 fire rangers were placed on unlicensed land at public expense. Shortly thereafter it became an obligation on the part of all licensees to participate in cooperative protection with the Government. . . ." The point to be noticed is the inadequacy of the fire system before the American Forestry Congress of 1882 was held.

The fact that in other provinces adequate machinery was not provided to make the provincial laws effective did not argue against the accomplishment of the congress. The congress could advise legislators, but it could not enforce legislation. Ontario's fire ranger system impressed the entire continent. Fernow was especially impressed with the provision of the fire protection law for the crown lands, woods, and waters, which involved cooperation between the state authorities and private interests in financial maintenance. New Brunswick and other provinces were gradually to see the worth of forest protection, but they were slow to secure enforcement for what legislation was enacted. These are but a few instances of the influences of the American Forestry Congress by popular education and instruction of public officialdom. Perhaps its most important consequence was that it brought Fernow, "the only professional forester in the membership," into prominence.

At the Montreal congress Nathaniel H. Egleston evaluated "the rising

[50] "The History and Status of Forestry in Ontario," *Canadian Geographic Journal* XXV, 3, Sept. 1942, pp. 111-114, 135. The Ontario fire protection service, with thirty-five men, was put into operation in 1885; New Brunswick passed a Fire Act in the same year.

interest in trees and tree-planting in America . . ." saying, "Hitherto there has been no adequate treatise on the subject of tree pruning in the English language. . . . The work of Des Cars, entitled, 'A Treatise on Pruning and Ornamental Trees,' has recently been translated from the French of the seventh edition by Professor Sargent, and published by the Massachusetts Society for the Promotion of Agriculture." John S. Hicks of Roslyn, New York, read before the Montreal congress a paper on "The Commercial Value of Pruning." But for forestry purposes there was no adequate work on pruning. To the third annual meeting of the United States Association of Charcoal Iron Workers held at the Vanderbilt House, Calera, Alabama, October 19, 1882, Fernow sent a paper which the secretary read on "Principles of Interlucation."[51] The paper was ordered published in the Association's *Journal*. The article later afforded the basis of another paper, "Pruning the Forest,"[52] which Fernow presented at the Saratoga meeting of the American Forestry Congress. Said Fernow, "Allowing that the young plantation has been started in accordance with the rules of a careful and rational forestry, the means of influencing its growth and yield are rather limited. In fact, in a large way an increase of yield can only be obtained by judicious thinnings. . . ."[53] Later he was to say, "Absolute rules as to the time for interlucations and their periodical repetition evidently cannot be given; the peculiar conditions of each individual case alone can determine this. The golden rule, however, is: early, often, moderately."[54] In 1882 Fernow discussed the physiological effect of interlucations. It was definitely a companion effort of his paper on "Conditions of Forest Growth." Much of what he said had special application to coppice management, with which he was concerned at Slatington.

On December 8, 1882, Rossiter Raymond wrote Fernow, "One thing is plain. We must start the new year on a basis which does not confine you at Lehigh Furnace on present terms and under present prospects. Mr. Hewitt once said that you must be given to understand that if that property was got rid of, you would be provided for." Even though Cooper, Hewitt & Company tried to keep Fernow in its employ, necessity compelled him to return to New York City. At some time, presumably within the first year, Fernow hung out his shingle as a "Consulting Forest Engineer." This was the pioneer professional forestry effort of this nature on the North American continent. One caller responded. That person, however, refused to become a client when Fernow informed him that he proposed to charge a fee for his advice. In 1883 Fernow became foreign correspondent for Stern Brothers Dry Goods store. The following year he served as a clerk in the New York Customs

[51] *Jour. of the U.S. Assn. of Charcoal Iron Workers* III, p. 282.
[52] *Report Am. For. Cong. for 1886*, pp. 84-89.
[53] *Jour. of the U.S. Assn. of Charcoal Iron Workers* III, 6, p. 345.
[54] *Report of the Div. of For. of U.S.D.A. for 1886*, p. 222.

House. But forestry was still his calling; he saw the needs and possibilities of forestry on the North American continent. His heart was wrapped up in the program of the American Forestry Congress.

Mrs. Fernow wholeheartedly encouraged his interest in forestry. In fact, when his work became burdensome, she assumed his secretaryship responsibilities as much as she could. It is easy to imagine what Fernow must have thought. In Europe forestry was an established institution; in America there were a few institutions which bore the name "forestry," a few which paid small salaries, but none with positions available. "I am a citizen of the world," Fernow would say, but that attitude did not feed his family. Fernow visualized forestry as an educational program, a business, a research institution, an art, and a potential science. Raymond, on January 2, 1883, proposed to send Fernow to the Pequest Furnace at Oxford, New Jersey, "to learn . . . the management of the blast furnace, with the understanding that it would be a good thing to have some one competent to take charge of Ringwood furnaces, when they should be blown in again." An arrangement was reached, but Peter Cooper died, and Hewitt was in congress and more than ever absorbed in politics. Raymond, of course, had to give first attention to mining interests. Fernow's employment with Cooper, Hewitt & Company had not been unsatisfactory, but both Raymond and Hewitt agreed that he deserved a better future. He continued to manage the Blue Mountain forest tract. In the little community along Trout Creek where they had resided, Fernow was known as an exceptionally able forest surveyor and an excellent furnace manager. The community regretted the departure of the Fernow family.

In 1884 Charles Edwin Bessey, a botanist and former student of Albert Nelson Prentiss and Asa Gray, and author of one of the most influential books in plant science history, *Botany for High Schools and Colleges*, had been asked by C. H. Gore and the chairman of the board of regents of the University of Nebraska to accept the deanship of the Industrial College and the chair of botany and horticulture.[55] At first he refused the offer. Bessey did not wish to leave Iowa Agricultural College at Ames, where he had created out of almost nothing a leading department of botany and a botanical laboratory for undergraduate instruction. This laboratory was among the first of its kind, if not the first, in the United States. On October 21, 1885, Charles Christopher Parry wrote Bessey that he had returned from a trip to Europe and was "not altogether surprised to hear of [his] removal to Nebraska, especially as under liberal auspices and less political interference it [was] likely to give a wider scope in useful pursuits." Asa Gray procured for Bessey from President Gilman of the University of California an invitation to deliver a course of lectures on Economic Botany, which "re-

[55] See A. D. Rodgers, *John Merle Coulter*, Princeton Univ. Press, 1944.

sulted in a delightful visit to the Pacific coast." It is said that Gray suggested that Bessey write the text *Botany for High Schools and Colleges.* When the latter went to Nebraska, he was appointed Dean of the Industrial College, professor of botany with a $5,000 grant to equip a botanical laboratory, and state botanist charged with the task of performing a survey of the state's floral resources. From this survey gradually emerged phytogeographic studies of direct significance to forestry.

Ecological investigation had had its real origin in Europe. Bessey and a group of brilliant students adapted or modified the methods to meet the needs of American study. At the University of Minnesota under Conway MacMillan, at the University of Chicago under Coulter and Henry Chandler Cowles, and elsewhere, ecology influenced botanical exploration, and at the beginning of the twentieth century it began to influence forestry research. In the early 1890's, Bessey said, so many "people became interested in forestry which [had been] regarded as a branch of horticulture, . . . [that] I blocked out a pretty full course of lectures and these were given to a class of about 20 or 30 students." On another occasion he explained more fully, "Early in the year 1891 in co-operation with Mr. [Robert W.] Furnas, Mr. E. F. Stephens and B. E. Fernow, the Chief of the Bureau of Forestry, a course of lectures in forestry was planned, to be given to the students of the University of Nebraska. This course was opened with a public lecture by B. E. Fernow, and was conducted for a period of several months in the second semester of the University year. In this course I gave ten or a dozen lectures, Mr. Furnas four or five; Mr. Stephens the same and Mr. Fernow two. . . ."

Bessey was a delegate to the St. Paul meeting of the American Forestry Congress.[56] There he met Robert W. Furnas, "one of the pioneer advocates of forestation in Nebraska." Furnas that year made an encouraging report of Nebraska tree planting on land which, when under the Indian title, had been "supposed to be a timberless region."[57] Nevertheless, there had been found "a narrow strip of valuable and well matured trees" along the Missouri River. In valleys of the Platte and other streams there was also found "a smaller and more recent growth of the same varieties." And, most remarkable, in the northwest part of the state was found a growth of white pine "of sufficient size to be used for lumber, but too young and immature to be of much value. After a time it was found by experiment that there was nothing in the nature of the soil or climate to prevent the growth of trees on the open prairie and away from the streams. Seedlings transplanted into well-prepared ground and protected from the prairie fires grew with vigor and rapid-

[56] *ibid.*, pp. 112-113.

[57] From Egleston's *Report of Division of Forestry for 1883*, pp. 448-449. Egleston's analysis is probably based exclusively on Furnas's report.

ity, and now," concluded Furnas, "tree-growing in Nebraska is universally conceded a success." By 1883 there had been planted 248,496 acres of forest. James T. Allan of Omaha, who spoke at the congress, estimated that forty-three million forest trees had been planted. Indeed, the Nebraska state constitution encouraged tree planting by exempting fruit and forest tree planted land from taxation.[58]

Dr. Hough told St. Paul citizens, "We want no parade—no excursions—banquets . . . ," and the congress's committee on arrangements complied with Hough's suggestion and induced the state legislature to grant the use of the State House chambers for its deliberations. Furthermore, General Herman Haupt, manager of the St. Paul (Northern) Pacific Railroad and grandfather of Professor Herman Haupt Chapman of Yale Forest School, invited the congress to go at the railroad's expense to Mandan, Dakota, to view the railroad's forest plantations made in large part by Leonard B. Hodges, author of the classic little *Tree Planter's Manual* and a pioneer in the forestry movement of Minnesota. Hodges had died that spring. Fernow for many years regarded Hodges as the man who was first to make forest plantations in the prairies. Hodges had assured Hough "that the people of St. Paul never do things *by halves*. [Hough had] said to him that our great want for the occasion is a *large attendance of earnest and active men*. We must try to get up a strong attendance of our own members, and see that they come prepared for work."

In this year Hough's *American Journal of Forestry*, and in 1886 the English *Journal of Forestry*, went out of existence. In 1884 Fernow began publishing his *Forestry Bulletin* from 9 Pine Street in New York City, but it lasted only three numbers. *Forestry Leaves*, leaflets of the Pennsylvania Forestry Association, soon began; but for a while there was in English only *The Indian Forester*, which was concerned primarily with tropical forestry.[59] In 1883 Hough had reason to urge that forestry needed more workers and more work.

F. P. Baker and Furnas, under government auspices, issued this year their *Preliminary Report on the Forestry of the Mississippi Valley and Tree Planting on the Plains*, a pamphlet of forty-five pages. Furnas's report of forest conditions of the Rocky Mountain and Pacific Coast states warned "that the consumption of the forests in the manufacture of timber [was] rapidly increasing, while their destruction by fire [was] both reckless and alarming." The introduction into southern California of the eucalyptus was encouraging. But since the opening of the Northwest by the Northern Pacific Railroad, lumbermen were "transferring operations from the nearly exhausted pineries of the lakes and upper Mississippi to the fir forests beyond the Rocky Mountains. The whole

[58] *loc. cit.*
[59] *Report of the Division of Forestry for 1886*, p. 183.

western coast of the American continent and the eastern coast of the Asiatic," observed Egleston, head of the forestry division of the federal department of agriculture, "offers a limitless market for the lumber of Puget Sound region, and the lumbermen seem eager to reap the offered harvest. But worse than the threatened consumption of the great forests of the Pacific slope of the Northwest by the lumbermen, is that of forest fires. These Mr. Furnas characterizes as 'simply fearful-criminal.' "[60] "California has no mine of wealth equal to [the redwoods] in value," said the report.

Maine, Massachusetts, Connecticut, New Jersey, Pennsylvania, Illinois, Wisconsin, Colorado—almost all of the great forested states—had taken practically no constructive action on behalf of forestry. Minnesota had the first of the state forestry associations. Ohio's forestry association was struggling valiantly to secure forestry legislation. In New Hampshire a commission of inquiry had been appointed. In New York a large mass meeting had been held and forestry leagues formed to procure proper legislation on behalf of the Adirondack forest. The rest of the states left the problem—if they regarded it a problem—to the state's agricultural or horticultural ranks.[61] Vermont was trying to inform itself of its forest problems by sending out a circular of questions. "In May, 1883," Hough told Joly, "I was sent home—nominally to make investigations by correspondence in certain states." From that time until June 11, 1885, when he died, his inactivity gradually caused him to lose interest in forestry, although, as he explained, he kept "doing what [he was] told . . . realizing the utter impossibility of *doing anything to please the Commissioner*—or of preparing anything that he would accept. . . ." Notwithstanding, Hough never was idle and hoped to his last year that he could "justify [himself] before [his] friends for having apparently done so little."

The addition at St. Paul of such members as Bessey, Budd, Northrup, and Baker was stimulating to the congress. Bessey urged each member to become a committee of one to answer the question, "Are the Concentric Rings Visible in the Wood a Correct Indication of the Age of the Tree?" Budd, Furnas, Bessey, Minier of Illinois, and others engaged in discussions on tree growth. Minier presented a paper "On the Measurement of Twenty-Two Varieties of Forest Trees." Budd brought news of his and Charles Gibb's trip to Russia in 1882 to investigate the trees and shrubs of northern Europe and Asia. They looked for species which might be introduced in America, especially hardy varieties which might be grown on the northwest plains of the United States and Canada. By the development of "physiological species" and by plantings from seeds and seedlings, new varieties might be obtained which would

[60] *Report of the Division of Forestry for 1883*, pp. 447-448.
[61] "Gleanings from the 'Forestry World,' " *Forestry Bulletin* 1, May 1884, pp. 1-3.

give a new impetus to prairie forestry. Budd's work at Ames, Iowa, was termed by B. G. Northrup as a "school of forestry." Northrup called for the education of youth in forestry. He was secretary of the Connecticut State Board of Education and had authored a work on *Economic Tree Planting*, published in 1878 at New York. Tree planting interest in Massachusetts and Connecticut, he said, had been spread with such effectiveness that almost every homestead, especially in Connecticut, had been beautified by tree planting during the past fifteen years.

The published reports of the St. Paul congress contained a paper by the authority in practical horticulture, W. C. Barry of Rochester, New York. This paper, on "New and Noteworthy Trees, Shrubs and Conifers," had been given earlier in the year before the American Association of Nurserymen, Florists, and Seedsmen at St. Louis, Missouri. Plant breeding at this time was of little significance to forestry, but geographical introductions of plant species were important, especially from the ornamental standpoint. In this phase of American plant study there already had been considerable work sponsored by the department of agriculture. Gibb was a Canadian and owner of an important experimental farm at Abbotsford in the province of Quebec. Although his work was primarily horticultural, it had importance to forestry. In 1883 he prepared a report for the Montreal Horticultural Society titled "Hasty Notes on Trees and Shrubs of Northern Europe and Asia." This was revised and enlarged for publication in 1884 in the *Proceedings of the American Forestry Congress.*

In 1883, giving expression to a long standing recommendation of its 1872 state park commission to retain ownership of a vast amount of miscellaneous tax-forfeited and undisposed-of state lands, New York prohibited further sales of between 600,000 and 800,000 acres situated in certain northern counties and of much of the forest lands which had been desolated by cutting and wastage. Ten thousand dollars were appropriated to purchase lands where the state owned jointly and partitions were necessary. Only a comparatively small area, 40,000 acres, had been available when the park commission, of which Horatio Seymour was chairman, had outlined a program of land acquisition and forest preservation. By 1883, however, the forest acreage in state ownership had enormously increased.[62] At the St. Paul congress Hough reported on the action taken up to that time on those lands which were situated north of the Mohawk River principally in the Adirondack Mountains. He sum-

[62] See C. R. Pettis, "Forest Provisions of the New York State Constitution," *Forestry Quarterly* XIV, 1 Mar. 1916, p. 51. See also Fernow's *A Brief History of Forestry*, 1911, pp. 489ff; Gurth Whipple, *Fifty Years of Conservation in New York State, 1885-1935*, N.Y. State Conservation Dept. and N.Y. State College of Forestry, 1935, pp. 18-20, 60, 63; Ralph S. Hosmer, "Fifty Years of Conservation," *Forest Leaves* XXV, 6, 277, April 1935, pp. 65-66.

marized his report, "This is only the beginning of a system of Forestry, since nothing was as yet provided for the management of the lands, except in one county only [St. Lawrence], where an agent has been appointed to look after the interests of the State in the forests of that county. The law relating to tree planting along the highways has been very recently modified, and the germs of something that may grow into a kind of forest management, may be found in several local laws in various parts of the State, which provides that waste land upon which taxes are not paid, shall become the property of the counties." There had been agitation for a convention to form a State Forestry Association. Nothing had been accomplished except to name three persons to attend the St. Paul congress. Of the three named, Hough was the only one to appear at the congress. Nevertheless there was every reason to be encouraged at the prospect of introducing forestry in New York. Fernow did not attend the St. Paul congress, but his paper, "The Management of Burned Forests," was read by Egleston. Fernow quoted Sargent, now an authority on dendrology, on the capacity of destroyed pine lands to reproduce again. Sargent's administration of the Arnold Arboretum at Cambridge, Massachusetts, had acquired for him an enviable prestige as a scholar in forestry. On September 16, 1884, the American Forestry Congress met at Saratoga, New York, and Hough presented a forceful paper on the "Duty of the State of New York with respect to the Management of its Waste Lands and the Encouragement of Forestry." During May of that year Fernow in his *Forestry Bulletin* presented an equally strong discourse entitled, "Two Burning Questions of the Day." One question concerned the preservation of the Adirondack forests, and Fernow noticed with delight that in April at New York City Carl Schurz had aroused "even in the bustle of the Metropolis a warm interest for the 'sacred woods.' " That year, 1884, New York State appointed Sargent chairman of a commission to investigate Adirondack forest conditions and report on a system of preservation.

In a letter to Joly on December 28, 1884, Hough despairingly commented on the New York situation, "Legislation failed last winter. It will soon be tried again. The hope of results is not strong. Too many unworthy men want the places as political 'dummies.' "

Hough did not single out New York for criticism. Maine's tree planting statute which exempted planted lands for twenty years had "led to no results" so far as he could learn. Neither commission of inquiry in New Hampshire and Vermont had accomplished anything. Of Pennsylvania Hough reported, "The Governor is considering what should be done. Nothing attempted beyond inquiries by a State Board of Agriculture. . . ." The "good results" of the work of the "State Forestry Association" in Ohio were "chiefly found in an enlightenment of public opinion. The practical results cannot yet be seen in legislation." In Minnesota the death of Leonard B. Hodges had taken the "soul" from the State Forestry Association whose principal function now was "the diffusion of information." Of Dakota Hough told Joly, "Hedge planting and windbreaks from necessity with a few tracts planted by settlers are about all that can be shown." Concerning Nebraska, "A considerable amount of planting in small tracts upon farms. Some interest taken at the State College at Lincoln. The Horticultural Soc. has tried to encourage planting, but in fact no systematic effort has been made. A trifling exemption from taxation by reason of increased value acquired from planting is all the law now extant." Hough believed that Iowa had "done more than any other in the way of planting." But the state's legislation which had allowed large bounties some years before had "led to evasion and fraud, and [had been partly repealed]. . . . The Horticultural Soc. [had] published Forestry Manuals for free distribution. . . ." In Kansas, also, the "Horticultural Soc. [had] published little manuals, and there are some very intelligent planters." A statute providing tax exemption for planting had been repealed. "In all the Southern States—I might truly say in *all* of the states the owners of the land have been in haste to clear off the forest and only here and there has a voice been raised against it!"

In the *Forestry Bulletin* of May 1884, in his column, "Gleanings from the 'Forestry World,' " Fernow added little to what Hough had said six months before. In Connecticut "forest planting [had] begun in a small way." In New Jersey the state agricultural board's reports had published a few forestry papers and the state's geological survey had published "a map of timbered area." In Pennsylvania a committee on forests of the state board of agriculture had reported during the past year. In West Virginia "laudable efforts to create a popular interest in forest preservation" were being made. In North Carolina forestry was being "taken up by the State Agricultural Department [and] simple and instructive papers on forestry [were being] given in its 'Monthly Bulletin.' " In Michigan, Volney Morgan Spalding reported, "Our statesmen are chiefly interested in maintaining the tariff to make what we have left of forest go the faster. A trespass agent is to prevent depredation on State lands." In Wisconsin J. C. Plum reported that the powerful lumber interests were "inimical to any interference or investigations. . . . We have a State Lumber Inspector to look after the stumpage from state lands and to prevent trespass or unlawful cutting on state lands." In Texas T. V. Munson said that an "Interest in artificial forest growing [was] growing weak. In the stock region [it was] not needed, in the timber region clearing [was] the only want." From Colorado it was reported that "very little public spirit [was] discernible. What we most want is experimental stations and instruction adapted to the peculiarities of the climate and conditions of soil." From Ontario province came the word, "The Ontario Fruit-growers Association for several years has been very actively forwarding the interest of forestry, and meant to change their name accordingly. Their Forestry Reports, issued with Government aid during the last three years, contain much valuable information, mostly gathered at the meetings of the American Forestry Congress, to which the Government detailed delegates; 3,000 members, holding three meetings a year, must needs be effective in spreading the information gathered. . . . The Government has recently established a 'Clerk of Forest Preservation' [R. W. Phipps, author of *Report on the Necessity of Preserving and Replanting Forests*, 1883, Toronto] with duties similar to those of the Forestry Division in Washington." Ontario was fortunate in its leadership, William Saunders and D. W. Beadle. In Illinois George W. Minier was endeavoring "to get the question before the Agricultural Society." In Minnesota, Iowa, and Kansas either the agricultural and horticultural society or the state college led in the work. Kansas was proud of its "promotion of artificially grown forests," a "*local*" interest which all states should emulate. Budd's experimental work in Iowa also drew praise.

But where were there any officially reserved lands under real forestry management? The federal timber-culture acts of 1873 and 1878 gave any settler a homestead in return for planting and maintaining a forest on one-sixteenth of his entry. But no knowledge of the species most likely to thrive, of the conditions required for most effective tree growth in various regions, or of how the forest area should be managed was either afforded or required. Correct forestry information issuing from forest experiment stations would improve this effort, which Fernow characterized as one "to encourage arboriculture in [western] treeless regions."

Fernow was more interested in "legislation looking towards the preservation of the remaining natural forests. . . ."

> We maintain that a forest administration for the State of New York, even on the basis of the present area of state forests should not only answer the purposes of protecting the water supply, but it should do so without any expense beyond a guarantee fund in the beginning, it should pay for itself with better salaries to its officers than those proposed [in a bill then pending to create a state forest commission], nay it should by and by yield a handsome revenue, decreasing instead of increasing taxation, following the example of European administrations. . . . Forests grow and are grown to be cut and to furnish valuable material to man. Their influence, climatic and hydraulic, is by no means destroyed or checked, by a well conducted, systematic forestry, which utilizes the ripe timber, taking care for its immediate regeneration and for the continuity of the forest as well as the timber supply. . . .

Protect the main waterways of the Empire State, said Fernow. Protect the water supply of the Erie Canal, the Hudson, and other rivers. Protect, also, the reservoir of these, the Adirondack forests situated at their headwaters. Introduce forestry management, log the timber, and provide for its reproduction according to sound principles of forestry.

William Saunders[63] read at the St. Paul congress a paper, "Insects Injurious to the White Pine." Saunders was a chemist and druggist by profession, a professor of materia medica, a public analyst, a pharmaceutical college president, a student of fruit growing, especially of experiments in hybridizing, editor of the *Canadian Entomologist*, and a botanist of gathering renown. He was author of a widely used text in agricultural colleges and schools, *Insects Injurious to Fruits*. Saunders' experimental farm near London, Ontario, where he conducted many noted cross breeding and fertilization experiments in agricultural and horticultural crops, would have been sufficient to earn for him an enduring place in the plant science history of Canada. His efforts put agriculture in Canada on a scientific basis and deserve even greater recognition. In 1885, the Canadian minister of agriculture selected Saunders to organize and direct a system of experimental farms to be established from the Atlantic to the Pacific. Saunders visited the United States and Europe to study the work of experimental farms already in operation. In 1886 he moved to Ottawa and there established the central Dominion Experimental Farm. Another farm was established at Nappan, Nova Scotia, for the maritime provinces; another at Brandon for Manitoba; one at Indian Head, Saskatchewan, for the Northwestern Territories (now Saskatchewan and Alberta provinces); and one at Agassiz for British Columbia. The Indian Head station acquired an early prominence, but forestry received attention at all of the Canadian stations, particularly as applied to forest planting.

Bessey, Sargent, Vasey, Mohr, and others had studied the geographical distribution of economically valuable forest species. Vasey over a period of years created singlehanded a botanical literature on forest tree taxonomy and geography. Sargent wrote his celebrated North American trees studies. Landscape gardening and the ornamental phases of horticulture and forestry were getting attention at Harvard University and elsewhere. Forestry, however, in Fernow's conception of the term, was developing almost no literature of its own. Books such as Saunders' *Insects Injurious to Fruits* had to be adapted to forestry. This work was regarded by Fernow "as a preparatory study of insect habits and of remedies against their ravages." Entomology was growing more rapidly than forestry. C. V. Riley sent to the International Forestry Exhibition at Edinburgh "a fine collection of forest insects." Fernow regarded

[63] See C. J. S. Bethune, "Dr. William Saunders, C.M.G.," *The Canadian Entomologist* XLVI, 10, 1914, pp. 333-336; also concerning the 50th anniversary of the Central Experimental Farm at Ottawa, see *London, Ontario, Advertiser*, June 6, 1936; and Louie M. Carling, *London Free Press*, Sept. 20, 1913.

Andrew S. Fuller's *Practical Forestry* as a book really on forest botany. These were valuable studies, but they treated phases of forestry rather than the whole. Nevertheless, fundamental groundwork was being laid.

The western and eastern problems in forestry differed in many respects. Timber culture, homesteading, and irrigation might occupy the attention of the West for some time. None of these phases was central to the natural resource problems of the East at this time. But East and West could join in one national enterprise, the introduction of approved forest management practices. Botanical and forestry problems were regional, but methods of solution could be universal. One state could become a model for the entire nation. Fernow approved of the selection of Saratoga, New York, as the location of the next congress. New York would be encouraged to introduce approved forestry methods in the management of its forest preserve.

At a special meeting of the American Forestry Congress held at the United States Department of Agriculture, May 7-8, 1884, Fernow reported on "The proper value and management of Government Timberlands." He argued that without expending vast sums of money indefinitely "a forest administration for the Government timber-lands, either of a State or of the United States, [could] be devised and maintained." Besides protecting water supply and climatic conditions, it would "pay its own expenses from the sale of ripe timber, . . . yield a handsome revenue and furnish sufficient means for acquiring and reforesting such localities as should be preserved in forest." This must have sounded like a large undertaking. Fernow realized that appropriations for many years would be necessary. Once the forest domain was under proper administration, however, it would become self-sustaining and profitable. No piecemeal reservations were contemplated. The entire publicly owned forest domain was held in view. Fernow believed that the elimination of timber depredations alone would save the nation millions of dollars.

Only a few persons attended these sessions in the Library Room of the department. "Lack of numbers," *Forestry Bulletin* reported, "is compensated by the enthusiasm and earnestness of those who with a public-spirited mind, without any direct personal advantage, will sacrifice the time and incur the expense incident to an attendance at a meeting. A respectable number, however, were present, coming from a wide reach of country. There were members and delegates from Canada, and there were representative men from Massachusetts on the East, and from Kansas and Nebraska on the West." That year the forestry division of the United States department of agriculture had been reorganized, with Nathaniel H. Egleston in charge. *Forestry Bulletin* characterized the amount of the annual appropriation made for the division's work as "meager." *Forestry Bulletin* asked why "no funds for the publication of material gathered during last year" had been provided? The division's—that is, Dr. Hough's—three published reports on forestry had contained "valuable statistical information." What action toward forest protection, preservation, and renewal had been stimulated? The forest resource was very valuable. The division's "working report" had fixed the "estimated value of our forest products at $700,000,000, which is more than the value of the corn crop, nearly twice that of the wheat product, ten times the output of the silver and gold mines or the value of the wool product, and three times the value of the output from all the mines of the United States put together. . . . *What efforts are being made by the general government to guard the continuance of this most valuable of all our industries?*"

Hough, Egleston, F. P. Baker, and Fernow spoke on the symposium program of the American Forestry Congress's Washington meeting. Baker, a resident of Topeka, Kansas, was one of the three agents appointed by Egleston to conduct inquiries for the department on the forest resources of the United States. His report on the forest conditions of the Mississippi valley and tree-planting on the plains, a supplementary report, and his suggestions in regard to the care and disposal of the public lands had been appreciatively received; and the special agents had been directed to continue their investigations. Baker presented a paper on "The Value and Management of the Timber Lands of the United States." This paper and that of George Vasey on the "Distribution of North American Forest Trees" left a lasting impression.

It will be seen, said Baker, "that when we come to speak of the *management* of Government timber lands we enter on a new field. There has been so far nothing that indicates the existence of a plan on the part of the Government having for its object the preservation of the forest still under its ownership and control." He formulated an original eight point plan, urging that foresters be trained at forestry schools, that forestry experiment stations be located in different parts of the country, that the forestry division be organized into an executive body. It should be organized, he said, into a "working force," and he outlined an elaborate scheme of duties and authorities. Trained, competent, and honest men, not mere land officers, should have the care of the government-owned forests. Railroad corporations should not be furnished tie-timber at the expense of the nation. Settlers' absolute wants should be confined to waste, fallen, and surplus trees. No more timber should be "slashed down," said Baker. Fire protection was urged. Land classification, based on surveys and descriptions, was recommended. "Government timber," he said, "should nowhere be sold at $1.25 an acre. If sold at all a price should be fixed upon it somewhere near its value." When forest surveys were made, the lands and the character and value of the timber should be shown.

Baker's speech was more important for its factual content than its recommendations. The government-owned Rocky Mountain forests, which Baker wanted withdrawn from sale or entry, would safeguard the agriculture of the lower regions of the Platte, the Rio Grande, and the Arkansas rivers, as well as the agriculture made possible by irrigation in Kansas, Colorado, Utah, and New Mexico, by preserving for these regions a controlled water supply at the headwaters. He pointed out that at that time the federal government owned about 85,000,000 acres of forest in two great regions—the east and west slopes of the Rocky Mountains and the parallel ranges in California, Nevada, Oregon, Washington, Colorado, Idaho, Montana, and Wyoming. There the greatest interest should be centered. Much of the land, mountain slopes of high altitudes, would never be wanted for homestead preemption. The federal government was not in the position of the State of New York which, confronted with the necessity of protecting the headwaters of the Hudson River and other streams having their sources within the Adirondack Mountains, would have to repurchase land the state had once owned. The federal government, Baker told his audience, could "withdraw tomorrow every acre of Government timber land from sale or entry," because the government still owned the land. True, 85,000,000 acres was a fraction of the "one billion, eight hundred and fifty-two million, three hundred and ten thousand, nine hundred and eighty-seven acres" that had once been the public domain. Yet he humorously observed that "eighty-five million acres of forest comprised in one body, would make a very respectable 'woodlot,' particularly when, at a low estimate, it was considered worth $212,500,000." These were figures based on the estimates of the 1880 census. Actually, neither the general land office nor the forestry division knew completely and satisfactorily the extent of the forests under the absolute control of the federal government. Up to that time the government had not differentiated sufficiently in its land-disposals between agricultural and forested lands. Huge areas under the vague title "swamp lands" had been disposed. Baker called attention to 23,000,000 acres of government land in the southern states, the larger part of which was supposed to be forest, most of it pine lands. Huge areas of unsurveyed public lands existed in Minnesota, Nebraska, California, Nevada, Oregon, Washington, Colorado, Utah, Arizona, New Mexico, Dakota, Idaho, Montana, Wyoming, Louisiana, Florida, Indian Territory, and Alaska. Indeed, large areas of surveyed lands in valuable timber states such as Minnesota and Wisconsin had passed out of government control. Immediate action with regard to the Rocky Mountain forest was most pressing. If the "preservation of the natural curiosities of the Yellowstone Park" justified a course of action on a small scale, the larger economic interests involved in the Rocky Mountain forest justified action on a larger scale. Little mention was made of forest utilization and real forestry management. That was regarded by Baker as a "new field." The leadership of Fernow would emerge at this and other points of forestry.

In the year of this meeting dedicated to forest management of government timberlands, a state forestry association was formed in Colorado. In the following year the office of state forest commissioner was constituted, but without adequate appropriations. In 1876 the Colorado state constitution had recognized the need of a state forest policy. Not until 1885, however, when Colonel Edgar T. Ensign was reappointed the first state forest commissioner in the United States, did the work with forest officers become effective.[64] Soon California, without granting administrative authority, created a forest commission, or state board of forestry, to study experimentally the requirements of various timber trees and other matters of forest culture. Three commissioners were appointed who "entered upon a wide range of duties of a practical nature with an energy and zeal which [encouraged] the expectation of beneficial results."[65] The chairman of this board, which began with "considerable power and ample appropriations," was Abbot Kinney, president of the Southern California Pomological Society, the Academy of Sciences, and mercantile and railway companies. Among a wide variety of occupations, not the least of which was that of an influential publisher, Kinney was known as a president of the state forestry society and water and forest organizations, and founder of Ocean Park. A business man interested in science, he served his state ably. The Ohio forestry bureau "was created in 1885, consisting of three unpaid commissioners, charged with the duty of ascertaining the forest conditions of the State, of investigating the causes of waste, suggesting legislation, and reporting" on these. In 1883, when the Ohio State Forestry Association, an outgrowth of the Cincinnati Forestry Club, was formed, proposed forestry legislation was immediately considered. One bill provided for the appointment of a state forester, another for an experiment station in connection with the Ohio State University, and still another, which finally became law, created a state bureau. The Ohio forestry bureau issued reports and created much forestry interest, but it did not endure many years. Both the California and Ohio forest policies were primarily investigative and educational.[66] That forest experiment stations were created by 1887 in different parts of California, especially the station located at Santa Monica, proved the wisdom of a policy of pre-

[64] See *Report of Div. of For. for 1887*, p. 139; *ibid. for 1886*, p. 174; *Proc. Am. For. Cong.* for Boston meeting, Sept. 1885.

[65] The first report was issued in 1886 by Secretary Sands W. Forman, San Francisco.

[66] *Proc. Am. For. Cong.*, Sept. 1885; Fernow, *A Brief History of Forestry*, pp. 490, 491; *Report of Div. of For. for 1887*, pp. 126, 146; Adolph Leué, *First Annual Report of the Ohio State Forestry Bureau*, 1885, introduction tells of the Bureau's founding; *Second Biennial Report of the California State Board of Forestry*, 1887-1888, especially p. 53, in which Lemmon describes his employment.

liminary field investigation. The California board employed John Gill Lemmon and Sara Plummer Lemmon to study forest trees and conditions of the Pacific slope. Lemmon was commissioned as botanist and his wife as artist. Others prominent in studying the botany of the state were enlisted, including Charles Christopher Parry and Edward Lee Greene. In 1886 John Lemmon was appointed California state forester.[67] This distinction, however, was nominal, for Lemmon was not a forester in the technical sense. In the 1870's the University of California gave some forestry instruction. In 1876 the United States department of agriculture, in its summary, "Progress in Industrial Education," stated that the "College of Agriculture and Mechanics at Berkeley" reported that the college farm was being planted with experimental crops to illustrate "the capabilities of the State for special cultures, as forests, fruits, field crops, etc." Since 1882, and doubtless before then, Eugene Woldemar Hilgard, California's first professor of agriculture, had urged forestry work there, by both state and federal governments.[68]

Cooperative forestry work between state and federal authorities awaited the establishment of agricultural experiment stations. Fernow later explained that when, as chief of the forestry division of the Department of Agriculture, he "proposed to start some cooperative work with one of the state agricultural experiment stations, the proposition was turned down as too paternalistic," and an educational period as to this, as well as to a forest reservation policy, was required. California, however, was among the first of the states to establish agricultural and forest experiment stations, and some cooperative programs between the state agencies were begun. On a small scale introducible forest species were tested regionally, and extensive groves of eucalyptus and acacias were planted in barren and special areas. Catalpa, locust, and other tree materials were distributed. A scientific and popular description of California forest trees was prepared, and their distribution and growth density mapped. As elsewhere in the United States, the characteristic native conifers and other economically valuable species were specially studied. Osier willow culture, there as elsewhere, received attention. A principal endeavor of the state forestry board was aimed at securing reforms in cutting methods on state and federally owned lands and the introduction of conservative management on private lands.

In New York the mass meeting held in April 1884 on behalf of the Adirondack forests, under the leadership of Carl Schurz, had been partly responsible for getting legislative efforts renewed within the state to obtain a forest commission. For some while the Chamber of Com-

[67] See Willis Linn Jepson, *Torreya* VIII, 1, Dec. 1908, p. 303. Lemmon did not have the title of State Forester at first, but he was active in the State Board of Forestry and soon acquired the title.

[68] Eugene W. Hilgard, "Progress in Agriculture by Education and Government Aid," *Atlantic Monthly,* April and May 1882, pp. 3-19.

merce, New York Board of Trade and Transportation, Brooklyn Constitution Club, and other organizations had lent their support to various legislative proposals for forest preservation and protection. Prominent citizens such as Morris K. Jessup had shared in some of the discussions at Albany. In the spring of 1884, Fernow, noticing that half a dozen legislative measures were before the senate and assembly, began urging in *Forestry Bulletin*[69] a forest policy which would not merely protect the state's water supply but be also revenue-earning and patterned after European forest administration. He wanted no "half measure" and besought the legislature and Governor Grover Cleveland to establish "if nothing else, at least a conservative policy with regard to the State forest property." Especially did he urge this when that year the legislature directed the state comptroller to appoint a commission to investigate a policy of forest preservation for the state, and Charles Sprague Sargent, D. Willis James, E. M. Shepard, and William A. Poucher were appointed.

This commission, with Sargent as chairman, themselves went to the Adirondacks and examined the state forest lands. While opposing further purchases of forest lands by the state, they definitely recommended management of the lands and forests already owned. Hearings were held by the commission, at which times the logging and saw mill interests were given an opportunity to express their opposition to changes of policy. No opposition to lumbermen as such was contemplated; rather, cooperation with the lumber interests was sought by the advocates of forestry. At the Saratoga meeting of the American Forestry Congress, Dr. Hough outlined several measures most or all of which, included in a bill drawn by him, were submitted to the legislature by the commission. This and other proposed legislation failed; and the need of a new or modified enactment, one which might reconcile the conflicting lumber, hydraulic, forestry, and other interests, was indicated.

The Sargent commission had performed an excellent service. More information on New York forest conditions was gathered together than had ever been available before. Previously the amount of state owned lands was known in a confused way. Knowledge of the value and location of a large part of the lands was indefinite, indicated on the comptroller's books by grants, patents, townships, and lot numbers. The Sargent commission encountered the lumbermen's arguments that fire was the chief cause of forest destruction, and that but a small percentage of the timber, even of the most valuable species, was being lumbered.

Fernow believed that New York, like European countries, with the

[69] May 1884, pp. 8-9; September 1884, p. 1; January 1885, pp. 3ff. (Report of Saratoga meeting, American Forestry Congress); "Pruning the Forest," *Rpt. of Amer. For. Cong.*, 1886, p. 84. See also references to footnote 62.

right kind of forest policy and management, could reduce, instead of increase, taxes. "Forests," he said, "grow and are grown to be cut and to furnish valuable material to man. Their influence, climatic and hydraulic, is by no means destroyed or checked, by a well-conducted, systematic forestry, which utilizes the ripe timber, taking care for its immediate regeneration and for the continuity of the forest as well as the timber supply." On the basis of existing state forest acreage, the state's water resources could be protected.[70] He had been in the United States less than eight years, and had had little business or direct political experience when he said this. America's democratic institutions quite obviously differed from the monarchic German political economy. But Fernow believed his premises predicated in scientific principles and economic laws common to all nations. America's first professionally trained forester was asked by Senator Lowe of New York to prepare the new legislation which, "while several other bills drawn for the same purpose were tabled," was passed by the legislature May 11, 1885, and four days later was signed by Governor David B. Hill. Fernow said[71] of this law: "It provided for a well organized system to suppress fires. Substantially the same law, with minor modifications," was later enacted in Maine, New Hampshire, Wisconsin, and Minnesota. This became the "foundational law of conservation" in New York and represented "the first comprehensive forest administration law in the United States."[72] By chapter 283 of the 1885 laws the legislature declared all lands owned or thereafter acquired by the state within the counties of Clinton (excepting two small areas), Essex, Franklin, Fulton, Greene, Hamilton, Herkimer, Lewis, Saratoga, St. Lawrence, Sullivan, Ulster, Warren, and Washington, to constitute and be known as a forest preserve; and placed its administration with a forest commission of three persons. These forest commissioners were to "have the care, custody, control, and superintendence" of the seven to eight hundred thousand acres of preserve lands scattered over the counties and were to "maintain and protect the forests now on the forest preserve, and to promote as far as practicable the further growth of forests thereon." A forest warden and other officers, including foresters, were to be appointed; and the net result was the establishment of one of the first efficient fire warden systems in the United States. The forest preserve area was to be enlarged by new portions added from the state's forest counties. By chapter 448 of the 1885 laws, the New York legislature on June 9 provided an amended procedure applicable to fifteen forest counties for the sale

[70] "Two Burning Questions of the Day," *op. cit.*, pp. 8-9.

[71] *Forestry Investigations* U.S.D.A. 1877-1898, *op. cit.*, pp. 25-26; 173.

[72] Gurth Whipple, *op. cit.*, p. 20; Ralph S. Hosmer, "Fifty Years of Conservation," *op. cit.*, p. 65; see also, *People of the State of New York vs. Benton Turner* 145 NY 451, judgment affirmed and 1885 laws held constitutional by U.S. Supreme Court. (1897) 168 US 90, *Turner vs. New York*.

of unpaid tax lands to the state, and for the state's collection of taxes from non-residents. Fernow's work must have had to do only with chapter 283. For the purposes of administering and enforcing this set of laws, $15,000 were appropriated. In 1915 he explained to a New York state constitutional convention that a technical management was intended but the lack of available technically educated personnel made the institution of a complete forest administration and management impossible for many years. Indeed trained foresters in quantity were not available in any state of the United States until toward the very last years of the century.

When the forest administration law of 1885 was enacted, Fernow wrote, ". . . the *economic* and watershed protecting aspect of the Preserve was uppermost. At that time, the tourist, private camp, and summer guest development was still in infancy. . . ." The park concept, therefore, was not written into the law. Years later the state began actively to purchase forest lands with money appropriated to enlarge the forest preserve; $25,000 in 1890 was jumped to $600,000 in 1895 and a million dollars in 1897. A forest preserve of state-owned land in the Adirondack and Catskill region gradually has evolved, and included within the preserve boundaries have been created the Adirondack and Catskill parks. Much of the park areas were privately acquired, but state-owned lands within the park area constitutes part of the preserve. State-acquired titles to lands have been vested in a state agency. While "the idea of converting the preserve into a park grew" through the last years of the century and into the new century, title to new lands was taken in a forest preserve board. The purposes of a park were essentially recreation and pleasure; the purposes of a preserve were the industrial and manufacturing ends subserved. In either case, watershed protection was afforded.[73]

In addition to the passage of the forestry legislation of 1885, two other major events occurred that year in New York, the formation of a state forestry association and the organization of the forest commission.

Warren Higley of Ohio, who had transferred his law practice to New York City, had become president of the American Forestry Congress at its Saratoga meeting in September 1884, replacing Commissioner of Agriculture Loring. Higley as president, Joly as first vice president, and Fernow as secretary, shared an aggressive leadership in the congress. Dr. Hough, still an officer, participated. On December 28, 1884, he wrote to Joly, "The succession of another man at the head of the Department of Agriculture is as well assured as in the office of President. Until then, nothing can be done. A bill is now before Congress for ap-

[73] Extracts from a letter written to the New York Constitutional Convention by Fernow, *Forestry Quarterly* XIII, 4, Dec. 1915, p. 584; Gurth Whipple, *op. cit.*, p. 63.

pointing a Commission to consider the reservation of woodlands—but it can only affect the Western and Pacific territory, where alone we have timber on the public lands. . . ."

In 1885 Grover Cleveland, governor of New York, became the twenty-second president of the United States. Hough's letter clearly indicated a dissatisfaction with Commissioner Loring. Perhaps there was represented also a dissatisfaction with Egleston as chief of the forestry bureau. Hough must have had in mind Senator Edmund's bill to "establish a Forest Reservation on the head-waters of the Missouri River and the head-waters of Clark's Fork of the Columbia River," a mountainous region consisting of about seven thousand square miles. Flood control and climatic influences were the reservation's justification in the minds of a committee of the American Forestry Congress, which approved the project by resolution at its Washington meeting in May 1884. Forest preservation of course was also a principal cause; and the preservation of elk, deer, and buffalo, as well as use for a pleasure-seekers' park, were not overlooked. Although the reservation was planned to secure and preserve a forest tract at the headwaters of important rivers, the idea of a park was also in line with a policy fixed by George Washington, who had "given his countrymen the ample parks adorning the National Capital." This bill was defeated in the House of Representatives. Paragraphs from *Forestry Bulletin* in behalf of passage show a trend of argument used during these years: "It imperils no personal interest nor infringes on railway lands or possessory rights of Indians, and seems absolutely without objections. . . . It is an act for preservation of natural forests, now fast being destroyed by fires kindled by vandal hunters, supplementary to the prayers of forestry men and statesmen which have secured to the nation White Sulphur Springs, the wonderful trees of the Yosemite, and the mountain park of the Yellowstone."

Hough told Joly:

> As I have repeatedly stated in your presence, our Government has passed the title without timber reservation to private owners, until there is none [of the public land] left, except in the remote territories. It cannot compel the reservation or planting of woodlands upon private lands. There is not the remotest prospect it will buy back lands to plant forests upon. It can *encourage* in various ways:
>
> By establishing Experimental Stations;
>
> By diffusing information broadcast;
>
> By offering premiums for best results, greatest quantity, on cheapest and best methods in planting;
>
> By promoting special education upon forestry in the schools, and in various other ways. . . .

This was a considered condensation of Hough's views, expressed during the last year of his life, of what the federal government might do in forestry. Joly had asked Hough to aid him to prepare a statement of what was being done "in the way of encouragement of Tree Planting in the United States." Hough answered,

. . . unfortunately it is a "Short Story soon told." The "Tree Planting act" of 1873 by Congress intended to encourage plantations upon the prairies produced some results, but although an immense amount of land has been entered, the law has very generally been evaded. An entry would be made in a rapidly-settling region with the intention of finding some one who would pay $200 to $500 for an abandonment, when the other party would at once enter by homestead or purchase title. I have known a man enter his quarter section each for himself, his adult children and various relatives none of them becoming actual residents and all of them being paid to retire their claims to give a chance to others. The radical fault of the act was, in not providing that a tract once entered for tree planting, *should never be held under any other form of title.* At the last session I think . . . there was a decidedly large party favoring repeal [of this act]. This is all that Congress has done in the way of direct encouragement. . . .

Hough then told of his appointment as a forestry investigator "upon the general questions of Forestry" in the United States, and of his preparation of three forestry reports and the beginning of a fourth report. Writing from his home at Lowville, New York, on December 28, 1884, he said:

I think I can foresee a time coming, which will educate our people upon the question of forestry, in realizing the want which *scarcity and high prices* must inevitably bring.

When our people find that they *must have* timber and that it can be got only by *cultivation,* they will plant for the profit of it—and will diligently study the ways by which it can be done to best advantage.

I regard our great railroad system as a *powerful* agency in hastening this time, by depleting distant timber regions to supply others already depleted.

I have an illustration within sight of my door. The whole eastern horizon towards the Adirondacks was once bristling with pine forests and vast quantities of lumber were sawn and sent off. We now get *all* our pine from Canada and Michigan. How long can we do this?

Hough believed that the states had done something by means of Arbor Days. "The planting done is trifling: but the public interest awakened in the subject is a *great deal.* . . ." Hough looked forward to the time when there would be a new commissioner of agriculture. In 1885 Norman J. Colman of Missouri became the new commissioner—the last commissioner, since before his term expired, agriculture became officially recognized by a place in the President's Cabinet.

The advanced nature of Hough's thinking was borne out by his recommendation to the Saratoga congress that plantations and nurseries be established in connection with educational institutions to supply seedling trees and seeds for reforestation. He suggested as possibilities the agricultural college of Cornell University or the state experiment station at Geneva, New York. In fact, he suggested that such institutions might be established independently on the state's land in the Adirondacks. Little did Hough realize that within another decade and a half some of the largest and most important forest nurseries of the world would be located in the Adirondack regions.

Commissioner Loring in his opening address to the Saratoga congress sought to encourage the spread of state forestry associations modelled after that in Ohio. The congress enacted a resolution approving the placement of an experiment station by the Ohio association in connection with the agricultural and mechanical college at Columbus, which today is Ohio State University. The forestry movement in Ohio took a leading position.

Forming their association on January 13, 1883, they had held bimonthly meetings and attempted to educate the public and secure needed legislation. Adolph Leué had laid before the St. Paul congress a plan of organization for such a station. The congress endorsed it wholly and recommended that all of the states and provinces of the United States and Canada adopt the program. Said Leué, "As the State of Ohio still owns certain tracts of land adapted to forest culture, it would not only be proper, but even advisable to utilize the same for experiment stations and model forest plantations."[74] Fernow rejoiced at this instigation of rational forestry methods, but prophetically he pointed out, "The difficulty will be found, however, in the selection of a director, who must not only possess a superior organizatory spirit, but besides having a comprehensive scientific education, must know to what points to direct investigation first, and what observations and experiments will bring practical results soonest." Fernow was correct; the station's reputation was based on its program rather than on results. Each state should have a forestry association, Fernow concluded. Government programs necessarily were built around forest commissions. Until the nation and states had trained foresters and skilled research men, there was no need of experiment stations.

On December 26, 1884, Fernow wrote to Joly:

I personally hope very much that you will find it possible to [attend the Executive Committee meeting of the Congress, January 10, 1885]. I am feeling especially gloomy tonight as to the prospects of our next meeting, as I just got an intimation of the proposed formation of a "Society for the Protection of Forests" headed by some big men and money bags of New York. I trust, however, that other than forestry interests will keep me in your esteem, should those get into other hands.

Again on February 12, 1885, he forwarded important information to Joly:

. . . We—i.e. Mr. Higley and myself—are very busy preparing a meeting at Utica for the formation of a New York State Forestry Association, which

[74] *Forestry Bulletin* 2, Sept. 1884, pp. 10-12.

we have undertaken as officers of the Congress. . . . Boston has been chosen for the place of meeting [of the next Congress] and we shall work hard to make [it] a rousing affair. . . .

This letter was written before Chapter 283 of the New York laws of that year, the forest administration law, was signed, establishing the state forest preserve. With the advice and approval of the senate, Governor Hill appointed as members of the newly created forest commission Townsend Cox, Sherman W. Knevals, and Theodore B. Basselin. Abner Leavenworth Train was named the commission's secretary. But the only one on this commission to acquire real distinction in the forestry history of New York was the assistant secretary, Colonel William F. Fox.[75] The most serious handicap which the new commission encountered was the lack of foresters to institute forest management in the preserve. A few untrained men, lacking field maps, notes, and often even survey records and property descriptions, had to deal with the complicated situation. The commission had sufficient money for the forest work of that time. But to spend it fruitfully and conservatively required trained knowledge and experience of forestry. The green timber of the preserve became known as "Adirondack Corn." Years were required to build up survey records, maps, field notes, line locations, title descriptions, and other essential data. The "law's delay" figured as a handicap. Land title litigation, often going to the state's highest tribunals, ensued. Former owners stampeded the courts in efforts to assert their equities of redemption or possession of previously owned lands. A "land boom" followed. Timber speculators fought the new legislation with so much determination that further legislation, the constitutionality of which had to be tested along with the older laws, had to be secured. These processes took time, especially when litigation went to the United States Supreme Court. Years passed before constitutional points of the 1885 laws were settled. By that time a large part of the softwood timber of the state had been lumbered, particularly the wood pulp lumber. Perhaps the most serious struggle of all arose in trespass evictions. Scandalous abuses took place. When in 1893 timber cutting on state lands was legalized and despoilment promised to be extended, there emerged from the constitutional convention of 1894 the much disputed Article VII, Section 7, which forbade the cutting of timber, dead or alive, on state-owned forest lands.

Fernow for many years insisted that he knew that this constitutional provision was framed by well-meaning persons who feared arbitrary and "tyrannical" action by the commission in its management of the beautiful Adirondack forests, or a fear that lumbering activities would

[75] G. Whipple, *op. cit.*, pp. 20, 188; Ralph S. Hosmer, "William F. Fox, Pioneer in Forestry," *Bulletin to the Schools, University of the State of New York*, XXVII, 7, (March 1941), pp. 219-221.

be permitted without adequate supervisory forestry personnel. They realized that competently trained foresters in the United States and Canada were not to be found. To use Fernow's words, the situation "as regards personnel was not changed [from what it had been in 1885], and it was wise enough to delay the attempt at forest management."[76] The forest situation had indeed become paradoxical. After creating a state forest preserve and a forest commission in 1885, a constitutional enactment in substance forbade forestry practice within the commission's jurisdiction. Within less than a decade forestry in New York State had been given real life, only to have its practice substantially limited to privately owned lands.

If New York had had at that time a forceful forestry association, subsequent embarrassment might have been saved. A forestry association might have activated the public mind so that the fear of unintelligent political interference in the management of the state owned forests might have been relieved. The people did not understand forestry, especially forestry as a part of a state policy. Forestry was naturally associated with watershed protection, with tree planting, and with Arbor Days. Forestry unfortunately seemed hostile to the lumber interests, whereas truly it only endeavored to assure a future timber and forest supply for lumber and all industrial interests. A strong forestry association might have educated the people in the values of forest fire protection, forest reproduction, and forest management for revenue. If the wealth of New York justified a huge park area as a recreation center and fish and game preserve, forest reservations and forest management were not necessarily outlawed. Foresters were not available, but proof of what they could accomplish would probably have brought about facilities for their education.

Fernow had tried to organize a forestry association:

> It was in 1885 after the [Saratoga] meeting of the American [Forestry Congress], that myself, as Secretary, and Judge Higley, as President, both residing in New York, considered it our duty as officers . . . to organize a State Association. I began by searching to find out whether anything had been done in this direction, and found that an attempt had been made two years earlier, by a lawyer, to bring together public-spirited people into such an association. He had worked out a constitution, and had the assurance of a number of influential men that they would join, but, owing to his preoccupation in other directions, the matter had been dropped. Just then Judge Higley and myself received an invitation to come the next Saturday to the Arsenal Building in Central Park, where a forestry association would be formed, the call being signed by E. B. Southwick, Entomologist of the Park. We, of course, went there, and found, besides seven reporters of the newspapers, two or three friends of Mr. Southwick, who in quite a cool manner proposed to organize the Association by proposing the name of Morris K. Jessup as

[76] See references of footnote 62 of this chapter, especially Pettis and Whipple (pp. 31-69). Quotation is from *Forestry Quarterly* XIII, 4, p. 584.

President.[77] Upon asking whether Mr. Jessup had been seen about the matter, we were informed that he had not, but that there was hardly any doubt but that he would accept. This seemed to us a rather childish proceeding, and we pointed out that it would be necessary to make more of a canvass beforehand and secure a wider representation in the State. Thereupon a committee was appointed by us, being "us." Andrew D. White, then President of Cornell University, having just come back from Berlin as Ambassador [he was actually Ambassador to Russia at St. Petersburg], we found, happened to be in town, and we immediately waited upon him to secure his interest and advice. We had made up our minds that there should be a rousing first meeting somewhere in the middle of the State, with prominent men to call the meeting, and we asked White to preside over this meeting. He informed us that within two weeks he was leaving for California, but, if the meeting could be organized as quickly as that, he would be willing to preside. Whereupon, we began telegraphing to various influential people in the State, and within less than a week we had a call in all the newspapers to bring together a meeting in Utica, signed by ex-Governors, ex-Judges, Senators, etc. The meeting took place within another week, but Andrew D. White failed us. Among those present, however, was the, then, youngest Assemblyman, Theodore Roosevelt, and he readily accepted the position of presiding officer. The meeting was quite fully attended, some hundred legislators being present. The Association was formed, a constitution which I had drafted was adopted, and Morris K. Jessup, who had been interviewed [was] made President and a Mr. Powers, Secretary. This was an unfortunate choice, for although this gentleman had been writing in the papers on forest conservation, he was unfit for the Secretaryship when he had to meet people, being without tact; and in a short time the Association was ashore. Mr. Southwick later on became Secretary, and for a few years some insignificant meetings took place in New York. I had lost interest and lost track of what became of the Association finally, which evidently died of inanition. . . .[78]

In this all too brief association Fernow became acquainted with Theodore Roosevelt. The good names of Abram S. Hewitt and Edward Cooper appear among the signatures of leading citizens interested in the formation of the Association. Hewitt, immediately after the Utica meeting, may have recommended Fernow for appointment as chief of the forestry division of the United States department of agriculture.

[77] As a committee chairman of the New York Chamber of Commerce, Jessup had been active on behalf of forest legislation.

[78] From a letter written to F. F. Moon, March 26, 1914. See also Fernow's article in *The Empire Forester*, student annual of the N.Y. State College of Forestry at Syracuse, and the review of it in *Forestry Quarterly* XIV, 2, p. 363.

CHAPTER III

Fernow as Chief of the Division of Forestry of the United States Department of Agriculture

On July 10, 1885, Fernow, as corresponding secretary of the American Forestry Congress, sent out an invitation to its members. "Allow me to call your particular attention to the Boston meeting of this Congress, which is designed to unite all New England forestry interested with a view of establishing a uniform policy in regard to her forests. . . ." By this time forestry associations had been formed in Minnesota, Ohio, Quebec, Manitoba, Colorado, and New York. Practically every society devoted to the interests of agriculture or horticulture had begun to give forestry a prominent place in its discussions. Forestry commissions or commissioners to inquire into the needs of or to manage forest domains had been appointed in Vermont, New Hampshire, New York, Pennsylvania, Ohio, Colorado, and California. Arbor days had been established in fifteen states[1] and in Canada. These facts gave the American Forestry Congress a justified sense of pride as it gathered on September 22 for its fourth annual meeting in the rooms of the Massachusetts Horticultural Society.

The congress was divided into sections as defined by its constitution and by-laws: forest planting, forest management, forestry proper, preservation of forests, forest economy, technology and statistics, applied science and climatology, general topics.

The congress was pleased with its welcome to Boston. "Our last two annual meetings have largely lacked the local support which must needs be enlisted to lend impressiveness to our proceedings. The welcomes which we have met in this center of intellectual life, and especially by the gentlemen of the Massachusetts Horticultural Society, must be . . . gratefully acknowledged." The congress now had eighty-nine members —twenty-one life members and sixty-eight annual members.

The Boston congress enabled Fernow once again to urge members to "produce at our meetings only work of some special value," to make a "concerted effort [to] establish the principles upon which the forestry we advocate is to be carried on. . . . We need definite well-authenticated local observations, arrived at by well-described scientific method; we need methodical work in establishing the conditions of growth for different species, their behavior towards the soil and towards each other in different soils, their rate of growth at different periods of life under different conditions." Basic to all work on a national scale was the need

[1] See *Report of Div. of For. for 1892*, p. 316.

to recognize that different conditions and therefore different problems were to be found in the eastern mountain regions, the treeless states of the West, the forest areas of the northern states, and the vast forest wealth in the South.

A high point of the meeting was the address by the new commissioner of agriculture, Norman J. Colman, who promised that some practical forestry work would be done by the department. Colman contrasted the fifteen thousand dollar annual appropriation for the forest commission of New York and ten thousand dollars allowed the forestry division of the federal department.[2] He urged the congress to help secure a fifty thousand dollar annual appropriation for the latter.

Fernow read a paper on the practicability of using the lumbermen's waste material as a fertilizer in both agriculture and forestry. He handed over the question "to experimenters and inventors."

Dr. Oliver Wendell Holmes sent a message to the congress expressing the hope that the congress would induce the country to retain "leaves enough to hide its nakedness, of which it is already coming to be ashamed." Holmes hoped that the meetings would provide "a powerful impetus toward the protection, the conservation, and wise utilization of our forest wealth."

In his report of November 20, 1885,[3] Nathaniel H. Egleston gave much space to the report of the New Hampshire forest commission, which had been studying forest destruction and the effects on streams, ponds, and rainfall. During four years the commission had been securing data from reputable inhabitants. The commissioners, pointing out that one-half of the state should produce wood and timber, appealed to farmers and the public and emphasized the economic functions of the forest in relation to water supply, crop production, and of course the rainfall influence. Egleston observed that "the proper storage and distribution of our water-supply are of much greater importance to us than the amount received."

A forestry congress of the southern states was held in 1885 in Florida. Prominent among the subjects discussed were the too rapid decimation of the forests and the destructive effect on forest growth caused by grazing domestic animals. Egleston, however, commented, "Happily the Southern States are so amply stocked with timber of valuable quality, having 50 per cent of their area clothed more or less densely with trees, that if the facts brought to view at the recent congress are properly set before the people of those States there is reasonable ground to

[2] The *Report of Div. of For. for 1886* places the sum made available to the New York forest commission at $32,500. The amount of state-owned forest land was said to be 715,267 acres. The California forest commission, recently created, was said to have a "moderate appropriation" of $15,000 to prevent forest fires, prosecute depredators, aid forest planters, and make a forest map of the state.

[3] *Report of Div. of For. for 1885*, p. 194.

think that the destruction of the forests may be arrested before it shall have gone so far as to imperil hopelessly the great interests of the country."[4]

The year 1886 was a turning point in the history of North American forestry. Probably as early as 1885 President Grover Cleveland consulted Abram S. Hewitt to ask if he knew of any man who might head the forestry division of the United States Department of Agriculture. That a new appointee was to be selected was not indicated by either Colman or Egleston in their November report of that year. Each, however, assured the president that the division of forestry recognized "a kindred work" and gave "whatever aid it could" to the American Forestry Congress. Fernow, obviously, was the leading figure of the congress. In 1884, the year of the Saratoga congress, Hewitt had been associated with Fernow in forming the New York State Forestry Association. Hewitt had seen Fernow and Higley accomplish what Verplanck Colvin and others in July 1883[5] had failed to do. At the Saratoga congress Charles Kendall Adams, then a professor of political economy at the University of Michigan and later a president of Cornell University, had presented a dynamic appeal for widespread public education in forestry. Fernow and Adams had joined together to refute by factual and scientific proof the lumbermen's denial of a connection between the forest and river-and-stream supply in the lower lands. A trip by rail, boat, and stage had taken members of the congress to Blue Mountain Lake and through a chain of lakes to Raquette Lake and the heart of the Adirondacks. There they saw the importance of forests at the headwaters of navigable streams. Egleston was so enthused that he argued in his 1884 report for the "reclothing" of the upper waters of the Ohio and Mississippi with forests, as well "as to expend millions in building dikes to check the ravages of the floods."[6]

Hewitt recommended Fernow to President Cleveland. Hough, in an address before the American Forestry Congress at Montreal, had recorded that an American student had been registered at one of the European forestry schools when he visited Europe. This student, however, must not have completed the course or did not return to the United States. Hewitt knew that there was only one man qualified for the position. Although Fernow was known as a Republican in politics and the administration was Democratic, Fernow was appointed. The new chief related:

In 1886, having resisted the tempter for half a year, because a politician and not a forester was needed in the position, I accepted the call to take charge of the forestry work in the Department of Agriculture. Dr. Hough, who had assiduously compiled three voluminous reports of information, had

[4] *ibid.*, pp. 199-200.

[5] See *Forestry Bulletin* 1, May 1884, p. 1.

[6] *Report of Div. of For. for 1884*, p. 163.

been superseded by a reverend, white haired gentleman, whose knowledge of the whole subject was even less than that of his predecessor, and he was at his wits end what to do with the munificent appropriation of $8,000 [exclusive of salaries]. I had the unpleasant task not only of superseding, but retaining as my assistant this old gentleman [Nathaniel H. Egleston of Williamstown, Massachusetts] together with another similar assistant, a former Secretary of the State of South Carolina. I found the two cosily, but by no means amicably, ensconced in a little garret room with two small oval windows, quarreling as to whom the credit of their performances really belonged. The introduction of a typewriter to our trio was an innovation highly resented by the two.[7]

Egleston had completed a fourth ponderous *Report upon Forestry* in 1884, a volume of more than four hundred pages.[8]

On April 6, 1886, Rossiter Raymond wrote to James T. Gardiner, director of the state [geological] survey of New York:

Mr. Bernhard E. Fernow, the new Chief of the Forestry Division at Washington, wants to get from some competent person a discussion of the hydrological (if that is the proper word) influences of forests, particularly as to floods and low water in large rivers. . . . I know Fernow well. He is a thoroughly trained forester (formerly of the Prussian service) and a man of great ability. If the politicians give him any chance he will do good work. And I am very anxious that the educated men of the country should help him in his effort. The Forestry Division has hitherto been little more than a sham. . . .

Fernow followed this letter with his own letter of April 23. He said:

There has been so much said and written on forest influences, pro and con, that I thought it a desirable undertaking to review the subject thoroughly and have it placed in a comprehensive and comprehensible form. The greatest difficulty is to find some one, unbiased and capable at the same time of doing justice to both sides and who can present the subject, without prejudice one way or the other, at once to the average reader and to the scientist. Engineers generally rely upon the meager and often untrustworthy measurements at hand, and fail to discern those influences, the existence of which the empiric, by simple reasoning and from historical evidence, believes to be sufficiently established. You know that methodical measurements were begun in Germany in 1868, which have so far yielded some positive data, the value of which engineers should be the most capable of judging if they are sufficiently broadminded. These data are little known or understood in this country, and should be critically reviewed, the possible inferences for this country made, the differences of our conditions from those abroad pointed out, and a plan developed, particularly adapted to our physical and constitutional conditions, by which the questions at issue can be experimentally settled.

[7] "The Birth of a Forest Policy," *op. cit.*

[8] In *Forestry Bulletin* 2, Sept. 1884, Fernow published a letter from Egleston referring to this report as the principal work of the Division during his incumbency: "Nowhere else will be found such an exhaustive account of the consumption of the forests by the railroads as will be found in the forthcoming report from this Department, prepared by Dr. Hough. . . ." The year of the report is variously given as 1884 and 1885. Egleston's report of Nov. 20, 1885, refers to it as published in the early part of the year. Especially important was the "very full report from six of the prairie States" on tree planting, cleared land, fire damage, forest destruction, etc.

I need not point out the immense importance of the subject to the country at large. While I believe the forest influences on climate and waterflow and general cultivation to some degree are beyond dispute, I consider the economic importance of the forests as vastly superior. At the same time it would be difficult to secure the action of the government on the latter account, and the interests of private persons in the forests are too ephemeral for them to study or even to consider the consequences of their reckless wastefulness.

Could, however, the general influences of the forest, even locally only, be established, the duty of the Government to preserve at least its present timber lands for the general good, would be a strong incentive for action which it ought really to take for merely economic reasons. . . .

He informed Gardiner that the appropriation for the fiscal year was "nearly exhausted." T. P. Roberts had written an article on the subject which would appear in the annual report of the American Forestry Congress.[9] Dr. Hough had "rehearsed" some of the experiments of Dr. Ebermayer in his first *Report on Forestry*. What was still needed, however, was a scientific and popular elucidation of the entire subject truthfully given. Fernow asked Gardiner to prepare it and on April 26 wrote him in care of the State Board of Health at Albany, saying:

I do not doubt you will find considerable difficulty in establishing the *quantitative* influence of a change in forest areas, since it is questionable whether anywhere such measurements have been made, which can form a reliable basis for deductions. But if all the material is sifted and sufficiently convincing deductions as to qualitative influences can be made, I shall be well satisfied. It will be rather more a philosophical study, than a mathematical one, and consequently reference to European data, which cover mostly longer periods of observation and perhaps are often more uniformly reliable will be of first importance. Should reliable data be found on this Continent, it would be a satisfactory addition, even if it were only for the State of New York. I will, however, say that in discussing river floods, it may be necessary to make a distinction between mountain rivers and rivers of the plains. . . .

Fernow believed that the conditions of streams in the East might not be found applicable to a study of the largest and most important drainage area of the United States, the Mississippi River system. Fernow's first attack as chief of the forestry division on forestry problems in the United States seems largely to have centered on the study of forest influences.

Fernow assumed his duties as chief of the forestry division on March 15, 1886. At that time congress allocated no specific appropriation to forestry work, which was included generally in the annual budget of the Department of Agriculture. With the end of the fiscal year on June 30, congress, allowing a special appropriation, elevated the division to a status not entirely at the mercy of the commissioner. The sum received,

[9] Thomas P. Roberts, "Relation of Forests to Floods," *Proc. Am. For. Cong. for 1885*, pp. 92-106. This paper was read at the Boston meeting in the absence of the author.

$10,000, was the same, and the division was made a permanent integral part of the Department, with statutory rank.

To prepare his first report, due on August 15, Fernow required the assistance of Egleston in statistical matters and George B. Sudworth in compiling notes for the list of timber trees published. Sudworth, who came to the division soon after Fernow's arrival, was a quiet studious individual, a graduate of the University of Michigan who had taught botany for a year at Michigan Agricultural College, and who, although appointed as a botanist in the division of forestry, was to contribute some of the most enduring work of the division. Soon an outstanding authority on the nomenclature of the arborescent and forest flora of the United States, a learned scholar of dendrology, he was to remain in federal forest work longer than any employee of the division and to acquire a knowledge of forest resources and conditions highly respected and praised by Fernow. Sudworth immediately began to familiarize himself with the geographical distribution of forest trees, especially with reference to special regions of economic significance. The division inaugurated a "new and important line of work—studies of the biology of our timber trees." To field botanists fell this task in most part, as we will show. But the ingenious direction of the work emanated from Washington, and Fernow as well as Sudworth took a special interest in its furtherance.

Fernow had been in Washington but a short while when there arrived an invitation to attend a public meeting in the Hall of the Historical Society of Pennsylvania. Action in the interest of forest preservation and reforesting of wastelands had been previously considered informally at the residence of Mrs. Brinton Coxe. A public meeting, however, was set for May 26. John Birkinbine was influential in this gathering, but Rothrock was the dominant figure. He told his audience that in every country of Europe, excepting England, there was a forestry school. But the main part of his address dealt with the forest situation of Pennsylvania, which already had lost its ship-timber industry to Michigan and Minnesota. The dire need of reforestation and the preservation of forests for fuel and to conserve water supply were stressed. Not to be disregarded were consideration of methods to fight the natural enemies of the forest. Rothrock was an authority in forest mycology and entomology, and Asa Gray had taught him botanical taxonomy. He had trained himself in forest botany and agricultural botany. In Europe Rothrock had acquired an amateur's knowledge of forestry which superseded his interest in "medical botany." As a doctor of medicine, he saw the forest in relation to hygiene and health. Rothrock believed that the way to attack the forestry problem of Pennsylvania was to exempt timberlands from taxation and to cultivate timber on the state's thirty-five hundred square miles of land which were known to be unfit for agricultural purposes. Fernow agreed and urged enlistment of the farmers' interest in the cause of Pennsylvania forestry.

At a meeting on June 2 it was decided to form an association. On June 10 a constitution was adopted. In the temporary organization, Rothrock was named president and Birkinbine secretary. A permanent organization was effected on November 30 in the auditorium of the Young Men's Christian Association of Philadelphia. Birkinbine presided at the meeting, owing to the illness of Rothrock. Fernow was present and held the audience "for an hour in a thorough exposition of the science and practice of forestry."[10] Fernow began to plead the cause of his forestry work for the federal government:

> The General Government has a Forestry Bureau, without forests, and with insufficient means to do much good. That it should, at least, take care of its remaining 70,000,000 acres of timber land and not let it be wasted, burned, or despoiled seems not to need any argument. The interest of the whole nation in the development of the Western agricultural lands demands a preservation in strong hands of the Rocky Mountain forests, and perhaps it seems desirable that operations should be extended to planting largely on the Military Reservations, on the treeless plains, if for nothing else than for the sake of the good example.

Fernow opposed a system of voluntary restrictions on the utilization of forest resources. He believed that constructive action was necessary. A use of the Canadian fire ranger system—the maintenance cost to be defrayed jointly by the state and lumber and private interests—was suggested as a possible solution. In any event, the Pennsylvania Forestry Association had been organized.[11]

Immediately the University of Pennsylvania became interested in the cause. In November the official publication of the Association, *Forest Leaves*, announced[12] that the organization, pursuing a policy with the university's scientific society, had arranged another course of forestry lectures. That spring a series of lectures had been given, one on "Our Forests" by Professor E. J. James, one on "Forests and National Existence" by Reverend John L. Lundy, and one on "The Sanitary Aspects of Forestry" by Dr. J. M. Anders. Fernow lectured on March 31 on "Forests and Forestry in the United States." Given in the University Chapel, an effort was made to have the lectures printed and published. Fernow discussed the influence of forests on soils and climatic and hydrological conditions. He treated the question of industrial supply. So interested in the forestry cause had the university become that at the organization

[10] *Forest Leaves*, April 1887, pp. 1-3; "Sketch of the Forestry Movement in Philadelphia," *ibid.*, July 1886, pp. 1-3; "Forestry Annals" etc. *ibid.* III, 11, pp. 140, 151-152; *ibid.* X, 10, Aug. 1906, pp. 153-157 (article by G. H. Wirt); letter of F. L. Bitler, May 4, 1917; intro. of Fernow's address (mss.) to Penna. For. Assoc., June 23, 1917.

[11] *Forest Leaves* XX, 4, No. 227, Aug. 1925, pp. 59-61, and references of footnote 10.

[12] *ibid.*, Nov. 1887, pp. 1ff.

meeting of the Pennsylvania Forestry Association, Dr. William Pepper, university provost, had suggested the propriety of establishing a chair of forestry in one or more colleges. The university trustees seriously considered the proposal. Had funds been available, the University of Pennsylvania might have founded the first chair in America devoted exclusively to the teaching of forestry. Professor James's report on "Government Forestry" for the United States, made soon after Fernow took office, had won Fernow's admiration.

Edmund Janes James was a professor of political economy and social science and connected with the Wharton School of Finance and Economy at the university. Later president of Northwestern University and the University of Illinois, he was also a founder and president of the American Academy of Political and Social Science, president of the American Economics Association, and the American Society for Extension of University Teaching. A teacher, editor, statistician, conservationist, and economist, he was a recognized scholar and honored for many attainments.

In the summer of 1886 Commissioner Colman instructed Fernow to investigate tree planting in the West. Fernow combined the journey through Kansas, Nebraska, and Colorado with an attendance at the American Forestry Congress held September 14-20 at Denver. Fernow saw the "need of aid by a systematic and rational distribution of suitable plant material" from experimental forests. He was not impressed with "the value and amount of the tree planting in Nebraska."[13] On December 9, 1887, at a meeting of the Pennsylvania Forestry Association, Fernow and Rothrock sharply disagreed on this point. Both were in agreement as to the value of the work when well done, but Fernow stood out as the champion of systematic forest management. In his first report, dated November 15, 1886, he wrote:

> The operations of . . . a forest department might be properly extended to the creation of new forests, so as to produce beneficial results upon the agricultural conditions of the arid and semi-arid regions of the Western States and Territories. . . . It has been shown that the climatic influences of the forest must be largely dependent upon its size and density, therefore no considerable change of the unfavorable climatic conditions of the plains can be soon expected, unless large tracts be covered with forest growth. The military reservations in the hands of the General Government form a most desirable basis for such extensive plantings. . . . If properly managed such Government forests would serve most admirably as practical schools, of forestry, as object lessons, as forest experiment stations. . . . It is *not* the control of the Government over private property, it is *not* the exercise of eminent domain, it is *not* police regulations and restrictions that have produced desirable effects upon private forestry abroad, but simply the example of a systematic and successful management of its own forests, and the opportu-

[13] *Forest Leaves*, Dec. 1887, p. 20; Feb. 1888, p. 25.

nity offered by the Government to the private forest-owner of availing himself of the advice and guidance of well-qualified forestry officials. . . .[14]

Fernow found at the Denver congress "diverging views as to the most desirable manner of procedure. . . ." The need for a change of policy "at least as regards the use of the forest domain of the Government was unanimously declared to be urgent."[15]

Bessey, a delegate from Nebraska to the Denver congress, had made a "special study of the western yellow pine (Pinus scopulorum) [which] showed that it had once been widely [scattered] throughout the northern, central, and western portions of [his] state." In explorations he came across kinnikinnick growing. From this it was an easy step to the suggestion that the sandhills of central Nebraska might be made to grow pines extensively. Bessey later wrote:

Once this thought was entertained, it was not long before the idea of forest planting reservations took shape, first as state reservations and later as reservations of the National Government. And so in my annual reports to the State Board of Agriculture I urged with as much force as I could command that such reservations should be made. . . . In 1886 I was appointed by the Governor of Nebraska to be one of the state delegates to the American Forestry Congress at Denver. . . .

Repeated and prolonged visits afterwards to the Rocky Mountains impressed upon me the great importance of the forest cover about the headwaters of the rivers that rise in that region. Here it was not man's vandalism, but man's carelessness that swept away the forests. Instead of destruction by the axe and saw, it was destruction by forest fires. . . . The destruction was as complete here as in the lumber regions of Michigan, but here the evil was more far-reaching. In Michigan there was the destruction of the trees, and the exposure of the ground under conditions unfavorable to reforestation, in the Rocky Mountains there was the same destruction of the forest with the similar adverse conditions as to reforestation, and in addition there was the destruction of the continuous water supply for the great rivers that rise in the mountains. And these rivers are those whose waters are carried out upon the plains in irrigation ditches to render them fertile. Living upon the plains, this phase of the forest problem became one of the greatest interest to me, and quite naturally, I became an earnest advocate of the conservation of the forests. . . .

In the summer of 1887, at his own expense, Fernow went again to the Rocky Mountain regions. The journey was made to acquaint himself with forest conditions and to attend meetings of the American Institute of Mining Engineers. "It was admitted everywhere," he recorded, "that the present conditions of administration have become insufferable and that the practical forestry work of the Government should first of all be directed to the protection and proper administration of its timber lands. The desirable legislation for such action on the part of the Government, outlined in my last year's report, has been more fully formulated after

[14] *Report of Div. of For. for* 1886 (Nov. 15), pp. 165-166.
[15] *ibid*, p. 179.

the personal inspection of local conditions afforded by my journey. . . ."[16]

Returning from his journey, Fernow wrote Joly:

I have just returned from an extended trip over the Rocky Mountains and find your letter of August 3, '87. By this time you will have received the call for our Springfield [Illinois] meeting in September. . . . I greatly wish such a meeting in Quebec as you propose—we need it, that is the Congress needs another such send off or revival, as Canada has given it before. There has been contemplated a meeting in Atlanta, Ga., to consolidate with the "Southern Forestry Congress," but whether that needs to be in one or two years has not been decided. . . . My journey West—undertaken at my own expense, though for the benefit and in the interest of my office!—has shown me that the important step to be taken is to reserve the Rocky Mt. forests and I shall try to concentrate my energies in that direction.

Fernow in 1886 had begun to draft what became known as the Hale bill in congress, and which was recommended for passage at the Springfield congress the following year. In essence[17] it provided a system of national forest administration and that all federally owned forest lands should be withdrawn from sale or entry until after a survey had been made and the commissioner of forestry had issued a certificate that the lands may be sold. Lands were to be classed: first, as distant from headwaters of important streams, covered by timber of commercial value, more valuable for forest purposes than for cultivation; second, lands partially or wholly covered by timber but suitable for homesteads, and more valuable for agricultural purposes than for timber; and, third, mountainous and other woodlands which, for climatic or economic or public reasons should be held permanently as forest reserves. The commissioner, with the approval of the secretary of the interior, was to determine what land should be held in reservation and what sold. The commissioner was to appoint inspectors and rangers and make regulations for the administration of the forests in such particulars as logging operations, grazing, and occupancy. The president was authorized to proclaim reservations and authorize land sales not exceeding twenty-five thousand acres. Military and naval units were to be utilized to enforce the law. Penalties also were provided for infringements.

Fernow later explained why he had placed the administration of the reservations with the Department of the Interior rather than the Department of Agriculture.[18]

When I formulated the first legislation in 1886, having in view the setting aside of the public timber domain and instituting a forest service for its administration, I located this in the Department of the Interior, although I occupied then the position of Chief of the Forestry Division in the Department of Agriculture.

There were then two good reasons for this location. In the first place, the

[16] *Report of Div. of For. for 1887*, p. 611.

[17] See *Forest Leaves*, Dec. 1887, p. 18; Jenks Cameron, *op. cit.*, pp. 202ff.

[18] Letter to H. H. Chapman dated March 10, 1916.

whole land business in the United States being transacted by the Interior Department, it seemed that the segregation of national forests could with less friction be done by leaving the matter in that Department. In the second place, at that time the Department of Agriculture was without administrative functions and appropriate machinery, which made it apparently easier to organize an administration in the Department of the Interior. . . .

At the time there was an objection raised against organizing this Service in the Department of the Interior because the function of the General Land office and its organization was for *disposal* of the public domain, not for permanent retention and continued administration of any part of it, least of all an administration based on scientific knowledge. This objection [was] valid. While it is possible to organize any kind of service in any of the Departments, there is such a thing as logical relationship and practical consideration which makes one department preferable for a given service than another. The reference to the Department of Agriculture of the forest service [would have been] logical. . . .

The last paragraph is not an admission of error; the other considerations were controlling. Furthermore, these considerations remained controlling for some time to come. It was very important that the new service work harmoniously with the general land office and with the United States Geological Survey. Since by 1905 all forest work as far as possible was centered in the forest service of the Department of Agriculture, Fernow could not be held responsible for the fact that later the administration of the national reserves was principally centered in the Department of the Interior. Although the Hale bill never became a law, it shaped the federal forest policies of the following years.

Widespread discussions and debates of the legislative proposals distributed forestry propaganda and tended to convince a disbelieving public of the need for adequate national forestry legislation.

During Fernow's first year of office there was published "A descriptive catalogue of manufactures from native woods, as shown in the exhibit of the United States Department of Agriculture, at the World's Industrial and Cotton Exposition at New Orleans, Louisiana," by Charles Richard Dodge. In the annual report for 1886, a first attempt was made to classify tentatively the American forest flora, which listed 97 species then believed economically important. Eastern timbers, particularly the conifers (spruce, hemlock, cedars, cypress), were studied. Fernow announced immediately: "With its present appropriation the Division, in my opinion, cannot satisfactorily undertake extended forest statistical inquiries, and should, therefore, confine itself mainly to the work of establishing the methods upon which forest planting and forest management can be carried on in our country with our native timber trees. . . ."[19]

[19] *Report of Div. of For. for 1886*, pp. 149, 175; for the "Specially Valuable Trees" see pp. 192-212. See also Fernow's résumé of the work of the Div. of For., *Yearbook of the U.S.D.A. for 1897*, pp. 149-150, Government Printing Office, Washington, 1898, containing a revised list of valuable trees.

Fernow wanted to stimulate forest planting. Distributing a sufficient number of seedlings, however, proved impossible because of lack of facilities. Fernow skeptically evaluated the departmental function of distributing seeds. "When I first went to Washington, in 1886," he later confessed in a Massachusetts address[20] "there was a requirement to distribute forest seeds; and I found that my predecessor had been distributing acorns, which he had had on hand for three years, to encourage tree planting. I found out this, that it is not easy to handle forest seeds, or to give instructions on how to handle them, without considerable demonstration. I found out also that the United States is so enormously big that it can do but a very little in this line. The distribution of a few hundred dollars' worth of seed is almost throwing away the money."

Fernow had a long-distance program of forestry, although he was aware that in the United States a dollar and cents economy with a ledger sheet balanced annually required proof of immediate results. Moreover, he was not unaware of the picturesque and romantic value of forestry. Forests were the setting of two centuries of romance in American history. But the public wanted no more government than necessary, especially paternalistic government.

Horticulture in the United States was then in transition from an art to a science. Nevertheless, although a strong scientifically-minded minority was protesting, the prevalent procedure of variety testing of species was dominant. Fernow wanted forest species, especially exotic introductions, studied experimentally in various regions. But this required seedlings as well as seeds, and to distribute seedlings extensively enough for adequate experiments required forest nurseries. Forest nurseries and their maintenance required funds. Nurseries could be made part of a program of a great forest department, or part of an administration of military reserves. The logic was clear. First must come the forest reservation policy, and then the details of adequate forest administration could be worked out. The immediate larger scale task was to acquaint Americans with their forest resources. It was more to the point to study the forests in their natural state in order to improve them than to attempt ineffectual programs of artificial afforestation. Reforestation inevitably was bound up with improving forests. Why should we create forest nurseries, Fernow asked, until we know what the needs of forest regions are?

Forest biological investigations were instituted immediately. Fernow wrote:

> To be able to give advice as to methods of forest management, the systematic study of the biology, the life history, of our timber trees must precede the formulation of specific rules. This work the Forestry Division has begun this

20 "A Forest Policy for Massachusetts," *51st Annual Report of the Mass. State Board of Agric.*, pp. 35-36.

year, and a number of able observers and botanists, with a practical turn of mind, have been engaged to make and compile in ready form the studies and observations on the life and behavior of our native species upon which the forester may proceed intelligently in his management. These studies will naturally require years for their satisfactory completion, as observations must be made in a great variety of localities through several seasons.

Of immediate consequence, of course, were thorough inquiries among the coniferous supplies. "As the coniferous trees are today, and will be for some time to come, the most important factors of our present forest wealth, and as their reproduction and management, especially with the unfavorable conditions under which our forests are worked, are among the most difficult tasks of forestry," wrote Fernow in his 1886 report,[21] "attention has been first directed to the study of the most important of these, namely, the white pine of the North, the long-leafed pine and the cypress of the South, the pitch pines of the Western mountain ranges, and the fast-disappearing hemlock, so important for our leather industry, soon to replace more largely the waning supply of white pine. The monographs on the white pine, by Prof. [V. M.] Spalding, Ann Arbor, Michigan; on the long-leafed pine, by Dr. Charles Mohr, Mobile, Ala.; and on the bald cypress, by Prof. A. H. Curtiss, Jacksonville, Fla., have been completed. It is proposed to take up gradually the other important conifers and deciduous trees. . . ." In the Division's report for the year 1887 (pp. 74-95), notes on trees, seed of which had been distributed by the Department, were published pursuant to the announced policy. Matters of geographic distribution, growth, soil and site, propagation, quality of wood and economic uses, and descriptive characters of twenty or more principal tree varieties were presented: white pine, red pine, short-leaved pine, bull pine, Calabrian pine, Norway spruce, Nordmann's fir, Douglas spruce, bald cypress, red cedar, California white cedar, Lawson's cypress, black locust, honey locust, hardy catalpa, osage orange, green ash, box-elder, broad-leaved wattle, blue gum, red gum, Jarrah, and sugar gum.

The more important studies were not the first farmed out. Fernow said,[22] "My attempt at organizing a volunteer service for phenological observations was the very first thing I devised—mainly for general educational purposes and to attract attention to the subject of forestry—I think within the first three weeks of my existence in Washington the schedules were printed and distributed among various colleges and universities and the Agassiz Society etc., etc." Observations of seasonal phases of plant development, the phenology of plants, had been supposed since the time of Hofmeister to give a better index of climatic differences than temperature and humidity. The phenomena of budding, leafing, blossoming, leaf fall, fruiting, and ripening, it was hoped, could be recorded

[21] p. 177.

[22] Letter to Raphael Zon dated July 11, 1908.

according to regions. But the failure of workers to keep recording comparative data year after year, the lack of a sufficient number of workers, and the lack of clerical assistance within the Department itself caused the enterprise eventually to collapse.

The only one in America to perform the work systematically and for a sufficient time to produce good results was Volney Morgan Spalding, who continued to use the schedules for years "as a very satisfactory means of directing his students to the observation of biological phenomena in the field. . . ." Years later an effort was again made to do this work. Fernow was by no means the first to conceive the plan. Dr. Hough had performed a similar work for the Smithsonian Institution, but he abandoned it. This work and the monographic life history studies did not appear to be essential to forestry at the time, even though the forest was involved. The work appeared to be primarily botanical. Yet the monographs formed the basis for some of the most notable taxonomic studies of the pines, cypress, and other economically valuable forest species. Fernow was indeed severe with one author whose work was confined to botanical phases of investigation.

That the most able students of forestry, members of the American Forestry Congress, and others, were pleased with Fernow's initial program is indicated by a letter written to Joly by John S. Hicks, of Roslyn, Queens County, New York, on January 21, 1887: "I have nothing new to tell about forestry. I saw Fernow in the summer and found him just the same interesting interested [person] and I see that he has an article in the Dec. number of Popular Science Monthly. No better testimony could be made to his character and ability than the fact that he being a strong Republican should have so good an office under Democratic administration. . . . The story is told that the commissioner of agriculture admitted he "had to appoint a Republican because he was the only man in the country who knew anything about forestry."

Fernow was consulted about irrigation matters in the West, about landslides and avalanches, about every economic phase connected with the administration of the nation's natural resources. His arguments were so skillfully drawn, his explanations so clear, vivid, and complete, his logic and argument so plainly truthful, that his reports of the division of forestry in 1886 and 1887 were regarded as the best works on forestry published up to that time. *Forestry in Europe*, a compilation of consular reports from Austria-Hungary, France, Germany, Italy, and Switzerland, issued by the State Department, was considered a valuable document. But Fernow's two extensive reports on forestry were the ablest and best reports that had been published by the Department. The 1887 report was especially widely commended.[23] That Fernow had

[23] *Forest Leaves*, Dec. 1887, p. 17. Fernow's 1887, or second, report was published

established for himself a reputation as an author and editor was attested by the fact that he had edited or published every report thus far of the proceedings of the American Forestry Congress.

Fernow did not seek to alarm the American public concerning the facts of forest depletion. He sought to arouse them to the need of forest restoration and care. In his 1886 report,[24] he argued, "While for more than a century alarmists have prophesied a dearth of timber, and by their clamor have induced more careful husbandry of forest resources in Europe, apparently their prophecies have not been fulfilled. But there can be no doubt that the conditions favorable for a fulfillment of such predicted danger are growing with the increase of the world's population and with the greater requirements of an advancing civilization. . . ."

Fernow realized that the demands for building materials, both in hardwoods and softwoods, might exceed the supply. By far the largest portion of the forest domain was owned by farmers and private interests. Speculation in the timberland of the West was still rife.

Restrictive and protective legislation was helping. In many of the states, especially in the West, "stock or herd" laws were enacted to save the young growth against incursions of grazing domestic animals and against the practice of firing the woods to produce fresh herbage. "Protective laws, directed against theft or the destruction of timber by man or cattle, and against incendiarism, are found in every State and Territory," said Fernow.[25] "These laws, however, have not exerted much protective influence." Yet substantial gains were evident. Massachusetts, for instance, in recent years had improved its forest fire laws and taken other measures promotive of the interests of its forests.

Where was the timber replacement of lumbered or burned areas to come from? Under the Timber Culture Act, it was calculated[26] on the basis of statistics of 1882 that at least 4,414,289 acres should be planted to forests. Fernow condemned the practice of counting trees and dividing the number counted by the number required under the timber culture act, and then inferring by estimate the present acreage of artificial forests. Through the statistical division Fernow attempted to arrive at some estimate, unreliable as it might be, and he discovered that in Vermont, Massachusetts, Virginia, Indiana, Illinois, Minnesota, Dakota Territory, Nebraska, Kansas, Iowa, Missouri, Washington Territory, Oregon, Colorado, Idaho Territory, Utah Territory, California, Arizona Territory, and New Mexico Territory, only 3,605 plantations of more than five acres each were reported.[27] Some of the states reported none,

---

as a separate publication (147 pp. with index) and in the department's annual report, pp. 605ff.

[24] p. 150. [25] p. 179. [26] p. 181.

[27] *Report of Div. of For. for 1887*, pp. 3-4.

or as few as one plantation. Obviously tree planting activities were not to supply the nation's future forest supply.

Nor could the nation rely on the custom of Arbor Day planting. By 1886 this observance had been extended to a number of eastern and southern states. In 1876 it had been reported that approximately a million and a half trees had been planted in Minnesota. Nebraska and other prairie states presented also glowing, often exaggerated, accounts of the extent and increase of tree planting interest. But this was not forest planting. Arbor Day and other plantings were frequently ornamental, along highways and in parks and yards. Fernow regarded Arbor Days as a "specially desirable means of forestry reform." Again and again he urged more states to adopt the observance. But neither tree planting nor Arbor Day plantings were at the heart of the forestry problems of the United States. Said Fernow, let the arboriculturist, the nurseryman, the landscape gardener, and the roadside planter deal with the problems of individual tree planting. Let the forester study the problems of the forests, forest management, forest utilization, and forest planting.

The western railroads had become interested in tree planting for purposes of lumber. M. G. Kern, agent of the division, prepared a report on the dependence of the railroads on the continuance of adequate forest supplies.[28]

In 1887 Fernow patented a tree planting machine he had invented. The machine was never manufactured because Fernow realized that few people would take an interest in planting twenty thousand trees in a day on plowed grounds.[29] If the support of individuals could not be enlisted in forest planting, there was one alternative—collective or community action. Since sixty to a hundred years are required to grow some trees to maturity, the investment of private capital in such undertakings could hardly be anticipated. Forestry could be made profitable, but generations were required to realize the profit. The only agencies that could be looked to were governmental. For the immense timber acreage owned privately, governments could present a helpful program of education. "It is a hopeful fact," observed Fernow in 1886,[30] "that nearly 39 per cent of the reported forest area, comprising 190,255,744 acres, seems to have been in the census year in the hands of farmers." State governments could not displace the corporate and private interests who owned the "bulk of the once endless forest areas." On a non-competitive basis, however, governments could profitably practice forestry.

[28] Bulletin 1 of the Div. of For. was published in 1887, titled "Report on the Relations of Railroads to Forest Supplies and Forestry, together with appendices on the structure of some timber ties, the behavior and the cause of their decay in the roadbed, on wood preservation, on metal ties, and on the use of spark arresters," by B. E. Fernow.

[29] *Forestry Quarterly* XIV, 3, p. 544. [30] *Report of Div. of For. for 1886*, p. 166.

Fernow told an amusing story in connection with his efforts to convince the public that forestry could be a profit-making business. One day he received an inquiry "asking whether private forestry was possible and as to methods of carrying it out. This letter was signed 'The Jabez Club.' In answer, I stated that I believed that I could carry it out if given 3,000,000 acres of southern pine land and a working capital of $2,000,000. In reply this correspondent said that he had one-half the required acreage and asked for suggestions where he could get the balance. The letter was signed as was the first and I replied that before going further I must know the name of my correspondent. This letter had no reply. I was unable to find the Jabez Club in any directory. Jabez is a name mentioned once in the Bible. . . ."[31]

In his 1886 report Fernow discussed the "General Principles of Forestry,"[32] including such matters as soils and their care, weeding, mixed plantings of species, what, where, and how to plant, and allied subjects. The whole led to an exposition on various types of forest management: (1) coppice management, (2) standard coppice, and (3) the timber forest. These categories grouped the various methods which might have been expounded under thirty or more titles. The topics discussed were treated more fully in the 1887 and subsequent reports.

In the 1887 report Fernow wrote the results of his examinations of the "Condition of Forestry Interests in the States."[33] Also he suggested a method of prairie forest planting which might supply timber for the lumber interests, firewood, material for fence-posts, tool stock, or ties and sills. Most interesting, his method suggested a way to establish shelter belts to protect farm lands from hot and cold winds and provide a forest cover to improve the soil.[34] Fernow studied the trades which dealt in or used timber. He considered the advantages and disadvantages of tariffs. His vision for the future, however, was formed by devising a systematic plan of forestry work, predicated on a scientific basis of forest management and sound economic and practical considerations. The entire conspectus furnished the foundations on which the fundamental structure of modern forestry has been raised. Its outline,[35] as it appeared in his 1887 report, is given below:

[31] Statement at a meeting of the New York section of the Society of American Foresters, July 30, 1919.

[32] pp. 187ff. [33] pp. 97ff. [34] pp. 95-96.

[35] *Report of Div. of For. for 1887*, pp. 50-51. Concerning the emergence of forest pathological research in the United States and Canada, more will be said later. Special attention should be drawn to the fact that Fernow and Roth, as a part of studies of physical and physiological properties of woods, began investigations in the biotic agencies, their description and life histories, which cause tree diseases. Such work has been characterized as a study of wood-destroying fungi, and the microscopical changes in wood cells induced by such, actually, a mycological study of woods, and a study in the cytology of decay. In this, neither Fernow nor Roth thought of themselves as forest pathologists, although each was interested in the larger subject known as forest protection and made pathological studies part of investigations into the life histories

A. SCIENTIFIC BASIS OF FORESTRY.

I. *Forest biology*—(Consideration of the growing crop.)

1. Timber and forest physiology. Life history of species in their individual and aggregate life.
2. Forest geography. Flora and their distribution.
3. Study of forest weeds in their relation to forest growth.

II. *Timber physics*—(Consideration of the grown crop.)

1. Anatomy of woods.
2. Chemical physiology of woods.
3. Physical properties of woods.
4. Influences determining the physical properties.
5. Diseases and faults of timber.

III. *Soil physics and soil chemistry*—(Consideration of the conditions for growing a crop.)

B. ECONOMIC BASIS OF FORESTRY.

I. *Statistics.*

1. Forest areas.
2. Forest products.
3. By-products.
4. Prices, trade, substitutes.

II. *Technology*—(Applied timber physics. Needs of wood consumers.

1. Methods of harvesting [lumbering] and preparation for market, including improvement of machinery.
2. Economy in the use of product.
   a. Utilization of waste material.
   b. Methods of increasing the durability of timber.
3. Special needs of consumers of forest products.

---

of forest species and forest biology. (See the chapter on the New York State College of Forestry at Cornell University.) One of America's first great forest pathologists, Emilio Pepe Michael Meinecke, in an article on "Forest Protection—Diseases" (*Journal of Forestry* XXIII, 1925, pp. 260ff.) has placed the origins of forest pathology with this work of Fernow and Roth. "The history of Forest Pathology in the United States," Meinecke said, "dates back to the years 1887 and 1888 when the first articles on tree diseases appeared in the *Reports of the Department of Agriculture*. They represent the first genuine attempts at scientific study of the subject in this country." As late as 1925, Dr. Meinecke maintained, forest pathology was not sufficiently advanced so that real consideration was given to "the effect of the disease on the tree itself as a growing and functioning unit." To that year, he said, "morbid physiology of the forest tree is a field which has remained almost virgin," although he admitted that researches on the white pine blister rust, hereinafter to be referred to, had resulted in a "workable system of control and protection." Without disclaiming the truth of these contentions, it may be pointed out, nevertheless, that Fernow's and Roth's studies were so planned that pathological physiology was to find a place in forest life history technological investigations. Dr. Meinecke said, "Forest pathology as a science did not originate in this country. It was brought to the United States from Europe by students of Robert Hartig." Again not disclaiming the truth of these assertions, it may also be pointed out that Fernow and Roth mapped their work "somewhat on the same plan which was pursued by the eminent German forest botanists, Dr. R. Hartig and Dr. O. Noerdlinger in regard to the German timber trees." *Report of Div. of For. for 1888*, p. 618.

III. *Forest policy*—(Determining the relation between forestry and the purposes of the State.)

1. Forest influences.
   a. Influence on temperature and electricity.
   b. Influence on humidity and rain-fall.
   c. Influence on winds.
   d. Influence on water-flow and water-level.
   e. Influence on soil, formation of avalanches, shifting sands, dunes.
   f. Influence on health and fertility (and ethics).
2. Commercial peculiarities, position of forestry in political economy.
3. History of forestry.
4. Forest police, formulation of the rights and duties of the State and of its methods in developing forestry; legislation, State forest administration, education.

C. PRACTICAL BASIS OF FORESTRY.

I. *Origination of the forest.*

1. Artificial afforestation.
   a. Procurement of seed and other plant material.
   b. Nursery practice.
   c. Choice of kinds for pure and mixed growth.
   d. Methods of preparing soil.
   e. Methods of forest planting.
2. Natural reforestation.
   a. From seed.
   b. From the stump.

II. *Management of the forest and forest regulation.*

1. Methods of improving and accelerating the crop.
   a. Cultivation.
   b. Filling.
   c. Thinning.
   d. Pruning.
   e. Undergrowing.
2. Methods of improving forest conditions.
   a. Road making and facilities of transportation.
   b. Survey, division into blocks, marking, and booking [describing] area.
   c. Protection against fire, water, shifting sands, climatic influences, insects, cattle, abuse of pasturage, etc.
3. Methods of management.
   a. Timber forest.
   b. Standard coppice.
   c. Coppice.
   d. Method of "selection" and other methods.
4. Forest regulation.
   a. Ascertainment of rate of accretion; methods of determining accretion in mass; value; yield.

b. Ascertainment of proper rotation and determining yearly or periodical cut.
c. Regulation of the use of forest by-products.

III. *Harvest.*

1. Methods of cutting, with a view to natural reproduction; progressive fellings.
2. Methods of securing most thorough utilization of product.

Fernow was thorough. In his 1886 report he listed the principal American publications on forestry to that time. In addition to the census investigations and the government reports on forestry, there were listed more than forty works by thirty-seven authors or institutions.[36]

"Standard coppice" was the method of smaller-scale management which Fernow favored. It "deserves most attention, especially in the Western prairie states," he said "where the production of fire-wood and timber of small dimensions is of first importance, but the production by the farmer of larger and stronger timbers at the smallest cost should not be neglected." He criticized certain walnut plantations in the West which had been started without the use of this plan. He outlined the method and the reasons for its use in a report on western tree planting.

The "timber forest method" was defined as that which grows "trees to full maturity for lumber [and] is reproduced entirely by seed or by planting nursery-grown or forest-grown seedlings. European practice, with its intensive methods of management, necessitated by a crowded population and with its tendency to routine and stereotyped procedure," said Fernow, "has developed a form of management which prescribes a clearing up of the grown forest and its reproduction by artificial planting (seeding only where, with less dense population, a small supply of labor or other local peculiarities recommends it); a method which has elicited the admiration of writers on forestry and pleasure seekers abroad, but which must be condemned as being contrary to nature and the best interest of the forest, not being a product of the observance of natural laws, but a child of seeming financial necessity."[37] Fernow found that there was a "desire to return to natural methods of reforestation [among] practical men, while the scientific pedagogues are still discussing the advantages of their pet method."[38]

In lumber camps in Canada and to some extent in Maine, a method of selecting trees of an arbitrarily fixed diameter was employed. This method, Fernow believed, would be satisfactory if the selections were made with due regard to reforestation and the aftergrowth. Too often, however, the method proved to be little less than a conservative lumbering which took no account of light requirements and shade conditions, or

[36] *Report of Div. of For. for 1886*, p. 226.
[37] *ibid.*, pp. 215-216.
[38] *ibid.*, p. 217.

of the effect of the cutting and clearing on the future condition of the soil. Too often it resulted in an indiscriminate slashing of both the mature and new growth. Not even if the clearings were made in strips were the disadvantages always eliminated.[39] The advantage of the method was in "exposing the soil less to the drying influence of sun and wind, and of making a natural reforestation from the remaining trees not entirely impossible if the species is a shade-enduring one, and conditions are otherwise favorable; and for this reason," Fernow wrote, "its adoption in our pineries (especially those of the white pine, to a considerable extent shade-enduring) would mark a desirable improvement upon the indiscriminate slashing of all growth."

For the "timber forest," where utilization and the growing of mature trees for lumber was contemplated, Fernow outlined several European management methods. That method, later to be known as the clear cutting and artificial replanting method, recommended itself, Fernow said, because of its simplicity; but there were objections and he presented them, adding: "To be sure, on the treeless plains, and on the cleared and denuded forest areas, we have no choice but to resort to planting; but wherever we are still possessed of natural forests our endeavor should be to reproduce them by natural seeding, supplemented only if necessary by artificial means.

"From a financial point of view this method of working for reforestation by the seed from the original timber growth is the only advisable one where soil and timber are cheap and labor difficult to obtain, as is the case in our lumbering regions, and especially so as the lumberman, after having taken what can be converted into cash, is not likely to make any expenditure upon the soil to provide for future growth."

From the foregoing, it will be seen that Fernow favored at this time those methods by which reforestation was achieved "by the seed from the original timber growth," particularly in those forest regions where extensive lumbering activities took place. Other outlined management methods for reforestation, each of which was characterized by care taken for the requirements of new forest growth, were: the selection method which Fernow regarded as the method of American lumbermen and which antedated the later more scholarly selection method elaborated for American conditions and needs by foresters Gifford Pinchot and Henry Solon Graves; management in echelons; and the regeneration method, so-called, both of which were described in his 1886 report.

When Fernow arrived in the United States he believed in keeping the forest in its natural state as much as possible, as was indicated in his address, "Conditions of Forest Growth." At that time he said: "Of all the methods of management, the timber forest with natural reproduction from seed trees is best calculated to maintain the vigour of the

[39] *ibid.*, pp. 217-219.

soil, for shade-enduring species, if the cutting is done with necessary prudence, so that the soil is exposed as little as possible. Next to this method comes absolute clearing, with immediate artificial reseeding or replanting. This is almost the only method advisable for light-foliaged trees."

He believed in the advantages of natural regeneration with as little interference by man as possible. Man should clean and thin and war against natural enemies of the forest—insects, harmful wild life, diseases, pests, fungi, and so forth. Man should protect, if necessary legislate, against unregulated grazing. Indeed, man himself as a user, should be regulated in his conduct toward the forest. If good morality was not sufficient, then more forceful measures would have to be applied. To solve the problems of reforestation "the most elaborate method, based and worked on the best scientific principles, for which, however, I am afraid our time has not yet come," said Fernow, "is that which we term the Regeneration Method." He explained, "This method presupposes the growing of timber to maturity . . . and depends for the reforestation upon the seed from the mature trees; but it acts upon the consideration of the conditions under which seeds are ripened and germinate, the requirements of the young plants during the first years, especially in regard to light and shade and their further development as a homogeneous crop. This method has been carefully elaborated, with much detail, for the different species forming European forests. But as its application in the near future in our forests cannot be expected, it may suffice to give the rationale underlying it. . . ."[40]

In 1905 Fernow again placed an estimate on this method, "Some twenty years ago when I was still young and an enthusiastic advocate of natural regeneration, but indifferently acquainted with conditions in the United States, I opposed the opinions of the well-known veteran horticulturist, Thomas Meehan, who held that the best policy for much of the American forest would be to remove it as rapidly as possible and supplant it by planting new forest. . . ." Fernow during the years had seen in the United States and Canada "thousands of square miles on which the highest skill [would] never produce anything worth having by natural regeneration, after having fooled away valuable time and energy." However, even in 1905, he retained the belief that "While there are conditions where luckily a combination favorable to natural regeneration exists, a much larger area of our mixed forest, in which valuable and undesirable species share, will be best replaced by a planted forest, when that becomes practicable. Two conditions must first be fulfilled to make this practicable: protection against fire which will make

[40] *loc. cit.*

people willing to risk their dollars in planting, and rise in stumpage values, which will make it easier to show the profitableness of investments in this direction. At least States, corporations, and similar long lived institutions may then see the advantage of using now useless soils in that way. . . ."[41]

Notwithstanding the fact that Fernow turned away from a belief in natural regeneration and took up a more extensive advocacy of forest planting, it must be remembered that the creed expressed in his reports of the division of forestry for the years 1886 and 1887 controlled his teaching and the practice of forestry on the North American continent for many years.

That the method of management must differ according to species and local conditions is evident; and especially in a mixed forest is the best skill and judgment of the forester required to insure favorable conditions for each kind that is to be reproduced. That such seedings are rarely satisfactory over the whole area, and that bare places of too large extent must be artificially sown or planted, is to be expected.[42]

Fernow's efforts to promote research on the tremendous subject of forest influences were not very successful. Dr. Gardiner was unable to write on the subject in accordance with Fernow's wishes. Fernow himself in 1886 had to begin writing summaries of the subject, published by the Department. As late as 1908 Fernow had to admit that not much more was known than that local conditions controlled in the solution of every problem. On April 22, 1908, he wrote:[43]

Without such local knowledge, I could only speak on the generalities involved in river regulation and especially that part of the subject in which I am most interested—the effect of reforestation. . . . Local conditions vary the forest influence to such a degree, that instead of the forest cover being beneficial it may under some conditions even become detrimental, or at least nugatory, as regards regulation of water flow.

To tell the truth, while we know much of the general philosophy of the influence of the forest cover on water flow, we are not so fully informed as to details of this influence as we might wish. Twenty years ago I compiled what definite knowledge was then in existence regarding these influences, and came to the following conclusions:

"The surface drainage is retarded by the uneven forest floor more than by any other kind of soil cover. Small precipitations are apt to be prevented from running off superficially through absorption by the forest floor. In case of heavy rainfall this mechanical retardation in connection with greater subterranean drainage may reduce the danger from freshets by preventing the rapid collection into runs. Yet in regions with steep declivities and impermeable soil such rains may be shed superficially and produce freshets in spite of the forest floor, and an effect upon water conditions can exist only from the following consideration.

[41] "Comments on the Minnesota Experiment," *Forestry Quarterly* III, 1905, pp. 99-113.

[42] *Report of Div. of For. for 1886*, p. 220.

[43] Letter to the Editor of *Canadian Enquirer*, Toronto, Ont.

"The well-kept forest floor, better than even the close sod of a meadow, prevents erosion and abrasion of the soil and the washing of soil and detritus into brooks and rivers.

"Water stages in rivers and streams which move outside the mountain valleys are dependent upon such a complication of climatic, topographic, geological, and geographical conditions at the headwaters of their affluents that they withdraw themselves from a direct correlation to surface conditions alone. Yet it stands to reason that the conditions at the headwaters of each affluent must ultimately be reflected in the flow of the main river. The temporary retention of large amounts of water and eventual change into subterranean drainage which the well-kept forest floor produces, the consequent lengthening in the time of flow, and especially the prevention of accumulation and carrying of soil and detritus which are deposited in the river and change its bed, would at least tend to alleviate the dangers from abnormal floods and reduce the number and height of regular floods. (Bulletin 7, Forestry Division, U.S. Dept. of Agriculture, Forest Influences, 1887 rpt.)"

Yet even today we have not very far advanced in the exact knowledge and must still remain doubtful as to the precise function of the forest, and all the general assertions that are found in literature on forest influences, except perhaps those on soil erosion, need more careful investigations.

The point which Fernow maintained in 1886, that local conditions govern in all research studies of the interrelationships of woods and waters, was still true twenty years later. Forest influences as propaganda were badly misused. Many claims which had no factual basis were urged. Fernow directed attention to the situation in the Adirondacks. In an address, "Woods and Water," delivered before a chamber of commerce meeting, March 9, 1888, he urged:

When we come to apply forestry principles to our specific case in the Adirondacks, it will be necessary first to study present conditions, physical, forestal, social and commercial.

We find the Adirondacks a region which, by its location forming the headwaters of streams, its climate, its mountainous character and its soils, is forever destined to be devoted to forest growth, there being no agricultural land worth cultivating with but few exceptions.

We find the forest originally composed of densely grown hardwoods, with spruce, pine, and hemlock mixed in. The soft woods are largely culled out, large areas are cleared and covered with worthless brush, others burnt over and laid waste, washed and bare rock.

We find hardly any local markets, and but little development by roads or railroads, water transportation being mainly relied upon for the wood product, leaving the great resource of hardwood almost unavailable.

The population consists of poor farmers, lumbermen, and guides, and a large number of pleasure seekers in summer.

State ownership is the only hope of saving or restoring the favorable forest conditions.

What is to be the policy of the State, when as proposed, it has got possession of the bulk of the important forest property, important mainly on account of its location?

It would be irrational and poor policy to simply reserve it, protect it against fire, and ravages and for the rest leave it to nature, as has been proposed, occasionally cutting out the old trees. What is wanted is a fully equipped rational forest management, of expert foresters, who will not only preserve, but improve its forest conditions and secure to the State not only a park, a health and pleasure resort, but secure it without any cost not only, but with a handsome revenue in addition. . . .

The forest Commission states that of the area to be reserved, 1,275,483 acres are virgin forest, and 827,955 acres lumbered over, the balance being waste, water, denuded, burnt, or improved land.

In 1888 Fernow wrote on "The Timber of West Virginia," another region which formed the headwaters of important streams to the Atlantic Ocean and tributaries to the Ohio. He had a faculty of generalization and a knack of reaching his audience by discussing a local situation of concern to them. His lecture, "Our Forestry Problem," given at the National Museum, April 2, 1887, and published in *Popular Science Monthly*, is a good example:

The Adirondack Mountains are within easier reach [than France, Spain, Italy, Greece or Palestine. In those countries] the thin cover of earth exposed to the washing rains is carried into the rivers, leaving behind a bare, forbidding rock and desolation, while at Albany the Hudson River is being made unnavigable by the debris and soil carried down the river; the Government has spent more than ten million dollars, I believe, and spends every year a goodly sum, to open out a passage over the sand-bar thus formed.

Go to the eastern Rocky Mountains, or to Southern California, and you can gain an insight into the significance of regulated water-supply for the agriculture below, and also learn how imprudently we have acted and are acting upon the knowledge of this significance by allowing the destruction of mountain-forests in the most reckless and unprofitable manner. Along the shores of Lake Michigan, and along the sea-coast, we are creating shifting sands by the removal of the forest-cover, to make work for the ingenuity of our children in devising methods for fixing these sands again. The vegetable mold with which the kind forest had covered the alluvial sands of the Southern coast-plain we are taking pains to burn off in order to replace it with expensive artificial fertilizers.

That the great flood of the Ohio, which cost the country more than twenty million dollars, was entirely due to deforestation, I will not assert, but it must have been considerably aggravated by the accumulation of minor local floods due to the well-known reckless clearing of the hillsides. . . .

That the vast stretches of land in the Northwest, from which the white pine has been cut and burned off, present the aspect of a desolation which sickens the heart, you may hear from every one who has seen these deserts unnecessarily wrought by man. Every traveler in this country, be it to the White Mountains, to the Adirondacks, along the Allegheny Mountains, be it through the Rockies, or the redwoods of California, can not but be startled by the desolate, sad aspect of many of these once beautifully clad mountain crests. . . .

Let the United States Government, which still holds some seventy million acres of the people's land in forests, mostly on the Western mountains, where its preservation is most urgently needed—let the Government set aside these otherwise valueless lands, and manage them as a national forest domain. . . . Let the military reservations on the Western treeless plains, which are still in the hands of the General Government, be planted to forests and managed as such; this would be no doubtful experiment, would interfere with nobody, would enhance the value of the surrounding country—and education, example, and encouragement are provided, as far as it is in the legitimate province of the General Government.

Fernow believed that legislation to provide proper reservation and administration of the mountain forests was an immediate national concern. "The Forestry Division, without forests, without means and opportunity to engage in active, practical forestry, can do but little. . . ." It was not sufficient to remain an advisory, clerical service, confined to a garret room in a government building in Washington. Words alone would not modify existing methods of forest treatment; something more was required. Working plans of foresters would make provision for good roads, adequate transportation facilities, recultivation of denuded areas, and other improvements.

The problem of the federally owned timberlands illustrated this. Fernow, like Carl Schurz and a very few others, wanted *all* the publicly owned forest lands reserved and placed under appropriate forms of management. Hough had urged the withdrawal of public timberlands and discussed principles for their management, but few had given his recommendations any serious attention. To many the proceedings of the American Forestry Congress had provided a happy source for magazine and newspaper feature stories. The forestry gospel was a vogue. Although everyone agreed that the forests were being rapidly destroyed, few really believed that a comprehensive program such as Fernow's would have to be instituted. Conservation did not seem to require reservations. Moreover, the connection of woods and waters was strongly disputed in many quarters. Inevitably, the entire subject reached congress, in whose chambers opposition began to gather.

The Hale bill, which Fernow authored, was destined, therefore, to become an instrument of education and not of law. Discussions, continuing for years before the committee on public lands, kept the matter before the eyes of legislators. Bulletin 2 of the division of forestry, "A Report on the Forest Conditions of the Rocky Mountains, with a map showing the location of forest areas on the Rocky Mountain range" was an important source of materials for debate. It contained an exposition by Professor E. J. James on "The Government in its Relations to Forests." Colonel Edgar T. Ensign's "Report on the Forest Conditions of the Rocky Mountains," Abbot Kinney's "Report on the Forests of Los Angeles, San Bernardino, and San Diego Counties," a dendrological analysis of the "Forest flora of the Rocky Mountains," by George B. Sudworth, and a map of the principal western irrigation ditches were included. In 1887 Colonel Ensign had been appointed a special agent of the division of forestry. For the first time a detailed account of forest conditions extending over a large area was available.

The sixth meeting of the American Forestry Congress was held at Springfield, Illinois. In the following year the executive committee's report at the seventh congress which met at Cleveland announced, "Illinois, after our Springfield meeting, fulfilled the object for which we met, by [organizing] a State Forestry Association." Fernow added, "Kentucky has joined . . . the number of States which think that their forestry interests need looking after. I was also present at the first occasion on which Tennessee during her first Chautauqua, chose to present the subject to her people, by invitation of her Governor." Fernow addressed both meetings. In Tennessee the division had completed a canvass of its forest conditions—part of a survey of the state's cooperage industry. A few years later, in 1892, Fernow would inspect Chickamauga National Park and report on its resources with recommendations for its development. In Kentucky Fernow placed before the state the same kind of plea he made in Tennessee. Changed conditions due to deforestation at the headwaters of streams would intensify floods and droughts, two of the most serious and dreaded foes of a permanent agriculture. An excerpt illustrates:

> Take for instance the several thousand square miles of rugged country in the eastern part of your State, now covered with a valuable natural growth of heavy timber, the great water reservoir from which your streams are fed, the Cumberland, the Kentucky, the Licking, and some of the branches of the Big Sandy. What is to be the future of these lands, of these waters? . . . Under the control of the State these areas may remain a continuous source of supply for valuable timber, which the fertile valleys below with an increasing population will need, and at the same time the safety of the agricultural and mining interests . . . may be insured. . . . We ought to discern in these influences the mere mechanical part of a forest and the physiological functions which a forest plays. We do not need to go into any deep scientific investigation to understand that either the cold northern blast or the hot southern wind is less felt behind a sheltering piece of wood; nor does it need a professor's skillful experiment to show that the rain washes off the loose soil from bare hills, that it must run off more quickly into the brooks and rivers, when the mechanical interference of foliage, trunks, leaf mould, roots, etc., does not impede its repair process. Every farmer in Kentucky I dare say is acquainted with the effect of the downpour of rains upon the soil, furrowing up the hillsides, washing off the fertile and exposing the unfertile soil; and maybe he has also observed in his own neighborhood the curious phenomena of a spring drying up, when the trees around it had been cut away. . . .

Fernow was indebted for some conclusions to the excellent work of Kentucky's pioneer geological survey which unfortunately had ceased before completing a canvass of the state's forest economy.

Michigan was also aided by Fernow in establishing a forest policy. Michigan, fortunately, possessed three great leaders in the forestry movement—Volney Morgan Spalding, Charles W. Garfield, and William James Beal. In Dr. Hough's *American Journal of Forestry* Spalding's article on "Forestry in Michigan—Outlook and Suggestions" had appeared. A forest commission to determine upon a forest policy for the state was the outcome. Garfield became the commission's director, and Beal and he collaborated in preparing a report of the forestry convention held at Grand Rapids. Fernow furnished a paper, "The Basis of Forestry Legislation and Practicable Forestry Laws for Michigan."[44] He argued for a rational system of forest management, for better protection of the forests and future growth, for such education and information as would "enable the people to utilize their forest growth to better advantage," for forest planting and reforestation, for a thorough canvass of the state's forest resources before legislation was enacted concerning these, and for a forest commission or board clothed with authority to enforce laws and control the state's forestry interests.

The first large municipal forests to be established in the United States were each located in coastal cities—one at Lynn, Massachusetts,[45] and the other at Griffith Park, Los Angeles, California.[46] The former, originating in the second town of the Massachusetts Bay Colony, was regarded by Fernow as prior to all others, although towns of New England had had a communal forest history which went into the early years of the eighteenth century.[47]

In 1888 Charles Sprague Sargent of the Arnold Arboretum of Harvard University began to publish his influential magazine, *Garden and Forest*, a journal of horticulture, landscape gardening, and forestry. Fernow answered many inquiries from correspondents of this magazine, and he contributed a number of articles. During the first year he wrote on such subjects as "Influence of Undergrowth on the Increase of Timber," on the forest laws of Italy, on European forest management generally, and on forest influences. In an article on "European State Forestry," he pointed out that communities, villages, cities, towns and "eternal" corporations such as colleges and churches had become pos-

[44] In his *Report of Div. of For. for 1888* (pp. 600-601) Fernow wrote, "A forestry convention was held early in the year at Grand Rapids. The Michigan State Board of Agriculture was constituted a board of forestry, for the purpose of devising and proposing needful forestry legislation. . . . The first report of the forestry commission of this State was published at the close of the year 1888. The commission was established by act of the legislature, in June, 1887, and organized in October of the same year, for the purpose of furnishing information necessary for the basis of legislation." *Forest Leaves*, March and April 1889 (p. 44), refers to the Michigan report as prepared by Beal and Director Garfield and says that the convention was held on January 26-27, 1888. See *First Report of the Directors of the State Forestry Commission of Michigan for the Years 1887 and 1888*, especially pp. 14-15, Lansing, 1888.

[45] B. E. Fernow, "Communal Forests," *Garden and Forest* III, 1890, p. 349; also *ibid.* II, Oct. 30, 1889, p. 526, on the Lynn Public Forest.

[46] *Forestry and Irrigation* X, p. 493, 1904.

[47] Richard H. D. Boerker, *op. cit.*, Ch. XVII, pp. 251ff., 258-259.

sessed of large tracts of forest land from which they derived a revenue by wise management.

By 1888 the movement to shape a scientific agriculture had crystallized in the passage by congress of the Hatch act, which provided federal funds to enable every state to establish an agricultural experiment station. Agricultural colleges and experiment stations were broadening their research programs, and in practically every unit work of incidental importance in forestry was being done. At Michigan Agricultural College there was an extensive arboretum, which included a virgin forest in which the college was located, sample grounds of timber trees, and a two-acre tract containing 215 species of trees and shrubs. In 1887 Professor Beal lectured on forestry daily for twelve weeks to a class of 25 seniors. At Kansas Agricultural College two authorized experiment stations grew, tested, and distributed tree species adapted to the soil and climate of that state.[48] At Iowa Agricultural College Budd was still introducing and testing fruit and forest species brought from Europe and Asia. Budd was also developing students who were extending the work to other prairie states. N. E. Hansen in South Dakota was one of these. The plant breeding phase of scientific research in horticulture and agriculture demonstrated its worth on the prairie and plains. Today some of the most valuable agricultural crops are hybrids which have been developed through breeding and genetic research. L. H. Pammel has said that Budd realized that "our fruits . . . would come from the hybrids of our American stock and the European types." Budd distributed thousands of new plants through the college nurseries, and such "trees as the May day tree, the Russian oleaster, the lilacs, caraganas or Siberian pea trees, the Colorado blue spruce, the Douglas fir, white fir, the laurel willow of Europe, are but a few of the illustrations of the types he sent out to be used [to ornament] our homes and make the state more beautiful."[49] Budd was the "father of Iowa horticulture," Pammel said, and he was among the first to shape professional work in horticulture and forestry. The interdependence of horticulture, forestry, and agriculture became clearer each year.

In 1887 Thomas Jonathan Burrill of the University of Illinois commented on conditions in his state, "Not many forest groves have been planted by individuals and none by corporations. Still, the number of trees for farm shelter is very great. In some localities individuals have intelligently preserved woodlands, but usually no such care has been taken; the native forests are gradually disappearing." In Missouri a brief period at the agricultural college was given over to forestry teach-

[48] *Forest Leaves*, Feb. 1888, p. 34; *Report of Div. of For. for 1887*, pp. 122-123, 133-134, 136.

[49] L. H. Pammel, "Joseph Lancaster Budd," *Prominent Men I Have Met*, Ames, 1926, pp. 9-14.

ing. It was reported that "Incidental private interest, unorganized, exists and shelter belts have been planted in the prairie region of the State."[50] In the vast arid regions beyond the Rocky Mountains and in the mountain states and territories, it was found that with the aid of irrigation, timber tree planting of barren regions could supplement the heavy forest growth in the mountains and valleys. A small but alert group was becoming more aware that technical soil study was much needed.

On October 17, 1889, Colonel Edgar T. Ensign presented a paper before the Philadelphia congress and confessed that Colorado thus far, during more than four years of forest administration, had had to confine its activities to tree planting of timberless regions. In that state the aid of irrigation was sometimes found beneficial:

> With the exception of the Yellowstone Park, there are no Government Forest Reserves in this country. Examining the forest conditions of Colorado, Wyoming, Montana, Idaho, Utah, Arizona, and New Mexico, I found that the entire forest area is upward of one hundred thousand square miles, but this includes all kinds of forest growth, light and heavy, valuable and inferior. I found that the forests existed chiefly upon the mountain slopes, and that they protected and nourished the sources of many important streams. It also appeared that the successful operation of the great and rapidly growing irrigation systems of the region depended upon the equable and continual flow of mountain streams. It was further found that owing to adverse local conditions, large portions of the coniferous forest, when once destroyed, would not be reproduced. Finding, therefore, that the relative forest area was small, say 14% or less of the entire land areas, and that every square rod of woodland served a useful purpose, I came to the conclusion that all the public timber lands, should, if possible, be reserved. . . .[51]

In Washington Territory, a heavy coniferous forest growth area, there was a comprehensive fire law and some timber planting. But laws, however good, did not enforce themselves, and forest fires took a heavy toll. In Oregon there was even less forest protection. In California the forest depletion through fires and wasteful lumbering was equally shocking. Hilgard had repeatedly warned the state and the nation of the indirect danger of forest fires to agriculture and horticulture. For, as Fernow warned, California's developing fruit industry was largely dependent on the water supply of rivers flowing from mountain areas whose forests were being depleted with no thought of replacement. Fernow was not an alarmist. His reports showed that "while the process

[50] "Condition of Forestry Interests in the States," *op. cit.*, pp. 127-128, 133, containing reference to Burrill's experimental forest plantation.

[51] Colonel Ensign's address, "Government Forest Reserves in the Rocky Mountain Region," *Forest Leaves* III, 1, April 1890; concerning the Philadelphia meeting see *Forest Leaves* II, 8, Dec. 1889, pp. 109ff. Ensign's address, "A Plea for the Rocky Mountain Forests" is in *Proc. Am. For. Cong. for 1888* (the Atlanta meeting), p. 31; see also Schurz's address to the Philadelphia congress, *Forest Leaves* II, 8, Dec. 1889, pp. 120-122; for a biographical sketch of Ensign see *Journal of Forestry* XVI, 3, March 1918, p. 374; for tree planting in Colorado see *Forest Leaves* III, 3, 1890.

of denudation has been carried on to an unhealthy extreme in the Eastern, middle, and a few of the Western states, the forest area still remaining in this country is a magnificent one. . . ."[52]

Fernow's ability to estimate forestry resource figures was uncanny. He estimated the timber producing area of the United States at five hundred million acres and the standing timber at twenty-five hundred billion feet. Years later, about 1909, a report of the conservation commission substantially verified these figures by a thorough canvass.[53] Furthermore, Fernow realized that the value of forest products was increasing about thirty per cent for every decade.[54] He saw no reason to be discouraged if constructive legislation could be obtained.

The Hale bill, written and sponsored by Fernow and endorsed by the American Forestry Congress, suffered modifications by congress at first, and later it was completely absorbed in another legislative proposal.[55] On April 24, 1888, Fernow wrote the Pennsylvania Forestry Association and described the situation:

> The Committee on Public Lands in the House of Representatives has reported a bill to the House which does not embody any of the recommendations made by the Forestry Congress or the Secretary of the Interior [Carl Schurz], and it is questionable whether the same can be so radically amended in the House as to provide for the administration which you have advocated in the bill offered by the American Forestry Congress.
>
> The only hope for legislation embracing the more radical and only rational reform lies, therefore, with the Senate. If the Senate passes the bill introduced by Senator Hale, on behalf of the Forestry Congress, before the House has had time to pass its Committee bill, the existence of such legislation may have some influence with the House, and if the House Bill should be passed first, it might be so amended in the Senate as to include the features you advocate. The bill of the Forestry Congress introduced by Senator Hale, No. 1779, is referred to the Senate Committee on Agriculture and Forestry, and awaits action on the part of that Committee. Other bills, partly for the same purpose, have been referred to the Public Lands Committee of the Senate, although neither of them are as thorough and radical, and, in the opinion of the writer, as practicable and desirable as the bill your Association has advocated.
>
> I ask, therefore, your Association, and especially your very active Committee on Legislation, not to withdraw their influence and active support in securing the consideration before Congress of the proposed National Forest Administration. . . .[56]

52 *Forest Leaves*, Nov. 1888, p. 89; for Fernow's analysis of conditions in California, Washington, Oregon, Colorado, etc. see "Condition of Forestry Interests in the States," *op. cit.*, pp. 97-147.

53 In a letter from Fernow to A. C. Frost, dated Nov. 23, 1909.

54 "Timber Lands as Desirable Real Estate," *Proc. of Nat'l Real Estate Congress*, 184, pp. 93-97, at p. 95.

55 "The Forest Reservation Policy," American Forestry Association, eight page pamphlet prepared for 55th Congress by Fernow as chrm. of asso. exec. committee. History of policy traced to 1887, 50th Cong., pp. 1-2.

56 *Forest Leaves*, June 1888, p. 64.

Pennsylvania was slowly coming to the foreground in matters of forestry Arbor Day had been inaugurated there in 1886. County forestry associations had been formed in Delaware and Montgomery counties. Lack of funds, not lack of appreciation, explained why no educational institution in the state had done anything worthwhile in forestry. Dr. W. A. Buckhout of the Pennsylvania (State) Agricultural College, however, had managed to get some consideration of forestry before the state's influential agricultural society. At its meetings on January 25-26, 1888, Fernow had spoken on "The forestry legislation practicable for Pennsylvania." Professor E. J. James, who did so much to prove statistically the value of the forest wealth in comparison with other basic industries in North America, and Thomas Meehan, who threw the weight of his influence in horticulture and agriculture to support the forestry cause, also addressed the meetings.[57] Fernow's strategy of appealing to states and regions to advance the cause of national forestry was wise, but it was not an easy task. On July 13, 1888, Fernow wrote Joly:

> Your kind and encouraging letter of June 20 came during my absence in Tennessee where I hope I have sown the first seed for a State Forestry Association. I do not despair so much of ultimate success in our movement, nor do I think that we have not had some encouragement during the time we have been at work, but I despair of my capacity to properly administer the movement, especially feel I despondent over my incapacity to properly prepare our meetings. The Atlanta meeting has received a setback by the announcement that the Piedmont Exposition is not to take place. The President of the Southern States F[orestry] Congress and our President met and decided upon November 12 as the best date—after the election is over. . . . Our meeting, besides intended to fraternize the two sections in this economic reform, is to exert further influence upon the National Congress to pass our Administration Bill which so far has had little show. . . .

The scars left by the Civil War had not completely healed. In forestry another link in the chain of national unity was being forged. By 1887 the Southern Forestry Congress had met twice at De Funiak Springs, Florida.[58] A letter written by Fernow indicated that the congress met in 1887 at Huntsville, Alabama. The members had discussed methods to obtain legislation for greater forest protection. The Southern Congress, moreover, agreed to combine with the national organization.

On August 16, 1888, the seventh annual meeting of the American Forestry Congress assembled at Cleveland and adjourned to meet again that year on December 5 at Atlanta. Called to order on that day by Pres-

[57] *Forest Leaves*, Feb. 1888, p. 26; "Condition of Forestry Interests in the States," *op. cit.*, pp. 108-109. Arbor Day seems to have been officially established in Pennsylvania early in 1887. *Forest Leaves* III, 11, p. 151. That E. J. James's influence was helpful to Fernow is shown in *Report of Div. of For. for 1886*, p. 162.

[58] For meetings of the Southern Forestry Congress see "Condition of Forestry Interests in the States," *op. cit.*, pp. 117, 119.

ident C. R. Pringle, the congress had barely been organized in the Georgia Hall of Representatives when a delegation from the Southern Congress, which had gathered in the Senate Chamber, appeared and presented resolutions to merge the two organizations. A few moments before four o'clock the members of the Southern Forestry Congress entered the Hall of Representatives to be greeted with "hearty applause." Honorable James A. Beaver, Governor of Pennsylvania, was elected president of the enlarged congress. In his message to the Pennsylvania legislature the governor, said Fernow, took "special pains to refer to the forestry work of the congress as well as the special commission appointed by him to examine and consider the subject of forestry in Pennsylvania."[59] An excursion to the Augusta exposition was a planned feature of the Atlanta congress.

In his report to the congress Fernow termed the past year "the crisis in its existence." Six years of propaganda, though they had not yet borne "fruit," nevertheless showed "fruit blossoms" which carried "the promise finally of a useful harvest." That very week the New York Academy of Science was devoting a meeting to the forestry problem. Revival of the New York Forestry Association was contemplated. The Adirondack Forest Commission was striving to inaugurate real forestry practice. Michigan was canvassing her forest conditions. It had not been encouraging to Fernow to say in 1887:

> No instruction in forestry is given [in Maine], but Prof. F. L. Harvey, of the State Agricultural College, properly remarks: "We are interested in establishing the distribution and rate of growth of our timber trees, the best age to cut them for the greatest yield of lumber, the succession of timber"; and he should have added, the best mode of accelerating the greatest yield from natural forests.

In 1887 Indiana had admitted that "no private or State interest in the matter of forests is reported." Of Arkansas Fernow had had to write, " 'To get rid of the timber' is the only forestry interest reported. . . ." But Dakota Territory and Kentucky reported forestry associations being formed. Tree-planting interest had been so enlivened in Texas that a State Forestry and Water Supply Association was added to expand what forestry work had been done by the Texas State Horticultural Society. Commissioner Ensign was developing a forestry system in Colorado. At the congress General A. W. Greely read a paper on the meteorology of the Rocky Mountain region. Greely's paper on the "Rainfall of the Pacific Slope and the Western States and Territories" had been published. Adolph Leué, secretary of the Ohio State Forestry Bureau, was active. The congress had seventy-one members. When Fernow prepared his *Report of the Division of Forestry for 1888*,[60] he

[59] *Report of Div. of For. for 1888*, p. 601. [60] pp. 598, 601, 640.

observed, "I have before me reports by the State Board of Forestry of California, by the Forest Commissioner of Colorado, by the Forest Commission of Michigan, by the Forestry Bureau of Ohio, by the Forest Commission of New York." Maine had had a forestry convention at which "a committee was appointed for the purpose of urging the President to use his influence with Congress for the purpose of securing the withdrawal of public timber lands from sale or occupation, and also to secure, by means of the next census, more ample and satisfactory information in regard to the forest conditions of the country. The State Grange [had] also taken similar action. . . . In Texas and Kentucky, State forestry associations [had] been formed during the last year. In Ohio interest in forestry [had] been stimulated during the past year by the exhibition of forest products which was made in connection with the Centennial Exposition at Cincinnati. . . . Much time was not unprofitably consumed by the Division in preparing an Exhibit for the Centennial Exposition, and, again for the International Exhibition of Paris."

After the valued 1880 census, no official census on a national scale was made until 1890. The Maine convention indicated the reliance which not only "forestry cranks" but also sound conservative businessmen were placing on the 1890 census to reveal the facts concerning forest resources. That the census authorities in 1890 slighted the forest industries[61] was inexplicable. Other basic industries were not slighted. In his 1888 report, Fernow clearly indicated that he counted on the 1890 census to aid the forestry cause, especially because no statistical approximations as to the forests and forest resources had been produced by official agencies since 1880. Only estimates had been possible.

Fernow summarized forestry progress in the United States in an article, "Forestry in the United States," published in 1891 in the fifth volume of the *Reports of the United States Commissioners to the Universal Exposition of 1889 at Paris*. He said, ". . . no system of forest management exists and no working plans have been even thought of. . . ."[62] The real forestry movement was only a decade or two old. "Tree planting, hardly forest planting, for the sake of climatic amelioration, has been practiced. Only here and there in the Eastern States, on the prairies and in California, are small plantations or groves of planted forest to be found; but forest management applied to natural forests is not known to exist anywhere. The necessity for the application of forest management and forest growing, however, is rapidly becoming more evident, and a system of forestry, adapted to American conditions, political, climatical, and floral; is gradually taking shape."

[61] *Report upon the Forestry Investigations of the U.S. Dept. of Agric., 1877-1898*, p. 22.

[62] Vol. V, p. 747, Dept. of Agric., Government Printing Office, Washington.

In October 1888 Fernow presented before the Buffalo meeting of the American Institute of Mining Engineers an address, "The Mining Industry in Relation to Forestry."[63] The address dealt largely with legislation in these two industries, which in many points had had a common origin. Reforestation to prevent avalanches and landslides, to prevent soil erosion on mountainsides, and to advance agricultural or other basic industries aided the mining industry incidentally. Timbers used in the mines were studied as a service to this industry. A coordinate interest in timber physics, in strengthening and making timbers more durable, was directed toward both utilization and conservation.

Fernow explained in another letter to Joly dated June 12, that his effort to institute a national forest policy was making slow progress:

> I must say in confidence to you, that I feel but little encouraged in this work and especially in the Congress: the fault lies perhaps with me, but I certainly have little aid from the members. They have been very kind in lauding me when I did not deserve it, but they have done little themselves to forward our interests, and now, that my time has become valuable in other directions, I shall have to insist upon my retirement from a responsibility that I have never been able to fulfill to my satisfaction. As I have always urged before, it takes a man who will assert himself and push more, than I am willing or capable of, to make a success of running a reform association. I have no doubt the political air of Washington has wiped out a considerable quantity of my enthusiasm. It would make this long letter too long should I begin to recount the whys and wherefores.
>
> As you have always taken an interest in my personal welfare, it will please you to hear that I am prospering in health and wealth—wealth of family, having just come from Brooklyn, where my wife in her mother's home had added a sturdy boy to our circle, wealth of purse by successful investments and a rich inheritance; the independence which this latter confers on me, I hope to use in *forcing* forestry reform upon the Government, which it is unwilling to undertake.

Fernow was somewhat embittered by the failure of congress to enact into law his Hale bill, but he was not completely discouraged. At the Atlanta congress he took the position that though "we struck a stone in our first thrust of the spade, [it] need not discourage us from continuing the digging. I may remind you that it took fifteen years to pass the Interstate Commerce Bill. There is still hope that a Forest Administration may be inaugurated before the national forest domain is all disposed of."

The Minnesota situation was encouraging. General Christopher Columbus Andrews, returned from his years as consul-general to Brazil,

[63] *Transactions of the Institute of Mining Engineers*, XVII, pp. 264-275. At the June 1889 meeting in Colorado Fernow spoke on "Avalanches," also published in *Transactions* XVIII, p. 583. In bulletin 2, Div. of For., U.S.D.A., "Report on the Forest Conditions of the Rocky Mountains," *op. cit.*, Fernow had included a study prepared by him on "Snow Slides or Avalanches, Their Formation and Prevention."

had renewed his lusty interest in forestry. In 1889, detailing tree planting progress in the state, he wrote,[64]

I have long been of the opinion that the government of the United States ought not to part with the title to any more of its pine timberland, but only sell the timber; and that it would derive great economical benefit from the adoption of a reasonably stringent system of forestry administration which would protect the timber from trespass and from fires, and promote its regrowth. . . ."

From the lake states to Texas, white pine was so abundant that its exhaustion was not seriously contemplated. Minnesota lumbering had been in its glory for about three decades. John Birkinbine and other thoughtful students reminded readers, "An army of 20,000 men can soon reduce the timber resources of the 39,000 square miles of wooded area of Minnesota, particularly if assisted by fires. . . ." In 1889 congress enacted the Nelson law, legislation prompted primarily to protect Indian titles in the vast Chippewa reservation situated in the northern part of Minnesota. Under this law the Chippewas ceded to the United States government almost a million acres of land and water surface; they were in turn made beneficiaries of a land disposal system which embraced areas around Cass Lake, Leech Lake, Lake Winnibigoshish, and other regions. Excepting lands comprising the White Earth and part of the Red Lake reservations, the huge areas in question were to be surveyed and divided into 40-acre tracts. Tracts containing no merchantable pine were to be classed as "agricultural land" and opened for settlement at a stipulated figure per acre under the homestead laws. Tracts containing merchantable pine were to be classed as "pine land" and sold on the basis of the amount and value of the pine. It is said that this was the first time that the United States government had ever sold its pine lands thus. The difficulties of estimating the amount and value of merchantable pine, and what 40-acre tracts contained merchantable pine, increased with the years and in 1902 made necessary the passage of another law, the Morris bill, which will be discussed later.

The point to be observed is that the system first put into effect on the Red Lake reservation employed land surveying, timber cruising, timber and land appraisal, and regulatory provisions of land disposal. Perhaps Fernow was consulted when the Nelson bill was written. This seems unlikely, however, since regulatory measures with regard to forest reproduction, which Fernow believed essential, were not contained. It was a land disposal, not a forestry, enactment. But a kind of forest management was predicated. The theory of the Morris bill separated land sales and timber sales and proved very advantageous financially to the Chippewas. By 1904 the Chippewas were receiving from timber sales more

[64] *Forest Leaves* II, 7, Nov. 1889, p. 105.

than the land and timber combined had brought under the law of 1889.[65]

In 1888 Samuel Bowdlear Green had left the Houghton Experimental Farms at Cornwall-on-the-Hudson, Mountainville, New York, and become professor of horticulture and applied botany at the University of Minnesota, and horticulturist of its experiment station. Green was a graduate of Massachusetts Agricultural College and had also studied abroad. He and Willet M. Hays carried on horticultural and agricultural research at the University of Minnesota, and included forestry in their program. At least as early as 1890, forestry courses were provided in the agricultural college of the university.[66]

For many years Minnesota had had some fire protective legislation. Even before its state forestry association had been founded, the state had sought to encourage tree planting and the growing of timber and shade trees. Almost a decade before Green went to Minnesota the state forestry association, subsidized by the state, had inspirited a wide tree planting interest. By lectures, by distributing a manual, by experimental tree cultivation, and by financial assistance, a real prairie forestry was so advanced that by 1887 it was estimated that there were "50,000 to 60,000 acres of planted forest in the State." Green integrated the academic phases in a statewide program of agricultural improvement. General Andrews developed forestry as an official part of the state's political economy. So far had Minnesota's recognition of forestry gone by 1889 that the state maintained a forestry fund, supported by a tax levy. Under this law, General Andrews estimated, 10,000 acres of new forest had been planted. Along the highways were fully six hundred miles of shade trees. Moreover, the state possessed valuable school lands—two sections of each township donated by the federal government—from which white pine and other timbers of a certain diameter and height were sold. Nor did stumpage sales vest the land titles.[67] In Minnesota federal and state forest work was conducted side by side, in some respects even cooperatively.

On April 23, 1889, the law committee of the American Forestry Congress met in the parlors of the Riggs House at Washington to consult regarding a proposed visit to President Benjamin Harrison. Fernow and his associate, Edward A. Bowers, then special inspector in the public lands service under appointment of Secretary Lamar, were among those

[65] *The Forester* VI, 12, Dec. 1900, pp. 283-285; H. B. Ayers, "Minnesota Woodsmen," *Forest Leaves* III, 5, Mar. 1891, p. 76; C. C. Andrews, "Forestry in Minnesota," *Forest Leaves* II, 7, Nov. 1889, p. 105; "Forest Management in Minnesota," *Forestry and Irrigation* X, 12, Dec. 1904, pp. 580-582; J. Cameron, *op. cit.*, pp. 228ff.

[66] "Forestry at the University of Minnesota," *Forestry and Irrigation* X, 10, Oct. 1904, p. 463; "Samuel Bowdlear Green," *Proc. Soc. Am. For.* V, 1, 1910, pp. 148-149. Green became Professor of Horticulture and Forestry in 1892 and became Dean of the Forest School when it was set up as a separate department.

[67] "Condition of Forestry Interests in the States," *op. cit.*, pp. 124-125; C. C. Andrews, "Forestry in Minnesota," *op. cit.*

present. Bowers was a lawyer by profession, a graduate of Yale University, who, beginning the practice in Dakota, became a city judge at Groton and public lands inspector and moved to Washington in 1889 where he became a member of the American Forestry Congress. The committee chose Nathaniel H. Egleston as their spokesman. Obtaining their audience with the president the next morning in advance of a host of office-seekers, Egleston expressed the committee's appreciation of being received ahead of the others.[68]

"Ah, gentlemen," replied the president, "had you waited, I fear, that these Washington forests, with which I am surrounded, would have grown so high and thick that you could never have reached me." Governor Beaver of Pennsylvania made an earnest plea for forestry, after the committee had presented the president with a memorial from the congress which urged adoption of an efficient national forestry policy. The American Forestry Congress, however, was not the only organization which petitioned the president. The California state board of forestry, which tried in 1887 to arrange that an American Forestry Congress be held in San Francisco, also supported a movement which sought to have the public forest lands withdrawn from sale and placed in custody of the army until a commission could determine what forest regions should be retained permanently under a national plan of forest management.[69]

Fernow obtained also a memorial from the American Association for the Advancement of Science by an address delivered before Section I in 1889. This address, "Need of a Forest Administration for the United States," attracted country-wide attention and was published in the Association's proceedings.[70] Delivered at Toronto, it appealed to the Association on grounds of political economy. It was the first time that action from this influential agency had been asked on behalf of forestry since the Association's memorial had been sent to congress and the state legislatures in 1873-1880. Said Fernow:

> Several states have from their own initiative or as a result of individual and associated effort begun to give serious consideration to at least the management of their remaining state forest property, notably New York, California and Georgia. Not so the United States.
>
> I, therefore, . . . call upon this Association, through whose influence the only action for the promotion of forestry by the general government was secured, to further exert its influence in securing the more needful and more important action necessary to effect the reservation and administration of the remaining timber domain.

Pennsylvania had always enjoyed an intelligent leadership in its forestry association. Each year the state forestry work had become more

68 *Forest Leaves* II, 4, May 1889, p. 58.
69 The formal petitions are given in *Report of Div. of For. for 1889.*
70 Vol. XXXVII, pp. 359-366.

definitely allied with the national movement. In February 1889, *Forest Leaves* had promised that the "probabilities are that the annual meetings of the American Forestry Congress and the Pennsylvania Forestry Association will form a notable assembly of the friends of Forestry in Philadelphia next fall." The Philadelphia meeting proved to be one of the strongest in the history of the American Forestry Congress. It was especially strong because the southern forestry elements were fused with other national elements to form the American Forestry Association and present a solidly united national front. A high point in the annals of organized American forestry was reached when Carl Schurz told of his past efforts to commit the government to a forest policy.[71] Held October 15-18, the meetings brought delegates from as far as Quebec, Colorado, and Florida. Governor Beaver commented that organized forestry was now unitedly American, embracing "all the North American regions, and, so far as that is concerned, all the South American States. . . ."

At the Philadelphia meeting Fernow read a paper on "The Practicability of Using Fires to Prevent Destructive Forest Fires," and called to attention the practice of the Indians who annually had burned the grass of forest lands to prevent too heavy accumulation of debris. Fernow knew the forest, but it was one matter to know the forests and forestry practice, and it was another to secure governmental forestry administration of publicly owned timber lands. The Philadelphia meeting must have encouraged him. To report a general increase of interest in forestry matters over the nation was always a satisfaction. But he also reported that the division of forestry, for want of money, had had to curtail the ambitious program Fernow had outlined in his reports of 1886 and 1887. Appropriations had never been sufficient to carry through extensive systematic investigations. The division seemed doomed to remain a bureau of information. Its educational function could never be adequately performed without adequate research. Increased appropriations the next year would launch a new era, "placing at [the division's] disposal for the first time funds sufficient to provide for following up in good earnest some special investigations."[72] Experiments to investigate the astonishing subject of artificially produced rainfall were authorized, and $2,000 was allotted to the division for the experiments. Immediately Fernow prepared a strong disclaimer and discussion of the subject, and in his 1891 report he reiterated, "Our present knowledge of meteorological forces and conditions does not warrant an assumption of results from the methods which it was proposed to pursue, and he [Fernow] was, therefore, excused from planning or conducting the experiments." Nevertheless, the division's appropriations

[71] *Forest Leaves* II, 8, Dec. 1889, pp. 120-122.

[72] *Report of Div. of For. for 1890*, p. 193; also Fernow's *Report upon the Forestry Investigations of the U.S. Dept. of Agric. 1877-1898*, pp. 8, 16.

showed an increase in 1891 and again in 1892 for timber physics investigation, although this was not stated in the appropriation clause. From 1883 to 1890 the total funds for all work of the division had been $10,000, of which $2,000 was for salaries and $8,000 for investigations.

The Philadelphia meeting's finale appropriately and impressively was celebrated in Fairmount Park, a landmark of pioneering silvicultural experimentation. Several hundred persons assembled to participate in a memorial tree planting ceremony. Fernow planted the first tree to honor the memory of François André Michaux. In 1889 civic interest in Philadelphia became so aroused that proposals were made to reclaim John Bartram's historic garden by placement of an arboretum there[73] and to establish a forestry station at Penn's Manor. Efforts to secure endowments for a chair of forestry at the University of Pennsylvania got well under way and before the year ended the university trustees at the request of the Pennsylvania Forestry Association and other organizations announced that this was granted. A chair was promised as soon as an adequate endowment would be secured.

The most noteworthy event of the Philadelphia meeting of the American Forestry Association was the passage of Fernow's resolution which recognized the National Academy of Sciences as the legitimate counsellor of the federal government in matters of scientific import and called on the Academy to appoint a group of eminent men to consider the urgent matter of forest conservation on the western mountain ranges. The plan called for a statement of the views of the group to the President of the United States; it was hoped that this would be followed by an act of congress which would withdraw temporarily from sale all forest lands owned by the United States. During three administrations the secretary of the interior had recommended this step. The national and state forestry associations often had urged such legislation. The commission was to examine the forests of the national domain and report on a plan for permanent organization of a forest administrative service. The resolution was adopted at the morning session on October 18. At the morning session of October 16, Fernow had read a paper on the "Relative Value and Limitations of Proposed Forestry Work." At that time he had proposed a resolution which requested the senate and house to withdraw from sale all the government-owned forest lands and to commit such lands to the guardianship of the army until a commission, to be appointed by the president, could examine the forests of the public domain and recommend to congress a scheme for their permanent management.[74] It is to be noticed that the plan finally formulated included selection of the

[73] Soon after this proposal the city of Philadelphia acquired Bartram's Garden as a site for a park. See *Forest Leaves* II, 3, March to April 1889, p. 33; III, 11, pp. 151-152.

[74] *Forest Leaves*, 8, Dec. 1889, p. 109; also B. E. Fernow, "The Forest: Forest and Floods," *Garden and Forest* III, 1890, p. 9.

commission's membership by the National Academy of Sciences; at least, as counsellor, the Academy was to recommend names to the president for appointment.

On April 21, 1889, the chairman of the senate committee on irrigation had addressed a communication to Fernow which requested information concerning the timberland area within the dry section of the United States west of the one hundredth meridian; also, the extent and effects of tree planting, and the influences of forests and forest culture on water conservation, and their known or probable effect on water distribution for irrigation purposes. Fernow replied on June 30 that statistics to answer the inquiries were meager and that what data were available made "direct and positive statements" almost impossible. Most of his report, therefore, aimed to discuss the relation of irrigation schemes to forest conditions, rather than the influence which the forest exerted generally upon water conditions.

By this time considerable publicity had been given to discussion of the claimed influences of the forest and reforestation upon climatic, soil, and water conditions. Early in 1888 Fernow's attention was called to an article written by Henry Gannett, geographer of the United States Geological Survey, on the question "Do Forests Influence Rainfall?" Gannett's answer was that the influence of forests in this regard was negligible. During the year Gannett prepared several articles advancing substantially the same conclusion. *Science*[75] had published the article which aroused Fernow. He addressed a letter to the publication and demanded its repudiation because, he contended, erroneously used data and erroneous conclusions were "being largely quoted by the unscientific press," and the public was being misled. Fernow offered to furnish a paper controverting Gannett's claim.

On February 13, N. D. C. Hodges, publisher of *Science,* replied to Fernow:

> As I remember Mr. Gannett's article, it was simply to the effect that the change in the amount of forest-covered land in any district did not show any increase or decrease in the rainfall over that district.
>
> If you wish to attack this position, I shall certainly be very glad to publish a communication from you, but I do not think that the letter you sent me was in such form as to help forward any discussion of the matter.
>
> As I stated in my last, and as you acknowledge, Mr. Gannett is a careful man, and not one to be extremely reckless in what he publishes. Mr. Gannett only gave the figures for certain districts, and it is perfectly possible that the figures for other districts may show other results. . . .

Fernow told Hodges that Gannett "should rather have advocated the establishment of a proper 'test of the theory' upon which such discussion may intelligently proceed, instead of drawing unwarranted conclusions

[75] Vol. XI, No. 257, Jan. 6, 1888, pp. 3-5.

and settling the matter before the investigation has fairly begun. . . ."[76]

That year one "of the most notable discussions on the subject of the influence which forests exert on rainfall occurred" before the Washington Philosophical Society. Three meetings were required to complete it. Fernow presented a paper before the society, and debate followed.

At the end of the year, therefore, Fernow was aware that the subject should be offered to the public in intelligible, condensed form. In the division's annual report[77] he gave sixteen pages to a constructive technical analysis. He evaluated Gannett's article and presented his own view. The report, including description of European experimentation, was so concisely and plainly tendered that laymen could easily understand it. Fernow deplored that the division could do no more than compilatory work. Still, "for obvious reasons," experimental stations, although recommended, had had to be held "in abeyance." He praised the work of some American scholars, particularly Mark W. Harrington, who, while he had not inquired into causative factors sufficiently, had arrived at results which seemed "to indicate an increase of rainfall over the same area with which" Gannett dealt. In research techniques, Fernow distinguished between what he called "wholesale methods" and what was really needed, "data upon which to discuss the question with precision and on a mathematical basis." Fernow argued that "whatever observations of rain-fall we have are absolutely unreliable and useless for the discussion of forest influences, since it is not the rain-fall but the catch of different rain-gauges which we compare, and the rain-gauges which are or have been in use are liable to errors of very considerable magnitude." Many factors studied at stations situated differently with respect to forest conditions should be compared. Air temperature, soil temperature, humidity, evaporation, transpiration, and composition, size, and position of the forest area must be taken into account. Gannett had taken rainfall and precipitation measurements recorded for other purposes than to study forest influences, and had studied changes in regions which were regarded as deforested or reforested. Fernow disputed the correctness of Gannett's method and the truth of his conclusions. In addition he disputed Gannett's factual materials. Fernow maintained:

In the first place, as regards the choice of localities which were to be compared in regard to the amounts of precipitation during different periods, the prairie region comprising Iowa, northern Missouri, southern Minnesota, Illinois, and part of Indiana seemed to offer a proper field because, as it is asserted, during the last thirty years this great area has been considerably reforested by natural growth. On the other hand, Ohio, originally heavily

[76] This letter, evidently returned by Hodges, was found among Fernow's papers, attached to the letter of February 13.

[77] pp. 602-618.

wooded, has, as is known, been quite considerably deforested, and thus promises to yield valuable data for comparison. A third area was chosen, comprising New England and parts of New York, which originally densely wooded, then almost entirely deforested, is said now to be largely grown up to wood again. The author then attempts to solve the question whether these asserted changes in the soil-cover have been accompanied by changes in the amount of precipitation.

Fernow set forth some of Gannett's precipitation statistics and even quoted his conclusions pointing to little or no forest influence. After explaining that the stations from which the statistics had been gathered were mostly "of recent origin" whereas European experimentation covered much longer periods, he challenged Gannett by saying:

It [is] doubted that the reforestation of the prairies, on the whole, [has] taken place to such an extent as to appreciably change its forest area. For the Ohio region it [is] to be remarked that the main deforestation took place at the end of the preceding and beginning of this century, while most of the stations are only ten or twenty years old [only three are older], and therefore do not present data covering a time of appreciably greater forest area. It [is] also doubted whether the waste lands of New England covered with a sparse brush-wood could be considered as forest areas exerting an influence.

Fernow did not intend to quarrel with Gannett, but he wanted adequate presentation of "both sides of the controversy." Almost at the same time, although its real connection seems improbable, congress increased the division's appropriation by allocating a sum to produce rainfall by artificial means. Fernow said:[78]

Since the influence of forests on climate and water flow formed such an important stock in trade of the forestry reformers, and since such extravagant notions under this head were being propagated in the newspapers and journals, I undertook early in my career to bring together what was really known on the subject and published it in a Bulletin on Forest Influences [Bulletin 7] in which naturally also the very doubtful influence on rainfall was touched upon. The result was curious. I had struggled in vain for several years to obtain the increase in appropriations which had been promised me when I accepted office. One morning, however, coming to the Department, I found that the Senate had increased my appropriation by five thousand dollars ($5,000), but the appropriation had an appendix to it, there having been added to the reading, "and for the production of rainfall."

Evidently I was not to be permitted to merely talk about rain, but to produce it. I tried to persuade the Secretary of Agriculture (J. M. Rusk) to let me write a report on the impossibility of artificially making rain, and to let me use the money in other directions, but this was not to be. I did, however, write the report, giving a short historical review of earlier efforts in that direction, and showing, like an Irishman, that in the first place it could not be done, and that in the second place the appropriation was too small.

[78] "Birth of a Forest Policy," *op. cit.*; for rainfall experiments see *Report of Div. of For. for 1890*, pp. 227-235; *for 1891*, p. 194; *Forestry Quarterly* X, 3, Sept. 1912, p. 570; J. Cameron, *op. cit.*, pp. 213-214.

The result was an additional $12,000 appropriation in the next budget.[79] . . .
The origin of this appropriation was also interesting. A syndicate of capitalists had built the capitol of Texas and had taken in payment some 3 million acres of land in the Panhandle. This land was found practically without rain and without opportunity for irrigation. Now, a civil engineer from Chicago [Edward] Powers, had about that time written a book on the *War and the Weather* in which he proved satisfactorily to himself and others that battles are usually followed by rain, just as Fourth of July cannonades are said to produce rain. One of the members of the syndicate had become a Senator, and, encouraged by this book, had secured the appropriation.
At that time I became known in Washington among my familiars by the name of the gapogari, the official rain-maker employed by the villagers in the East Indies, who is well treated and well fed if he performs his office satisfactorily and whipped if he fails. I naturally refused to perform this office, being afraid of my reputation as a sane man and a forester. A bolder man was placed in charge of the appropriation and, as the Secretary of Agriculture afterwards reported, his explosions were quite successful—as explosions.

Nevertheless, the net educational result of the publicity given this amusing episode and the public explanation of the forest's influences on climate, soils, waters, hygiene, and even rainfall created favorable opinion toward efforts in forestry and irrigation. In his 1891 report Fernow spoke of the subject of water management as "the problem of the future,"[80] saying:

Hitherto water management in many districts has mainly concerned itself with getting rid of the water as fast as possible, instead of making it do service during its temporary availability by means of proper soil management, horizontal ditches, and reservoirs—drainage and irrigation systems combined. It seems to have been entirely overlooked that irrigation, which has been considered only for arid and sub-arid regions, is to be applied for plant production in well-watered regions with equal benefit and profit, if combined with proper drainage systems and forest management. To pave the way for a better utilization of water supplies in the Eastern States seems as much a proper function for the Department of Agriculture as the development of irrigation systems in the Western States; and a comprehensive collection of water statistics and forestry statistics with reference to their mutual relation seems to be a desirable task for the cooperation of various branches of this Department and the State Agricultural stations.[81]

On January 20, 1890, President Harrison forwarded to congress the memorial of the American Association for the Advancement of Science. This memorial, signed by President Mendenhall, Secretary Fernow, Hilgard of California, Bessey of Nebraska, Saunders of Canada, and

[79] Fernow excluded the appropriations of $5,000 and $12,000 for artificial rainfall production as "not germane to the work of the Division and not expended under its direction." See *Report upon the Forestry Investigations of the U.S.D.A. 1877-1898*, p. 7.

[80] pp. 194-195.

[81] See also Fernow's "Statement of the Relation of Irrigation Problems to Forest Conditions," before Special Senate Committee on Irrigation and Reclamation of Arid Lands, 51st Cong., 1st session, Senate Report 928, IV, 1890, pp. 112-124.

other committeemen, urged the withdrawl of public forest lands from sale or entry and requested creation of a commission to study the forest situation and recommend constructive legislation. On August 25, 1891, this memorial was followed by another, this time to the Department of Agriculture, which requested the Department to cooperate in a nation-wide agricultural program of coordinated water management.[82]

In 1889 Fernow had made another trip to the West, evidently going by way of Denver and Salt Lake City to San Francisco. From San Francisco side trips were taken into Oregon and Washington to the Puget Sound country, to the redwoods regions of California, and into the Sierra Nevada Mountains. Rossiter Raymond wrote Fernow on May 22:

> The trip to Monterey (and a little one up to the Russian vine country if you chose to take it—2 or 3 days would do it) will show you the peculiarities of the Coast Range pretty thoroughly. The 90 miles of staging into the Yosemite will give you an excellent idea of the Sierras. A visit to the Mariposa grove of Big Trees—the largest grove, I believe, will show you as to them all that you could see in a summer. But if you wanted to see more of the Sierras, you could leave the car at Truckee or Colfax. . . . The date of the Monterey excursion is not fixed. . . . Possibly you may feel that the Monterey trip and the Grand Cañon trip are not fairly parts of your official route. . . . But the Yosemite and Big Trees trip certainly does belong to your duty. . . .

So, presumably, Fernow went to the Mariposa "grove," the Yosemite, and what is now Sequoia National Park. He may have visited the picturesque regions around Monterey and Santa Cruz. Returning via Mohave, the desert and forest areas along the Santa Fé Railroad interested him. The forests near Santa Fé, and Denver doubtless absorbed his attention. Fernow must have travelled westward over the continental divide from Denver to Salt Lake City via either the new Denver and Rio Grande Railroad, or by what is now the Union Pacific Railroad through Cheyenne. In either event, great forest areas of government timberlands could be seen.

The occasion of the trip was to attend the Denver meetings of the American Institute of Mining Engineers, held in June of that year. Fernow spoke on the subject of "Avalanches."[83] The journey was hurriedly made, only seven weeks being allowed for the entire circuit. Fernow may have travelled with Rossiter Raymond and others in their private car, either the "Mascotte" or "Iolanthe." For part of the route, however, he had government passes and may have gone alone. At Berkeley, California, he probably visited Hilgard.

[82] See Secretary Noble's address, "Our National Parks and Timber Reservations," delivered before the Chicago meeting of the Am. For. Ass., Oct. 18-19, 1893. Also Proc. 51st Cong. 1st session, S. ex. doc. 36. Concerning the memorial of August 25, 1891, see *Report of Div. of For. for 1891*, pp. 194-195.

[83] See note 63 of this chapter.

In 1889 Fernow wrote a "Report on the Section of Forestry Collections in the United States National Museum." These collections had been organized in April before his departure for the West. In this report Fernow compiled "two statistical tables[84] [which gave] in briefest manner an idea of the forestry interests of the United States; two half-sections of Douglas Fir, and Sitka Spruce from the northwest (228 years old and 7 feet in diameter) show the rapidity and immense dimensions of the growth in that section; while a historic chart adapted to a section of Tulip poplar (5 feet in diameter) from the Mississippi Valley brings to the mind of the beholder by referring the annual ring growth to historical data the long periods of time which are required to produce our forest giants in the East and which form the basis of calculation" of the forester.

When Fernow reported in the early summer to the senate committee on irrigation, he acknowledged the aid which had been given him by Abbot Kinney of the California state board of forestry, by Colonel Ensign of Colorado, and G. C. Brackett of Kansas, who was to serve notably the pomological interests of the country for a generation. Professor Harrington also had furnished some valuable meteorological data.

Fernow wanted facilities to enable the division to make a more careful survey of the forest conditions of the nation, particularly in the West. He insisted that such surveys were more needed than the currently authorized irrigation surveys. First examine the forest conditions, said Fernow, and then study the supplementary irrigation necessities. In his 1890 report Fernow stated his argument for forest surveys:

> There are three reasons implied why the Government has been induced to establish this Division, and to appropriate funds for forestry work. The first is that, owing to the heavy drains to which our virgin forest supplies are subjected without any provision for recuperation or reforestation, the future of wood supplies may be endangered. The second is that the methods at present followed in utilizing the natural forest areas are destructive, not only of the future forest resources, but also of the cultural and water conditions of the denuded and adjacent territory. A third reason is the desirability from economic considerations (for climatic ameliorations) of encouraging tree growth on the large treeless areas of the United States in the West and on the many places in the East and South which have been made so by irrational treatment on the part of man.
>
> While in regard to the soundness of the third reason there can hardly be any doubt, there has never been a thorough investigation as to the validity of the former two, the work for the Tenth Census being the nearest approach to it.

[84] Fernow also prepared "a series of 30 photolithographs from the work of the French Forest Administration, illustrating the effects of deforestation in the alpine districts of Southeastern France, and the methods applied to counteract the torrential action thus produced."

"Reforestation on the plains and forest preservation on the mountains," said Fernow, " is of greater national concern than the location of irrigation reservoirs."[85] Water problems would be better served if attention were given to forestry in connection with irrigation systems. Forest preservation and extensive reforestation were not only irrigation "coadjutors," but they supplied partly the conditions which irrigation and reservoirs were designed to produce. Neither forestry nor irrigation for some time to come could appeal to private investment. Both were matters for government action, but the government could continue to assist private enterprise. Both irrigation and forestry were long-time investments, and on the scale required only the government could afford the large sums necessary to locate, construct, maintain, and manage proper facilities for either. Vegetation depends, said Fernow, not on any one factor among the conditions of growth, but on all factors balanced favorably for reproduction and fruitful development. Fernow wrote:

> Vegetation does not, as is often stated, depend on rainfall—certainly not on the mean annual rainfall—but on conditions of atmospheric as well as soil humidity and conditions of transpiration or evaporation respectively.
>
> The simple mechanical impediment, then, of a timber-belt or even a single row of trees opposed to the progress of a drying wind is sufficient to affect the crop under the shelter of the windbreak, by lowering the rate of evaporation and transpiration.
>
> Therefore, agriculturists in regions with plenty of rainfall yet find it advantageous to have recourse to irrigation, in order to supply the exhaustion by rapid evaporation and transpiration. The wonderful growth of the Sequoias on the Pacific Coast and Sierra Nevadas finds certainly not its explanation in the amount of rainfall, which in the former locality is less than on the Atlantic side and occurs nearly [all] in winter with hardly any in summer. But the mists and fogs coming from the ocean reduce the rate of evaporation and help to economize the moisture of the soil during the long period of vegetation. One of the most important studies in connection with irrigation problems will be that of the rate of evaporation and of the influences promoting or retarding it.

Fernow pointed out that as yet little data were collected. "If, as is claimed, there has been observed in the Plains region any effect of tree-planting on water supply," he continued, "it is most likely this mechanical effect which the timber-belt or windbreak exerts, allowing a better utilization of the moisture by the crops." The forest, like irrigation, was an agency which conserved moisture. If tree planting on the plains had not made this truth more evident, the error had been in failing to plant forests. Management in the Rocky Mountain and California forests was needed to help solve the water supply and irrigation problems of the lower regions. It was believed that not only had an interdependence of moisture and vegetation been experimentally proven; those persons

[85] "The Relation of Irrigation Problems to Forest Conditions," quotations taken from Fernow's original manuscript, and an article on Frederick Haynes Newell, *Forestry and Irrigation* XIII, 4, April 1907, p. 193.

"who doubt the existence of [the forest's influences on climate, soil, and water conditions]—some of which are proved beyond doubt—should not forget that the first conception and rational explanation of the existence of forest influences originated with the profoundest student of Nature that this century has produced—Alexander von Humboldt—and such able observers as Buffon, Boussingault, and Becquerel sided with him; and in our own country the ablest writer on the subject, George P. Marsh." More certain, moreover, were the advantageous mechanical influences supplied by a forest cover, such as in retarding snow-melting and heavy water drainage from the mountain-sides. Fernow said, "Complaints that the snows do not lie as long into the summer as they used to before the forest cover was removed may be heard all along the eastern Colorado Slope, where irrigation has been practiced in the most rational manner and the waterflow best observed." Lessons in flood and drought control from combined forestry and irrigation efforts could be far-reaching.

In 1890, however, confusion had become so widespread in the administration of the irrigation surveys that congress no longer made provision for their continuance. Nevertheless, skillful engineers such as Frederick Haynes Newell, a graduate of the Massachusetts Institute of Technology and a friend of Fernow, had been connected with the survey under Major John Wesley Powell in Colorado and other Rocky Mountain regions. Powell, directed in 1888 by congress to determine the extent to which arid lands in the West could be reclaimed by irrigation, and Newell, first employed by the geological survey under Powell,[86] contributed valuable ideas to the government program of land reclamation. Irrigation thus commenced a struggle for federal recognition along expanded well organized lines. The pattern was partially supplied by forestry; the organization of a National Irrigation Congress and gradual expansion of an organized federal service with increased financial support and authority was a similar development. The federal congress did not overthrow entirely the work in irrigation completed by 1890. The government agency was partly reorganized, and Newell was placed in charge of a service to measure streams and to select and survey reservoir and ditch sites. Newell had an outstanding reputation in the East as a "hydrological" engineer, owing mainly to his study of the Adirondack Mountains. From the standpoint of forestry, the furtherance of irrigation was very important. After 1886, when Abbot Kinney had "called upon [him] to state briskly [his] views in regard to the influence of forest vegetation on water supply" to an irrigation convention which evidently took place in California, Fernow became increasingly identified with the related movement for irrigation.

[86] See "Major John Wesley Powell," *Forestry and Irrigation* VIII, 2, Feb. 1902, p. 59; also *ibid.*, 7, July 1902, p. 269.

CHAPTER IV

New Forestry Legislation

ON NOVEMBER 14, 1889, Colonel Ensign, Warren Higley, and Charles C. Binney,[1] as representatives of the American Forestry Association, had met with a committee of the American Association for the Advancement of Science in the office of Assistant Secretary of Agriculture Edwin Willets, formerly president of Michigan Agricultural College. These men, together with Fernow, Bowers, and Egleston, conferred with the new Secretary of the Interior, John W. Noble, on the matter of reserving and protecting the public forest lands of the government. Major Powell and Colonel Hinton of the United States Geological Survey asked to be present at the conference.[2] A disparity of views and policies between the geological survey and the forestry division was openly discussed at the conference. Fernow wrote:

> In Mr. John W. Noble, Secretary of the Interior, under Harrison's Administration, we found a gentleman of broad views to whom our efforts did not appear without merit. We had arranged for a Committee of the Forestry Association, then in session at Washington, to wait upon the Secretary in order to argue the reservation policy. Major Powell, the Director of the Geological Survey, asked permission to be present, which, of course, was politely granted. Before we had an opportunity to state the object of our visit, Major Powell launched into a long dissertation to show that the claim of the favorable influence of forest cover on water flow or climate was untenable, that the best thing to do for the Rocky Mountain forests was to burn them down, and he related with great gusto how he himself had started a fire that swept over a thousand square miles. He had used up our time, when our chance came to speak. We consumed not more than two minutes, stating that we had not come to argue any theories, but wished to impress the Secretary with the fact that it was under the law his business to protect public property against the vandalism of which the Major had just accused himself.[3]
>
> I can still see the twinkle in the Secretary's eye with which he met this short, pointed thrust, and the result was gratifying. At midnight on March 3, 1891, the Secretary managed to get a rider into a bill, then in Conference

[1] On Nov. 29, 1889, Fernow wrote to Joly, "Mr. Binney . . . with Dr. [Henry M.] Fisher and Mr. [Herbert] Welsh [both of Philadelphia were] the moving spirits of the Congress and [were] engaged to put it on a better basis."

[2] See the Report of the Committee on Legislation, *Proc. Am. For. Ass.*, Washington, 1891. The meeting was held on Dec. 30, 1890; at that time there were 196 members, a considerable increase over the past year.

[3] This is Fernow's account. Both he and Powell were zealous for their respective causes, and an account giving Powell's point of view may be found in *The Story of the Great Geologists* by Carroll Lane Fenton and Mildred Adams Fenton, Doubleday, Doran and Co., New York, 1945, pp. 232ff. Powell was an able administrator and a respected scientist; on his Rocky Mountain expeditions of 1867 and 1868 he was accompanied first by T. J. Burrill and then by George Vasey, both greatly interested in forests.

Committee, the rider giving power to the President to set aside forest reservations. Thus, most important legislation, which changed the entire land policy of the United States, was enacted without any discussion, or, indeed, without direct participation in framing it by either House or Senate.[4]

A second notable piece of national forestry legislation, therefore, had been obtained as a rider to legislation which had another principal object in view. Again direct debate of forestry issues had escaped the floors of congress.

Section 24 of number 162 of the public laws, approved March 3, 1891, authorized the president to proclaim extensive forest reservations irrespective of special economic value. Fernow concisely described the bill as one "to abolish timber-claim planting." The new legislation probably did not empower the president to reserve the entire national forest domain at once. He could not have followed the course for which Fernow and the American Forestry Association had been striving. The authority read that "from time to time" the president could set apart public reservations.

Neither the memorial of the American Association for the Advancement of Science, nor the petition of the American Forestry Association, nor the provisions of a bill prepared by the committee on legislation of the Association and transmitted to congress with the Association's memorial was responsible for the enactment of the new legislation. Later, referring to his Hale bill, in modified form the Paddock bill, and the effect the new legislation had on these measures in congress, Fernow wrote:[5]

> Of this radical, yet reasonable, legislation, all that could be obtained was the enactment of a brief clause, inserted at the last hour of the 51st Congress into "An Act to repeal Timber-culture laws and for other purposes." The credit for securing this recognition belongs to the then Secretary of the Interior, Hon. John W. Noble.

Still later, when he was asked who had drafted section 24 of the act of March 3, 1891, Fernow answered,[6] "I do not know who drafted the exact clause, but I know it would never have been inserted, if we—that is those who were actively carrying on the forestry propaganda—had not educated the Secretary of the Interior to the propriety of this move. Indeed, Secretary Noble was generous enough to admit as much more than once in public speeches—one of which should be found in the report of the meeting of the American Forestry Association in December 1901[7]. . . . I remember very well that Mr. Edward A. Bowers and my-

[4] "Birth of a Forest Policy," *op. cit.*

[5] "The Forest Reservation Policy," a pamphlet prepared by Fernow as chairman of the Executive Committee of the Am. For. Ass. for the 55th Cong.

[6] Letter to George B. Grinnell, dated April 12, 1910.

[7] *Proc. Am. For. Ass.*, 1893, pp. 36-41; *ibid.* for Dec. 1891. This action of Congress, though accomplished under Secretary Noble, was the culmination of the efforts of

self, representing the Association, more than once called on Mr. Noble to argue the point of reservations. . . . The section, by the way, was not added by the Committee on Public Lands, but inserted in Conference Committee in the last hour of Congress by the insistence of Mr. Noble, that he would not allow the bill to be signed by the President unless the clause was added. . . ."[8]

In 1891 congress repealed the timber culture law and the preemption law. It amended the homestead law by requiring or permitting commutation only after fourteen months of residence and cultivation of the land by the homesteader. Congress abolished public sale of government lands, and sought by new legislation to eliminate the perpetration of frauds—under the desert land laws. Under the Permit Act of 1891, a permit cutting system was also established. Within another year the Timber and Stone Act would be extended to all public land states. The most important revision of the 1891 land laws, therefore, was section 24 by which the long sought reservation policy—authority to set aside forest reserves—was put into effect. This read: ". . . the President of the United States may, from time to time, set apart and reserve, in any State or Territory having public land bearing forests, in any part of the public lands wholly or in part covered with timber or undergrowth, whether of commercial value or not, as public reservations, and the President shall, by public proclamation, declare the establishment of such reservations and the limits thereof."

The President was not slow to proclaim reservations under this authority. Nor was the public slow to sense in the Permit Act something to be had for nothing. The law seemed to license the felling of the forests. Apparently it was left to the discretion of the secretary of the interior what restrictions, if any, and penalties for violations were to be imposed. Applications for "permits" flooded the general land office so that a special force had to be employed to attend to them. The secretary complained that more was left to his discretion than should be required of an executive officer, certainly since his office changed with every change of presidents. Nothing determined when the cut timber had to be used or prohibited its being cut and stored. With the value of forest products increasing, the secretary sensed it would take but a small percentage of the population to exhaust the public timber resources, and the likelihood was that as more people learned of the situation, the pressure would increase.

Hough and Fernow in their earlier reports, especially Fernow's report of 1886 (pp. 164ff.). The reservation policy had been definitely linked with the forest management program before this time.

[8] *Forestry Quarterly* IX, 1, 1911, p. 185. See also a quoted letter from Fernow to this effect in John Ise's *The United States Forest Policy, op. cit.*, pp. 99, 109, 114-119. At p. 115, note 187. Jenks Cameron, *op. cit.*, pp. 204ff. *Forestry Investigations*, U.S.D.A., 1877-1898, *op. cit.*, pp. 191-201.

Fernow had an answer. Now that a federal forest reservation policy had been adopted, forest management and administration was implied. Why have forest reservations unless provision for this management was implied? Certainly the Paddock bill, a rewritten version of the Hale bill, would not have to pass congress before a rational policy of forest management could be introduced. In the interim, what was to happen to the lands reserved? Were all public timberlands, not specially withdrawn from sale or entry, now opened to unrestricted use? What kind of management, if any, was to be applied to lands which were reserved? Common sense management, Fernow said, must provide "(1) Proper organization and efficient service. (2) Protection against theft, fire, or other damage of the property. (3) Regulation of the occupancy and the use of the reservation by citizens. (4) A system for cutting the crop and marketing it according to the needs of the population. (5) Reproduction of the crop and maintenance of proper forestry conditions."[9]

Fernow pointed out that in the one million square miles of the western mountain states, not quite three million inhabitants were to be found, or only three to the square mile, and if we deduct the population of our cities, a little more than three to every two square miles.

Unfortunately the law of March 3, 1891, had "opened up to almost unrestricted use all timber lands not so reserved." Fernow drafted a strong argument in support of a liberal construction of section 24. Pointing out that the presidential authority was given unconditionally and the objects were left unexplained by the law, he argued:

> There can hardly be any doubt, however, as to what objects and considerations should be kept in view in reserving such lands and withdrawing them from private occupancy. These are first and foremost of economic importance, not only for the present but more specially for the future prosperity of the people residing near such reservations, namely, first, to assure a continuous forest cover of the soil on mountain slopes and crests for the purpose of preserving or equalizing waterflow in the streams which are to serve for purposes of irrigation, and to prevent formation of torrents and soil washing; second, to assure a continuous supply of wood material from the timbered areas by cutting judiciously and with a view to reproduction. Secondary objects, such as can and will be subserved at the same time with those first cited, are those of an aesthetic nature, namely, to preserve natural scenery, remarkable objects of interest, and to secure places of retreat for those in quest of health, recreation, and pleasure. Both objects are legitimate, but the first class is infinitely more important, and the second is easily provided for in securing the first.
>
> Since there have arisen misconceptions in regard to these propositions it may, perhaps, be proper to emphasize the fact that the multiplication of national parks in remote and picturesque regions was not the intent of the law, but it was specially designed to prevent the great annual conflagrations,

[9] This and the following quotations are taken from Fernow's *Report of Div. of For. for 1891* (pp. 224-229), in which he argued strongly for a liberal construction of section 24.

to prevent useless destruction of public property, to provide benefit and revenue from the sale of forest products as needed for fuel and lumber by residents of the locality, and altogether to administer this valuable and much-endangered resource for present and future benefit. These, I take it, are the objects of the proposed reservations.

Forest management, such as contemplated, does not destroy natural beauty, does not decrease but gives opportunity to increase the game, and tends to promote the greatest development of the country.

Fernow did not deny that the army might afford "admirable protective service . . . over the period of insufficient civil administration." The goal, however, was a trained forestry personnel.

In 1890 congress had created the Yosemite National Park, the Sequoia National Park, and the General Grant National Park—all in eastern and middle southern California. Congress had also amended its irrigation law of 1888 to permit withdrawals from entry of certain public lands for reservoir sites.

Following enactment of the law of 1891, President Harrison promptly proclaimed a forest reservation on the White River Plateau, at the headwaters of the White, Grand, and Yampa rivers, situated in northwestern Colorado, and north of the right of way of the Denver and Rio Grande Railroad. Another reservation was created at the headwaters of Pecos River in New Mexico, a heavily forested locality near Santa Fé, and along and north of the right of way of the Santa Fé Railroad. The president also enlarged the boundaries of Yellowstone National Park.

The Yellowstone National Park timberland reserve was established September 10, 1891 to consist of 1,239,040 acres. The White River Plateau timberland reserve was established October 16, 1891, as consisting of 1,198,080 acres. The Pecos River forest reserve was established January 11, 1892, as of 311,040 acres.

Fernow's division of forestry had collected information concerning a number of forest tracts of the national domain. After the December 1891 meetings of the American Forestry Congress held at Washington had adjourned, members of the congress presented to the president another memorial. Judge Higley spoke for the congress. The petition was referred to the secretary, who sent investigators to the proposed reservations:

(1) The Flathead and Marias River region, occupying the rugged and mountainous continental divide in northwestern Montana.

(2) The rugged slopes of Pike's Peak, in Colorado.

(3) The mountain region northeast of Santa Fé, N. Mex., at the head of the Pecos and the Canadian rivers.

(4) The Tulare region, comprising much of the western slope of the Sierra Nevada range in eastern and southern California.

(5) The Crater Lake region, in southeastern Oregon.

(6) The Turtle Mountain region, in Bottineau and Rolette counties, N. Dak.

(7) The Lost Park region, in Colorado.

(8) The unoccupied lands about the headwaters of the Mississippi River in northern Minnesota.

Fernow foresaw that much of the lands had to be surveyed. Much would be found to be included in railroad grants, since railroads traversed or were near the proposed reservations. Fernow wanted all the remaining timberlands reserved. He wanted "interspersed parcels" brought up to constitute compact reserves. He realized that management would have to be "common sense management and . . . leave the development of better forestry methods to future years. . . ." An opportunity to obtain knowledge and experience was at hand.

Seventeen forest reservations were proclaimed by President Harrison. In his 1892 report Fernow listed most of these according to states.[10] Practically every one had been set aside to secure favorable water conditions for agricultural land along rivers at the headwaters of which the reservations were situated. Lands with and without irrigation projects were included. In some states, North Dakota notably, irrigation and forestry were officially joined. Fernow observed, "The primary object of these reservations [was] to insure favorable water conditions in the regions which depend for their fertility upon irrigation. . . ." Eventually it would be found neither practicable nor wise to exclude these areas and their resources from utilization. Under a conservative but profitable system of management, their timber and other natural resources would be used. The reservations were described as follows:

In Arizona—Grand Cañon Forest Reserve, in Coconino County, containing about 1,851,520 acres.

In California—San Gabriel Timber Land Reserve, in Los Angeles and San Bernardino counties, containing 555,520 acres; Sierra Forest Reserve, in Mono, Mariposa, Fresno, Tulare, Inyo, and Kern counties, containing about 4,096,000 acres; San Bernardino Forest Reserve, in San Bernardino County, containing 737,280 acres; Trabuco Cañon Forest Reserve, in Orange County, containing 49,920 acres.

In Colorado—White River Plateau Timber Land Reserve, in Routt, Rio Blanco, Garfield, and Eagle counties, containing 1,198,080 acres; Pike's Peak Timber Land Reserve, in El Paso County, containing 184,320 acres; Plum Creek Timber Land Reserve, in Douglas County, containing 179,200 acres; The South Platte Forest Reserve, in Park, Jefferson, Summit, and Chaffee counties, containing about 683,520 acres; Battlement Mesa Forest Reserve, in Garfield, Mesa, Pitkin, Delta, and Gunnison counties, containing 858,240 acres.

In New Mexico—Pecos River Reserve, in Santa Fé, San Miguel, Rio Arriba, and Taos counties, containing 311,040 acres.

[10] *Report of Div. of For. for 1892,* p. 313 (national parks), p. 318 (forest reservations), p. 319 for following quotation; *for 1893,* p. 324 (areas and dates of national parks and forest reservations).

In Oregon—Bull Run Timber Land Reserve, in Multnomah, Wasco, and Clackamas counties, containing 142,080 acres.

In Washington—The Pacific Forest Reserve, in Pierce, Kittitas, Lewis, and Yakima counties, containing 967,680 acres.

In Wyoming—Yellowstone National Park Timber Land Reserve, lying on the south and east of the Yellowstone National Park, containing 1,239,040 acres.

NOTE—The areas given are the estimated aggregate areas lying within the exterior boundaries of the reservations. The lands actually reserved are only the vacant, unappropriated public lands within said boundaries.

In his attention to the matter of forest reservations, Fernow had not forgotten the need for forest planting, as distinguished from tree planting. In 1889 life-history monographs of the eastern pines, the shortleaf, loblolly, and Cuban species, by Mohr; of *Pinus strobus,* the white pine, by Spalding; of the Norway and pitch pines, *Pinus resinosa* and *Pinus rigida,* by William Flint; of the hemlock, *Tsuga Canadensis*, by Albert Nelson Prentiss; of the two northwestern spruces, *Picea nigra* and *Picea alba,* by Kate Furbish, were regarded by Fernow as "the most valuable work in the division within the last three years." These monographs were valuable for their fundamental knowledge, especially their botanical systemization. But excepting the work of Mohr on the southern pines and that of Spalding on the white pine, the treatises were not complete for the purposes of forestry analysis. It was planned that eventually these monographs would be printed, together with technological field studies of the southern pines being pursued by Filibert Roth.

In his 1889 report for the division Fernow defined what he regarded as the requirements of the tree planting movement. He commented, "Altogether . . . the amount of tree planting is infinitesimal, if compared with what is necessary for climatic amelioration; and it may be admitted, now as well as later, that the reforestation of the plains must be a matter of cooperation if not of national enterprise. . . . I would . . . propose to seek the cooperation of the Experiment Stations now existing in the treeless regions, and that of private individuals, who can offer special facilities in order to establish . . . experimental plantations upon a uniform and centrally directed plan."

At the Quebec meeting of the American Forestry Association in the summer of 1890, special consideration was given to forestry work sponsored by the Dominion government on its experimental farms and on the western plains of Canada. Dr. William Saunders, the director and chief speaker, was a close friend of Fernow and an admirer of his work. Since 1887 at the Central Experimental Farm, since 1888 at Nappan (Nova Scotia), Brandon (Manitoba), and Indian Head (Saskatchewan), and since 1889 at Agassiz (British Columbia), practical work had been under way. Within these few years the results obtained promised to justify the most ambitious program for agricultural advancement ever undertaken by any government. In the spring of 1888 some twenty thousand trees had been planted at Indian Head.[11] Afforestation still dominated the forestry work of Canada. In the province of Quebec, Joly and Gibb tested in northern latitudes such valuable species as the black walnut, including American, European, and Asiatic varieties. There were counterparts of this work in the prairie states and northern New England. Among the prairie states the outstanding authority on the special relation of these studies to forestry was Charles A. Keffer.[12]

In an article on "Prairie Forestry" published in 1890 in *Garden and Forest* Fernow wrote:[13]

> Allow me to make a brief rejoinder to Professor Keffer's remarks in regard to forestry on the plains. . . . To be sure, without tree-planting in a treeless country, there can be no forestry; yet, while trees and the planting of trees is the necessary basis for forests and forestry it should be now understood and urged that the planting of trees alone does not constitute forestry. . . . It is the manner of planting which constitutes the difference between mere tree-planting and forest-planting. . . . What we do now on the prairie in regard to forestry bears the same relation to forest planting proper that the crude unscientific scratching of the ground for a food crop, by the Indian or Mexican, bears to the highly intensified methods of the New Englander or European. . . . The first and the lasting object and leading thought of the forester is to create and maintain forest-conditions. Such conditions are afforded by dense growth, mixed growth and undergrowth, which combination alone can shade the ground effectually and continually. . . . We must have a knowledge of the life-history of our forest trees, their requirements, their rate of growth and development during the various stages of their life. . . . I hope I have made clear my proposition—that it is the absence of forestry principles and forestry methods, and not the deficiency in volume of planting which deprives our tree-planting in the west of its right to the title of forestry, although in the end, for climatic effects, the volume alone will tell. I agree most readily with Professor Keffer that it is the enormous evaporation and dissipation of moisture, due to the unchecked winds much more than to the deficient rainfall, that makes agriculture precarious on the western plains, and hence the more need of creating extensive forests and forest conditions in that region.

[11] W. Saunders, "Forestry on the Western Plains of Canada," *Proc. Am. For. Ass.*, 1890, pp. 81-83. The planting at Indian Head was begun in the summer of 1887 and the first planting in the shelterless area occurred in the spring of 1888. The farm at Brandon was selected in the summer of 1888 and planting was started in the spring of 1889. Also, Saunders' "Forestry at the Dominion Experimental Farms," *idem.*, pp. 78-80.

[12] *The Prairie Farmer*, June 25, 1887, said, "The Regents of the Dakota Agricultural College have selected a good man for Professor of Horticulture, in the person of Charles A. Keffer. Mr. Keffer graduated in Horticulture under Prof. Budd, at the Iowa Agricultural College in 1883. He was for a time the managing partner in the nursery firm of Lawrence & Keffer (now Lawrence & Vincent) of Lamars, Iowa. For two years he has been associated with Prof. Porter in the Minnesota Agricultural School, as Assistant in Horticulture. For the present we understand his work will be Horticulture and Forestry, with the addition of Botany." He had also taught horticulture and forestry in South Dakota and Missouri.

[13] p. 146.

At the fifteenth annual meeting of the American Association of Nurserymen on June 4, 1890, Fernow spoke on "The Relation of Nurserymen to the Forestry Problem." He maintained the thesis that nurserymen, to understand real forestry, must study trees in the forests and in groups. They must learn there their characteristics of growth in relation to light, climate, water, and soils. The discussion which followed his address indicated that profitable trees for forest planting were the white ash, the yellow and black locusts, the green ash, walnut, chestnut, and basswood.[14] During the next years Fernow was in much demand as a speaker before state horticultural societies. On January 19, 1892, he addressed the Minnesota State Horticultural Society at its annual meeting on "Foresting the Great Plains!" in which he pleaded for study of "the changing conditions through many years and the changing relations of the different parts of the crop, the behavior of the trees toward each other during their growth." But the incongruity of the situation seriously concerned him. "While we are discussing here the reforesting of the plains at great expense," he said, "in the northeastern parts of your State, you allow the irrational devastation of natural forests, by which thousands and millions of acres are turned into barren brush and waste lands. As long, therefore, as the Association does not see its way clear to inaugurate a reforesting plan, it would be well to support a plan, by which to prevent deforesting, where it can do no good, but infinite harm." In March of that year he wrote to the editor of *Forest and Stream*, "I do not know whether you are aware that three reservations have already been proclaimed and about a dozen more are under examination. One in northern Minnesota comprising areas from three to six million acres deserves especially your attention. . . . While these reservations are not asked for game preserves or parks, but for economic forestry purposes, there is no better method of preserving game than a well conducted forestry administration which secures a proper natural or artificial reforestation of the areas that are cut over." At the annual meeting of the Iowa Horticultural Society on January 21, after reminding his audience that the success of the peach and apple crops of Michigan and northern New York were threatened by the increased force of winds caused by forest denudation, Fernow urged, "In your prairie State there is no natural forest to be managed or to be kept from devastation, with but a few exceptional cases. . . . Reconstruction—reforestation is your need. . . ."

If he had discussed forestry in relation to horticulture in any wooded states, he said, he would have "shown that by the absence of a rational forest management horticulture [was] harmed inasmuch as insects in-

[14] *Forest Leaves* III, 2, 1890, p. 30; also an abstract in *Garden and Forest* III, Jan.-Dec. 1890, p. 302.

jurious to the orchard find in the rotten wood, half burned trees and branches, that are left by the lumbermen, most favorable breeding places. . . ." Fernow had discussed this subject in a paper entitled "The Effect of Forest Mismanagement on Orchards," which was presented before the American Forestry Association at Quebec and published in part by *Garden and Forest*.[15]

Again he discussed the windbreak influence of reducing evaporation. Earth culture and forest conditions, whether of climate, soil, or water conditions, were shown to be closely related. In his Iowa address, however, Fernow presented a plea for the "forest belt" rather than the windbreak:

> A series of properly placed windbreaks alone will do much to secure successful growth of plants otherwise suited to the climate. That a forest belt will do better service in breaking the force and thereby the evaporative power of the winds, than the windbreak of one or a few rows of trees may be readily admitted. But a forest-belt, if only large enough, will do more; it will modify other climatic conditions and thus permit the horticulturist to extend the range of his plant material. That this is true, experience has shown beyond a doubt. . . .
>
> Forest areas to serve as climatic factors must be large, and they must be dense. The best success in forest planting, anyhow, is attained by a dense stand—not less than 8,000 to 10,000 seedlings to the acre most of which are not to develop into trees of size, but to serve as cover of the soil to prevent evaporation and these may be of inferior kinds, that keep a dense foliage—and for climatic effects success is attained in proportion to the success of shading the ground.

"If, then, forest planting," concluded Fernow, "must be considered an important aid to horticulture in widening the range of its possibilities, it is but proper for horticulturists to pay attention to systematic forest-planting." He offered to send them copies of his Bulletin V, "What Is Forestry?" which had already been presented as public addresses before the state boards of agriculture of Kansas and Nebraska and the chamber of commerce of Rochester, New York. In this bulletin appeared articles by A. M. Thomson and J. W. Smith on tree and forest culture on the Dakota plains. Fernow said:

> From Professor Bessey I learned only today that my theory regarding the former forest cover of the plains is borne out by the discovery of pine forests buried in the sand hills of northern Nebraska, and that he found the same kind of pine naturally growing in eastern Nebraska, which covers the Black Hills and Rocky Mountain slopes, namely, the bull pine (*Pinus ponderosa*). . . . If I were to direct planting in Nebraska I should use largely the bull, the Scotch, and the Austrian pines, with the Douglas spruce, and for undergrowth the hardy and shady juniper. . . .[16]

At this very time the forestry division under Fernow's supervision

[15] 1890, p. 462.
[16] Washington, Gov't Print. Off., 1891, pp. 39-40.

was conducting an experimental plantation in the southwest corners of Holt County, Nebraska, on land made over for the purpose by Hudson Bruner of Swan. The "Bruner plantation" was planned to study methods for the reintroduction of conifers. In 1890-1891[17] Fernow arranged for this prairie forestry experiment, in which "ten kinds of evergreens and six kinds of deciduous trees in varying combinations" were planted. The evergreens used were bull, banksian (which was found the most promising species for the plains), red, white, Scotch, and Austrian pine, Engelmann and blue spruce, Douglas fir, and arbor vitae. With these were mixed locust, box elder, cherry, birch, hackberry, and red oak. From six to ten thousand plants were placed on four plats in loose sand with a good supply of damp subsoil.[18]

This provided a basis for future experimental study both in forest growing and forest protection on the prairies. Eventually four national forests in non-agricultural regions where extensive timberlands did not exist—the Niobrara, the Dismal River, the North Platte reserves in Nebraska, and the Garden City reserve in Kansas—were created. Forest nursery projects were added.

Possibly Bessey stimulated Fernow to found the "Bruner plantation." Bessey had noticed bearberry growing on the sand hills.[19] "That," he said, "has been one of my foremost guides in urging the sand-hill planting. I never saw the bearberry growing where the yellow pine did not or could not grow."

Fernow had visited Nebraska to deliver addresses. When he decided to locate the "Bruner plantation" in Holt County, he arranged a contract whereby the United States Department of Agriculture agreed to furnish "plant material for forest purposes." The owner agreed to furnish the land and labor and to use the plant material "in the manner indicated by the chief of the Forestry Division." The plantation management was to be "controlled by the Department of Agriculture for not less than five years, or so much of that time as may seem necessary to pass the plantation beyond the experimental stage."[20] Within twenty years the success of the venture was definitely assured. Long before the twenty year period had passed Fernow knew that the plantation had been worth the experiment, although for some years the results were not

[17] *Report of Div. of For. for 1891*, pp. 206-207, in which Fernow said that in the spring he had planned and in part directed the forest sand hill plantation but had not been able to supervise the planting. So far as was known "no real forest-planting experiments [had] anywhere been undertaken with a view of ascertaining [the best planting methods on prairies and plains] by comparison." He elaborated the theory that the sand hills had once extensively supported *Pinus ponderosa* and other varieties of pine. The "Bruner Plantation" must not be confused with the federal nursery at Halsey, the Bessey Nursery.

[18] E. R. Sandsten, "Forest Planting on the Plains," *Forestry Quarterly* I, 4, July 1903, pp. 140-144.

[19] *Proc. Soc. Am. For.* X, 1, Jan. 1915, p. 114.

[20] *Report of Div. of For. for 1891*, pp. 206-207; *for 1892*, pp. 298-301.

very encouraging. Fernow realized that forestry would gain by such cooperative work.

In 1897 Fernow, reporting on cooperative work of the division with state agricultural experiment stations, evaluated the accomplishments of his administration. He reported that stations in Montana, Utah, Colorado, Texas, Oklahoma, Kansas, Nebraska, South Dakota, and Minnesota were engaged in direct cooperative work with the division. In addition there were planting stations located in the forest regions—one in Minnesota at Grand Rapids and another in Pennsylvania at Ridgway.[21] Planting operations in these instances were not large and were closely supervised. Methods to reforest cut over, brush, and waste lands were being improved and standardized. Close supervision was necessary; in some of the work the federal division did practically everything except to furnish the labor and land space. The "Bruner plantation" was not planned to anticipate ecological research in the sand hill region, but its results were as indicative as though it had been so planned.

Fernow held a scientist's attitude toward the "Bruner plantation." Interested from the economic aspect, he eagerly hoped and believed that scientific answers to the forest problems of the sand hill regions would be found. To his last year as chief of the division of forestry he believed in the work and recommended that it be "persistently continued."[22]

In 1896-1897 Bessey launched a definite movement to induce the state and national governments to investigate the possibilities of starting a productive forest in the sand hills. His ambitious program to develop plant science on the prairies had always embraced an interest in trees and forests. In early state agricultural and horticultural reports he had expressed an interest in reforestation. He appeared before the Nebraska State Horticultural Society on behalf of the productive forest project, and *Garden and Forest* in its issue of February 3, 1897, endorsed it. This led first to state reservations and then to national reservations. Years were required to overcome doubts and opposition, but the movement won. The comment of *Forest Leaves* in April 1904 expresses typical satisfaction. "[There is] little room for doubt that the adaptability of sand hills to timber-growing will ultimately be proved. On April 16, 1902, two forest reserves were created in the State of Nebraska. The Dismal River reserve includes an area of about 86,000 acres, lying between the Loup and Dismal Rivers; the Niobrara reserve includes 126,000 acres near the centre of Cherry County, lying between the Niobrara and Snake Rivers. Both are in the sand hill districts of northwestern Nebraska. . . ."

[21] B. E. Fernow, "Division of Forestry," *Yearbook of the U.S.D.A. for 1897*, pp. 155-157; also *The Forester* VI, 9, Sept. 1900, p. 213.

[22] See *Reports of Div. of For.* during these years; also the references of footnote 21 and *Forestry Investigations* 1877-1898, *op. cit.*, pp. 22-24.

In about 1890 an organization known as the Adirondack League Club in New York purchased "a large area of virgin timber lands (some 93,000 acres) in the southwestern part of the Adirondacks with the stated purpose of placing it under forest management. As a proof of the bona fide intention of the club, I may say," reported Fernow that year, "that the direction of the forest policy of the club was confided to the present writer. I deem this move such an important one, and the opportunity of teaching forestry principles in their application to a definite object so welcome, that I . . . reproduce . . . such parts of my report to the executive committee of the club." This report was submitted on November 15 in New York City. Fernow examined the forest property which was located in Hamilton and Herkimer counties and reached by what is now the Adirondack division of the New York Central Railroad at Big Moose. From there a drive to Inlet was made, over a road constructed by the club.

Fernow regarded the club's intention to be one of "practically applying for the first time in the United States forestry principles to the management of its woodlands. . . ." He congratulated the club "on the excellent opportunity for such application offered in its valuable property, combining as it does the three essential conditions which may render profitable forest management in the United States at the present time possible, namely, a sufficiently large and compactly situated area, a large amount of available and valuable material uninjured by fire or otherwise, and proximity to large centers of consumption, to which it can be made accessible. . . ." Presumably the club had had to acquire title to the property subject to the provisions of a contract "under which a certain lumber firm obtained the right to cut during the next fifteen years all the spruce above 12 inches in diameter on any part of the property without any restrictions. . . ." Unfortunate from the standpoint of forest policy as this was, since logging operations were turned over to a lumber company and the club thereby had made no "advance upon methods already existing," Fernow pointed out that forestry science might be applied by cutting lumber "with a view to favor reproduction. . . . As the aims of the technical part of forest management can be summed up in two words —natural reproduction—so can the financial policy be formulated as consisting in wise curtailment of present revenues to secure permanent and increasing revenue for the future. . . ." Fernow discussed the subjects of forest fire protection and the organization to be effected. The latter would consist of officials and a service force to map the property, locate a road system, and develop a "proper and profitable forest management [which was] dependent upon the possibility of marketing inferior material . . . with permanent and easy means of transportation. . . ." He explained why he had prepared such a full report:

I have dwelt at length on some elementary considerations, because with the present movement in the State of New York to establish in the Adirondack region an extensive State park it is desirable that the members of your club should be fully imbued with proper conceptions as to what is or ought to be involved in such a proposition. The State of New York has hitherto been incapable of grappling with the question of forest preservation in the Adirondacks solely because of ignorance as to what forestry and forest conservation involve, and, secondly, because the question was not treated as a business proposition. The club will fail in the same way, as far as forest management and forest conservation are concerned, unless it is placed upon a business basis.

The great State of New York, with 3,000,000 or 4,000,000 acres of woodlands reserved as a State park as proposed, ought to be able with such a park not only to protect its watersheds and to furnish hunting, fishing, and health resorts to its citizens, rich and poor, but with only half the area productive and large amounts spent for improvements and recuperation of burnt areas such a forest property should not only pay its maintenance expenses and interest on purchase money, but by and by return to the treasury and relieve of taxation its citizens to the amount of several million dollars. . . .[23]

Garden and Forest[24] announced that "if the recommendations in [Fernow's] report are adopted, the people of the United States will have for the first time a practical object-lesson in the management of their woodlands, according to the established principles of forestry. The tract offers a favorable field for such an experiment, for it is sufficiently large, and it contains a large amount of available and valuable material uninjured by fire, and within an accessible distance of good markets." The article was probably written by Sargent, the editor, who said, "Let us have one example of a forest managed as a permanent investment. . . . [We may hope that the club will] not be diverted from its purpose to carry on its proposed experiment."

Three recommendations made by Fernow to the club bear a special significance. "I advise especially," he wrote, "that you do not precipitately contract away the soft pulp woods without reference to the simultaneous utilization of the hard woods. . . ." From this general forest policy for Adirondack privately-owned lands would develop a decade later a strenuous controversy on the problem of hardwood utilization. It was soon found that in applying a policy of logging hardwoods to increase softwood supplies, special treatments were necessary, special solutions had to be found.

Another recommendation of particular interest was in the matter of fire protection. "The whole fire question in the United States," wrote Fernow, "is one of bad habits and loose morals. There is no other reason or necessity for these frequent and recurring conflagrations. . . . The club can afford to employ its entire income for several years solely to

23 *Report of Div. of For. for 1890*, pp. 215-223.
24 Feb. 18, 1891, p. 73.

this object of showing its determination to break the spell and to make the appearance of fire the exception and not the rule. . . ." He outlined a proposed fire prevention system.

Nor did Fernow neglect to recommend advantageous connections with manufacturers—pulp mills, manufacturers of small woodenware, furniture, carriage materials, and industries using charcoal.

In publishing in his 1890 official report the practical forestry features contained in his recommendations to the Adirondack League Club, Fernow had in mind "inducing other proprietors of woodlands to apply as far as practicable similar principles." *Garden and Forest* complimented the presentation as clearing away much false understanding as to what real forest management meant. Fernow's recommendations and working management plan became in essence a "lesson in forestry."

In a supplementary report of a meeting of the executive committee of the American Forestry Association, held at Washington on December 30, 1890, the club's organization was announced and notice was taken of the belief that the league's plans constituted "the first attempt at permanent forest management in this country on any large scale." A summer resort and hunting ground, a tree farm, and mature timber utilization under management were contemplated. Judge Warren Higley spoke at the meeting and described both the plans of the club and the movement of the Adirondack Park Association which was seeking to have the state set aside and place under "proper forest administration" three million acres of Adirondack forests.

The Adirondack League Club prospered during the 1890's and the early 1900's. Residents of Utica, Syracuse, Rochester, Buffalo, and other cities, purchased camp and cottage sites. An elaborate central club house was built and a forester was employed. Stumpage was sold to the Moose River Lumber Company. At one time Judge Warren Higley was president of the league, which took quite an interest generally in Adirondack forest preservation.[25] There is also reason to believe that Colonel William Freeman Fox[26] was interested in the league's activities.

In November 1885 Colonel Fox had been appointed assistant secretary of the New York State Forest Commission, created by the law of that year which was written by Fernow. To Fox belonged no small share of credit for the field work of the commission's first years. Colonel Fox held several titles during various reorganizations of the commission, but through the years of our immediate concern he was superintendent of forests of the forest, fish, and game commission. In the forest commission's reports he published several important articles on forests and lumber industries of the state, one on Adirondack spruce. Had the

[25] *Forestry and Irrigation* VIII, 1, Jan. 1902, p. 4.

[26] Ralph S. Hosmer, "William F. Fox, Pioneer in Forestry," *Bulletin to the Schools*, The University of the State of New York, XXVII, 7, March 1941, pp. 219-221.

Adirondack League Club forest management program complied from its inception with all of Fernow's recommendations, it is reasonable to suppose that Colonel Fox would never have advocated during 1896 and 1897 the establishment of a demonstration forest within the Adirondack Forest Preserve. The league's forest was privately owned, while the preserve was the property of the state. Yet for demonstration purposes Colonel Fox might have regarded the league's experiment sufficient for the time being. On the other hand, success of the league's venture might have prompted the state to establish a similar demonstration area on the publicly owned forest lands of the preserve.

The Adirondack preserve became in 1894 subject to a clause written into the New York state constitution which forbade the cutting of timber, dead or alive, on state lands. Fernow became so alarmed at the implications of this constitutional limitation that he questioned whether even forest planting was legal on the lands concerned.[27] Obviously the intention of the clause, Article VII, section 7, was to keep the lands in a state of wild nature. This article of the New York constitution—today, Article XIV, section 1—has played a much disputed role in the forestry of the state. Forest utilization as a source of revenue to the state has been practically negated. The type of systematic forest management which Fernow offered the Adirondack League Club, therefore, must be regarded as a working plan offered to private concerns, although the club's forest holdings were located within the Adirondack Forest Preserve.

A few years later a real example of forest management was put into practice in the East. At the suggestion of a consulting forester, the multi-millionaire George W. Vanderbilt in 1891 decided to place under practical forestry management the portion of his renowned Biltmore estate which was not already devoted to agriculture and landscape gardening. Situated among the beautiful mountains of western North Carolina and along the French Broad River above the mouth of Swannanoa River, lands in forest and waste were dedicated to forestry "in order that from the result of such forest management conclusions might be drawn as to the practicability of introducing forestry at the present time and under the present condition of the lumber market of the United States." The estate was situated about two miles from Asheville. To the southwest was located the Pisgah forest, of which Mount Pisgah was a part. It was decided that after the estate's experiment had been started on a small scale, the Pisgah forest would be subjected to forestry practice and extensive lumbering. Logs were to be floated down the river to Asheville, there to be mixed with the timber taken from the estate.

The estate and forest covered an immense acreage, but the experiment began on about 3,600 acres. A system of improvement cuttings was in-

[27] *Forestry Quarterly* VII, 3, Sept. 1909, pp. 305-312.

troduced. This would improve the forest quality and at the same time realize a sustained yield financially from the sale of firewood and lumber. From the beginning a system of forest drives and rough wood paths was laid out.[28]

The first forest plantations on this estate were made as early as 1889.[29] These were planted under the supervision of Frederick Law Olmsted, landscape architect. The Olmsteds, father and son, interested in gardening and arboriculture, aided Sargent materially during his early years of developing the Arnold Arboretum at Harvard, and in landscaping the Boston park system, a work Fernow regarded as a model for other cities.

In 1890 on the Biltmore estate planting and seed sowing forest operations on 300 acres were performed under contract by the Robert Douglas and Son Nursery of Waukegan, Illinois. The species chiefly used was northern white pine. These plantations were probably the first of real worth.[30] In 1895 Gifford Pinchot added more plantations. During this year Dr. C. A. Schenck was brought from Germany by Vanderbilt to take charge of forestry work. Since 1892, however, Pinchot had had systematic forest management under way, and to him goes a large share of credit for placing the forestry work of the estate on a sound basis.

Gifford Pinchot was born at Simsbury, Connecticut, August 11, 1865. He was graduated from Yale University in 1889. His father, James W. Pinchot, a lumberman of extraordinary wealth, interested his capable son in forestry. Henry Solon Graves has written: "The elder Mr. Pinchot merits a high place among those who contributed to the founding of forestry in this country. He was familiar with the forest system of Europe, especially of France. He had frequently discussed the need of forestry with his friend, the elder Frederick Law Olmsted, and with others who perceived the necessity of reforming the methods of handling our forests. He encouraged his son to study forestry as a profession. . . ." Gifford chose forestry as a profession, and studied in France, Germany, Switzerland, and Austria. But before beginning his studies, he consulted Fernow who told him to go to Europe for his forestry education. Fernow believed that in the United States there was not offered as yet "in any manner a substitute for at least one year's sojourn at a French or German Forest Academy and forest station." In 1890, discussing "Forestry Education in the United States,"[31] Fernow com-

28 George H. Wirt, *Forest Leaves* VIII, 1, Feb. 1901, pp. 8ff.; the announcement of the school in *The Forester* IV, 1, Jan. 1898, p. 4, and about the Pisgah Forest and Biltmore Estate on pp. 37-38.

29 Invitation of the Biltmore Forest School to attend "the 20th anniversary of forestry at Biltmore together with the 10th anniversary of the Biltmore Forest School," held Nov. 26-29, 1908.

30 Ferdinand W. Haasis, "Forest Plantations at Biltmore, North Carolina," Appalachian Forest Experiment Station, *U.S.D.A. Misc. Pub. 61*, Jan. 1930, pp. 1, 2, 8, 11, 30.

31 *Forest Leaves* III, 2, June 1890, pp. 25-28. Quotations given here are taken di-

mented that "the first American student of forestry has begun his studies at the Forest Academy of Nancy, France,—a native of Pennsylvania [the famous forest estate of the Pinchot family is located at Milford] and a graduate of Yale. He advised with me, and followed my recommendation, and is now after half a year's trial thoroughly convinced of the wisdom of his move. The only mistake was, that he knew almost nothing of American forest conditions and but little of the fundamental natural sciences. These, however, he will as readily learn there and on his return he will be able quicker to acquaint himself with our peculiar conditions." Pinchot, while in Europe, also studied under direction of the renowned German forester, Sir Dietrich Brandis, who won a reputation for his forestry work in India.

Fernow advised Pinchot to go to Europe because there were no object lessons in any section of the United States. "I would consider it almost an impossibility for a professor of forestry to be successful in his teaching without an opportunity to show its application," wrote Fernow. "My advice would be therefore to send young men well grounded in all they can acquire here of botanical and practical knowledge for one year to Europe to imbibe the spirit of forestry, which they cannot do here and by personal observation to acquire and bring home for application the essential features of forest management." Fernow's article on education replied to an article by Burnet Landreth, who proposed a curriculum for a chair of forestry planned to be established at the University of Pennsylvania. Fernow complained that Landreth gave too little attention to the "practical education of the young forester." As yet there was not sufficient professional business to warrant education of many trained foresters. Fernow believed more in what "the popular lecturer, the wandering teacher" could do. Scientific forestry teaching was to be found in Europe. "I should, therefore, propose," argued Fernow, "that the money raised be utilized to endow a lectureship, employing a man who is thoroughly versed in the science of forestry. . . ."

American schools were not adequate to educate professional foresters. The agricultural colleges of Vermont, Rhode Island, Massachusetts, New York at Cornell University, Pennsylvania, Texas, Michigan, Minnesota, Missouri, North Dakota, South Dakota, Kansas, Illinois, Oregon, Utah, Colorado, and California gave forestry instruction as part of their botanical, dendrological, agricultural, horticultural, physiographic, landscape gardening, or experiment station work. Forestry instruction was attached to the most convenient course. Most of the teaching dealt with ornamental trees and shrubs, with tree species suitable for

---

rectly from Fernow's written manuscript. Other material on Pinchot was taken from R. S. Hosmer's article on the seven charter members of the Society of American Foresters, *Journal of Forestry*, Nov. 1940. Also, Gifford Pinchot, *Breaking New Ground*, Harcourt, Brace and Co., New York, 1948, an autobiographical account.

planting in various locations on the farm, and including the propagation and cultivation of ornamental and useful species. Attention was given to species identification, including those of the forest. Occasionally life histories of forest species were examined. Almost no forestry of the European style was taught. Studies of tree functions in health and disease awaited the development of plant physiology and mycology and their extension to forest species. A few states, notably Massachusetts, Minnesota, South Dakota, and Texas, provided leadership in instruction. The leadership was more in the instructor than in the facilities afforded. Although no one of them could claim schooling or training as professional foresters, a number of eminent plant students taught forestry: S. T. Maynard, B. M. Watson at the Bussey Institution of Harvard University, A. N. Prentiss, W. J. Beal, S. A. Beach, S. B. Green, C. A. Keffer, E. A. Poponoe, T. J. Burrill, C. S. Crandall, and others. These were mostly botanists and horticulturists. In California even Hilgard, who was a staunch advocate of forestry instruction, included forestry in a course in economic botany.[32]

Egleston wrote an article on "The Duty of the Agricultural Colleges and Experiment Stations in Relation to Instruction in Forestry,"[33] and he also addressed the agricultural colleges and experiment stations. But there was little response. In 1890, before President Harrison proclaimed the first forest reservation on the White River Plateau in Colorado, that state, said Egleston, was the only one in the Rocky Mountain and Pacific regions which made forestry a part of its university instruction. The professor of botany and horticulture lectured on the subject. The three-year-old Oregon Agricultural College at Corvallis provided some forestry instruction under E. R. Lake. Egleston pointed out that probably one-fourth of the total area of the United States was in woodlands. Five hundred million dollars annually were contributed to the wealth of the nation by forests. Forty colleges, from land sales, already had a fund of more than seven and a half millions of dollars at their disposal. Five million more dollars were represented in their plant equipment. The experiment stations were receiving annually about three quarters of a million dollars. Forty colleges, fifty experiment stations, and about seven hundred instructors doing work in agriculture and horticulture should be doing more for forestry.

The secretary of the interior was endeavoring to prevent irresponsible lumberman from devastating the new national forests and public timberlands. As he had feared, he was finding it much more difficult to enforce departmental regulations than laws having the force of congressional

[32] *Report of Div. of For. for 1890*, pp. 223-225.

[33] *Forest Leaves* II, 10, Feb.-March 1890, pp. 153-156. It is said that some forestry instruction was given also in Maine, New Hampshire, and Connecticut. See also *Forestry Investigations*, U.S.D.A., 1877-1898, p. 190.

enactments. Enforcing the requirement that a permit be obtained before timber was cut was of itself an enormous task. In 1891 at Washington Secretary Noble informed the tenth annual meeting of the American Forestry Association of his thorough sympathy with their aims.[34] He welcomed suggestions as to proper management of timberlands. The commissioner of the general land office, Thomas H. Carter, also expressed a cooperative intention. A committee of the association outlined suggestions for a bill which would protect prior rights on the reserved lands, return agricultural lands to entry, license prospecting for minerals, permit parties to hunt, fish, camp, and otherwise use the reservations legitimately, license the cutting of timber under regulations, protect the reserves from fire and theft of timber, and secure such organization as, with the cooperation of state authorities, would realize the objects of the reservations. The Association urged the secretary to exercise his authority under law, and withdraw from settlement and entry temporarily during examination all tracts recommended to be reserved by the Association. At the same time the Association recommended that forestry be made a part of the curriculum of all agricultural colleges and of the work of the experiment stations.

At the same meeting President Charles Kendall Adams of Cornell University read a paper on "The Needs of Forestry Education in the United States."[35] Gifford Pinchot, returned from his studies abroad, read a paper on "The Development of a Protective Forest Policy in Europe." Fernow again made an urgent plea on behalf of "The Proper Administration of Forest Reserves."[36] He proposed that "whatever scheme of administration [was] devised, it must be simple, tentative, capable of development into a more comprehensive system, with the application of finer methods of forestry added as experience shall teach them." He was aware that forest management for reproduction of species in all the timberland territory which he hoped would be reserved would be difficult and require "careful study and experiment in the field." Barren slopes and burnt leaf-mold reduced "the chances of germinating seeds and young seedlings" on all but the western slopes of the Pacific mountain ranges. He proposed experimental investigation.

In 1891 the American Economic Association published three papers read at a joint session with the American Forestry Association at Washington, D.C., December 30, 1890. These were "Government Forestry Abroad" by Gifford Pinchot, "The Present Condition of the Forests on the Public Land" by Edward A. Bowers, secretary of the American Forestry Association, and "Practicability of an American

[34] *Forest Leaves* III, 8, March 1892, p. 115.
[35] *Forest Leaves* III, 9, May 1892, p. 126.
[36] See an abstract of this address in *Garden and Forest,* Jan. 13, 1892, p. 20.

Forest Administration" by Fernow. Fernow's address was also presented in the ninth volume of the forestry association's *Proceedings*.

Fernow's address on "The Forest as a National Resource," read at the September 1890 meeting of the American Forestry Association at Quebec, was accompanied by the entrance of an old Huron Indian chief, Thomas Siouhi, and his son. In an unplanned episode, the sagacious elderly chief, clad in Indian costume, spoke after Fernow had finished: "We are the children of the forest, and are come to welcome the friends of the forest. Since I was sixteen years old, the forest has been my country. I have lived in it and hope to die in it. We are not numerous; we are gradually disappearing like the great trees of the woods. Protect us and our forests and you will have the prayers of the Hurons and the gratitude of their hearts." This address, an extension of his discussion "Need of a Forest Administration for the United States" before the section of economic science and statistics of the American Association for the Advancement of Science, summarized the special considerations influencing state action, dealt with the forest as a producer of material and as a condition of culture, and stressed that "national wealth consists not in what we have but in what we maintain." One generation should not be spendthrifts and despoilers of their children's heritage. "Forestry," concluded Fernow, "engenders and requires permanence, continuity of plans, management and conservatism." No radical departure in either political or economic doctrine was contemplated. The exhaustible, but restorable, nature of the forest resource made plain the duty to posterity. Forests as financial investments were less desirable to private than public agencies on the long-time basis.

In 1887 Fernow had delivered at Massachusetts Agricultural (State) College the first lecture course on forestry, including technical forestry, delivered on the North American continent by a single lecturer. The contents of these lectures were remarkable for their originality, for their functional point of view in forestry research, for their fullness of analytic and synthetic conception, for their emphasis on physiological investigation of forest and tree growth, and for their understanding of what today has given rise to ecological forest research.

The titles of these famous lectures indicate their scope: "How Trees Grow," "How Forests Grow," "Accretion and Its Measurement," "Timber Physics," "Sylviculture, Afforestation, Natural Regeneration, and Improvement of the Crop," "Forest Protection and Forest Exploitation," and "Forest Survey, Forest Regulation, Forest Finance."

Early in 1891 Fernow was asked by Bessey at the University of Nebraska to plan a course in forestry and give the initial lecture. Similar requests came from other sources. As a result Fernow prepared a standard "Scheme of One Hundred Forestry Lectures,"[37] which embraced "more or less fully the whole field of forestry in a condensed form." When one considers that these lectures laid the cornerstone of the immense structure of forestry education that was built during the next two decades, one realizes that Fernow is unquestionably the founder of forestry education in the United States. Four lectures were devoted to such introductory points as "What is a forest?" and the "Object of forestry and its methods in general," and to treating the forest as a resource. Twenty-four lectures embraced elementary phases of forest botany and soil physics. Fifteen lectures were devoted to forest planting. Twelve lectures dealt with phases of forest management. Eight lectures described forest protection and survey. Twelve lectures treated forest regulations and forestry mathematics. Fifteen lectures presented timber physics and technology, and ten lectures considered forest policy and history. Fernow gave several lectures at the foot of the great Pike forest at Colorado Springs, where Bessey at a summer school also presented a lecture series in botany.

The most significant introduction in the federal forestry work of this period, 1886-1892, however, was that of timber physics and wood technology.

When Fernow became chief of the forestry division, one of the first inquiries conducted was on the relation of forestry to certain basic industries using forest supplies and forest tracts of land. These were primarily the mining and railroad industries. The linkage of forestry to farm work, especially since a large part of forest lands was in the hands of farmers, had to be canvassed and studied. Nor was the lumber industry omitted. "Railroad forestry," however, quickly took a prominent place in the division's activities. In his 1886 report, Fernow had said:[38]

> A report on the dependence of railroad construction upon forest supplies by Mr. M. G. Kern of Saint Louis, agent of the Division, has been completed, giving in a number of Appendices important practical information to railroad managers regarding possible economies in the use of timber. Among these will be found the original investigations into the structure and use of certain railroad ties by Mr. P. H. Dudley, C.E., of New York, experiments in regard to the adhesion of spikes and the economy of different methods of fastening, a review and practical elucidation of different methods for the preservation of timber by Col. H. Flad, C.E., of Saint Louis, and Mr. H. Constable, C.E., of New York, and an exhaustive report on metal ties.
>
> A report on the relation of charcoal iron works to forestry has been prepared by Mr. J. Birkinbine. . . . Reports on the use of timber in mining enterprises and on the state of wood manufactures are in preparation. . . .

In 1887 Fernow announced that Bulletin I of the division had found

[37] An outline of these lectures is given in *Report of Div. of For. for 1891*, pp. 196-197. See also Jenks Cameron, *op. cit.*, p. 200.

[38] pp. 175-176.

a "most appreciative reception among railroad men and civil engineers. . . . The first issue of 2,500 copies not satisfying the demand, a second edition of 2,500 was ordered. . . . [It was] contemplated to issue from time to time such information of practical value as may aid in forest preservation and reforestation on the part of these most important consumers of forest products. . . ." He requested E. E. Russel Tratman, associate member of the American Society of Civil Engineers and a member of the American Institute of Mining Engineers, to investigate the possible use by railroads of metal instead of wooden ties and to study generally timber resources and their preservation. In 1889 Tratman made a report of progress in the research. It was published as a bulletin, giving considerable space to practical economies in the uses of woods which the railroads might employ to their advantage. To this was added a report of experiments in wood seasoning, conducted by the Chicago, Burlington and Quincy Railroad. Research in the use of preservative processes in roadbed construction and tie renewal was presented comprehensively within five years by reports and circulars. This enlisted active support of forestry by the railroads. Bridge trestle construction, the use of chestnut oak for ties, preservative processes, metal ties and their fastenings, metal tie-plates, the railroad's track, rolling stock and traffic, and ways of increasing the life and efficiency of wooden ties were discussed.[39] The work was an educational service, but it was more important as a business service. Fernow made a special point of informing business organizations and educational institutions of the work.

Fernow appealed to the nation's sense of economy, discussing forestry in relation to wood exports and imports and the tariff. Secretary Schurz had already expressed Fernow's view on the controversial issue of the tariff. On March 20, 1890, at a forestry convention held at Lancaster, Pennsylvania, Fernow quoted Schurz approvingly:

> If I had the power to choose for the country between an immediate reduction of tariff duties on the one hand and the introduction of an effective forest policy on the other, I should say: let the people be burdened a little longer by protected interests, for at a future day they can change their system and retrieve their losses, rather than let the destruction of our forests go on at the present rate, for that destruction may bring on a train of disaster from which the country may never recover.[40]

In an address given in Michigan in 1907 on the subject of woodland taxation and the tariff Fernow said, "I remember a committee of lumbermen waiting on me at Washington to ask me to assist their tariff agitation by an argument which should show that a tariff of $2 per 1,000

[39] E. E. R. Tratman, in *Report upon the Forestry Investigations of the U.S.D.A. 1877-1898*, pp. 396ff. See also in the same volume "List of Publications Relating to Forestry," p. 40.

[40] *Forest Leaves* III, 1, pp. 2-4.

feet would promote forestry. I promised to do so if they in turn could vouch that at least one-half of this tax on the public would find its way from their pockets into the woods for improved practice. . . ."[41]

In 1887 Fernow's rough estimates as to mill capacity satisfied him that "we have entered upon the road to exhaustion of lumber supplies; that we are squandering our capital instead of living on the interest which our forest area, if properly managed, might yield forever; that the need is at hand for a wiser policy which will dictate greater economy, fuller utilization, better protection, and recuperation of our forest lands. . . ."[42] But the tariff was not the solution. "An unbiased weighing of the arguments advanced on both sides leads to the conclusion that the removal of the tariff on lumber would have no appreciable effect upon the price to the consumer, nor be detrimental to the lumbermen's or saw mill business, nor in the least affect the laboring man; but at the same time no appreciable benefit towards preservation of forests and forest supplies need be expected at this date from such removal. Possibly positive local advantages may be gained if, by such competition, local manufactures were encouraged and the shipping of raw material made less profitable."[43] In a letter years later,[44] Fernow said, "As regards the trade extension work . . . let me call attention to the fact that I recognized the importance of this side of the business, namely, the marketing of the forest crop, early in my connection with forestry work. The whole timber physics work was laid out with that development in view. . . ." "Timber physics" was a term invented by Fernow.

Forestry in North America progressed through three principal phases during Fernow's years as chief of the division of forestry: (1) the forest reservation policy; (2) the introduction of forest management practice; (3) the timber physics program.

The supply of his first, or 1886, forestry division report, in a separate printing of 1,300 copies, had so quickly proved insufficient for the demands that by the time of his 1887 report, he had begun to prepare leaflets, circulars, charts, and other miscellaneous publications on special topics and for special groups or interests. For instance, during this period Fernow prepared for the national Grange special leaflets on agricultural forestry, and the substance of these was contained also in his annual reports. The first important bulletin on "Timber Physics" would not appear until the early 1890's. But, before then, several preliminary writings on the subject appeared. As early as his 1887 report, he described timber physics study and wood technology. Fernow divided forestry investigations into two main branches of inquiry—scientific inquiry and economic inquiry.

[41] *Forestry Quarterly* V, 4, Dec. 1907, p. 382.
[42] *Report of Div. of For. for 1887*, pp. 30-31.
[43] *Report of Div. of For. for 1887*, p. 33.
[44] Oct. 10, 1916.

Scientific research embraced three fields: forest biology, timber physics, and soil study. The economic basis was formed in investigations of forest and timber statistics, wood technology, and forest policy. His program was an elaborate effort to evaluate and apply all timber knowledge. Only a brief reference to the number of industries dependent on timber and its by-products is necessary to convey an impression of the importance of the work. Fernow grouped the industries: those using manufactured lumber and shaped wood principally; those using wood directly from the forest, unshaped or without special shaping; and those utilizing forest by-products, turpentine, tanning materials, maple sugar and other saps, fruits, leaves, and so forth. Other derivative materials and chemical by-products included wood alcohol, wood acids, gas, tar, pitch, pearlash, and the like. There was a great demand for posts, poles, piles, stakes, fence material, paving blocks, and other small materials, as well as for firewood and charcoal. He mentioned cooperage products, shingle manufacture, baskets and boxes, and other manufactures of measures, as well as matches, tooth-picks, skewers, tree-nails, shoe-pegs, pencils, excelsior, and many other small items. The cabinet-making and wood-shaping industries relied on the forest for their materials for house-finishings, sashes, doors, blinds, windows, and window frames, moldings, looking glasses, picture frames, and a host of other articles. There were also carriage and wagon manufacture, furniture and its veneers, carving, turnery, and bent work, musical instruments, box manufactures such as packing boxes, coffins, cigar-boxes of special construction, as well as a wide range of small woodenware, domestic and agricultural implements, tool stock, handles, mill-work, and other instruments. Of course, no one overlooked the large scale uses: house building, building construction, railroad building, mine timbering, ship and boat building, canal building, river improvement, bridge and trestle building, piling, scaffolding, et cetera. Steel and other metals today have displaced many of these wood uses, but new uses have arisen. The chief of the division of forestry did not underestimate the magnitude of his task. He initiated a program of study which related these wood uses and industrial arts to forest growth and forest improvement.[45]

"Technology of woods, or the adaptation of wood and other forest products to various industrial arts," said Fernow, required "special consideration, based upon the knowledge gained by the investigations into timber physics." Timber testing up to this time had been almost exclusively a work of engineers, almost none of the work being regarded as in the domain of forestry. In his work on the "Forests of North America" for the 1880 census, Sargent had established a department to study experimentally the nation's wood supplies, first, as to fuel value,

[45] *Report of Div. of For. for 1887*, pp. 43-44.

and second, the value of the principal timber trees as material for construction. Stephen Paschall Sharples, chemist, was appointed the department's special agent. Fuel value was arrived at by "a determination of the specific gravity and the ash of the absolutely dry wood, supplemented by a determination of the actual chemical composition of the wood of some of the most important trees; the value of our woods for construction," their report said, "has been obtained by experiments made with the United States testing machine at the Watertown arsenal." A report of nearly 250 pages was published, and the specimens used were deposited at the national museum at Washington and the Harvard college arboretum. When these results were announced in the ninth volume forming the final report of the tenth census (1884), this was regarded as "the only comprehensive work in timber physics ever undertaken on American timbers," but, since in the mechanical tests only a few select pieces were used to examine each forest species, the results were given little recognition. The comprehensiveness rather than the completeness of investigation prompted Filibert Roth later to point out that while no less than 412 species were examined in over 1,200 specimens, the purpose was more to study "all the arborescent species" than furnish "fuller data of practical applicability on those from which the bulk of our useful material is derived." Sargent and Sharples claimed for their conclusions only that "The results obtained are highly suggestive; they must not, however, be considered conclusive, but rather valuable as indicating what lines of research should be followed in a more thorough study of this subject."[46] The tree's locality and soil—in some instances its diameter and layers of heart and sapwood—and other data were arranged in tabular form. Specific gravity, mineral ash content, fuel value, comparisons of weight and strength, and other matters were given. But the specimens were examined "in most cases from the butt cut and free from sap and knots." The objects of the study were followed up by a number of investigators who, preparing "compilatory works, for use in practice and for reference," extended the research in very important ways. Valuable experimental investigation had preceded the work of Sharples. At the Stevens Institute of Technology, at Cornell University under R. H. Thurston, at the Massachusetts Institute of Technology under Gaetano Lanza, at the University of Pennsylvania, at Maine State College, at the University of Iowa, at the University of Minnesota, and at Yale University timber testing had been carried out, but foresters did not take part in any of

[46] Filibert Roth, "Development of the Science of Timber Physics and Methods Employed—American Work," *Report upon the Forestry Investigations of the U.S.D.A. 1877-1898*, pp. 381-383, containing bibliography; "The Work in Timber Physics in the Division of Forestry," *ibid.*, pp. 330ff. Also "The Woods of the United States," *Report on the Forests of North America*, 47th Cong. 2nd sess., H. misc. doc. 42, part IX, pp. 247-481, by Sargent and Sharples.

this work. Botanists and plant physiologists such as George Lincoln Goodale at Harvard University and Joseph Trimble Rothrock of the University of Pennsylvania contributed in minor fashion. The work was principally an effort by engineers "to work out the general laws of relation between physical and mechanical properties" of timbers. But Fernow wished to learn not only quantitative but also qualitative timber properties, related so far as possible to each timber's conditions of growth in the forest. Field work as well as laboratory research would advance the interests of forestry in America.

Fernow insisted that timber physics should embrace the sciences of engineering, chemistry, physics, botany, and forestry. The engineer who understood the processes of iron and steel manufacture and their uses, for example, was not equipped by virtue of that knowledge to study wood and wood uses and to develop the forest products industries. Nor would a knowledge of chemistry alone suffice, although the chemical industry was making wide use of wood as a raw material.[47] In his conception of the study of the forest's influences Fernow wanted the meteorologist, geologist, hydrologist, engineer, botanist, and forester to cooperate in coordinated research.

First, said Fernow, it was necessary to devise a scientific taxonomy which described the species with complete detailed accuracy. The forester would need to know more than the botanist or engineer about his product. The forester would have to know the soil, climate, and other environmental factors which influenced the tree's quality, as well as the part of the tree taken for analysis, the treatment of the material after felling, the manner of seasoning and drying, the arrangement of cell elements and grains, and moisture content, the specific weight, and other important factors. Engineers had often tested timbers in groups, not discriminating between special varieties of a genus. Sometimes a yardman, neither engineer nor timber expert nor botanist, selected the materials from a lumber yard. Fernow complained that "no attempt [was] made to make sure of the species; in fact, the means for doing so are usually not at the command of the professor; no knowledge as to the conditions under which the material has grown [existed]. . . . In short, the whole performance [was] more or less blind. . . ." In the absence of standardized test procedures, the examination had only limited significance. Fernow believed that the first purpose of timber physics research should be to ascertain laws and principles. No test could be complete without proof of the timber's strength, its flexibility, compression

[47] Fernow realized the importance of research in the chemistry of woods and woodpulp; he was interested in developing the uses of cellulose and in producing fibers and other products by removing "wood nitrogenous substances, resins, gums, and [mineral] ash" from wood. In 1890 he predicted that electrical processing would "eventually supercede all other processes."

characteristics, and cohesive factors. The effects of age, locality, moisture, shrinkage, kiln-drying, high-temperature and high-pressure processes employed, and of immersion required study.

In an atmosphere of ignorance and prejudice, Fernow announced the work. On April 23, 1892, before the Washington Philosophical Society, he explained the origins:

> I wish to introduce you tonight to a new word and to explain what its meaning and origin is, and besides the word itself, present a systematic arrangement of the subject matter. . . . Out of this attempt has grown what may be differentiated as a new branch of natural science. To this I propose to give the name "Timber Physics," under which name the knowledge of all phenomena exhibited by wood as dead material are comprised. I have used the word first in 1887, in schematizing the science of forestry. . . . It comprises . . . not only the anatomy, the chemical composition, the physical and mechanical properties of wood but also its diseases and defects and a knowledge of the influences and conditions which determine structural, physical, chemical, mechanical, and technical properties. . . .

The new science would develop on the one side "upon the basis of physiological botany, molecular physics and chemistry, and, on the other side upon the basis of mechanics and dynamics. . . ."

Fernow defined the work as scientific, but matters of economic utility were involved. In his 1887 report, he argued:[48]

> The properties upon which the use of wood, its technology, is based should be well-known to the forest manager if he wishes to produce a crop of given quality useful for definite purposes. Our ignorance in this direction has been most fruitful in fostering a wasteful use of our natural forests, and the same ignorance misleads even the forest planter of to-day in choosing the timber he plants and the locality to which he adapts it.
>
> How the Black Walnut has been sacrificed for fence material, how the valuable Chestnut Oak has rotted in the forest unused, how the Hemlock has been despised and passed by when it might have been successfully used to lengthen the duration of White Pine supplies, how timbers are used in unnecessarily large sizes and applied to uses to which they are not adapted while other timbers are neglected for uses to which they are adapted—all these unfortunate misapplications are or have been due to lack of knowledge of the technological properties of our timbers. Every day almost brings to light a new use for this or that timber, every now and then lumber papers are weighing the serviceability of this or that wood. Instead of proceeding on a sure and scientific basis in recommending the application of any wood to a particular use, opinions pro and con are brought to bear and the proper development and use of our resources is thereby retarded. Yesterday it was Redwood that needed commendation in the market, to-day it is Cypress that must be praised in order to receive due appreciation. . . .

Timber tests had not yet "duly appreciated" the qualities of woods. Woods valuable for manufacturing purposes were consumed as fuel. Valuable and scare wood varieties were used for coarse work even

[48] pp. 37-39.

though cheaper and more abundant kinds were available. "Crude 'experience'," said Fernow, "has been our guide, and 'crude' has remained our knowledge. Thus we hear of 'second growth' ash, hickory, etc., a very vague term indeed, as furnishing the only acceptable wood for many of the purposes to which it is put; and of the comparative uselessness of 'second growth' pine; while the difference lies simply in the condition under which the 'second growth' has grown, in the one case increased light influence, or in its age in the other case. The differences made in trade as to localities where timber is grown, as also the differences made or not made as to qualities of timber used interchangeably, are often without any proper foundation."

Timber physics would be valuable to the forest planter wishing to grow a wood of certain quality. He would be able to learn the soil conditions, climatic influences, and other factors which would tend to produce the desired result. The manufacturer also, from the study of anatomical structure of woods, would be able to form "a ready estimate of quality." "The chemical composition, hardness, cleavability, and minor qualities, such as the grain, color, susceptibility to polish etc., also the faults or the effects of diseases of timber, will form an object of these investigations. Lastly, this investigation will have to be so conducted as to determine the factors which produce difference of quality in the individuals of the same species and of different species. . . ." For example, it was to be found that the Cuban and long leaf pines were twenty-five per cent stronger than was assumed. Furthermore, in the pines, it was learned that the "variation in weight, hence also in strength, from center to periphery depends on the rate of growth, the heavier, stronger wood being formed during the period of most rapid growth, the lighter and weaker wood in old age."[49]

Soils research was attached to the work almost a decade before it became an established agricultural study. Said Fernow:

The elements which determine mechanical conditions of the soil—its looseness, depth, granulation, and consequent capacity for moisture—seem to be more important for forest growth than chemical constituents, although we shall not be justified in omitting such chemical investigations into the dependence of quantitative and qualitative wood formation on certain minor constituents as would teach us the use of fertilizers in the growing of seedlings at least, or as might influence our choice of species for certain soils in

[49] Filibert Roth summarized the work from 1890-1896 in "The Work in Timber Physics in the Division of Forestry," *Report upon the Forestry Investigations of the U.S.D.A. 1877-1898*, pp. 330-395; in the subsection on the work's development, *op. cit.*, are quoted Fernow's bulletin 6, a preliminary report (1892), and his annual report (1890); in the main presentation of the factual findings and principles deduced are quotations from circular 12, "Southern Pine: Mechanical and Physical Properties"; circular 15, "Summary of Mechanical Tests in 32 Species of American Woods," and much other valuable data on southern and northern oak, bled and unbled pine, distribution of resin in pine, strength of large beams and columns, tests of maximum uniformity, relation of compression, and endwise strength to breaking load of beam.

mixtures or in a change of crop. . . . The physical improvement of soils by other means than manures which latter can hardly become practicable in general forest growing, must be based upon a thorough knowledge of soils and their properties. . . .[50]

For example, it was necessary to investigate the belief "that all manure is hurtful in growing conifers."

In 1888 Fernow began to write extensively on timber physics. In *Forest Leaves*[51] there appeared an article, "Increasing the Durability of Timber," a review of a *Forestry Leaflet.* Causes and preventive methods of wood decay, timber uses to induce better preservation, natural factors which influence durability, and many kindred matters were discussed. Where durable timbers were scarce, it was recommended, to prevent decay and render woods stronger and more durable, that factories be established to impregnate woods by processes described in the division's bulletin 1.

Fernow described aims, objects, and methods of research in timber physics, or "the science of wood." Filibert Roth, however, was to be the real technician to develop the actual laboratory methods and practice. Within less than a decade after his work had been started, he could claim confidently, "On the whole, it is in no way boastful to assert that this work has already furnished practical data enough to more than pay the expenses incurred ten times over; that its fruits are not half gathered, and that for more than a quarter of a century its results will serve as a basis for the user of wood and as the guide to the teacher and experimenter." Some idea of the contribution made by this work to forest conservation could, furthermore, be indicated by Fernow when, referring to the proof "that the strength of our longleaf pine is from 20 to 25 per cent greater than had hitherto been supposed, by this knowledge an annual saving of at least $6,000,000 worth of this material alone could be effected. The demonstration by the division," Fernow maintained, "that the bleeding of this same species for turpentine does not deteriorate the timber value of the trees has added at least $2,000,000 annually to the product of the pineries of the South."[52]

Filibert Roth[53] was born April 20, 1858, in Wilhelmsdorf, Württemberg, Germany. He later said that his birthplace was "in one of the best forest districts of Germany, in Oberant, Ravensburg." Roth's father Paul had studied at Göttingen and Tübingen, was a naturalist and linguist, and took Filibert on long foot tours in southern Germany and

[50] *Report of Div. of For. for 1887*, p. 41.

[51] Feb. 1888, p. 41. See also circular 20, U.S.D.A., Div. of For., "Increasing the Durability of Timber" (1898), 5 pp.

[52] Filibert Roth, *op. cit.*, p. 377; B. E. Fernow, "Division of Forestry," *Yearbook of the U.S.D.A. for 1897*, p. 154.

[53] Much of the material concerning Roth has been furnished by his daughter, Mrs. O. W. Boston, of Ann Arbor. Some of the quotations of Roth are taken from his testimony in the Brooklyn Cooperage Case. See footnote 56.

in the Swiss cantons near Lake Constance. Roth's mother was born in Switzerland. She was especially talented in the art of growing flowers, and she gave the boy a deep and lasting interest in gardening. Young Filibert received his education in the *Realschule* of Ravensburg, and in accordance with the usual procedure of the progressive school at Wilhelmsdorf, he was sent to Neuchatel, Switzerland, as an exchange student. There Roth learned the French language. At the scientific academy at Neuchatel the young student formed concepts of plant study and was impressed by the well-managed forests. "I became familiar," Roth said, "with the operations as they are carried on in the German forests in the same manner that a farmer boy becomes acquainted with the ordinary operations of farming by plowing, sowing, harvesting. . . . I had then seen the forest nurseries. I had seen people plant forests. I was familiar with the manner in which those people harvested their crops."

In the early 1870's Paul Roth brought his family to the United States because he admired the republican form of government. Filibert made the journey alone, arriving with a tag on his coat lapel saying, "Send me to Ann Arbor, Michigan." The family, excepting the eldest daughter, settled in Ann Arbor. While still quite young, Filibert went to Sauk City, Wisconsin, to reside on a farm. There he learned more of forestry and agriculture. Two of his playmates were the Oschner brothers, who became famous in medicine and surgery. Roth said of his early Wisconsin lumbering experience:

> I became familiar by observation not only with the distribution by transporting lumber on a very large scale by means of rafting on the Wisconsin river. I saw there each year a million feet of lumber rafted, and became in this way, by observation, familiar with the lumber business as it was there carried on. Then later, I got out lumber under contract in helping to build Fort McKinley in Wyoming. I also worked with a man who built and repaired the bridges at the three forks of the Missouri, and became familiar there by actually working with a portable sawmill, . . . by helping to put up a mill and running the mill and getting out timber for the mill. In 1883 I worked in Wausau, Wisconsin, which was then one of the large pine producing centers of Wisconsin. I worked in the sawmill of Leahy & Beebe and I became familiar there with different parts of the work, putting the logs in the pond, of driving the logs to the yard, and the . . . piling and sorting etc. of the lumber.

Another account says:

> [When Roth] was only 16 years old he felt self-sufficient to such a degree that he "hit it out West." On the western frontier, along the eastern edge of the Rockies where the forest and plains meet, from Montana to Texas, he spent the greater part of the next eight years of his life. . . . He aided in the extinction of the buffalo (although he said that he usually took care of camp rather than indulge in the slaughter); saw the quelling of the numerous Indian outbreaks; . . . witnessed the first plowing of the prairie which had

been prairie for ages. . . . He saw the railroads stretched across the country. . . . His seven or eight years were spent thus, as cowboy, hunter, wolf trapper, Indian trader, prospector, etc., making his living after the fashion of the frontiersman.[54]

Paul Roth had bought a ranch where Ft. Worth, Texas, is now located. Almost as soon as the family arrived, however, Paul Roth died. Young Filibert found employment in stock raising for a while. Hunting occupied him from 1876-1879 and took him into Wyoming and Montana. From 1879-1880 he engaged in farming, lumbering, and some bridge building in Montana. While on the Gallatin River his labors were mostly farming and timber work. From 1880 to 1882 he was employed by a company known as Edwards and Monforton in the capacity of sheep herder. He became familiar with matters pertaining to grazing. He travelled extensively through the mountains of Wyoming, Montana, and Idaho. In 1883 Roth returned to Wisconsin. For two years his summers were given to sawmill and woods work and his winters were occupied in teaching country school to earn enough money to go to college. At a teachers' institute meeting at Wausau he met and fell in love with Clara Hoffman, a daughter of John Jacob Hoffman, a Lutherman clergyman.[55]

Roth entered the University of Michigan in 1885. There he studied botany and forestry under Spalding. In 1887 he was made curator and custodian of the University Museum. The following year he married Miss Hoffman. "From 1888 on," he said, "I was engaged in investigating into the technical principles of timber, and took up in earnest the study of forestry by reading. The work that I did in this investigation was under the direction of Dr. Fernow."

Roth was destined to become not only Michigan's first great forester but, more important, America's first great student from the forestry standpoint of "the technology of our timbers and especially . . . the conditions upon which the qualities of our timbers depend."[56] Late in 1887 Professor Spalding of the University of Michigan and Fernow planned, as an adjunct to life history studies of important conifers, "an investigation into their technological characters and qualities and the conditions under which these qualities were attained. . . . Several students at the botanical laboratory of Michigan University were engaged [to study] microscopically the structure of various pines" under Spalding's

[54] Reprint from *The Michigan Forester*, 1923.

[55] Based on Roth, *op. cit.*, and on a chronological list prepared by him; also a mimeographed sheet, *Ass. of Mich. Foresters,* Dec. 1925.

[56] Quotations of this and the next paragraphs are based on *Report of the Div. of For. for 1888*, pp. 618-621; Roth's testimony in *People of State of New York vs. Brooklyn Cooperage Co.* (205 NY 531) Vol. 28, clerk's office, New York Court of Appeals, Feb.-March 1912, pp. 300-318, folios 1196-1268, especially 1254-1258; letter written by Roth to Fernow April 18, 1912; references to footnote 49, *op. cit.*, pp. 331ff. and footnote 53.

direction. Roth has explained how the new work was placed under him and how he and Fernow became acquainted. "Professor Fernow," he said, "had then undertaken a large investigation into the technical operations of the American woods and he had enlisted in this a number of men of repute, among them Professor Spalding of the University of Michigan. He was professor of botany, and he had undertaken the study of the white pine in cooperation, or rather under the direction of Dr. Fernow, and also the study of woods from the standpoint of structure and specific weight and shrinkage and the like. Professor Spalding came to me and said: 'I cannot possibly do this work for the forestry division on account of my many other duties. Will you take up this work?' And I did, and it was largely . . . a study into the technical quality of the wood itself. The wood was collected through Dr. Fernow, or under Dr. Fernow's direction, and a goodly portion of it was collected by Dr. [Charles Mohr] of Mobile, Alabama. . . . They sent me a wood up to Ann Arbor to examine. I was a student in natural history there at the time. About that time I took up reading books on forestry: in German and English; including the works of Dr. Fernow. And that was under the direction of Dr. Fernow. In 1890 I got a permanent appointment in the division of forestry; at that time I think my position was termed special agent. I stayed right there in Ann Arbor, at the University of Michigan." In August 1888 Fernow visited Ann Arbor and on August 26 Spalding wrote to Erwin Frink Smith of the section of vegetable pathology of the United States Department of Agriculture: "Fernow was here a week ago last Saturday, looked over Roth's work and was much pleased apparently. I think he will have him go right on with it and furnish the necessary material." Thus began Roth's famous strength and durability tests of economically valuable timbers. The work was divided into the study of (1) the anatomy of woods, and (2) the chemistry and physiology of woods. Newton B. Pierce, also a student of Spalding and later with the division of vegetable pathology at Washington, supplied wood samples of the northern pines from his home at Ludington, Michigan. In his annual report for the year 1888, Fernow announced, "The timbers thus far brought under investigation by Mr. Roth have been, of Northern pines, *Pinus strobus*, and partially, at least, *Pinus resinosa*; of Southern pines, *Pinus cubensis, mitis, taeda, glabra,* and also *Taxodium distichum.*"

Of Roth's several very important publications from the division of forestry, the first would be bulletin 10: "Timber: An Elementary Discussion of the Characteristics and Properties of Wood" (1895). Very important was his comparative study of three southern pines, the long leaf, the short leaf, and loblolly. By 1896, when the mechanical, physical, and structural study of the four principal southern pines was completed, the results were based on more than 20,000 mechanical tests and over

50,000 weighings and measurements. The timber physics progress report of 1893, bulletin 8, would publish Roth's conclusions as to the effect which bleeding for turpentine has on timber, the results of laboratory study and field work in the southern pineries in 1892. On July 18, 1893, Fernow appointed him "Special agent and expert in timber physics," and he and his family then moved to Washington.

Roth, however, believed that the real work in timber physics, though fully planned before, began when studies and tests were made to determine the value of southern, as well as northern, oak for carriage construction purposes. As early as 1889, in the Washington University laboratory of Professor J. B. Johnson of St. Louis, Missouri, tests were made on northern and southern white oak. The following year, at the Indianapolis meetings of the American Association for the Advancement of Science and the Society for the Promotion of Agricultural Science, Fernow and Roth met and drew up their "first plans in Timber physics." In 1890 the University of Michigan conferred on Roth a bachelor of science degree. This was the year Professor Spalding, informing Erwin F. Smith of the work of his class in plant physiology, told of the "admirable piece of work" Roth had done on a thesis or special report, "Ascent of Water in the Stems of Tall Trees." During 1885-1893 while at the university, he studied botany, zoology, and geology as well as forestry. Dr. J. B. Steere, his teacher in zoology, accompanied him to Indianapolis.

There Fernow and Roth, pleased with the results of Roth's examinations of bald cypress and the more important lumber pines of the south and lake region, pleased with the tests and examinations made of northern and southern oak at the request of the carriage manufacturers' association, pleased with the response of railroads which offered free transportation of logs used for beam and other tests, pleased with recognition from the engineering profession, mapped out a "comprehensive plan . . . to study systematically our more important timber trees." At first the work had been hampered by lack of funds and facilities. But by 1890 the appropriation being increased, a detailed arrangement was entered upon between the forestry division, Roth, and the test laboratory of Dr. J. B. Johnson of Washington University at St. Louis. For five years the St. Louis laboratory and its facilities were used. Fernow announced the immediate plans in his annual report:[57] "For the present it has been decided to study the pines, especially the white pine and the three southern lumber pines." Mohr, furnishing a complete description of the conditions of growth of each test specimen or disk, was to collect the material to be studied, Roth was to examine the disks to determine their "physical and physiological features," while

[57] *Report of the Div. of For. for 1890*, pp. 193, 198-199, 209-214; *Forestry Investigations*, 1877-1898, pp. 8, 331-332, 346, 377ff.

the logs, and later special parts of the disks, were to be sent to Johnson. At this laboratory, "for the first time, a systematic series of beam tests," Fernow announced, "will be made and compared with the tests on the small laboratory test pieces. Such tests with full length beams in comparison with tests on small specimens promise important practical results, for a few tests have lately developed the fact that large timbers have but little more than one half the strength they were credited with by standard authorities, who relied upon the tests on small specimens." Forest technological investigations, as well as timber physics examinations, were thus provided. Purely scientific as well as practical conclusions were held in view. "We know," said Fernow, "that the width of the annual rings, their even growth, the closeness of grain, the length, number, thickness, and distribution of the various cell elements, the weight, and many other physical appearances and properties of the wood influence its quality, yet the exact relation of these is but little studied. . . . We know, in a general way, that structure and composition of the wood must depend upon the conditions of soil, climate, and surroundings under which the tree is grown, but there are only few definite relations established. We are largely ignorant as to the nature of our wood crop, and still more so as to the conditions necessary to produce desirable qualities, and since forestry is not so much concerned in producing trees as in producing quality in trees, to acquire or at least enlarge this knowledge must be one of the first and most desirable undertakings in which this Division can engage."[58]

The thoroughness of the work pleased Fernow. He quoted an authority in engineering who said, "Inasmuch as what passes current among engineers and architects as information on the strength of timber is really misinformation, and that no rational designing in timber can be done until something more reliable is furnished in this direction, the necessity for making a competent and trustworthy series of such tests is apparent. This is a work which the Government should undertake if it is to be impartial and general." Fernow added:

> A careful record of all that pertains to the history and conditions of the growth from which the test pieces come, and of their minute physical examination, will distinguish these tests from any hitherto undertaken on American timbers.
>
> The disk pieces will be studied to ascertain the form and dimensions of the trunk, the rate and mode of its growth, the density of the wood, the amount of water in the fresh wood, the shrinkage consequent upon drying, the structure of the wood in greatest detail, the strength, resistance, and working qualities of the wood, and lastly, its chemical constituents, fuel value, and composition of the ash. . . .

[58] 1890 report, *ibid*, pp. 209-211.

The utmost care was to be taken to be certain that the wood specimen was, in fact, the botanical species to be studied.[59]

Three railroads offered free transportation for the test logs. For the first test series it was estimated that fifty trees would be studied, involving thousands of tests "and a large amount of laboratory determinations." The growing scarcity of hickory and ash suitable for carriage manufacture had induced this industry in 1888 to investigate timber supplies. A report that southern grown white oak was unfavorable for carriage making had resulted in the cooperative investigation arranged by Fernow and members of the National Carriage Builders' Association. October 1890 found Fernow addressing a formal communication to the organization to announce that not only had a plan been drawn and work begun, but also that "the ultimate object" of the investigation would be "to find, if possible, the relation of qualities of the various timbers to the conditions under which they have grown." He urged a theory which he admitted the investigation might disprove. He thought that environmental conditions effected a growth rate which, in turn, determined height and diameter of the tree. "Upon this," he said, "is dependent the kind and character of the cell elements of which the wood is composed, and *upon size and arrangement of the cell elements depend ultimately the qualities* of the wood. . . ."[60]

One of the achievements of the division was to convince the railroads that chestnut oak, which was cut for bark in the Appalachian region, was suitable for railroad ties. By 1909 the railroads had "accepted chestnut oak on a par with white oak."[61] During 1891 fifty-nine oak trees from Alabama, twenty-two trees of white pine from Wisconsin, ten trees of short leaf pine, and fifteen trees of loblolly had been collected, partly tested, and examined. To determine the influence of tapping for turpentine upon the quality of long leaf pine, 149 trees furnished three to four thousand test pieces. A study to determine the influence of the amount and character of seasoning also had been started.[62] In time the work became organized in four departments: (1) collecting; (2) mechanical tests; (3) physical and microscopical examinations of test materials; and (4) compilation and discussion of results. Fernow soon issued his comprehensive Bulletin VI on the subject. Statistical inquiries concerning the nation's forests, timber supplies, and consumption had been displaced by these more scientific investigations. The financial appropriations for the division had not been sufficient to attempt more. Forest reservations from the public domain totalled seven-

[59] *Report of Div. of For. for 1890,* pp. 210-211; also Fernow's "Scientific Timber Testing," *Digest of Physical Tests* I, 2, April 1896, p. 90.

[60] Letter, October 11, 1890. See also *Report of the Div. of For. for 1888,* p. 629; for 1889, *op. cit.*; and references of footnote 57.

[61] *Forestry Quarterly* VII, 3, p. 354.

[62] *Report of Div. of For. for 1891,* p. 192.

teen million acres, and the secretary of agriculture as well as Fernow was urging that the reservation policy "should be followed by a well-considered supervision of the same, and the remaining timber lands on the public domain should be withdrawn from disposal."

In his 1892 report Fernow told the nation that no less than 6,800 tests of various kinds had been performed in Johnson's laboratory at St. Louis, that it had been established that pine timber quality was not impaired by turpentine bleeding, and that, therefore, the value of the southern pine forests had appreciably increased. It was also said:[63]

It is very gratifying that this first venture of original investigation by the Division of Forestry has found general favor, not only in a part of this country, but also has been highly commended by the technical press of the Old World. The calls for special investigations into the qualities of the timbers in various sections of the country have grown very numerous, and it is to be regretted that the scant appropriations made for this work will not allow an expansion, such as might furnish at least preliminary knowledge in regard to all the timbers which appear on the market. There is a special demand for the tests of such kinds as are still more or less unknown, they being now drawn upon to eke out the deficiency of supply of the better-known kinds. The Douglas spruce, the cedars, the sugar-pine of the West, the bald cypress of the South, and other conifers ought to be tested without delay. If Congress had appropriated the necessary funds which were asked for in the special bill introduced during the last session, it was the intention to establish a test laboratory at San Francisco, and another one at Washington. . . .

In his report of November 20, 1893, Secretary of Agriculture J. Sterling Morton of Nebraska commented:[64]

Members of the American Forestry Association, and all other citizens interested in the conservation of woodlands and reafforestation of denuded areas of lands not suitable to tillage, will be pleased to read in "Dankleman's Zeitschrift, September, 1893," the deserved compliment which the reviewer of the United States timber examination work (instituted by B. E. Fernow, in charge of forestry interests) has unreservedly awarded this Department. The judgment of Mr. Fernow's work in this division, in his scientific investigation of the several varieties of timber, as to strength, durability, and general utility, in relation to the conditions of growth, is all the more valuable because the gentleman who gives it is himself in charge of forestry work of a similar character for the Prussian Government. And it is, therefore, a matter of congratulation, among all those who realize the importance of forestry work in the United States, to read the following unequivocal and merited commendation of the work of this division in the Department of Agriculture.

"This plan of work is as remarkable for its scope as for consistent pursuit of an eminently practical result. Although Germany has accomplished a

[63] *Report of the Div. of For. for 1892*, pp. 294-296 (including descriptions of cooperative investigations with Division of Chemistry on tannic contents and their distribution in woods, etc., and with Division of Section of Vegetable Pathology on "bluing" of timber). Concerning federal forest reservations and management, see *Report of Sec'y of Agric. for 1891*, pp. 47, 223ff., and references to footnotes 9 and 10 of this chapter; also *Report of Sec'y of Agric. for 1893*, p. 31.

[64] *Op. cit.*, p. 32.

great deal in some directions of this field, especially in investigating the laws of growth and wood structure, we are yet far from having such a comprehensive and indispensable knowledge even of our most important timbers. We must admit, with a certain sense of humiliation, that the Americans show us what it is we really ought to know, and that they have already by far surpassed us in the elaborate organization for these investigations."

If, in less than a decade, Americans have in a forestry specialty surpassed Germany, why can not we a generation hence rejoice in the most efficient forestry system of the world?

In 1892 Fernow told the Washington Philosophical Society that he proposed to enlarge the systematic study of American timbers. Physical and mechanical examinations would be conducted with such care "in marking the test pieces and describing the conditions in the field surrounding the study material, that it will be possible for any later investigator to use this material. . . ." The intention was to "establish the laws of qualitative wood growth." Moreover, the division of forestry was cooperating with the division of chemistry in the study of woods, including the chestnut and various oaks, to supplement or find new sources of tan extracts and help solve the problem of a decreasing supply of tanbarks; and with the division of vegetable pathology to inquire into the cause and prevention or control of the "bluing" of timber, especially southern pines, tulip poplar, and other softwoods.

Although Fernow regarded the timber physics work as "the most valuable and promising in which the division [had] been engaged since its creation," at the same time he regarded the rise of the wood pulp industry, as "the most important development in the use of forest products." He wrote:

It can be said, without fear of contradiction, that in no field of industrial activity has a more rapid development taken place within the last few years than in the use of wood for pulp manufacture. The importance of this comparatively new industry for the present, and still more for the future, can hardly be overestimated. Its expansion during the next few decades may bring revolutionary changes in our wood consumption, due to the new material, cellulose, fiber or wood pulp. Though rapid in its growth, the industry has by no means reached its full development. Not only is there room for improvements in the processes at present employed, but there are all the time new applications found for the material. While it was in the first place designed to be used in the manufacture of paper only, by various methods of indurating it, its adaptation has become widespread: pails, water pipes, barrels, kitchen utensils, washtubs, bathtubs, washboards, doors, caskets, carriage bodies, floor coverings, furniture and building ornaments, and various other materials are made of it.[65]

Anyone having a superficial knowledge of the rise of these industries in the United States realizes instantly how prophetic were these observations made by Fernow in 1890. In that year Canada reported having

[65] *Report of Div. of For. for 1890*, pp. 199-208.

only thirty-three pulp mills. California reported one; Massachusetts, Pennsylvania, West Virginia, and North Carolina three each; Virginia, Ohio, Minnesota, and Oregon two each. New York led this list with sixty-seven mills. There were twenty-three manufacturing "chemical [soda] fibre" and twenty-nine making "chemical [sulphite] fibre." Spruce and poplar were chiefly used, although pine, fir, hemlock, bass, cypress, gum, buckeye, maple, cottonwood, tamarack, and aspen were also utilized. The entire study of these woods for pulp lay before the division.[66]

During 1890-1891 Fernow did some popular writing, endeavoring to increase the public's interest. The most noteworthy articles were "Tracts on Tree Topics," published in *Kate Field's Washington* and of which a few reprints were issued. Later when Sargent inquired of these for bibliographical reasons, Fernow replied:

> You could not have surprised me more in the bibliography line than by your inquiry after the Tracts on Tree Topics. These were short articles written in a breezy style to suit the journal in which they were published, namely, Catefield's Washington, the short life of which you may remember. . . . You will, therefore, understand that these ebullitions were of absolutely ephemeral character, and I can hardly see what bibliographic value they may have. I considered them so lightly that at first I did not even take a clipping.

Fernow counted as more valuable his analysis, written August 7, 1891, on the red cedar for manufacturing pencils, statistics concerning its consumption and export, its habitats in the far southern states, and the agencies that may attack its growth. During this year Fernow also wrote for the *American Garden*[67] on the cost of forest despoliation and the benefits of forest management. His thesis was, "It is the number of trees that yield the best result, not the greatest number, that we try to keep growing."

Most of Fernow's writings dwelt on science or economics in special relation to forestry. The study of forest tree seeds was practical. When he had taken office as chief of the forestry division, he had gone before the American Nurserymen, Florists, and Seedsmen's Association and the American Pomological Society and discussed "Forest Tree Seeds" and the influences which affected their quality. He had presented a resolution which favored the Association's active participation in the matter of seed control. In 1887 Fernow sent to the Association a paper entitled, "Objects and Workings of the Seed-Control Stations."[68] Forest seed testing had been performed at state agricultural experiment stations in Connecticut, Maine, New York, North Carolina, and Ohio; but the

[66] Attention should be called to Fernow's evaluation of what was termed "electro pulp." He foresaw that forest management would have to furnish supplies near ample water power when commercial plants were established for electrical processing.

[67] Sept. 1891, pp. 519, 587.

[68] *The Prairie Farmer*, June 25, 1887, p. 407.

work had not been "systematically carried on in the sense of establishing a continuous control and a possible guarantee of the seed-material in the market."

The division of forestry already afforded facilities for taxonomic research. The seed control stations could study the seed's life processes —fructification, seed-ripening, germination, development, and weed eradication. The work of both could be coordinated. By 1890 the forest botanical herbarium contained several thousand specimens. The seed collection of different species numbered 360, and a special collection of 1,200 buds of 100 forest species had been preserved in alcohol. Fernow realized that a check list of forest species was needed. Accordingly, in 1891, he wrote in *Garden and Forest*,[69] "The discussion with reference to the establishment of a stable botanical nomenclature has a special interest to me from the fact that, in a short time, I propose to have published for this division a check list of the arborescent flora of the United States, containing both botanical and [common] names; and while Mr. [George B.] Sudworth is working out the botanical synonymy, it will fall to me to decide muted points."

Forestry in North America developed regionally. Fernow had not led in the first years of development of forestry in the Middle West. As chief of the division at Washington he had focussed attention on the problems of the West. Always he had kept a watchful eye on the East, especially the Adirondack Mountains. No region entirely escaped his attention. Now, however, he turned southward to the forests which Roth and Mohr had studied. Roth had travelled there doing turpentine field investigation. He also had studied the sawmills of the South. Mohr presented a thorough account of the growing naval stores industry, which was published in the division's 1892 report.

During 1892 Fernow wrote for the *Manufacturers' Record,* a weekly southern industrial, railroad, and financial newspaper. A series of articles pointed out clearly the forestry needs and possibilities of the southern states. He said:

> Within the last decade or so the center of lumber production has gradually but surely gravitated toward the South as the result of the steady and rapid decimation of supplies which the Northern lumber States, especially Michigan, Wisconsin, and Minnesota, have yielded in enormous quantities during the last fifty years. It would be hazardous to prophesy when the day of utter exhaustion of Northern forests, even of white pine alone, will be accomplished. Many contingencies entirely beyond computation enter into this calculation and forbid the present solution of the problem. Nevertheless, the weakening of our great staple, white pine, and other kinds in the North is undeniable, and it is to the South, we shall presently look for making up the deficiency. Hence the review of Southern timber resources proposed in these papers may be considered timely. It is proposed to present this in a

[69] p. 213.

series of papers, the present giving a general picture of conditions, the next dealing with the forest flora from a botanical standpoint, to be followed by a discussion of the pines and hardwoods in particular, and finally an account of the development of the lumber industry in the South.[70]

Fernow won the manufacturers by appealing to their business sense. The word "forestry" does not appear once in the introduction. Fernow discovered that of 160 genera of North American forest trees, about 77 grow within the southern states. While the hardwood industry had grown more slowly than that of the pines, by 1892 the manufacture and sale of southern hardwood lumber was "exceeding the wildest dreams of twenty years ago." Fernow discussed the more valuable timbers and their distribution. The cypress steadily was increasing in importance as a timber tree. Throughout the papers he argued the need for more careful management.

Fernow had begun by pleading, "There is still a rich resource left to the South, which we hope, almost against hope, will be utilized in a more rational manner and with more profit to the present and future generations." He concluded:

> We see then that the solution of this great problem of a rational development of these great resources is not attainable by the single man or firm, but calls for associated effort, which will bring about those social and commercial changes that predicate improvement all around. When this general spirit of improvement that is beginning to show itself in some quarters, is more fully developed, we may expect a better future for the great Southern forest. At present it is as recklessly slaughtered for present gain, as irrationally treated and cut with as little concern for its continued revenue producing capacity as has been the fate of the Northern forest.

If the test of forestry was to be found in the forests, where in the entire United States was there a bright picture to be seen? In the vast public timberland domain there were reserves but no management. In the Adirondacks there was a state preserve but little or no rational management. In New England forests efforts were being made to enforce fire laws. Commissions were studying forest conditions, but practically no forest policies had been adopted by the states. The situation was general over the entire United States, and the South was especially weak. Here and there was a bright spot of management or planting activity, but it was all forestry in embryo. The division of forestry was doing its part, although still laboring with inadequate finances. Not until 1892 were special appropriations allowed for timber physics research. Even then the appropriation for such purpose was more implied than expressed. Evidently the amounts ranged between five and ten thousand dollars annually. The division warned against future forest ruin if large scale constructive action was not made possible, but congress

[70] *Manufacturers' Record*, June 10, 17, 24, July 1, 8, 1892, Baltimore.

refused to pass the division's and the American Forestry Association's forestry bill.

In 1892 Fernow spoke before the section for economic science and statistics of the American Association for the Advancement of Science. The topic of his address, "Economic Conditions Antagonistic to a Conservative Forest Policy," culminated in a plea for the federal government to place in reservations its fifty or sixty million acres of forest land under "a circumspect management by which, while the needs for timber of a growing population are subserved, forest conditions are kept in favorable condition." At this time there were pending before congress several proposed legislative measures, but the one of which the American Forestry Association took cognizance and endorsed was a bill (S. 3235) introduced by Senator Paddock of Nebraska "To provide for the establishment, protection, and administration of public forest reservations." In the next chapter we will discuss a forestry measure (H.R. 119) introduced by Representative McRae, which several times modified was later sponsored by the forestry association when it "became apparent that the original bill (the Paddock bill), although most desirable, was too elaborate." When the association's committee on forestry, of which Fernow was secretary, reported favorably on the Paddock bill, it had been favorably reported out of committee and placed on the calendar. At that time the President had reserved five distinct tracts of public timber lands, and several large areas were being examined before being reserved. Fernow prepared a twelve-page statement for the first session of the fifty-second congress to accompany the bill's presentation.

At the eleventh annual meeting of the American Forestry Association held on December 20, 1892, arrangements were concluded with the secretary of the interior to confer concerning additional reservations to be set apart from the public lands, and further, to take up such pertinent matters as were necessary with the public lands committee of the house of representatives. Fernow was named as a member of the Association's committee which was to consult with the secretary and the lands committee.[71]

[71] Statements in Report 1002, 52nd Cong., 1st sess.; Jenks Cameron, *op. cit.*, p. 206; John Ise, *op. cit.*, pp. 122ff.; Fernow, "The Forest Reservation Policy," *op. cit.*; *Proc. Am. Asso. for Adv. of Sci.* XLI, 1892, pp. 329-335; "Management of the National Forest Reservations," *op. cit.*; and unpublished memoranda found in Fernow's collection of documents, etc. See also *Proc. Am. For. Asso.* (10th, 11th, and 12th meet., 1891-1893), 1894, Washington; *Forestry Investigations*, 1877-1898, pp. 192ff.

CHAPTER V

The Division of Forestry and Forest Administration

On December 20, 1892, Fernow delivered a lecture before the National Geographic Society on "The Battle of the Forest,"[1] which dramatized the role of the forest in the evolutionary fight for survival. Exhibiting a wide knowledge of paleobotany and considering both low and high forms of vegetation, Fernow anticipated much ecological research that has since been performed. He had a deep interest in forest history and forest distribution, geographically and botanically, but he was more interested in man's participation in the forest scene. The popular lecture, illustrated with slides, was often repeated through the years and was revised many times.

Fernow informed the public of its responsibilities to the forest. The forest had served man and man must serve the forest. He said:

> There is no use talking about the introduction of fine forestry systems from Europe until we have educated our people to appreciate the value of forest property and to respect property rights and laws, which exist in every state and province against forest incendiaries, but cannot be enforced for lack of proper moral support in the communities. . . . The forester is in the same business as the lumberman, namely, to supply wood material to the community. He is not after the beauty but after the substance of the tree; he also uses the axe to harvest the crop, nay, he utilizes the forest even more closely than the lumberman, but in this utilization he introduces one new point of view, namely that of the economic use of the soil for *future* crops. He is not satisfied with the mere harvest of what nature has accumulated, leaving it to nature to do as it pleases in re-establishing the forest, but he feels himself obligated to provide systematically for a new and, if possible, better crop. Under his care the trees will also be cut and removed, but the forest will persist. He is the preserver of the forest, not in the manner in which the public is often made to believe, namely by preventing the use of the wood, but as all life is preserved, by removing the old and fostering the young growth. He is a sower as well as a reaper, a planter as well as a logger, and to him forestry is, with regard to wood crops, precisely what agriculture is, with regard to food crops.

In this address Fernow indicated a change of attitude more favorable to the forest management method known as "clear cutting" of inferior forest areas and replanting with more valuable stock. This method was applied to mismanaged virgin woods; sometimes it was the only method possible. It was used in Germany, the old timber being systematically cut and replaced by another crop of superior character. But the selection of

[1] Given at Washington, D.C., and published in the *National Geographic Magazine* III, 1892, pp. 127ff.; given also before the A.A.A.S. on Aug. 21-22, 1894; printed in *Nature,* Vol. 51, pp. 130ff., 1894; later presented at meetings of the Am. For. Ass. and other organizations.

management methods was "a complicated problem, in the solution of which politics, public and private, financial and other interests, play an important part."[2]

Reputable journals, especially those of the trades, were beginning to regard the forestry movement as a "craze." Fernow replied strongly to one editor, "There is no doubt that the writer is in the main correct in two propositions, namely, that there is much, too much, amateur writing on American forestry by those who do not know or appreciate economic conditions, and, secondly, that these conditions are or seem to be antagonistic to a more rational forest management than prevails at present." Fernow recognized that reforms could not be readily effected under existing social and economic conditions. In 1892 his article, "Economic Conditions Antagonistic to a Conservative Forest Policy,"[3] had been published. In his 1892 report for the division of forestry he had confessed that he realized that the farmers, who held thirty-five to forty per cent of their property in forests, were a "safe and conservative" class. "No doubt," said Fernow, "whatever attempt at rational forest management exists in the United States may be found among the farmers. It is probable, however, that a large part of their forest property is held only for speculative purposes. . . ." This circumstance he viewed as an advantage to forest conservation. The waste in logging operations was a source of primary concern to Fernow. He believed it possible for lumbermen to work the forest with more regard to future conditions. In a letter he pointed out:

> An attempt in this direction is successfully made in Maine and the lumbering operations in many lumber camps of Michigan are carried on in a much more rational and conservative manner, than in New York or, as far as I know, in most New England States. Canadian methods are also in some respects superior to ours. . . . Now as to the "forestry craze." When it is divested of its crude, more or less unintelligent interpretation by uninformed friends—such as every reform movement must count in its ranks—it is not to stop lumbering or to introduce European management or to advocate anything irrational. On the contrary, its object and ultimate goal is to advance more rational use and treatment of our forest resources; to aid in insuring continuous supplies for the lumber business; to stop only wasteful practices, especially destruction by fire by methods such as the State of Maine has last year devised by wise legal enactment. . . . In the case of New Hampshire, while perhaps under the political conditions existing, the capacity of the State to manage its forestry interests in a broad statesmanlike manner, may not be most promising, the principles upon which the purchase by the State of the mountain forests is asked, remain certainly correct if we admit their value not only for lumber supply, but for water conditions and most espe-

[2] In an article, "Sand Dunes," in *Garden and Forest*, 1892, p. 190, Fernow wrote of the reforestation and cultivation of sand dunes in Europe. In his lecture on the "Battle of the Forest" he said, "How this succession of plant life takes place can be studied even now in all its stages, for instance on the sand dunes of Lake Michigan. . . ."

[3] *Proc. A.A.A.S.* XLI, 1892 (abstract), pp. 329-335.

cially for their beauty as a mountain cover, which attracts to the State hosts of visitors, and with them annually a large influx of money and increase of development, which in taxes should pay the interest on the purchase money for the forest lands.

But even these immediate considerations did not constitute the chief cause of concern. In his address, "Economic Conditions Antagonistic to a Conservative Forest Policy," Fernow concluded, ". . . The United States Government owns some fifty or sixty million acres of forest land under conditions where forest preservation is a necessity, where inducement to conservative forest management on the part of individual owners is even less than in our eastern states, where dire calamities are bound to follow a policy of neglect and forest destruction. . . ."

Fernow did not exaggerate. The old claim of forests in relation to public health, he admitted, was supported by scanty scientific evidence; but no one disclaimed a hygienic significance. When writing on the forest influence on climate, Fernow did little more than delineate the results of European experimental research in the hope of stimulating similar research in America.[4]

At a special meeting of the American Forestry Association held in connection with the World's Columbian Exposition of 1893, the division of forestry displayed an elaborate exhibit. In an address, "Forest Conditions and Forestry Problems in the United States," delivered before the meeting, Fernow pleaded for a liberal support of the division's work, for wise tariff legislation on forest products, for the nationalization of Arbor Day, and for a chair of forestry to be located in the United States Military Academy at West Point. He believed that efforts should be concentrated on aiding states to adopt conservative forest policies. He deplored that in states like California and Colorado, which were among the first to recognize officially the advantages of forestry organization, "political decrepitude" had set back the progress previously made. On the other hand he congratulated Pennsylvania, which had instituted a systematic procedure to investigate its forest conditions and construct an intelligent program of forest preservation. The value of timber was fixed by its future use. Government action was imperative to enforce a program which would protect the timber product of the future.

Canada also was realizing more and more the good to be attained by forestry. At the Chicago meeting of the American Forestry Association, Aubrey White, commissioner of crown lands in the provinces of Canada, spoke on "The Forest Resources of Canada and the Management of Government Timber Lands." William Saunders, director of the Dominion's experimental farms, spoke on "Forest Conditions on the Plains

[4] *Garden and Forest,* 1893, pp. 34, 147.

and Prairies of Canada." Canada was rich because of its forest wealth, but it had not gone far in forestry work. Fire protection, some districting, some afforestation, and restrictions on logging operations especially in Quebec and Ontario provinces still dominated the Canadian system. It was management of a sort, but it was not full scale. Ontario's fire prevention system was admired over the entire North American continent. Restricting logging operations to trees of an arbitrarily prescribed diameter accomplished a conservative lumbering result but was not intelligent forestry. Fernow could see reasons why under certain conditions a tree of thumb-sized diameter should be cut. He told this to a committee of New York men who consulted him. Denuding a forest did not improve the forest unless intelligent provision was made for reforesting the lands.

Fernow deplored a forestry of rigid rules not adaptable to conditions and needs. Consistently he contended that nature unaided should perform as far as possible the work of the forest. Rules found their origins and verification in man's experience. Rules were formed to improve the forest for man's uses, present and future.

During 1890-1895 the first timber reservations of the Dominion of Canada were set apart by executive order of the minister of the interior. Located in thinly timbered areas of the West, the reservations were established more to protect water supply for lower agricultural regions than to perpetuate a timber harvest for the future.

In 1893 at the Chicago World's Fair meeting of the American Forestry Association, Secretary Noble, introduced by Fernow as the man most responsible for securing the first United States forest reservations, described these reservations as located "chiefly at the sources of great rivers and among the mountains and all in regions almost altogether unsuitable for agriculture." Added to the reservations already listed were the Afognak forest and fish culture reserve of Alaska, established December 24, 1892; the Ashland forest reserve established September 28, 1893, consisting of 18,560 acres in Oregon; and the Cascade Range forest reserve established the same day, of 4,492,800 acres. Secretary Noble referred also to the Hot Springs, Arkansas, reservation established by special act of congress. The total timber reservations comprised more than seventeen and a half million acres. Colonel Ensign also spoke on "Forest Reserves in Western Mountain Regions."

It is interesting that at this time the protective argument was dominant—protection of water supply and preservation of the forests. Afforestation, reforestation, planting of waste, barren, cut-over, and burnt-over lands were secondary. Even in the states the water supply reason was most persuasive. In 1893 a permanent commission in New Hampshire was formed and authorized to purchase two tracts, one in the Mount

Monadnock region near Dublin in the southwestern part of the state, and another, a tract in the center of the White Mountains which includes what was known as "Beecher's Cascade." An article[5] pointed out that in the White Mountains "are the headwaters of the Saco, Ammonoosuc, and Merrimack rivers. If these sources are not protected, the flow will be lessened in times of drought and the flood increased. The Merrimack river turns more machinery than any other river in the United States; what an immense loss it would be if these great mills should be closed. . . ."

To prepare the exhibit in forestry at the World's Fair, Fernow had requested that the states permit the national government "to develop and teach forestry as a science." Cooperative exhibits were not excluded, but matters pertaining to forest botany and geography, technology, forest culture, management, and forest economy were to be embraced in the federal sphere.

A large share of educational work was passed to the states, particularly that having to do with regional forestry.[6] Around the Lumber and Forestry Building, a colonnade of tree trunks with their natural bark, lent an appropriate atmosphere. Each state furnished a typical tree. The building thus symbolized the governmental structure of the United States.

To Fernow came an honor which pleased him highly. The German government invited him to prepare its exhibit. Secretary of Agriculture J. Sterling Morton granted Fernow a furlough. For the first time since his arrival in America in 1876, Fernow returned to Germany. He was barely on board of the steamship *Aller* when a friend handed him an article by Henry Gannett which had appeared in the *Washington Evening News*. Attacking efforts to inaugurate a rational forest policy in the United States, Gannett urged that timber consumption was not exceeding natural timber growth and that any claimed relation between forest growth and climatic, soil, and water conditions had little, if any, significance. On April 5, 1893, Fernow answered, addressing a letter to the secretary of agriculture. He said of Gannett, "One can not but deeply regret that men whose position before the public imposes upon them the responsibility of leading public opinion intelligently and upon the basis of well-established facts should thus be found ignoring their responsibility."

At the last census Gannett and Fernow had quarreled. The latter had maintained that it would be proper for the census to gather forest statistics. Gannett had objected. In his letter to the secretary of agriculture

[5] "Forestry in New Hampshire," *Forest Leaves* VII, 1, Feb. 1899, p. 9; see also E. M. Griffith, "The Forestry Agitation in New Hampshire," *The Forester* VII, 4, April 1901, p. 79.

[6] *Forest Leaves* III, 7, Jan. 1892, p. 95.

Fernow rejoiced that Gannett, who always had asserted that fifty per cent of the United States was wooded, now said thirty-seven per cent. "As far as Mr. Gannett's estimates and calculations of woodland areas are concerned," said Fernow, "they are wholly irrelevant to the question at issue, namely, the question of timber supply; for he overlooks entirely the character of such wooded lands as timber producers. . . . Regarding his knowledge of the relation of forest cover to climate, soil, and waterflow, the same lack of familiarity with the real facts and their significance is apparent."[7]

This controversy between Fernow and Gannett struck at the vitals of the forestry movement. In 1896 Gannett organized the division of geography which in 1897 was reorganized as the division of geography and forestry and was charged with mapping and surveying the new reserves. The divisional and departmental setup became complicated; and overlapping of work was not infrequent. The administration of the land laws was becoming more involved each year, and some unravelling was required. At this time Gannett prepared a study of the forest resources, published as part of the geological survey's report of 1898, a work highly commended by Pinchot.[8] In 1893 Fernow was compelled to admit that there existed "no absolutely correct data" to meet the statistical information advanced by Gannett. The chief reason was the inadequacy of the appropriations allowed the division of forestry. The failure of the 1890 census to follow the precedents of the two previous censuses in gathering "forestry statistics" was attributable, Fernow charged, to "Mr. Gannett's voice in shaping the policy of the last census."

Fernow visited the forest departments of Prussia, Saxony, Saxe-Weimar, Bavaria, Württemberg, and the leading forest academies and forest schools of Eberswalde, Munich, Tharandt, Giessen, Eisenach, Tübingen, Münden, and Zürich.[9] Once again he visited with his aristocratic and wealthy German relatives. He returned to the United States and discussed in his reports the subject of forest management. He believed that the forestry system of the Germans was excelled by no other nation. It is said that he admired especially the system of the Prussians. Fernow was probably not altogether fair to French forestry,

[7] Gannett's statement, according to Fernow, that the wooded area of the United States covered "approximately 1,113,000 square miles" did not accord with the figure of the Forestry Division which "by correspondence with well-informed residents in each State some years ago, ascertained the area under forest to be below 500,000,000 acres. But we may readily concede the larger area," wrote Fernow, "simply remarking by the way that the failure to arrive at more certain figures is perhaps chargeable to Mr. Gannett's voice in shaping the policy of the last Census. . . ." See Fernow's comments on the 11th Census in his report for the Division in 1890. The controversy between the two men had begun in 1888.

[8] Jenks Cameron, *op. cit.*, pp. 215n., 220-224, 238.

[9] *Report of Div. of For. for 1893*, pp. 326, 359.

but he sought to be impartial. He submitted his manuscripts to qualified authorities. Fernow was somewhat ignorant of the methods of the French; he later confessed to no practical experience in the forests of France and only a reading acquaintance with forestry there. It is unfortunate that on visiting Europe in 1893 Fernow did not visit the French forest academies as well as those of the Germans and Swiss. It must be remembered, however, that he had to make a hurried visit, staying but a few weeks. For the entire time he was employed by the German government. He was interested always in any European work which had special or potential application to American conditions. When he studied the forestry system of Sweden, he compared it to Canadian conditions. The latest knowledge of felling budgets, yield calculations, evaluation methods, methods of harvesting and transporting materials would all have application to forestry in North America. In 1893 one progressive measure seems to have caught his special interest—the introduction of exotics. The great plant introduction enterprises being developed by agricultural exploration were becoming important in forestry.

In July 1889, David Fairchild had left his association with his uncle, Byron David Halsted of the New Jersey state experiment station, and accepted at Beverly T. Galloway's invitation a position in Washington with the United States department of agriculture. Fairchild has described[10] the working conditions of the few pioneers who were gathered together in the red brick building with the mansard roof situated in a park south of Pennsylvania Avenue. In those years the science of bacteriology, for example, was in infancy, especially in its relation to plants. Forestry was still usually viewed as a propagandists' program. Even in plant introduction work the forest was given scant attention. Tree planters were testing varieties of tree species in different parts of North America. The era of horticultural variety testing had not yielded to more scientific experimental work. Exotic introductions in American agriculture were neither extensive nor systematized.

Plant introduction, the work which was to bring Fairchild worldwide renown, was not the cause of his going to Washington. Botany and horticulture had captured the imagination of the young graduate and son of the president of Kansas State Agricultural College. This college had not been altogether lax in its forestry interest. A student schooled there in the plant sciences was graduated with a thorough understanding of the scientific fundamentals on which forestry could be based. Fairchild became one of the new group which made up the section of plant pathology (and physiology when it was added) of the United States

[10] David Fairchild, *The World Was My Garden*, Scribner's, New York, 1938, pp. 107, 291, 439. The next two paragraphs (and the two quotations) are based mainly on this book.

Department of Agriculture, and Fernow and he became acquainted. Fairchild became impressed with the fact that Fernow's "interest in the problems of American forestry was that of a thoroughly trained scientist."

Fairchild left Washington to study advanced morphology and cytology in Europe, but he remained a special agent and investigator for the department. From Europe were coming such discoveries as the Bordeaux mixture, tremendously valuable to agriculture and horticulture. A new scientific agriculture was being developed, aimed toward improving the quality, health, and quantity of field, garden, and forest products. Fairchild studied and examined plant work from Germany to the gardens of Corsica. The Mediterranean and Asiatic areas challenged a corps of agricultural explorers who emulated Fairchild and went in search of unknown exotic plant wealth. The movement did not originate with Fairchild. William Saunders of Washington, D.C., had worked along the same lines, but Fairchild organized the search on a large scale. The policy, encouraged by Secretary of Agriculture Morton, was enlarged by his successor, James Wilson. When Fairchild returned to the United States about 1897, a new section of the department of agriculture was authorized—that of foreign seed and plant introduction. There was, Fairchild relates, an interim between the time when arrangements to create the section were made and when the appropriation could be obtained. During this interval Fairchild was employed as a special agent of the division of forestry to prepare under Fernow's direction a bulletin on "Systematic Plant Introduction," Bulletin XXI (twenty-four pages) published in 1898. Fernow was so eager to have someone acquainted with European procedures and advancements in this work that while Fairchild was journeying across the Pacific via Hawaii to Vancouver and completing his first world tour of study and exploration, Fernow arranged in 1897 with Fairchild to accept the special agency in the forestry division.

Complying with a request from the secretary of agriculture to determine what trees were best adapted to growing in southwestern United States and the arid regions west of the 100th meridian, Fernow devised a scheme to locate arboreta at various strategic places in the dry regions. The arborescent flora of the world were to be gathered and tested. A "competent gentleman" was secured to put the plan into effect, but since the introduction of a specific line of exotics was contemplated, the work was absorbed by the plant introduction section within the seed division.[11]

The 1894 American Forestry Association meeting was especially notable. Beginning on the evening of August 21 at Brooklyn, New York, with Fernow's lecture on "The Battle of the Forest," August 22

[11] *Forestry Investigations of the U.S.D.A., 1877-1898*, pp. 22-24.

and 23 were spent in hearing discussions of forest conditions in Alaska, the Adirondacks, New Jersey, and other regions by such persons as William H. Dall, Verplanck Colvin, J. S. Smock, and John Gifford. A lecture on the "Petrified Forests of Arizona" provided interest. L. H. Pammel, botanist, horticulturist, professor at Iowa State College, and leader in the plant science research of the middle and northwest plains, read a paper on "Prairie Forestry." The discussions were concerned with regional forestry progress, but general scientific advancement was not neglected. Franklin Hiram King, professor of agricultural physics at the University of Wisconsin and one of a half dozen leading scholars developing the valuable study of agricultural chemistry, presented the results of numerous experiments which pointed to the effectiveness of windbreaks to prevent evaporation from soils.[12] He urged the special utility of windbreaks to protect light soils. A. D. Hopkins of the University of West Virginia discussed the "Relation of Insects and Birds to Present Forest Conditions."

Nor were state forestry interests neglected. In 1893 the Association had adopted a recommendation of its executive committee to accept an invitation to aid the New York forest commission to secure desirable legislation in the management of the new Adirondack Park. A committee was named to arrange a meeting in New York, preferably at Albany. The meeting was finally arranged in Brooklyn. In 1894 the Association joined with the American Association for the Advancement of Science to take advantage of the invitation of the New Hampshire forestry commission to visit the White Mountains with the purpose of persuading the state to preserve the mountain forests, secure legislation to form a fire protective service, and induce lumbermen to apply rational methods in their logging activities. Thursday, August 23, the members enjoyed an excursion up the Hudson River to West Point. From there they journeyed to Plymouth, New Hampshire, and began in earnest to study the White Mountain regions. Several days were spent visiting lumber camps and sawmills in the Pemigewasset Valley. Flume House was visited. From Profile House the party took a tramp through the forest and climbed Mount Washington. Almost a full week, August 21-27, was consumed by the meetings. After a trip through Crawford Notch to Glen Station and by carriage to Wentworth Hall in Jackson, New Hampshire, the meetings were ended as they had begun. Owing to the absence of Rothrock, who was scheduled to speak, Fernow repeated his lecture, "The Battle of the Forest." A wide area in central and northern New Hampshire had been investigated.

At another meeting of the Association that year at Washington, D.C.,

[12] *ibid.*, pp. 313-314, concerning Bulletin 42 of the Wisconsin Experiment Station and the University.

John Gifford, who was coming into prominence in forestry deliberations, told the Association that a forestry organization of one hundred members had been formed in southern New Jersey.

As a part of the program of the Washington meeting, the members of the American Forestry Association went to the White House to commend to President Grover Cleveland the work of their organization. The president listened attentively, expressed increasing interest in the work and promised to give whatever aid he could to the cause. When President Harrison had left office, some thirteen million acres of forest lands had been reserved and a total area of about fifty million acres of public lands, classed as timber lands, remained. Soon after beginning his second term of office, President Cleveland had begun proclaiming new reservations, and before 1894 between four and five million acres had been added to the reserved areas.

At the Brooklyn meeting Fernow had spoken on the "Condition of our Public Timber Lands and Forest Reservations." Each year since 1887, the year of the Springfield congress, Fernow had appeared to urge the passage of a federal law which would commit the government to a forest reservation policy. His Hale bill (S. 1779, 50th congress), which would have realized both a reservation and administration policy for the publicly owned timberlands of the nation and which had been endorsed at the Springfield congress, had fallen under the weight of debate and maneuvers and become a part of another senate bill (S. 2367, 51st congress and S. 3235, 52nd congress), the Paddock bill.

The Paddock bill from a forestry standpoint was a worthy piece of legislation, but it first had to be settled whether the secretaries of the interior, by virtue of the law of March 3, 1891, had implied authority to manage the reserves once the president had proclaimed them and the reservation had been established. "In the absence of specific legislation, the Secretary of the Interior," Fernow disclosed, "construed the reservation of these lands as a withdrawal not only from sale and entry, but from all use whatsoever, the Department being powerless to protect or utilize the same."[13] From the forester's viewpoint this situation disastrously minimized the significance of the reservation policy. Some legislative authority to manage the reserves had to be obtained. Should the general land office perform the work of administering the reserves? Should a separate bureau in the department of the interior or the department of agriculture be created? Or should an independent bureau be created? It was not easy to settle the question. Nor was it easy to decide what permanent regulations should be framed to prevent fire, regulate occupancy, regulate timber cutting, and fashion policies for general and

[13] "The Forest Reservation Policy," *Science* V, new series, 1897, pp. 489-493, 868-869. This article was reprinted for the executive committee of the Am. For. Ass. to be presented to the 55th congress. Fernow was author as chairman of the committee.

special administrative ends. Policies for water reservoir lands, for national parks, and for military reservations supplied a partial but not complete precedent to aid in solving problems presented by forest reservations. Temporarily the army could protect the reserved areas. Permanently, however, a trained forestry personnel was required to keep the forest reservations in the condition necessary to accomplish the objects of their creation.

The American Forestry Association discussed these questions in 1891. The hope that all the public timberlands would be reserved had not been shattered. By 1893, however, at the Washington meeting held in December, another forestry bill pending before congress was occupying their attention. In Representative Thomas C. McRae of Arkansas Fernow had found a firm friend of the forestry movement. McRae had been reared in a heavily wooded state. Until he had travelled in states barren of forests he had believed that the nation's timber supply was inexhaustible. But once convinced of the inevitable consequences of deforestation, he had become an ardent supporter of real forestry. He became the author of a bill introduced in the house which virtually absorbed the architecture of the Hale bill. It contained "the features upon which all subsequent legislation regarding forest reserves [was to be] based."[14] The Hale bill, the Paddock bill, and the McRae bill, therefore, may be conveniently grouped under a term which Fernow used, "our administration bill." There were other forestry measures under consideration in the senate and house during this period. Fernow's "administration bill," regardless of its title or location, was the legislation for which he fought.

Fernow was the mover behind the congressional scenes. He related the story of his actions:

> . . . at last, we found a chairman of the democratic House Committee on Public Lands fully alive to [our administrative bill's] need in Mr. McRae, member from Arkansas. He adopted our bill, which thereafter went by his name, and pressed it for passage. One day he telephoned me to come to the Capitol, when he told me that, if I could condense the whole bill into a short paragraph he might be able to get it as a rider into a bill then in Conference. I did so not only, but made it germane to the bill. Unfortunately, this bill was made to carry too many riders and broke down under the load when reported back to the House for passage, not standing the scrutiny of the watch dogs. . . .

In 1893 at the Washington meeting of the American Forestry Association the McRae bill was referred to a committee on resolutions to clear it of some misrepresentations. In August 1894 at the Association's Brooklyn meeting Fernow brought the bill to the Association's attention

[14] *Forestry Investigations of the U.S.D.A., 1877-1898*, p. 26.

again by offering a resolution to approve the efforts of the house public lands committee and its chairman McRae to secure its passage.

Great was the jubilation that same year at another Washington meeting of the Association. The house of representatives had passed the bill! By resolution the Association urged the senate committee, to which the house bill had been referred, to report the bill to the senate for passage at an early date. Fernow's vigorous sponsorship promised fulfillment.

In his report of 1893 for the division of forestry Fernow, after listing the twenty-one national forest reservations comprising a total of 17,564,800 acres, and the more than three million acres of the four national parks, had said, "The present great need of providing protection and suitable administration for these reservations is to be met by the enactment of a law (H.R. 119) which, while less comprehensive than that contemplated in the 52nd congress (S. 3235), contains the essential features for a first step toward a more thorough organization, and recommends itself on account of its simplicity." The efficiency of the army's protective service demonstrated in the Yellowstone National Park justified the contemplated use of the army in the reservations. The secretary of the interior was to be authorized to regulate the use and occupancy of the reserved areas, thus settling their legal status. Fernow commented:

> The sale of ripe timber from reservations and other public timber lands under such supervision as to insure the inviolability of the forest cover is also permitted, in the discretion of the Secretary. This provision, which has been severely criticized, is most important and essential to any kind of successful forest policy. Its absence from the statutes hitherto has been the fruitful source of depredations and forest destruction, for, the resident population must be provided with wood material, and, in the absence of legal methods and fair means to do so, it is driven to supply its necessities by unfair means. As soon as a value is placed on the timber of the public domain it will be possible not only to dispose of it advantageously, but also to control the manner of its use without injury to the forest conditions and the future, and an interest in the same will grow up. In this or a similar provision, which attempts a rational use of the forest resources, lies the only salvation of our Western forests and of the soil and water conditions dependent on the same. The funds derived from the sale of ripe timber and other income are to be set aside for the purpose of establishing gradually a more amplified and effective system of forest management, so that the forest itself shall pay for its own protection.

The argument carried weight. A bill providing for management of the huge forest reservations passed both the house and the senate. But it never became law! Fernow explained why.

> In the next session[s] of Congress (1894-1895) we secured passage of the bill in both Houses without any irregularity, and yet it did not become law owing to one of those little accidents which make history. The bill had been

rewritten in the Senate Committee, although the provisions remained practically the same, but when it was sent over to the House, Mr. McRae, who knew of its conditions, was absent, being called home by the sickness of his daughter. If he had been present, the bill would have been referred to Conference Committee and the differences, if any, would have been straightened out and the bill would have become law. As it was, the Senate bill was referred to the Public Lands Committee, and as it was in the last days of Congress could not be reported back to the House, and died with the Congress.

On another occasion, Fernow officially explained the result: "Several bills providing for the administration of these forest reserves were also formulated and supported by arguments before the Public Lands Committee of both House and Senate, and the passage of one of these in both Houses was secured in 1895, failing to become a law only from lack of time to secure a conference report."[15]

The entire blame could not be placed at the doors of congress. The forestry ranks themselves became divided. It was difficult for the few members of the American Forestry Association, who gathered in 1895 at the summer meeting at Springfield, Massachusetts, to understand why no law had been passed. At that time the progress made in congress seemed to be satisfactory. At the Springfield meeting there intervened a proposal, the substance of which Fernow had sponsored in 1889 at the Philadelphia meeting. Gifford Pinchot had not appeared at an Association meeting as a leading spokesman since 1891. In 1890, on his return from forestry study in Europe, he had addressed a joint meeting of the American Economic Association and the American Forestry Association. In 1893 he had addressed a meeting on the mutual interests of lumbermen and foresters. Pinchot thus far as a forester had been primarily a consultant and student. Until 1895 he had given his best efforts to forestry on the Biltmore Estate in North Carolina. The New York board of trade and chamber of commerce had enacted a resolution which urged congress to create a commission of three members to examine and report on the nation's forests and their condition. R. U. Johnson of *The Century Magazine* presented the resolution at the Springfield meeting of the American Forestry Association, explained its substance, and urged the Association to endorse it. Pinchot then followed Johnson and read a paper on national forest conditions and the urgent need of constructive action to protect the forests of the national domain. Since the efforts of the Association to a large degree thus far had been ineffectual, argued Pinchot, the need for action was immediate, and the proper procedure was through a forest commission, as proposed by Johnson.[16]

15 "The Birth of a Forest Policy," *op. cit.; Forestry Investigations of the U.S.D.A., 1877-1898*, p. 26, 191.

16 *Garden and Forest* VIII, 394, Sept. 1895, pp. 369-370; also *Proc. Am. For. Ass.* of the summer meeting at Springfield, 1895. The same volume presents the proceedings

Fernow bitterly opposed the proposal. There was no necessity for further investigation. The division of forestry and the department of the interior had been investigating since 1886. Congressional action was needed. Forestry, divided against itself, could not triumph as effectively as if it presented a united front. Fernow correctly believed that congress would enact a law providing forest administration for the reserves. Years ago the appointment of a commission had been frowned on. If a commission now were asked for, most especially if its appointment were procured, congress, Fernow argued, would be more hesitant to pass the forestry legislation then pending.

In spite of these arguments the Association suspended its rules and adopted a resolution which joined with the New York board of trade and chamber of commerce in advocating the creation of a commission which should investigate thoroughly the public forest lands and recommend measures for their "treatment and disposition." Meanwhile the McRae bill became lodged in the senate with the committee on forest reservations and was not reported out for passage. Another bill took its place, got to the calendar, but went no further.

Fernow has interpreted these events:

When we came so near securing a full committal of the government to not only the reservation policy, but to a complete forest administration, Mr. Pinchot, who up to that time had kept aloof and had not shown any spirit of cooperation with these efforts, appeared at one of the meetings of the Association (Springfield, Mass., 1895), and read a harangue in which he charged the Association with failure of recognizing its duty and of having accomplished anything. In utter ignorance of the circumstances he asked that legislation be called for, to appoint a Commission to formulate the very legislation we had nearly secured. It was explained that such a Commission had before been asked for by us, but the Public Lands Committee having found out that our bill was in existence preferred to deal directly without such a Commission. Nevertheless, the meeting, poorly attended especially as regards real working members, instructed the Executive Committee to formulate and introduce a commission bill.

The Committee not wishing to stultify itself in this manner sought to meet the demand by inducing the then Secretary of the Interior, Mr. Hoke Smith, to sign a letter prepared by the committee, calling upon the Academy of Science, the legally constituted adviser of the Government, to express its views on the needs of a forest policy. The Academy was not prepared to give such advice, but asked for an appropriation of $25,000 to inform itself. . . .[17]

That the forestry movement in America was pleased with the progress made in these years was shown by a leading editorial written by John

of the annual meeting at Washington, D.C. The following editorial from *Forest Leaves* refers to the Washington meeting. See the complete account in *Forest Leaves* V, 7, Feb. 1896, p. 100.

[17] "The Birth of a Forest Policy," *op. cit.* See also Fernow's "The Forest Reservation Policy," *op. cit.*, pp. 3, 4, 8.

Birkinbine in *Forest Leaves*,[18] then the official organ of The Pennsylvania Forestry Association and the American Forestry Association:

The annual meeting of the American Forestry Association, of which through the courtesy of Mr. F. H. Newell, Corresponding Secretary, we are able to give a record . . . was of a most encouraging character. There was no large attendance to produce this encouragement, for a mere handful of earnest workers were present at the business sessions, but the evening meeting was a decided step in advance, and evidenced the efforts of Mr. B. E. Fernow, chief of the Forestry Division.

The National Geographic Society, by acting conjointly with the American Forestry Association, endorsed the efforts for forest reform in an emphatic manner, and an audience of probably five hundred of the most intelligent citizens of Washington, by their presence and attention in the height of the social season at the capital, showed their interest in the efforts to preserve and propagate forest growth. . . . When the Chairmen of the Committees on Public Lands, in both the United States Senate and in the House of Representatives, and a member and former chairman of the latter committee, stand before an audience of the character which faced them, and plead for forest reserves or protection against forest devastation; and when a member of the Cabinet, the Secretary of Agriculture, presides at such a meeting, and is supported by such men as the Director of the United States Geological Survey, the chief of the Forestry Division, and by other government officials, we claim there is great reason for encouragement. . . .

This meeting was significant for its emphasis on the immediate connection of forests and water supply. William E. Smythe called for an entire revision of the land laws applicable to the West. The homestead law was characterized as a farce, and the desert land law as an instrument of fraud. Over the entire nation the theme of woods and waters was being carried to the people. State forestry associations, particularly in Minnesota, and other organizations called on governments to extend the policies of creating and maintaining forest reserves and establishing reservoir systems at the headwaters of important streams.

In the spring of 1896 Dr. Rothrock spoke at a large meeting in Philadelphia on "Forest Reservations as Affecting the Water Supply of Philadelphia." Fernow spoke at meetings in New Jersey and in Pennsylvania. At a meeting in Philadelphia at the Franklin Institute, John Gifford argued that just as the horticulturist improves the quality and quantity of the yield of an orchard, the forester increases the productivity of the forest. To be successful, the system must be perpetual, and an amount equivalent to the increment is the annual harvest. The principal is bequeathed from generation to generation.

To the first numbers of *The New Jersey Forester*,[19] edited by Gifford,

[18] V, 7, Feb. 1896, p. 97.

[19] I, 1, Jan. 1895, pp. 2-3; also the issue of May 1, 1896, pp. 45-46; and "Are Forest Fires a Necessary Evil?" in I, 4, 1895, pp. 48-49. For the Franklin Institute meeting, March 6, 1896, at which Gifford spoke as forester of the New Jersey Geological Survey, see *Forest Leaves* V, 8, April 1896, p. 123; for the meeting of the N.J. For. Ass. at

Fernow contributed two articles, "What Are We After?", and "The Palisades Park." In the first he urged that "forestry is not what its first advocates in this country believed it to be, the preventing of the use of the forest. . . . Forestry is exactly the same as agriculture. . . ." The question was whether the state or community had reached such a level of development as to warrant the introduction of forestry methods which at first would have to be "crude but commonsense treatment of the virgin woods" and gradually permit of "finer methods."

Concerning the Palisades Park adjacent to the Hudson River, which had once been the summer home of the botanist, John Torrey, Fernow said, "There is no more hopeful sign of the arrival of a more highly civilized condition in our communities than the movement for open space, for parks, for protection of historic or picturesque and interesting places for reservations in general. [But] why not call a spade a spade? . . . I do not see why the Palisades Park, to be created for the purpose of satisfying the esthetic sense of the people, should be called a forest, albeit a forest growth may be maintained in it. . . ." He regarded the Boston municipal parks in the same light. If a park or reservation was to be created, he recommended management by military authorities and the introduction of forest management methods. The states, like the federal government, as yet had no trained forestry personnel. Military management was recommended because it was the "only permanently stable and systematic organization in our government." Then, too, the site was near West Point Military Academy, and Fernow favored the introduction of forestry instruction there.

John Gifford of May's Landing and Princeton, New Jersey, was assembling the first valuable forestry library used for lending and circulating purposes in North America. Gifford was to rank among the first of America's forestry educators. He said that forestry was a part of Fernow "as much . . . as was any organ of his body." Fernow and Gifford remained firm friends and co-workers for many years.[20] A graduate in science from Swarthmore College in 1890, he was also, before going to the University of Munich to obtain a doctorate in economics, a special student at the University of Michigan and Johns Hopkins University.

Fernow wanted the place of forestry defined in American life. He believed that the American people had made two great mistakes: the first was moral, in its treatment of the Indians; the second was economic, in its treatment of the forests. His educational program had

---

Plainfield, May 21, 1896, including a speech by Fernow and one by B. D. Halsted on "Diseases of Trees," see *Garden and Forest*, 431, May 27, 1896, p. 220.

[20] *The Forester* IV, 1, Jan. 1898, p. 7. The Giffords became connected with the Department of Forestry and Protection of the Palisades of the New Jersey State Federation.

begun to reach far corners of the land. For example, in 1896 the West Virginia Academy of Sciences,[21] under the leadership of A. D. Hopkins and L. C. Corbett, held a meeting to inquire into the subject of forest protection and draft legislation to spread a system of forest reservations in the middle Allegheny mountains, principally in West Virginia, and also in parts of Maryland, Virginia, Pennsylvania, and North Carolina, at the headwaters of such important rivers as the Monongahela, Elk, Gauley, Guyandot, Big Sandy, Potomac, James, and Tennessee.

In response to a frightful year of forest fires, Minnesota had enacted a fire law and chosen General C. C. Andrews to execute it. Wisconsin passed similar legislation. "These laws, as well as the one so satisfactorily inaugurated in Maine," commented Fernow,[22] "are modelled more or less closely after the forest-fire law of New York, which it was my privilege to draft in 1885 [for Senator Lowe], who incorporated it in the general legislation for the Adirondack forests inaugurated that year. . . ."

During this decade important range research studies began at Abilene and Channing, Texas, under the supervision of Jared Smith of the department of agriculture. Later this work was enlarged to include studies in range management, much of it to take place on the national forest reservations. Leadership was assumed by Bessey at the University of Nebraska and Pammel at Iowa State College in this growing "prairie forestry."

In 1895, pursuant to recommendations of the secretary of agriculture, congress had provided a special appropriation for a division of agrostology within the department. This division was organized on July 1, with F. Lamson-Scribner as chief and Jared Gage Smith as first assistant chief. Scribner was a graduate of the Maine State College of Agriculture, had taught botany, and served in the botanical division of the U.S. department of agriculture, under Coville, as its first appointed special agent in charge of its mycological section. For a brief period he had been chief of the newly created section of vegetable pathology, immediately preceding B. T. Galloway, and then had gone to the University of Tennessee at Knoxville as professor of botany and director of the state agricultural station. Smith had received two degrees from the University of Nebraska, Bachelor of Science and Master of Arts, and from 1888-1890 had been assistant agrostologist of the Nebraska agricultural experiment station. For at least a year he had been associate botanist of the Shaw School of Botany in St. Louis, Missouri, and from 1893-1895 botanical assistant of the Missouri Botanical Gardens. These

[21] The meeting was held at Morgantown on February 11, 1896. See *Forest Leaves* V, 8, April 1896, p. 122; *Garden and Forest*, 425, April 15, 1896, p. 152.

[22] *Garden and Forest* VIII, 1895, p. 242. *Forestry Investigations*, 1877-1898, p. 183, adds New Hampshire and Pennsylvania.

two men, therefore, were well equipped to forward investigations in the "natural history, geographical distribution, and uses of grasses and forage plants, their adaptation to special soils and climates, the introduction of promising native and foreign kinds into cultivation, and the preparation of publications and correspondence relative to these plants."

Two experimental grass stations, to study the growth and value to agriculture of about 400 different varieties including the "true buffalo grass of the Western plains," were at once established. Range management studies were supplied with valuable scientific knowledge from these investigations which were outlined in the department's *Yearbook for 1895* (pp. 44, 525), and forestry research incidentally benefited.

Fernow had not neglected the farm aspects of forestry. In the *Yearbook of the United States Department of Agriculture* for 1894 appeared his instructive treatise on "Forestry for Farmers," the next year reprinted separately by the department. The booklet outlined general principles for small timber tract and woodlot owners. The rules of practice applied mainly to "the conditions prevalent in our northeastern states."

It was a large task to keep abreast of all the developments in state forestry, as well as to advance forestry work in the national government. The gathering of fairly reliable statistical information was a heavy burden on the industrious shoulders of the division's small corps. The lack of such information must have worried Fernow considerably. Sargent at Harvard also watched with interest the work performed in the states. During the years 1895-1896, *Garden and Forest*[23] gave publicity to the work being done in Minnesota by S. B. Green and H. B. Ayers. They were studying how the cut-over pine lands might be most effectively reforested and developed and the young growth preserved. A comment in the magazine said: "That American forests may be restocked as they are in Europe by logging in such a manner as to provide with certainty the necessary conditions for a second growth there can be no doubt; but how far nature can be expected to restore forest growth under the methods of lumbering now practiced is quite another question, and its answer will be awaited with interest."

The same periodical[24] noticed "that many wealthy men in various parts of the country are getting possession of large blocks of forest land, either as permanent investments, as game preserves or places of summer residence. Leaving aside the immense tracts set apart by the National Government and by the state of New York in the Adirondacks and the Catskills, clubs and private individuals now own nearly a million acres of forest preserves in [Massachusetts] while in Maine, especially in the Rangeley Lake country, in the upper White Mountains of New Hampshire, and along the tributaries of the Connecticut and Androscog-

[23] 451, Oct. 14, 1896, p. 412. [24] 462, Dec. 30, 1896, p. 530.

gin rivers there are many large preserves. Blue Mountain Park, which was established by Austin Corbin in the southwestern part of New Hampshire, covers thirty-two square miles, while the estate of Mr. George W. Vanderbilt, of Biltmore, contains a forest of 100,000 acres, which will be the field of systematic experiments in practical and scientific forestry. . . ." To this list might have been added the Girard estate[25] in Pennsylvania. Located near Pottsville, in Schuylkill and Columbia counties, its tree planting and forest protective work had been commenced as early as 1877.

Soon Pennsylvania,[26] under the leadership of its first forest commissioner, Rothrock, would start purchasing tax-forfeiture and other land titles to locate state-owned forest reservations at the headwaters of its three important rivers, the Delaware, the Susquehanna, and the Ohio. The principle was made plain. If the headwaters of western streams which benefited arid and irrigated lands should be protected by forest reservations, reservations should also protect the headwaters of eastern streams in the Appalachian and eastern mountain ranges, where floods menaced the lower lands, where droughts occurred, and where irrigation in the humid agricultural regions was a possible solution to the problems presented by dry land areas.

Pennsylvania by 1895 was a leader in state forestry. In 1892 the state's Chautauqua Association had set apart a "Forestry Day at Mount Gretna"[27] and placed its program in charge of the Pennsylvania Forestry Association. The Paddock bill was then pending in the federal congress. On July 23 Fernow had secured the Association's endorsement of this proposed legislation. He addressed the Chautauqua on the "Forestry Problem," warning that at the present rate of consumption and exclusive of the unpredictable consideration of new forest growth the existing supplies might be adequate only for sixty to seventy years more. The "graver consequences" in regard to changed water conditions due to "altered forest conditions" were stressed. Deforestation was the deleterious factor, and reforestation of the watersheds and stream banks was the hopeful solution. Soil erosion and the impairment of water regulation by the forest were disturbing the natural balances. He doubted that American legislatures could be persuaded to compel restrictive and regulated forest management of lands owned privately. Private capital was invested for the sake of realizing profits more or less immediately. Again and again Fernow emphasized that on a community

[25] Hugh P. Baker, "Forestry on the Girard Estate," *Forest Leaves* XI, 8, April 1908, pp. 119-120; Jay F. Bond, "Notes on the Girard Estate Forest Plantations," *Forestry Quarterly* VI, 1, March 1908, p. 34; *Forest Leaves* VIII, p. 138. Planting may have begun as late as 1879; see *Forest Leaves* XI, 5, Oct. 1907, p. 78.

[26] "Forestry Commission, Pennsylvania," *Forestry Investigations of the U.S.D.A., 1877-1898*, pp. 177-180.

[27] *Forest Leaves* III, 11, Oct. 1892, pp. 146-147.

basis extended from one generation to another forestry could become profitable, especially when secondary results were properly evaluated.[28]

In 1892 Rothrock resigned his position as professor of botany at the University of Pennsylvania to become secretary of the Pennsylvania Forestry Association and coordinate forestry interests within the state. During the winter of 1892-1893 the state legislature authorized the appointment of a forestry commission. Two years later the commission reported. Rothrock, who principally authored this report of the state's second forest commission, thereupon resigned as general secretary of the Forestry Association and became botanist of the forestry commission. That year, 1895, the state created a department of agriculture and directed its secretary to obtain and publish information concerning the extent and condition of the forests, and to enforce all fire and protective laws. Two years later the movement to create state forest reservations became fully effective. The force behind the entire development was Rothrock.[29]

By the years 1894-1896, when the McRae bill proponents struggled so valiantly to have its provisions enacted finally into law, forestry within the United States had already become an integral part of American life. Fernow believed that forestry was at last permanently established in America, and in 1895 he joined in a proposal to make possible a school of forestry within the United States department of agriculture. On February 16, 1895, Fernow appeared before the committee on agriculture of the house of representatives in connection with house bills 8389 and 8390. One bill sought to amend further the Morrill Act which gave land grant aid to state agricultural and mechanic arts colleges by applying "a portion of the proceeds of the public lands to the more complete endowment and support of the colleges" to support forestry courses there. The other bill sought to "establish and maintain a national school of forestry." Five thousand dollars were to be appropriated for each college to enable it to provide forestry instruction and object lessons in the field. The "National School of Forestry" was conceived not as a separate institution of the nature of a college with set school methods, but rather as an opportunity to pursue special studies. Divison of forestry officials and officers of other divisions were to give courses related to "forestry science"—soil physics, botany, vegetable pathology, and so

[28] Fernow also appeared before a meeting of the Pennsylvania Forestry Association at Philadelphia on April 10, 1896, to urge the passage of the McRae bill. See *Garden and Forest*, 425, April 15, 1896, p. 159. By this time Rothrock was State Forest Commissioner.

[29] *Garden and Forest*, 1892, p. 612; *Forest Leaves* X, 10, Aug. 1906, pp. 153-157; *Report of Div. of For. for 1893*, p. 325; *Forest Leaves* V, 7, Feb. 1896, p. 99; *Garden and Forest*, #489 (July 7, 1897), p. 261; *Forest Leaves* VIII, 1 (Feb. 1901), p. 6; *ibid.*, 2, April 1901, p. 24, concerning Rothrock's reappointment as forestry commissioner and the creation of a department of forestry within the department of agriculture; *Forest Leaves* IX, 9, 1904, p. 129; VI, 10, 1898, p. 161; VI, 11, 1898, p. 178; VIII, 1, p. 6.

forth. Travelling scholarships were to be provided. Obviously Fernow now believed that the time had arrived when there was need of professional instruction. National forest reservations and the promise of forestry management would soon offer the necessary object and field lessons, as well as the places of employment for trained foresters. These ventures in forestry schooling as proposed, however, were not ideal programs. Neither wholly graduate or undergraduate, they were adopted to meet a difficult situation. If the army took over the responsibilty of protecting the reserves from fire and theft, army personnel must have instruction in forest ranging. "Everywhere," said Fernow, "we see that knowledge is wanting, and it is to supply this want that the Government is now called upon to exercise its educational function." Forest managers were to be educated: first, at the agricultural schools of which forestry was a part; and post graduate instruction at the "National School" might be afforded after a student had received the necessary elementary training. The entire scheme, which had the support of the colleges and forestry professors and the American Forestry Association, was planned to meet the "emergencies of the future." Since General Andrews's early effort of 1880-1882 to secure authority to have a national forestry school placed at St. Paul, other forestry school projects had been discussed, especially one proposed in the Adirondack Preserve.

In the West the acute need of foresters was most evident. Struggling with small monetary appropriations, the University of California at Berkeley was striving to maintain a state forestry system, and doing "a great deal of profitable work. . . ."[30] Experiment stations at Santa Monica and Chico were still functioning, and recently the state legislature had established another station "on the slopes of Mount Hamilton in order to discover what hardwoods [would] grow best on the rough lands of the Coast Range. . . ."

The national parks, to be sure, were not conceived for purposes of forestry. Forestry was based on forest utilization, not on pleasure or scenic beauty. But even in the parks a soldier or an engineer was not a forester, and some forest management was needed in the parks. Aside from Yellowstone Park in Wyoming and the Yosemite Park in central California, there were in California also the Sequoia and General Grant

[30] *Forest Leaves* V, 8, April 1896, p. 116, quoting *Northwestern Lumberman.* Concerning General Bidwell's gifts and the Chico Forestry Station, see Charles Howard Shinn, "The Story of a Great California Estate, Rancho del Arroyo Chico, the Home of the late General John Bidwell," *Country Life in America* I, 3, Jan. 1902, p. 81. On May 15, 1895, Hilgard sought Bessey for the professorship of botany at the University of California, to replace Edward Lee Greene. Hilgard wrote to Bessey, ". . . both Dr. LeConte and myself consider it especially desirable that the lines of physiological and economic botany, which heretofore have been altogether subordinated to the systematic study of California plants, should be strengthened as they would be by securing you as head of the department. . . ." The University was in charge of the forestry station. Concerning the Santa Monica station, see *Botanical Gazette* XXVII, Jan.-June 1899, p. 498.

parks in Tulare and Fresno counties. These park areas covered more than three million acres. In 1896 huge forest reservations, such as the Cascade Mountain Range reserve of Oregon, stretching from the Columbia River nearly to the borders of California, and the Sierra Forest reserve along the Sierra Nevada mountains from Yosemite Park to the mountains east of Bakersfield, notably Mount Breckinridge—each comprising between four and five million acres—had no more protection from fire, timber-thieves, and sheep-herders, than non-reserved lands.[31]

A decade earlier a group of men connected with the University of Southern California had tried to place a school of foresty in the forest at Tulare. The plan had failed.[32] Abbot Kinney, prominent in the early forestry history of California and for many years a co-worker and friend of Fernow, had been a leader of the plan. There was real need for a practical school. Some of the most magnificent forest growth of the region lay to the southwest and west of Mount Whitney, and in these forests were contained the headwaters of the Kern, the Tule, and Kaweah rivers.[33] Military protection was afforded Sequoia National Park, but the use of the military for a purpose for which it was not intended was criticized severely.

In 1861 a clearing of Douglas firs at what is now Seattle, Washington, had made way for the construction of a building, in sight of the harbor, to be known as the University of Washington. Three decades later, the state legislature provided a new campus, and another building was constructed—Denny Hall, completed in 1895. The president of this progressive institution, which early permitted elective courses in its curricula, was Mark Walrod Harrington, formerly chief of the United States weather bureau, professor of astronomy at the University of Michigan, and editor of the *American Meteorological Journal.* The professor of history was Edmond S. Meany, a graduate of the University of Washington in Seattle, who gave a course in the history of Washington and Washington forestry. These subjects in time became part of a course in northwestern United States history. Of course, part of the study of Washington forests was transferred to the botany section of the department of biology. Meany consulted with Fernow who was delighted at the prospect of forestry instruction, however meager, in the Pacific northwest. Fernow promptly sent copies of the publications of the division of forestry, together with a selected list of books and the names of leading workers and writers in the forestry movement. Among the works procured was Sargent's great *Silva of North America.* When at length the purchases were made known to

[31] *Garden and Forest,* 423, April 1, 1896, p. 131.

[32] *Cardinal and Gold, a History of the University of Southern California,* General Alumni Assoc., 1939, p. 29.

[33] *Garden and Forest,* 460, Dec. 16, 1896, p. 502.

Fernow, he replied, "You have assembled out there one of the best collections of works on forestry to be found anywhere in the United States." An arboretum was provided; exchanges of plant materials were arranged. For years the forestry curriculum was maintained in conjunction with botany and horticulture. The work was original in that it emphasized the forest and apparently minimized the agricultural and plant science aspects. At perhaps four places on the west coast in the early 1890's a respectable knowledge of forestry principles could be obtained, but no graduate or student who left these institutions could call himself a forester.[34] Toward the end of the century state forestry associations in Oregon and Washington were formed. Eventually the far northwest became a stronghold of organized forestry.

When Fernow in 1897 reported to the American Forestry Association the "well-planned course of lectures on general forestry topics being instituted" at the University of Washington, he told also of "a more specific course on the technical questions of forest planting" started at Kansas Agricultural College, and of his recent course of forestry lectures, attended by from eighty to one hundred and fifty students and professors, and presented at the school of economics of the University of Wisconsin.

Fernow and Pinchot were the outstanding professionally trained foresters in America. Schenck, of course, was at Biltmore. There may have been others, but they were of far lesser importance. Henry Solon Graves, an Ohioan by birth who received his preparatory education at Phillips Academy, Andover, Massachusetts, had graduated in 1892 from Yale University. A close friend of Pinchot, he had begun to study forestry after a year of teaching at King's School, Stamford, Connecticut. Becoming much interested in the subject, he went to Harvard and studied a year in related scientific courses, especially geology and botany. Much of his work was with Charles Sprague Sargent and John G. Jack at the Arnold Arboretum. In 1894, Graves spent the summer and autumn in field research, studying, among other tree species, the white pine. Results of this were later included in a small book, *The White Pine*, a study with tables of volume and yield, prepared by Gifford Pinchot and Graves and published in 1896 by The Century Company. In a preface to the work written March 7, 1896, Pinchot characterized this as the "first systematic description of the growth of a North American tree." He accredited Graves with preparing the silvicultural notes, and the calculation and tabulation of results of his research in the woods. By 1896, to complete his forestry education, Graves, like Pinchot, had

[34] Edmond S. Meany, "Genesis of the Forestry Idea at the University of Washington," Univ. of Wash. *Forest Club Quarterly* IV, 3, November 1925, pp. 19-22; also *Proc. Amer. For. Asso.* XII, 1897, fifteenth annual meeting, exec. committee report by Fernow.

gone to Europe, but had chosen a German university, the University of Munich. He, like Pinchot and others, received guidance in his studies from the famous forester, Sir Dietrich Brandis. Such celebrated foresters as Robert Hartig, Heinrich Mayr, and others increased the stature of knowledge and aided in the education of this man who was to contribute greatly to forestry education and practice on the North American continent. Returning in 1895 from his studies in Germany, Graves became associated with Pinchot in his activities as consultant in forestry. An early investigation by Graves was of forest fires in southern New Jersey.

In 1897, visiting many mining towns, Graves reconnoitered the Black Hills of South Dakota by pack-horse for the United States geological survey. There he saw the public lands problem in relation to forestry and economic progress in the United States. Years later he prepared an unpublished manuscript, "The Public Land Laws from the Standpoint of Forestry." A nation of small agricultural homesteads was an attractive picture, and to this idea he dedicated his energies for many years. He soon realized that public lands administration had failed to recognize lands valuable for forests as a classification distinct from either agricultural or mineral lands.

Graves, early in his career as a forester, sought also to demonstrate the value of forestry to owners of private forest lands. Both he and Pinchot, as students of the Adirondack forests,[35] became consultants on valuable privately owned forests in these regions. In New York, by reason of the historic Article VII, section 7 of the constitution of 1894, which forbade commercial forest utilization of the publicly owned forest preserve, forestry practice, except on private forest lands, seemed stopped, temporarily at least. In 1895, at the Springfield meeting of the American Forestry Association, Colonel Fox and Judge Higley each explained that the plans and work of placing state-owned lands under management, including provision for disposing of ripe timber for revenue, had ceased because of the constitutional amendment.

Educating the public as to the real purpose and value of forestry was to continue. Colonel Fox announced that 80,000 acres of new lands would be added to the preserve as soon as possible. In 1896, as superintendent of forests of the state forest, fish, and game commission, he began in his annual reports to recommend placement of a demonstration forest in the Adirondacks to show what real forest management might accomplish. Each year Fernow's writings had been reaching every state of the nation, and forestry progress made in New York had been always considered. To advance forestry interests there he had both written and spoken. May 10, 1892, before the Genessee Valley Forestry Association

[35] *Forestry and Irrigation* IX, 4, April 1903, p. 175.

at Rochester, he had spoken on "The Profitableness of Forest-culture," and *Garden and Forest* published extracts from this address. The Springfield meeting, however, became absorbed with the suggestion of Pinchot and others that a forestry commission be established to investigate the public forest lands and recommend procedures. Fernow opposed this from a belief that the chances for securing passage of legislation then before congress would be weakened. There was no need for further study. The real need was congressional authority to institute forest administration in the reserves, and to delay management in the reserves might threaten the entire forestry outlook. But Fernow bowed to the wishes of the majority.

"To satisfy the parties which held with Mr. Pinchot," Fernow later explained,[36] "I dictated a letter, and [Edward A.] Bowers secured the signature of the Secretary of the Interior [Hoke Smith], calling upon the [National] Academy of Sciences, scientific adviser of the government, to express an opinion. It was then that a committee of that academy made its junketing trip through the West, and recommended all that we had recommended; also an extension of the reservations to double the then size. We had avoided increasing the reservations on account of the ill feeling which existed, because they were simply withdrawn from all use. . . ."

On February 15, 1896, Secretary Smith signed the letter addressed to President Wolcott Gibbs of the National Academy. It read as follows:

Sir: I have the honor, as the head of the Department charged with the administration of the public domain, to request an investigation and report of your honorable body, as is provided in the act incorporating the National Academy, and by article 5, section 5, of its constitution, upon the inauguration of a rational forest policy for the forested lands of the United States.

Being convinced of the necessity of a radical change in the existing policy with reference to the disposal and preservation of the forests upon the public domain, I particularly desire an official expression from your body upon the following points:

1. Is it desirable and practicable to preserve from fire and to maintain permanently as forested lands those portions of the public domain now bearing wood growth for the supply of timber?

2. How far does the influence of forest upon climate, soil and water conditions make desirable a policy of forest conservation in regions where the public domain is principally situated?

3. What specific legislation should be enacted to remedy the evils now confessedly existing?

My predecessors in office for the last twenty years have vainly called attention to the inadequacy and confusion of existing laws relating to the public timber lands, and consequent absence of an intelligent policy in their administration, resulting in such conditions as may, if not speedily stopped, prevent a proper development of a large portion of our country; and because the evil grows more and more as the years go by, I am impelled to emphasize

[36] Letter to H. H. Chapman, dated Jan. 4, 1912.

the importance of the question by calling upon you for the opinion and advice of that body of scientists which is officially empowered to act in such cases as this.

I also beg to refer you to the proposed legislation which has been introduced into Congress for several years past at the instance of the American Forestry Association, supported by memorials of private citizens and scientific bodies, and more especially the memorials presented by the American Association for the Advancement of Science in 1873, which led to desirable legislation, and again in 1890, 1892, and in 1894.

As I believe that a speedy change in the existing policy is urgent, I request that you will give an early consideration to this matter, and favor me with such statements and recommendations as may be laid before Congress for action during this session.[37]

President Gibbs at once appointed a committee consisting of Charles Sprague Sargent, chairman; General Henry L. Abbott, who had served as chief engineer of the United States Army; Arnold Hague of the geological survey; William H. Brewer of Yale University; Gifford Pinchot; and Alexander Agassiz.

Congress on June 11 approved in its Sundry Civil Appropriation bill the sum of twenty-five thousand dollars, as requested, for the investigation and report to the Academy. On July 2 the committee members, except Alexander Agassiz, journeyed west and traversed "large areas of unreserved forest,"[38] visiting all of the reservations established prior to 1897, except six, which were "either of limited extent or well-known to the members of the committee."

Fernow then and later charged that the money was spent "very unnecessarily." It was rumored that he resented not being made a member of the committee, but it would not have been proper for him to be a member. As the chief forestry employee of the government, the government's policies had been of his making. Had he been made a committee member, a charge might have been justified that the commission had added little or nothing to what already was known or had been done. As events turned out, the report of the committee, in whom the National Academy, congress, and the president had confidence, told the nation in effect that the division of forestry's work had been sound.

That Fernow did not covet a place in the committee's membership seems further substantiated by his report as executive committeeman of the American Forestry Association at its fifteenth annual meeting, held in Washington on February 5, 1897.[39] This report was given a few

37 "Committee on Forest Policy," in Frederick W. True (ed.), *A History of the First Half Century of the National Academy of Sciences*, Washington, 1913, pp. 315-316. In 1891 Fernow had renewed his recommendation for a National Arboretum at Washington, claiming that a great institution like Kew Gardens could be established there. He used as part of his argument a memorial sent by the A.A.A.S. to government authorities. See *Report of Div. of For. for 1891*, pp. 202-203.

38 "Committee on Forest Policy," *op. cit.*, p. 316.

39 *Proc. Am. For. Ass.* XII, 1897. It was announced at this meeting that the Associa-

days after the committee of the Academy had made its preliminary report to Secretary of the Interior David R. Francis, and the day before the committee's report was forwarded to President Cleveland. It said:

Your committee, in securing the appointment of [the Academy's forest commission] did not expect that its recommendations would be essentially or strikingly different from those made and advocated by your Association, but hopes that the weight of the opinion of the eminent gentlemen composing the Forestry Committee and of the body from which it was selected will do much to arouse more generally public interest and to secure the passage of desired legislation.

During the last session of Congress, the McRae bill, H.R. 119, was again passed in the House of Representatives, with amendments, to be sure, which do not meet the approval of your Committee. Nevertheless, we would prefer the passage of the bill for the good that is in it, rather than favor the continued lack of a definite legal status and of all protection for the existing forest reservations, hoping for improvements by later legislation.

In the Senate Mr. Allen has reported and placed on the Calendar a bill from the Committee on Forest Reservations (S. 2118) which is in the main the same as the House Bill, with further undesirable amendments added.

The hope of passing this legislation, which would mark a first step towards an administration of the existing forest reservations, during the present session of Congress, depends on the willingness of Senator Allen to change his bill in form, so that if passed it can be sent to conference.

Meanwhile the policy of forest reservations has not only been kept in abeyance, but has become discredited and objectionable with the people of the States where they are situated, since thereby large areas have been absolutely withdrawn from any, even rational, use and are left without protection.

The forest reservation policy had strong support in West Virginia, Minnesota, New York, and Pennsylvania. State forestry associations had been organized in Washington and Oregon. Michigan was preparing to revive her earlier forestry interest. Montana was becoming interested in forestry. There were many encouraging signs of increasing action among the states.

But the federal government stood unmoved. Six years earlier the federal government had embraced the forest reservation policy. For six years it trifled with the matter of forest management and administration while the public timberlands remained unused and deteriorating. The McRae bill could not be taken up by the senate during the current session; it had been pigeonholed, lost from sight in the senate committee on forest reservations. Senator Allen's bill, placed on the calendar, was never to receive further action.[40] The states where the reservations were located were antagonistic to the forest policy of the government.

---

tion was incorporated. See also Fernow's "Recent Legislation of State Forestry Commissions and Forest Reserves," Circular 17, 1897, p. 15; and "Forest Fire Legislation in the U.S.," Circular 13, 1896, p. 8, U.S. Div. of For.

[40] Senator Allen was from Mississippi. Senator Teller from Colorado and Senator Dubois of Idaho had also proposed legislative measures. Senator Dubois, chairman of

Fernow, the division of forestry, and the American Forestry Association had been proceeding cautiously in advocating the creation of new reservations. From the initial stages of the movement to set apart for forestry purposes the nation's public timberlands, Fernow had wanted all the government owned forest lands reserved under a uniform system. Experience, however, had taught him that if the government's settled policy was to have the president proclaim separate reservations, wisdom urged caution. Wisdom's role certainly was not to arouse unnecessary hostility to the reserving of forest land areas. Already bitter denunciation was heard in the states where the reservations with their timber and other valuables were wasting. Consequently the report of the committee of the National Academy astounded many of the forestry ranks.

The committee recommended the establishment of thirteen new forest reservations, covering more than twenty-one million acres of forest land. On Washington's birthday, February 22, President Cleveland, nearing the end of his second term in office, proclaimed the new reservations. Early in February Chairman Sargent had addressed a letter to President Gibbs of the Academy and recommended "the creation forthwith"[41] of the reservations. Secretary of the Interior Francis had furnished a "favorable recommendation."[42] It is surmised that President Cleveland acted possibly "without consulting, or even notifying, the representatives of the states affected. . . ."[43] Fernow has told how he reacted:[44]

President Cleveland heroically and, as it seemed to us at the time, injudiciously, carried out the first part of the program [of the report of the committee of the Academy which] recommended a further extension of the forest reservations and an administration for them such as we had before formulated. With éclat [he proclaimed] all on one day, Washington's birthday, February 22, 1897, some 20 million acres as forest reservations, in addition to the 18 million already reserved.[45]

The reservation policy had never been favored by the Western Representatives and Senators, who saw in it an impediment to settlement and development of the Western country, and now when without previous announcement or even competent investigation this large block of territory was suddenly withdrawn from entry or disposal, the storm broke loose.

---

the senate committee on public lands, was regarded as "among the pronounced friends of forest reform." (*Forest Leaves* V, 7, 1896, p. 97.) In the House of Representatives, Johnson of California also had introduced an enactment. No results accrued from any of these. See John Ise, *op. cit.*, pp. 128-129, n. 19.

[41] Jenks Cameron, *op. cit.*, p. 207.

[42] "Committee on Forest Policy," *op. cit.*, p. 317.

[43] Jenks Cameron, *op. cit.*, p. 207, n. 65. The complete report of the committee on forest policy was transmitted to Gibbs and Secretary Francis on May 1, 1897 for printing by the government.

[44] "The Birth of a Forest Policy," *op. cit.*

[45] The contents of this paragraph have been rearranged by the author, but not changed.

In a session of the Senate which lasted two days, including a Sunday, the proposition of impeaching the President and of annulling not only the reservations made by him but all of them was hotly discussed.

We were on the point of losing all the toilsomely achieved success through the overzealous interest of our friends. . . .

It is difficult to say, how exactly the disaster was averted; there were many conferences and influences brought to bear, but it is to the credit of the then Speaker of the House, Joseph Cannon, to have manfully assisted in preventing rash action. The Congress came to an end on March 4 without action, but also without having passed the appropriation bills for the government, so that it became necessary for the President to call immediately an extra session.

The new Congress was in not much better mood, although considerably smoothed down, and in the Sundry Civil Appropriation Bill, passed June 4, 1897, suspended President Cleveland's proclamations of forest reserves, made upon recommendation of the Academy of Science and "the lands embraced therein [were] restored to the public domain the same as though said order and proclamations had not been issued," but this suspension was to last for only one year or until the reservations had been examined and revised. . . .

In these troublesome times a new ally had arisen in the person of the Director of the Geological Survey[46]—not because the Survey at that time had any except possibly rather antagonistic interest in the forestry movement, but the forest reservations might furnish an object for the extension of survey work in that direction. An organized survey party was just then running out of work, and it was desirable to provide a new field for it. Hence the Director busied himself to secure, in the same sundry civil bill, an appropriation of $150,000 for the purpose of surveying and investigating the reservations with a view to delimiting any agricultural or mining lands that might have been included.

Of course, this could not be done within the year and not for $150,000. Eventually, not less than [one and a half] million dollars were spent on this work, and by 1905, when it was turned over to the Forest Service hardly one-third of the investigation was finished. A magnificent set of volumes, describing the reservations, has been the result. Needless to say, the forest reservations remained in force and only here and there their boundaries were changed.

In that appropriation bill also, as part of the appropriation for the survey of the reservations, the provisions of the McRae bill substantially were incorporated, providing for an administration of the forest reservations by the Secretary of the Interior.

Thus it happened that not only the reservation policy itself but the inauguration of a forest service and administration came into existence as by accident, or at least only as a rider to an appropriation bill for a survey. Forest supervisors and rangers, etc., were appointed and rules and regulations for the management of the reservations were formulated by the Commissioner of the General Land Office and [within a decade] this business [was] handed over, as it should be, to the Forest Service in the Department of Agriculture.

A story persists that Henry Gannett persuaded Sargent to choose Pinchot rather than Fernow as a committee member of the National

[46] Henry Gannett was Geographer of the U.S. Geological Survey and was charged with the examination of the forest lands. Early in 1898 a large corps was at work. See *Forest Leaves* VI, 7, Feb. 1898, p. 114.

Academy of Sciences' commission. Aside from the fact that President Gibbs selected the members, the credibility of this story may be discounted by the plain truth that there existed no antagonism between Sargent and Fernow. Moreover there is little evidence to indicate that Gannett had any special influence in naming the committee. Sargent's interest in science and his hearty support of the forestry movement from its beginning were such that it seems most likely that he would not have denied Fernow a place on the commission had he believed Fernow wished such an appointment.

The committee of the National Academy of Sciences recommended a forest administration policy substantially like that of the Hale bill, the Paddock bill, and the McRae bill—the creation of a forestry bureau within the department of the interior, and the use of army personnel pending the organization of a permanent service. There were other important recommendations—for example, the division of western forest areas into departments in charge of inspectors. The form of organization was patterned after that of Germany. An advisory board consisting of a director, an assistant director, and four inspectors was to "pass on general matters relating to the forests. The actual care of the forests was to be intrusted to a corps of foresters, assistants, and rangers." The committee's report began with a review of Gustav Wex's researches on the relation of stream-flow to forests in central Europe, and argued for intelligent attention to forest preservation in the United States.[47] The chapter which depicted fire devastation, unregulated sheep grazing and its effects, and illegal timber cutting in the reserves was especially noted. The form of administrative organization was framed to eliminate each of these as far as possible.

The American Forestry Association thanked President Cleveland for his bold action in support of a federal forest reservation policy. John Gifford wrote after a meeting with the president:

> I remember at one time when I was on a committee of three from the American Forestry Association appointed to thank President Cleveland for setting aside so many reservations. When we entered, the waiting room was full. About to turn away, an aide asked our errand. When we told him our mission he said to wait. He would see the President at once. He quickly returned and ushered us in ahead of everybody. We received many black looks from waiting politicians. "Take your time to it," said the President, "there is no hurry. This is refreshing. It is the first time anybody has thanked me for anything for a long time. Let that bunch of favor seekers rot in their chairs." Then for an hour or more he talked, told how he had worked for forestry while governor of New York state, how he had set aside twice as many reservations as would hold. "A Republican President will probably succeed me and he will undo half of what I have done, so to be safe I have

[47] "Committee on Forest Policy," *op. cit.*, pp. 318-320.

done aplenty." By the time he finished the day was over, and the waiting room was empty. . . .[48]

William McKinley became president in March 1897. Secretary of Agriculture J. Sterling Morton was succeeded in his office by James Wilson, who was to hold the secretaryship longer than anyone had theretofore or has since. He was to champion the cause of forestry, becoming automatically, as was the custom, president of the American Forestry Association. McKinley was reelected to a second term of office but, as everyone knows, his tragic assassination deprived forestry of a great friend. Vice-President Theodore Roosevelt moved into the office of president. President Cleveland's fear that a Republican president would undo half of what he had done proved unwarranted. On March 2, 1898, President McKinley exercised his prerogative under section 24 of the act of March 3, 1891, and proclaimed the Pine Mountain reserve in southern California, comprising 1,144,594 acres of land situated almost entirely in Santa Barbara, Ventura, and Los Angeles counties. "With this reserve," commented *The Forester,* "all the mountain land in Southern California is practically reserved. The reserve was made at the request of the Californians themselves, who have learned the meaning and value of the reservation policy." By the beginning of the century, President McKinley had reserved between six and seven million acres of forest lands.

The Forester, which was founded, edited, and published in New Jersey by Gifford, was transferred in 1897 to the American Forestry Association to become its official organ. In July 1898 this publication announced two important events:

As we are going to press we learn that the Conference Committee on the Sundry Civil Bill has finally agreed to abandon the Senate amendments which were designed to abolish the forest reservations proclaimed on February 22, 1897. . . . The Association and its friends are to be congratulated at the success over a strong opposition. The individual efforts of members, as well as the persistent and splendid campaign of the press, backing up the conferees of the House and their advisers, Messrs. Lacey and McRae, have undoubtedly been responsible for the victory. . . .

On July 1, Mr. Fernow having resigned his official position as Chief of the Forestry Division, which he has held for twelve years, also resigned the chairmanship of the Executive Committee of the Forestry Association, and withdraws with the present number of *The Forester* from its editorial management to devote his whole attention to his new duties at Cornell University. Mr. Fernow has served the association actively as an officer without compensation since 1883; first as its Secretary until 1888, and since then as Chairman of its Executive Committee.[49]

On January 25, 1897, the American Forestry Association had been

[48] An unpublished manuscript, "Reminiscences Relating to the Early Days of the American Forestry Association," by Gifford, lent to the author by the Association.

[49] p. 139.

incorporated by seven persons, Fernow and Bowers among them. The year 1898 however was to bring to a close Fernow's eighteen active years of service to this first great North American forestry organization. For many more years the Association would retain Fernow's name as first vice-president, an honor which he fittingly accepted.

By 1898 the job on which Fernow had set his heart at Washington was completed. First, the federal forest reservation policy was permanently established and had withstood a severe test, Second, the forest reserves were provided with adequate authority for the introduction of rational adminstration. Under authority of a law of June 4, 1897, the general land office of the department of the interior within a month had issued rules and regulations by which the reservations were to be managed. The enabling authority was written in the form of "provisos" into a sundry civil appropriation bill, but Fernow regarded the "provisos" as embodying "the most important forestry legislation thus far enacted by Congress. These had been in the main formulated in a bill known as the McRae bill. . . ."[50] Fernow had virtually become the author of the clause which inaugurated rational forest management in the forest reserves. The forestry movement, he said, had cause to celebrate its "silver jubilee" one quarter of a century after the Haldeman bill, the first true forestry bill introduced in congress, had been lost.

Fernow had cause to be gratified that his battle of more than a decade was won. Adequate legislation now authorized the secretary of the in-

[50] *Forestry Investigations of the U.S.D.A., 1877-1898*, pp. 192-193. Fernow wrote, "The sundry civil appropriations bill passed June 4, 1897 (see Senate Doc. No. 102), set aside the proclamations of February 22, 1897, suspending the reservations, which were made upon the recommendation of the committee of the academy, until March 1, 1898, presumably to give time for the adjustment of private claims and to more carefully delimit the reservations, an appropriation of $150,000 for the survey of the reservations under the supervision of the Director of the Geological Survey being made. The provisos attached to this appropriation embody the most important forestry legislation thus far enacted by Congress. . . . The law authorizes the Secretary of the Interior to permit the use of timber and stone by bona fide settlers, miners, etc., for firewood, fencing, buildings, mining, prospecting, and other domestic purposes. It protects the rights of actual settlers within the reservations, empowers them to build wagon roads to their holdings, enables them to build schools and churches, and provides for the exchange of such for allotments outside the reservation limits. The State within which a reservation is located maintains its jurisdiction over all persons within the boundaries of the reserve. Under the above enactment, the Commissioner of the General Land Office has formulated rules and regulations for the forest reservations, and a survey of the reserves last proclaimed is being made by the United States Geological Survey, the appropriations for such a survey having been continued for the year 1898; and the date for the segregation of agricultural lands and their return to the public domain open for entry having been deferred. The appointment of forest superintendents, rangers, etc., although not with technical knowledge, to take charge of the reservations marks the beginning of a settled policy of the United States Government to take care of its long-neglected forest lands. . . ." Also *ibid.*, pp. 202-204, in which is shown that one "proviso" suspended the reservations and restored them to the national domain, but the effect of this was saved by the next "proviso," which restored all undisposed-of reservations on March 1, 1898, to the force and effect of the President's proclamation. See John Ise, *op. cit.*, pp. 132ff; Jenks Cameron, *op. cit.*, pp. 207-208.

terior through the general land office to administer the reserves, to "make such rules and regulations, and establish such service as will insure the objects of such reservations, namely, to regulate their occupancy and use and to preserve the forests thereon from destruction," et cetera.[51] But the work of surveying, mapping, classifying and describing the reserves was placed with the United States geological survey. Technical and scientific responsibility remained with the division of forestry in the department of agriculture. Most serious of all, so far as the department of the interior was concerned, the act failed to supply adequate funds for the administration. Only $18,000 was available for the care of the reserves during 1897-1898. Under the Sundry Civil Act (the law of June 4, 1897) the set of rules and regulations framed by the special service division of the general land office (published on June 30, 1897) functioned quite satisfactorily for a number of years. Filibert Roth affirmed this in 1902.[52] Nevertheless few field agents could be employed during the first year, 1897-1898. The care of the reserves remained about as it had been before. The Sundry Civil Act for the fiscal year 1898-1899 provided appropriations which were much more adequate, and the general land office then organized a real force to manage the reserves.

The Act of 1897 was not devoid of clauses which worked unplanned-for consequences. A discussion of these is not necessary to a biography of Dr. Fernow. Yet, as a part of the problems confronting future forestry management of the reserves at the time he left government service, some reference to the so-called "forest-lien" and "non-export"

[51] At the American Forestry Association's sixteenth meeting, held at Washington at the Cosmos Club in December 1897, Fernow told the members that at an extraordinary session of the 55th congress an "amendment prepared by your committee was introduced in the Senate, and after some changes . . . was passed. . . ." The complete report of the committee of the National Academy of Sciences, which was sent on May 1, 1897, to the Academy's president and was forwarded by him to the secretary of the interior, "did not mature in time to have any influence on this legislation except by its absence to precipitate it." The reservations, which under the law of June 4, 1897, were suspended for a year, might have been permanently wiped out, had the President signed the appropriation bill when it contained a clause annulling the effect of President Cleveland's proclamation of February 22, 1897. The President, however, refused to sign the annulling legislation, and the senate committee later abandoned the amendments designed to abolish the reservations. See *The Forester* IV, pp. 9, 139.

[52] Filibert Roth, "Administration of the U.S. Forest Reserves," *Forestry and Irrigation* VIII, 5, 1902, pp. 191ff.; *Forestry Investigations of the U.S.D.A., 1877-1898*, p. 194 sets forth the appropriations 1872-1896 to employ agents to protect timber on public lands. At p. 202, setting forth the act of 1897, it is said, "This law enables the Secretary of the Interior to formulate a plan for the proper administration of the forest reservations, but its provisions can hardly become operative without a sufficient appropriation to carry it into effect." Jenks Cameron, *op. cit.*, p. 209, says that the preliminary work began with timber agent appropriations. At p. 204, *Forestry Investigations, op. cit.*, may be found the act of June 30, 1898, appropriating $75,000 for "care and administration of the forest reserves." In 1897 (*Yearbook*, p. 160) Fernow urged "the ultimate transfer of these reservations and their administration to the Department of Agriculture. . . ."

clauses enacted in 1897 has pertinence.[53] The "non-export" clause, which in effect confined forest reserve lumber shipments to intrastate commerce where the timber had been cut, would be changed in 1907 to permit interstate shipments. At first, domestic needs proving disproportionate to available timber supply, much good, matured, utilizable timber was wasted on the reserves, a waste remediable only by sound forest management and adequate markets. More serious as a continuing threat to the reservation policy was the deplorable homestead claim situation brought about by the "forest lieu" clause, a situation further complicated by Congress's suspension for almost a year of the effective date of President Cleveland's proclamation of the extensive new reserves. Intended to relieve homestead claimants who found their lands within a reservation withdrawn from settlement, the clause privileged homesteaders to select in lieu of their unperfected bona fide claim or patent within closed reservations other lands from unreserved areas of the public domain. Within a few years Congress restricted these selections to vacant, non-mineral, and surveyed public lands open to homestead entry. But, enabled for a while to select the more as well as less valuable lands in unreserved areas, and while the President's proclamation was suspended even in the new reservations, homesteaders, many of whose claims became owned by large corporate interests, obtained some of the government's best undisposed lands in exchange for worn and worthless lands, valueless railroad grants, lands denuded of timber or for other reasons found of inferior value. The government was a heavy loser.

Nevertheless, despite its defects, the Act of 1897 defined the lines along which the government's forest policy was to be developed during the next decade. Secretary of Agriculture James Wilson, in his report published in the *Yearbook U.S.D.A. for 1908* (pp. 175-176) observed that "For Americans ten years ago forestry had neither a practical basis nor practical interest. On July 1, 1898, there were two professional foresters in the employ of the Government, less than ten in the whole country, no school of forestry on the Western Hemisphere, no scientific knowledge of the first principles of American practice in existence. The very word forestry was usually meaningless except as it was misunderstood. The foundations of the present National Forest policy had, it is true, been laid. Yet so feebly were these foundations supported by popular approval and so dubious was the prospect for rearing a proper superstructure upon them that there was no security for their permanence. President Cleveland had by his proclamation of February 22, 1897, turned at a single stroke over 21,000,000 acres of public land into

[53] Jenks Cameron, *op. cit.*, pp. 208-209, 233-234; John Ise, *op. cit.*, pp. 139-141, 176-190, 292, 331. Cameron, at pp. 210-211, gives an appreciative estimate of the contributions made by Dr. Fernow in establishing forestry science and practice in the United States and Canada. Many foresters believe this to be the most fair estimate of his work thus far published.

National Forests, but because of the belief that this action meant their withdrawal from use a storm of protest had led to the suspension of the effect of the proclamation for a twelvemonth, during which the whole reserve policy hung in the balance. The law of June 4, 1897, which accomplished this suspension, also laid down the lines along which the government's forest policy has ever since developed by defining the purpose for which forest reserves could be created and authorizing their protection and administration; but not until more than half a decade afterwards was there an application of anything actually approaching forestry. . . . The Department employed but 14 persons in 1897 in this work. Not an acre of land, public or private, at that time was under its care or receiving the benefit of its advice. There was no equipment for field work and frequently no information available upon which to base practical advice concerning forest management. The National Forests, with a total area of 39,000,000 acres, were about to receive for the first time some organized administration and protection through the General Land Office."

This statement, interesting for its condensed factual content, made no effort to describe or evaluate the "foundations" of United States forest policy but rather progress since 1897-1898. At the turn of the century all work of the department of agriculture expanded greatly in importance. Government forestry work, under the able leadership of Gifford Pinchot as chief forester, participated in the expansion. By 1908 beginnings were being made to establish forestry experiment stations in connection with the national forests. By 1908 efficient organization of the forest service in districts would be functioning, and all national forests be placed under the department of agriculture rather than as in 1898 three units of the department of the interior and one of agriculture. By 1908 the forest service personnel would be figured in thousands, its expenditures in millions of dollars, and the national forest area would be increased to almost 168,000,000 acres. By 1908 were again functioning effective organized programs of forest products research.

Forester Pinchot took up his task in 1898 with rare ability as an administrator, statesman, and student. The creation of a strong, efficient forest service serving both private forest owners and the government agencies was to be his accomplishment deserving of all the honors and tributes accorded him; and Fernow, as we will show, was among the readiest of foresters to honor him and his achievements.

In 1896, and probably before, Fernow had considered resigning his position as chief of the division of forestry, and when in 1898 an opportunity to perform a professional service more consonant with his scholarly attainments became available to him, he did resign to be made director of the New York State College of Forestry at Cornell University. Academic instruction in silviculture, taught and studied with regard to American forest conditions and needs, was now wanted. Qualified foresters to take up the practical task of managing scientifically and economically the enormous forest areas under reservation would soon be needed in increasing numbers. Among many other reasons, moreover, which called for professional forestry education now, none perhaps convinced Fernow and Roth of the need more during the years 1896-1898 than the compulsory discontinuance of timber physics investigation within the division of forestry.

In 1896 Fernow prepared an article, "Scientific Timber Testing," for a progressive little journal, *Digest of Physical Tests, A Résumé of Practical Tests Made in the Laboratories of the World.* In this he dispassionately considered the work's weaknesses and accomplishments. Not every plan had produced results. For example, the research to ascertain the moisture content of woods and wood products had not been entirely satisfactory. But scientific testing, he said, sought "to find out what the capabilities of materials are, what causes the properties, how they are related to each other, and how they may be produced or influenced; it attempts to develop *laws* of strength and to furnish data for *general* application."

"I hear," wrote Fernow, "some 'practical' engineers say that in practice it would be impossible to apply such refined knowledge, and hence the test data should refer to conditions only which occur or are usual and recognizable in actual practice." This was the sharp issue of "pure versus practical science." "To such," he replied, "my answer can here only be brief. This paper is not written for them; they need some instruction in the history and philosophy of scientific work as applied to practical results, when they will learn that progress, improvement of the practice, can be expected only from applying the opposite of their practical methods. The more refined, the more careful and systematic the methods by which a scientific investigation is carried on, the more likely will it produce results useful to the practice. . . ."

To engineers he still said, "Most of the testing done in the past has been done by engineers who were not at the same time botanists, or rather physiologists, and who failed to study and to appreciate, or to allow for the variability of this fickle material. Not only is it necessary to distinguish between the many different species—engineers are rarely capable of recognizing more than the genus, if one may judge from the engineers' tables of strength, in which mostly generic names only, spruce, fir, pine, oak, etc., are used—but one must know also to distinguish differences in development of the species, and take into consideration physical as well as chemical properties of wood. . . ."

Roth was well qualified to perform scientific timber testing. Transfer of Roth from Washington meant a transfer of the work. Fernow saw a need to train foresters for the field work which was inevitable with the development of the new federal forest reservations and with the extension of state forestry. Those persons who regarded forestry as principally an economic method to protect and preserve the forests, as a practical art which did for the woods what horticulture did for the garden, as empirical tree culture based on botanical investigation, naturally did not regard timber physics research as "germane to forestry." For that matter, neither did those persons who clung to the historical view that timber physics research was mechanical or chemical engineering. Research which established that seasoned timber is sixty to seventy-five per cent stronger than fresh material, that southern oak for industrial purposes compares favorably with northern oak, that chestnut oak could be utilized in railroad ties, that turpentine-bled pine could be safely included in building specifications, that the longleaf pine is twenty to twenty-five per cent stronger than was believed, and many other conclusions and proven results, was gratifying to Fernow. Engineers were furnished with dependable strength-test results of America's most important lumber trees, and much of the data was at once incorporated in such standard engineering manuals as John Cresson Trautwine's. Fernow and Roth maintained that to test timbers expertly, timbers, unlike iron, brick, cement, and stone, should be known from forests to laboratory. The tester should be a "rare combination of engineer, botanist, and physicist."

For an unexplained reason, however, timber physics research in Washington was curtailed in 1896 at the height of its usefulness. During a period when the work was receiving recognition and high praise and commendatory notices from technical journals of the lumber industry, of engineering science, of architecture, of carriage manufacturers, and of all branches of industrial woodworking, when societies of engineers and architects and other groups had written the secretary of agriculture and members of congress urging its continuance and enlargement, in 1896 over strenuous protests from Fernow and others who realized its potentialities, the work was ordered to be discontinued as "not germane to the subject of the division."[54]

On March 21, 1896, Fernow had confided to Joly:

> I am happy in the possession of such appreciative words as yours, although I deserve them only in part and at the same time feel that the appreciation I receive here in the Department is not what it should be: for I am hampered in my work instead of being supported, especially under the present administration. But for the leaden anchor which we always have to carry around, and which has lamed me so that I have lost much of my enthusiasm and vigor, we could have done more and more valuable work. It is true I am still

[54] *Forestry Investigations of the U.S.D.A., 1877-1898,* p. 16.

here, but have been more than once on the point of leaving because the office became too burdensome.

The threat to timber physics research within the division could not at this time have been the source of Fernow's discouragement. In 1896 appeared the great monograph, Bulletin XIII, "The timber pines of the Southern United States," prepared by Dr. Charles Mohr with a discussion of structure by Roth. This was "the first attempt in the United States of a comprehensive statement, from a forestry point of view, of the economic, technical, and sylvicultural conditions and requirements of four species of forest trees." In April 1896 Fernow had announced in his article, "Scientific Timber Testing," that "The Division of Forestry has entered upon a series of tests and investigations in timber physics carried on with the precautions outlined for the purpose of determining not only more thoroughly the range of values for our various species, but especially of determining the effect of the variables affecting strength and furnishing rules of inspection. The work has progressed slowly on account of deficient funds. During the last four years, however, over 30,000 tests have been made with thorough examination of the test material, and at least for the four Southern pines the data based on over 18,000 tests are already well established." Descriptive and technical publications continued to appear during 1897 and 1898.

Timber physics investigation sought "to remove, once for all, ignorance so fatal to a conservative use of our forest resources. . . ." Engineers, wood consumers generally, and even farmers realized how little was known of wood and how important it was to secure reliable information. But by 1897 timber physics research had been abandoned. That year Fernow prepared for the *Yearbook of the Department of Agriculture* a review of the entire forestry work of the division, which *The Forester* considered a "valedictory." In the *Yearbook,* moreover, was contained a list of the one hundred trees most important for timber, with notes of their distribution, cultural requirements, and their character and use.

The chapter on "Forest Technology and Timber Physics" expressed the realization "that as far as the enormous business of harvesting and marketing forest products and of wood manufactures [was] concerned, the forestry interests [lay] in the hands of other men than the farmers, who own only a limited portion of the great forest areas." The value of forest culture for persons growing wood for profit, among these were the farmers, was dependent most certainly on "knowledge of the qualities of our products and its serviceableness for different purposes."[55]

[55] Bulletin 10 of the Division, "An Elementary Discussion of the Characteristics and Properties of Wood," prepared by Roth under Fernow's supervision, and another study

Even after timber physics investigation had been abandoned at the division of forestry, Fernow pleaded for more research.

Everybody knows how the black walnut has been squandered in fence rails and been burned without the knowledge that it could have been kept for a century (in logs, if not standing), with increase in value and without danger of decay. Who does not remember how millions of feet of hemlock, from which the bark was taken, were lying rotting in the woods, because the value of the wood was unappreciated! And even to-day millions of feet of most valuable chestnut and oak are left in the woods unused after the bark has been taken by the tanner. While this may be in part due to economic conditions, the transport of the wood being too difficult and too expensive, there is no such reason for leaving the excellent hemlock of the Pacific Coast uncut in the woods.

In some portions of Washington and Oregon about one-half the forest growth consists of hemlock trees 300 feet and more in height and 3 to 4 feet in diameter, furnishing a magnificent material for many purposes. Yet, such is the ignorance regarding its value that it can not be marketed, and it is left standing. This would at first sight appear an advantage for the future; but it is not, for the trees, suddenly placed in different conditions, even if the fires that follow the logger should spare them, die as the consequence of the exposure by removal of their neighbors, and thus one-half the value of the forest growth is lost. Examples of this kind could be multiplied from all sections of the country. The other kind of ignorance, namely, regarding the properties of the woods which we do use, exhibits itself in their wrong and wasteful application.

There has been so little systematic and reliable investigation on our timbers that until a short while ago the sizes which architects, builders, and engineers prescribed for use in structures were formulated upon the data furnished by European investigators on European timbers, which are by no means of the same quality as ours. The use of unsuitable woods in places where liable to decay, and the absence of proper handling of woods used for such purposes, occasion a large wastage, due to the necessity of replacing them; and many a disaster, from the break of a wagon pole to the collapse of a building in which large amounts of property and even life are destroyed, may be traced to ignorance in the use of woods.

On April 14, 1897, Fernow prepared an estimate of coniferous supplies then apparently on hand at the request of the senate (senate doc. no. 40, 55th cong.) in which, "hedging as much as possible," he arrived at the conclusion that with the existing usage there was probably not more than "sixteen years' supply standing in the Eastern States . . . and that the supply of the Pacific Coast would not suffice to lengthen this period of plenty beyond thirty years, even if this supply were not largely destroyed by fire."[56] Years later, in a letter dated September 23, 1916,

by Roth, "The Uses of Wood," published in the *Yearbook of the U.S.D.A. for 1896*, pp. 391-420, were intended for the use of the farmer as well as "every other citizen who builds a house or uses a spade."

[56] Senate Document 40, 55th Cong., 1st sess., "White Pine Timber Supplies," letter of Fernow to Secretary of Agriculture, 1897, p. 21. See also *Yearbook of the U.S.D.A. for 1897*, p. 153.

he discussed the matter. "To be sure, there is now more definite knowledge to be had and the changed usage has had much to do to lengthen supplies, as well as the Canadian importations." Dean Clifton D. Howe of Canada has added, "Neither [Dr. Fernow] nor anyone at that time could have foreseen the extent to which Canada would contribute its pulpwood and its pulp and paper products to the States or could have anticipated the extent to which abandoned farm lands in New England and New York State would furnish second growth white pine."[57] Fernow was fully aware of the fallacies of statistical information. With a small corps and small appropriations to finance all work in the division of forestry—the total annual appropriation under Fernow's direction at no time exceeded $33,520—statistical accuracy could hardly be expected. Fernow maintained that the total appropriations of the division represented "not much over 1 per cent of the appropriations for the entire Department of Agriculture during the same years, a ridiculously small and disproportionate amount when the relative magnitude of the agricultural and the forestry interests are considered."[58]

In "Considerations in Gathering Forestry Statistics," an address presented May 27, 1897, and printed in December of the following year, Fernow honestly confessed to the American Statistical Association the undependability and the difficulty in employing adequate techniques to assemble data on the forest. His address sought a preliminary method to procure a "tolerably satisfactory statistical inquiry into our forest conditions and forest resources to produce as a basis for statistical purposes." December 15, 1897, he went before the National Board of Trade to warn them that industries representing capital in billions of dollars were dependent for their continued existence on forest supplies and forest products. The forests were almost as basic to national life as agriculture.

Fernow addressed the American Paper and Pulp Association on February 16, 1898, on the subject, "Woodpulp Supplies and Forestry."[59] He introduced his subject, saying "The discussion of forestry before an association of business men like the paper and pulp manufacturers, who have invested in their mills and plants over 200 million dollars, producing annually over 300 million tons of material, worth over 100 million dollars, means largely a discussion of the future of supplies for the woodpulp and paper trade. . . ." He had begun to urge on industry the importance of restocking the land with trees. Reproduction can be aided, he said, by planting and judicious thinning. In

[57] "Bernhard Eduard Fernow—An Appreciation," *Illustrated Canadian Forestry Magazine*, March 1923, p. 168.

[58] *Forestry Investigations of the U.S.D.A., 1877-1898*, p. 8.

[59] *The Forester* IV, March 1898, p. 52. This issue is largely devoted to woodpulp supplies and their treatment. Fernow, Pinchot, Roth, and others contributed.

this address Fernow referred to his studies of "Financial Results of Forest Administration in Saxony, Bavaria, and India." His scholarly analysis of "Forest Policies and Forest Management in Germany and British India" was published as part of house document number 181, of the 55th congress, the 3rd session, and was reprinted separately in 1899. This work is still regarded as authoritative.

While Fernow was chairman of the executive committee of the American Forestry Association, the Association joined with the National Irrigation Congress of 1897 to reiterate a belief that extensive forest reservations and real forest management were imperative in a healthy national economy. Fernow had written articles for the lumber journals, and he contributed the chapter on "American Lumber," which appeared in *One Hundred Years of American Commerce*,[60] edited by C. M. DePew in 1895. Business men had confidence in Fernow even though he expressed such opinions as that with "the end of the century the lumber industry will have reached the climax of its development." Fernow's versatility was shown by the fact that he could appear as a business consultant, a scientific scholar, a forester, a government official, lecturer, teacher, and citizen. As vice-president of section I of the American Association for the Advancement of Science, the section on economic science and statistics, he was called on to deliver an address on "The Providential Functions of Government with Special Reference to Natural Resources."[61] This lecture became the basis of the first chapter of Fernow's book, *Economics of Forestry* (1902), a series of lectures to students of political economy delivered at the University of Wisconsin, which conferred on him the honorary doctor of laws (LL.D.) degree. In 1895 Fernow prepared an exhibit for the Cotton States and International Exposition, held at Atlanta, Georgia, which depicted in graphic style the statistical facts concerning the lumber production of the South. There were a number of articles of lesser consequence written by Fernow that appeared in current periodicals. Most of them dealt with matters such as profit in forestry. Fernow was occasionally charged with maintaining a "negative" forestry, but this was merely the skepticism of a research scientist. He offered no more than he confidently believed he could prove. He strove to be exact because he wished to preserve the unquestioning confidence of the public.

The year 1897 saw the appearance of Sudworth's "Nomenclature of the Arborescent Flora of the United States," the division's Bulletin XIV, which analyzed six thousand names applied to our five hundred forest species. This work was followed by a more condensed list in

60 Chap. XXX, pp. 196-203. See also Fernow's "Wood Chopping to Forestry," *Lumber Trade Journal*, Aug. 15, 1897.

61 *Proc. A.A.A.S.* XLIV, 1895, also reprinted, 20 pp. Concerning the forestry exhibit at the Atlanta exposition, see *Yearbook U.S.D.A. for 1895*, pp. 519-522.

Bulletin XVII. Fernow held throughout his life a steady interest in forest nomenclature. "Forest Terminology" was one of the first subjects taken up when he began to edit *Forestry Quarterly*. Notes, special articles,[62] and reviews of current literature on the subject were included.

Fernow's botanical interest was clearly portrayed in his address, "The Forests and Deserts of Arizona,"[63] presented before the National Geographic Society on February 5, 1897. He knew that "some of the most interesting mountain forests—botanically speaking—are to be found there, and the most lovely and most extensive, as well as most economically important pineries that exist between the great forests of the Pacific Coast and the western border of the Atlantic forest in Texas and Arkansas, a thousand miles away in either direction. . . ." As an article it was illustrated by a picture of the San Francisco Mountains, the present site of the Coconino National Forest. Fernow considered Arizona regions botanically, historically, and geographically, as well as from the forester's point of view.

Had scientific horticulture been started in America earlier, the linkage of the practical art of horticulture and the botanical laboratory would have been more complete. Plant breeders strove in their experimental gardens to ascertain laws of plant variation and the responses of plants to climates and soils. A few scholars in horticulture investigated breeding from the point of view of plant physiology and plant pathology. But the physiological study of tree growth had not gotten far in America. Even today plant breeding in tree species is not widely accepted as fundamental in forestry research. Very important work is being done by some in this field, particularly at the Institute of Forest Genetics at Placerville, Californa. "From forest biology," Fernow said in his 1893 report, "we learn what are the various conditions under which forest trees and forests develop as living beings; from timber physics, we learn what are the results in the wood material of the influence of various conditions. In the practice, then, or art of forestry the knowledge gained from these sciences is applied to attain certain proposed results, to produce a desired crop, which in quality and quantity correspond to the soil and climate and to the art of man in directing the same to best advantage. . . . The methods of crop production or forest culture, being based on the natural laws of the interrelations of plants to soil and climate, must, at least in principle, be alike all over the world. Here pure forestry science finds its application and development."

Fernow saw there were two forces behind the forestry movement—science and economics. While he urged physiological investigations, he

[62] III, 3, Aug. 1905, pp. 255, 360.
[63] *National Geographic* VIII, 7-8, July-Aug. 1897, pp. 203-226.

kept a steady eye on plant introductions which might serve forestry interests. The same forces that were making a scientific horticulture and agriculture could be harnessed to forestry. Under his direction the division of forestry published in 1895 a bulletin on "Some Foreign Trees for the Southern States." To increase silvicultural knowledge for the forest producer, experimental tests were made and special strains of basket osiers, tan bark wattle trees, cork oak, and eucalyptus seed were introduced on a small scale. A bulletin on "Osier Culture" was prepared and published in 1898 for the division by John M. Simpson under Fernow's direction. Bamboo was studied as a substitute for wood. Since in practically every instance the division furnished everything except the land and labor for trial plantations, the work could not expand enormously because of the lack of money. Cooperative work with the state agricultural experiment stations supplied such constructive advancements that Charles A. Keffer was brought from Washington to take charge of the division's entire trial plantation work with stations and private individuals. Keffer, as assistant chief of the division, prepared and published in 1898 under Fernow's direction Bulletin XVIII, which reviewed the division's "Experimental Tree Planting in the Plains." The Bruner plantations received special consideration.

Regional forestry applications were related to forestry development generally. Fernow hoped that the work of "plant acclimatization [would] be extended to all kinds of plants with liberal appropriations from Congress. . . ." The division of forestry would have "the satisfaction of having assisted the farmer by taking the lead in this work, though in a direction not exclusively its own."[64] Soils problems were kept in view. Describing a farmers' bulletin on "Washed Soils: How to prevent and reclaim them" and his article, "The Relation of Forests to Farms," in the 1895 *Yearbook*, Fernow reiterated his belief that water management, by irrigation in arid and subarid regions and proper distribution and use of available water supplies in humid areas, was the "great problem of the future" and that no rationally successful water management is possible without forest management.

Classification was fundamental in timber physics investigations. One sought to classify timbers according to durability. One classified the most lasting, economical, and valuable preservatives. And so on. Every objective analysis required systematic procedure. There Fernow came squarely against the problems of taxonomy used in wood analysis. He saw the advantages and disadvantages in a taxonomy based on the most refined anatomical data. For the silviculturist concerned with a few economically valuable tree species there were obvious advantages. However

[64] *Yearbook of the U.S.D.A. for 1897*, pp. 158-159; *Forestry Investigations of the U.S.D.A., 1877-1898*, pp. 22-24.

he confessed also that "The most convincing proof of the difficulty of using anatomical data for recognition of species came forcibly to my attention during the timber physics work when a competent investigator, who had constructed a good wood key based on anatomical characters, found in . . . samples, carefuly collected in the woods . . . of the four Southern commercial pines, 16 species represented. We have fortunately arrived at a period in the world's development, when the call is general for a scientific basis of our practice. But, I fear, that our enthusiasm in that direction sometimes slops over and leads us to expect at once more results than it is practically possible to obtain."[65]

The "scientific basis" of practice in forestry was years in arriving. Protests were not enough to induce the government to revive the timber physics work. The Hurley bill (no. 518) in the house and the McBride bill (no. 2587) in the senate both called for an appropriation to permit the division of forestry to continue timber testing. *The Forester*, in January 1898,[66] announced this, but in the June number of the same year,[67] the publication observed that the transfer of Roth from Washington to Cornell University suggested "that probably the valuable work in timber physics, which has given to the forestry division an international reputation, will also be transferred to Cornell University from the department of agriculture."

On November 2, 1898, Fernow spoke before the 32nd annual convention of the American Institute of Architects at Washington. By this time he was dean of the New York State College of Forestry at Cornell. Secretary Wilson had named Gifford Pinchot as chief of the division of forestry. No announcement that timber physics investigation was to be revived was forthcoming. None would come for several years. Roth had gone with Fernow to Cornell, and in June 1898 *The Forester*[68] announced that he would "lecture on the branches of technological character, such as timber physics and wood technology, exploitation, and forest protection." *The Forester* assured its readers that Pinchot could "make the Division what it should be, namely, an executive bureau in charge of the Federal timberlands and reservations." The interpretation that timber physics research had been transferred to Cornell University was not subscribed to by Fernow, who persistently argued that the work should be reestablished at Washington. He told the American Institute of Architects:[69]

[65] B. E. Fernow, Discussion of I. W. Bailey's paper on "The Role of the Microscope in the Identification and Classification of the Timbers of Commerce," *Journal of Forestry* XV, 1917, pp. 176-191, at pp. 188-189.

[66] p. 6.

[67] IV, 6, June 1898, p. 116.

[68] *ibid.*, p. 116; *Forest Leaves* VI, 7, Feb. 1898, p. 113.

[69] A pamphlet titled "Some Peculiarities of Wood." See also "Relation of the Strength of Wood under Compression to the Transverse Strength," *Am. Inst. Mining*

Yet it is possible to study wood in a scientific manner with the assurance of practical results as has been shown by the extensive and fruitful series of studies which one wise administration of the United States Department of Agriculture authorized and another wise(?) administration discontinued just when most promising progress had become possible and the first important results had been announced. If no other fact of value for the practitioner had been obtained than the discovery that the "strength of a beam at the elastic limit is equal to the strength of the material in compression," the value of the work could not be denied, while as to the propriety of the government undertaking the study of this difficult and complex subject there could be hardly any dissenting voice, especially when it is admitted that it is the function of the government to secure a conservative policy in the treatment of our forest resources and presumably also of the material which the resource furnishes.

Fernow adhered tenaciously to his belief in the necessity for timber physics research, saying, "I am inclined to think that twenty to fifty per cent more efficiency can be secured in the use of wood materials than is now obtained by merely applying the knowledge now in existence. . . ." Strength and durability tests were not the only phases of the work. He explained that there were other desirable fields for experimental study, such as the reduction of rot and fire dangers in timbers, the field of wood-preservatives, and the entire field of wood specifications in construction and for other purposes, in which matters pertaining to shrinking and swelling of timbers, sizes to be used, and many other questions were presented. Had these investigations proceeded on the biological bases which Fernow advocated, without interruption and with increased facilities, a true forest pathology might have been constructed. Forestry might not have had to await development of plant pathology by botanical science. The same might be observed with regard to forest soils research. Fernow's real "valedictory" was a report to congress on the *Forestry Investigations of the United States Department of Agriculture* for the years 1877-1898. Roth prepared Chapter I, "The work in timber physics in the Division of Forestry." Of the publication's 401 pages, completed and forwarded in December of 1898 and published by the government in 1899, sixty pages were devoted to delineating the scope, methods, aims, and accomplishments of timber physics research. This report evidently had little influence on the timber testing which was revived in 1902 under the leadership of engineers who possessed little or no training in the plant sciences.

It is interesting to observe that the subject of "Forest Influences," another branch of forestry research which Fernow wanted conducted by men of biological training, was given only two dozen pages in

Eng. XXVIII, Feb. 1898, pp. 240ff. Fernow regarded "the important discovery of the relation between the strength in compression and in cross breaking" as the investigation's "crowning result," putting the designing of beams upon a surer footing and saving much future useless wood testing. *For. Inv., op. cit.*, p. 17.

Forestry Investigations, 1877-1898, although the subject is occasionally mentioned throughout the book.

Fernow was neither a money raiser nor a politician. The government work had been difficult for him. He gladly turned to the necessary work in forestry education. He must have realized that no one with the possible exceptions of Pinchot and Schenck, both of whom were offered the position, could direct the New York State College of Forestry with the same experienced leadership.

The division of forestry now found the leader it had needed. Young, aggressive, with initiative and extraordinary capabilities as administrator and organizer, Gifford Pinchot took up the leadership of the forestry division. During Fernow's incumbency salaries had increased from $2,000 to $7,820. The rainmakers' research fund had increased the division's investigation fund from $8,000 to $10,000. But even with funds for timber physics research, funds for investigation did not exceed $15,056.85.[70] During the last five years, 1894-1898, the research fund was increased to $20,000, in one year to $25,000, and the total salary allowances aggregated $8,520. But contrast these sums with the appropriations obtained after Pinchot became chief. Immediately the sums annually allowed to forestry were doubled and more; and the personnel were increased so that within eighteen months the working force had been enlarged four hundred per cent.[71] On May 25, 1900, President McKinley signed an appropriations act for the department of agriculture in which $80,000 were allowed to the division of forestry for the fiscal year ending June 30, 1901. This sum was said to have been "just twice as large as the annual appropriation for 1899-1900, which, in its turn, doubled the appropriation for the previous year."[72] Within the next decade the amounts increased annually by leaps and bounds until they were figured in the hundreds of thousands of dollars, and eventually in the millions. There were many events that proved the rare administrative ability of Gifford Pinchot.

Under Pinchot forestry became regarded throughout the nation as a strong influence in the progress of agriculture. The economic side of forestry had to be emphasized. Beginning with approximately forty million acres of reserved forest land,[73] the amounts in reservations were expanded to one hundred million acres and more. During Pinchot's administration the division of forestry became a bureau, not precisely that contemplated by the committee report of the National Academy of Sciences, but a bureau within the department of agriculture. The for-

[70] *Forestry Investigations of the U.S.D.A., 1877-1898*, p. 8.

[71] *The Forester* V, 12, Dec. 1899, p. 290.

[72] *ibid.*, VI, 6, June 1900, p. 139.

[73] As of June 30, 1898, there were 40,719,474 acres; see *Forest Leaves* VII, 6, Dec. 1899, p. 91. As of August 1901, there were 46,828,449 acres; see *ibid.* VIII, 4, p. 59.

mation of a complete forest service within the department was achieved. Fernow assisted in its establishment.

In 1898 the National Board of Trade adopted a resolution which advocated that all forest work should be centered in the department of agriculture. It was cumbersome to have the general land office administer the national forest reserves, the geological survey map and describe and recommend new boundaries, and the department of agriculture have charge of all professional forestry work. It became apparent that the forestry functions of the department of the interior, the geological survey, and the department of agriculture would have to be integrated. Even though the department of the interior had built up a strong forest work, it had to secure technical working plans for the reservations from the department of agriculture. At the eighteenth meeting of the American Forestry Association, held in Washington on December 13, 1899, the matter was thoroughly discussed. Some members favored transfer of all forestry work to the department of the interior. Others, contending that forestry is a phase of agriculture, argued that all forestry work should be centered in the department of agriculture. With the turn of the twentieth century the function of the government with respect to its public lands had almost completely changed from what it had been when the division of forestry was created. Whereas its principal business had been to dispose of the lands under existing laws, it now functioned to impose obligations to conserve and utilize its publicly owned domain, which had largely been withdrawn from entry or sale. The interdepartmental confusion was corrected by a special act of congress, approved February 1, 1905, which transferred the management of the federal public forest reservations from the department of the interior to the department of agriculture. The consolidation was hailed as the greatest advance made on behalf of the national forests since the act of March 3, 1891.[74] In the process of securing the 1905 legislation, the cost was the loss of an efficient forest management service within the department of the interior, but to effect the consolidation, Secretary Hitchcock, Pinchot, and other high ranking officials in land and forest matters cooperated.

When Fernow left Washington to go to Cornell University, many shared the viewpoint of a bright American-born wife who devotedly had helped her husband. Mrs. Fernow wrote at a later date, "Events [in forestry do not relate] the difficulties that had to be wrestled with, the small money appropriations, the hard work necessary to get Congress interested, the political red tape. But they were all so successfully wrestled with that, when my husband left Washington for Cornell,

[74] *The Forester* VII, 4, April 1901, p. 93.

Forestry stood firmly on its feet and a comfortable position was ready for Mr. Pinchot."

President Cleveland, by proclamation, had reserved the central portion of the Black Hills of South Dakota, the Big Horn Range in Wyoming, the Jackson Lake country south of the Yellowstone National Park in Wyoming (later known as the Teton Forest Reserve), the Rocky Mountain forest of Montana (the Flathead reserve north of the Great Northern Railway's right of way and extending to the Canadian boundary), the Sun River reserve south of the Great Northern Railway (the Lewis and Clarke Forest Reserve), the Priest River reserve in northern Idaho and northeastern Washington from the Great Northern Railway to the Canadian boundary, the Bitter Root Mountains reserve on both sides of the boundary lines of Montana and Idaho, the Washington reserve (the Cascade Mountains of northern and southern Washington to the Canadian boundary), the Olympic Mountain region in northwestern Washington, the Stanislaus Forest Reserve (the summits of the Sierra Nevada Mountains in California north of Yosemite National Park), the Mount Rainier Forest Reserve (an enlargement of the old Pacific Forest, along both slopes of the Cascade Mountains nearly to the Columbia River, in Washington and Oregon), the Uinta Forest Reserve of northern Utah embracing most of the Uinta Mountains, and the San Jacinto Forest Reserve of southern California.[75]

President McKinley did not neglect the federal forest reservation policy. In his last annual message in 1899 he pointed out that since June 30, 1898, the number of reserves had been increased to thirty-six and the total estimated acreage augmented by almost five and a quarter million acres. The Trabuco Canyon Reserve in California and the Black Hills of Dakota Reserve had been enlarged. The Mount Rainier reserve of Washington had been reduced; and six new reserves were created, the San Francisco Mountains of Arizona, the Black Mesa of Arizona,

[75] *Garden and Forest,* Nos. 470 and 471, Feb. 24, March. 3, 1897, pp. 80-81. The list as compiled by Fernow in *Forestry Investigations of the U.S.D.A., 1877-1898,* p. 192, follows:

1. Black Hills Reserve in South Dakota	967,680 acres
2. Big Horn Reserve in Wyoming	1,198,080
3. Teton Forest Reserve in Wyoming	829,440
4. Flathead Forest Reserve in Montana	1,382,400
5. Lewis and Clarke Forest Reserve in Montana	2,926,080
6. Priest River Forest Reserve in Idaho and Washington	645,120
7. Bitter Root Forest Reserve in Montana and Idaho	4,147,200
8. Washington Forest Reserve in Washington	3,594,240
9. Olympic Forest Reserve in Washington	2,188,800
10. Mount Rainier Forest Reserve in Washington	1,267,200
11. Stanislaus Forest Reserve in California	691,200
12. San Jacinto Forest Reserve in California	737,280
13. Utah Forest Reserve	705,120
Total estimated area	21,279,840 acres

Lake Tahoe of California, the Gallatin River of Montana, the Gila River of New Mexico, and Fish Lake of Utah. In December 1898 the aggregate acreage had been placed at 43,597,714 acres.[76] By 1903 the number of federal forest reservations would be increased to fifty-two, totaling 61,218,525 acres within the boundaries of Alaska, Arizona, California, Colorado, Idaho, Montana, Nebraska, New Mexico, Oklahoma, Oregon, South Dakota, Utah, Washington, and Wyoming.[77]

Among the reserves not already mentioned were the Alexander Archipelago Forest Reserve of Alaska; the Prescott, the Santa Rita, the Santa Catalina, the Mount Graham, and the Chiricahua Reserves of Arizona; the Santa Inez Reserve of California; the San Isabel Reserve of Colorado; the Madison and the Little Belt Mountains Reserves of Montana; the Lincoln Reserve of New Mexico; the Wichita Reserve of Oklahoma; the Payson Reserve of Utah; and the Crow Creek and Medicine Bow reserves of Wyoming. By 1902-1903 eight forest reserves had been created in the Hawaiian Islands and one in Porto Rico.

In 1907, while a bill was before the senate and house of representatives to require congressional approval of presidentially proclaimed reservations, a virtual repeal of the act of March 3, 1891, President Roosevelt endorsed a proposal, submitted by forester William T. Cox and transmitted to the president by Pinchot, to set aside sixteen million more acres of mountain forest lands before the senate and house enacted the new legislation.[78] On March 2, 1907, two days before the act became effective, President Roosevelt created twenty-one new reservations with an aggregate area of over forty million acres.[79] Today the United States forest service administers 152 national forests, comprising about 180,000,000 acres in forty states, Alaska, and Puerto Rico. During and following Fernow's years as chief of the division of forestry, most of the public timber domain—in the 1880's, fifty to seventy million acres—was placed in reservations, largely in response to the educational pleas which he initiated.

At the sixteenth meeting of the American Forestry Association in 1897 it was announced that Pennsylvania, principally through the efforts of Forest Commissioner Rothrock, had passed laws which provided for formation and management of state forest reservations, and for an improved system of fire prevention administration. Pennsylvania and its forestry movement had been fortunate in the leadership of four able governors—Hartranft, Beaver, Pattison, and Hastings. In August 1898 *Forest Leaves*[80] announced that tracts of 39,000 acres of "un-

[76] *Forest Leaves* VII, 6, Dec. 1899, p. 91; *The Forester* IV, 12, p. 235.

[77] *Forest Leaves* IX, 2, April 1903, p. 25.

[78] Gifford Pinchot, "Roosevelt's Part in Forestry," *Journal of Forestry* XVII, 2, Feb. 1919, pp. 122-125.

[79] Jenks Cameron, *op. cit.*, pp. 244-245.

[80] VI, 10, Aug. 1898, p. 161; VI, 11, Oct. 1898, p. 179.

seated" lands had been secured and reserved. By autumn these tracts had been increased to 48,865 acres by purchases and tax forfeiture titles. By winter more than fifty-five thousand acres had been acquired. That autumn Governor Hastings appointed a commission to examine and select reservations of not less than 40,000 acres each, one at the headwaters of the Delaware River, one at the headwaters of the Susquehanna, and one at the headwaters of the Ohio. Within three years Pennsylvania established a forestry division in its department of agriculture, and the total reserves were increased to 97,962 acres, with more than 113,000 soon authorized to be acquired. "Pennsylvania," boasted *Forest Leaves*,[81] "is the only State in the Union, we believe, which has recognized the importance of forestry to the extent of making a separate and distinct State Department in its interest." The American Forestry Association in 1897 acknowledged that Pennsylvania, through the work of its forest commissioner and its adoption of a forest reservation policy, stood foremost in recognizing its duty to its forests. Even New York and the federal government were not excepted.[82] In its issue of July 7, 1897, *Garden and Forest*,[83] commenting on the act providing forest reservations at the headwaters of the state's important rivers and an act remitting taxes to encourage private owners to preserve growing forests, as well as the prospective distribution of 17,000 copies of the forest commissioner's report on the condition of woodlands, observed that "Half a dozen years ago no sane man would have hoped that any one of the forest laws enacted by the last Pennsylvania Legislature would pass. . . . It is very plain, too, that the report of the Forestry Commission which was published last year has done much educational work in that state, while the influence of its Forestry Bureau, created the year before, has been constantly exercised for good."

In 1898 Rothrock formally petitioned the University of Pennsylvania and Pennsylvania State College to include in their curricula adequate forestry instruction. The setting apart of state forest reservations had made available lands for the practice of forestry. Rothrock wanted in addition lands for a school of forestry practice to train foresters for work in the Pennsylvania forests. He had seen the forest academies of Europe. The vision was soon to be realized. As early as June 1898 *Forest Leaves*[84] asked, "When will Pennsylvania start her school of which there are rumors in the air now?"

The division of forestry of the federal agricultural department, under Filibert Roth's leadership, had investigated Wisconsin forests to aid a state commission there. Wisconsin was the first state to pursue an official

[81] VIII, 2, April 1901, p. 24; VIII, 1, Feb. 1901, p. 6.
[82] 16th meeting, Dec. 8, 1897, see *The Forester* IV, 6, Jan. 1898, p. 13.
[83] p. 261.
[84] p. 158.

systematic inquiry into its forest resources.[85] From this investigation issued the division's Bulletin XVI, prepared by Roth and titled, "Forestry Conditions and Interests of Wisconsin."[86] A map of the state's forest distribution was included, as well as a discussion by Fernow of the objects and methods of forest statistics. The northern counties of Wisconsin, twenty-seven in all or more than one-half of the state, were visited during three and one-half months. The entire work was done with the state geological survey. In 1878[87] the legislature had set aside state lands in twenty-three townships in Iron and Vilas counties, some 50,000 acres in a lake region including headwaters of important rivers such as the Wisconsin, as a state park, where no one was permitted to cut or destroy timber. In 1897, however, another legislature took the progressive position of creating a forest commission to draft plans to utilize and protect the state's forest resources, to organize a forestry department for the state, and to create a forest reserve; but with strange inconsistency, the same legislature sold out its beautiful state forest park to lumbering interests. Lumbermen had supported the legislation enacted in Pennsylvania, but not in Wisconsin. The situation became more astonishing when the Wisconsin forest park land had to be repurchased after the valuable timber was gone. The lands were practically denuded. The reason for the repurchase was that the state park was so situated as to afford protection to the state's rivers and a great natural reservoir of lakes and swamps. From these lands, cut-over and burnt-over tracts, Wisconsin's first state forest reservation, nevertheless, was to be developed during eight years of a well-organized and efficient forestry department.

In October 1897, in the presence of Fernow, D. M. Riordan, C. A. Schenck, and others, a state forestry association was organized in North Carolina. With a membership of about fifteen persons, the first annual meeting was held at New Bern.

Schenck[88] had been born March 25, 1868, at Darmstadt in Hesse, Germany. Educated in this city, he had studied at the University of Tübingen, and in 1888 he had taken the forestry course at the University of Giessen. He graduated from this institution in 1891 and then spent some time in military service, after which he went on to further study. He was given the state examination and appointed *Forstassessor* to the government of Hesse-Darmstadt. In 1895 he obtained a doctorate in philosophy from the University of Giessen. Mr. Vanderbilt asked

[85] *The Forester* IV, 6, June 1898, p. 127; "Wisconsin" in *Forestry Investigations of the U.S.D.A., 1877-1898*, pp. 181ff.

[86] Published in 1898.

[87] The materials dealing with Wisconsin forestry history have been taken mainly from a copy of a manuscript, "History of Forestry in Wisconsin," prepared by State Forester Griffith and found among Fernow's collected documents.

[88] *Forestry and Irrigation* IX, 4, April 1903, p. 174.

Sir Dietrich Brandis to recommend someone to manage his North Carolina estate. Sir Dietrich recommended Schenck, who took up his work at Biltmore in 1895. Under Schenck's direction the "greater part of the planting" of the forest estate was done.[89] Schenck left in 1909 and C. D. Beadle became superintendent. Schenck has related in a letter to Mrs. Fernow how he and Fernow met:

> It was in 1895 that I first met your husband in Washington. I was fascinated by his personality, his endless enthusiasm, his courage, his eloquence: later on, we had the first meeting in Wilmington, N.C. for a Forestry Association, about to be created in North Carolina. I did not know English, and, frightened, that I was of any public necessity to make my little address revised by an associate at Biltmore, it had to be put in print by me, before I came down to the meeting. Helas! En route to the meeting from Biltmore, a bottle of North Carolina claret which my wife had placed in my valise, close to the addresses, began to leak; and when I tried to unpack them in Wilmington, the printed sheets were all spoiled by claret. Then, at the meeting after an eloquent address by your husband, I was almost dragged by him to the speaker's rostrum to deliver *some* kind of a speech. I did. I related the accident which had befallen my finely prepared address: Dr. Fernow and the whole audience roared. I became bold and bolder; and, when I was through Dr. Fernow almost embraced me, assuring me that I was actually in possession of the gift of gab. From that moment on, from that first public utterance on, from the encouragement and self-confidence then in me established by your husband I began my public career, small as it was, comparatively speaking. . . .

In September 1897 a special autumn meeting of the American Forestry Association began at Washington and journeyed by way of Lookout Mountain to Nashville, Tennessee. En route from Washington to Tennessee, the Association members stopped at Biltmore, where Dr. Schenck showed them some thirteen thousand acres of old farm fields and mountain, brush, and forest land being treated in accordance with the principles and practice of European forestry. Forest growth in various stages of development, methods of regenerating, cutting, thinning, and planting forests, forms of nursery practice, tools and appliances, forest roadbuilding, soil erosion prevention, and other kindred work were demonstrated. Meetings were held and special consideration was given to a forest policy that would aim to replace the rapidly disappearing southern timber growth. Although the Biltmore experiment was distinctively private, the work exemplified what could and should be undertaken by governments for the forests of the South.

Aside from the early forest reservations to supply timber to the old wooden navy, federal forestry in the South may be said to have originated formally with the organization in 1899 of an Appalachian Park Association in North Carolina. Reservation of at least one forest region

[89] Ferdinand W. Haasis, "Forest Plantations at Biltmore, North Carolina," *op. cit.*, p. 2.

in Florida had attracted interest. Agitation to create forest reservations in the watersheds of large rivers along the mountain ranges north into New England followed the action in North Carolina. The federal government began to examine 9,600,000 acres in the southern Appalachian region—mapping and classifying lands, and learning the probable cost of their purchase—with a view to acquiring the lands as forest reserves. By 1901 Secretary Wilson was ready officially to inaugurate a campaign for their acquisition, a campaign entailing work which was to last for years.[90]

Already the federal government had established a precedent to purchase new, as well as reserve old, lands for forest reservations. In 1896 six hundred thousand acres had been acquired from the Blackfeet Indians, and the following year these lands had been placed in the Flathead reserve. President McKinley had favored acquiring lands for forest reservations in the eastern watersheds, and President Roosevelt made this the subject of a special message to Congress.

In 1898 at a meeting of the American Forestry Association held at Omaha, Nebraska, amalgamation of the Association with the Irrigation Congress was urged. F. H. Newell, who had served the Association as secretary for several years, rejoiced in the belief that at last few persons, especially among farmers, doubted the close connection between forestry and irrigation. But he added, "After a united effort we have succeeded in getting a number of men together in the East to form an American Forestry Association. We have about 1,000 members, but my experience has been that it is exceedingly difficult to bring in the Western men. . . . The Western politicians say this is an Eastern organization and does not know about the matters of the West. . . ."[91] Unity of action was needed, and no stronger natural bond could be established than that between irrigation and forestry interests. Within three years *The Forester*, official publication of the American Forestry Association, and *National Irrigation*, official publication of the National Irrigation Association, were combined to produce *Forestry and Irrigation*, a publication devoted to both interests.[92] Floods, especially the great Johnstown flood of the Ohio and floods of the Mississippi River, had impressed the nation with the need to reserve or acquire and manage such forest areas as were necessary to preserve equable waterflow in the East and provide continuous and adequate water supply in the West. Irrigation progress had trailed forestry progress throughout the nation and in the states,

[90] "The Appalachian Forest Reserve, the Subject of a Special Message to Congress by President Roosevelt," *Forestry and Irrigation* VIII, 1, Jan. 1902, p. 12; Jenks Cameron, *op. cit.*, p. 233; Chase P. Ambler, "Our Mountain Forests," *Country Life in America* II, 1, May 1902, p. 3; George F. Weston, "Biltmore etc.," *ibid.* II, 5, Sept. 1902, pp. 180ff.

[91] *The Forester* IV, 11, Nov. 1898, pp. 217-224.

[92] The announcement was made in December 1901; *The Forester* VII, 12, p. 295.

but in years just before the turn of the century these movements, more closely working together with increased unity of purposes, acquired new vigor. The new strength proved beneficial to the south and east as well as, of course, the west.

On December 1, 1898, Fernow observed, "Nine States have special forestry commissions or other agencies charged with taking care of the forestry interests of their States, or else to investigate and report on desirable legislation, and three or four other States have charged some existing commission with similar duties. In many, if not most, cases the legislation leading to these commissions has been either formulated or suggested by the writer, or at least supported by arguments and facts drawn from the Division."[93] New forestry associations had come into being—in 1895 in Utah, and in 1896 in Connecticut. In June 1898 Fernow addressed the National Park and Outdoor Association at Minneapolis on "The Aesthetic Side of Forestry."

Up to December 1, 1898, the division of forestry, Fernow said in his letter to Secretary James Wilson transmitting *Forestry Investigations, 1877-1898*, had experienced "the period of propaganda and primary education. We have during this period made the beginnings for a new departure, for an economic reform. We have laid the foundations upon which it will be possible to build a superstructure."[94] Rothrock must have agreed with this interpretation, for early in 1901 he was quoted as saying, "Up to the commencement of 1900 much of the work done has pertained to what might be called the period of agitation of the cause of forestry. It was necessary before our people could be induced to enter upon a new work that they should be convinced that it was necessary. This has been accomplished, and the task now before us is to begin the practical work of restoration."[95]

How was this to be done most effectively? The authorities in the United States were not in agreement. Schenck was dominated by that type of forestry which emanated from Germany and stressed revenues. In America forestry stressed conservative management. The private forest was of prime importance. Forestry thus became a branch of economics. The underlying sciences, botany, engineering, et cetera, were of secondary importance. When Schenck early in 1898 decided to found a school to train foresters and rangers (it is said that private instruction was begun in 1897)[96] he planned to give only a one-year course of forestry practice.

Forestry to Fernow had attained the stature of a science and was gathering prominence as a profession. He had seen the mining industry

93 *Forestry Investigations of the U.S.D.A., 1877-1898*, p. 25. See a discussion of fire laws and forestry commissions created to the year 1897 in *ibid.*, pp. 172-189.

94 *ibid.*, pp. 26-27.

95 *The Forester* VII, 1, Jan. 1901, p. 6.

96 Jenks Cameron, *op. cit.*, p. 262n.

in America pass through a transition from empirics to science. He had brought forestry in America through much the same transformation. A more elaborate scientific basis and direction was necessary for the future of forestry. A school with a one-year course and no prerequisites to entrance could not satisfy the standards he had set.

The Biltmore school later taught botany, silviculture, and dendrology. Gradually Schenck brought his students from the forests into the classroom. Practical forest work remained basic, for Schenck was just what he represented himself to be, an excellent manager in the woods. The school produced during its span of a decade and a half many able foresters who found prominent places in government and private services. In 1909 the school became involved in an "embroglio," in the course of which Schenck hurled charges and was strongly answered even by some of his former students. But for a number of years Schenck exercised an influence in forestry in America. Fernow and he were not always in agreement, nevertheless they gave each other credit for ability.

The Biltmore experiment offered facilities to the landscape gardener, the arboriculturist, the dendrologist, the botanist, the horticulturist, the agriculturist, and the forester. The nursery, covering about one hundred acres of ground, was devoted principally to the production of ornamental and forest trees. The forest department represented "one of the first instances on the continent where scientific forest control [had] been applied to a large area."[97] The "Great Herbarium," originated by Frederick Law Olmsted and enlarged by C. D. Beadle represented fifteen thousand species of local and world flora. Five hundred thousand specimens of flowering plants were included. A part of the famous botanical collections of Alvan Wentworth Chapman, for many years the acknowledged authority on the botany of southeastern United States, especially of Florida, was purchased, adding a distinctly southern significance to the work. Dr. Schenck's school immediately captured support from all students of plants and the forest.

Rothrock supported Schenck.[98] While there is little reason to believe that the professional relations of Rothrock and Fernow were not cordial, the two men had engaged in an academic dispute on the "Relation of Trees to Light and Shade as the Basis of Sylviculture."[99] Rothrock believed that Fernow in his bulletin, "Forestry for Farmers," had given too much space to the subject, whereas Fernow had replied that he regarded the relationship so fundamental that he had been tempted to define silviculture as the "art of managing light-conditions in the

[97] George F. Weston, "Biltmore etc.," *Country Life in America* II, 5, Sept. 1902, p. 180.

[98] *Forest Leaves* VI, 9, June 1898, p. 146. Rothrock wrote, "There can be no question as to [Schenck's] fitness for this important work."

[99] *Forest Leaves* V, 8, April 1896, p. 124; V, 9, June 1896, pp. 140-141; VI, 10, Aug. 1898, p. 172.

forest." Fernow said that "if any one should ask me what he should do to acquire the first practical knowledge of sylviculture, I would answer: 'Go into the woods and observe the behavior of the trees with regard to the light conditions under which they grow. Find out what degree of shade each one can endure under the same soil and climatic conditions.' . . ." Rothrock argued that Fernow narrowed forestry to wood production, when he might have discussed agricultural forestry, the need to return certain agricultural lands to forests for nitrogen and fertility. Rothrock held that "the object of forestry is to produce the largest quantity of wood, of any desired quality, at least expense in a given area." He objected to "placing an old science in a new land without adapting it to produce the largest results in that region. . . ."

Rothrock presumably had reviewed Roth's bulletin on "Timber." At least, the reviewer in *Forest Leaves* had stated that "quite a large portion of the information contained [in the bulletin had] been briefly but clearly stated in earlier publications in our own country." Fernow replied and asked the reviewer to name the American publications on the subject. "With the exception of the chapters on structure contained in the text-books of botany, and a meagre collection of stray papers on some of the points touched," commented Fernow, "the writer knows of no attempts to discuss the physics of wood in anything like a comprehensive or even discursive manner. In fact, the only book in the English language with which he is acquainted, is one by Thomas Laslett, an Englishman, *Timber and Timber Trees*, which, while very useful in certain directions, namely, as a reference book to the useful timbers of the world, does not satisfy the inquirer after the nature and behavior of wood in general. . . ."

Fernow had been a pupil of G. Heyer. Nearly fifty years had passed since that "grand master of modern forestry science [had written] his classic little treatise on 'the relation of forest trees to light and shade,' which [placed] this knowledge as the key note of the entire structure of sylvicultural teaching, and especially of its most important chapter, that on 'thinning.' " Familiarity with the principles of forest growth and light "in all its bearings," Fernow argued, would enable anyone to practice silviculture in any country, "after a brief period of observation of the behavior of the species with which he has to deal, for this principle does not apply to German and French conditions only, where it was first worked out, but to American, Australian, or Indian conditions as well—in fact, it applies in all parts of the world where trees grow, for it is simply the interpretation of nature. If we have not observed our native species sufficiently to indicate their behavior and relative position with reference to light and shade endurance, it would be a most useful task for the interviewer to discuss the errors, and to add his observations, for the basis of American forestry practice can be laid only by an accumulation of such observations."

Rothrock and Fernow disagreed as to the fundamental emphasis in forestry—the scientific or the economic. It is strange that Rothrock, who had done so much to advance the interests of laboratory investigation in botany, should not have entertained the same point of view in forestry. In his discussions of the scientific questions of forest influences, the influence of forest removal on rainfall, stream-flow, water supply, and the disturbance of the "balance of nature" one may discern a scientist's interest in forestry. But Rothrock was dealing with legislatures. Immediate monetary returns on forestry investments made by the state presented a strong argument. The arguments of the advantages to a state in having its own academy teaching its own practice for its own forests were plain common sense and good business. Rothrock's silviculture was that of the botanists. His great teacher in botanical taxonomy had been Asa Gray, who, although his sympathies and interests in plant study were wide, was first and foremost a taxonomist. DeBary in Europe had been a second Asa Gray to Rothrock, teaching him to carry forward physiological and anatomical laboratory research in plants. Rothrock's interest in forest mycology and pathology may be traced directly to DeBary's teaching and to his own experience as a doctor of medicine. Rothrock was a biologist in plant study, but he had not become a technician in wood products research, a professionally trained forester, or a silviculturist as European foresters understood the term.

Years later Rothrock acknowledged to Fernow that Fernow had come to forestry in America as a "Godsend" and done more than anyone to develop a great public interest. Working plans, Fernow insisted, should not be first concerned with reduction of the forest cut but with reproduction of the crops by skillful methods. Working plans should not be aimed to take a dollar today in preference to two dollars tomorrow. Rothrock was thoroughly in sympathy with this point of view. Some magnificent secondary forests in Pennsylvania today are the best proof of this principle. Fernow's views of forestry were more rounded and complete. He had arisen in the service of the federal government, while Rothrock had served a state.

Pennsylvanians steadfastly kept their faith in Fernow. John Birkinbine, president of the Pennsylvania Forestry Association, in an editorial in *Forest Leaves* in June 1898,[100] commented, "Every friend of forestry will be gratified to learn of the selection of Mr. B. E. Fernow as the head of the forestry school being established in connection with the Cornell University. . . . We all recognize that Mr. Fernow has made the Division of Forestry what it now is. . . ."

[100] VI, 9, p. 146.

CHAPTER VI

Progress in Forestry Education: Cornell, Yale, Biltmore

IN HIS 1892 report of the division of forestry Fernow had indicated the unsatisfactory forestry conditions in the United States. "The ownership of the forest area," he said, "is for the most part in the hands of private individuals. The policy for the single States of the United States to own lands, except for building, etc., and for eventual disposal, has not been germane to the spirit of the institutions of the country. School lands, indemnity lands, swamp lands, and other lands which the General Government has given to the States, or which they have owned otherwise, have never been held for an income, except by their sale. The State of New York seems to be the first to make an exception, having set aside an area of nearly 1,000,000 acres in the Adirondack and Catskill mountains as a forest reserve; and a movement to extend this reserve over a larger area—3,000,000 acres, more or less—is strongly advocated. The administration of this reserve is, however, confined to protection without utilization, and forest management in any sense does not as yet exist, although the staff of the three forest commissioners includes, besides a secretary with assistants, a superintendent with assistant, inspectors, and surveyor, eleven foresters, who constitute, in fact, however, only a police force."[1]

Mentioning two attempts known to him of "private enterprise having in view the introduction of forest management," Fernow further observed, "The one in the Adirondacks, contemplated by the Adirondack League Club, in which over 100,000 acres of excellent virgin timber land are to be brought under systematic management, has not yet progressed far enough to speak of it as a fact; the other, begun in the mountains of North Carolina by a rich private owner, lacks, unfortunately, the opportunities of serving the contemplated purpose, namely, to be an object-lesson of the profitableness of forestry. Being applied to a forest area severely culled and away from markets, that might take inferior material, such demonstration can hardly be expected in the near future."

In the following year Fernow's report[2] of forestry advancement in New York was still critical. He mentioned that "New York has passed new legislation having in view the final establishment of a compact State forest and also introducing some methods designed for the utilization of the spruce in the present State forest reserve. This last pro-

[1] On public forestry, p. 313; on private forestry, p. 318.
[2] *Report of Div. of For. for 1893*, p. 325.

vision is faulty in that it is based on the misconception that restriction of the cutting to certain sizes is sufficient to preserve acceptable forest conditions." A group of gentlemen from New York, who proposed to secure the passage of legislation which would restrict lumbermen in the state "from cutting below a certain diameter" had called on him, "as an expert, to tell them what, under proper forestry principles, would be the right diameter to lay down as a law. Great was their astonishment," wrote Fernow later, "when I declared that any diameter which paid best, even down to the size of the little finger, would satisfy the demands of forestry."[3] Fernow insisted that primarily what distinguished the lumberman from the forester was the latter's provision for replacement by nature of her removed timbers. "Continuity is the keynote of forest management by the forester," he said. New York, like Pennsylvania, was to have several governors who would befriend forestry. As late as 1898, Fernow could say:[4]

The State of New York is the first and only State in the Union to have entered upon a definite policy of forest conservation, acknowledging the necessity and duty of the State to assume the protection of its most important watershed and of the forest cover thereon. . . . Such a policy, now firmly established, presents a number of problems. . . . The main and fundamental one, the problem of ownership, has been practically settled by various acts of the Legislature, namely, in 1883, when the State determined to retain the forest lands which it then owned; in 1885, when it placed them in the care and custody of a Forest Commission; in 1890, when the first act authorizing the purchase of additional lands was signed by a democratic governor, with the memorandum affixed that the act was good but inadequate; and finally in 1897, when the Legislature and a republican governor created The Forest Preserve Board, giving it authority to acquire for the State, by purchase or otherwise, control of the entire region within an outline comprising three million acres more or less, or as much thereof as might appear desirable. The acquisition of lands has proceeded cautiously and slowly. . . . The next problem is that of the administration of the property. . . . At first a forest commission of three unpaid commissioners was charged with this duty of the "care, custody, control and superintendence of the forest preserve," and the law declared that "it shall be the duty of the Commission to maintain and protect the forests now on the forest preserve, and to promote as far as practicable the further growth of forests thereon"; also, to "have charge of the public interests of the State with regard to forests and tree planting, and especially with reference to forest fires in every part of the State."

In 1893 the number of the Commissioners was increased to five, with additional powers as to acquisition and lease of lands, and especially the specific power, with certain restrictions, "to sell the standing spruce, tamarack and poplar timber, the fallen timber and the timber injured by blight or fire." Another change was made in 1895, when an amalgamation of fisheries and game interests with the forestry interests was provided and the [five] Commissioners of Fisheries, Game and Forests were installed. . . .

[3] B. E. Fernow (ed.), "Forestry," *Recreation*, 1903-1904, p. 151.

[4] "Adirondack Forest Problems," *Report of N.Y. State Fisheries, Game and Forest Commission*, 1898, also printed separately, pp. 3ff. See also *Forestry Investigations of the U.S.D.A., 1877-1898*, pp. 172-177.

The first legislation, instituting the Forest Commission, had in view the application of forestry methods to the management of the property; but the Commission failed to devise such technical management, and the people, as is well known, by constitutional amendment restricted the activities of the Commission by forbidding the cutting of trees on State lands, and thereby ruling out a large share of forestry work. Knowing the history of this amendment we can assert that it was intended, not to establish a policy of non-use, and to exclude forever the application of such forestry work as requires the use of the ax, but rather to delay it until conditions should be more favorable for the employment of technical forestry management. . . .

In other words, the intention of much debated Article VII, section 7 (now Article XIV, section 1), of the New York constitution was to allow sufficient time to elapse to permit the education and training of foresters. Some said that the amendment expressed a distrust of members of the state commission. Others said that it was the production of sentimentalists interested first in preserving the scenic beauty of the Adirondack forests. Fernow, knowing the amendment's history, repudiated such opinions. As the years went by and the amendment was interpreted and reinterpreted by the courts, he pointed out that the state was depriving itself of a large revenue which might be realized through forest utilization and that the progress of forestry in the state was being seriously impeded.

At the summer meeting of the American Forestry Association held in conjunction with the American Association for the Advancement of Science on September 4-5, 1895, Judge Warren Higley and Colonel Fox spoke on the subjects of the Adirondack preserve and forestry in New York. Both men in years before had spoken on these subjects to the association. Now Judge Higley believed the state policy to be "to buy and maintain these forests without the aid of revenue from the sale of forest products," and Colonel Fox, confessing disappointment since the "forests could undoubtedly be improved by cutting," added that "a rational system of forestry must be held in abeyance for the present." The constitutional convention had spoken for the state and said that no timber on lands owned or acquired by the state could be cut, dead or alive, much less lumbered and sold for a profit. Fernow later raised the question whether, since the amendment sought to preserve the forest in its natural state, forest planting was outlawed. Reforestation, however, was found to be within the purview of the amendment. New York found itself in the anomalous position of having a forest commission and a forest preserve board, appropriations aggregating millions for land acquisition,[5] and comparatively no forest management which might be practiced on its lands owned or acquired.

In 1897 *Garden and Forest*[6] joined in the protests of forestry inter-

[5] Gurth Whipple in *A History of Half a Century of the Management of the Natural Resources of the Empire State*, p. 189, says that, during 1895-1900, two large appropriations totaling $1,600,000 were made for acquisition of land.

[6] 468, Feb. 10, 1867, p. 52.

ests against the effect of the New York constitutional enactment. Referring to a preliminary report made the year before by the state's commissioners of fisheries, game and forests, the publication joined the outcry against letting the state preserve "go to waste" when it might provide "a source of revenue and still more an instructive example of what [could] be done under scientific management." The reservation "should be put under the charge of skilled professional foresters to make it a model for our New World conditions, and be an object lesson in forest economy for the whole country." The comment charged that the framers of the constitutional provision which forbade the use of the axe in any of the "lands of the state, now owned or hereafter acquired, constituting the forest preserve," knew of no such thing "as rational or conservative forestry, or if they did know it, they felt that the people of this state were too ignorant to organize and develop any system of forest practice in an intelligent and scientific way, or that they were too corrupt to administer such a trust without official knavery." Since purchases of large additional wooded areas were contemplated, it was suggested by the commissioners led by Colonel Fox that a sum should be appropriated to acquire a tract of virgin forest in the Adirondacks to be used as an experiment station where the practicability of scientific forestry might be demonstrated. "We hardly see how this can be accomplished under the constitution," observed *Garden and Forest*, "in which it is stated that this forest preserve shall be forever kept as wild forest." It was suggested that forest land not part of the preserve and not subject to the constitutional exaction, be purchased. The commissioners believed that to establish such a demonstration forest would bring about the long advocated establishment of a forest academy.

New York's forest policy, inaugurated formally in 1885 by legislation written by Fernow when the state owned between seven and eight hundred thousand acres of forest lands, was to embrace within twenty-five years two preserves with an estimated acreage of more than a million and a half acres. Created from scattered portions of sixteen forest counties, the forest preserve has consisted of two preserves, the Adirondack preserve (since described as "the state owned land within the Adirondack park"[7]) of fourteen counties, and the Catskill preserve of two counties.[8] On April 1, 1909, the Adirondack preserve was esti-

[7] Ralph S. Hosmer, "Fifty Years of Conservation," *Forest Leaves* XXV, 6, April 1935, pp. 65-66, in which the Adirondack Forest Preserve as of that time was given as 2,145,733 acres and the Catskill Forest Preserve as 223,491 acres. C. R. Pettis, "Forest Provisions of the N.Y. State Constitution," *Forestry Quarterly* XIV, 1, March 1916, pp. 51ff., estimated that the State Forest Preserve increased in twenty years from 720,744 acres to "more than 1,800,000 acres."

[8] Gurth Whipple, *op. cit.*, pp. 20-64.

mated[9] at 1,529,354 acres and the Catskill preserve at 106,473 acres.[10] During those years more than three and a half million dollars were expended by the state for these purposes. Not all the lands added by way of purchase were acquired by fee simple title sales. Almost eight hundred thousand acres were possessed by original ownership or were acquired by tax title purchases, resales of bonded lands, or other methods of title acquisition. Much the same methods were pursued by Pennsylvania and other states to acquire lands for forest reservation purposes. If the lands were not originally owned by the state, the lands were acquired by tax forfeiture or outright purchase. The differences were principally in the sums of money paid.

At the Washington meeting of the American Forestry Association held December 8, 1897—the year forestry fever was at its height due to President Cleveland's precipitous proclamations and the repercussions in congress over the new national reserves—Fernow in the executive committee report said that "partial State ownership of forest areas [had become] an indispensable part of a State forest policy." This important departure from the original practice of reserving only lands owned by the state was shown by the fact that New York had appropriated one million dollars to increase its holdings in the Adirondacks and that Pennsylvania had authorized the purchase of three 40,000-acre reservations on the watersheds of three river systems, with provision also to increase these holdings.[11]

On December 23 the New York state forest preserve commissioners met to consider their annual report to the legislature. They had spent an appropriation of a million dollars,[12] and they planned to ask the legislature for another million to continue purchasing during the next year. Among the additions made this year were 18,625 acres bought from W. Seward Webb,[13] 42,000 acres from the Indian River Company, and 23,873 acres from W. W. Durand. During the summer of 1897,[14] at the instance of Dr. Webb, Gifford Pinchot examined Adirondack spruce on the property to acquire knowledge of the laws of growth of the tree. The results of this and other studies were included in an address given before the American Paper and Pulp Association on "The Sustained Yield of Spruce Lands."

In its February 1898 issue,[15] *The Forester* gave space to Governor Black's message to the New York legislature, which recommended that

[9] Letter from A. B. Straugh to Fernow, dated Oct. 11, 1909.

[10] See footnote 7 of this chapter.

[11] *The Forester* IV, 1, Jan. 1898, p. 12.

[12] *ibid.*, p. 7.

[13] Gurth Whipple, *op. cit.*, p. 35, "The William Seward Webb purchase of 75,000 acres, acquired in 1895 by special act of the Legislature, for which $600,000 was agreed to be paid, was the largest single transaction in the history of the Forest Preserve."

[14] *The Forester* IV, 3, March 1898, p. 56.

[15] IV, 2, Feb. 1898, p. 27; IV, 3, March 1898, p. 50; IV, 5, May 1898, p. 95.

since the state already had acquired, or in the interim would acquire, one million acres of forest lands, an experimental forest area should be set apart to study "the proper treatment of the woods." "This is good," commented the journal, "but Governor Black should also have recommended the establishment of a forestry school at the same time, and in connection with this experimental area. . . ." Next month the same publication announced, "The proposition of the Governor of New York, to which we referred in our last issue—namely, to set aside the experimental forest area for the State of New York—has taken definite form by the introduction of a bill in Albany, providing that the Forest Preserve Board use part of the $500,000 to be devoted to additional purchases for the Adirondack Preserve to secure not to exceed 30,000 acres for such experiments." This legislation, which became chapter 122 of the New York laws of 1898, was introduced into the legislature early in February, received the governor's signature the following April, and, by the middle of that month, definite organizational procedures pursuant to its provisions to establish a college of forestry in connection with Cornell University were instituted.

Colonel Fox, Fernow has indicated,[16] proposed the idea of a demonstration forest tract in the Adirondacks. At first it was not proposed as a college venture. Ignorance of what forest management really implied, Fox believed, was the chief reason why the unwise timber-cutting limitation on public forest lands had been written into the New York constitution. Purchase lands outside of the Adirondack Preserve, *Garden and Forest* suggested, basing its article on the reports of the commissioners of fisheries, game and forests.[17] Such lands might not be subject to the constitutional prohibition, and assuredly they would provide the long-needed forestry object lesson. Colonel Fox's proposal, presented elaborately in reports of 1896 and 1897, "would probably have passed without attention like so many other good things in such reports but for a small incident," Fernow wrote:[18]

A dealer in Adirondack real estate . . . came into Colonel Fox's office while he was occupied with his part of this report and the Colonel read the pertinent passages to the dealer. The dealer pooh-poohed the idea but, seeing the possibility of a deal, returned after a while to ask what kind of a tract would be needed, and having been informed, is said to have secured an option on the specified tract. He then saw the Governor and warmed up his interest in such a demonstration. Governor Black soon after went on a fishing trip in the Adirondacks in the company of Colonel [Charles Spencer] Francis [later ambassador to Austria-Hungary]. In the course of their conversations the Governor mentioned the proposition, but expressed the fear that politics

16 "The Intimate History of the Rise and Fall of the New York College of Forestry at Cornell University," unpublished manuscript by Fernow found among his papers.

17 Gurth Whipple, *op. cit.*, p. 189, says that during the period 1895-1900 Colonel Fox "was appointed Engineer, and also given charge of that part of game administration related to deer. . . ." But it seems undoubted that he remained "known as superintendent of forests" until 1909. See Ralph S. Hosmer's study of Fox, *op. cit.*, p. 220.

18 "Intimate History of the College of Forestry etc."

would interfere with carrying it out to a successful issue. To avoid this, Colonel Francis, who was then on the Board of Trustees of Cornell University, suggested that the university might be charged with conducting the experiment. President Schurman was called into consultation and, I believe, it was he who suggested that a College of Forestry be instituted at the university to carry on the demonstration. He then called upon the writer . . . to elaborate a scheme for such a college. Bills were introduced in the State Legislature in which, it is understood, the legal provisions were supervised by the Governor himself and the technical provisions were formulated by the writer. The bills enacted, the writer was invited to become Dean and Director and to organize the college and inaugurate the demonstration. . . .

On March 31, 1898, Fernow addressed a communication to President Schurman and applied for the position as director of the college. It seems that the letter was written as a matter of form. On the next day, April 1, the board of trustees of Cornell University accepted the provisions of the state law which authorized the creation of the New York State College of Forestry and an experimental forest. During the spring, probably in April, President Schurman had called at the home of Abram S. Hewitt and consulted him concerning Fernow's fitness for the position as director. Hewitt, at Schurman's request, placed in writing his recommendation of Fernow. "That letter I received before I had made any selection of Dr. Fernow, while I was inquiring from different parties about him," Schurman later disclosed. Schurman received letters of recommendation from Judge Warren Higley, from Professor Johnson of Washington University at St. Louis, who enclosed a letter from Professor Fuertes of the College of Engineering of Cornell University. Dr. Leland O. Howard[19] of Washington also recommended Fernow. On April 16 President Schurman, describing Fernow as by "far the best man in the United States for the directorship and one of the best in the world," announced Fernow's acceptance of the position. Schurman appointed a committee of six to obtain the demonstration area. On May 3 there was held a meeting which was attended by the governor, members of the forest preserve board, and a committee of the trustees of Cornell University. It was decided that a tract should not be finally selected until a joint examination of the several tracts offered or considered had been made by representatives of the board of trustees. Fernow's appointment as director was not to become effective until September. It was decided, however, immediately to employ Fernow to examine the various tracts.[20]

[19] See a study of Howard by Bernard Jaffe, *Outposts of Science*, Simon and Schuster, New York, 1935, pp. 281-316. Howard was well known in Ithaca, having been a student at Cornell and a member of the Ithaca Natural History Society. He was also acquainted with Fernow and his work in Washington. Howard was long connected with the Entomological Division of the U.S.D.A.; and his entomological work, even during his first years of public service, ranked in importance with that of C. V. Riley.

[20] See President Schurman's testimony in *People of the State of New York vs. The Brooklyn Cooperage Company and Cornell University*, p. 468, section 1871, at the office of the Clerk of the Court of Appeals of New York at Albany.

Fernow related:

The first thing to do was to secure the demonstration area. Here the first trouble arose. The purchase price of the 30,000 acres was to come out of the funds provided for the Preserve Board charged with land purchases for the State Reserves, and this Board had the say as to the price of the land. The writer would have selected a virgin township which at that time could have been bought for around $12 per acre, but this the Board vetoed.

An important choice lay between two other tracts. "The Blue Mountain tract, located in the center of the mountains, had been turned down by the writer on account of its inaccessibility. On complaint of the owner at the first examination, made entirely without guidance, that the examination had not covered the whole tract, a second examination was arranged in company with Colonel Fox and 'the Commodore,' the owner's agent. The examination did not change the opinion of the writer, although, if it had done so, he might have secured free of charge a valuable cottage site on one of the beautiful lakes."

The Blue Mountain tract was situated in Hamilton County. On June 9 President Schurman announced that Fernow had completed an inspection of Adirondack forest lands situated in three townships of Franklin County and two townships in Hamilton County. A Franklin County tract was reported unfavorably. The Hamilton County tract was placed second on the list. Township 26, excepting Follensby Pond tract, with enough of the adjacent property to bring it up to 30,000 acres, was recommended. That a second examination of some of the properties had to be made did not alter Fernow's opinion, who reported again in August. By letter of November 14, Colonel Fox as superintendent of forests informed President Schurman that the forest preserve board at a meeting on October 24 had passed a resolution directing the purchase of lands offered by the Santa Clara Lumber Company. This "Hobson's choice," as Fernow called it, made the university the owner of 30,000 acres of land located in Franklin County. It consisted of the west half of Township 23, with a small parcel of 300 acres in the southeast corner of the township, and so much of Townships 26 and 27 east of the Raquette River as was necessary to make up the complete acreage.

Tupper Lake, a village of two railroad terminals, was situated three miles from the western boundary of the college forest. Road and river facilities were available. At the center of the forest was located the village of Axton. To the north was the region of Wawbeek and Upper Saranac Lake. To the northeast was Ampersand and to the east Ampersand Peak. To the northeast was Lower Saranac Lake with its steamboat landing, and to the east Middle Saranac Lake. The site selected for the college forest was both scenic and practical. Favored with high elevations, slopes "of varying aspect," with valleys and river bottoms, one half consisted of virgin timber and one half of culled over pine and spruce lands. Part of the tract was burned over.

"The tract had some points to its credit," said Fernow. "Although mostly lumbered for pine and spruce, it contained still virgin areas, and altogether, represented a variety of Adirondack conditions, thus making it possible to demonstrate a variety of sylvicultural methods. It was within reasonable distance of railroad connection at Tupper Lake, an industrial center, and was in large part isolated from tourists' resorts, and tourists' travel. There were also buildings that could be readily adapted for use of the college."[21]

Fernow, in his report of the college dated January 15, 1899, said:

A water power of eighty feet fall, in which a quarter interest goes with the property, may offer opportunity for establishing small wood manufactures to use up inferior wood materials usually wasted. The property has been secured at a very reasonable price [$165,000] and appears desirable in every respect for the purpose which it is to serve. As soon as the property is turned over to the College and the weather permits, it is proposed to make a forest survey and ascertain the amount of timber standing and the annual growth, as a basis for working plans and to determine the amount of material which should be cut annually. For this purpose a small amount of the original appropriation of $10,000 has been reserved. Active operations in laying out roads, in establishing nurseries and beginning logging operations will have to wait until other appropriations become available.

At that time, from the $10,000 appropriation for the quarter year, there was an unspent balance of $5,644.33.

Under chapter 122 of the New York laws of 1898, the "title, possession, management, and control" of the Adirondack experimental forestry tract was vested in the board of trustees of Cornell University for a period of thirty years, at the expiration of which time the property was to be "conveyed to the people of the State of New York . . . without further price or consideration therefor, and the same" thereupon was to "be and become a part of the forest preserve. . . ." The negotiation of the purchase terms, the drafting of the deed from the Santa Clara Lumber Company to the university, and every matter pertaining to the college forest, excepting the selection of the site by Fernow, was performed by the forest preserve board. Although the date of the deed conveying the property read December 21, 1898, the trustees did not actually get possession of the tract until March 1, 1899. At that time the trustees began to exercise a voice in the demonstration.

Executive matters relating to the college forest took much of Fernow's time during the first year of the school's operation. The larger task of getting the school started on the campus at Ithaca was even more difficult. Fernow was quartered in Morrill Hall, the first of the university buildings, which was named for the author of the most im-

[21] "Intimate History of the College of Forestry etc."

portant law in the agricultural history of the United States, the Morrill Act of 1862 which granted federal land-grant aid to the nation's state colleges of agriculture and mechanic arts. True to the conceptions of its founders, the university gave instruction in the classics as well as the arts and sciences. On the campus was a state-supported veterinary college and an unexcelled college of engineering. The state supported one of its agricultural experiment stations there. There was also special meteorological work. The department of agriculture had not yet been made over into the New York State College of Agriculture, although the state in appropriating a large sum of money to build a dairy industry building presumably had settled a policy of making Cornell University its center of agricultural education. The entire university had grown so rapidly that it had outgrown its building facilities. The university treasurer in charge of room assignments told Fernow that he was unable to find room space for the "newcomer," the New York State College of Forestry. Fernow himself had to locate empty room space. Quarters were at first shared with the department of political economy and Sibley college of engineering. In 1899, however, spread over three buildings, the facilities were "somewhat improved." Roth was given a room for his wood laboratory. Fernow was allowed new, though still cramped, quarters. A small basement room housed demonstration material and collections. The need of "convenient and permanent lecture and laboratory rooms" was plain from the beginning, and as soon as he was convinced that the college was fairly well established, Fernow began to ask for a building worthy of the Empire State, of two stories and a basement, and not to exceed $50,000 in cost. Professional forestry education in the United States, nevertheless, began at ten o'clock on the morning of September 22 or 23, 1898, in a classroom located in Morrill Hall. Fernow went promptly to the lecturer's desk and, gazing pleasantly at his small group of students, said: "You are the first students of silviculture in America; I congratulate you."

In September 1898 the New York State College of Forestry issued its first bulletin, "Aims and Methods of the College of Forestry," which was published both as a reprint and in *Science*.[22] *Forest Leaves* quoted portions from the bulletin in its article on the college and also published an extract from the *Railroad Gazette* which approved the location of the demonstration forest near the Saranac Lake region.[23] The forest, said the article, had "navigable water connection with the railroad, and its average distance from the Adirondack Division of the New York Central and Hudson River Railroad [was] about eight miles." The *Gazette* regarded this as very important since it was "a fixed fact that no successful hardwood lumbering [could] be done without cheap transpor-

[22] New series, VII, 198, Oct. 14, 1898, pp. 494-501.
[23] *Forest Leaves* VI, 12, Dec. 1898, pp. 204-206; VII, 3, June 1899, p. 40.

tation. . . . It is generally true that the birch, beech, maple and black cherry in the Adirondacks cannot now be profitably taken out unless the teams can make more than one trip a day. Throughout this tract there is a short team haul to water, where flatboats can take the logs to the railroad. . . . The chances of success in this have nothing to do with the case. The tie-timber, the cabinet woods, as well as the soft woods, are disappearing from this country, and unless the cuttings can be at least partially replaced by new growth, there is a great problem surely but slowly looming up; one which seriously affects the economic condition of many industries." The *Gazette* described the forest as "an experiment station" at which Fernow would have charge of "the cutting, marketing, and subsequent planting of the timber trees." So enthused was this leading journal over this "experiment of scientific forestry" that it believed Fernow's venture to be "the first trial ever made in this country to determine the commerical results of cultivating timber under conditions which will cause the results obtained to be of general practical value. In saying this we are not unmindful of Mr. Gifford Pinchot's interesting development of the Biltmore property in North Carolina, and of his valuable report upon it, but the conditions under which that development has been made were special and not general. . . ."

At the August meeting of the American Forestry Association held at Boston in 1898 Fernow had read a paper on the college and its plans. This was published by *The Forester*[24] and formed the basis of the bulletin on the college's aims and methods. The bulletin announced that three teachers of forestry were provided. Fernow of course was one. The organization of the forestry school, he said, "was effected by calling in the services of two assistants, Mr. F. Roth who had added to his practical experience in woods and mills [by devoting] eight years to the timber physics investigation in the United States Division of Forestry and by assiduous reading had acquired the theoretical knowledge of forestry. Dr. John Gifford had been in charge of the forestry work of the New Jersey Geological Survey."[25] Through the generosity of Gifford who had given land typical of the famous "pine barrens," near May's Landing, New Jersey's first forest reservation, the state's agricultural experiment station was enabled to investigate profitable forestry methods by a series of regional tests. Gifford, after organizing forestry as a movement in New Jersey, had gone to Europe to study. "Soon after I received my doctor's title in forestry in Munich," he wrote, "I received a letter from Fernow saying that he had been appointed head of the New York College of Forestry at Cornell University and that together with my old friend Roth he invited me to join the faculty.

[24] IV, 9, Sept. 1898, pp. 185-192.
[25] "Intimate History of the College of Forestry etc."

The joy and distinction of an academic career appealed to me, so I gladly accepted."[26]

Fernow announced in the bulletin on aims and methods that a four years' course leading to the degree Bachelor in the Science of Forestry (later changed to the degree Forest Engineer) was established.[27] "In this course," he said, "the first two years are entirely given up to studies of the fundamental sciences, while forestry subjects and supplemental studies are left for the last two years. . . . The required fundamental and supplemental courses comprise altogether about 1,270 hours, to which 450 hours' supplemental work are added as elective but desirable, while the forestry branches represent about 600 hours, of which 130 are optional, making an average of about 17 hours per week of required and elective work." Botany, chemistry, geology, and the allied sciences constituted the fundamental branches. Considerable time, however, was given to mathematics, entomology, political economy, and engineering, especially map-making and road building. Courses in fish culture and game preservation were contemplated. An attempt was made to introduce a course on business law taught by a member of the law school's faculty, but a teacher was not available at that time.

Immediately the director arranged for ample library facilities. Leading German, French, and English forestry journals, some periodicals of the lumber trade, and other valuable reading matter were made accessible to students at the forestry school. More than "five hundred numbers" of books and articles on forestry and kindred sciences, "comprising the leading works in English, French, and German languages," Fernow said, were placed in the university library and stamped as the property of the New York State College of Forestry.

During the first term Roth gave courses in timber physics which, curiously enough, were attended by ten students of engineering and one forestry student. Roth was called on to lecture three times on "Wood as a Material of Construction" to a large junior class in Sibley college of engineering. To a "Seminary" in marine engineering he lectured on the "Fireproofing of Wood." To another Sibley college class he lectured on the "Strength of Wood and Timber Testing," and to a botanical seminar he lectured on fungous diseases of wood. By the second year the college of architecture had made Roth's course in timber physics required for all students. The college of agriculture at the same time made Gifford's course in silviculture compulsory.

On November 8, 1898, Roth told Erwin F. Smith: ". . . I feel quite at home here, have a class of 13 in timber study this term and next,

[26] Gifford's "Reminiscences," unpublished; see also *The Forester* IV, 6, June 1898, p. 116.

[27] pp. 5-8. See Fernow et al., "The Training of Professional Foresters in America," a symposium in *The Forester* V, 5, May 1899, pp. 103ff.

GIFFORD PINCHOT

HENRY SOLON GRAVES

CLIFTON DURAND HOWE

FILIBERT ROTH

SAMUEL J. RECORD

forest mensuration next term and spring, besides two other courses, lecture to 100-150 engineers on wood; gave lect[ure] on fireproofing; study fungi (systematic but also morphological) especially wood destroyers, have nice excursions and generally good times. Fell in with a good set here and have made many pleasant acquaintances. Feel a new man, feel like work, and feel that my few words are not to be pocketed in unread yearbooks; have living ears, interested eyes to talk to and show. In spite of lateness in starting, there are about 35 students working toward forestry, and no doubt there will be more next year. As you notice Fernow set his requirements high, which perhaps he may in part alter." Inadequate laboratory facilities and financing held back the new timber physics work; but development of the demonstration area required Roth more. That Roth alone was qualified to teach timber physics was attested by the fact that when later he returned to federal forestry work in Washington, Fernow said, "In certain directions, it will be impossible to replace him, notably in the line of timber physics, in which subject he is the foremost man in the country." The vacancy was filled by a student of Roth and Fernow, Judson F. Clark,[28] who took charge of the biological course, including timber physics, dendrology, forest mensuration, and silviculture.

Fernow's bulletin on aims and methods was about equally divided between matters of the school and the demonstration forest at Axton. As early as 1898, therefore, he announced their silvicultural policy:

> It is to be the endeavor to change from the present condition of hardwoods with an admixture of spruce to spruce with an admixture of hardwoods, the admixture being considered desirable for various reasons, among which specially counts the danger to which the shallow-rooted spruce is exposed from winds, which is alleviated by association with other species.
>
> To carry out this policy it is evident the hardwoods must be numerically reduced, the conditions for the reproduction of spruce made favorable and the young growth of spruce favored by subduing its competitors—operations which require the highest skill of the silviculturist. . . .

The college forest's management was to be for spruce, "the most valuable timber, with the other conifers desirable concomitants, the hardwoods, although now in preponderance, being less readily marketable." Spruce for paper pulp promised good markets, since few substitutes of a desirable character were then known.

Reforestation by planting, at first, was merely to supplement the several management methods which would be applied in various portions of the college forest. Fernow said:

> Cutting away the old growth and planting a new crop just as wanted appears the simplest system. Yet, aside from other flaws which adhere to this

[28] Clark, a specialist in plant physiology and forestry, spent six months in "practical forestry studies in Germany" before taking up his work. See the *Fourth Annual Report of the N.Y. State College of Forestry for 1901*, p. 7.

method, it would under our conditions of labor be too expensive to employ. Planting is only to be resorted to on such areas as are now denuded or devoid of desirable species, or else for demonstration of methods and results. In such cases other species adapted to the locality and promising both silvicultural and financial success, among which especially is the white pine, would be favored.

The other class of management for reproduction, which depends upon natural seeding from the trees on or near the area to be reproduced, offers several methods. Among these the method of selection in which mature trees here and there are selected through the forest, or certain parts of it, resembles most the lumberman's present method, except that he is influenced only by the marketableness of his trees, while the forester keeps foremost the benefit to the young growth that is left. This method is especially adapted to those portions which are situated on the high elevations, crags and heads and wherever it is dangerous to expose the soil. Modifications of this system, for instance, one in which groups of trees are removed and the reproduction, therefore, is secured by clumps rather than by simple individuals, may be acceptable in other parts of the property, and finally for the sake of demonstration all other systems of management, such as the strip system, the nurse-tree system etc., may be practiced on smaller or larger areas.

Fernow realized from the start that the demonstration area was not to be merely a business forest, nor a park or luxury forest, nor a fish and game preserve, nor a forest nursery. It was to be all of these, although the aesthetic phase, and most certainly the amusement phase, were to be secondary. The forest was to produce, harvest, and reproduce wood crops and earn a self-supporting revenue. Its statutory dedication made it an area to demonstrate the advantages and methods of sound forest management. It was to be an experimental area for the whole Adirondack forest preserve. Above all, it was to be an educational project as part of the New York State College of Forestry.

In March 1899 Roth went for the first time to the experimental forest. He returned to Ithaca and in April went again to the college tract to remain until autumn. Roth became the forest's manager. He began to lay out forty-acre tracts and to start plantations which would include fifty thousand trees.

December 20, 1899, by letter, Roth told Erwin F. Smith of the year's progress at Axton and the beginning of some management problems in the college forest. 1899 was the year that Fernow accompanied the Harriman expedition to Alaska, an honor we will further discuss later, and during his absence Roth served in his place. Roth's letter to Smith was a concise summary of important advancements made, but it was tinged with a suggestion of impending difficulties: "We are at work," Roth wrote, "our college has about 16 regulars. I had two classes this fall studying wood (32 students in all). Our work in the forest is progressing. My summer in the hills was a hard one, but a very instructive one. We started a seed bed, nursery, set out 67,000 trees (pine and spruce), made quite a survey of the land, dividing the one half into 40 acre tracts, the other by contour lines into irregular bodies, built and repaired camps and are now cutting timber, chiefly firewood on burned-over ground which we mean to re-stock. Dr. Fernow left the bus[iness] of starting things to me and went to Alaska, as you know, but returned just in time to get a smell of the fires we had and to find what it was to stop and how difficult to squelch these things. Had quite a bit of trouble, quite a number from lightning. Shall go up in April and stay till June. Hope to go to Europe if I can. . . ."

Roth did not go to Europe. His valuable services in the college forest were too much needed. He was the real founder of the famous nurseries at Axton. Guiding the school's destinies through its second year and managing the forest property redounded greatly to his credit. Fernow always retained control and direction of the logging operations and the responsibility for policy was his. The fact that, for years after the school was discontinued and the college work in the experimental forest surrendered, an unexpended working capital or fund of something like $8,000 plus a valuable investment of merchantable timber, especially spruce, were available demonstrated Fernow's ability in this direction.

In Fernow's second annual report for the college, he stated the two main considerations held in view when forming the college forest policy: "Two objects, it would appear, were in the mind of the legislature when connecting the management of this forest property with an educational institution, namely, that it serve as a working laboratory for the students of such College, and also that it be so managed as to secure experience, which might be applied to other forest properties and especially to the holdings of the State." He found it "desirable to set apart certain limited portions to be treated solely with reference to the educational object. For instance, it would hardly be considered desirable in the Adirondacks to rely upon coppice management. Yet for demonstration purposes small areas may be treated under such a system. Or, thinnings in young woods and other silvicultural operations may be instituted where, under present business conditions, practical considerations would exclude them. The work required in these special demonstration areas will be performed as much as possible by the students themselves, under the direction of the professors, as part of their practical education during the spring terms, or at other times. As to the second object, namely to secure experience that may serve other forest owners and especially the state in its Adirondack Reserve, the problem may be formulated as follows: to show how a wild woods in the Adirondacks may be treated, cut and utilized, not only without impairing but actually improving the productive capacity, changing it into a more useful and better investment for the future, into a continually revenue-producing civilized forest."

The selection system was first applied, and in portions of the forest where no logging operations took place no change in silvicultural procedure was ever made. When in 1899, however, Fernow began to plan to change *within the logging areas* to a policy of removing gradually all standing timber including hardwoods of marketable value and, where seed trees and natural reproduction would not replace a valuable forest, to replant the clear cut areas with a valuable conifer growth, he did this more because in his opinion as a forester this policy would more effectively enable the management to comply with the legislature's directives and at the same time realize the objectives of serving the state educationally and create in from fifteen to thirty years a valuable forest of sustained yield. This silvicultural method, known as the clear cutting and replanting system, was, moreover, to be supplemented by demonstrations of other silvicultural methods: the storage forest so-called, the shelterwood system, coppice management; we will see that Fernow had in mind demonstrations of about thirty silvicultural systems. Almost half of the completely stripped acreage, Fernow estimated, would remain covered by a natural growth. He planned to replant, systematically, at appropriate intervals, over many years, and in accordance with needs, the balance of the cleared areas with tree stock from the seed beds and nurseries. In 1899, however, planting was still more or less confined to special areas, largely due to the cost and difficulty of importing material. The college was to train foresters for private consulting work and for government service: and in a direct and real sense was to serve the State of New York by ascertaining from scientific experiments and demonstrations what recommendations most efficiently might be applied in managing its forest properties.[29]

Nothing analogous to the Cornell forest demonstration had yet appeared on the forestry scene in America. It was a pioneering venture in every sense, and still occupies a unique place in the history of forestry in America. Perhaps the chief criticism today it that it attempted too much. Perhaps the American public was not yet prepared and failed to grasp the true import of the educational intention. Surely the venture did much to promote forestry education and showed why it was so much needed. The last episodes of the college forest experiment took place almost a decade after the college's active management had ceased. This fact, however, does not lessen the significance of the venture, and what was accomplished for forestry during the years of college management, because the reasons for the discontinuance were distinguishable from the main educational objectives. It is easier at times to magnify fault than to discern right. Almost before Fernow had settled in 1899 on his

[29] See the testimony of Fernow and Roth in *People of the State of New York versus Brooklyn Cooperage Company, loc. cit.*

forest management policy, criticism began to be directed toward the college forest.

During this year it became necessary to decide the silvicultural method to be generally applied when full logging operations would get under way. Fernow favored and announced that a forest management for spruce and pine most readily appealed to good business sense. Marketing these species, to be floated on navigable streams, was less difficult than marketing the hardwoods, for the reasons the *Railroad Gazette* had presented in its article on the forest. Nevertheless Fernow set about to find a way to use and market the hardwoods, to introduce a management policy which would embrace both soft and hard woods, and at the same time to employ conservative lumbering practices and to utilize all the forest's productions and eliminate forest waste.

No criticism attaches to those foresters employed by owners of private forests within the Adirondack forest preserve area, or limited otherwise by such special circumstances as lack of adequate water, rail, or road facilities from forest to market, who recommended a practice which logged the softwoods to a prescribed diameter and applied conservative lumbering methods to the hardwoods. Enough seed trees of the softwoods were left to allow for natural reproduction. The policy was so formed as to provide that at a future time a return could be made to the region for another cutting. When the merit of this silvicultural policy in its application to all Adirondack forest regions, including the college forest, became a subject of controversy in *People of the State of New York versus Brooklyn Cooperage Company*, the claim being that Fernow should never have changed from the selection management method to the clear cutting and replanting policy within logging areas. Charles S. Chapman, expert witness for the state in this legal action and at the time with the United States forest service, described the selection method applied on other Adirondack and privately owned areas thus:

> The system that was followed was to cut out the spruce to a diameter limit of ten inches, market that and leave the hardwoods, for the reason they were not readily marketable, with a view to reproducing spruce from the seed trees that were left and to leaving the smaller trees to come on and form a part of the next crop with the idea [of] cutting over the land again for a second crop after a given number of years. That was devised by Gifford Pinchot and Professor Graves. . . . The plan of selection was devised and begun on the Whitney and Webb tracts about 1898 and 1899. 1899 was the time that the report of Professor Graves was published on that: I think the plan was started directly after that. . . .[80]

The value of the policy could not be tested on state-owned land of the Adirondack forest preserve because of the constitutional amendment

[80] *ibid.*, folios 1994, 2026, 2035, 2104.

which prohibited cutting. Forestry practice on privately owned lands centered on three properties, that of Dr. W. Seward Webb at Ne-ha-sa-ne Park, of W. C. Whitney at Long Lake, and that owned by the Delaware and Hudson Railroad, a property later referred to as having similar conditions to the college forest. During the first half of the year 1899, Gifford Pinchot's work on *The Adirondack Spruce* was reviewed by prominent forestry journals. Not always, but many times during these years, the lack of forestry education in this country could be seen in the amount of attention and space given to diameter-limit recommendations, a practice which obtained more among lumbermen than foresters. Far more important from the forestry standpoint was the amount of work begun in practical assistance to farmers, lumbermen, and others. In his article "Progress in Forestry in the United States," published in the *Yearbook of the U.S.D.A.*,[31] Pinchot quoted an extract from his annual report for that year which was reviewed by *The Forester* in January 1900. Over the nation a vast amount of work was being done by the division, which was now composed of four principal sections: working plans superintended by Henry S. Graves, economic tree planting by James W. Toumey, special investigations, and office work. The report for the year 1899 said in part:

During the year applications were received from 123 owners in 35 States for the management of 1,513,592 acres. Of these applications, 48 were for large tracts covering together 1,506,215 acres, the remainder being for wood lots.

Personal attention on the ground was given to 41 tracts, covering about 400,000 acres in 19 States. The contribution of private owners to the expenses of this work was about $3,000.

It was found possible for the owners of a majority of these tracts to carry out the working plans without personal assistance, but 15 of them required the active participation of the Division. On two of the latter, comprising 108,000 acres, the working plans were put into execution early in the year, and the first year's work has been successfully completed. The second year's work is being pursued under very favorable conditions.

As a result of a calculation, based on exact measurements, of the amount of lumber wasted by the prevailing practice of cutting high spruce stumps in the Adirondacks, there has been a decided change for the better on certain tracts, and at the same time a great reduction in the amount of young spruce cut for road building has been brought about. These are important changes.

In connection with the preparation of the working plans for the two large tracts in the Adirondacks, a special study has been made of the growth and production of the spruce on the eastern side of the mountains and of birch and maple on the western slope.

Of the total amount of land submitted for working plans, about 1,200,000 acres have not yet been examined. These tracts will be considered during the ensuing year. . . ."

That year saw publication of Graves' important bulletin XXVI, "Prac-

[31] 1899, pp. 293-306, quotation at p. 302.

tical Forestry in the Adirondacks." In the *Yearbook of the U.S.D.A.*[32] there also appeared his study, "The Practice of Forestry by Private Owners," in which, distinguishing the division's conservative lumbering recommendations, he described the practice followed on the Webb and Whitney tracts. "Not only is there a diameter limit for the cutting," he said, "but all trees are marked to be cut, and seed trees above the specified size are left when necessary." Eight rules for the lumbering were set forth, and special precautions were taken to protect against "unnecessary damage to youth growth." All merchantable logs "as large as 6 inches in diameter at the small end" were to be utilized, and no stumps were to be cut "more than 6 inches higher than the stump is wide." Diameter limits in these connections were construed as guiding diameters aimed toward a light cut of the softwoods. Restrictions were placed on the uses to which spruce might be placed in the forest; and precautions were taken to eliminate waste.

At the beginning of the century the New York legislature appropriated $2,000 for field studies in the state forest preserve, and the fisheries, game and forest commission requested the United States division of forestry to examine its lands and submit forest management recommendations. This action was highly significant because it marked the beginning of cooperative studies between the state and national governments. Ralph Sheldon Hosmer and Eugene S. Bruce were placed in charge of the preliminary field work which began in June 1900 and continued until 1901. The working plan called for a study of forest conditions, the lumbering possibilities, the fire problem, and other forestry matters. In 1900 *The Forester* commented: "The investigation of the forest from a forester's point of view is to cover the stand of timber, the reproduction of the most important kinds of trees, and the extent and distribution of the forest types. . . . The study of the possibilities of conservative and business-like lumbering will require a complete familiarity with the conditions of transport by water and rail, with the marketable stand of timber in amount, quality, and distribution, and with the state of the market. . . ."[33] Bulletin 30, "A Forest Working Plan for Township 40 of the New York State Forest Preserve in Hamilton County," was issued recommending the logging of softwoods and conservative lumbering of the mature and overmature hardwoods. The bulletin, issued by the United States division of forestry, aimed to show how forestry methods should be applied in an Adirondack region, especially one served as this one was by the Raquette Lake Railway and by tributaries to a large important lake. The technical forest work directed by Hosmer won commendation. Bruce's analysis of the lumber-

[32] 1899, pp. 415-428, at pp. 420ff.; Gurth Whipple, *op. cit.*, p. 82.

[33] "Forestry for the New York Preserve," *The Forester* VI, 7, July 1900, p. 164; Bulletin 30 is discussed in *ibid.* VI, 10, Oct. 1901, p. 258.

ing possibilities was so well received that he was brought into notice, and a secure career in forestry was his from that time forward. F. H. Newell, hydrographer of the United States geological survey, conducted the examination of the forests in relation to water supply, and in a bulletin he discussed the influence of conservative lumbering on the water supply of the township.

Another working plan was prepared for the region south of Raquette Lake, Townships 5, 6, and 41 in Hamilton County, consisting of about 70,000 acres. It was completed in 1901. This report was published by the New York forest, fish and game commission.[34]

Fernow knew that financial and market considerations, management for sustained yield, incremental growth maintenance, crop continuance, and even-aged rather than many-aged timber stands, often made the selection system the best and perhaps only silvicultural procedure. Other leading scientific management procedures had instances of most appropriate use. Management methods for natural regeneration and artificial reforestation could be combined in a variety of ways. The forester, more than the lumberman, managed more with a view to the young crops; and sometimes conservative lumbering plus adequate provision for forest reproduction was the forester's wisest recommendation. But the Cornell forest was intended to exemplify not only good business methods, not only to demonstrate the leading silvicultural procedures, not only to school foresters to serve private industry as well as governmental agencies, not only to conduct experimental forestry research, but all of these, and very important, to earn a revenue. Chapter 122 of the New York laws of 1898 imposed upon the University and College the obligations to "conduct upon said land such experiments in forestry as it may deem most advantageous to the interests of the state and the advancement of the science of forestry, and may plant, raise, cut and sell timber at such times, of such species and quantities and in such manner, as it may deem best, with a view to obtaining and imparting knowledge concerning the scientific management and use of forests, their regulation and administration, the production, harvesting and reproduction of wood crops and earning a revenue. . . ."

Fernow fully realized that special forestry problems were presented. Furthermore, merely to lumber conservatively, he knew, tended to permit the hardwoods to crowd out the young softwood growth. Fernow knew that to cut clear the hardwoods and to leave enough softwood seed trees to reproduce a secondary growth was not always dependable, unless the ground was "scarified," or other precautionary measures were taken to provide against various contingencies.

In his 1886 report of the division of forestry Fernow had said that

[34] Gurth Whipple, *op. cit.*, p. 82.

the management policy must be fitted to the forest's needs. There was not one, but several, management systems to apply: coppice management for wood production of small dimension including firewood, tan-bark, and charcoal; standard coppice management for small wood and woodlot production in western prairie states; and for timber forests, where the object was to grow mature trees for utilization, the selection method, the regeneration method, management in echelons, and clear cutting and replanting each embraced to greater or less extent scientific procedures to secure effective natural reproduction and reforestation. Depending on differences of management objectives and policy, of varying requirements of forest species, of regional differences in forest soil, climate, and the whole range of environmental factors, each method served proper functions, each had a place, each had advantages. The forester's business was to choose the appropriate method. Fernow was now an educator. On the Cornell tract, he wanted, when facilities permitted, to illustrate these and other methods. But such demonstrations could not be inaugurated at once or even in years. Beginnings were made with the selection method. When logging commenced, his forester's judgment pointed to the wisdom of a policy of clear cutting areas, leaving seed trees for natural reproduction, and, where natural reforestation could or would not occur, or at least could not be depended upon, to supplement with artificial planting, similar to that planting work early started in waste, culled, or burned areas. Planting work and nursery practice, therefore, at first was begun on a limited scale. In 1899-1900 Fernow in New York and Schenck in North Carolina began to import seedlings from foreign sources.[35] Perhaps earlier, Schenck, through nurserymen, had imported materials from foreign lands. The question of the Adirondack forest work, however, was proving to be, how could the most and best spruce and pine be effectively produced at the least expense?

During the first year Fernow sent a circular letter through the university agricultural extension service to the farmers of New York and invited them to improve their woodlot management by securing advice from the college. Many students had to be refused admission to forestry classes, especially Roth's timber physics classes, because of inadequate facilities. To anyone not familiar with the work, it naturally seemed that not much space or equipment would be needed. Forestry was an out-of-door subject, and the college had a huge forest tract in the Adirondacks. Professorial colleagues, however, were cooperative. The professor of political economy, Jeremiah W. Jenks, permitted Fernow to share his lecture room; but the room, not adapted to laboratory work, was not adequate. Not even the laboratory facilities of the department

[35] Facts taken from the correspondence of Fernow and Haven Metcalf, pathologist in charge of the Bureau of Plant Industry, U.S.D.A., Oct. 1916.

of botany were sufficient for forestry laboratory experimentation. Fernow could not gather together at any one place all of his forestry demonstration materials. Liberty Hyde Bailey, the professor of horticulture, offered for plant and soils investigation the use of his department's forcing house. Each year, in report after report, Fernow stressed the school's acute need for more adequate facilities: lecture rooms, laboratories, storage space, apparatus, and materials. On the campus the only satisfactory facility was four acres of ground for nursery work.

As serious as the problem of inadequate facilities was proving to be, the problems in the demonstration area were more serious. What of the topographic survey, the boundary survey, the forest survey, and the timber estimate? When the trustees took possession of the forest a boundary survey by the state engineer still had to be completed. The topographic survey and the forest survey or timber estimate became the school's work. The forest survey was organized in May. The topographic survey was arranged for in June, with the aid of Professors Ogden and Mott of the college of civil engineering. Through the spring and the summer Roth sought to prepare the forest for the school's practical instruction. Sowing and planting in the nursery, making improvement cuttings and thinnings, marking out regeneration cuttings, measuring trees, drawing up yield tables, surveying, laying out roads, subdividing, drafting working plans for limited areas, and a host of other silvicultural operations were planned for the Juniors and Seniors who would be transferred to the forest for the entire spring term. A simple dormitory to house and board students at Axton was to be built. Removal of brush, stock-taking of resources, reconditioning of one hundred acres of farm property—buildings, barns, a store, and post office—and numerous other tasks confronted the management composed of less than half a dozen persons. Supervising the work of ten to thirty-five timber estimators required much time. Before the end of 1899 two serious forest fires had been fought. These were caused by hunters and parties not directly concerned with the forest management. One of twenty-acre extent required "110 labor days and the hauling of water with a team for three days" to subdue. Another required fending four or five miles of frontage.

"The work performed," Fernow summarized in his report of January 15, 1900, "is shown to have consisted, besides the preparatory work of survey and stock-taking, mainly in planting fifty acres of slash, clearing for next year's planting a like amount, establishing a nursery for plant material, containing some 1,500,000 seedlings, building portions of a highway, and opening and making accessible the Wawbeek District, in which operations over 1,000 cords of stove wood and (——) feet of logs have resulted; repairing and painting buildings and building a new camp." The planted material consisted largely of white pine and Norway spruce, with Douglas spruce and Scotch pine.

Seventeen students were enrolled. In addition to the regular forestry courses, a course in fish culture was given by B. W. Everman of the United States fish commission. The zoology department of the university arranged a course under H. D. Reed on the morphology and classification of fishes, birds, and mammals. Cyrus P. Whitney gave a course in timber estimating. Gifford, whose work was primarily silviculture, gave a course in game preservation. W. H. Wetmore presented a short course on marketing the forest crop. There were a number of novel and distinctive features, some of which were used to advantage by other colleges on the Cornell campus.

During the first years the school's staff found their way through a maze of perplexing but not unexpected problems. One entirely unforeseen event, however, presented a serious obstacle. A railroad which was planned to follow "largely the valley of the Raquette River" and to cut south across the college forest and the Adirondack state park had to be abandoned because of a decision of a New York state court. Fernow explained the management's embarrassment in his report:[36]

This projected railroad—the continuation from Tupper Lake of the New York and Ottawa Railroad, proposing to connect at North Creek with the Adirondack Railroad, and making a short line through to eastern ports—has, unfortunately, by the short-sighted policy of the State, enjoined in the Constitution, in not permitting State lands to be granted for such purposes, been prevented from being built, thereby hampering considerably the development of the College Forest. . . .

It is . . . the reduction and removal of the old hardwoods, which alone assures success in the silvicultural program of re-establishing and giving advantage to the conifers. If this program be conceded as correct, then it might appear even good business policy to be satisfied if only the cost of removal of the undesirable material were covered by its sale. To find a market for the hardwoods, minor material as well as logs, is the key to the solution of the silvicultural problem: increase in the proportion of the more valuable spruce and pine.

In hardwoods, at least in the Adirondacks, the proportion of log material is much smaller than that of mere cordwood material, the latter averaging probably more than double in cubic contents of the former. The cordwood market, therefore, . . . is even more important than that for logs.

Under present conditions of means of transportation and in the absence of a local market, neither cordwood nor logs can be sold with the expectation of leaving a margin, unless cheap means of transportation, i.e., direct railroad transportation, can be had.

It had been expected, and the tract was located with that expectation, that the extension of the New York and Ottawa Railroad from Tupper Lake would furnish that opening, but . . . the courts have denied the right of way

[36] "Beginnings of Professional Forestry in the Adirondacks," *First and Second Annual Reports of the Director of the N.Y. State College of Forestry*, Feb. 1900, Ithaca, N.Y., pp. 24, 30; reviewed in *Forest Leaves* VII, 8, April 1900, p. 126.

for a portion of the road, without which it cannot be built, under the constitutional clause forbidding the taking of State lands for such purposes. The necessity, therefore, arises of constructing independently the needed railway tracks to connect with through lines, in order to market the hardwoods. Even then, while logs and the better classes of firewood may be disposed of with a slight margin of profit, the bulk of the latter would remain unsalable and its disposal, the burning of the debris after logging, would entail a disproportionate expense.

The solution of the market question, then, appears in the establishment of manufactures upon the tract, which would utilize all the wood and ship the manufactured article. The most economical use of fuelwood consists in the distillation of the same for acetic acid and wood alcohol. The most economical use of hardwood logs is in the manufacture of staves with modern machinery. . . .

Fernow had calculated the distances of the forest from tidewater. He had taken into account the time element and changes in conditions necessary to make such manufacturing on or near the college forest profitable. He announced, "At present writing, negotiations are pending with responsible parties for the erection of such plants, under contracts which require the furnishing for a term of years of all raw material, contingent upon the ability of the trustees to enter upon such contracts, the contingency being dependent upon the action of the legislature in providing the necessary continuous appropriations for working capital." Fernow in his first annual report had asked that an appropriation of $12,000 be allowed for the college work, and $30,000 for the demonstration area. Now he asked for more.

In his second report he stated his silvicultural policy, "The aim and business policy . . . of the management should be within the thirty years, or sooner, as quickly as possible, to have cut all the old growth, or nearly so, giving chance for the volunteer young growth, and reproducing a crop of superior composition, and also to plant up the waste places." If manufacturing plants should be brought to or near the forest, it could in time become self-supporting as well as "secure the silvicultural object":

In case such contracts materialize, the most difficult question of forest management in the Adirondacks, namely, the market for hardwoods, will be solved and the attention of the manager can be entirely devoted to the silvicultural problems, the carrying on of logging operations in such a manner that the volunteer young growth of both hardwoods and conifers may be saved and given opportunity for development, and additional spruce and pine be reproduced assisted by artificial planting wherever necessary.

As late as the beginning of 1900, logging in the college forest had not really begun.[87] Fernow had first sought to find a hardwood market among "the neighboring owners of summer camps. This brought no re-

[87] *Third Annual Report of the N.Y. State College of Forestry for 1900*, transmitted to the Legislature Jan. 21, 1901, J. B. Lyon, State Printer, Albany, pp. 16-17.

sponse. The possibility of establishing a mill in Tupper Lake for the logs was considered, but that," Fernow found, "left the cordwood undisposed of, Tupper Lake itself being amply supplied with such from near-by sources. The New York cordwood market and the brick-kiln market were also investigated, with negative results from the financial point of view. A wood alcohol manufacturer was then invited to look over the tract with a view [to] establishing a plant. His proposition was also objectionable from the financial [standpoint], besides requiring that the log-wood be cut into cordwood. . . ."[38]

On or about May 5, 1900, Cornell University and its board of trustees, on behalf of the New York State College of Forestry, entered into a contract with the Brooklyn Cooperage Company, whereby the latter agreed to erect and maintain on or near the college forest two or more factories, one to manufacture staves and headings, and another to manufacture products of wood distillation. The hardwoods, maple, birch, and beech, and the softwoods, spruce and pine, were to be cut by the college according to agreed diameters and delivered to the manufacturers. The Cooperage Company was to provide railroad facilities. Trees in leaf along streams, ponds, rivers, highways, and fire lines, to a width of not to exceed twenty-five rods and altogether not comprising more than 1,500 acres of the college forest, were to be reserved at the university's discretion. This was done for aesthetic and protective considerations.[39]

There was some anticipation of opposition of wealthy camp-site owners in the Upper Saranac region. The shelter areas were set apart to forestall any formal protestations from groups or individuals to whom the noise, smoke, and unsightliness of logging operations might become a nuisance. Fernow had planned to begin logging in an area remote from tourist resorts and the luxurious camps of the lake regions. When it became known that the planned railroad extension across the state-owned lands of the Adirondack preserve, which was to connect Tupper Lake and North Creek, could not be built, the college forest management was compelled, in order to avail itself of the only possible transportation facilities, to choose a logging site nearer the summer residents. This selection, in the Wawbeek section of the college forest, started real trouble for the New York State College of Forestry.

Some persons, among them the chief forester of the division of forestry at Washington, believed as a matter of sound business judgment that Fernow by arranging the contract with the Brooklyn Cooperage Company had signed the instrument which would spell ruin for

[38] "Intimate History of the College of Forestry etc."

[39] See the testimony of the Brooklyn Cooperage case; also *Third Annual Report etc.*, pp. 14-16.

the forestry experiment in the Adirondacks. Fernow had explained the difficult situation in which he found himself in the reports of the college made to the university and the state. He later explained further:[40]

> It was possible to interest the Brooklyn Cooperage Company—a concern making at that time 25,000 barrels a day. This company was induced to associate itself with a wood alcohol manufacturer to establish both a wood alcohol and cooperage plant using both logs and cords and to build the railroad to the woods, the switches to be built by the College.
>
> At the beginning of the negotiations it had been proposed to cut over the tract in the thirty years for which Cornell University was to be in charge of the tract for the purposes of the demonstration; but the representative of the Company objected to this proposition because it would not furnish sufficient wood material to justify the establishment of a plant. The Company was persuaded to buy an adjoining tract of some twenty odd thousand acres on its own account, and the period of delivering the crop from the College forest was reduced to fifteen years. By that time, it was argued, the demonstration would have been sufficient, the tract would have become accessible in all its parts, and the remaining timber left under the contract alongside of roads, and waters, could have been cut over for a small home market, or additional territory might have been acquired. At any rate, the most difficult problem, the market for the hardwoods, was solved. The contract prices were $2.04 per cord and $6.00 per M feet for logs, both delivered in the woods at rail. Later, a market was found even for rotten wood, hard and soft, at the lime kiln in Vermont, which, while not lucrative, would at least pay the cost of getting rid of undesirable material.
>
> It might be of interest to explain the peculiar contract figure of $2.04 for the cordwood. Every condition of the contract had been agreed to and the price was stipulated at $2.00 per cord, but when the lawyers submitted the instrument it was specified that the cordwood length was to be made 50 inches, two inches above normal, which, it was claimed, was usage for retort wood. A wrangle ensued which nearly put a stop to proceedings. Finally a compromise was reached by splitting the difference and increasing the price as for one inch. Since the contract called for 8,000 to 10,000 cords, besides the logs that would fall with them, this meant an annual addition of around $400. To be sure, it also entailed some difficulty with the wood choppers.
>
> The meticulous forester would ask here what kind of a working plan had been elaborated; what method of determining the felling budget had been applied; what had become of the sustained yield management, which to the academician is the *sine qua non* of forest management. Well, in a practical proposition like the present case, the mill requirement dominates everything and is the felling budget and it should not be overlooked that this becomes the sustained yield budget by merely adding enough area to make it so. For the rest, the elaboration of academic working plans was to be the privilege of the students. The only thing to decide upon was to be on the silvicultural policy. This too could only be generally outlined as it would be desirable to try out various methods as the various conditions of the stands to be cut should suggest. For the areas to be cut at first, hardwoods with the conifers removed, it was decided to replant conifers and expect natural regeneration of hardwoods from the left trees to add to the composition. The one felling area so treated [was to prove] the success of this procedure.

[40] "Intimate History of the College of Forestry etc."

The next thing was to secure appropriations to carry out the contract and on this behalf the writer repaired to Albany to appear before the Legislative Committees. The miserly appropriation of $10,000 for the college was readily secured, but for the woods work an annual appropriation would have been too risky: it was necessary to argue for a working fund which needed no annual appropriation, and to which could be joined the income from the sale of wood. A fund of $50,000 was asked.[41] One member of the Assembly Committee, a wise lumberman, doubted that this would be sufficient; nevertheless the appropriation was cut down to $20,000, and only as a result of a second visit to the Capital was increased to $30,000. It was a question whether to go on with the project, risking success in securing further appropriations, or abandon the plan and lose the promising start. With much hesitation it was decided to go on.

An interesting incident in this appropriation campaign may be worth while relating. Colonel [Theodore] Roosevelt, with whom the writer had had social relations in Washington, was then Governor and the writer called on him in a friendly way. Towards the end of the conversation, the Governor asked, "Can I do anything for you?" "No," was the rejoinder, "except not to veto my appropriations." "Have you got them?" "No, I am here to argue them before the Committee." Impulsively, the Governor pulled out a card and wrote a few words on it and, handing it over to the writer, said, "Show this to the Chairman; it will do some good." Outside, the writer read, "This will introduce Dr. Fernow. What he says goes." Needless to say, the writer did not use the card for fear of introducing political attitudes.

The troubles in organizing and operating the woods work came mainly from home sources. A steering committee of the Board of Trustees seemed to be instituted mainly to curb the enthusiasm of the Director, to act as a brake, so that matters should not proceed too smoothly, and that the Director should not direct too much.

The Director foresaw, even before the Cooperage Company contract was thought of, that a competent local superintendent would be needed to direct the work, for it would become impracticable to superintend it closely enough from Ithaca on a tract two hundred odd miles away to be reached only by a long day's journey or a night with change of cars at one in the morning. The Committee thought that the two Assistant Professors, who were fully occupied with their lecture work, could do the superintending. The writer insisted that either a competent logging boss with an open mind to acquire the forester's attitude or a competent forester who could acquire knowledge of the logging business should be employed. The former would be expensive, the latter non-existent or not available unless imported. Accidentally, at that time, a Swiss forester, highly recommended, made application for a position. He could have been here a year before the logging operations were to begin, ample time to become acquainted with American conditions or to show that he was not the man for the position. But the Director was overruled and Prof. Roth was charged with the superintendence. This was all right for the summer. He prepared the nurseries, made the first plantations, superintended

[41] In the Second Annual Report of the College, dated Jan. 15, 1900, Fernow asked for $50,000 to erect a building on the campus at Cornell, $10,000 for working expenses, and $50,000 as a working capital for the college forest; in the Third Annual Report he again asked for the new building, $12,000 for working expenses, and $50,000 as a working fund for the forest. The latter request was dated Jan. 15, 1901.

the topographical and boundary survey, subdivision, etc.; also during the first winter inspect[ed] a small logging operation. . . .

Eventually . . . the committee "caved" on the superintendence question and allowed the Director to import the Swiss forester. But by the time Mr. Haggar arrived, the preparatory year had passed, operations on a large scale in the logging camp were going on, which he was not competent to supervise for lack of acquaintance with American usage. A tactless bookkeeper in charge and a logging foreman with sixty to ninety men [were] frequently at "loggerheads." The Director had a hard time, on his frequent inspection trips, to keep them at peace.

Mr. Haggar, after the winter was over, proved himself most competent in superintending nursery and planting work. But when the Philippine Forestry Bureau called for assistants, he left for the Islands.[42]

It was only when the cart was nearly in the mud, due to lack of competent superintendence, that we secured a really competent man to take charge, in Mr. Horace Field, an experienced lumberman. . . .

Just to give a glimpse into the narrowness of the attitude of our steering committee, one incident will suffice. The Director wanted to buy a pair of horses which were urgently needed for carrying on the work of Prof. Roth. The committee "did not think that forestry involved livestock business," and "all the teaming that was needed could be hired." The Director, returning from a three months' outing with the Harriman Alaska expedition, found that the bill for horse hire had already grown to the price of a team. He, therefore, immediately purchased on his own account a team to rent to the University if the committee could not see the propriety of owning it. Needless to say, the livestock business increased as the logging operation took shape. . . .

The invitation to accompany the Harriman Alaska expedition honored Fernow at a time he was deserving of recognition. In 1899 Edward H. Harriman, in conjunction with the Washington Academy of Sciences, invited a group of twenty-five scientists and three artists to go at his expense by special train and the steamship *George W. Elder* to Alaska. Harriman was a railroad magnate, wealthy, and interested in opening up the far northern country's vast natural resources. His intention was not that of an exploiter; he wanted this comparatively unknown United States possession to be scientifically studied.

The eastern members of the group left New York for Seattle by special train on May 23. The entire party sailed from Seattle on May 30 and was gone for two months. In the course of their voyage they travelled nine thousand miles. "From Puget Sound to Juneau and Lynn Canal the vessel threaded her way northward among the forested islands and fiords of the 'inside passages'; at Sitka she entered the open

[42] Complying with a cable request of the Taft Philippine Commission, the division of forestry of the U.S.D.A. selected from its personnel two trained lumbermen who had knowledge of forestry. In April 1900 a bureau of forestry under Capt. George P. Ahern of the Ninth Infantry of the U.S. Army had been established. Not long afterward the bureau was reorganized to consist of a senior officer, an inspector, a botanist, ten assistant foresters, thirty rangers, and a considerable clerical force. See *The Forester* VII, 3, March 1901, p. 74; "Forestry in the Philippines," *ibid.* VII, 9, Sept. 1901, p. 230.

ocean and took a northwesterly course in front of the stupendous glaciers and snow-capped peaks of the Fairweather and St. Elias ranges; at Cook's Inlet she changed her course from northwest to southwest and skirted the Alaska Peninsula and Aleutian Islands, touching the emerald shores of Kodiak and the Shumagins; at Unalaska she again turned her prow northward, entered the troubled waters and treacherous fogs of Bering Sea, called at Bogoslof Volcano, the Pribilof or Fur-Seal Islands, and the islands of Hall, St. Matthew, and St. Lawrence; and, finally, after visiting Eskimo settlements on both the Asiatic and American coasts, and peering poleward through Bering Strait —the gateway to the Arctic—she put about and began the homeward voyage."[43]

While the members of the party learned much of the flora and fauna —special systematic attention was given to fungi, marine algae, vascular plants, small mammals and birds of the coast region, marine animals, seaweeds, and insects—the party did not go far into the interior at any point. Not a great deal was learned of the forests and forest growth. Camping parties went ashore at Glacier Bay, Yakutat Bay, Prince William Sound, Kodiak Island, the Alaskan Peninsula, and the Shumagins. A side trip was made from Skagway at the head of the Lynn Canal to the summit of White Pass by way of the newly constructed White Pass and Yukon Railroad. The interests of the party were various. Frederick V. Coville, William Trelease, DeAlton Saunders, and Thomas H. Kearney, Jr., were botanists; William H. Brewer was a botanist and a student of forestry; Fernow was the only forester. There were others in the party with forest interests: John Burroughs and John Muir, naturalists; Wesley R. Coe of Yale University; William H. Dall, paleontologist; Henry Gannett, geographer; G. K. Gilbert, geologist of the United States geological survey; W. B. Devereux, mining engineer of Colorado Springs; Daniel G. Elliott of the Field Columbian Museum of Chicago; Benjamin K. Emerson, geologist of Amherst College; Charles A. Keeler and William E. Ritter of the California Academy of Sciences; C. Hart Merriam, chief, and A. K. Fisher, of the United States biological survey; Robert Ridgway, curator of birds of the United States national museum; George Bird Grinnell, editor of *Field and Stream*; Tresor Kincaid, zoologist of the University of Washington; and Dr. Charles Palachi, mineralogist of Harvard University.

This journey must have been most pleasant for Fernow. In crossing the United States side trips were taken to Shoshone Falls, Boise, and Lewiston, Idaho. At Lewiston a steamer was boarded and the party was escorted through the Snake River canyon to the junction with the Columbia River, where the train trip continued. On the northward

[43] John Burroughs, John Muir, and George Bird Grinnell, *Alaska*, Doubleday, Page & Co., New York, 1902; *The Forester* VI, 11, Nov. 1901, p. 291.

journey, a visit to the Colonial Museum, Vancouver Island, British Columbia, provided an opportunity to view many historic and scientific objects of the West. In the midst of these rich forest regions Fernow must have realized more and more the tremendous forestry possibilities and needs of the western coast from the northwestern states and territories to Alaska.

Numerous papers issued from the expedition. Systematic studies in geology, botany, paleontology, and zoology appeared for a number of years after the first volumes, containing papers of general interest, had been published. In these volumes were contained, among others, Fernow's paper on the Alaskan forests and Henry Gannett's study of the geography of Alaska. Whether or not the discussion which ensued was a repercussion of their differences at Washington, Gannett and Fernow clashed. Fernow felt constrained to come to the defense of his article.[44]

Fernow presented his claims to science and the profession. He observed that some of Gannett's conclusions on the composition and character of forest areas indicated "that two people may see the same thing and yet not see it in the same way." Conclusions which Fernow had drawn had been founded on explorers' reports, theories of plant distribution, geologic history, climatic factors, and other reputable sources. He admitted that in his twenty-page illustrated study of the "Forests of Alaska" he had not always been able to avail himself of primary sources:

> In the lately published volumes of the Harriman Alaska expedition there is to be found a curious divergence of statements or opinions regarding the forests of Alaska. The writer, who accompanied the expedition, prepared a longer article on the subject for the above publication, the conclusions of which Mr. Gannett, a few pages further on, seems to negate entirely, both as to the character and the value of both the interior and the coast forest.
>
> Neither the writer nor Mr. Gannett had any opportunity of inspecting the interior forest. They could, therefore, only interpret second-hand information. . . .

Fernow then proceeded with a new analysis and a further explanation of his published work.[45]

In 1899, at Washington, in the home of Pinchot, Henry S. Graves and he had concluded that, based on the premise of an immediate and widespread expansion of forestry activities on the North American continent, another forest school soon would be needed. Being graduates of Yale University and familiar with the need of foresters in federal, state, and private work, they promulgated a plan for a new school at Yale, and thus brought to effect forestry pleas from such prominent alumni as Egleston, Brewer, Bowers, and others.

[44] "The Forests of Alaska," *Forestry and Irrigation* VIII, 2, Feb. 1902, pp. 66-70.

[45] B. E. Fernow, "Forests of Alaska," in *Alaska, Harriman Alaska Expedition*, New York, Doubleday, Page & Co., 1902, Vol. II, pp. 235-256.

In February 1900 *The Forester*[46] quoted from an address delivered by President Hadley of Yale University before the Cleveland alumni association. Hadley said:

> Of all the needs at present, the thing we feel the need of most is the intelligent teaching of forestry, which stands out prominently. We need it for the sake of the rainfall of the country, for the health of the country, for the future life of the country. I hope I shall see established at Yale in the not distant future a school of forestry, which shall be not a school of a kind of botany as are some of the schools at present in the country; not modeled on German fashions, as is the case with the remainder; but as a school adapted to the needs of America, teaching in the studio and the laboratory, the principles of botany and surveying, the laws of economics necessary to the understanding of the subject, and giving the men a chance to go out into the fields, and do practical field work, and work into positions with the United States government, work into positions of private influence also, which are bound in the immediate future to increase very greatly in importance. Such a school of forestry I believe we have at hand and before us.

During the following months the same publication announced that Yale University had received from Mr. and Mrs. James W. Pinchot and their sons, Gifford and Amos R. Eno, a gift of $150,000 to found a school of forestry as a department of the university. The gift was to be utilized in connection with the gift made by Professor O. C. Marsh of his beautiful residence on Prospect Hill to locate a botanical garden for the university. Henry Solon Graves was appointed Pinchot Professor of Forestry. The school's governing board was to consist of the president of the university, ex-officio, Dr. William H. Brewer, professor of agriculture, and Gifford Pinchot, special lecturer on the state and national forestry.

On May 22 the Yale Corporation announced that James W. Toumey had been secured to teach forest botany, outlines of forestry, forest planting and sowing, forest technology, lumbering, and forest protection. Toumey, a graduate and former assistant in botany at Michigan State College, was an authority on tree planting. No "tree-planter" of the old forestry movement type, Toumey had invigorated this phase of forestry work while superintendent of tree planting in the division of forestry of the United States department of forestry.[47] He expanded Fernow's policy of cooperation with the state agricultural experiment stations. He changed the practice from one of almost complete supervision and financing to one of supplying working plans and other directive assistance. Toumey's program required applicants to provide their own planting materials, their own financing, and the maintenance

[46] *The Forester* VI, 1900, pp. 38, 71, 83, 147. See also *The First Thirty Years of the Yale School of Forestry*, especially H. S. Graves, "The Evolution of a Forest School," pp. 1-26.

[47] J. W. Toumey, "Progress in Tree Planting in the United States," *The Forester* VI, 9, Sept. 1900, p. 213; also *ibid.* VI, 6, June 1900, p. 147.

responsibility was left with the station, institution, or individual planter. Thus the division was enabled to widen the work's effectiveness enormously and to include many programs in many states. Toumey, of course, profited from Fernow's experience. Indeed, he carried out many ideas which Fernow had wanted to institute. Toumey concentrated on developing forest nurseries over the country. Extensive reforestation was accomplished, especially on denuded lands in the Southwest. Toumey had been professor of botany and horticulture at the Arizona Agricultural College. For a while he had served as acting director of the state's experiment station. After going to Yale Forest School he emerged as a strong proponent of scientific forestry in America.

The Yale Forest School was inaugurated with a brilliant group of men. F. H. Newell gave a course in forest hydrography. About 1902 Edward A. Bowers began presenting a course in forest law. During the school's first year a four hundred acre tract of land including the Maltby Lakes was made available for study of silviculture and management. The board immediately planned a summer school to be commenced at Grey Towers, the estate of the Pinchots at Milford, Pike County, Pennsylvania. Nothing pointed to any displeasure on Fernow's part at seeing another school of forestry established, but he resented the charge that the New York State College of Forestry was "modeled on German fashions." Years later Fernow would answer this in an address delivered at Yale University.

When Yale Forest School was founded, Gifford Pinchot's position as chief forester of the federal bureau of forestry and Graves's and Toumey's experience with the division gave the school authority in the immediate work of training foresters for the tasks close at hand, especially in government forestry. By 1901 the federal appropriation for forestry had leaped almost to two hundred thousand dollars, more than six times as large an amount as Fernow's division had during his last year at Washington. Naturally Fernow fully realized that the Yale school would be a forceful competitor.

The New York College of Forestry graduated its first student in 1900. Ralph C. Bryant was graduated with the degree of Bachelor of Science in Forestry after completing a thesis on working plans for a hypothetical 24,000 acre tract in the Adirondacks, and for a selected tract of 120 acres. Both plans were drawn with reference to certain specific formulas and conditions. In 1900 Cornell University had twenty-four forestry students, four of them seniors. At Biltmore there were nine students. Yale began with seven students.[48]

[48] Concerning the Department and the appropriation for the Division of Forestry, see *The Forester* VI, 6, June 1900, p. 139; VII, 2, Feb. 1901, p. 46; VII, 4, April 1901, p. 120. Concerning the N.Y. State College of Forestry and other schools, see *The For-*

The demand for foresters was increasing. At a meeting of the American Forestry Association in 1899 Fernow presided in the absence of Secretary Wilson, the president. He expressed pleasure that a new generation of members would begin to carry forward the policies born of struggle and experience. Forestry, like botany and other basic scientific research, was spanning the continent and invading insular possessions of the United States. By September 1901 the Philippines bureau of forestry had taken three graduates of the New York school, one from Biltmore, and others of varying backgrounds.[49]

During the first years of the century the United States bureau of forestry gave technical advice concerning about fifty million acres of federal and state forest lands, in addition to approximately four million acres owned privately. A large part of the latter was situated in the South.[50] The legislatures of Virginia, North Carolina, Tennessee, South Carolina, Alabama, and others voted that an Appalachian forest reserve be created in the eastern states by the national government.[51] In the West the work of establishing and delimiting new federal forest reservations continued. The United States geological survey persisted diligently with its function of surveying, mapping, and describing the reserves.[52]

At the American Forestry Association's last meeting of the century, held December 13, 1899, at Washington, D.C., state forestry progress was reported from California, Pennsylvania, Minnesota, Michigan, Georgia, Wisconsin, Nebraska, Nevada, and other states. During the first years of the new century, Indiana established a department of a state board directed to buy land for a state reservation, nurseries, et cetera.[53] Furthermore, by an almost unanimous vote, the California legislature voted an appropriation of $250,000 to purchase redwood forests in the Big Basin of the Santa Cruz Mountains, a cause for which botanists, particularly Asa Gray, and foresters had fought, and which helped to clear the way for other reservations of big tree areas.[54] The forest preserve board of New York reported in 1900 that the Adirondack preserve area was 1,357,576 acres, the Catskill preserve area, 96,205 acres, and that the average purchase price per acre since the first of the year had been reduced from $4.26 plus to $2.88 plus.[55] This was considerably more than had been paid in Pennsylvania, which re-

---

ester VI, 5, May 1900, p. 120; VII, 1, Jan. 1901 (on the 19th Annual Meeting of Am. For. Ass.); VII, 12, Dec. 1901, p. 304.

49 "Forestry in the Philippines," *The Forester* VII, 9, Sept. 1901, pp. 230, 233.

50 *Forest Leaves* VIII, 6, Dec. 1901, p. 87; *The Forester* VII, 8, Aug. 1901, p. 204.

51 *Forestry and Irrigation* VIII, 1, Jan. 1902, p. 12; "Growth of Interest in Forestry," *The Forester* VII, 4, April 1901, p. 120.

52 *The Forester* VI, 1, Jan. 1900, pp. 2-6.

53 *Forest Leaves* IX, 2, April 1903, p. 25.

54 "Growth of Interest in Forestry," *The Forester* VII, 4, 1901.

55 *Forest Leaves* VIII, 3, June 1901, p. 46.

ported that year a total forest reserve area of 324,000 acres.[56] Tennessee was still a fertile state for forestry expansion. Organized forestry effort there had gathered momentum since the state's first centennial celebration. An initial meeting of a Tennessee Forest Association gathered at Sewanee on August 7, 1901, and Charles A. Keffer, now a professor at the state university, presided as temporary chairman.[57] In the East and West forest experiment stations were to be found, in most instances but not always, working with a state agricultural experiment station. Occasionally, an aggressive scholar, working alone or under the bureau of forestry, was advancing some special form of research. Range research students from the University of Nebraska, Iowa State College, or other western institutions were developing that phase. Among these was C. S. Crandall, who was interested in the horticultural and agricultural aspects. Later we will consider more fully the growing research in forest ecology. In Texas at this time federal forestry work was represented by William L. Bray, organizer of a department of botany at the University of Texas, among the first graduate students to obtain a doctorate in botany at the University of Chicago, and who had also studied abroad. The magnificent publications of the United States geological survey, presenting topographic features, soil conditions, conditions of climate and rainfall, and exact analyses of forest conditions, fire destruction, and lumbering within the federal reservations, were valuable contributions to the American literature on forest distribution. In their preparation the valuable services of such students as John G. Jack, John B. Leiberg, Ayers, Sudworth, and others were employed.[58] But the interpretation was economic. The addition of trained ecologists to the American forest scene permitted the inclusion also of more purely scientific techniques in forest scholarship. When the students of Henry Chandler Cowles of the University of Chicago began to study the eastern forests of the United States from Michigan to Maine and from Tennessee and Mississippi to Florida, and even went west into Montana, Arizona, Colorado, and other states, a new type of forest scholarship arrived. It has already been pointed out that from the University of Nebraska a very important group of scientists, ecologists produced under the leadership of Bessey, had begun to develop the science of prairie and forest, with the emphasis on regions. More and more forestry in North America would gain by utilizing the productions of ecological learning.

In 1901 for the use of its state forestry commission the legislature of Michigan set apart 100,000 acres of forest land around Houghton and

[56] *Forest Leaves* VIII, 5, Oct. 1901, p. 67.

[57] *Forest Leaves* VIII, 5, Oct. 1901, p. 78; *The Forester* VII, 6, June 1901, p. 138.

[58] *Botanical Gazette* XXXI, Jan.-June 1901, p. 210; *The Forester* VII, 1901, pp. 112, 131.

Higgins lakes in Crawford and Roscommon counties. An experiment station was to be established there, and to it were to come both foresters and ecologists.[59] Since 1898 northern Michigan had been a favored ground for ecological research, almost as favorable as the sand dune regions in the southwest portions of the state. For a number of years exemplary natural history surveys would be conducted throughout the entire state. The state forest reserve was centrally located. A group headed by Professor Charles A. Davis, former student at the New York State College of Forestry, investigated the tract's possibilities. Within a few years Burton Edward Livingston's study of vegetational distribution and its controlling factors, entitled, "The relation of soils to natural vegetation,"[60] would issue from this region. This study was begun in 1901 in Kent County.

The horticultural societies of the Great Lakes states, especially under the leadership of Spalding, Garfield, and Beal, and in Minnesota under the direction of Hays, Green, Chapman, and Andrews, had renewed their fight for forestry during the last years of the past century, and they had rejoiced to find that their years of work had not been in vain. Minnesota's fire warden system was widely praised. The state now had a law which enabled tax-delinquent lands to be set aside for purposes of a state forest reserve. Prairie states were also active. Toward the close of the century a park and forestry association was organized in Nebraska. Iowa's association, organized at the turn of the century, was soon issuing *Proceedings*.[61]

At this time Minnesota was probably the center of forestry interest. A Minnesota national park or reservation in northern Minnesota was proposed. The suggested area, for a while at least, comprised seven million acres of land lying at the divide of the headwaters of three of the nation's most important streams—the St. Lawrence, the Mississippi, and the Red River of the North. This movement culminated in the passage in 1902 of the famous Morris Act, already explained, which created a forestry reserve of 200,000 acres and where the benefits of forest management were to be convincingly demonstrated.

In 1899 Minnesota had created a state forestry board to study and report on most effective methods to reforest denuded areas, to prevent forest fires, and to encourage citizens to preserve and restore their forests. Five years later the board was still pleading for funds and opportunities "to go to work."[62] Three million acres of wasteland unfit

59 *The Forester* VII, 11, Nov. 1901, p. 275.

60 *Botanical Gazette* XXXIX, Jan.-June 1905, p. 22.

61 *Forest Leaves* VII, 6, Dec. 1899, p. 79 (the Nebraska Ass.); *Forestry Quarterly* I, 1, Oct. 1902, p. 32 (the Iowa Ass. and the first issue of its *Proceedings*).

62 *Forest Leaves* VII, 3, June 1899, pp. 14, 41; X, 4, Aug. 1905, p. 50; VII, 7, Feb. 1900, p. 105; IX, 4, Aug. 1903, p. 57; VIII, 10, Aug. 1902, p. 155; *Forestry and Irrigation* X, May, Sept., 1904, pp. 228, 379; *Garden and Forest*, 439, July 22, 1896, p. 300; *The Forester* V, 2, Feb. 1899, p. 47, and 3, March, pp. 49, 63.

for agriculture in scattered localities which might be planted with pine was still undeveloped. Nevertheless, much had been accomplished. In 1899 S. B. Green's *Forestry in Minnesota,* a local forestry manual published by the state forestry association, had appeared. Three years earlier H. B. Ayers and others had persuaded the state horticultural society to encourage authorities to set apart a small area of timbered land to be administered by the university with a view to demonstrating the value of good forest management. The state during the first years of the century received millions of dollars from timber sales from lands given by the federal government, but not much money was reinvested by the state in its forest lands. The state was slowly being awakened. On a donation of one thousand acres of cut-over pine land in Cass County, the gift of Governor John S. Pillsbury, a survey and a preliminary working plan for the land's management were completed. There the board located a forest nursery, where seedlings, especially spruce, were grown. Valuable demonstration areas exhibiting reforestation methods were maintained on these and other lands, and these afforded the university forestry work excellent out-of-door laboratories. When in 1904 congress granted the state 20,000 acres of third and fourth rate lands for forestry, a rugged forest and lake country was selected in the Vermilion Range about twelve miles west and northwest of Ely. The state board began to prepare plans for a survey, a map, timber estimates, road building, and other facilities. It may be said, therefore, that while Minnesota for a quarter of a century had taken a leading part in the forestry movement of America, forest management on state-owned land did not get a real start until early in the twentieth century.[63]

Early in 1901 the New Hampshire society for preservation of forests was organized at Concord. There was hope of further governmental action in New Jersey,[64] a state long "lumbered out," whose forestry problems, while statewide, centered northwest and southeast and were critical for water supply, wood-lot and sand dune recuperation, and fire protection.

Forestry education was expanding. Forestry courses were being established from southern California to New Hampshire. The legislature of North Dakota authorized the establishment of a school of forestry at Bottineau.

Forestry interest was still running strong in Canada. In 1899 the report of the clerk of forestry for the province of Ontario observed,[65]

[63] *Forestry and Irrigation* X, 9, Sept. 1904, p. 379; "Forestry in the University of Minnesota," *ibid.* X, 10, Oct. 1904, p. 463.

[64] *The Forester* VII, 3, March 1901, p. 68; VII, 4, April 1901, p. 104 (on New Hampshire); VII, 5, May 1901, p. 125; *Forest Leaves* VIII, 3, June 1901, pp. 40-41 (on New Jersey).

[65] *Forest Leaves* VII, 8, April 1900, p. 124.

"In considering the progress of the movement in the direction of rational and scientific forestry methods in Ontario, it is difficult to overestimate the importance of the legislation introduced by the Commission of Crown Lands in the Legislature of 1898, styled the Forest Reserve Act, by which power was given the government to set aside areas of the crown domain to be kept perpetually for growing timber. . . ." This was the course of action of a province; the Dominion government also protected forest lands within its jurisdiction.

Canada,[66] like the United States, had begun to conserve its second most valuable industrial resource by establishing national parks—the Rocky Mountain Park in 1887 and Glacier Forest Park in 1888, the former consisting of 2,880,000 acres of land in the Northwest Territories and the latter of 18,720 acres in British Columbia. The creation of both of these parks accompanied construction of the transcontinental Canadian Pacific Railroad; and for the Dominion government's aid in building the railroad, British Columbia transferred to the Dominion a belt of land of twenty miles on each side of the railway's main line.

After the creation of parks there had followed the setting aside of timber reservations, at first made principally to protect the water supply. In the middle 1890's, particularly in 1895, Dominion reserves had been established by executive order number 5 of the minister of the interior. In Manitoba, the Turtle Mountain Reserve of 75,000 acres near the international boundary, the Riding Mountain Timber Reserve of 1,215,000 acres, and the Lake Manitoba West Timber Reserve of 159,460 acres had been set apart in 1895. That year in the Northwest Territories the Waterton Lakes Forest Park of 34,000 acres had also been established.[67] In Ontario, Algonquin Park of 1,109,383 acres[68] situated 150 miles north of Toronto, and Rondeau Park had been set apart in 1893-1894 as game preserves. In 1895 Laurentides Park of 2,531 square miles was set aside in Quebec, and in 1898 the Spruce Woods Timber Reserve of 190,000 acres was established in Manitoba.

There was created in British Columbia in 1901 the Yoho Park of 530,240 acres. The Foothills, or Bow River, Preserve in the Northwest Territories, the Cooking Lake Timber Reserve of 109,000 acres in northern Alberta southeast of Edmonton, and the Moose Mountain Timber Reserve of 103,000 acres in eastern Assiniboia had been set

[66] R. H. Campbell, "Forest Reserves in the Dominion of Canada," *Forestry Quarterly* I, 4, July 1903, pp. 159-162.

[67] Changes were made from time to time. Lake Louise Forest Park and Mount Stephen Forest Park, set apart under the Dominion Lands Act in 1895, were included in Yoho Park. Sand Lake Forest Park was another reserved area.

[68] Today Algonquin Park is said to consist of 2,721 square miles ("Playgrounds in Ontario," issued by the Canadian National Railways, 1941 (?), p. 27) and "measures 71 miles from east to west by 55 miles from north to south" (*Toronto Star Holiday Guide*, 1945, p. 2). The park was conceived partly as a breeding ground for game, and shooting is prohibited, though fishing is permitted.

apart in 1899. In 1901 the Beaver Hills Timber Reserve of 170,00 acres was established. In 1902 in Manitoba the Duck Mountain Timber Reserve of 840,000 acres was designated. Practically all of northwestern Manitoba had been reserved from settlement.

In 1901 in Ontario the great Timagami Reserve, a magnificent forest of 1,408,000 acres of pine, spruce, and other timbers, was established. Forty-five thousand acres on the north shore of Lake Superior, Sibley Reserve, and the Eastern Reservation of 80,000 acres in the counties of Addington and Frontenac were also designated, the latter in 1899 and the former in 1900. Not until 1902 would any action be taken with reference to New Brunswick lands. At that time, authority to select and set apart a reservation was granted. In 1902 in British Columbia the Long Lake Timber Reserve of 76,800 acres was set apart.

On March 8, 1900, in the house of commons at Ottawa, the Canadian Forestry Association had been organized with Sir Henri Joly de Lotbinière as president and William Little as vice-president. Canadian forestry's true friend, Sir Henri, had received the order of knighthood at Lord Aberdeen's recommendation, "evidently," he told his son Edmond in a letter of December 6, 1901, for his part in promoting harmony between discordant elements of the Dominion population in Quebec and Ontario. Invited at a Quebec banquet to address audiences in Ontario, he went to Toronto and Kingston and, offering a message of peace for Canada, was soon asked to return to receive an honorary degree from Kingston University along with Lord Aberdeen. An insistent opponent of national and religious prejudice, a staunch believer in schools and education, an organizer of forestry associations in the provinces of Manitoba and Quebec, first president of the latter, often a presiding officer of the American Forestry Association, he was still its vice-president, representing Canada. Soon to be appointed lieutenant governor of the province of British Columbia, he was to maintain at Victoria an experimental garden to test the introduction of eastern Canadian tree species to western Canada and send seeds and seedlings of western species to eastern localities including his estate at Point Platon on the St. Lawrence. To his son he commended participation in the Canadian and American forestry associations and an interest in forestry as "a fine work, one for which you are well fitted in every way. Take it up," he urged, "for its own sake as well as for the good you may do. . . . I think I owe more to Forestry, which gave me so many friends and so many opportunities, than to Politics."

In 1899 a forestry bureau had been established in the Dominion's department of interior. Elihu Stewart, placed in charge, had made an official trip through Manitoba and British Columbia and investigated the forest conditions of western Canada. As chief inspector of timber and forestry of the department, Stewart reported to the American Forestry Association meeting at Washington that the Bow River Reserve was being districted, fire protective measures were being taken, and the afforestation program of the Dominion experimental farms in the West was going ahead. The Dominion's fire protection system, however, was not to be compared with that of the province of Ontario. The provincial clerk's report for the year 1899 indicated that almost two hundred rangers had patrolled licensed lands during the season of 1898.

During 1898-1902 the loud cry was for forest management and trained foresters. Management on privately owned forest lands was growing. In a report[69] Henry S. Graves, superintendent of working plans in the division of forestry at Washington, had expressed genuine admiration for the forest situation he found on the historic Stephen Girard estate, located twelve miles north of Pottsville, in Schuylkill and Columbia counties, Pennsylvania. He was especially impressed by the forest planting and fire protective features of the management. Graves admired also the fire protection system maintained on the 40,000 acre tract of Dr. W. S. Webb in the Adirondacks. In his study, "The Practice of Forestry by Private Owners," published in the department's *Yearbook for 1899*, he described this together with other instances of early forest practice on private tracts in the United States, forest planting, and conservative lumbering procedures.

As all the features of forestry management—afforestation, reforestation, protection, and utilization—were embraced in the numerous private and public forest programs in the United States and Canada, the demand for foresters became more insistent. Only the professional forestry schools could supply the men necessary to meet the demands. But caution was necessary not to place forestry in public disfavor.

Graves's wide experience with forest and woodlot owners had convinced him that lumbermen generally had a strong prejudice against scientific forestry. By virtue of his position and his close relationship with Pinchot, Graves probably knew more about working plans and proper management for regions throughout the United States than anyone. Fernow had initiated working plan concepts. The next administration, however, developed the concepts and applied them.

Graves befriended research without ignoring the claims of lumbermen and private interests. "Forestry," wrote Graves, "is a science in that its practice is based on scientific facts and principles, but it is essentially an art and a business. The fact that forestry is scientific has proved a serious obstacle in the way of its adoption by many forest owners in this country. Lumbermen have a strong prejudice against scientific forest-

69 *Forest Leaves* XI, 8, April 1908, pp. 118-120.

ers, for they believe the latter are theorists and that they can offer nothing practical. . . ."[70]

Graves attributed this prejudice to a lack of knowledge of the real nature of forestry. He urged, "Experiments in silviculture are of great value and are very much needed in this country." He believed that every encouragement should be given to experiments which studied the lives and behavior of trees. As dean of the Yale Forest School, Graves realized that education would have to give a place to practical management systems as well as scientific theory.

At the turn of the century the United States department of the interior applied to the department of agriculture for complete working plans for all of the national forest reservations in the West.[71] The intention was to transform the reserves into revenue producing agencies. Since 1898, when Frederick V. Coville had prepared a bulletin on forest growth and sheep grazing in the Cascade Mountains, interest had steadily heightened in all phases of forest protection and preservation, including protection from fire and domestic animal grazing. It was realized that a whole range of problems needed study.

The leaders competent to perform the gigantic task of solving the problems presented by the vast variety of conditions were few. Roth was summoned to Washington from the New York State College of Forestry. In 1901 Fernow said,[72] "That finally the Federal Government must institute a full-fledged management of its 40 forest reserves, comprising over 46,000,000 acres, is self evident. . . ." Roth, who on August 5, 1898, had resigned from his position with the division of forestry at Washington, tendered his resignation to Cornell University in the spring of 1900 to return to the division as an expert in forest investigations. Roth was profoundly needed in both places. On May 21, 1900, President Schurman addressed a letter to Roth, who then was at Axton:

> I am in receipt of yours of the 18th instant resigning your position as assistant professor. If this question is still open to reconsideration on your part, I should desire not to present the letter of resignation until I have had an opportunity of conferring with you. We have highly appreciated your services, and are unwilling to lose so good a man. . . .

Roth's bulletin on "Timber: An Elementary Discussion of the Characteristics and Properties of Wood," published in 1895 had contained what Fernow described as "information never before published in English in systematic and accessible form and with special application to American timber." His bulletins on Wisconsin forest conditions and resources (1898), on the "Bald Cypress" (Circular 19), on "The An-

[70] "The Study and Practice of Silviculture," *The Forester* VII, 5, May 1901, pp. 105-112.

[71] *ibid.* VI, 3, March 1900, p. 71.

[72] *ibid.* VII, 10, Oct. 1901, p. 238.

nual Ring" (Circular 16), and his timber physics reports, bulletins, and circulars (1895-1899), such articles as "The Uses of Wood," presented in the *Yearbook of the United States Department of Agriculture* for 1896, and other laboratory and field studies had given him a wide reputation in forestry. In 1902 he issued his study of "Grazing in the Forest Reserves" and his "Forest Reserve Manual for the Information and Use of Forest Officers," as well as his intelligent and popular text, *First Book of Forestry.*

Roth left Cornell and went to Washington, where he soon established himself as perhaps its most valuable officer in the field. Much of his time was spent in the reserves locating boundaries and directing and aiding survey work. On July 1, 1901, he received a promotion in the bureau. By that time Secretary of the Interior Hitchcock had organized a force of rangers for fire protection. Roth aided in the placement of technically trained men in the work. The position of head ranger was created. Moreover, the secretary of the interior decided to set up a bureau of forestry in the general land office of his department. To the position as chief of this bureau he called Roth in November of 1901.

Fernow, who had once proposed legislation which would have allocated a forestry service in the department of the interior, now favored the unification of all forestry work within the bureau of the department of agriculture. He said, before Roth was constituted chief of the interior department's bureau,[73] "At present the General Land Office is still in charge of [the reserves] but already the Secretary of the Interior has recognized that technical management of these timber lands is necessary and has called on the Bureau of Forestry to prepare the necessary plans. As soon as such plans are formulated, their execution should also be left with the Bureau, for technical supervision of the cutting of timber is as essential as technical plans, and it is questionable whether the General Land Office, which was instituted simply to dispose of the public domain, could be so organized as to furnish this technical supervision and continuous management. . . ." Notwithstanding the growing belief that the technical forestry management of the federal forest reservations "should be under the direction of the Bureau of Forestry,"[74] an announcement during the summer of 1901[75] said that Secretary Hitchcock was planning to create a bureau within his department to protect, extend, and introduce an improved forestry system within the forest reserves. Forest utilization, reforestation, and other incidents of a progressive forest management were contemplated. The appointment of Roth as chief may have palliated Fernow's objections, but it was an anomalous situation—the trained forestry personnel in the department of

[73] *loc. cit.* [74] *loc. cit.*
[75] *Forest Leaves* VIII, 4, Aug. 1901, p. 59.

agriculture had little more than advisory authority. Opposition to the arrangement was expressed by almost everyone including the president of the United States. Immediately Roth began to carry out provisions for intelligent forestry administration and extension of the reserves. In 1902 he urged the American Association for the Advancement of Science to memorialize congress again to enact legislation for the withdrawal from entry and for administration of all public lands. His article, "Administration of United States Forest Reserves," which appeared in *Forestry and Irrigation*[76] that year, stands as a classic in the forestry literature of this country.

Roth predicted that timber work soon would be foremost of the government duties of administration. Improvements of the "free-use" and sale under application systems would occur. The ranger, to deserve his title, would have to be a scaler, estimator, and general timber surveyor.

Roth pleaded for "a thorough study and description of many of the forests of the reserves. . . ." Only thus could the dangers of overcutting be averted. Only thus could there be a judicious disposal of the mature and overmature timbers. Protection of the forest would remain the guiding principle. He wrote:

> So far, the forest work in the reserves has been little more than a modification of ordinary lumbering, restricted to local, urgent demands. It has been limited to such timber as could be spared without injury to the protective forest, and at the same time secure an economic use of the material; also a cleaning up of debris, such as any orderly farmer demands in his woodlot, thus avoiding the dangerous fire traps of the ordinary logger's "slash." In addition, a few attempts have been made in other directions. In some of the reserves fire lines have been cut for the protection of the timber, and also a few preliminary experiments have been made of reforestation of burns and chaparral lands. So far, the results of these experiments are too few to warrant further description. To what extent reforestation of bare lands and similar work in practical forestry will be introduced is difficult to state now. That there are a number of localities where a reasonable expenditure of money for the purpose would be well repaid, there is not the least doubt. . . . Grazing in the forest reserves today is of greater importance, financially, to the people of the respective districts than is the timber business.[77]

As yet there was almost no reforestation of bare lands in the reserves. Grazing, mapping, districting, and general protective work occupied attention. Generally, sheep and goats were forbidden to graze on the

[76] *ibid.* VIII, 1902, pp. 191, 241, 279.

[77] Chief Forester Pinchot also regarded grazing as "decidedly the most important problem of the National Forest Reserves. At present only in rare instances does the value of timber annually taken from the forest reserves approach the value of the forage yearly consumed by grazing animals. Perhaps only in a single instance—that of the Black Hills—is timber cutting distinctly the more important industry. . . ." *The Forester* VII, 11, Nov. 1901, p. 276. See also Pinchot's "Notes on Some Forest Problems," *Yearbook of U.S.D.A. for 1898*, pp. 181-192, at p. 187.

reserves. Sheep grazing was permitted in eight of the forty-six reserves. In 1901 a limited number of horses and cattle were permitted on nearly all of the reserves. Since the reservations were protective forests, every possible precaution was taken to prevent timber despoliation and soil erosion and depletion.

Theodore Roosevelt had followed McKinley as president of the United States. While yet vice-president elect and governor of New York, he had kept a steadfast interest in natural resources and their conservation and had written to the National Irrigation Congress held at Chicago, November 21-24, 1900:

> The problem of the development of the greater West is in large part a problem of irrigation. . . . We are just getting to understand what is involved in the preservation of our forests. Not only is an industry at stake which employs more than half a million of men, the lumber industry, but the whole prosperity and development of the West, and indeed ultimately of the entire country, is bound up with the preservation of the forests. Right use of the forests means the perpetuation of our supply both of wood and of water. . . . I venture to point out that without the attainment of the following objects your plans must measurably fail:
>
> First: Government study of the streams upon which your plans depend.
> Second: Government construction and control of great irrigation plants.
> Third: The preservation of forests by the extension of the forest reserve system, and hence of government control of the forests.
> Fourth: National protection and use of the forests under expert supervision.
> Fifth: I want you to see to it that private owners of forests in the West and East alike understand that timber can be cut without forest destruction (the Department of Agriculture will tell them how) and that the ownership of water rights in the arid country, and of forest lands anywhere, entails public as well as private duties and responsibilities.
>
> The East is interested in the commercial development of the arid lands of the West, just as the West is interested in the proper development of our harbor system and of our commerce on the high seas. . . .[78]

Secretary Wilson said what Fernow, Bowers, and many others interested in conservation of natural resources had said for years, "The water problem, like the forest problem, is essentially and primarily one of conservation and use."

During the first decade of the century the states and the federal government began to take affirmative legislative action with respect to their water problems. Again the technique of invoking commissions to investigate and administer was utilized.

President Roosevelt's first message to congress definitely placed him with those presidents who had aided the causes of forestry and irrigation. Natural resources and their problems included more than woods

[78] *The Forester* VI, 12, Dec. 1900, p. 289.

and waters now. Broken down into separate parts, the land problem presented problems of the forest cover, the soil, small plants, the forest's wild life, disease prevention and elimination, mineral resources, and many other factors.

Revenue was primary and research was still secondary. The grazing consideration was important. The act of 1897 had not specifically granted authority to charge grazing fees on the reserve areas. Neither had it prohibited them.[79] When Pinchot had become chief of the forestry division, one of the first problems on which he took action was the matter of grazing privileges, a difficult subject for which he found an effective solution. A representative of the grazing industry was brought into the federal forestry personnel. This provided a cogent argument for rational forest management and further proof of the business acumen and astuteness of Pinchot. Pinchot has told[80] that soon after President Roosevelt entered the White House a decision on grazing impended. Representatives of the industry, the chief forester, and the president arrived at a point of agreement, and future progress was made the more certain.

In 1900 at Washington, D.C., the Society of American Foresters[81] was formed by seven charter members—Gifford Pinchot, Henry S. Graves, Edward Tyson Allen, William Logan Hall, Ralph S. Hosmer, Overton Westfeldt Price, and Thomas Herrick Sherrard. On March 26, 1903, President Roosevelt broke with tradition and spoke in a private residence before the Society. Congratulating foresters on having "created a new profession of the highest importance, of the highest usefulness to the State," he dared to be specific on the matter of grazing. He discussed the relations of the mining and lumber industries to forestry, and said, "Even the grazing industry, as it is carried on in the Great West, which might at first sight appear to have little relation to forestry, is nevertheless closely related to it, because great areas of winter range, available and good for winter grazing, would be absolutely useless without the summer range in the mountains, where the forest reserves lie. . . ."[82] President Roosevelt's address became the first number of the valuable *Proceedings of the Society of American Foresters*, begun under the able editorship of Dr. Graves. Fernow was elected to membership in the Society on December 15 at the third meeting when eight foresters, some not then residents of Washington, were

[79] Jenks Cameron, *op. cit.*, pp. 220-223, 243-244.

[80] "Roosevelt's Part in Forestry," *Journal of Forestry* XVII, 2, Feb. 1919, pp. 122-125.

[81] Ralph S. Hosmer, "The Society of American Foresters, An Historical Summary," *Journal of Forestry*, Nov. 1940; Theodore Roosevelt, "Forestry and Foresters," *Proc. Soc. Am. For.* I, 1, May 1905, p. 3.

[82] For a general reference on grazing and range management, see R. H. D. Boerker, *Behold Our Green Mansions*, Chaps. IX, X.

added to the charter membership. These were E. M. Griffith, James W. Toumey, C. A. Schenck, F. E. Olmstead, George B. Sudworth, Horace B. Ayers, Filibert Roth, and Fernow. Gifford Pinchot became the Society's first president and retained the office for many years.

Foresters in America, Fernow believed, were prematurely claiming the prerogatives of an American forestry. Forestry had regional attributes, of course, but forestry was a science, an applied science, and should know no continental or national boundaries. Since 1882, when at the Montreal congress he read his paper on "Conditions of Forest Growth," Fernow had furthered regional studies of American forest species. He admitted then that he was not sufficiently familiar with American species to outline a comprehensive program, but he called for a "complicated system of elementary knowledge which [could] be gathered by local observations, based on a correct understanding of the physical forces at work" in the forest. His organization of rules of good forest management and his definitions of growth conditions had been general. Specific data, however, would create the architecture of forestry. With sufficient knowledge, an "American forestry" would come into being. But as yet research had neither uncovered nor authenticated enough data to inform the world of the special conditions in America. In his report for 1900 on the New York State College of Forestry, he elaborated:

> Three primary essentials must be the basis of an American system of forestry:
>
> 1. Better protection of forest property, including rational methods of taxation—a subject of legislation.
> 2. More thorough utilization of the forest crop—a subject of wood technology and development of means of transportation and harvesting.
> 3. Silvicultural methods of harvesting, so as to produce a desirable new crop, or artifical reproduction, if that is more effective and cheaper —the main concern of forestry.

At the college forest at Axton Fernow attempted to choose the most desirable felling areas, to use the best methods of felling, to discover the most advantageous methods of obtaining natural or artificial reproduction, and like matters. The scientific advances issuing from the academies, universities, and laboratories of Europe were taught. Europe led the world in medical study, in plant science research, in fact, in all the natural sciences. With the beginning of the century, Americans in a few fields of knowledge began to claim leadership. Practically every great American student of plants, however, if he did not go to Europe and study, was at least acquainted with European literature. What was true of the older branches of plant study in America was more true of the youngest branch, forestry.

The final contract of Cornell University with the Brooklyn Cooperage Company was not concluded until July 1900. The construction of the college forest railroad from Tupper Lake's railway connections and mills to a point in the forest known as the divide near the Wawbeek section, had retarded full scale logging. The college had had to build a spur of more than 1¼ miles. The manufacturers who located their factories at Tupper Lake laid out and completed during 1900 a track of more than four miles. These ventures had been necessary, but they were expensive and time-consuming.

Soon after the contract with the Cooperage Company was concluded, Fernow took a sample cutting "to gain an insight into methods and results," and that year an "analysis of the results of a sample felling [brought] out the basis for calculating yield and cost of logging of culled hardwood lands in the Adirondacks. . . . The business side of the College Forest," announced Fernow in the report for 1900, "is fully established, the market for the old crop having been secured and logging operations on an adequate scale for its harvest having begun. The expectation of making the experiment self-supporting from the start by means of this harvest promises to be realized. . . ." Planting operations had been continued, especially from May until June, and by the end of the year ninety-five acres on burnt areas had been treated. Fernow elaborately reported on the work of the nurseries, one at Axton and the other in the Wawbeek district. The college had an enrollment of twenty-five students; and for their schooling and accommodation at the forest, as well as for other management purposes, buildings had to be remodeled, repaired, or new ones provided. Plans for a lecture hall, dormitory, library, and housing facilities had to be abandoned because of the insufficiency of the legislature's appropriation for that year. But getting large-scale logging operations under way, if only for a short while, was a real satisfaction. By September a crew of thirty to sixty men was at work. By the end of the year eighty men, plus cordwood cutters, were employed. The wettest weather in six years, however, had impeded the summer work. And the winter was worse. Continuous full-scale logging and the completion of facilities were slowed in December because of heavy snowfall and other adverse circumstances. Harvesting remained difficult nearly all winter.

Not until 1901 did full-scale operations under favorable circumstances get under way. Deep snows on unfrozen ground delayed the completion of the college forest railroad, and this was costly. If sufficient funds had been available to have built the railroad to forest regions remote from the camp-site and residential section of Upper Saranac Lake, or if the proposed railroad facility across the preserve from Tupper Lake to North Creek had been sustained by the court and been built, Fernow would have been able to carry out his original working plans. Nevertheless, a stave factory was being built and an alcohol distillery was under construction.

The cost of hauling logs to Camp Foresters, the point to which the railroad was completed in 1901, or of hauling logs and cordwood to the stave factory or distillery "entailed unusual losses in all directions." Logs lay shrunken and unused. But the harvest of 36,274 hardwood logs, plus about 8,000 cords, 128,328 feet, board measure, of hemlock and spruce, and 38,000 logs on skids awaiting better hauling weather, was encouraging. The planted area by 1901 was increased by 160 acres to a total of 255 acres—105 acres in the cut-over area and 55 acres of old fields and burns around Axton and in the Wawbeek district.

This year the "farm" was managed, not rented, and a sizable crop of hay and potatoes showed a good profit. A boarding house was established.

Green timber two hundred feet wide screened "all highways and other avenues of travel,"[83] and preserved the forest's natural and scenic beauty to outsiders. But the wealthy summer residents had to enter the woods near the college area. To them the presence of the manufacturing plants between Tupper Lake and the forest, the railroad, and the logging operations were inconsistent with the fashion and splendor of a forest preserve which was to them, and was called on maps and in the public prints, a park. Immediately there were rumbles of protest. Those of the Association for the Protection of the Adirondacks[84] and other organizations were strong, and they added to Fernow's worries. The Association for the Protection of the Adirondacks had been formed in 1900 and "took over the leadership formerly exercised by the New York Board of Trade and Transportation. . . ."

From the first year the weather had been difficult—rain and snow, to say nothing of fires from dry weather, and other troubles had retarded efficient forest operations. To the end of 1901, only five hundred of the thirty thousand acres had been logged. Not even five hundred acres had been so cleared as to require replanting, and during the first two years 169,500 seedlings were set out. Moreover, shipments of plant materials had been received from a number of outside sources.

The planting material used had been Norway spruce and Scotch pine, which exhibited the most vigorous development, Douglas fir, which as yet showed no certain adaptability, white pine, European larch, basswood, ash, black cherry, and black locust. Riga and red pines, Colorado white fir, and white spruce made part of a total estimated 232,000 seed-

[83] Ralph C. Bryant, "Silviculture at Axton and in the Adirondacks Generally," *Journal of Forestry* XV, 7, Nov. 1917, p. 891.

[84] Gurth Whipple, *op. cit.*, pp. 77-79.

lings planted by 1901. At least sixty per cent of the planted stock everywhere, and eighty per cent in places, were believed living. That year most of the materials came from the home nurseries which now could furnish all necessary stock. On hand were a million and a quarter seedlings of different ages, more than could be used.

Fernow wanted a working fund of $150,000. With this the management could effectuate the type of "liberal, far-sighted policy which [had] made the forest properties of Germany what they [were], the best paying investments in the country." He argued, "The curtailment of working funds by the legislature, which cut the amount asked for from $50,000 down to $30,000, has considerably hampered the management and prevented the inauguration of many things that it would have been proper to do, and also has made it necessary to postpone some desirable silvicultural operations. While the legislature had not circumscribed the appropriation which was made in 1900 by any limitations as to its expenditure, the management planned not to rely upon further appropriations, but to treat this appropriation as a working capital, to be kept intact and to be replenished by sale of log and wood harvest, and so far as possible to use only the profits for improvements, salaries and conduct of the business generally. This wise business policy was in part determined upon as meeting the requirements of the law, which called upon the college to show how to secure a revenue, and in part it was dictated by the necessity of delivering regularly under contract for the next fifteen years the annual harvest, the logging operations requiring, therefore, an assured working capital and hence independence of uncertain appropriations. . . ."

The building of the railroad spur, the equipping of the college forest, in fact, the entire "initial outlays incident to the starting of [the] business enterprise" which the statutory directives contemplated, made "most careful financiering" imperative. There was a harvest of "about 2,500,000 feet of logs," "over 8,000 cords of wood," a "railroad of 1.4 miles extent" which connected with the main line, nurseries, plantations, et cetera, but weather had held the spring planting to 105 acres that year; and severe culling of hardwoods below a diameter of fourteen inches, in addition to damage to the forest due to wind and snows, had necessitated costly replanting of about three hundred acres with conifers. Good forestry could and would utilize broken and fallen timbers, but a necessary corollary was adequate transportation, which included roads as well as railroads. The college forest policy as to tree-size required before cutting was to be flexible, and shaped foremost with a view to the interests of crop-replacement. Diameter limits, ranging from eight to ten inches and upward, depending on purposes and circumstances, are mentioned in the school's reports. As late as his 1902 report, however, Fernow said, "no hardwood trees below fourteen inches and softwoods below twelve inches are cut, unless they are defective and not fit to grow into the new crop, or likely to damage the young crop by shade or being thrown by winds."

This was the situation which existed when the decision to introduce the clear cutting and replanting silvicultural policy was adopted. "It is only the less experienced who clings to one prescription," wrote Fernow. "The man of wider judgment varies it according to the varying conditions. . . ." Immediately he answered criticisms, charges of contemplated denudation of the whole forest area as well as some involving an alleged silvicultural issue. "The choice of method," he said, "is partly influenced by natural conditions, partly by the objects and conditions of the owner. In a protective forest and in a luxury forest, the selection system, which culls here and there and leaves the forest as a whole undisturbed, may be most satisfactory on account of the objects in view, which necessitate a constant soil cover of grown timber, but in a business forest, which is managed for revenue, the first or any of the intermediate methods of gradual removal, or a combination of natural and artificial means of reproducing the crop, may be preferable, because cheaper or more successful in final results of a useful timber crop. . . ."

The silvicultural policy was described as "a mixed system [consisting] in concentrated logging, in which all young volunteer growth and sapling timber of promise is saved as far as practicable, and the valuable conifers are planted in (or sown as the case may be) at the rate of 500 to 1,500 plants per acre, according to needs. Moreover, clumps of trees have been left on elevations and otherwise scattered over the area, to act as seed trees to fill in the crop with hardwood and native spruce. Besides, as the annual cuts are not strung together, but widely separated, the margins of the cut area also provide seeds for that purpose for several years. In other words, a mixed natural and artificial system has been chosen, which promises most success in the reproduction, and probably at the least expenditure, the result being a mixed forest of hardwood and conifers, in which the latter are given the preference." This was not saying that of two silvicultural systems, the selection or the clear cutting and replanting, the latter was being selected. But wide publicity was given to the belief that Fernow planned to clear cut the forest and replant it with a new growth. Fernow did not say this. The most that he said was that *within the prescribed statutory period*, or about fifteen years, in the entire demonstration area both hardwood and softwood might be clear cut and, where nature did not provide new desirable growth, planted with profitable crops. The silvicultural problems could not be dodged. The college could not go into business on the lumbermen's basis, since the purpose was to demonstrate the advantages of forestry management. No reflection on lumbermen in general was imputed, for some were employing forestry methods. These were few at this time, however.

Moreover, the clearing method with artificial replanting, said Fernow, permitted a "tolerably accurate statement of cost."

The harvesting is concentrated and the element of its cost can be readily figured, as also can the cost of planting, and a complete success of the young crop can almost be forced. With the gradual removal and natural seeding methods, an area 10, 20, 30 times as large must be taken into operation simultaneously, to secure the same felling budget annually; that is to say, means of transportation for the harvested crop must be spread and must be maintained over a much larger area in order to secure the single annual felling budgets by gradual removal during a given number of years. . . . The larger the area to be harvested over, the more expensive does the harvest become. . . . Every logger knows that the difference is considerable and will go far to offset the direct money outlay for planting. Finally, the result in a naturally regenerated young crop is by no means as assured as the theorist who discusses the natural regeneration methods *on paper* takes for granted. It is dependent on many uncontrollable or only partially controllable circumstances, among which the occurrence of seed years, proper weather and especially proper soil condition at the time of seeding and germination, proper light conditions during early development, should be mentioned. The result, especially in a mixed forest with species of unequal value, even in the most skillful hands, is not as absolute as with artificial reproduction, which practically is controlled by the purse alone. . . .

In the college forest there were many considerations—high railroad freight rates, low quality of some of the timber, the distance to good markets, the fewness of management personnel, and the amount of supervision required. Roth had left Axton and Ithaca and returned to Washington. Fernow was alone with the problem.

In the Adirondack forests there was not only the tendency of the hardwoods to crowd out the softwoods; regeneration of certain valuable forest species was uncertain. Spruce was an illustration. Rossiter Raymond later put in a letter to Fernow the substance of a discussion which they may have had at this time. Raymond wrote:

I have a very clear and positive recollection of your once saying to me that spruce could not be relied upon for natural replanting, because the seed did not send out a vertical shoot which would penetrate the covering of dead leaves upon the ground. According to my recollection, you said that some other seeds could do this, but the spruce could not . . . [that the fallen seed] would die without taking roots. Also, that spruce trees could not be safely left by culling the forests of the Adirondacks for the purpose of a natural reseeding, because isolated spruce trees could not stand against the winds of that region. . . .

To which Fernow replied:

You are right about spruce regeneration excepting that you overlooked the little saving clause of the expert. I did explain why in nature the reproduction of the spruce when mixed with hardwoods as in the Adirondacks natural re-seeding is difficult, because the spruce seed falls after the foliage of the hardwood trees is shed in the autumn and rarely finds good germinating chance. But, of course, if you want to have it reproduce you can scarify the ground and secure that chance. Again the chance of windfall when spruce trees are isolated must at least influence the method of procedure in securing the natural regeneration, and makes this difficult, although not impossible. . . .

There was another circumstance in the college forest which decisively influenced policy. "It stands to reason," said Fernow in his 1901 report, "that in the systems of natural regeneration only those species can be reproduced which are present in sufficient numbers, hence, if we wish to have in the new crop species which are absent or poorly represented, we must resort to artificial means. In the Wawbeek district, not only has the most valuable part of nature's original crop, the White Pine and Spruce, been previously most severely culled, leaving few or no trees that could be utilized as seed trees, but the young volunteer growth of these species is poorly represented or, as in the case of the White Pine, mostly absent. These species which are recognized as most desirable would have to be, therefore, supplied artificially. . . ."

In the contract of the university with the Brooklyn Cooperage Company, Fernow had reserved for the college the right to prescribe the silvicultural policy. It is true that in a hearing before the United States Industrial Commission in Forestry, the testimony of which was published in 1901 in Volume X of the commission's reports and republished as Bulletin 6 of the college, Fernow admitted that the policy was "to replace the old decrepit natural forest by a new, more valuable forest more or less rapidly." Other similar pronouncements might have been made. However, not until his report for 1902 did Fernow affirm the new policy *in extenso*. At that time, he made it clear that any contemplated denudation would be confined to restricted areas. The annual logging area would comprise five hundred to eight hundred acres. Probably one-half of the acreage would require replanting. Five to eight hundred acres on a thirty thousand acre tract, it would seem, was not extravagant, especially since under the contract no more than "one-fifteenth of the wood standing on the College Forest" was to be cut each year, and thus the clearing of the hardwoods and small quantities of the softwoods would extend over as much as from fifteen to twenty years during which time natural regeneration and artificial replanting would replace parts and the whole with a new and more valuable forest growth.

Fernow should have stated his policy explicitly. It was not simply to clear cut the decrepit, mature, or overmature hardwoods, nor to log the hardwoods to increase the softwood growth, nor to leave the thrifty hardwoods and conifers which were windfirm, to burn the brush economically, to reduce the fire danger by most approved methods, to plant the logged over, burned over, waste, and barren areas, to utilize the inferior material, to educate foresters. It was all of these and more. Fundamentally, he sought to discharge his obligation under the law—to "cut and sell timber at such times, of such species and quantities, and in such manner as it may deem best, with a view . . . of harvesting and reproduction of wood crops and earning a revenue therefrom. . . ." He pleaded for "financial assistance to increase means of prevention of forest fires, at least of the young plantations which are to replace the old crop." But he met difficulties.

Fernow was accused of forest devastation in an era when forest conservation meant forest preservation. His policy of hardwood utilization was condemned as "iniquitous" by at least one scholar. The charge was made that Fernow contemplated "reckless and wholesale denudation, to the detriment of the water-flow and climate. The public prints," wrote Fernow in the hope of silencing the opposition, "also contained statements contrary to fact, as, for instance, that Cornell University derived financial benefits from the sale of the wood, that the company to which the harvest [was] contracted was itself cutting the same down to hoop-poles, that no attempt at reproduction was made, and that the whole State Forest Preserve was being rapidly denuded." He answered that the college of forestry did not control the state forest preserve and had no voice in its management, although certain accomplishments of the college forest were being put into practice within the preserve area, so far as Article VII, section 7, of the constitution permitted. The college forest, Fernow believed, was only secondarily a protection and luxury forest, similar to the preserve. The college forest was primarily a business forest.

The first plantation of the college forest, made in 1899, had gratifyingly demonstrated that it was possible to reforest waste brush lands without extraordinary expenditures. As a result the forest, fish and game commission procured a special appropriation of $4,500 for similiar work. Indeed, the college management had anticipated the result and grown the large amount of plant material needed for the commission's purposes. In his report for 1902 Fernow said:

> Under the superintendence of three graduates of the College employed by the Commission, over 500,000 seedlings grown in the College nurseries and sold to the Commission at nearly cost price were set out this last spring in waste brush land, the area planted—rather thinly—being reported as 700 acres. . . .

In his 1901 report he had rejoiced that during the year

> . . . a surplus of stock was on hand—partly on account of the inability to get the planting area [of the college forest] in condition—and the College had

the gratification of disposing of this surplus to the State Forest, Fish and Game Commission, which intends to follow the good example of the College and recover some 300 acres of waste brush land in its Preserve next spring. For this purpose, the College has sold to the Commission 420,000 seedlings of various descriptions at a slight increase in the cost of producing the same, namely $3 per thousand in the average, including stout transplants and two year seedlings. The incentive to this movement was furnished by a gift of some 6,000 plants from the College nurseries to the Assistant Superintendent of Forests, who, with the assistance of volunteers, planted the same on a bare slope in the Catskills. In this cooperation, which should continue until all the burnt and waste brush lands in the Forest Preserve are restored to useful production, the College sees its first influence for good realized. . . .[85]

The nursery and forest planting policy of the college forest was getting away to an excellent start. Its value and implications for the future were appreciated, but the silvicultural policy was not so well understood. Fernow quoted Austin Cary, forester of the Berlin Mills Company of Brunswick, Maine, "the first and only forester actually practicing in the United States under similar conditions to those prevailing in the Adirondacks," who had written in an article on "Management of Pulpwood Forests":

As for conservative cutting of spruce woods, I will say most emphatically that we find it a difficult and risky process, one that is likely to bring more loss than gain. . . . The winds are continually damaging our native *uncut* stands, and the thinning of woods in all exposed situations, on ridges and mountains, is either entirely impracticable, or must be done with the greatest caution, to ensure that what is left standing will not blow down. The key to success is variation of the cutting according to the stand and lay of the land. The critical matter, the thing that must be continuously thought of, is the safety from wind of what is left. . . . Lastly, we do not hesitate, when we think that it is the proper thing to do, to cut clean.

The college forest had proved that, when hardwoods were cut at all, it was unwise to hold over spruces eight inches or more in diameter. The dangers from windfall, fire, insect infestation, and other considerations, made the diameter criterion sometimes impractical. Each was a factor among the physical conditions which governed the cutting. The tree-height was especially important, for it, said Fernow, "furnishes the leverage to the wind. Another point in favor of clearing, followed by artificial planting, or at least of severe opening of the crowncover, is that the accumulation of duff in many localities is inimical to a satisfactory natural reproduction, which, at least for the conifers, requires that the seed come into contact with mineral soil."

To Fernow forestry was "a technical art, wholly utilitarian, and not, except incidentally, concerned in esthetic aspects of the woods; it is

[85] Evidently the Catskill plantation was located on Wittenburg Mountain between Woodland Valley and Cross Mountain streams in Ulster County. A second plantation made in the fall of 1901 was located by the Commission on Timothyburg Mountain in the town of Shandaken, Ulster County. See Gurth Whipple, *op. cit.*, p. 88.

engaged in utilizing the soil for the production of wood crops, and thereby of the highest revenue attainable. To make the soil produce the largest amount of the most useful wood per acre is the foremost aim of forestry." Sustained annual yield from the forest was not regarded as an inherent and necessary condition of sound forest management, although it was "the ideal to be worked for always and everywhere." Perhaps these were the fundamental doctrines which involved the college forest in controversy. Perhaps Fernow's silvicultural policy, evolved to comply with the statutory injunction "to earn a revenue," might more wisely have been formed with a view to the public's reaction, specifically the reactions of organizations and individuals interested in the Adirondack park and the private lands within its confines. Fernow admitted that time might prove him to have been in error. Since inherently the decision as to silvicultural policy was a matter of opinion about which foresters might differ, he had adhered to no rigid inflexible formula for the entire college forest. The selection method was not applied in the logging areas. Adhering to a gradually enlarging policy of clear cutting and replanting the areas to realize sustained annual forest yield and a desirable secondary forest growth within the experimental period of from fifteen to thirty years, he provided a pretext for controversy which invaded the capitol at Albany, the campus at Ithaca, and finally ended in a toilsome bitter law suit which lasted more than a decade. After a vehement widespread discussion of the wisdom of the new silvicultural policy, it was resolved amid seven discouraging years of a court battle, judgments from which were twice reviewed by the highest court of New York. How persistently the silvicultural question confronted the several courts who heard the arguments of fact and law involved may be deduced from the opinion of the last appellate court whose judgment was affirmed by the Court of Appeals. "For the first two years under this contract [of Cornell University and the Brooklyn Cooperage Company] the selection system was adopted. Thereafter, the clear cutting system was adopted. Nothing in this contract, however, prevented the adoption of either system or of any system which might be found most in accord with scientific forestry. . . ."[86] It cannot be too much stressed that Fernow believed that at least thirty silvicultural methods might have been applied within the college forest area.

President Schurman, in his letter to Governor B. B. Odell, Jr., which transmitted the college's 1902 report, related that the school's attendance had increased from seven students in the first year to seventy, fifteen of the number holding bachelors' or masters' degrees from col-

[86] *People of the State of New York versus The Brooklyn Cooperage Company,* 147 Appellate Division 267, affirmed 205 NY 531.

leges and universities. In response to the unfavorable criticism of the college forest management, a committee of the board of trustees of Cornell University, "consisting, along with the President, of the Hon. S. D. Halliday and Mr. E. L. Williams, who [were] in charge of the University's western timber lands, and Mr. F. C. Cornell, the son of the founder [who located those lands], and a gentleman who also had large experience in the management of western timber lands, visited the Adirondack demonstration area of the College in the month of October, and spent two or three days in a thorough examination of all the operations which the Directors had conducted, or had then in hand, or proposed for the future."

> After a thorough discussion they reached the unanimous conclusion that the Director's policy was a sound one and that, whatever might be good forest management elsewhere, in areas like those now being treated in the demonstration forest, where all the valuable softwoods had already been removed by the lumbermen, and only hardwoods, mostly rotten, remain, the wisest policy was practically to denude and then to replant, as is the practice, indeed, with more than 80 per cent of all the forests in Germany. What the critics of this policy have overlooked is that clear cutting, or what they call denudation, is only a means to an end, and that the end, which is the all-important thing, is the reproduction of wood crops. . . . It is the proud boast of Cornell University never to have failed in anything it has undertaken. It intends, too, to make this great State experiment in forestry a success. The University would not tolerate, nor could it afford to be responsible for, any other result. But it proposes to achieve this result in its own way, i.e., by securing a plan from the most eminent scientific forester in America and then adhering to it, even though ignorant critics who know nothing about forestry think that some other way should be followed. And in pursuing the policy which has been laid down for itself the University has the right to ask of the public a certain amount of patience.

President Schurman also informed the governor that the trustees' committee had voted "at a meeting held in the forest itself that wherever tracts were denuded they should be replanted with the utmost possible speed." Alas! President Schurman's request that "the Legislature . . . soon make adequate provision for the erection of a State Hall worthy of the aims and work of the College" was soon lost from sight in a smear of disputation which covered up the real issues of science and education.

Authorities at this time seem to have been more concerned about the wisdom of Fernow's silvicultural policy than about the nature of Cornell University's legal title to the forest lands. Everyone connected with the forest management, including university officials, seems to have been confident that the university held a good legal title, a title which gave the college the rights of a private owner until the end of the experimental period of thirty years when the title would return to the state. No one seems to have been openly disturbed as to whether the title was impressed with the attributes of a public trust. But the opponents of utilization of lands directly or indirectly connected with the Adirondack forest preserve went behind the discussions of silvicultural policy and brought forth the question of the university's title and rights.

When in 1901 Governor Odell had vetoed a bill to appropriate two hundred thousand dollars to purchase forest lands for the state, chiefly within the boundaries of the proposed Adirondack park, he had urged that "in [his] judgment the time [had] arrived to consider what the policy of the state [was] to be with reference to the acquirement of land in the Adirondacks for the forest preserve. Over $2,000,000 have already been expended for that purpose, and as yet no comprehensive plan [had] been finally determined upon as to the State's policy and the amount that shall be expended in carrying out the improvement for the preservation of the State's forest and water supply. Until a definite scheme shall have been adopted it seems to me unwise to make small appropriations annually."[87]

By 1903[88] the report of the forest, fish and game commission showed that almost eight hundred thousand acres of Adirondack lands were held by about sixty owners or by clubs. The holdings ranged from three hundred to seventy-nine thousand acres in single blocks.[89] New York had been first to espouse forestry in a system of public forest administration, but unobtrusively the state's leadership was going over to a park administration with a qualified forest administration for its remaining public forest lands. The state which had provided an annual appropriation to its forest administration which had been the envy of even the forestry division of the federal government was more and more circumscribing its forestry work. It was not even encouraging the maintenance of a state forestry association.

Fernow had authored the first state forestry administration law. The influence of Dr. Hough had been thrown behind the preserve concept with forest utilization as part of the program. Fernow had watched the law weaken under the weight of circumstances, and its importance dwindle. This had taken place although Governor Hill, Governor Flower, Governor Black, and Governor Roosevelt in strong language had embraced both utilitarian and aesthetic concepts. Each had said that the state-owned forests might and should provide a large source of revenue to the state, as well as protect water supply and provide summer homes and sanitariums and pleasure resorts. Moreover, forestry was sponsored by governors of both parties and was presumably nonpartisan.

[87] *The Forester* VII, 7, July 1901, p. 178.

[88] See an editorial in *The Independent*, Dec. 24, 1903, a reprint of which was found among Fernow's papers.

[89] See also Gurth Whipple, *op. cit.*, pp. 168ff.

Comparatively the Cornell forest covered a very small fraction of the entire Adirondack forest preserve. Its logging area thus far, a part of which had been replanted, was a very small fraction of the college forest. Nevertheless the fire danger, the noise and smoke nuisance, and other considerations prompted a group of property owners near Upper Saranac Lake to organize and file an application with the forest, fish and game commission to have the state's purchase of the demonstration forest area declared void.[90]

The application was brought in the name of Eric P. Swenson, representing the association of property owners, and the petition was signed by such prominent and influential citizens as ex-Governor Levi P. Morton, Jules S. Bache, Sidney M. Colgate, Charles Peabody, Isaac N. Seligman, F. S. Bangs, Alfred L. White, and others. The association was represented by James F. Tracey and John G. Agar, both of whom, the latter especially, remained as counsel in the long years of battle in the courts which followed. Agar at one time served as president of the Association for the Protection of the Adirondacks. Tracey was an attorney of Albany; and Agar, who was also associated with David Wilcox, was of New York City. Cornell University was represented at the hearing by Fernow, President Schurman, and State Civil Service Commissioner Cuthbert Pound.

The applicants questioned the constitutionality of the law under which the college forest administration was created and charged the college with committing an *ultra vires* act in cutting and selling timber from the forest. The courts of New York had sustained a series of precedents quite favorable to the state in its efforts to effectuate forest administration within the preserve.[91] The claim that the college had exceeded its authority was supported by Lieutenant-Governor Timothy L. Woodruff, who argued that since he was a member of the state forest preserve board when the tract was bought, he knew that Governor Black and the legislature had never contemplated authorizing such a program of forest denudation as the college had inaugurated. Although Fernow took the stand and explained the forestry objectives of the college forest, the arguments of the applicants were unyielding. Counsellor Agar charged that the school intended to lay bare the entire tract. The hearing was adjourned to permit both sides to submit briefs.

[90] For accounts of the hearing on this application see *Forestry and Irrigation* VIII, 2, Feb. 1902, p. 47; also report of the college for 1902, p. 24. During 1902 the planted area was increased to "about 275 acres," the year's new planting being necessarily confined to wasteland. Until January 1903 only "about 1,500 acres" had been logged; and of this, 500 acres could be said to be "denuded." A total of 105 acres of the cut area was replanted, but more than a million seedlings in the two large nurseries were ready to plant in the balance.

[91] Gurth Whipple, *op. cit.*, p. 35.

The opponents of the college forest were not content to go to the forest, fish and game commission. They went also to the attorney-general of the state. During the summer of 1902 Attorney-General Davies rendered his opinion[92] that the college had not violated any provision of law, constitutional or otherwise. No cause to warrant commencement of an action before a judicial or quasi-judicial body to dispossess the college of its forest tract was shown. The opinion of this attorney-general was very important since it reflected the current opinion concerning the law at the time. It established by the highest public authority obtainable that every action thus far taken by the university and the college had the stamp of legality. When these questions reached the courts, years were consumed before an answer was finally obtained. The attorney-general's opinion read:

> The contention rests entirely upon the assumption that the lands in question are "the lands of the state" and this assumption is wholly unwarranted. The lands are the property of Cornell University. The act in pursuance of which they were purchased provides that the "university shall have the title, possession, management and control of such land" for a period of thirty years. . . . The doctrine of equitable ownership and resulting trust has no application. Any corporation or individual owning lands within the forest preserve may cut and destroy the timber upon it at will. It is only the lands of the state which are protected.[93]

The attorney-general rejected the argument that since monies of the state were unlawfully used in the purchase of the college forest area the state was the equitable owner of the demonstration area. Had the contention been sustained, the college forest would have become state lands subject to the provison of the constitution which forbade timber cutting.

Fernow's course of business conduct was legally sustained. That another attorney-general later arrived at a different conclusion does not impugn the soundness of Fernow's actions. When the next opinion was rendered, there was another fact presented which was not part of the picture in 1902. Fernow knew that competent legal counsel had drawn the contract signed by the Brooklyn Cooperage Company and the board of trustees of Cornell University. The question of the nature of Cornell University's title to the college forest at that time was necessarily passed on and settled to the satisfaction of counsel. According to Fernow, some time was consumed by counsel deciding whether, in point of law, the board of trustees had sufficient authority to enter into the contract with the Cooperage Company. The Cooperage Company probably also had

[92] *Forestry and Irrigation,* July 1902, p. 273.

[93] Fernow expressed this view in his 1902 report (p. 25), saying, "The College of Forestry does *not* control the State forest reserve, has not even a choice in its management, nor is it operating on any State lands, the tract at its disposal having been deeded directly from the owners to Cornell University. . . ."

counsel, since it was investing large sums of money to build mills, railroad tracks, and to purchase more land.

It is said that Fernow was approached with an offer of compromise—the New York State College of Forestry was to be richly endowed and the college was to remove the objectionable features of the demonstration area. Private capital was to purchase the entire Cooperage Company, or at least the company's rights to the contract with the university. Fernow saw at stake the obligations to the state, the college, and, most of all, to forestry. He walked away from the offerer, saying vehemently, "No compromise."

As might have been expected, opposition to the college forest also resounded in the state legislature. In 1902 a special committee of the legislature was appointed to visit the Adirondacks, examine the state's property, and report to the assembly in 1903.[94] They returned with recommendations submitted to the forest preserve board and, incidentally, with criticism directed toward the management of the college forest. The thoroughness of their investigation on the college forest tract was, to say the least, inadequate. Fernow presented to the senate committee on March 2, 1903, a seven-page pamphlet written on behalf of the college and entitled, "Brief Statement Concerning the General Policy and Practice on the College Forest." He reiterated his outline of silvicultural policy presented in the college's report for 1899 and stated that experience had caused the management to decide that "the two methods of natural regeneration and artificial replacement [would] be used simultaneously according to the various conditions found on the ground; some parcels [would] be entirely denuded and replanted, others containing sufficiently young crops [would] be merely thinned." The large intention was to cut over and *reconstruct* the forest. It was true that only "1,500 acres [had] been cut over, of which approximately 40% [needed] replanting." But did these facts sustain the extravagant and exaggerated—indeed, the false—claims that the forest lands were being denuded? The land was never to be denuded. Fifteen to thirty years were to be used to apply the policy of gradually removing the available timber harvest. During that period, a young crop—the product of natural regeneration and artificial replacement, and a much more valuable forest, an admixture of conifers and hardwoods—would be covering the tract and replacing the old with a new harvest. But the committee and Fernow differed as to the area extent which required replanting.

The committee found only 275 acres replanted and brush and debris strewn over the balance of the cut area. This Fernow explained:

Owing to difficulties in getting the cordwood cut and removed, the planting

[94] *Forest Leaves* IX, 3, June 1903, p. 38.

areas could not be got ready in time, so that only 105 acres of the cut over area have been planted, but in addition about 170 acres of burns and wastes outside the cut area, or altogether an equivalent of nearly half the cut acreage has been planted, with altogether round 250,000 plants and over 50 pounds of seed.

The delay in delivery of cordwood, together with other circumstances, has also cut down the expected profits, from which the planting operations were to be paid for, while the close economy forced upon the management by curtailing the initial working fund has prevented its use in that direction.

Estimating the harvest now ready for delivery, there have been cut and delivered, wholly or partially, approximately 7 millions feet of logs and 10,000 cords. About 10,000 cords of the logged area remains still uncut and uncorded.

The committee stated, to quote *Forest Leaves*' interpretation of the report, "that if it was necessary to remove the trees, in order to substitute a better class of timber, it would have been better to burn it off, thus saving the money which it is claimed is being lost in carrying out the lumber contract, requesting that the existing contract be canceled, and the work of removing the old forests be stopped, the efforts being directed for a period to the management of nurseries for seedlings and the replanting of waste-places." This does not imply that *Forest Leaves*[95] endorsed the report, although it did commend the committee for its "intelligent appreciation of the value of forests and anxiety for their preservation and care." But it was not admitted that money was being lost under the contract with the Brooklyn Cooperage Company. Fernow admitted that he did not regard the reconstruction work "in all respects satisfactory. The reason, however," he said, "does not lie in errors of policy or method, but in the lack of financial background." Fernow had never found it advantageous to seek cancellation of the contract. He had fretted and sought more money but never resorted to this extreme.

Delivery of the logged material at the railroad siding to the Cooperage Company under the contract, together with an unexpected and unprovided-for rise in costs, had taken so much of the college forest's capital that all the brush and debris could not be removed or destroyed immediately. This presented a difficult problem. Fernow had frequently recognized the fire risk and pleaded for adequate facilities to guard against it, but he had had little luck. In 1903 there occurred a disastrous fire. 1903 was one of the most disastrous fire years in the history of the Adirondack forests. Fernow would never have followed the committee's recommendation to burn off rather than log the trees to be removed in order to substitute a better class of timber. He candidly admitted:

The poor character of the old crop, coupled with unfavorable market conditions, makes it doubtful whether it is possible to reconstruct a severely

[95] See John Birkinbine's editorial criticism in *Forest Leaves* IX, 4, Aug. 1903. p. 49.

culled forest in the Adirondacks by means of profits from the sale of the old hardwood crop alone.

But his confidence was set forth in his conclusion:

Since satisfactory planting in the Adirondacks can be done, as demonstrated by the College, for less than $10 per acre, if we allow a cut of only 6,000 cubic feet of timberwood equal to 120 standards in the 80th year, the investment of $10 would have paid an interest of nearly 4%, even at present stumpage prices, while a rise of prices of more than 2% may be confidently anticipated, as demonstrated by the experience in this and other countries. Expenditures similar to those practiced by the European nations are bound to produce similar results.

Perhaps a 30,000 acre demonstration tract was too large an area for a first experiment in forestry, but Fernow was dissatisfied because he could not place it on the basis of the European forests which were often many times larger.

Fernow has told of other confusions which had found their way into the assembly chambers at Albany, stories equally exaggerated and which must have reached the governor:

It appears that the false relation at the start with the Preserve Board had engendered some inimical attitude bound to make trouble in every way possible. At the time the Director was charged on the floor of the Senate with using oleomargarine in his camps contrary to law. It looked as if they had him on this charge for he was actually using it in the camp. Fortunately a flaw in the wording of the law saved the situation. The law provided severe penalties for manufacturing or selling certain described butter substitutes in the state, and also for feeding materials "in contravention to this law" to employees. Since the material used had neither been manufactured nor sold in the state, being bought in Pennsylvania, it was not in contravention to the law. The danger was averted. Another similar trumpery was made in the same place, when it was claimed that the College was keeping ferrets in camp, undoubtedly for the illegal purpose of hunting. The bill book, however, revealed in a saddler's bill the purchase of a pair of "ferrets" for fifty cents. Some one had taken the pains to look over the bills in the auditor's office and was so anxious to find something wrong that he did not stop to read carefully.

These trivial annoyances were to be followed by more serious troubles. It had been planned to begin logging operations in the furthermost corner of the property, away from public observation and private summer camps; but the severe curtailment of the working fund prevented the extension of the railroad to these parts, and forced the beginnings to be made in the more conspicuous part adjoining the summer camps of wealthy New York bankers. These, especially two of them, who had used the tract for hunting purposes, took umbrage at the operations and began proceedings to stop them. First, a newspaper war criticizing the methods of management was begun; then the Attorney General was interpellated to interfere, but without success; then a legislative committee of inspection was secured and, without advising the College authorities or their superintendent, was taken around by the bankers, dined and wined and provided with a disapprobation report. Finally the Governor was "seen." No additional appropriation for the woods work had been asked for. The bill providing appropriation for the College was passed without debate. After the Legislature had adjourned, the Governor vetoed the bill "because serious criticism had been made of the College Forest Management." . . .

Perhaps a few words might be added regarding the legality of the purchase of the tract by State money and its deeding to the University for thirty years to carry out the demonstration. It was a "contingent" purchase. There were many precedents in purchases of land for the Adirondack park where the contingency was the removal of the spruce by the former owner. These precedents might have appeared natural to apply to the present case.[96]

Three appropriation bills were presented to Governor Odell. The plantation of the state forest preserve inspired by results obtained on the college forest had been so successful that an appropriation of $6,000 had been allowed by the legislature to further the project of planting up wastelands of the state. Press, public, and Adirondack residents had given the measure their hearty support. The governor, however, vetoed the bill! A second bill of a similar nature which granted $5,000 for a special demonstration on the Cornell forest tract was approved by the legislature. By this time two large nurseries, "capable," Fernow said, "of producing one million plants of 2-3 year old pines, spruce, and other species," were established at Axton. The astounding fact was that the governor signed this bill. The third bill presented the annual appropriation of $10,000 for the school. This bill had passed the legislature without opposition. No criticism or complaint had ever been directed toward the work of the school on the campus at Ithaca. At its last registration the New York school was said to be "larger than any French or German forestry school." The governor, however, vetoed this bill. An unsubstantiated story purported to account for this inexplicable situation by intimating that the governor got the bills confused. Intending to do away with the demonstration forest and its logging activities, he crippled the planting work of the forest, fish and game commission, an organization unaffiliated with the college forest. Even more astonishing, he did away with the New York State College of Forestry. Perhaps the governor believed he was following the recommendations of the legislative committee. On at least two occasions Fernow charged in published statements that he was influenced by two wealthy New York bankers, owners of estates near the college forest. Governor Odell may have believed that the college forest should be confined to nursery work and wasteland planting. He may have believed that Cornell University was involved in a contract which meant certain increased financial losses to the management, and therefore indirectly to the state. He did not say so. What cause did he have to deny to the school its annual appropriation which had been granted for four years without serious protest or question? The school was now flourishing as

[96] "Intimate History of the College of Forestry etc."

the largest and most extensive forestry institution of its kind in North America.

Justifying his action, the governor was reported to have said that ". . . the operations of this college of forestry have been subjected to grave criticism, as they have practically denuded the forest lands of the State without compensating benefits. I deem it wise, therefore, to withhold approval of this item until a more scientific and more reasonable method is pursued in the forestry of the lands now under control of Cornell University."[97]

Obviously the governor was unacquainted with the history of the college forest, with the intentions or plans of the management, or with the accomplishments thus far. Presumably he had fallen victim to the erroneous propaganda which had been directed at the forest and its management. If he disapproved of the silvicultural policy in the forest, he had that privilege as a citizen of the state. He had the right to disagree with Fernow. But why should he have pursued an arbitrary irrational course which did violence to the school? It is useless to conjure up explanations. The fact was that the New York State College of Forestry inevitably would go out of existence unless the board of trustees of Cornell University, or even Fernow alone, could save it as a private institution. The next decision fell to Cornell University.

Fernow pursued a dignified course. He had received the news of the governor's veto at a dance, but he did not let it spoil the party. *Forestry Quarterly*, which Fernow edited and which was an official publication of the college, said:[98]

> Ostensibly the Governor's veto of State aid was applied, because a legislative committee had expressed its disapproval of the technical methods employed in the College Forest; and the University abandoned the College because of the Governor's veto and its helplessness to continue the College on its own motion.
>
> It appears that the report of the legislative committee was made unaided, as far as known, by professional advice, and was secured directly or indirectly by a group of camp owners on Saranac Lake, who did not like the logging operations on the College tract (adjoining their properties), on which they had exercised hunting privileges. Having failed to secure from the Attorney General an opinion, that the College forest experiment was unconstitutional, having failed in spite of a vigorous campaign in the newspapers through two years and in spite of the adverse report of the committee (which came into the woods without advising the University authorities of their intention and under the guidance of the camp-owners), to influence the legislature, and not being able to stop the operations in the woods, they secured directly or indirectly the Governor's aid. *The closing of the College, which, however, does not bring about the stoppage of logging operations, only withdrawing the technical supervision of the same, is presumably intended merely as an entering wedge to force the legislature to a closing of*

[97] *Forestry Quarterly* I, 4, July 1903, p. 156. [98] *ibid.* II, 1, Nov. 1903, p. 42.

the entire demonstration by buying out the contracts under which the University is otherwise forced to continue logging operations.[99]

The College being a state institution, it was natural for the University to obey the Governor's injunction to close it, although it had been generally hoped that, knowing the circumstances which led to the veto, the Board of Trustees would maintain this very successful educational branch, especially as it promised to become self-supporting. The President's report to the Trustees emphatically defends the methods of management criticized by the legislative committee, closing the arguments with the words: "The University stands by its expert"; but the report then pleads inability to carry on the work of the College for lack of means or, indeed inability to do otherwise than discontinue: "the action of the state authorities seems to give the Trustees no alternative."

Some legislators voiced disapproval of the silvicultural policy. Fernow, however, summoned to his aid the authority of European foresters, especially those of Germany. Furthermore, no serious discussion among American foresters arose to support the action of the governor. The profession on numerous occasions protested the action of the governor. Fernow offered to carry on the school, financing it by the tuitions. The students actively supported the offer. But on June 17, 1903, at the annual spring meeting of the board of trustees of Cornell University, further instruction in the college was ordered suspended. The suspension, the trustees added, would hold until the state saw fit to provide funds again to take up the work. In the interim, all appointments to the instruction force, including that of the director, were vacated.[100] The New York State College of Forestry did not go out of existence. The charter was not surrendered. Mynderse Van Cleef of the board of trustees was constituted director. By chapter 599 of the laws of 1903, the legislature had granted and the governor had approved five thousand dollars for the college to be used in a reforestation demonstration. The authorities thus had a small working fund, but in June 1903 all planting of the logged over, barren, waste, and brush areas ceased. Evidently the fund was used to clear up the land and plant some new trees. After this time the university trustees requested no further appropriations for the forestry college. Since July 1, 1900, when the working fund appropriation of thirty thousand dollars and the income from the logging contract and other sources had become available, no specific legislative appropriations had been made for the college forest. In his report for 1902, which was transmitted to the legislature on January 21, 1903, Fernow had asked for "a substantial increase of appropriations for both and a building to house the college. . . ." His financial statement showed an unexpended balance of $11,173.13. Indeed, for a number of years thereafter, while testimony was being taken

[99] Italics mine.

[100] *Forestry and Irrigation* IX, 7, July 1903, p. 319.

in the cause, *People of the State of New York versus Brooklyn Cooperage Company* impleaded with Cornell University, an unexpended balance of working capital of upwards of eight to nine thousand dollars remained.

The courts later found that the "expenses of cutting and delivering timber to the Brooklyn Cooperage Company under terms of [the university's] contract [had] proved so great, no profit was derived therefrom by Cornell." But the intention of the experiment had not been to enable the *university* to make money. Fernow in his 1902 report, which reached the legislature and the governor during the fateful year 1903, had explained:

> It will be remembered that the amount asked for working fund (*not* annual appropriation!) was $50,000, while only $30,000 were allowed by the Legislature three years ago. As stated in last year's report, expenditures for permanent investment in railroad, roads, nurseries, buildings, equipment, absorbed about $12,000, leaving only $18,000 to carry on the logging and forestry operations, which involve the cutting and delivery of 8,000 to 10,000 cords and 2,500,000 feet of logs, besides an uncertain amount of pulp wood. . . . While it has been possible to keep the working fund with which the operations started unimpaired or nearly so, the absence of profits has necessarily prevented an extension of the planted area to the desired amount.

Fernow had asked for "an increase in working fund or else annual appropriations for silvicultural work. . . ." He expatiated on many matters which had reduced profits—unfavorable labor conditions, wage increases, increases in living costs, difficulties in securing woodchoppers, inability to install effective modern machinery and apparatus to reduce logging costs and cordwood splitting costs, unfavorable weather conditions, and other factors. "At present," wrote Fernow to the authorities, "the necessity of 'making both ends meet' prevents the development of the experimental side, and hampers silvicultural work. I can only urge that the work in the College Forest should be considered as it was intended by the legislative act establishing it, as an *experiment*, even though it is carried on like a *business* on business principles. . . . If properly conducted and without stint, the expenditures of the present will be repaid with interest in the future, as has been the case with all European State forest administrations."

John Gifford wrote:

> Dr. Schurman, president of the University, said in a letter to me that he had personally seen the governor and that there would be no appropriation for the college. He said that the state authorities were determined to stop the work and "force an issue." Some said the trouble was that Fernow was not liked by the politicians who could not use him. The real issue was probably money. Although the professors would have worked a couple of years for half pay or nothing rather than see such a healthy and successful institution die such an unnatural death many have felt that it was to Cornell's

discredit that they did not find a way at least for its temporary continuance.[101]

Fernow offered to continue the work without salary. He later gave voice to another rumor: "A creditable rumor has it that for thus gracefully submitting to the whip of the Governor, the University secured the Agricultural building. . . ."[102] In other words, Cornell University, without intending or planning to do so, traded the New York State College of Forestry for the New York State College of Agriculture which was established in 1903 and for which Roberts Hall was built.[103] Dr. Liberty Hyde Bailey, who became at this time dean of the New York State College of Agriculture and director of the state's agricultural experiment station, with Speaker Nixon of the New York State Assembly, also visited the Cornell forest at Axton and sustained Fernow's work as proceeding in the right direction. Moreover, Bailey pleaded with the Cornell board not to disband the college of forestry. Bailey, like Fernow, however, was overruled.

What actually prevented the trustees from giving encouragement to a proposal later officially offered by Governor Odell to reestablish a college of forestry at Cornell University was that the university was involved, or soon was to become actually a party, in the most widely discussed litigation in the history of forestry in the United States.

The Brooklyn Cooperage Company had continued to cut timber on the Cornell forest. Another attorney-general, Julius M. Mayer, had come into office. In 1905 at the request of the association of residents of Upper Saranac Lake, he rendered another opinion in the matter of the Cornell forest, there being the added fact that now the New York State College of Forestry was pursuing no technical forest management. Mayer examined the contract of the Brooklyn Cooperage Company with Cornell University, and said:[104]

There is no suggestion that the authorities of Cornell University entered into this contract through other than good motives. It seems that they had been advised by the forestry expert in their employ that the best method of experiment was to denude the tract, in order that the result of reforestation could be ascertained within the life of men then living. So far as the testimony and arguments before me disclosed, no official of the State of New York was consulted, directly or indirectly, in regard to the agreement above referred to. It cannot be said, therefore, that the state was in any way responsible for this contract, or that it acquiesced in the terms thereof. In my opinion it was never contemplated that under any circumstances Cornell was to be permitted to make a contract for the stripping of the forest within a

[101] "Reminiscences etc."

[102] "Intimate History of the College of Forestry etc."

[103] This is discussed more fully in the author's *Liberty Hyde Bailey, a Story of American Plant Sciences*, Princeton Univ. Press, 1949.

[104] *Forestry and Irrigation* XI, 7, July 1905, p. 295.

possible fifteen years on a tract of land which was dedicated to an educational experiment of thirty years.

The attorney-general brought an action to enjoin the alleged "waste of land" being perpetrated by the Brooklyn Cooperage Company and to stop further cutting under the contract. Obviously, if the forest was held to have become part of the state forest preserve, the land was made subject to the restriction as to cutting embodied in the constitution. In January 1906 at Albany, a court at a special term overruled a demurrer to the complaint of the state. From this decision an appeal was taken by the Cooperage Company and was transferred from the third to the fourth judicial department for lack of a quorum of members qualified to hear it. That year Cornell University was impleaded with the Cooperage Company. The decision was against the company, and an appeal then went to the highest court, which held the act creating the college and experimental tract constitutional, but that the facts of the state's complaint stated a cause of action. Thus far, the cause had been tried on the pleadings, the complaint and answer or demurrer.[105]

Not until 1908 did the suit come on for hearing *on the merits* of the controversy. The issues were now joined and the court was now ready for the relevant testimony. The questions were whether the claimed land-wastage should be restrained and the property reconveyed by the university to the state.

It should be noticed in passing that by the time the forest situation was considered by the courts on its merits, "less than half of the timber had been removed." The Cooperage Company, moreover, had expended "upwards of $350,000."[106] The situation in 1908 was very different from what it had been in 1898-1903. To use the language of Presiding Judge Smith, "From 15,000 acres of the 30,000 purchased a large part of the timber had already been removed. From that part it was necessary to remove still further in order to conduct the experiment of reforestation. And upon the balance it was necessary to remove substantially all of the timber." Of course, the denuded areas, which had been logged since the college had ceased its technical management had not all been replanted. The Brooklyn Cooperage Company had assumed no obligation to continue the reforestation experiment. Even the high courts were not disturbed by the fact that ". . . the contract called for the clearing of all the land. . . ." Since the court decided the cause on the basis

[105] 187 N.Y. 142, affirming 114 App. Div. 723, argued Dec. 19, 1906, and decided Jan. 8, 1907. Judgment in the Appellate Division of the Supreme Court in the 4th judicial department had been entered on order of the court on Aug. 7, 1906.

[106] See the majority opinion, 147 Appellate Division 267, rendered in 1911 and based on evidence introduced at the trial on the merits 1908-1910. This judgment of the Appellate Division of the Supreme Court was affirmed the next year, 1912, by the Court of Appeals without opinion, 205 NY 531, on authority of its former, or first, decision, 187 NY 142.

of the university's title to the forest premises, this was an *obiter* finding, and therefore inconclusive. No criticism from a legal point of view is implied; but from the forestry standpoint it may be noticed that, while the contract bound the cooperage company to erect stave mill and wood alcohol manufactories, and its railroad facilities, to take from the property and utilize the logs and cordwood harvested and delivered by the college in accordance with the contract (which included provision for an annual notice as to the amount needed required to be served by the company on the college), in no year was the university obliged to cut "more than one-fifteenth of the wood standing on the College Forest." The courts of New York construed this as the "most important subdivision of the contract." Fernow in his "Brief Statement Regarding the General Policy and Practice on the College Forest" prepared for the Senate committee in 1903, described this as requiring the cutting and delivery at rail of "not to exceed 1/20 of the hardwood timber standing, useful for the specific manufacture, or as much as needed by the manufacturer." Further, he pointed out that the university retained "the right to reserve and leave uncut whatever under good forestry practice should be so reserved and left uncut." More than this, the university was vested with a discretionary privilege to decide as to the uncut timber to be left "alongside of rivers, streams, ponds, highways, and firelines, to a distance of 25 rods, and also to leave the timber uncut wherever else for reasons of good policy it [was] desirable to leave the woods undisturbed, as on mountain knolls and steep slopes. Furthermore, a reservation [was] made of wood required for local needs, to the amount of 1500 cords per annum."

During the next fifteen to twenty years, the hardwoods (maple, beech, birch, etc.) were to be logged and it may be added that "small quantities" of softwoods (spruce, pine, etc.) were sold in amounts as these were found necessary to remove under "proper forestry management." Nevertheless, without much regard for the fundamental intention of marketing primarily the hardwoods, the view of the last court to submit a written opinion was that irrespective of whether the contract called for complete, or substantially complete, clearance of the forest to "accomplish the purposes of the experiment thereupon," this fact of itself "was in complete harmony with the purposes of the act, and with the powers given to the university thereunder, both express and implied. . . ." Nor was the court disturbed over the representation that "the experiment could have been carried on with a smaller acreage. . . ."

Evidently the strong argument made against the college forest was the disastrous fire of 1903. Fernow testified in the law suit several times. He prefaced his explanation with a description of his forestry training in Germany:

We left the brush in the forest. We protected the forest from fires by forest rangers and by having proper morals in the neighborhood. . . . We could keep from having fires such as occurred on Lot 23 in the Adirondacks, among the brush because the morals of the community [were good]. The people had free range of those forests. . . .

Fernow hoped that the courts' decisions would point answers to several forestry matters involving law. The qualifications of a forester required to testify as an expert in a legal action needed definition. Although Charles S. Chapman, then an assistant forester of the United States forest service, admitted that he had never conducted a working plan in the Adirondacks, he testified that the Cornell experiment had shown "that clear cutting and transplanting could not be successfully carried on in that locality. . . ." He maintained that "a forest of beauty could [not] be produced on that land in thirty years." He questioned whether "the material grown on the land would have any market value at the end of thirty years. I refer," he said, "to spruce as well as pine." Early in 1908 Fernow wrote Graves, "I have just returned from . . . a three days' session in the court at Albany. . . . It is an interesting case as it seems to hinge mainly on definitions, what is forestry? what is an experiment? what is an expert? who is an authority? . . ."

On March 5, in an address, "Present Condition of American Silviculture,"[106a] Graves took official notice of this lawsuit before the members of the Society of American Foresters. Seemingly, as much as Fernow, Graves expected that the court's decision might help to clear away some of the disagreement concerning fundamental silvicultural policy with respect to state and privately owned forest lands in the Adirondacks. This address again will be referred to in the next chapter in connection with Graves' important two-fold advocacy before the society and in government forestry circles of the need for, first, more forest management experience in American forests, and, second, scientific research and practice of the sort very soon afterward commenced at forestry experiment stations established in connection with the national forests. For forestry in North America, his intention was the shaping and realization of definite aims, clearly understood policies, and reasonable agreement among foresters upon underlying principles of silviculture. Graves' comments with regard to silvicultural practice in Adirondack forests are pertinent at this point in our narrative because these disclose a widespread, almost official, interest among foresters in the questions of policy introduced in the testimony of the law suit. Graves was never a witness in the case nor did he seek to influence either testimony or the decision. But he used this situation to argue to foresters the need for settling constructively, as far as possible, matters of principle and policy in silvicultural practice. Graves complained that

[106a] *Proc. Soc. Am. For.* III, 1, pp. 29-40, at p. 33.

foresters "[are] not agreed as to the proper silvicultural treatment of State forests in the Adirondacks, and this disagreement has led to a notable suit now in progress of the State against the Brooklyn Cooperage Company, a suit which hinges on what constitutes correct silviculture on the State forests of New York. It is equally true," he added, "that there is emphatic disagreement as to the principles of handling large private tracts in the Adirondacks and elsewhere, disagreements not of details of marking timber, but of fundamental silvicultural policy." Graves commented on the applicability of the selection system for present conditions in American forests. Two years later, in a formal paper,[106b] "The Selection System," he defined the applicability and limitations of the system as a silvicultural policy.

Fernow's attitude was shown by a letter written during the middle of the summer of 1908 to Hugh Potter Baker where he said, "I have just returned from the hearing in the Cornell case at Albany, where Mr. C. S. Chapman was pitted against me as an expert in forestry matters. I do not think that even his own attorneys could fail to have become doubtful as to the width of his experience, which is the basis of expertness, of the young gentleman. He claimed that selection forest was the only experiment worth trying, to which the simple reply is that no experiment is necessary if it is known that there is only one way of doing it."[107]

As a forester Chapman represented a viewpoint not at that time in agreement with Fernow's but must have been convincing as a witness. In later years he occupied positions of responsibility with the forest service and with private forestry agencies. Foresters today are not entirely in agreement on points of policy. His views then were given as conclusions of opinion. He spoke within his rights. Nevertheless, in 1917, Ralph C. Bryant and a group of eminent American foresters, many of them former students of Fernow, gathered at Tupper Lake and examined the forest conditions of the Cornell forest approximately fifteen years after the management experiment. Although no care had been taken of the premises for a number of years, although fires had damaged many of the valuable plantations—among them the most valuable one planted in 1901 at Cross Clearing—the conferees outlined a policy of silvicultural management agreed to by all present. Bryant wrote an article[108] on the subject, saying that while many foresters regarded

[106b] *Proc. Soc. Am. For.* V, 1, 1910, pp. 1-17.

[107] See B. E. Fernow, "The Results of Scientific Forest Management," *Forestry Quarterly* VI, 3, Sept. 1908, p. 229, where Chapman was referred to as an "expert of the Forest Service"; also, "A Place Adequate to Meet our Needs for Wood Timber," address before the Society for the Protection of New Hampshire Forests, *For. Quar.* XI, 3, Sept. 1913, pp. 307f., *American Forestry*, Aug. 1913, and reprint.

[108] "Silviculture at Axton and in the Adirondacks Generally," *Journal of Forestry* XV, 7, Nov. 1917, p. 891; see also Fernow's "Axton Plantations," *ibid.* XV, 8, Dec. 1917, p. 988.

the college experiment as a failure, "as a matter of fact time [had] shown the policy to have been right. *There is no better vindication of Dr. Fernow's policy than the present condition of the logged-off areas near Wawbeek. All plantations which were made under twelve different conditions have proved entirely successful. . . .*" Bryant very much resented the discontinuance of the college, and he told Fernow so. On September 11, 1917, Fernow wrote to R. H. Campbell, saying, "You may have heard . . . of our visit to Axton to inspect the various plantations which have proved themselves entirely successful after 15 years. . . ."

Fernow confidently believed that the law suit, *People of the State of New York versus The Brooklyn Cooperage Company,* would be decided against the state. He confided to others his expectations. But the decision on the merits was in favor of the state. The testimony of Fernow, Filibert Roth, Clifford Pettis, and other witnesses of distinction amounted to little. While in *obiter dicta* the court passed on a number of issues, the basic legal point was decisive. The lands of the Cornell forest were held to be state lands. Cornell University did not appeal from the decision on the merits as delivered in 1910. The appellate division, when reviewing the case on the pleadings, had held that *it seemed* that the university held the title to the forest land as trustee for the state. When the cause on its merits was reviewed, the court affirmed the judgment of the Albany Special Term that the people of the state were equitable owners of the college forest land, and, therefore, both the university and the Cooperage Company were enjoined from cutting any more timber. The university, moreover, was required to convey the lands to the state. This judgment in turn was reviewed by the state's highest court and affirmed without opinion on March 19, 1912. The court,[109] consequently, made the law of the case the decision of the Appellate Court. No federal question was found to be involved. The Cornell forest was found to be state land and the court, indicating no liability on the part of the university to the Cooperage Company by virtue of their contract, said in effect that if the Cooperage Company had any recourse for its losses, its reimbursement by the state would have to be voluntary. Fernow condensed his version of the law suit in a paragraph:[110]

[109] In 187 N.Y. 142 the court had found no constitutional infringements in the act creating the College of Forestry (chapter 122, N.Y. laws of 1898). Since the legal title of the college forest lands had never been vested in the State, Article VII, section 7, of the constitution had no application. When Cornell University as "a subordinate governmental agency" or "trustee" for the State was ordered by the court to convey the legal title to the State, the college forest lands obviously became part of the Adirondack Preserve, and the constitutional provision became effective. Up to this time, even on maps of the Adirondack Preserve, the college forest had occupied a unique place. The decisions are almost impossible to harmonize, embodying a number of difficult distinctions.

[110] "Intimate History of the College of Forestry etc."

A three-cornered lawsuit extending through many years between the Cooperage Company (which had spent around a quarter million dollars on its plant), the State, and the University ensued and finally, most iniquitously, the Company was ousted of its contract . . . and the tract was added to the State Forest Preserve. Thus ended the first attempt at introducing forestry methods in the State of New York as a demonstration and nothing is left of it but the plantations as far as these have not been burned up."

The Brooklyn Cooperage law suit had done more to make the state and the nation forestry-conscious than any single event for some time. Fernow conducted himself as a professional forester and educator through the long years of conflict. Again and again during the law suit and afterward he objected to any construction which narrowed silvicultural method to a choice between the selection method and any other one method such as the clear cutting and replanting. In a letter written March 5, 1912, to R. M. Parker, president of the Brooklyn Cooperage Company, Fernow said:

I had supposed that the spectre of the silvicultural systems had been laid; evidently it is still alive. . . . There are not three but more nearly 30 silvicultural systems or methods, none of them bad, worse or worst, but really more or less readily applicable and desirable according to conditions, natural and economic, and to be applied according to the forester's judgment.

I am certainly not on record anywhere as having advocated the selection system as preferable to any other. Economic conditions may force us to the use of this system, recognized as fit only where better systems cannot be, as yet, used. It is the least intensive method of reproducing a crop. . . . We did not practice [the selection method], and did not contemplate practicing it in those places where we did our cutting, whatever we might have done elsewhere, simply because it was not desirable.

When the Brooklyn Cooperage Company suit was at its height, E. A. Sterling, a former student of Fernow at Cornell, for a while employed by the New York forest, fish and game commission, later prominent as an American authority on "railroad forestry" as forester of the Pennsylvania Railroad, and for some time, along with Graves, Fernow's most generous and able aide in publishing *Forestry Quarterly*, wrote:

At two hearings in the case of State of New York vs. The Brooklyn Cooperage Company and Cornell University, this question of natural regeneration vs. artificial reforestation was the pivotal one, on which the operations of the Cornell College of Forestry were to be adjudged; the expert of the Federal Forest Service and others maintaining that the selection forest was the only proper method to apply, while Dr. Fernow claimed that all methods were to be "experimented" with, but that under the local conditions where the operations were begun, artificial reforestation with conifers with the aid of natural regeneration of hardwoods was the rational method.[111]

Fernow had said that diameter limits in logging operations should be guiding diameters conforming to needs and conditions. The applica-

[111] "Artificial Reproduction of Forests," *Forestry Quarterly* VI, 3, Sept. 1908, p. 211.

bility of the selection method was similarly regarded. In the course of the law suit the soundness of Fernow's financial and time computations had been challenged. None of these matters, however, were specifically passed upon by the courts, although in the recital of facts some reference to some of them was made by the law court, including the pronouncement that for the first two years of the management of the college forest the selection method was applied and then a change was made to the clear cutting and replanting method. The final judgment of the highest court, the court of appeals, was divided in the close ratio of four to three members.

Four judges, Messrs. Gray, Haight, Werner, and Chase, agreed in the majority conclusion which sustained the judgment of the appellate division of the third judicial department. With presiding judge Walter Lloyd Smith writing the appellate court's opinion, the appellate division in 1911—practically a half a dozen years after the cause had been formally started and more than eight years since Fernow had been on the scene of the logging operations at the Cornell forest—had affirmed, also by a divided court, the first and really only judgment reached upon the merits of the controversy. Not until the year 1910 was the offering of testimony, written and oral, of both sides, completed in the trial court. First, two tedious years, 1906-1908, had been required to secure a final opinion from the state's highest tribunal on the legal issues raised by the beginning trial court's overruling of the demurrer to the complaint. Two more years had had to go by before the second trial judge, Alden Chester, rendered his Supreme Court opinion based on the law and the evidence, saying:

> At the Special Term the contract between the University and the Cooperage Company . . . was held in an unreported opinion to be void. . . . The trial has been had, but I fail to see that the evidence produced in support of the allegations of the complaint are very materially different from the facts alleged therein, which were admitted for the purpose of the demurrer, or that the evidence of the defendants makes any very substantial change in these facts. Of course they are greatly amplified by the evidence, and there is a vast amount of testimony by experts on forestry as to their differing theories on opinions regarding the science of forestry; but the controlling facts were before the Court of Appeals on the demurrer, and the conclusions it reached leave me but little latitude in framing the judgment which must follow the trial.

As a matter of fact, the opinion of the Appellate Division of the fourth judicial department, affirming in 1906 the judgment of the Supreme Court overruling the demurrer, had been concurred in by all judges and written by Judge Frederick William Kruse, who later was a presiding judge of this court.

Notwithstanding the weight of several opinions favorable to the state's claims, the dissents from the majority result in the court of appeals in 1912 were strong. Judge Frederick Collin, appointed, though a Democrat, to the court by Republican Governor Charles Evans Hughes, and elected in 1910 to a term lasting until 1920, dissented from the majority conclusion. Judge Willard Bartlett, on the court since 1906 and later its chief justice, favored modifying the majority result in accordance with a dissenting opinion offered by Judge John M. Kellogg of the appellate court of the third department. On the theory that in the absence of proven law violations by either the university or cooperage company only the New York legislature, and not its attorney-general, could change a "fixed public policy of the State" at least for the thirty-year period defined by the laws of 1898, and in view of the losses suffered in timber and wood, mills, and improvements on the college forest area, these judges favored so modifying the judgment as to take therefrom the immediate "requirement that Cornell University convey the lands to the State" and so qualify the injunction clauses "that they shall real until the Legislature shall make further appropriations therefor." Chief Justice Edgar Montgomery Cullen in 1912 dissented from the majority conclusion but did not accompany his dissent with a formal opinion. In 1907, while dissenting from the majority result reached by Judges Gray, O'Brien, Werner, Chase, and Edward T. Bartlett, he agreed with the court's views given in an opinion written by Judge Bartlett so far as these held that chapter 122 of the New York laws of 1898 authorizing the university to create a forestry school and demonstration forest area did not violate any provision of the New York constitution. From 1904 until 1913 he was chief justice of the court and the nominee of both parties, Republican and Democratic, for the position.

Worthy of notice, also, was the caliber of attorneys-at-law who participated in this legal action, particularly when presented to the court of appeals. After the state's first victory before this court, Julius M. Mayer went out of office as attorney-general of New York, and some years later was appointed by President Taft judge of the federal district court for the southern district of New York. By 1912 Thomas Carmody was in the office of attorney-general and with him, on behalf of the state, as of counsel, was the noted New York lawyer John Giraud Agar, and also James Francis Tracey and J. A. Kellogg of Albany. Representing Cornell University, along with its university attorney, Mynderse Van Cleef of Ithaca, was Edward Wingate Hatch of the New York law firm, Parker, Hatch and Sheehan. Edward M. Shepard appears to have been counsel for the Brooklyn Cooperage Company in the first proceedings before the court of appeals. But the appellant's counsel in 1912 were D-Cady Herrick of the law firm of Herrick and Herrick with offices in Albany and New York, and James Montgomery Beck of New York, who already had been assistant attorney-general of the United States and later was to be United States solicitor-general. Other lawyers might be mentioned, but these are sufficient to indicate the array of legal talent which participated in this celebrated case in the history of forestry.

Although instruction at the New York State College of Forestry at Cornell ended in June 1903, some twenty students returned that year, some to pursue other studies, some to continue undergraduate work and prepare for graduate study in forestry elsewhere, and some took Fernow's courses in forest regulation and forest finance given privately at his residence on Cornell University's campus. Fernow exercised his privilege to live one year in his campus residence. A reunion of the Cornell Foresters' Club at Fernow's home brought together seventeen old members.

At a meeting on December 15, the Cornell foresters presented Fernow with a large silver loving cup, gold lined, with stag horn handles. Karl W. Woodward presented the tribute. Fernow replied, saying there was "no sweeter reward to a teacher, outside of the success of his students in the world, than the expression of their appreciation of his labors with them and of their loyalty to him as a man who has devoted himself to their interests like a father to his sons. . . ." He accepted the gift as a professional honor. Forestry as a profession was "still largely built on empirics" and was still trying to establish itself. Proof of this was shown in the many journals which commented on the college forest experiment and its outcome. Some had bitterly attacked the management policy; others had defended it. Widespread interest, especially among the agricultural groups, had been enlisted. Rossiter Raymond and the *Engineering and Mining Journal* and other valuable industrial and scientific journals had become aroused. Fernow was pleased with the aggressive response which indicated an improved understanding of forestry and its potentialities.

CHAPTER VII

More Progress in Forestry Education; Forestry in the West

WHILE the New York State College of Forestry was still giving instruction, professional forestry teaching in America was centered in it, in the Yale Forest School, and the Biltmore school. When the school at Cornell closed, students transferred to Yale to complete their postgraduate instruction. Some remained at Cornell to take other work or prepare for forestry work in the future. Some went to other institutions. By the autumn of 1903 another valuable course of forestry instruction was available under Roth at the University of Michigan.

Early in 1903 *Forestry Quarterly* had deplored an event which had taken place in Washington. Filibert Roth had resigned as chief of the division of forest reserves of the general land office of the department of the interior. The *Quarterly* interpreted this as "a severe blow to the honest and rational management of the forest reserves."[1] Roth's staff resigned with him, and on February 6 the division gave him a silver cup. He had been urged to return to Michigan for the good of the state and its university by Volney Morgan Spalding and others. He returned to Ann Arbor, and in March the university board of regents elected him professor of forestry.

Roth and C. A. Davis instituted the work as planned with an enrollment of eighteen students—three seniors, five juniors, three special graduate students, and seven undergraduates. The course consisted of two years of graduate work and was administered as part of the graduate school. The university had access to a large forest reserve. A gift, the Saginaw Forest Farm, increased the department's facilities. Woodlots, nurseries, and experimental plantations were planned. Roth, furthermore, became warden of the state forest preserve. There had been forestry instruction before Roth's return to his alma mater; Spalding and Garfield had induced the board of regents to renew forestry courses at the university. But not until 1903 was a department organized, the predecessor of the present-day school of forestry and conservation. Fernow later ranked this school along with Yale.[2]

[1] *Forestry Quarterly* I, 3, April 1903, p. 116; also *Forestry and Irrigation* IX, 12, Dec. 1903, p. 579.

[2] *Forestry and Irrigation* IX, 9, Sept. 1903, p. 422; IX, 5, May 1903, p. 215; *Forestry Quarterly* II, 1, Nov. 1903, p. 45; II, 2, p. 75; Dow V. Baxter and Leigh J. Hunt, "Glimpses of Saginaw Forest, Eber White Woods, Stinchfield Woods," a pamphlet issued to the School of Forestry and Conservation of the University of Michigan, 1946.

Samuel Newton Spring graduated from the Yale Forest School in 1898. After three years of business with J. B. Farwell Company of Chicago, he returned to Yale and received his master's degree in 1903. Officials of the University of Maine at Orono, which was the state's agricultural college, that year consulted Dean Graves with a view to establishing forestry instruction. The state that year had appropriated funds and the university took Spring from a position as a field assistant with the United States forest service. The college work was so arranged that it was placed under the control of the state's forest and land commission. Spring laid out a course consisting of general forestry, forest botany, silviculture, forest measurement, lumbering, and forest management. The work compared with that of other agricultural colleges and introduced there the technical instruction given at Yale. Spring aided in the state agricultural extension work. He attended grange meetings and lectured on the care of woodlot and farm forest lands. The forests of the state and their system of administration were also studied. One of Spring's students, H. L. Churchill,[3] became a pioneer in relating the development of forestry to holdings of the pulp companies.

At this time the nation was experiencing a tremendous expansion in agricultural education. Moreover, no agricultural curriculum was complete without adequate forestry instruction.[4] In Michigan the state agricultural college at East Lansing had recognized this and enlarged its forestry course to include four years of study. The University of Minnesota some years before had assumed a leadership in combined agriculture and forestry. The University of Nebraska was also performing a notable function farther west. The University of California at Berkeley was seriously contemplating inaugurating a forestry school.[5] On November 19, 1902, Burrill of the University of Illinois had written to Bessey at the University of Nebraska, "[Forestry] is not of such immediate importance to Illinois as in most of the other states but it is coming to the front everywhere to such an extent that we must undoubtedly do more than we have been doing, either by simply enlarging our courses of instruction or by organizing a department."[6]

Forestry and Irrigation in March, 1903, announced:

[3] Concerning forestry at the University of Maine, *Forest Quarterly* I, p. 157; *For. and Irrig.* IX, Dec. 1903, pp. 575-576. Concerning Churchill and the Finch, Pruyn and Company see A. B. Recknagel and S. N. Spring, *Forestry*, Knopf, New York, 1929, pp. 137ff., especially p. 141.

[4] *Forestry Quarterly* II, 1, 1903, pp. 44, 45; I, 2, p. 155; *Forestry and Irrigation* IX, 5, May 1903, p. 223.

[5] Early in 1902 President B. I. Wheeler of the University of California sought an endowment fund to found a school of forestry at Berkeley (*Forestry Quarterly* I, 1, Oct. 1902, p. 39). Late in 1889 the University of Southern California at Los Angeles had established a short course in forestry, a part of a projected forestry program (*The Forester* V, 2, Feb. 1899, p. 66).

[6] See Ralph S. Hosmer, "The Progress of Education in Forestry in the United States," *Empire Forestry Journal*, April 1923.

Toronto University, the State university of the Province of Ontario, is realizing the importance of the subject of forestry. President Loudon has pointed out that the Crown forests of Canada exceed those of the United States and Russia put together. The Senate of the University has provided a curriculum for a course in forestry, and at its last meeting of the Alumni Association, believing that the scientific study of the subject was of the utmost importance to the prosperity of the province, passed a resolution which was sent to the Premier and the Minister of Education, and which urged that the government give effect to the state provision authorizing a School of Forestry at the earliest possible date. . . .

In the next chapter we shall consider why this action primarily resulted from a group of forestry lectures delivered by Fernow at the School of Mining, Kingston, Ontario, January 26-30, 1903. At the twenty-fourth annual meeting of the Ontario Agricultural and Experiment Union, held December 8-9, 1902, at Guelph, the home of the agricultural college of the province, Fernow had presented an illustrated address on "The Evolution of the Forest" and read a paper on "The Farmer's Woodlot." A very favorable impression had been made.

Furthermore, in 1903 Harvard University permitted students to register for the degree, Bachelor of Science in Forestry. Provision at first was made only for juniors and seniors; two technical forestry courses—silviculture and forest mensuration, both given by R. T. Fisher—were offered. A course in dendrology, also, was provided by J. G. Jack. For many years plant science study at Harvard had deservedly occupied a place of leadership. The Bussey Institution, its agricultural college, from its inception had forwarded scientific progress in agriculture. While its leadership was not as steadily maintained as in a few other institutions, of its original contribution in the movement to develop a scientific agriculture in America there can be no doubt. In landscape gardening and in arboriculture and dendrology Harvard excelled, largely through the able leadership of Charles Sprague Sargent at the Arnold Arboretum. The forestry department which was soon organized presented a four-year course similiar, in part, to that which had been offered by the New York State College of Forestry. The department's formation was welcomed by the American Forestry Association as an "offset" to the loss of the New York school. Forestry work at Harvard on its own and as an adjunct to the work of the Bussey Institution gained renown under Fisher, who became one of America's leading foresters. An extraordinarily proficient field man, Fisher took a prominent role in developing the forestry of the New England states. Nor was his sphere of influence limited to this region. He had studied woodlots of New England for the bureau of forestry. Today the famous Harvard forest at Petersham, near Amherst, Massachusetts, a research station and demonstration forest of 2,000 acres established since 1908, is a celebrated institution in American silvicultural research. Its origins trace to Fisher. In the next chapter we shall discuss another phase of wood and forest research which notably has been furthered at Harvard, laboratory work in wood technology.

An important announcement concerning forestry education was made by *Forest Leaves* in October 1903: "We are glad to advise our readers that the proposed Forestry School at Mont Alto, Pennsylvania, for which an appropriation was made at the last meeting of the Legislature, is now in successful operation."[7] At last Rothrock had accomplished his purpose to include academic instruction in Pennsylvania forest work. The forest academy idea in a sense was new. The closest analogy, of course, was the Biltmore school in North Carolina. We have seen that forestry work in the United States and Canada—the United States schools were supplying a few foresters to private concerns in Canada—had grown so much that real forestry education involved both undergraduate and graduate schooling. No one of the colleges, however, could be called an academy in the strict sense, although at Berea College in the mountains of Kentucky, S. C. Mason as a professor of horticulture and forestry had been giving forest ranger instruction as part of agricultural education. This type of pioneering forestry schooling was badly needed.

Under the influence of Rothrock, George Herman Wirt had crystallized the idea of a forest academy for Pennsylvania. Rothrock in securing state forest reservations had intended to show how forestry works. When management was started, he wanted foresters to take charge of the cut-over areas. Never favoring political appointments, Rothrock wanted trained men who understood the forest. Pennsylvania, rich in natural resources, heavily wooded, should have its own forestry school. Neither the university at Philadelphia nor the agricultural college in Centre County had established even a chair of forestry, although some forestry instruction was offered.

Dr. Rothrock, as a physician, had brought George Herman Wirt into the world. Asa Gray, the father of modern American botany, had visited Rothrock at McVeytown, their home city. Rothrock told Wirt's father, "I can't get help at the University of Pennsylvania or Pennsylvania State College. I need trained foresters and wish your boy would take up the study of forestry at Biltmore." Rothrock had envisioned the forest as a health center. Interested in founding boys' camps in the forest, he had also visualized forests as great out-of-door sanatoria. One of his sons suffered from tuberculosis. Indeed, at one time Rothrock for

[7] Before this announcement was made, "Forestry at Mont Alto," extracts from a letter of George Herman Wirt, had appeared in *Forest Leaves* VIII, 10, Aug. 1902, p. 151. See also *ibid.* VIII, 5, Oct. 1901, p. 68.

reasons of health had left his wife and family and embarked on a temporary but notable career as a botanical explorer.

In 1900-1901 Wirt, at Rothrock's persuasion, went to Biltmore. While home on vacations the young student spoke of the master's schools of Germany, of which Biltmore was really a prototype. Rothrock said, "All right, we'll establish an academy." Wirt completed work at Biltmore and was taken into Pennsylvania's department of forestry as the first trained forester employed by the state.

Wirt was given odd jobs to perform during his first year with the department. Finally, however, a suitable unit on which forestry practice might begin was ready and he was sent there. The location was in the South Mountains of Pennsylvania, south of Chambersburg, cut-over and burned-over land, the site of an old charcoal iron furnace. Wirt had prepared a bulletin on how to propagate commercial trees in Pennsylvania. In the summer of 1901 he had assisted in a land survey of Monroe and Pike counties. With a degree of Bachelor of Forestry from the Biltmore school and a preliminary education at Juniata College, Wirt was fitted to do more than establish a forest nursery at Mont Alto and inaugurate a management of the forest there. One student assistant, a colored lad, had gone with him. Soon three other assistants arrived. In May 1902 they laid out a forest nursery of white pine, red spruce, and some locusts and catalpas. The following year the state legislature approved the creation of a state forest academy at Mont Alto. Wirt was chosen to be its director.[8] He began with a class of thirteen boys, most of whom had lived in the farm and forest regions of the state. During 1902 and the early part of 1903, Wirt's student assistants worked half a day and studied at night. These students became part of the first class, organized in September 1903; and of the thirteen, six completed the course in August 1906 and were placed in the state forests at forestry work. Rothrock, to secure his appropriation for the school, prepared a stipulation that the school's purpose was to train forest rangers. The real intention, however, was to train foresters for work in the Pennsylvania forests. Fernow never criticized the academy so long as the ranger training dominated. When, however, the academy concept was expanded and a curriculum, modelled after those of Yale, Cornell, and the forestry schools of Europe, was prepared by Director Wirt and approved with minor changes by Rothrock, Fernow told Rothrock that the change was a mistake. But Rothrock, telling Wirt there was enough glory in forestry for everyone, held his ground.

When all hope of resuscitating instruction at the New York State

[8] For biographical sketches of Wirt, see *Forest Leaves*, March-April 1941, p. 3; and H. S. Clepper, *Journal of Forestry*, 43, 9, Sept. 1945, pp. 687-688. Wirt's article, "A Half Century of Forestry in Pennsylvania," appeared in the Oct. 1943 issue of the *Journal of Forestry*.

College of Forestry was gone, Fernow decided to retain his residence in Ithaca and do literary work. *Forestry Quarterly*, the school's official publication, was dedicated "mainly or entirely" to "professional or technical" forestry interests. Other publications interested in the forests were more devoted to "propagandism." The *Quarterly* was to provide a medium of communication for those who were "building up the science and art" in the United States. His capacity as editor-in-chief could be continued to advantage. When first issued in October 1902, the journal's board of advisers from the faculty and alumni had consisted of Fernow, Gifford, and Walter Mulford. From April 1901 Mulford had served as forester of the Connecticut agricultural experiment station, and from July of that year he had filled the office of state forester of Connecticut, being chosen for the distinction of occupying the first such position legislatively created in the United States. This was a part of a state forestry program enacted by the general assembly at its January session.[9] After suffering at Ithaca from a severe case of typhoid fever, Gifford left and joined the United States forest service at the invitation of Chief Forester Pinchot. He was sent to the Luquillo forest reserve in Puerto Rico. With Gifford in Puerto Rico, with splendid work being performed by the Philippines bureau of forestry, with Ralph Sheldon Hosmer, a Harvard graduate in agriculture and a Yale graduate in forestry, soon to begin work in the Hawaiian Islands, forestry systematically was expanding its orbit in the western hemisphere and within the United States insular possessions.[10] Forestry as a world institution, Fernow realized, was more and more to develop conventional segments. A tropical forestry of global importance was being shaped. A technical forestry journal was needed. Fernow transformed his capacity as a forestry educator to that of an editor, author, and consultant in forestry.

When Rothrock had reviewed Roth's *A First Book of Forestry*, he announced that "American forestry [had] passed the amateur stage, and entered upon the professional. The books of Pinchot, Sargent, Graves, Fernow, Green, Gifford, and Roth," he said, "are now available, and any one desiring to understand true forestry can do so by a study of their writings." In addition to Roth's recent book, Gifford had written a book on *Practical Forestry*. Sargent had completed the first part of *Trees and Shrubs*. The great *Silva of North America* was making a profound impression. Combined with Fernow's *Economics of Forestry*, Pinchot's *Primer of Forestry*, and Graves and Fisher's *The*

[9] *The Forester* VII, 11, Nov. 1901, p. 269; *Forestry Quarterly* I, 3, April 1903, p. 81; *ibid.* I, 4, July 1903, p. 158; *ibid.* III, 1, 1905, p. 86.

[10] Concerning the Philippines see *The Forester* VII, 9, Sept. 1901, p. 230. Concerning Gifford's appointment to Puerto Rico see *Forestry Quarterly* I, 3, April 1903, p. 157, and *Forestry and Irrigation* IX, 7, July 1903, p. 323. Concerning Hosmer's appointment to Hawaii see *Forestry Quarterly* II, 2, Feb. 1904, p. 135.

Woodlot: a handbook for owners of woodlands in southern New England, there was a growing American literature of forestry, in addition to bulletins of the governmental forest services and the schools.

Another recent event promised forestry development. The proponents of irrigation and water conservation had marshalled their forces and secured in 1902 the passage of the National Reclamation Act. The future of the federal forest reservations was now truly assured. The entire West would prosper as lands were reclaimed, reservoirs were built, forest reservations improved and utilized in great schemes of reclamation and conservation. In 1903 Edward A. Bowers presented an address on "The Future of Federal Forest Reservations."[11] He still hoped for passage of "the proposition originally advanced by the American Forestry Association in a bill drawn by its executive committee as far back as 1887," a law "reserving from all disposition public lands more valuable for timber growth and forest uses, including water conservation, than for agricultural, mineral, or other purposes." Once the permanent boundaries of the reservations were determined "in accordance with the topography of the country" and made to conform "to the mountain ranges or drainage areas rather than to the arbitrary township range and section lines of the public-land surveys," once the agricultural lands were segregated and the boundaries properly marked, future greater development "in forestry proper" would be possible. The study of forest reproduction would be freed of "rude" procedures at first made necessary because of the cost. Game preservation, the preservation of unusual or strange natural phenomena, the equalization of stream flow to supply the farm areas, the maintenance of natural water conditions to extend irrigation, and other phases would be administered so as to enhance the program. Public education was still needed to "appeal to the intelligence of our people and educate them as to what the *real* purposes" of the forest reservations were. Bowers believed that "the important irrigation projects" then being commenced by the federal government would perhaps prove to be the "strongest single ally in the maintenance and extension of the existing [forest] reservations."

By 1903 Walter Mulford had begun to demonstrate forestry's value at a state agricultural experiment station.[12] A detailed forest survey of a typical forest region of the state had been commenced. Study of the state's forest conditions, of nursery practice, seed care, species-testing, planting methods and costs, seed-sowing methods, woodlot treatment, thinning and improvement cuttings, of reforesting burned over and barren areas, and of the best methods to reclaim lands, together with an advisory and informative service similar to that offered to private

[11] *Forestry and Irrigation* X, 3, March 1904, pp. 131-135.
[12] *Forestry Quarterly* I, 3, April 1903, p. 81.

forest owners by the United States bureau of forestry, was providing an excellent illustration of what a forestry department in an agricultural experiment station might do in a state where the forest owners were predominantly farmers. Two experimental tracts were established, one in the Connecticut valley and another in the northern part of the state. "It is hoped," wrote Mulford, "that in the near future the State will go much further, and engage in forestry on a sufficiently liberal basis to accomplish something in the way of regulation of the flow of our smaller rivers, and to insure to future generations a home-grown supply of large-sized timbers. The regulation of stream flow of the smaller rivers is of peculiar importance to Connecticut, because of the large number of manufactories depending upon water power."

Mulford had graduated from Cornell University in 1899 with the degree of B.S.A. He next had secured an F.E. degree from the New York State College of Forestry. While living in New Haven as an employee of the Connecticut agricultural experiment station, he taught for a while at the Yale Forest School. In 1904, however, he entered the United States bureau of forestry to take charge of commercial tree studies in the southern Appalachian Mountains. He then spent several months in Europe in preparation for a permanent position with Roth's forestry department at the University of Michigan. Mulford's position in Connecticut was taken by Austin F. Hawes and later by Samuel Newton Spring.

In the spring of 1902 Forester Ernest A. Sterling of the Pennsylvania Railroad Company put into effect a plan to plant black locust on unused land acquired by the railroad at Vineyard, about fifty miles east of Altoona, Pennsylvania. During the following five years more than a million and a half locust trees were set out. A forest nursery was begun at Hollidaysburg, also near Altoona. Red oak, pin oak, Scotch pine, tamarack, chestnut, and European larch were tried. Hardy catalpa was tried on fertile well-drained bottom land. Norway spruce was raised for snow fences. Arborvitae, grown in the nursery, was used as screens, for decoration, and for other purposes. Sterling realized that timber demands by railroads would exceed available supplies. Neither the early work of the division of forestry nor other work had solved all the timber consumption problems of the railroads. There was still a large place for "railroad forestry."[13] Sterling was demonstrating how special wasteland areas could be made productive.

Western railroads such as the Santa Fé and Southern Pacific made beginnings, especially in setting out small forest plantations. The Louisville and Nashville, the Michigan Central, the Illinois Central, the Big

[13] *Forest Leaves* XI, 4, Aug. 1907, p. 50; XI, 9, June 1908, p. 142; XII, 3, June 1909, pp. 36-37; *Proc. Soc. Am. For.* IV, 1, 1909, pp. 30ff.

Four, the St. Louis and San Francisco, and probably others attempted plantations of various tree species. In 1908, in his *Forestry Quarterly* article, "Artificial Reproduction of Forests," Sterling listed paper, lumber, railroad, iron, coal, coke, and other wood-using companies which coordinated artificial reforestation work with forests maintained as a part of their business. As a matter of fact, Western railroads were among the first investors in eucalyptus plantations. Many times, however, railroad authorities did not provide experienced forestry personnel. Knowledge of proper site location, adaptability of the species, and other imperatives in plantation work were requisite. We have already alluded to the other general phase of "railroad forestry," the tie preservative processing. Several railroads, among them the Rock Island and the Northern Pacific, financed treating plants and laboratory facilities to improve practice. It must be said, however, that no railroad in the United States has used forestry to better advantage than the Pennsylvania Railroad, which began the work on one main division and expanded it to include the entire system. Forester John Foley is still employed by the company. The work has been extended to ornamenting station grounds, and nursery practice has been much enlarged.

At this point, the early work of a few other forestry students should be considered.

Abraham Knechtel,[14] after graduating from Michigan Agricultural College in 1900, had taken the F.E. degree at the New York State College of Forestry in 1901. During the next seven years he was connected with forestry work of the New York forest, fish and game commission. The history of forest nursery and plantation work portrays the steady and persistent influence of the work which Fernow and Roth exerted in the state. By 1910 New York excelled all other states and even the federal government in this special application of forestry. Adirondack forest planting financed by an agency created by the state began in 1899 at Axton in the Cornell forest. In that year "the first coniferous nurseries" were established. The first recommendation for reforestation activities by an official agency, the forest, fish and game commission, had been made in 1898,[15] the same year the New York State College of Forestry was created and Cornell University was authorized to plant, raise, and sell timber. In accordance with the planting authority, Fernow and Roth had laid out in 1899 the forest nurseries at Axton and Wawbeek. It will be recalled that the initial Catskill plantations—one located on Wittenburg Mountain in Ulster County and one on Timothyburg Mountain in Shandaken, Ulster County, in 1901—drew their nursery stock of Norway spruce, white pine, and Scotch pine from the

[14] Clyde Leavitt, "Abraham Knechtel," *Proc. Soc. Am. For.* XI, 1, Jan. 1916, p. 155.

[15] Review of "Tree Nurseries in New York State," *Southern Lumberman*, Aug. 13, 1910; *Forestry Quarterly* VIII, 4, Dec. 1910, pp. 557f.

college nurseries. There had been private plantations before these years in the Adirondacks. After the success of forest planting was demonstrated, lumber companies, railroads, West Point Military Academy, and municipalities (notably Rochester) made plantations. The same year, 1901, that the commission located a four-acre hardwood-softwood nursery in Ulster County south of Brown's Station, a coniferous nursery of two and one-half acres at Saranac Inn, later increased in area, was established by the state.[16] "In 1901," writes Gurth Whipple, "the Forest, Fish and Game Commission drew particular attention to the planting of trees and advised the establishment of a small tree nursery in charge of a professional forester and that seeds be gathered from local forests in order to reforest the waste lands of the Forest Preserve. A year later the Commission planted a large area of land near Lake Clear Junction with white pine, Scotch pine, Norway spruce, Douglas fir, European larch, and black locust. This was the first plantation in the Adirondacks set out by the Commission. Abraham Knechtel and Clifford R. Pettis supervised the planting. E. A. Sterling remained at the Axton nursery where he prepared transplants for shipment. . . ." By this time the New York Central Railroad had become so interested in encouraging forest planting operations and fish stocking of the Adirondack lakes that it furnished free transportation to those engaged in the work. Knechtel, after further study in Europe, was to become a forester in the Dominion forestry branch to carry on forest planting and administer a fire protection service in the prairie provinces of Canada.

Ralph C. Bryant, it will be remembered, was the first appointee from the New York State College of Forestry to a position under Colonel Fox of the New York forest administration. Bryant proved to be a very able forester. However, Colonel Fox, seeking a trained forester, could well have been compelled to employ Bryant since he held the only Bachelor of Science in Forestry degree from the college of forestry.[17]

In 1901 Pettis received the F.E. degree as a member of the New

[16] See Samuel N. Spring's review of Clifford R. Pettis's Annual Report of the Dept. of Forestry of the N.Y. Commission, in *Forestry Quarterly* VIII, 4, Dec. 1910, p. 472. See also Gurth Whipple, *op. cit.*, pp. 88f. Whipple gives 1902 as the date for the establishment of the four-acre nursery at Brown Station, Ulster County, and for the selection of the seven-acre site for the nursery at Saranac Inn.

[17] Ralph Clement Bryant was the third generation of his family to be interested in trees. His grandfather, Arthur Bryant, brother of the poet William Cullen Bryant, had done a great deal of experimental planting and had published in 1871 one of the first volumes on forestry in America, titled *Forest Trees for Shelter, Ornament, and Profit.* His father, Arthur Bryant, had owned extensive nurseries and conducted experiments in tree planting in cooperation with the University of Illinois. Young Bryant entered the University of Illinois in 1896 and took his work in science, which included a course called "forestry" but which was really dendrology. His degree from the New York State College of Forestry was said to have been Forest Engineer. See a biographical account in *Yale Forest School News* XXVII, 2, April 1939, p. 22.

York school's second graduating class. The school, largely through Gifford's influence, had decided to grant the degree of Forest Engineer. For a year Pettis served as a field assistant with the federal bureau of forestry, and in 1902, commencing eight years as state forester of New York, he began to evolve the celebrated nursery practice of the state. Under his direction and supervision the state's reforestation program was greatly expanded. He had been schooled by Fernow and Roth. The fundamental principles and patterns were the results of combined effort. Yet, under Pettis, the New York work became a model for other states. Especially noteworthy was his work in the nursery-growing of conifers. Following the death of Colonel Fox in 1909, State Commissioner Whipple appointed Austin Cary to Fox's position. Fernow told Cary that he had confidence in his ability, but in 1910 Cary resigned and became professor of lumbering in the college of forestry at the University of Minnesota. Pettis was promoted in May to the position of superintendent of the New York state forests. Ralph Sheldon Hosmer has commented, "Mr. Pettis was the first man who had received technical training as a forester to hold a responsible position under the State of New York. For almost 25 years he served the Conservation Department and its predecessors, the Conservation Commission and the Forest, Fish and Game Commission." His department for a while was known as the division of lands and forests. It is said that at the time of his death in 1927 the annual forest nursery output in New York was between twenty-five and thirty million trees. Probably the largest forest nursery in the world, at Saratoga Springs, New York, was started by Pettis.[18]

During the college year 1901-1902, forty students, or nearly three times the number of fourteen remaining from the previous year, had been registered. Furthermore, in 1901, of six graduates and six special students and two seniors who then had left the college, four had found employment with the United States department of agriculture, one with the United States general land office, three with the Philippine bureau, two with state agencies, and four in private employment.

The first student to complete the four years' course of the New York State College of Forestry was Willard Weld Clarke.[19] As a student he did field work in Arkansas, New York, and Tennessee for the bureau of forestry; and after graduation, like Bryant, he joined the Philippines forestry service. Later he and Bryant returned to the United States, Clarke to become a forest assistant and Bryant, after a period with the United States forest service, planned and taught a course in lumbering at Yale Forest School.

[18] "Clifford R. Pettis, Forest Builder," Bulletin to the Schools, *The University of the State of New York* XXVIII, 7, March 1942, pp. 238ff.; "James S. Whipple, Forest Administrator," *ibid.* XXIX, 7, pp. 252ff.

[19] *Proc. Soc. Am. For.* IV, 2, 1909, p. 229.

Raphael Zon has had, perhaps, the most novel career of any forester of the United States. He as much as anyone has influenced the development of scientific forestry within the United States forest service; certainly he has had much to do with placing the work on an enduring basis. Zon was born in Simbirsk, Ulianorsk, Russia. As a boy he was acquainted with Lenin, during 1884-1893 when he attended the classical gymnasium. While quite young, Zon formed a lasting interest in the Russian forests. But after receiving an equivalent of a bachelor of arts degree, he elected to study medicine and accordingly entered medical school. After a year he transferred to the natural sciences division of the physico-mathematical department. Comparative embryology and biology were his interests. His thesis was written on the "Sexless Propagation of Worms," a study selected for its merit and published in the *Scientific Transactions* of the Imperial Kazan University. His promising career in Russia was suddenly ended when, a few months before graduation, all liberal students were jailed by the government, and Zon spent nine months in prison. After being exiled to northern Russia, in 1897 he was smuggled out of the country by way of Kaunaus and Tilsit, Germany. He went to Brussels, where he attended lectures on political economy and sociology at the Université Nouvelle. He moved to London and worked for a while in the British Museum on a translation from German into Russian of Reele's *Critical Philosophy*. In the summer of 1898 Zon crossed the Atlantic and began to work on a Russian daily newspaper in New York.

Anticipating free tuition at the New York State College of Forestry, he applied for admission only to find that he had to be a citizen of the state to be entitled to such help. His clothing was packed and he was ready to return to New York City when Fernow arranged that his second forestry student should pay his tuition by signing promissory notes. While at Ithaca, Zon translated for Professor John Henry Comstock of the department of entomology a study of "The Development of Wings in the Phryganids," and for Professor Tarr a work on "The Origin of Loess." He assisted Professor Jeremiah W. Jenks in preparing for the United States industrial commission his "Investigation of Trusts."

In 1900 Zon was offered a position with the division of forestry at Washington. Fernow was much interested in him and induced him to remain at Ithaca. Together they investigated the structure and lives of forest trees. A book was planned and written in German, "Bau und Leben Unsere Wild Wald Baume." Zon received his F.E. degree in 1901, having been a forestry student at the college since the spring of 1899. On July 1, 1901, he became a student assistant with the United States bureau of forestry and worked on a tract of the Great Northern

Paper Company in Somerset County, Maine. He was promoted to assistant forest expert and made chief assistant to the computer in January 1902. That spring he began a study of the chestnut in Maryland and his results were published in a forestry bulletin. That summer he took up a study of balsam fir in the Adirondacks, a study which was extended to Maine during another year. In connection with the Kirby Working Plan in Texas, he investigated the silviculture of the longleaf pine. A later study of the loblolly pine in southern Texas was issued in a forestry bulletin. In 1903 Zon received another promotion, this time to the post of agent, and he was chosen to prescribe the treatment of Mohegan Park in Hamilton County, New York.

Zon showed unusual ability in evaluating forest conditions, resources, and problems; he has been an ardent and militant worker to promote scientific progress in the profession. Some of the most constructive suggestions concerning forest mapping and other fundamental procedure have come from him. He early became a contributor to *The Forester* and *Forestry Quarterly*, which he served in responsible capacities.

Philip Ayres, after one year as a special student at the New York State College of Forestry, became forester of Dartmouth College, and later, when the influential Society for Protection of New Hampshire Forests was organized, he began a long and valuable period of service as its forester.[20]

Clyde Leavitt had been a student at the University of Michigan where he had earned the degree of Bachelor of Arts. Nine months had been spent in military service in the Spanish-American War, and he had become acquainted with Captain A. E. McCabe, who helped him to arrive at an important decision. Leavitt had begun a career as a school teacher in his home town, Bellaire, Michigan. Hearing that Captain McCabe after the war had been assigned to the bureau of forestry in the Philippine Islands to straighten out lost land titles, he was persuaded to try to secure a teaching position in the Islands, and so wrote to McCabe. The latter replied and suggested that he study forestry. Up to this time Leavitt knew nothing of forestry. He had grown up in the Michigan north woods, had seen huge forest areas cleared, had watched log sleighs come in on the snow and ice in winter, and in the summer he and his playmates had ridden the logs. Leavitt had worked on farms, but forestry was never decided on until one day he conferred with McCabe in Petoskey, Michigan. At the time he considered studying at Cornell under Fernow or at Yale under Graves and Toumey. He also

[20] See James F. Colby, "The Forestry Legislation of New Hampshire," *Proc. Am. For. Ass.*, 1896, pp. 147-158; *Forest Leaves* VII, 1, Feb. 1899, p. 9; E. M. Griffith, "Forestry Agitation in New Hampshire," *The Forester* VII, 4, April 1901, p. 79.

considered the school at Biltmore, but he discovered that no training in the basic sciences was given there. He concluded that the Biltmore school was "subprofessional, little more than a rangers' course." He really did not have to investigate thoroughly since there was a good reason why he should select Cornell University. His father had been a student in the arts and sciences college there, was a close friend of John Henry Comstock, and had been one of a group interested in the natural sciences, particularly entomology and mycology. Comstock consulted Fernow, who wrote to Clyde that he might have a position as a secretary to the director at twenty cents an hour. Leavitt's father was a lawyer and had taught his son the use of the typewriter. To accept Fernow's offer all he had to do was to learn shorthand. He had worked his way through college. He went again to Ann Arbor and studied in a small business college. In 1902 he became Fernow's secretary. Controversy over the clear cutting and replanting policy intensified that year. The next year, in June, the college was closed.

Leavitt returned to Ann Arbor where Roth gave him the same position he had held with Fernow, this time at a stipend of one hundred dollars a year. Leavitt found in Roth another great teacher and scholar in forestry. Roth's estimate of Leavitt as a forestry student and as a forester also must have been high, since when Roth again was offered a position as a forestry professor at Cornell University, he sought to arrange a place for Leavitt on the forestry faculty of the University of Michigan. For many years Roth's bulletin, *Timber: An Elementary Discussion of the Characteristics and Properties of Wood*, served as the standard and really only American text in the important subject of forest products. Similarly enduring was his and Mohr's bulletin on southern United States timber pines. Roth had earned a reputation as a teacher while on the staff of the New York State College of Forestry. Leavitt graduated from Roth's classes at the University of Michigan in 1904. He took the civil service examination and became a forest assistant in the United States forest service.

That same year W. B. Greeley also entered the forest service. Greeley later disclosed in a letter to Fernow, "You may have forgotten the incident at Berkeley, Calif., in the summer of 1901, when a gangling youth called on you to ask advice about entering the forestry profession. You remarked that he was well qualified for it with his long legs. At any rate I have never forgotten it, for at that time my determination to cast my lot with the foresters was made. . . ."

In 1901 Fernow was asked to deliver a course of lectures at the University of Chicago.[21] He must have spoken also at the University of California or taught in the summer school, more likely the former, since

[21] *The Forester* VII, 6, June 1901, p. 154.

the Chicago lectures were placed in the summer quarter. Fernow was appointed to be a lecturer on forestry at the next summer session at the University of California during July and August of 1902. He was to instruct and present illustrated lectures.[22] These events were the predecessors of the summer school inaugurated in 1903 by the University of California.[23] The school became an annual summer event at Idyllwild, San Jacinto Mountain, California. During the 1903 sessions, among other features, Dr. Willis Linn Jepson of the department of botany discussed the life histories of a number of indigenous forest species.[24] Arnold V. Steubenrauch, a former student of the New York State College of Forestry, dealt with a number of forestry problems of the state. R. S. Hosmer, then investigating the forest resources of southern California for the bureau of forestry, lectured, and Chief Forester Pinchot was also listed as a lecturer.

With evident progress throughout the United States, with student numbers increasing, and with new interest showing in many educational institutions, forestry needed a technical journal. Accordingly, with its second volume, *Forestry Quarterly* entered upon an "independent career." In November 1903 its board of editors consisted of Fernow as editor-in-chief, Henry Solon Graves of Yale University, Filibert Roth of the University of Michigan, John C. Gifford of Princeton University, Richard T. Fisher of Harvard University, Walter Mulford, Ernest A. Sterling, Stuart J. Flintham, Clyde Leavitt, and Frederick Dunlap.

In 1892 Dr. and Mrs. Fernow had suffered a sad bereavement; their only daughter, Miss Gordon Fernow, died of blood poisoning. Four sons, Rossiter, Edward, Fritz, and Karl mourned her loss with their parents. Fernow was able to rise above this sorrow and carry on his work. He believed that creation was the product of energy, that mortals return to energy. He found room for the concept of Providence. In that time of theological dogma, such a belief was thought to be atheistic. His belief was a kind of fatalism.

Fernow had personal resources which never failed him. He found retreats from the world of reality which helped him through critical periods. Mrs. Fernow would read to him in the evenings. He was an artist at heart in many ways. He loved to dance, Scotch dances and dances of his fatherland folk, especially with groups of his friends and colleagues. He enjoyed the intellectual companionship with his students during Sunday evening gatherings at his home. He was a skilled horseman, and he found release from care in music. By the hour he played

[22] *Forestry and Irrigation* VIII, 3, March 1902, p. 95.

[23] *Forestry Quarterly* I, 4, July 1903, p. 158; *Forestry and Irrigation* IX, 9, Sept. 1903, p. 424.

[24] Jepson's lectures were not confined to local species.

the études of Chopin, the sonatas of Beethoven, the masterpieces of Mozart, Brahms, Liszt, Bach, and others.

During the period of 1903-1907 Fernow engaged in two special types of work—literary, and consulting forest engineering. "For four years," said Roth, "Fernow worked as consulting forester; kept several timber cruisers and surveyors going summer and winter; did more forest consulting work than had ever been done by any forester in the United States; examined large properties; carried his work into Cuba, Mexico, the South and the Northeast, and demonstrated, in a way quite surprising to some of his acquaintances, his great versatility, and his capacity in business which had long secured for him a standing among large business men, such as no forester had ever enjoyed. . . ."[25]

In this period he maintained an office at 42 Broadway, New York City, which was quite a contrast to his consulting office of about two decades before. He served a number of influential and wealthy clients, lumber concerns mainly, and although he maintained his legal residence and home at Ithaca, his range of forest investigations covered a wide area from the pulp lands of Cape Breton, Nova Scotia, to Colima, Mexico, and the Sierra Madre oak forests on the south.

Occasionally a forest investigation was made for scholarly purposes. On August 18, 1906, Fernow sailed from New York with Norman Taylor of the New York Botanical Garden to spend several weeks among the mountains of Santiago, Cuba. On this timber exploration Fernow was accompanied by "four woodchoppers and a very intelligent storekeeper." His expedition began about seventy-five miles west of Santiago and he went by horseback and on foot the entire journey along the shore and in the mountains. He found the trip "rough traveling, indeed so rough that [he] could not see most of the property which [he] was to inspect." He told E. W. Nelson, field naturalist of the bureau of biological survey of the United States department of agriculture, "I had interesting side lights on other resources and an especially interesting exhibit of how foolish capital can be in relying upon imperfect information. The property approached by Chirivique Harbor, of 500,000 acres, had once before been handled as an iron property, and cost some good American investors a loss of one and a half million dollars. The timber proposition was not of any better character."

From the journey Fernow produced two interesting and valuable articles, "Forest Conditions of the High Sierra Maestra in Cuba," published in *Forestry Quarterly*,[26] and "The High Sierra Maestra," presented in the *Bulletin of the American Geographical Society*.[27]

These treatises contributed to the growing field of tropical for-

[25] *American Forestry*, April 1920.
[26] IV, 4, pp. 239ff.
[27] XXXIX, 5, pp. 257ff.

estry. There was a strong movement to extend exploratory and experimental research, including the establishment of laboratories to study wild and cultivated tropical plants in health and disease, and this included forestry. In 1903 Chief Forester Pinchot, speaking at the eleventh annual meeting of the National Wholesale Lumber Dealers' Association, expressed faith in world forestry. He had returned from a world tour studying forest conditions in the tropical regions of the Philippines, in the far northern forest regions of Siberia and Russia, and again he had examined forest regions in Europe. The lumbermen's committee on forestry urged, among other matters, sufficient appropriations for timber testing and a timber census of the United States.[28] Pinchot reassured them in agreeable language, "You are the axe that does the work; we are the helve that serves to give it direction. . . . We must consider from now on that the forest is a crop; that methods of renewing it are just as vital to you, who are interested in cutting it down, as to those who are interested in building it up." Replacement of destroyed forest areas, of course, was secondary to the protection and preservation of mature forest areas. The realization was common to both foresters and lumbermen that they must work together to preserve the forests.[29]

Pinchot was not the only American forester who had returned to Europe to examine methods and procedures. Graves had returned for further study of forestry methods. In addition to the increasing number of forestry students going to Europe to complete their education or do special work, the growing consciousness of a world forestry was being shown in Europe, which was now sending foresters to North America to study. Prominent German foresters visited the Cornell forest. Having examined reports of the New York State College of Forestry, Dr. Schwappach, who in the 1890's had been among those who professed such admiration for Roth's and Fernow's timber physics research, now defended the college forest management policy by concluding; "It is impossible [professionally] under the stated conditions to prescribe or do anything else." During the autumn of 1904 two officers of the Prussian Forest Service were sent by their government to inspect forest conditions in the United States and learn if possible a satisfactory explanation of why the New York State College of Forestry had collapsed. These foresters of world eminence were Oberforstmeister Riebel of the Forest Academy of Eberswalde and Forstmeister Dr. Jentsch, professor at the Forest Academy at Münden. They published in 1905 a review of this forest situation in *Zeitschrift für Forst und Jagdwesen*, and said

[28] *Forestry and Irrigation* IX, 4, April 1903, pp. 202-204. The committee's report was titled "Lumbermen Favor Forestry."

[29] "The Forester and the Lumberman," *Forestry and Irrigation* IX, 4, April 1903, pp. 176ff.

in part,[30] "It cannot be doubted that from the standpoint of rational forestry the clearing system was justified, and was suited to secure the desired aim, namely to establish, under the existing conditions, quickly, surely, and cheaply a conifer forest with an admixture of broadleaved trees. . . ."

Late in 1902 at Washington Fernow had presented before a section of the American Association for the Advancement of Science his analysis of the "Outlook of the Timber Supply in the United States."[31] He pointed out that varying methods of the various censuses and the "variable success of enumerators in securing information" had rendered the data of uneven value, so much so that comparisons led to erroneous conclusions. The Lumber Dealers' Association in their convention[32] had heard their committee on forestry report that only the 1880 census had given definite and reliable information. Had the conclusions of this census proved correct, they said, the entire white pine supply would have been out of existence in 1890, "while now, twelve years subsequent to that date, there [had] been a production in three states of over five thousand million feet." No attempts to collect timber statistics, they pointed out, had been made in the eleventh or twelfth censuses. Fernow discussed the data presented by the last census and prognosticated a consumption increase per capita "not less than 3 to 5%"[33] and an exhaustion of supplies "in less than thirty years if this rate of consumption continues, and of the most important coniferous supplies in a very much shorter time." Canada as a prospective source of future supplies was not reassuring. Forest reproduction on existing forest areas under proper management to protect against fires and unnecessary waste was the constructive procedure. Fernow was an authority on the lumber industry, and he was not usually a prophet of doom. But his and other warnings helped to prevent a national disaster. Timbers of smaller diameters are being cut today. Supplies have not been exhausted, but they have been diminished, and new markets have been found. Fernow analyzed the lumber problem scientifically even in his popular writings. This is illustrated in an article on "American Lumber" which appeared in *The Chautauqua* in February 1899, and which was reviewed in *The Forester* of the following month. Articles in business encyclopedias were patterned after it.[34]

Later Fernow suggested that the variable character of forest statistics

[30] *Forestry Quarterly* III, 1, pp. 32-38; II, 1, Nov. 1903, p. 42.

[31] *ibid.* I, 1903, pp. 41-49, 87-93.

[32] *Forestry and Irrigation* IX, 4, April 1903, pp. 202-204.

[33] Two years later, in another address before the same body, Fernow, allowing for a price rise of 1½%, placed the quantity consumption at not less than 1½%; *Forestry Quarterly* III, 1, Feb. 1905, pp. 18ff.

[34] Toward the end of the 1890's Fernow wrote other articles warning that if the methods in use continued the nation's lumber supply might not last sixty more years.

lay in the "premises as regards the standard log in use at a certain period. It can be fairly asserted," he said, "that if the standard which prevailed in 1879 had been continued in future logging operations in the White Pine territory the government estimates would have been found practically not far from the truth. Similarly, the amount of standing timber on the Pacific coast based on a standard of 20 inches now still in vogue, would probably have to be quadrupled if the standard sinks to a 12 inch log. In addition, there are other changes which make calculations as to the supply of any species and especially as to the time of their exhaustion hazardous. By others, I think my own guesses as to the probable amount of standing timber, have been again and again abused by using them for a mathematical calculation of the time at which a timber famine may occur. There never was any such use in my mind when I produced the figures. All that they were intended to show and to accentuate was that natural timber supplies are exhaustible resources, and that their exhaustion must be expected within a measurable period. . . . By changing standards, cutting more closely, by avoiding waste in logging and sawing, by avoiding extravagance in the use of the materials, we may lengthen the time during which these stores may last, but unless they are replaced by production, they must give out within much less time than it takes to grow a log tree. . . ." Fernow said this to Ellwood Wilson as late as November 26, 1909.

Fernow believed that the United States would have to rely for its lumber supply on its own resources and whatever Canada might spare from its transatlantic trade. In "The Movement of Wood Prices and Its Influence on Forest Treatment"[35] he elaborated this theme before Section I of the American Association for the Advancement of Science, saying that "... all the evidence seems to lead to the conclusion that knowledge of available supplies is increasing and exercising its influence and that a more rapid rise of wood prices than in the past is to be anticipated. . . ." Actual knowledge, not "surmises and guesses, opinions and sham opinions," as to future supplies was still needed. Wood substitutes had not yet reduced the quantity consumption of timber.

It was hardly to be wondered at that people interested in forest supplies more and more looked to the tropics. In December Fernow appeared before a Section I meeting of the American Association for the Advancement of Science and read a paper on "Tropical Wood Supplies."[36] Again he urged the further opening of the timber resources of the tropical countries to the south, warning, however, that the conifer areas in the woods and forests of tropical countries were limited and of inferior character when compared to the North American supplies, and

[35] *Forestry Quarterly* III, 1, Feb. 1905, p. 18.
[36] *ibid.* V, 1, March 1907, p. 51.

it would be much more expensive to lumber and market. "In the year 1900," he said, "the long predicted timber famine made its entrance into the United States, if a sudden rise in prices is the characteristic of dearth. It came on time, exactly as predicted. In that year the price of White Pine lumber, up to that time our principal staple, jumped all at once to almost double its previous value, and all other lumber staples increased in price rapidly, and have crept up ever since." Fernow foresaw "little comfort [to be] expected in dealing with our timber famine, approaching and in progress, by securing supplies from our southern neighbors. While the increase in wood prices will perhaps make the profitable exploitation of favorably located tropical forests possible, neither the character of their woods, nor the quantity they can supply promise to satisfy our needs readily." Tropical forestry, like tropical botany and horticulture has developed technically and expansively. Samuel J. Record, the late dean of the Yale Forest School, organized and published a journal entitled, *Tropical Woods*. Research, exploration, and improved transportation and communication have widened the forestry circumference since Fernow's years.

By 1903 the annual appropriation of the bureau of forestry of the United States department of agriculture amounted to approximately $300,000, and the bureau's work was organized as forest measurements, forest management, dendrology, forest extension, and forest products and records.[37] The work of each department had been started under Fernow, but it was now so modernized and expanded that each department's activities bore slight resemblance to the old. Of course in such fundamental work as dendrology under Sudworth, the familiar patterns had continued. The progress, however, was attributable more to the ability of the department personnel than the extent of the financing made available. Under Fernow's direction A. K. Mlodziansky had prepared a bulletin on "Measuring the Forest Crop," a seventy-page description of methods of measuring standing trees and forests and of devising ratios of tree and forest growth. Dr. Graves produced a text on *Forest Mensuration* which was to be among the most valuable of forestry literary productions offered to students in America. A monograph which typified persistent literary improvement was that of "The White Pine (*Pinus strobus* Linnaeus)," prepared as early as 1888 by Volney Morgan Spalding and several times revised but never fully completed by him.

Before Fernow and Roth had left the division of forestry in Washington, five species of conifers—the four southern timber pines and the white pine—had been studied with sufficient thoroughness to permit the publication of two bulletins. In 1896 Mohr's and Roth's bulletin

[37] *ibid.* II, 2, Feb. 1904, p. 81.

XIII had appeared, and, while Fernow added a discussion of forest management applicable to woodlands to Birkinbine's bulletin XXIII on "The Uses of Wood in Mining and in the Charcoal Iron Industries," his last real work for the division had been a revision and enlargement of Spalding's monograph on "The White Pine," a work to which Roth also contributed. All told, a decade of research by several workers went into bulletin XXII, which was completed in 1898 and published and reviewed in *The Forester*[38] the next year. This had materials on geographical distribution, on history of the white pine lumber industry, on botanical description and observation of the species including its morphological and histological characters and its seeding and forms, its right utilization, its rates and conditions of growth, and its silvicultural characters. A very important part was a paper by F. H. Chittenden on "Insect Enemies of the White Pine." Forest management here and abroad was also treated elaborately. Field measurements were performed by Austin Cary and Mlodziansky. The latter supplied materials on growth rates.

The bureau's valuable field studies among other softwoods have already been mentioned. On November 2, 1901, when Chief Forester Pinchot before the Society of American Foresters had outlined "The Immediate Future in Forest Work,"[39] among his plans were included study of important hardwoods in the Smoky Mountains on the Cumberland plateau, study of second-growth hardwoods in New England, study of hickories, oaks, ashes, elms, chestnuts, beeches, and sweet gum, principally in the South. Nor was he unmindful of the need to study the western yellow pine in Arizona or the sugar pine in California and Oregon. Many forest species were in need of special study.

Research was not limited to a descriptive study of tree species. Under the title of forest investigations, life history studies of insects harmful to trees of the East, South, and West were pursued. In view of the magnitude of the problems connected with the federal forest reservations, matters pertaining to forest management and forest extension received the largest share of attention. The problems dealt with for the most part were economic, not scientific. But laboratory research in conjunction with the bureau of chemistry—dendrochemical investigation—was maintained, particularly in the important field of wood-preservatives. Although the work had been started earlier, in 1903 Dr. Hermann von Schrenk was appointed chief of a division of forest products to coordinate certain work of the bureau of forestry, the bureau of chemistry, and the bureau of plant industry.

Since 1898 von Schrenk had been with the United States department of agriculture as pathologist in charge of the bureau of plant industry's

[38] V, 12, Dec. 1899, p. 294.

[39] *Forestry and Irrigation* VIII, 1, Jan. 1902, p. 18.

Mississippi Valley laboratory located at St. Louis, Missouri. In 1901 he had been made a special agent and chief of a division of forest products in the bureau of forestry. His energies, however, had not been given exclusively to either work, since from 1896 until 1903 he also taught plant diseases at the Shaw School of Botany and Washington University. The plan of the Mississippi Valley laboratory was evolved while Beverly Thomas Galloway was chief of the department's division of vegetable physiology and pathology and later first chief of the newly created bureau of plant industry. Diseases of agricultural and horticultural crops of the central West were studied. But more specifically because of von Schrenk's presence the work included the investigation and special study of timber diseases and timber preservation. Von Schrenk at no time lived in Washington except temporarily for purposes of consultations with either Galloway or Pinchot, or some other official connected with the department. He, perhaps, has rightful claim to the distinction of being America's first forest pathologist. Haven Metcalf in 1907 was appointed principal pathologist in charge of forest pathology within the department of agriculture. Metcalf, nevertheless, was primarily a botanist and had begun his connection with the bureau of plant industry in 1906 as a plant pathologist. George Grant Hedgcock, also constituted a forest pathologist in 1907 with the department, began as a botanist and plant pathologist, and became an authority on tree fungi, especially the rusts.

From 1902 until 1909 von Schrenk was a lecturer at the Yale Forest School on diseases of trees and timber preservation. From 1906 until 1914 he was to lecture on timber preservation at the Biltmore Forest School and in 1909 on plant pathology at the University of Wisconsin. But in 1907 his career as a consulting timber engineer for several railroads and the National Lumber Manufacturers Association (1914-1918) began to exceed in importance his connections with academic and research institutions. In 1895, after obtaining his bachelor of science degree at Cornell University under George Francis Atkinson and his master of science degree under William Gilson Farlow at Harvard, von Schrenk had studied with Robert Hartig at the royal forestry experiment station at Munich, Germany.

Emilio Pepe Michael Meinecke, born in California but educated in Europe, and who was not until 1910 to begin his eminent career as a forest pathologist with the United States department of agriculture, was an acquaintance of von Schrenk in Germany. Meinecke obtained his doctorate of philosophy in 1893 from the University of Heidelberg. Von Schrenk secured his degree of Ph.D. in 1898 from Washington University. Both men were highly respected by Fernow for their abilities as scientists. Meinecke also studied at the Universities of Freiburg, Leipzig, and Bonn, and took postgraduate work at other European universities. His career as a working pathologist, moreover, was started in Europe. In 1893 an assistant in the botanical institute of the University of Munich, in 1894 again at the University of Heidelberg, Meinecke served, too, as an assistant at the forestry academy of the University of Munich between the years 1898 and 1902. At the University of La Plata of the Argentine Republic, South America, he was professor of botany from 1907 until 1908-1909. In 1918 he became a pathologist with the U.S. department of agriculture and for many years was a consulting pathologist to the forest service in western districts. His book on *Forest Tree Diseases Common in California and Nevada* (1914), his study on *Forest Pathology in Forest Regulation* (1916), and other treatises and articles, were valuable contributions.

Von Schrenk's publications, *The Decay of Timber and Methods of Preserving It* (1902), *Seasoning of Timber* (1903), and *Diseases of Hardwood Trees* (1909), and several other lesser important studies of fungous diseases of trees, preceded the work of other American forest pathologists, although it should be pointed out that some very able American scientists, preeminently plant pathologists, began studies in forest pathology during the first decades of the new century. A few whose work may be mentioned were: William Codman Sturgis, whose special contribution to forestry will be considered later in this book; George Perkins Clinton, whose studies and published writings on the chestnut bark disease and white pine blister rust made him world famous; Frederick De Forest Heald, later in 1912-1914 to serve as pathologist of the Pennsylvania chestnut tree blight commission; Perley Spaulding, later pathologist of the Northeastern forestry experiment station located at Amherst, Massachusetts, and others. Sturgis and Clinton both had studied under Farlow and Thaxter at Harvard and thus were influenced by Farlow's pioneering academic interest in the study of forest tree diseases. But not until almost the turn of the century did forest pathology in America begin to emerge as a recognized independent research field. B. T. Galloway and Albert Frederick Woods had written for the *Yearbook of the U.S.D.A. for 1896* an article on "Diseases of Shade and Ornamental Trees." Specialists had written on diseases of various economically valuable tree species, as, for example, von Schrenk's studies of cypress, redwood, and ancient races of conifers. Von Schrenk's studies of cellular and structural changes in wood fibers induced by fungous agencies were of present and future value. Fernow and Roth both encouraged him in his researches. Entomologists early had aided foresters with separate studies. As early as the 1895 *Yearbook* L. O. Howard published "The Shade-Tree Insect in the Eastern United States," a study partly built around a reply made by Fernow in December 1893 to the Tree Planting and Fountain Society of Brooklyn, which had asked several experts to name nine of the most valuable trees for planting there. Fernow analyzed nearly fifty varieties as to endurance, recuperative power, cleanliness, beauty of form, shade, leaf form, rapidity of growth, persistence and other qualities. Howard took the large and medium-sized trees listed, and analyzed their specific rating for immunity from insect pests.

Many studies were primarily of economic significance, and only incidentally involved scientific study. Perhaps the most outstanding achievement of the bureau of forestry was the discovery of a new method to obtain crude turpentine and rosin by the so-called cup and gutter system. Tried early in 1902 on a turpentine farm near Ocilla, Georgia, within a little more than a year three-fourths of the southern pine belt had introduced the method profitably. This discovery revolutionized the naval stores industry of the United States and increased its annual output and income by millions of dollars.

By this time the leadership of the old division of forestry under Fernow, except Sudworth, had gone into teaching. Keffer, after a rather brief stay in Tennessee, went to New Mexico. In a few years every state and territory was said to have an agricultural college and experiment station. Yet more professorships in forestry, apart from horticulture and agriculture, were needed.[40] Forestry was gaining, even in the West. Railroads were more interested in forestry. In 1901 the Baltimore and Ohio Railroad[41] requested the bureau of forestry to make a working plan for its tract of 125,000 acres in Nicholas and Pocahontas counties, West Virginia. The interest in wood preservatives and the species adapted to processing was so widespread that special bulletins were being issued to inform industry of new results in dendrochemical research. Special bulletins, such as Edward T. Allen's bulletin on *The Western Hemlock* or that of the Kansas Agricultural College on *The Hardy Catalpa* were of both general and special value. In 1903, before the New York Railroad Club, von Schrenk and Fernow read papers on the growing relationship of railroad development and forest supplies and timber uses.[42] Railroads were but one instance of industrial expansion. Remote from urban life, forests were being utilized not only from profit motives but also for recreational and scenic advantages. That the Pocono Manor Association possessed seven hundred acres of forest land on Little Pocono Mountain in a region of rustic beauty about twenty miles north of Delaware Water Gap was worthy of special notice in *Forestry and Irrigation*.[43] Nor was scholarly interest in the forests subsiding. Old interests were finding new expression. An illustration could be found in the numerous articles on special forest flora—

[40] Samuel B. Green, "Forestry in the Agricultural Colleges and Experiment Stations," *Forestry Quarterly* VIII, 2, June 1910, p. 187.

[41] *Forest Leaves* VIII, 6, Dec. 1901, p. 92.

[42] *ibid.* IX, 4, Aug. 1903, p. 62.

[43] X, 11, Nov. 1904, p. 493.

many on a regional or state basis—being prepared by botanists and foresters.

There were many reasons why Fernow insisted that every forester should have the best of engineering knowledge. While director of the New York State College of Forestry, he had delivered on June 26, 1901, to the Western Society of Engineers an illustrated lecture entitled, "The Forester, an Engineer." He believed that the forester should know machinery used in forest logging operations. The forester should know the machines which mill and manufacture the forest product. He should be familiar with the transportation facilities from the log site to the lumber stack in the mill yard. Fernow believed that the educated forester should know the apparatus of timber testing, the equipment of the timber physics laboratory. Conversely, the engineer should have a knowledge of forestry. In forest engineering he believed there was a real field for the future. His early student, Asa S. Williams, gave promise of becoming an authority in this field. The forest railroad, whether narrow or standard gauge, the skidder, the wagon or truck, the forest road and bridge, the loader, surveying and mapping equipment, and of course all of the machinery of the mill were but a few points common to both engineering and forestry. In the Cornell forest a standard gauge with a forty pound steel rail had been used on the spur track, and a forty-six pound rail on the main rail line. Over these had gone a twenty-seven ton engine. Unquestionably a full-scale mechanical engineering knowledge rendered the forester's services to the large lumber or forest operator more valuable. Occasionally the knowledge was imperative. Fernow did not forsake his belief in the necessity of timber physics research and study. In the concluding paragraph of his address on "The Forester, an Engineer," he urged, "The science of wood, timber physics, which forms a branch of forestry knowledge, as it teaches the characteristics and the causes of these characteristics of the forest crop, this science, so far only poorly developed, although wood has been used so long, is indispensable to the intelligent engineer. . . ."

In December 1902 *Forestry and Irrigation*[44] quoted the annual report of Secretary of Agriculture James Wilson, which read, "In cooperation with the bureau of chemistry and in response to urgent demands, the series of tests to determine the strength of the principal merchantable timbers, discontinued in 1896, have been taken up."

F. E. Olmsted, assistant forester of the bureau of forestry, that year published in the *Yearbook* an important article, "Tests on the Physical Properties of Timber," in which he outlined the timber-testing work of Europe, the work accomplished in the United States under Sharples in connection with the tenth census, under Johnson, Roth, and Fernow in

[44] See also *Forestry Quarterly* II, 2, Feb. 1904, p. 81, where the annual report is reviewed. See also *Yearbook of the U.S.D.A. for 1902*, pp. 39, 78-80, 321-332, 533-538.

the division of forestry, the work under Gaetano Lanza at the Massachusetts Institute of Technology, and the new investigations now planned by the bureau of forestry. In 1900 H. S. Betts had graduated from the Stevens Institute of Technology. After two mechanical engineering positions with gas and electric companies, he applied for work testing timber for the bureau of chemistry, and was appointed. The work was to consist in part of road-materials research established in December 1900, in cooperation with the office of public road inquiries. In 1902 Secretary Wilson told of cooperative investigations of the bureaus of chemistry and forestry in "economic forest products such as tannin, gum, rubber, and wood pulps." A laboratory was also "now equipped for the testing of road materials of every description, as well as cement and concrete for drains and highway bridges." Into this work Betts went as an engineer in timber tests. His assistant was Prevost Hubbard, who was later an important asphalt engineer.

This laboratory, which lasted four years and was located in the basement of the bureau of chemistry building at Fourteenth and B Streets Southeast, tested timbers in conjunction with the division of public roads under Logan Walter Page. With the equipment available a few beam tests were tried. Experiments were started to determine the effect of moisture on strength, and for the purpose a soaking yard was located nearby. Facilities to season timbers were part of the equipment. Several series of tests were made on various species of southern pines. A system of sketching woods before testing to locate defects such as knots and checks was worked out, together with procedures, used for many years, of plotting results on graph paper. During this time Dr. Harvey W. Wiley, chief of the bureau of chemistry, acquired much interest in timber-test work. In the 1902 *Yearbook*, William H. Krug, chief of the dendro-chemical laboratory, reviewed results and suggested possibilities for a departmental program for "chemical studies of some forest products of economic importance." Wood and bark chemical composition of various native trees and turpentine adulteration were principally elaborated.

Another similar wood-testing laboratory was set up at New Haven in 1902 in the basement of Marsh Hall, then the domicile of the Yale Forest School. The reason which prompted the selection of New Haven as a laboratory site was, among others, that Professor Toumey was to aid in a series of tests on southern pine. Part of this work was also done at Washington. Neither Toumey nor his chief in Washington, Frederick E. Olmsted, knew how he was to do his job. Betts himself had to employ a helper to select southern pine in the New Haven lumber yards.

In 1902 Betts directed the New Haven laboratory at Yale Forest School. Among his pupils was William Buckhout Greeley, graduate in science from the University of California, who was to obtain his master of forestry degree in 1904.[45] In 1903 Betts returned to Washington and began more comprehensive test work, especially on the effect of moisture on wood strength. Storage yard and other new facilities and equipment were added. Harry Donald Tiemann, another graduate of Stevens Institute, who secured his M.F. degree in 1903, took charge of the Yale laboratory and remained until 1909, when he became senior physicist of the forest products laboratory at Madison. As a lecturer on forest products, as a research student of the technology of woods and their structure and properties, and notably by improving commercial methods and practice in kiln-drying lumber, Tiemann has made very valuable contributions to forestry.

Other laboratories in different sections of the country were established. In 1903 under Loren Hunt's direction at Berkeley in cooperation with the University of California a laboratory was established to determine mechanical properties of Douglas fir in structural size and in small pieces.

The St. Louis World's Fair was responsible in 1904-1905 for another laboratory. There a number of tests to determine the effects of steaming on the strength of wood were made. An episode in this connection is told. The laboratory was under the direction of Hermann von Schrenk, who at the time was doing some consulting work for one of the railroads. A fence post demonstration was wanted. Tanks with creosote were set up, and posts were put in. Some attendants were left to watch the processing and remove the posts when heated. The attendants fell asleep. The fire went out. The posts cooled. Von Schrenk returned. Looking to see the effects the bath had had, he was astonished to see that, on cooling, the creosote had penetrated the posts. Thus, by accident, the hot and cold bath method of treating timbers was discovered. Another laboratory was operated in 1905 in conjunction with the Exposition held in Portland, Oregon, test work there also being carried on for demonstration purposes.

The main laboratory of timber testing during this period was located in 1904 at Purdue University under Dr. W. K. Hatt's direction. A series of tests of hardwoods was made. Dr. Hatt was a professor of engineering. Fernow believed, however, that few of the men connected with the new work had the requisite knowledge in the biology of plant life. He said this of Dr. Hatt and of another student who became a leading figure in the work. The new work had taken over that part of timber physics research under Roth which had been principally performed in Dr. Johnson's laboratory at St. Louis. But little or no effort was being made to correlate conditions of growth of the timbers tested or establish any fundamental botanical systemization. Neither Fernow

[45] Most of this material is based on an unpublished manuscript lent by Betts.

nor Roth, however, protested. They were delighted to see timber testing reestablished with more ample funds than had been available before.

The year 1905 ushered in an expanded program dealing with the strength and related properties of American woods. A dendrochemical laboratory, not connected with Yale Forest School, was commenced at New Haven in one of the buildings of Sheffield Scientific School. For a while timber testing in Washington had again been discontinued, not for want of funds but to permit Betts and his aides, before moving to improved quarters, to collect samples of woods of the southwestern United States and to enlarge their program. Samples were collected as planned, and fuel wood samples were tested by the United States geological survey to determine their calorific value. The expanded program of 1905 emphasized technological research. Betts went to Charleston, South Carolina, where about ten miles distant at the mill of the E. P. Burton Lumber Company a laboratory was equipped with a 100,000 pound testing machine to test the effects of knots on the strength of structural materials. There Betts was assisted by McGarvey Cline. "The Charleston laboratory," Betts has written, "was operated in 1905 and 1906. It was during the operation of this laboratory that the idea of a central forest products laboratory of wide scope was conceived. The plan was largely Cline's. . . ." At the Burton Lumber Company the participants "worked out principles for the logical grading of commercial materials." The more the work continued, the more it was realized that it was better to bring timbers to the testing machines rather than to take testing machines to the forest. William L. Hall, in charge of "a further expansion of forest products work," was consulted. Not only strength tests of woods, but also further study of wood seasoning, wood preservation, pulp and paper manufacture, wood distillation, and other research phases were proposed. Other universities were to be brought into cooperative arrangements.

In 1906 a laboratory was commenced under Rolf Thelan's direction at Seattle in connection with the University of Washington. This was to test and determine the mechanical properties of woods of the Northwest, particularly Douglas fir and western hemlock. There had been several studies of northwestern timbers. For example, Henry S. Graves had written on "The Douglas Spruce of Northern Oregon."[46] Structural strength and commercial preservative treatment were in need of thorough physical study. During 1906 and 1907 a laboratory similar to that at the University of Washington was operated at Eugene, Oregon, in cooperation with the University of Oregon, under the direction of J. B. Knapp. Physiological investigation was incidental. Emphasis

[46] *The Forester* V, 3, March 1899, p. 52.

was placed on learning the mechanical and structural properties of the timbers of great forest regions.

Wood chemistry was not neglected. During 1906 and 1907 a chemical laboratory was operated at Boston under A. L. Dean, whose headquarters were at New Haven.

Until this time timber testing in the various laboratories had been done more or less separately, without regard for the work of others. To correlate the work, therefore, a central office with two engineers and suitable assistance was created in Washington, D.C. In May 1907 R. S. Kellogg reviewed in *Forestry and Irrigation*[47] "The Timber Tests of the Forest Service." Special importance was attached to the work on longleaf pine, loblolly or North Carolina pine, Douglas fir, western hemlock, Norway pine, and tamarack. He was impressed that the tests brought out clearly "the effect of rate of growth, knots and other defects upon strength." Mechanical and physical properties, studies of wood structure, wood preservation, derived products, and statistics continued to be the main branches of the work, and many experiments were made in cooperation with various industries for specific purposes. Such a study as that of the preservation of wood blocks for paving proved of immense value.

When Kellogg lectured on forest products research in Nebraska, Ohio, Illinois, and doubtless other states, the work was still being established. By 1913, however, when forest service investigations were reviewed in a two-volume report, fully one-third to one-half of its space was devoted to forest products. Within fifteen years these investigations achieved enormous expansion in many new important directions and a new emphasis was placed on the necessity for reforestation to supply the vastly increasing forest utilization demands. A tree would be viewed as "a national product . . . a plant which grows cellulose," and the suggestion was made that "some day we may change the forester's title to cellulose propagator." The establishment at Madison, Wisconsin, in 1910, of a great forest products laboratory, for several years "the only institution of its kind in the world," would indeed prove to be epoch-making.

A laboratory was located in 1908 at Boulder in cooperation with the University of Colorado. This laboratory made special tests on mine timbers and telegraph poles to secure a basis for design values. Full sized materials were used, including fire-killed and green-cut timbers. A

[47] XIII, 5, May 1907, p. 256; XIII, 3, p. 161; XI, 1, 1905, p. 26a. See also John Ise, *op. cit.*, pp. 311-313; Jenks Cameron, *op. cit.*, pp. 287-291; Howard F. Weiss, quoted in A. B. Recknagel and S. N. Spring, *op. cit.*, pp. 30, 225; "Review of Forest Service Investigations," issued March 11, 1913, G.P.O., Washington, I, pp. 17-27, II, pp. 33-48; Herbert A. Smith, "Forest Products Laboratory," Brazil Centennial Exposition, 1922-1923, G.P.O., Washington, 1922.

small treating plant was located near Norris, Colorado. A wood utilization office at Denver was maintained.

Another laboratory at Washington, D.C., was established in 1908, the Pennsylvania Avenue Pulp Laboratory, which tested the pulping qualities of several wood species. Study was pursued to determine the pulping qualities of corn stalks and several fibrous materials. In 1911 another pulp laboratory was located at Wausau, Wisconsin, and as part of its program technicians sought to define the pulping properties of a number of woods by the grinding process. They also determined the effects of various modifications on the resultant pulp induced by stone, pressure, speed, temperature, et cetera.

The last university laboratory prior to the location of a great central laboratory was put into operation in 1909 at Moscow, Idaho, in cooperation with the university there. This laboratory was to test the mechanical properties of ponderosa pine. At this time Betts, who from 1906 had worked at the Purdue laboratory with John Newlin, and who later was "the outstanding timber mechanics engineer in this country," had headquarters in the West, principally in Denver. Betts' influence in developing timber testing research had persisted from his first year with the forest service. With a helper he took up field study of ponderosa pine. Going to the Coconino and Tusayan national forests, he tested materials near Flagstaff, Arizona, and investigated the species as a source of naval stores. He found that nearly as much turpentine and rosin were obtained as from the southeastern pines.

On November 16, 1906, there had been held at Washington an important conference[48] of representatives of the National Hickory Association, the National Wagon Manufacturers Association, the Carriage Builders National Association, the National Association of Box Manufacturers, the Western Wheel Manufacturers, the National Lumber Manufacturers Association, the National Hardwood Lumber Association, the United States Forest Service, and the American Forestry Association. The conference unanimously passed a resolution endorsing enactment by congress of a bill which would appropriate $200,000 to establish a great central timber-testing laboratory. Chief Forester Pinchot was present and explained that he was not in a position to secure passage of the legislation but that the conferees and their friends might secure its enactment. William L. Hall presented a very brief history of timber testing in the federal government's forestry work.

Hall had graduated in 1898 with a Bachelor of Science degree from Kansas State Agricultural College at Manhattan. The following year

48 "For a National Wood-Testing Laboratory," *Forestry and Irrigation* XII, 11, Nov. 1906, p. 510.

he had obtained a Master's degree in forestry and horticulture. For a number of years he had been in charge of forest planting activities of the division of forestry. In 1905 he had taken charge of the branch of forest products of the forest service.[49] Hall showed complete knowledge of the timber testing then being pursued, but he had small knowledge of the work of Fernow and Roth. Hall was an able executive. His task was to coordinate and direct the new work and to bring business interests into closer contact with the work of the forest service. Hall considered Dr. Hatt to be the "man who prepared the plans and who [had] had charge of practically all of the work done in timber testing since [1902 when] plans were devised for beginning this testing work again."

The task of the period had remained one of business extension, not of science. If science had been put in the foreground the immediate appeal to the manufacturing interests would have been decreased. The manufacturers were impressed with the work being done in developing wood substitutes and with information which explained the most appropriate timber for a specific use. They wished the scope of the work enlarged. There now seemed to be no question as to whether the function was "germane" to governmental forestry. Between 1898 and 1905 the chief forester had performed the huge feat of integrating the division's field and administrative work, and after 1905 he coordinated the work of the forestry bureau of the department of the interior in building up a great forest service. Pinchot had had to be executive, propagandist, economist, and forester. With each year his interest in scientific forestry had heightened. Pinchot had not tried to imitate the work of Fernow. While Fernow's accomplishments had furnished the fundamentals and a foundation, the architecture of the United States forest service was Pinchot's. Many of Fernow's students were employed by the forest service. Occasionally they consulted with Fernow.

From Washington on August 24, 1908(?), Frederick Dunlap wrote to Fernow:

> My work here is going slowly during the summer while there is a new laboratory under way. I have a clear field in the pure physics of wood with a practical annex in dry kiln operation. I am contemplating increasing some specific heats this winter and to follow this up with studies of Heat conductivity and its changes with moisture content etc. [H. F.] Weiss [a former student of the New York State College of Forestry] and myself with a few others in the Forest Service are doing our best to develop the scientific study of wood in a systematic way, a line of work new to the past policy of the Service and the Bureau before it. Our work here has been almost entirely for immediate, practical results. I believe a certain amount of painstaking scientific investigation would be quite as profitable. . . .

[49] See the biographical sketch of Hall in R. S. Hosmer's historical paper on the Society of American Foresters, *Journal of Forestry*, Nov. 1940.

Dunlap also had been a student at the New York State College of Forestry. In 1902-1903 he came to the school "a riper man than the average," said Fernow, "and applied himself thoroughly. He was a good all-round student, promising to make a success of whatever he undertook." As the years went by Fernow was more and more pleased with Dunlap's work as a forest assistant in the forest service. In his capacity as physicist of the forest products laboratory, a position which he held until 1912, he contributed notably to the advancement of science in wood research. Some of his notes and articles published in *Forestry Quarterly* gave a definite impetus to a line of research which had been struggling for recognition for a number of years. In 1912 Fernow recommended Dunlap and helped him to secure a professorship of forestry at the University of Missouri. Evidently Dunlap kept Fernow informed of his progress. On November 4, 1908, he notified Fernow, "The wood utilization laboratory with which my work is connected may be moved from Washington and I with it. . . ." Some of the office work went to Chicago. There remained still the creation of a great central laboratory for both wood utilization and timber testing.

Forest service officials doubtless had realized that while Roth had initiated timber physics study under Fernow's direction and Professor Johnson's laboratory at St. Louis had furnished the first engineering facilities, Fernow had not been able to convince the American people and their representatives in congress that "pure science" in time would more than pay its own way. But today everyone recognizes the tremendous value of the work which has been developed at the forest products laboratory, an enormous institution which in the autumn of 1909 was established in small but commodious quarters at 1610 Adams Street in Madison, Wisconsin, under McGarvey Cline's direction. Cline supervised the building of the laboratory, which was erected on the campus in cooperation with the university. He then resigned to go into business, and Howard Weiss became director.

The University of Wisconsin was chosen as the site of the laboratory which was to unify the work of all but two of the branch laboratories. Other universities and institutions were consulted, notably the universities of Michigan and Minnesota. Roth was also consulted. The University of Michigan might have had the laboratory. Roth, however, believed that forestry, like botany and horticulture, was a form of agriculture. The site selection and the plans were largely the work of Pinchot, Graves, Betts, Hall, and Cline. The building was not officially dedicated until 1910. The University of Wisconsin, Betts said, "offered to do anything we wanted if the Forest Service would establish its laboratory as a cooperating institution of the university. We asked them to build a laboratory from our plans and to furnish us light, heat, and power. This they readily agreed to do. Our contribution to the University was a series of lectures and the opportunity for post graduate work." Accordingly, the year after its original establishment, the laboratory was moved into a building built by the university from plans furnished by the forest service.

The formation in 1907 of the American Society of Agronomy, the publication in 1906 of Hilgard's classic work on *Soils*, the elaboration at the University of Illinois, Cornell University, and elsewhere of methods of soil treatment to develop a "permanent agriculture," and a triangular debate between leaders of soils research as to the comparative importance of analyses stressing physical elements and chemical composition[50] had brought agronomic investigation into prominence. In forestry, however, there had been shaped a type of soil study which, while it included many agronomic features and covered a wide geographical range, was more linked with land reclamation and irrigation. During this period of forest soils study, the immediate and practical considerations had to prevail over the strictly scientific. The work was almost entirely confined to the field rather than the indoor laboratory.

The 1902 federal land reclamation law had inaugurated what George Hebard Maxwell, a leader in the western irrigation movement and the organizer in 1899 of the National Reclamation Association, had described as "a broad national policy of water conservation, through forest conservation and flood-water storage."[51] The following year Maxwell and his associates of the National Irrigation Congress and the National Irrigation Association, together with other forces, had organized against western land frauds and speculation. They urged repeal of the Desert Land Law, the Timber and Stone Act, and the commutation clause of the Homestead Law. They wanted to leave on the statute books the privilege of homesteading a 160-acre tract and the procurement of title after five years of residence.[52] By reason of the National Reclamation Act of June 17, 1902, land restoration in the West became an immense public business comparable to that of the national forests. A reclamation fund aggregating millions of dollars made up mainly of

[50] In their review of Bulletin 22 of the U.S. Bureau of Soils ("The Chemistry of Soil as related to Crop Production," *Forestry Quarterly* II, 1, Nov. 1903, p. 30), M. Whitney and F. K. Cameron said, "What many foresters, if not all, have long known of their crop, namely, that the physical conditions of the soil especially with reference to water conduction are of infinitely more importance in wood production than the chemical composition, seems from the investigation here reported to hold good for agricultural crops, also. . . ." Although Hilgard was supposedly in wide disagreement with this view, that he was not is shown by his major study, *Soils*. See F. H. King's review of Hilgard's book in *Science*, new series, XXIV, pp. 681-684.

[51] *Forestry and Irrigation* VIII. 1, Jan. 1902, pp. 15-17.

[52] *Forestry and Irrigation* X, Jan. 1904, p. 41; XI, Jan. 1905, pp. 24-26b. The number of forest reserves was placed at 61, and the total area 63,348,656 acres. Concerning Maxwell see *ibid.* VIII, 10, Oct. 1902, p. 403; concerning Walcott, *ibid.*, p. 443; concerning Hitchcock, *ibid.*, p. 442.

proceeds from disposals of public lands and from fees and commissions earned in the states was set aside. Under the act, the cost of surveys and construction of irrigation projects, including reservoirs and other reclamation agencies, was to be defrayed by the completed works, returned to the fund in installments, and reinvested in new projects. Within a year the federal reclamation service had gone into the thirteen states and three territories named in the act.[53] Already it was believed that in the great mineral-producing states of California and Colorado the yields from irrigated agriculture had surpassed the value of products from the mines. Indeed, Maxwell had quoted an authority to this effect even before the Reclamation Act was passed. At the American Forestry Association meeting in 1904, the directors reported that the reclamation fund was then about twenty-five million dollars. They emphasized the mutual importance of sound forest and water management, especially the forest functions of protecting irrigation works from floods, from washing of earth from hillsides, from silt, and at the headwaters of streams from the force of rains and run-off water in storms and thaws. *Forestry and Irrigation*[54] called for "the best technical administration obtainable," especially where the success of irrigation depended in part on the character of forest reservation administration. The slogan, "Save the forests and store the floods," was a sound statement of the plea, and to this was added, reclaim and build homes on the land.

For fourteen years Frederick Haynes Newell, at this time chief of the division of hydrography of the United States geographical survey, had had charge of irrigation development in the West. He[55] and Charles D. Walcott, director of the geological survey, had begun in 1902 to examine the extent of arid land which might be reclaimed, to measure the streams, to select reservoir sites, and to obtain all the data necessary to construct irrigation facilities. Each year the sum set aside for the projects was increased several millions of dollars. By 1905 the amount of land to be irrigated was approaching two million acres. Projects under construction[56] were on numerous western rivers—the Salt, Yuma, Uncompahgre, Minidoka, Huntley, Ft. Buford, North Platte, Truckee-Carson, Hondo, Belle Fourche, and Shoshone. Projects approved by the secretary of the interior were at Klamath Falls and on the Malheur, Milk, Palouse, Payette-Boise, Bismarck, and Buford-Trenton rivers. These projects, moreover, were additional to the great navigation projects which for years the federal government had under-

[53] Letter of President Roosevelt, dated Sep. 15, 1903, *ibid.* IX, p. 475.

[54] *ibid.* VIII, 7, July 1902, p. 278; XI, Jan. 1905, p. 26d.

[55] *ibid.* XIII, 4, April 1907, p. 93. Some of Newell's important writings were: *Agriculture by Irrigation* (1894), *Hydrography of the Arid Regions* (1891), *The Public Lands of the United States* (1895), *Irrigation in the United States* (1902), *Principles of Irrigation Engineering* (1913), and *Irrigation Management* (1916).

[56] *ibid.* XI, 10, Oct. 1905, pp. 442f.

taken on larger streams, among them the Missouri and Mississippi. These enterprises which attracted mills and manufacture and developed agriculture changed the industrial organization of the western half of the United States. In January 1902 Maxwell said[57] that two-thirds of the whole western half of the United States actually belonged to the government and that nine-tenths of the people lived in its eastern half! Five years later, when Newell was appointed director of the federal reclamation service, a tremendous task still lay before him. New towns had sprung up in the desert. New branch railways had been built. Thousands of people had begun to make the desert areas their homes. Yet more remained to be performed, much more, and forest work would play a principal part.

The United States geological survey was interested in the water problems of the nation from more than one angle. The water resources of eastern and southern states, both surface waters and underground waters, were being examined. At first glance the connection of forestry to underground waters may seem remote. We must recall, however, that many years earlier Fernow had predicted that water management as a problem of the future would be coordinated with forestry. Examinations of water resources beginning in the West did not minimize the inherent problems in the East. Water surveys already were linked with soil and forest surveys in some eastern states. Eventually forestry and irrigation projects would be combined in special developments of eastern regions. The report of the National Academy of Sciences for 1908 summarized the relation of forest and water conservancy in the eastern states:

> *Whereas* the headwaters of all important navigable streams to the west of the Mississippi River are now protected by national forests, while the Appalachian Mountains, which form the waterheads of many navigable streams of great importance, are entirely unprotected and are being damaged to a menacing extent by the wasteful cutting of the forest, unrestricted fires, and injudicious clearing; *Resolved,* That the council of the National Academy of Sciences heartily favors the extension of the national forest system to the Appalachian Mountains for their protection and permanent utilization. *Resolved,* That we urge upon Congress the passage at the present session of a bill to acquire in the southern Appalachian Mountains and the White Mountains such forest lands as are necessary to protect the navigable streams which have their sources therein and to make permanent the timber supply of the eastern part of the United States. . . .

In 1902 Charles Sprague Sargent, Henry L. Abbott, and William H. Brewer had comprised a committee of the Academy which, at the request of the chairman of the committee on forest reservations of the United States senate, had considered a message of President Roosevelt

[57] *ibid.* VIII, 1, Jan. 1902, p. 17.

transmitting a report of Secretary Wilson on the advisability of creating a "National Appalachian Forest Reserve" in the southern Appalachian mountains. Their report favored the reservation's establishment but recommended certain further study.[58]

These eastern forest reservations were eventually created under authority of the Weeks law. State-owned reservations were also set apart to conserve forest and water supplies. Of the large forest reserves in which Fernow for many years was interested, there were some which were shaped as parks, created by gifts of wealthy citizens. One of these was the Palisades Interstate Park, the gift of Mrs. E. H. Harriman and others, which was established by the joint action of New York and New Jersey to include the western side of the Hudson River from Fort Lee nearly to Haverstraw, and the Hudson forest reserve (a smaller strip farther north from West Point to Cornwall).[59] Fernow's primary interest in forest utilization, however, naturally directed the major portion of his attention to the real forest reservations.

Fernow and Roth always had recognized the importance of studying forests in relation to the soil cover. Soil study, however, was of more significance to agriculture than to forestry. By 1903 the United States bureau of soils had surveyed 33,785 square miles of lands and during the year contemplated surveying 27,850 more square miles distributed generally throughout the United States. "These surveys," said *Forestry and Irrigation* in June 1903,[60] "are valuable, particularly in the West, where the soil types, with their origin and processes of formation, are described, with recommendations as to crops grown, possible yields, adaptability of certain soils to crops, special soil problems, irrigation and drainage, location, origin and composition of alkali, and reclamation of lands from alkali, swamps, or sand." Drainage systems were being installed that year in Yakima Valley, Washington, and at Salt Lake City, Utah, and Fresno, California, to demonstrate the flexibility of drainage.[61] Map-making was an important function of the bureau of soils. Some students such as Hugh Potter Baker spent some time in soils work before becoming actively associated with forestry teaching and research. The bureau of soils examined the land resources principally with a view to agricultural improvement.[62] Since the examination stressed the soil's physical attributes, grading the land according to productivity, the work was specifically useful to forestry. Hilgard had

[58] *History of the First Half Century of the National Academy etc.*, pp. 93f., 323-325.

[59] E. L. Partridge, *Country Life in America*, Sept. 1908; *Torreya* VIII, 1908, p. 275; X, 1, 1910, p. 28; Gurth Whipple, *op. cit.*, pp. 161f.

[60] *Forestry and Irrigation* IX, 6 June 1903, p. 276.

[61] *ibid.*, IX, p. 380.

[62] The bureau of soils was also making studies of soil chemistry. See Howe's review of Bulletin 53, "The Isolation of Harmful Organic Substances from Soils," in *Forestry Quarterly* IX, 1, March, 1911, p. 99.

early recognized the interrelationships of soil and the plant cover. The plant indicator doctrine, so useful to forestry and agriculture, originated from soil scientists and many ecologists who considered physical and chemical soil constituents. Fernow considered both techniques useful in forestry. Years earlier he had discussed this subject and kept it alive in forestry research. The development of a study of forest soils as a special branch of research was tardier than Fernow wished. He encouraged every worker who sought to develop experimental forest soils study and forest pathology.

During the early years of the twentieth century there came upon the forestry research scene in America a new type of investigation, its techniques developed primarily by botanists—ecology. In the April 17, 1903, issue of *Science*[63] was published an article by Fernow entitled "Applied Ecology." Ecology's methodology would enlarge the scope of forestry research in matters of physical environment, soil, climate, water relations, et cetera, and also in chemical analysis. The methods would prove especially useful in attacking problems of forest tree diseases. Fernow wrote:

> Ecology as a special branch of botanical study has been segregated from the broader field only in recent times, the name having been first suggested by Häckel some twenty-five years ago. But like many phases of human knowledge, practically, the study of ecology, that is, of the adaptation of plants to their surroundings, has occupied man these hundreds of years. Long before the study of ecology assumed the dignity of a science did practitioners not only study but apply their knowledge for practical purposes in the production of plants. Agriculture, and still more so, silviculture, is based upon the recognition of the ecological relations of plants. The agriculturist goes so far as to create . . . the environment. . . . He can create an environment desirable to any plant. But the silviculturist has not the opportunity to the same extent to fit the environment to his crop; he must study the fitting of his crop to the environment, and as his crop is required to persist for a century or so, adapted to both the stable and variable conditions of the environment, the adaptation must be studied with great care, so that the changes in environment may not prove detrimental to his crop. . . .

Fernow sought to enlist botanists to aid practitioners of silviculture in solving the problems of silvicultural requirements of species. Definite knowledge regarding species and their adaptations to conditions was still needed in forestry. "There are many botanists, even those devoted to ecological studies," said Fernow, "who have not given thought to all the factors of importance in the environment which need consideration with a plant of such long duration as a tree. That trees are plants, unique in character and differently situated, as regards ecological factors, from the low vegetation, has hardly been realized. . . ."

[63] New series, XVII, pp. 605f. See also Fernow's "The Education of Foresters," *Canadian Forestry Journal* III, 4, Dec. 1907, pp. 143-153.

Fernow differentiated between stable environmental factors—soil and general or local climate—and the unstable or variable factors—seasonal variations and certain climatic conditions, plant and animal associations, and light. He was "not aware [that any] extended investigation" had been made of American trees to determine what chemical constituents were necessary to the growth of various forest species. So far as Europe was concerned, investigation had revealed that the presence of mineral constituents in the transpiration current or other parts of the tree was "simply fortuitous." "The physical conditions of the soil, especially with reference to water conductivity and water storage capacity," Fernow wrote, "are the more important of the edaphic factors."

The adaptive factors in need of research were the root systems, "gross as well as minute," and the mechanical and physical adaptations to soil and atmospheric conditions. The tracing, shallow-rooted system was regarded as "best adapted mechanically to the shallow soils, but since it must supply itself from the surface, its chances of securing sufficient supplies, are limited, hence these species are, relatively speaking, not adapted to dry soils or dry atmospheres. On the other hand, the deep-rooting species (with tap or heart root) can secure water from great distances below ground. . . ." Most plants, Fernow observed, "love neither dry nor wet conditions, although some are more capable of enduring such extreme conditions." Some species found in driest soil were also found in swamps. Some thrive better under one condition or the other. A study of those species capable of modifying their root systems was needed. It was urged that a closer study of tree species, their silvicultural requirements, and their appropriate locations would aid farmers, nurserymen, and all forest owners. Such knowledge was imperative to the forester. An unfavorable site often permitted the better adapted species to crowd out the desired species.

The next factor considered was climate. "The climatic range of a species in the natural field gives, of course, a first clue to its climatic adaptation, but we know now very well," Fernow continued, "that mechanical barriers to progress, inefficiency in transportation, and mere competition with other forms [are] sufficient to exclude species from a wider field. . . ." The black locust was used as an illustration. A new study of plant distribution brought about by local topographic and climatic differences was urged. "Our species so far have remained largely unstudied from this point of view," Fernow pleaded. "Among the minor variable features of local climate it is specially the frost phenomena which are of importance, and knowledge as to what species are liable to suffer or capable of withstanding these, and under what conditions."

Of the variable environmental factors in the "forest association," light and the species' adaptability to varying light conditions was "of the utmost interest to the silviculturist and should be to the plant ecologist. Although the physiological relations of light to plant growth have been studied by botanists, the ecologic relations have been hardly recognized. On this field the ecologists owe an apology to the silviculturists for having failed to perceive the importance, which the latter have pointed out and appreciated for the last hundred years. Almost the whole art of the silviculturist is based on the recognition of the photic adaptations of the different species. . . ." Supporting this, Fernow analyzed the great classic of Schimper on plant geography and pointed out that while the physiological influence of light had been dealt with, almost no attention had been accorded its ecologic character. An expanding field in "the topographic importance of light" lay ahead. "The relative tolerance or endurance of light among the tree species within a given climatic range," Fernow claimed, "is probably the most important ecologic factor which determines the character of the association. The tolerant, if adapted to climate and soil, must ultimately drive out or reduce in number the intolerant or light-needing, even though perfectly adapted to climate and soil. This accounts for the sporadic occurrence in the mixed maple-beech-hemlock-spruce forest of such light-needing species as the black cherry, the ash, the elm. It accounts for the existence of the most intolerant bald cypress or larch in the swamps, where their competitors could not follow. It accounts for the change of forest type under the influence of man, the alternation of species observed on burns and slashings. An ecological study of the relative shade endurance of our important species is the most important need of the silviculturist."

This study was written while Fernow was yet director of the New York State College of Forestry. In this interest for many years his position among foresters was quite unique, but through his editorial work he enlivened the interest of many a forester in ecology and many a botanist or ecologist in forestry. He suggested that "we might enumerate any number of problems of practical importance for the solution of which the practitioner is waiting. And as in other sciences, which were first deduced from empirics and now direct the practice, so for ecology has come the time to direct the practice." It is clear today that ecological methods have greatly advanced scientific forestry in North America.

Fernow led in transfusing ecology into forestry. Ecology originated in Europe under such great masters as Griesebach, Warming, Schimper, Wiesner, Drude, and others. Asa Gray's and Sir Joseph Dalton Hooker's studies of geographic plant distribution definitely aided its introduction to the United States and Canada. Three universities in the United States were mainly responsible for the formal beginnings on this continent—the University of Nebraska, the University of Minnesota, and the University of Chicago. Its methods, principally directed toward study of the living plant and the laws and factors of plant origins, growth, reproduction, and environment, immediately began to intensify and widen research in field, forest, and garden. We have commented upon the part of Bessey and others in developing this branch of learning in the United States. Its methods have been elaborated in both the plant and animal sciences. In the plant sciences the leaders were Henry Chandler Cowles, John Merle Coulter, Roscoe Pound, Conway MacMillan, and others soon to be referred to. They began to examine the physical and biologic factors of plant habitats, including the forest cover.

In 1899 Frederic Edward Clements made a reconnaissance of the subalpine and alpine Colorado front range regions at Pike's Peak to arrange "primarily by formation fascicles showing proper [evolutionary] sequence" the data of his ecological researches. When in 1905 Clements' famous *Research Methods in Ecology* was published, Fernow welcomed the work and recommended it to foresters as "the first of its kind in the English, and perhaps in any language. . . ."[64] Fernow liked "the benefit of such systematic procedures as the book advocates and elucidates." Henry Chandler Cowles, reviewing the book in the *Botanical Gazette*,[65] said, "The true ecology, the ecology that is to be, is developed only by the most arduous and long-continued work. The dilettante ecology is to pass away, and one of the foremost causes for this change will be this new book of Clements. . . . One can scarcely praise the work too much; it is what is needed to prevent ecology from falling into a swift and merited disfavor. . . ." Cowles liked "the ingenious and multiform methods that have been employed by the author in the study of the Nebraska and Colorado vegetation. . . ." Moreover, *Forestry Quarterly*,[66] in review of Clements's *Plant Physiology and Ecology*, welcomed this worthy textbook on an applied phase of silviculture. Fernow's point of view was not altogether in harmony with that attributed to Clements, that is, ". . . . that physiology and ecology are essentially the same, and that a study of the vital activities of protoplasm, or of the living organism should properly be merged with a study of the living plant in its relation to the factors of the habitat and its adaptations to these factors. . . ." While thoroughly in sympathy with ecological objectives, Fernow did not want the segregated values of

[64] *Forestry Quarterly* IV, 1, March 1906, p. 24.

[65] *Botanical Gazette* XL, July-Dec. 1905, pp. 381, 394.

[66] *Forestry Quarterly* V, 4, Dec. 1907, p. 405. See also the author's book, *John Merle Coulter*, Princeton Univ. Press, 1944, for more detail on this subject.

forestry, particularly silviculture, to be confused.[67] Clements had not written the first real studies in ecology. Among the first of merit had been a study by Conway MacMillan of the Lake-of-the-Woods region in Minnesota. Clements, however, distributed herbaria from the Colorado mountains in 1901 and illustrated by formation and succession the dynamics of plant association. In 1904 a pamphlet on this subject, also reviewed by Cowles, was made available. Cowles and Clements both saw that the physiological basis "distinguished the new ecology from that of other days." The addition later of a new plant anatomy also promoted specific advances.

In its first studies Cowles selected the sand dune areas in northern Indiana and in the vicinity of Chicago rather than a forest region. In a sense the sand dunes may be considered forests. Fernow most certainly was interested in these wide desolate areas. In his lecture on "The Battle of the Forest" he said, "How this succession of plant life takes place can be studied even now in all its stages, for instance on the sand dunes of Lake Michigan." Fernow traced the stages from the sand grasses to the climax forest. But there can be no question of the significance to forestry of the ecological studies pursued by Cowles and his group of students in northern Michigan. The field work spanned several years at the turn of the century, and from it and other work came forth the valuable studies of Cowles and Harry Nichols Whitford. When Whitford's "The Genetic Development of the Forests of Northern Michigan; a Study in Physiographic Ecology," was published in 1901 in the *Botanical Gazette*,[68] Fernow's *Forestry Quarterly* had not yet come into existence. For three summers, 1898, 1899, and 1900, Whitford studied Michigan forests. He spent the first two summers under the direction of Cowles, who also in 1901 wrote a similar study of the origin, development and classification of plant societies within the vicinity of Chicago. Whitford extended his ecological researches to Montana[69] and the Philippines. Although he was a botanist by profession, he had a strong interest in forestry. In the last chapter we will consider a professional fellowship in forestry between Fernow and Whitford.

In eastern America during this period another investigator began to publish the results of a number of years of careful experimental study. In 1905 in the *American Naturalist* Edgar Nelson Transeau's illuminating paper on "Forest Centers in Eastern America" was published. In

[67] In his review of *Research Methods in Ecology*, Fernow wrote, "We cannot agree with the author in attempting to make this study co-extensive with botany, or to identify ecology with physiology. . . ."

[68] *Botanical Gazette* XXXI, Jan.-June 1901; Cowles's study on p. 73; Whitford's study on p. 289.

[69] *Forestry Quarterly* III, 2, May 1905, p. 192, an abstract of Whitford's "The Forests of the Flathead Valley, Montana," *Botanical Gazette*, Feb., March, April, 1905, pp. 99, 194, 276.

Forestry Quarterly[70] Fernow reviewed it as "a very interesting paper on zonal forest distribution in Eastern America based not on mere description but on ecological and evolutionary considerations." Transeau's rainfall-evaporation ratios permitted the construction of a climatic map and a further differentiation of forest centers than had previously been possible. In this and other studies a basis was found for a world-wide agriculture and forestry. *Forestry Quarterly*[71] (presumably Fernow) remarked on the "new spirit of testing all of the old theories and practices of silviculture by scrutiny on a scientific basis and by careful experiment." During 1905 an entire section of the *Quarterly* was given over to the "Relation of Silviculture to Ecological Investigations" based on a series of articles which had appeared in *Botanisches Centralblatt.* Fernow realized that a transition in America of silviculture from an empirical to a strictly biological basis would be gradual. Ecology had stirred up a hornet's nest of disputation in Europe, especially in Germany, where forestry was advanced, and the lesson to foresters in America was moderation.[72] So impressed with Transeau's study was Fernow, however, that he wrote to Transeau and said, "You have set the egg on end just as Columbus did."

Fernow was an intense individual, but he was also cautious and somewhat slow to advocate sweeping changes. In 1905 the secretary of agriculture issued regulations and instructions for the administration of the national forest reservations. Fernow congratulated Chief Forester Pinchot for the simple common-sense management program which characterized the beginnings of national forest administration. Evolution, rather than revolution, was Fernow's doctrine.[73] He found a place for its application in both economic and scientific forestry. He did not like "one-sided" data. When some foresters in America charged that it was unfortunate that we could claim "no science of silvics, but only a collection of rules applicable to limited conditions,"[74] the elder forester advised not to accept all conclusions "without specific verification."

While Fernow was chief of the division of forestry he had been confronted with huge economic tasks—forest reconnaissances, stock-taking of resources, surveys, the preparation of charts, maps, drawings, statistical tables, and other responsibilities. Always with less than a dozen aides, he performed his duties with the facilities available to the best of his ability. He wrote about more than he was able to inaugurate. He was never satisfied, and not until he became editor-in-chief of *Forestry Quarterly* was he able to tell, and to show with materials at hand, what he really knew.

[70] *Forestry Quarterly* IV, 1, March 1906, pp. 38, 40.
[71] *ibid.* III, 1, Feb. 1905, p. 56.
[72] *ibid.* III, Feb. 1905, p. 56.
[73] *ibid.* III, p. 275.
[74] *ibid.* V, 2, June 1907, pp. 174-189.

Fernow regarded silviculture as applied ecology. As reviewer of Transeau's "Forest Centers in Eastern America" he commented:

> Instead of basing his zones like Merriam on the single factor of temperature, [Transeau] secures his basis much more rationally for floral forms, on a combination factor, namely, rainfall-evaporation ratios, the nearest approach to what the reviewer has claimed years ago as the principal factor in the distribution of arborescent forms, the transpiration factor. . . .

Forestry Quarterly[75] early in 1904 had recommended Transeau's "On the geographical distribution and ecological relations of the bog plant societies of North America." Neither Clements' nor Transeau's studies, however, escaped criticism. For that matter, neither could Fernow claim a unique place as an exponent of ecology in forestry research.

In 1902 Ernest Bruncken, then secretary of the Wisconsin State Forestry Association and later teacher at the Biltmore forest school, wrote on "Forestry and Plant Ecology."[76] Bruncken urged a number of forestry reforms. He advocated cooperation of foresters with lawyers to arrive at new methods to appraise damage to forest property. Fernow in an article, "Considerations in Appraising Damage to Forest Property,"[77] presented methods of evaluating damage to forest property from a *forester's point of view.* An interesting introduction was the federal decision, *Munn vs. Illinois,* which reflected on the matter of public interest in forests and which laid the basis for our law pertaining to industries vested with a public interest. It also considered in rate cases whether valuation should be fixed on the basis of a fair return upon a fair property value or on the basis of the property's reproduction cost less depreciation. The discussion was prompted by a suggestion from Bruncken.

Much as ecology might aid forestry, Fernow believed that, like botany, forestry would remain a separate profession. In a letter to William S. Cooper on October 24, 1910, he said:

> If you have in view to secure material for a history of Ecology in the United States, I should think that the *Botanical Gazette* is the only means of securing it. If history in Germany is of interest to you I may refer you to my own publication, which, I think, you will find in the Library of the University, entitled, "A Brief History of Forestry" etc. To be sure, as this is mainly a history of the development of forest policies, you will not find very much on the ecological side, excepting short references. It is a subject in which not much has been written. You might also inspect the *Forestry Quarterly* which would here and there have references to the newer development in silvical ecology. For the ecological features of different species, I would direct you to the *Silvical Leaflets* issued by the United States Forest Service.

That the *Botanical Gazette* and *Silvical Leaflets* were regarded as the

[75] *ibid.* II, 2, Feb. 1904, p. 94.
[76] *Forestry and Irrigation* VIII, p. 251.
[77] *Forestry Quarterly* III, 2, May 1905, pp. 119ff.

principal sources of forest ecology indicates the coordinating nature of the new science. That Fernow later was instrumental in procuring for forestry service in Canada two thoroughly trained ecologists, Whitford and Clifton Durand Howe, demonstrated his respect for this field, but he remained a zealous guard of the profession of forestry. He never wished silviculture and ecology confused.[78]

Fernow expressed confidence in "The Minnesota Experiment"[79] as an example of the application of scientific silviculture to forestry. In the Minnesota national reservation, on 231,400 acres including 200,000 acres of pine land administered for the benefit of the Chippewa Indians, timber was being harvested profitably by the United States forest service. Planned natural reproduction, 5% of the mature white pine trees being left for natural seeding, was being demonstrated. The young growth was being protected.

Herman Haupt Chapman was principally responsible for this constructive plan. Chapman was a graduate in science at the University of Minnesota. Always interested in farming, he had enjoyed a casual interest in forestry. In 1881 he had seen the Northern Pacific Railway's forest plantations set out at Mandan, North Dakota, by Leonard B. Hodges under the direction of his grandfather, Herman Haupt. Young Chapman had managed to complete three years of high school in a year, and he immediately studied practical farming. His university courses included dairying, animal husbandry, and agronomy.

By 1896 there had been established a forest experiment station at Grand Rapids, Minnesota. One day Willet M. Hays summoned Chapman to his office and asked, "What do you know about forestry?" Chapman replied, "Not one thing." Hays answered, "You must learn all about forestry." Chapman was not the first director in charge of the station, but he was the first to give its work a distinguished reputation. He went to Grand Rapids and set out to demonstrate what a forest station could accomplish. Part of the work was cooperative forest planting with the division of forestry, but the station, an integral part of the department, had for its main purpose, so Fernow said in his 1897 report, "to experiment on practical methods of reforesting cut-over waste brush lands." Chapman was superintendent there from 1898 until 1903. In 1899 he received the degree of bachelor of agriculture from the university, and his work took him into several other positions.

In 1899 Chapman secured a student assistantship in the East with the division of forestry. He began to study forest mensuration. Thus he became acquainted with Graves, Pinchot, Overton Price, E. T. Allen,

[78] For further information on this subject see H. de Forest, "Recent Investigations in Ecology," *Proc. Soc. Am. For.* IX, 1914, pp. 161-176.

[79] *Forestry Quarterly* III, 2, May 1905, pp. 99-113; *Journal of Forestry* XV, 7, Nov. 1917, p. 929; *Forestry and Irrigation* IX, 9, Sept. 1903, pp. 428-431.

Smith Riley, and other foresters. After three months Graves suggested that Chapman interview forestry pioneers in the United States. He journeyed about the country and conferred with Fernow, Rothrock, Roth, Fox, Schenck, and George H. Moses. Moses was secretary of the forest commission of New Hampshire which had investigated forest conditions and sought progressive forestry legislation. In the course of his travels Chapman examined importations of white pine in bundles. Similar importings brought the white pine blister rust into the United States. One winter he worked scaling logs. The next winter he decided to obtain an education in forestry. He chose the Yale Forest School.

While at Yale University he interviewed Congressman Page Morris, the man for whom the Morris bill was named. He presented a plan of administration for the Minnesota national reservation. With minor modifications his plan was incorporated in the legislation, a part of which formed the basis of the "Minnesota Experiment." Chief Forester Pinchot lent his valuable support to the plan and gave Chapman substantial credit.

From an aggregate 600,000 acres of the Chippewa national reservation, congress authorized the selection of 225,000 acres around Cass Lake to comprise a forest reserve under a management which provided for present and future timber harvesting and white pine reproduction on a large scale by the "seed-tree method."[80] Eugene S. Bruce, lumberman of the United States bureau of forestry, became the manager under Chapman's plan. In a paper, "Work and Policy of the Bureau of Forestry on the Minnesota National Forest Reserve," read before a large gathering of foresters at the summer meeting of the American Forestry Association in 1903 at Minneapolis, Bruce expressed the opinion that if 25% instead of 5% of the mature merchantable trees were left for natural seeding, plus all the young growth above a guiding diameter, "better results" would yield. S. B. Elliott, forest commissioner of Pennsylvania, brought the subject into discussion on the theory that "forestry methods and practice throughout the remaining White Pine region of our country" were concerned. A delay of a year in publishing an article written by Elliott on the subject enabled Fernow to make "a personal visit to the experiment under discussion and to ventilate his ideas on the general questions involved." This was some years before Chief Forester Pinchot issued to a "technically educated staff" the regulations and instructions for *Use of the National Forest Reserves*,

[80] *Forestry and Irrigation* IX, 9, Sept. 1903, pp. 428-431; IX, p. 496; VIII, 1902, p. 311; *Forest Leaves* IX, 4, Aug. 1903, p. 56. See Raphael Zon's conclusions in "Results of Cuttings on the Minnesota National Forest under the Morris Act," in *Proc. Soc. Am. For.* VII. In *For. and Irrig.* VIII, 1902, p. 311, the results of the law, as to 830,162 acres, are shown: water surface, Indian allotments, forestry lands (231,000 acres), islands, and that open to settlement.

which Fernow praised for their "simple common sense." Replying to Elliott, Fernow distinguished the Cornell forest experiment from the experiment in Minnesota on the basis that the former was part of the work of an educational institution. He confessed himself not to be "in the counsels of the Bureau of Forestry." He suggested a few improvements, principally of a protective nature, such as fire lanes or ditches around the cut or burned areas, a distribution of felling areas, and the like. He said:

> I may say at the outset that I was pleased with what I saw and glad that at last a beginning like this has been possible. I have seen nothing more hopeful for the introduction of forestry methods in the United States, nothing that will teach the lumbermen so readily the two important lessons; namely, that brush should be burned and can be burned at little expense, and that reproduction can—under conditions—be secured on no present outlay. I do not wish to be understood that what is being done is ideal or even what a great government ought to be able to do, but it is sufficient for a first attempt under crude conditions. . . . It is, indeed, a compromise not only with the public, but with economic conditions; yet it is a justifiable compromise. . . . The main value of the experiment is not so much in the demonstration that pine can be reproduced by natural seeding, which every forester at least knows, as in the demonstration that brush can be burned with ease, without danger, and with little expense, thereby increasing the chances for young growth to establish itself.

Fernow realized that the question of artificial versus natural reforestation was not settled, even in Germany. Yet, "to a large extent" he believed artificial "new forest" would have to supplant the old natural forests on thousands of square miles of land where "the highest skill [would] never produce anything worth having by natural regeneration after having fooled away valuable time and energy." He foresaw that with fire protection demonstrated and with rise in stumpage values, governments and long-lived institutions more than ever could be persuaded to invest in forestry. In the final analysis forest conditions controlled. Four entirely distinct types of forest were involved in the "Minnesota experiment": red or Norway pine, jack pine, white pine, and mixed pine. The intention of the federal legislation enacted for the Chippewa Indians in 1902 had been to encourage them to become farmers on those lands fit for agriculture and to make them financially independent by a forest administration maintained for their benefit. Whatever silvicultural method produced "the largest amount of the most valuable material in the shortest time" would be correct unless financial considerations limited or indicated a wiser procedure.

As early as 1904 New York began to realize that its work in forestry, once regarded as the best in any state, was losing its prestige by not keeping abreast of the progress made in other states. Fernow attributed the cause to "the absence of a serious and honest forest policy,"[81] the same cause which had been responsible for the collapse of the New York State College of Forestry. Legislators were ignorant of forestry. The attitudes of governors toward forestry varied. The railroads were arrogant. Some wished that Theodore Roosevelt were again governor of New York.[82]

At the December 1903 meeting of the American Forestry Association encouragement had been found in legislation which promoted forest fire protection and forestry administration in Minnesota, California, Washington, and New Hampshire. Maine had appointed a state forester. Forest reservations in Pennsylvania and Indiana had been increased. At the Minneapolis meeting that summer the Association had discussed the new federal reserve at Cass Lake and the Itasca Park state reservation in Minnesota. The Minnesota state legislature, however, was still performing such unusual acts as to direct the state forestry board to purchase land for forestry purposes at a stipulated figure and then failing to appropriate the money. Nevertheless other valuable state forestry work was being carried on. The entire white pine belt was aroused. When Filibert Roth read a paper on the possibilities and methods of reforestation in the white pine region, he called attention to the Michigan farmers' objection to forest reservations owing to the tax burden. This was so even though the university had under its control a forest reserve of several thousand acres where reforestation values were being demonstrated. Roth took comfort from the fact that tremendous opportunities lay before forestry in Michigan. Wisconsin had recently abandoned its policy of letting go its tax title and publicly owned lands and had begun to segregate its poor lands for forestry purposes. Fernow commented:[83]

> The latest forestry legislation in Wisconsin is still largely of a tentative character, suggesting indefinite and impracticable or unnecessary experiments with inadequate appropriations, toying with the situation, instead of instituting at once a well devised, professionally conducted management of the State's important forestry interests.

In 1897 a forestry commission had been created in that state, but not until 1903 was a forestry department formed. Fernow may have given to the department the advice that it needed, because for eight years thenceforward the department proceeded diligently to care for its cut-over and burnt-over tracts and to produce a thrifty young forest growth.

[81] B. E. Fernow (ed.), "Forestry," *Recreation*, 1903, pp. 469-472. For a concise statement of state forestry progress during the last decade of the nineteenth and first decade of the twentieth centuries, see "State Conservation Activity," by John Ise, *The United States Forest Policy, op. cit.*, pp. 144-147.

[82] *Forestry and Irrigation* X, 3, March 1904, p. 119.

[83] B. E. Fernow (ed.), "Forestry," *Recreation*, 1903, pp. 470f.

"The need of the hour," said Fernow in 1903, "is the realization by Legislatures and officials of the immediate seriousness of the situation, the establishment of well-organized forestry bureaus in each State, conducted by professional foresters, and, above all, an efficient fire police. To this end, the Association should have a carefully chosen committee, which should be ready to assist State authorities in formulating adequate legislation." Replacement of the increasingly diminishing timber supplies was, indeed, a greater need than ever. "In spite of the heroic efforts of the Federal Government to induce private owners to adopt a more conservative management of timber lands, in spite of the extension of the forest reservation policy, in spite of the beginnings of a forest policy in several States, these efforts are still embryonic and nowhere in proportion to the magnitude of the interests involved. The eastern wooded States in which there is any beginning at all of a forest policy comprise less than about one-third of the forest region and a really serious, although still inadequate, beginning can hardly be said to exist on more than one-fifth of the territory." At a meeting of the Association the following year, its board especially commended the cooperative study being made between the federal bureau of forestry and the state authorities in the White Mountains and other New Hampshire regions, as well as in Massachusetts. Forestry in New England was on the eve of great developments.

For a number of years the Society for Protection of New Hampshire Forests employed a state forester. Nine years of organized study of the forests and the presentation three times to the legislature of an advanced forestry measure were required before New Hampshire in 1909 enacted legislation which provided the appointment of a state forester, the establishment of a state and town fire warden system, and the creation of state forest parks. Congress extended a helping hand in 1907, and the White Mountains[84] of New Hampshire began to claim equal distinction with the Appalachian mountains as sites for forest reservations. On the basis of forest service surveys and watershed conditions, Secretary of Agriculture Wilson in 1908 recommended the purchase of areas in both regions as forest reserves.[85]

On November 10, 1904, at Montpelier, before the Forestry Association of Vermont, Fernow delivered an address entitled, "Fundamentals of Forestry." "The report of your Forest Commission of 1882," he said, "contains much common sense and many good suggestions; yet it has remained, as far as I know, all these years without any

[84] *Forestry Quarterly* I, 3, April 1903, p. 117. The New Hampshire legislature had passed a bill authorizing $5,000 to be spent for state and federal work in the White Mountains. See Philip W. Ayres, "Forest Problems in New Hampshire," *ibid.*, p. 121; and concerning Vermont see *ibid.* II, 3, May 1904, p. 202.

[85] *Forestry Quarterly* VIII, 1, March 1910, p. 81; VI, 1, March 1908, pp. 64f.

practical consequence." He did not allow New Hampshire to escape criticism, "Your neighbor to the east, New Hampshire, has also for many years supported a Forest Commission without much result, waiting for private charity to create a State Forest Reserve. Massachusetts has this year created the office of State Forester and thus has at least recognized this interest as a State matter, as have also the States of Maine, Indiana, Colorado, and California in a similar manner. . . ." He outlined what he regarded would be a desirable forest policy for the state, embracing briefly fire law improvement, a state forester, financial aid for associations and educational institutions, forest reserves of brush, stump, and wasteland, improvement of private woodlots and planting of waste places, and encouragement of towns by advice and state loans to acquire town forests, the state credit to be used to guarantee the public domain fund of the town.

Vermont's state forestry commissioner, Ernest Hitchcock, thought so highly of this address that for two years pamphlet copies of Fernow's address were made available to interested persons. When on January 24, 1906, Fernow spoke in Burlington, Vermont, on "Government Activity in Forestry," the address was issued as Bulletin 2 by the commissioner. In 1909 Austin Hawes, who had been state forester of Connecticut since 1904, was made state forester of Vermont and professor of forestry in the university. Both natural and artificial reforestation were studied. For these purposes sample plots were laid out, and the character and adaptability of vegetation examined.

In June 1904 Alfred Akerman, who became in 1906-1907 the founder of the Peabody department of forestry at the University of Georgia, had been appointed state forester of Massachusetts, and soon afterward Ralph C. Hawley was selected to assist him.[86] On December 2, 1903, Fernow had spoken before the state board of agriculture of Massachusetts on "A Forest Policy for Massachusetts."[87] He had advanced substantially the same policy recommendations which he later advanced to New Hampshire. But to Massachusetts he stressed a special point:

> There is no State in the Union that has enacted more far-reaching legislation regarding the care and preservation of shade trees and for securing public parks. The tree warden is a Massachusetts institution, of which the State may be proud; the trustees of public reservations are a most useful lever for securing the preservation of historic and scenic places. But I must strenuously insist that these are matters which have absolutely nothing to do with the care and rational treatment of the forest areas of the State. This last is an economic question, pure and simple; while the arboricultural pursuits of tree wardens, park superintendents, and the absolutely misnamed

[86] In 1906 Hawley became an instructor at Yale Forest School (*Forestry Quarterly* IV, 3, Sept. 1906, p. 234).

[87] *51st Annual Report of the Mass. State Board of Agric.*; *Forestry Quarterly* II, 2, Feb. 1904, p. 49; *Woodland and Roadside* II, 4, Dec. 1903, pp. 2-4.

"city foresters," which your law so miscalls, are of aesthetical nature. Much harm to the forestry movement has been done by not keeping these two laudable movements more distinctly separate.

I close with the hope that Massachusetts will soon do at least as well by her forests as she has done by her shade trees.

As early as 1890 Fernow had been consulted by a Massachusetts board ordered to inquire into forest conditions of the state, and as a start in the direction of protecting and improving this interest he had urged the appointment of a state forester. In 1906 Frank William Pane, agriculturist, horticulturist, and forester, a graduate of Ohio State and Cornell Universities, who had taught in West Virginia and New Hampshire, began a service of many years in this office. Massachusetts in 1908 created a state conservation committee to cooperate with the national committee appointed by President Theodore Roosevelt in response to the historic conference of governors called at the suggestion of the inland waterways commission. The chairman of the state committee was F. W. Rane, the state forester during whose administration wise and generous legislation was obtained.

One more point in Fernow's address delivered in 1903 to the Massachusetts board of agriculture is deserving of attention. He explained his opposition to forestry teaching in the high schools. He did not fear a glorified Arbor Day pedagogy. He believed that high school curricula were already overloaded. If he favored any general forestry instruction, it was in a kind of agricultural extension program which would include "agriculture, mining, and all other pursuits of man." Professional forestry teaching, however, exacted high standards, both in agricultural and forestry schools.

In 1904 the senior class of Yale Forest School numbered thirty-four students.[88] H. H. Chapman, who had decided to complete his forestry education while attending the Minneapolis meeting of the American Forestry Association, was graduated in that year. Chapman entered the United States bureau of forestry, was assigned with J. Fred Baker to forestry work in the Palo Duro Canyon near Amarillo, Texas, and later was sent again to Minnesota, this time to compile yield tables for Norway and jack pine. The Texas work was an extension of the idea that the world was to be converted to forests. The project promised failure, and the state purchased the land for a state park. The Minnesota work, however, proved very valuable, since the yield tables prepared were among the first produced for the species in this country. In the spring of 1906 Chapman was chosen to give a course on state forest policy at Yale. He had no intention of becoming an instructor in forestry, but after doing some field work at Waterville, New Hampshire, he was made a member

[88] *Forestry Quarterly* II, 3, May 1904, p. 203.

of the Yale Forest School faculty. Chapman continued silvicultural study among the southern pines, one of his noteworthy contributions being the development of a technique to promote growth by burning over the land at the right season and right age of the seedlings.

At this time the Yale Forest School was unquestionably the leading forestry institution of the western hemisphere. By 1904 a practice of inviting authorities to lecture on various subjects had been expanded. That year Overton Price lectured on special methods in use at the bureau of forestry. B. W. Evermann of the New York fish commission also lectured.

Fernow was signally honored. While Dean Graves made a world tour, Fernow was appointed to give Graves's courses. During the winter term, 1904-1905, the former director of the New York State College of Forestry gave two courses at Yale Forest School: forest management, and a new course in the history of forestry.[89] For the latter course he prepared his lectures in written form. These lectures became the basis for his book on the history of forestry in foreign lands. The history of forestry on the American continent was completed at a later time. So impressed with these lectures were his students that many wrote him and requested that the lectures be placed in book form.

The American Forestry Association, in which Fernow still was influential, was now composed of a membership of 2,200 persons representing every state except one, as well as Canada and the insular possessions.[90] Fernow was selected to serve as one of the directors of the tremendous American Forestry Congress held at Washington in 1905. There were other honors which showed no lessening of Fernow's leadership.

In the autumn of 1904 Iowa State College provided an associate professorship of forestry in a combined department with horticulture, and Hugh Potter Baker, a graduate of Michigan State College and the Yale Forest School, was selected for the chair.[91] During the next year Pennsylvania State College[92] planned a forestry department with Dean Buckhout in charge. That year, 1905, the Colorado School of Forestry at Colorado Springs and Manitou was organized, and within three years it developed a full forestry curriculum. Dean Graves examined its facilities and expressed confidence that the summer course afforded an excellent opportunity for practical ranger instruction. In 1906 J. Fred Baker went from Mont Alto Academy to Colorado College to serve as a forestry instructor. Later Baker returned to his alma mater, Michigan

[89] *ibid.* II, 4, Nov. 1904, p. 279; *Forestry and Irrigation* X, 12, Dec. 1904, p. 559.
[90] *Forestry Quarterly* II, 3, May 1904, p. 201.
[91] *Forestry and Irrigation* X, 9, Sept. 1904, p. 397.
[92] *Forestry Quarterly* III, 3, Aug. 1905, pp. 333, 415.

State College, to conduct that institution's forestry department. Fernow, at Baker's invitation, lectured there.

On October 22, 1908, Dean William C. Sturgis of the Colorado School of Forestry wrote to Fernow that he was "desirous of securing an instructor in forestry to take charge of a Course for Rangers . . . and also to give some instruction in our regular course under our Prof. Winkenwerder. We are to have the assistance of some of the Government officials in the Rangers course, but our own instructor should be a man well qualified to direct the work. . . ." In the next chapter we will relate how Fernow became director of a faculty of forestry at the University of Toronto. Dean Sturgis's letter was received after Fernow had gone to Canada. Fernow referred him to Clyde Leavitt to suggest a man. "I may only add," said he, "that here we have nobody as yet ready for such work. . . . The pressure for good men is indeed great, I myself being out fishing in that direction."

In 1906 Dean Graves's scholarly *Forest Mensuration* was published. Fernow characterized this book as "the first professional text book on one branch of forestry . . . a thoroughly good American manual." For many years it occupied a place among a few forestry literary productions of first merit in America. In 1905 Edward Tyson Allen[93] was appointed state forester of California. At the same time he was to serve also as forest inspector in the United States forest service. A son of a Yale University professor, Allen, after completing his grammar school education, had been tutored by his father and in 1898 entered forestry work in the United States department of the interior. He was appointed in 1906 as an inspector of the national forests in Washington, Oregon, and Alaska, and in 1908, district forester for the North Pacific region. A year later he was employed by the influential Western Forestry and Conservation Association, an organization which promoted forestry growth and expansion in the West. Ralph Sheldon Hosmer has said of Allen, "He organized western timberland owners for forest protection, and developed cooperative efforts between federal, state, and private agencies in five western states. He [was] the author of considerable forestry legislation, and of numerous periodical articles. . . ." By 1914 there were thirty timber-owners associations in the United States.

In the East, the position of state forester of Maryland was created in 1906 and was filled by Fred W. Besley.[94] Forestry of the lake states benefited in 1905 by the appointment of Walter Mulford to a position as assistant professor in Roth's department at the University of Michigan. The next year *Forestry Quarterly* reported extensive forestry progress in the Michigan state forest reserve.[95] An expected en-

[93] *ibid.*, p. 332.
[94] *ibid.* IV, 3, Sept. 1906, p. 233.
[95] *ibid.* IV, 2, June 1906, pp. 178, 181.

largement of the reserve area and experimental plantings from the reserve nursery numbering over two million trees gave promise of management demonstration. One railroad had requested the university to establish a forest nursery and plantations. Mulford took charge of the Saginaw forestry farm. The experimental plantings of varieties of pine, catalpa, and black locust were highly praised. By 1906 western forest reserves covered practically every important watershed and included many drainage basins.[96] In 1907 President Theodore Roosevelt summoned the governors of the states and territories of the United States to confer at Washington from May 13-15[97] to give formal cohesion to a movement which had been gathering strength for more than three decades—the "most weighty question now before the people of the United States," the president said—the conservation of natural resources.[98] At last an organized effort to revise the western land laws had brought about enactment of the forest homestead law of June 11, 1906,[99] which opened to farming millions of acres of land within the national forests. An enactment to preserve places of historical and scientific interest was also secured.[100] When Fernow set about to write the United States section of his *History of Forestry*, he must have noticed with satisfaction that practically every essential point of "primary education and propaganda" for which he had striven was at least partially recognized. Fernow was not alone responsible, but his leadership had brought results.

[96] *ibid.* IV, 4, Dec. 1906, p. 352.
[97] *ibid.* VII, 2, June 1909, p. 162, a review of the conference's *Proceedings.*
[98] *Forestry and Irrigation* XIII, 12, Dec. 1907, p. 629.
[99] *Forest Quarterly* IV, 3, Sept. 1906, p. 236; John Ise, *op. cit.*, pp. 166-168, 255f.
[100] Jenks Cameron, *op. cit.*, p. 249. There was also an effort to rewrite the old Homestead Law, to allow the settler a 160-acre homestead and require a five years' residence to secure title. Repeal of the Desert Land Law, the commutation clause of the Homestead Act, and the Timber and Stone Act was sought (*Forestry and Irrigation* X, Jan. 1904, p. 41). Since 1903 the American Forestry Association and kindred organizations had formally been seeking modification of the mineral land laws, the lieu land-selection law, and repeal of the Timber and Stone Act (*ibid.* XI, 1, Jan. 1905, p. 24). These efforts followed the act of 1891 which repealed the still older timber culture laws and amended the Homestead Act.

CHAPTER VIII

Canadian Forestry; Fernow at Pennsylvania State College

THE first forester of a Canadian province was Judson F. Clark. When the New York State College of Forestry was disbanded, Clark had entered the United States bureau of forestry. In 1904, however, he had left federal service in the United States and accepted a position as forester of the province of Ontario. Clark was a graduate of Ontario Agricultural College, having received a degree as bachelor of science in agriculture in 1896. From 1896-1898 he had taught at the province's agricultural college at Guelph. Obtaining a master of arts degree from Cornell University in 1899, he had taught botany, first as an assistant and then as a fellow, in the college of arts and science of Cornell. A doctorate of philosophy was conferred on him in 1901 by Cornell University. Clark turned his full attention to forestry when Roth left Fernow and Gifford to return to Washington and federal forestry work. He had taken courses in the New York State College of Forestry, and he was chosen to take charge of the courses in forest measurements, forest mapping, and wood technology. Proving capable as a teacher and able as a forester, Clark was to bring to Canada the latest and best forestry methods of the United States. Before taking up his position, he visited Europe and examined the principal forests, spending six months in study as a final preparation for his new task.[1]

Canada's forestry history had been similar to that of the United States. Officially organized in the Dominion government and in the separate provinces, forestry had begun as a movement without professionally trained foresters. The tremendous significance of the forests to the national economy had expressed itself in the formation of a Canadian Forestry Association.[2] Elihu Stewart, Dominion superintendent of forestry, had taken initiative. In 1899 Stewart had been appointed chief inspector of lumber and forestry for the Dominion. Impressed by the accomplishments of the American Forestry Association in the United States, he believed a separate organization might accomplish similar results in Canada. He summoned a group together, in part composed of Sir Henri Joly de Lotbinière, who had served many years as first vice president for Canada of the American Forestry Association, J. R.

[1] An announcement was made that Clark was to go to Europe. See *The Forester* VII, 7, July 1901, p. 180.

[2] E. G. Lotbinière, an address in *Report of the Canadian Forestry Convention* (Jan. 10-12, 1906), Ottawa, Gov't Printing Bureau, pp. 17ff. and reprint, or "Letter," prepared in 1905 and circulated in 1906 among members. Copy found in Lotbinière archives.

Booth, James Smart, William Little, Thomas Southworth, William Pearce, T. C. Keefer, C. H. Keefer, the venerable Canadian naturalist John Macoun and his son, W. T. Macoun, and Dr. William Saunders, director of the Dominion experimental farms.

In Chapter VI we have seen how, in 1900 at Ottawa, a meeting[3] was held and the Canadian Forestry Association formed with Lotbinière as president, William Little as vice-president, and the governor-general of Canada was invited to serve as the association's honorary president. Before the end of the year the membership numbered 369 persons. *Rod and Gun*, a sportsman's magazine, gave space to the Association in its monthly issues for articles and notices. A constitution and by-laws were adopted. For a number of years the Dominion government financed the publishing of reports of the Association's annual meetings. The provincial governments of Ontario, Quebec, and British Columbia each annually granted six hundred dollars to the Association. Canadian banks lent financial assistance. Supplemented by a revenue from membership fees, the organization immediately flourished.

In 1901 forest tree planting activity of the Dominion was reshaped to promote two objectives; the first was educational, and the second was designed to benefit the settlers. On application and after inspection and preparation of a working plan, trees and seeds from the experimental farm nurseries at Brandon and Indian Head were furnished for the planting of shelters, forest plantations, and windbreaks. The intention was to improve the agriculture of the Dominion. Between 1901-1905 more than 5,100,000 trees and a huge quantity of seeds were distributed. Furthermore it was estimated by Stewart in 1905 that eighty-five per cent of the trees planted were thriving. The deliveries were made under a standardized system. A government inspector visited the region to be planted and after examining the soil and environmental conditions prepared systematic recommendations. In this period the United States government also carried out planting.[4] The Dominion government proudly pointed to its replanting of a part of the sandhills of the spruce timber reserve in Manitoba, a region which Fernow would later visit.

A report of the Canadian Forestry Association for 1904-1905 read:

The tree planting scheme under Federal management in Manitoba and the North West Territories continues to develop. During the year 1904, 1,-800,000 trees were distributed to 1,027 settlers, an average to each of 1,752 trees. In 1905 the distribution will be 2,000,000 trees to 1,120 settlers. The

[3] *The Forester* VI, 4, April 1900, p. 86.

[4] James M. Fetherolf, "Forest Planting in National Forests," *Forestry Quarterly* VII, 2, June 1909, p. 127. In 1909 Pinchot's report showed that in 1908 about 700,000 trees were planted in forests in Nebraska, Kansas, Colorado, New Mexico, Arizona, Utah, Idaho, and California. At the planting stations there were more than 2,200,000 trees being grown, ready for 1909. Enough seed was sown in 1908 to produce 4,600,000 seedlings. See *Torreya*, 1909, p. 85.

Forestry Branch has so far sent out about 5,000,000 trees and 2,000 pounds of tree seeds.

A nursery to supply farmers was being set apart at Ontario Agricultural College at Guelph. Lectures on forestry were being given at farmers' institutes. The program was one of agriculture, and principally concerned with tree planting as distinguished from forest planting. The movement reached into the heavily forested province of British Columbia. In 1906 Dr. William Saunders addressed the Canadian Forestry Convention on "Forestry at the Experimental Farms," stressing the advancing importance of tree planting in regions of British Columbia.

By 1905[5] the Dominion timber reserves had attained a total area of 9,686,880 acres. Water and timber protection, as well as fish and game protection, were contemplated. The objects of the Canadian Forestry Association had been described as being:

> The preservation of the forests for their influence on climate, fertility and water supply; the exploration of the public domain and the reservation for timber production of lands unsuited for agriculture; the promotion of judicious methods in dealing with forests and woodlands; re-afforestation where advisable; tree planting in the plains and on streets and highways and the collection and dissemination of information bearing on the forestry problem in general.

In addition to the Dominion timber reserves there were those of the provinces. The crown forest reserves of Ontario alone aggregated more than nine million acres. A department of crown lands had been established. Fire ranging service in Ontario in 1904 had cost substantially more than eighty thousand dollars, and of this amount approximately one-half had been paid by the department and the balance by the licensees. More than thirty thousand dollars had been spent on forest ranging, about one-third on the forest reserves and one-third on the parks. In 1904 more than three hundred fire rangers were seasonally on duty in the forest reserves and Algonquin Park, and twenty rangers patrolled the right of way of the Temiskaming and Northern Ontario Railway. Contrasting these figures with those of 1885, when about thirty-seven men were employed at a cost of nearly eight thousand dollars, half of which was later refunded to the government by the licensees, there was a showing of definite progress. But considering the tremendous publicly-owned forest area, as well as that owned by private interests, Ontario should have had one of the best fire protection services in North America. Ontario had thousands of square miles in reservations,[6] mostly

[5] See references of footnote 2. The 1904-1905 report of the Canadian Forestry Association mentioned is a mimeographed or typewritten sheet found in the Lotbinière archives.

[6] See references to footnote 2. Also *Forestry Quarterly* III, 4, Nov. 1905, p. 410, where the reservations are listed: Algonquin Park Reservation, 1,466 square miles, January 1892. Rondeau Park Reservation 7⅘ square miles, 1894. Eastern Reservation, 125 square miles, April 1899. Sibly Reservation, 70 square miles, February 1900. Timagami

along the higher watersheds. In his 1903 Massachusetts address Fernow had praised the Ontario fire protective system. The fire risk being greater in some regions and at some seasons, he approved of special and general patrols according to the requirements. He believed that in forest regions towns should be included in the arrangements between the government and the timber limit holders, providing a chief fire warden and subordinates, as suggested by the systems of New York, Maine, Wisconsin, and Minnesota.

Quebec also had an advanced forest fire protection policy, and its forest reservations totalled 3,622,000 acres in 1905. The Gaspesian forest reserve of a million and a half acres had been set aside in 1904. A large area, 422,000 acres, had been added to Laurentides National Park, which previously had comprised nearly 1,700,000 acres. Further additions were contemplated. In 1907 William Little of Montreal would walk into the office of *Forestry and Irrigation*[7] and hand over a clipping from a Canadian newspaper of February 15 which read: "At the end of 1907, the Province of Quebec will have a larger forest reserve than any other country in the world, and an efficient protection will be given to the sources of the wealth-giving water powers of the Province."

The province of Quebec in 1907-1908 set about in earnest to institute a rational forest policy by reserving practically the entire remaining commercial timber area not under licenses. For land under license it

---

Reservation, 5,900 square miles, January 1901. Mississage Reservation, 3,000 square miles, February 1904. The Nipigon Reservation will be considered later.

[7] *Forestry and Irrigation* XIII, 4, April 1907, p. 173. In December 1907 the same publication (XIII, 12, Dec. 1907, pp. 511f.) described the Quebec reserves as containing 116,700 square miles, about one-half of the entire land area of the province. See also *Forest Leaves* XI, 5, Oct. 1907, p. 77, where the total area of the Quebec reserves was given as 165,474 square miles, the largest being the Saguenay and Labrador reserve of 109,360 square miles. The creation of national parks and forest reservations in Quebec had all transpired in a little more than a decade. See also Fernow's review of the "Report of the Minister of Lands and Forests of Quebec for 1907" in *Forestry Quarterly* VI, 2, June 1908, p. 162, where he says that the forest reserves in 1907 had been increased to twelve, comprising almost 108,000,000 acres, almost all of the St. Lawrence River and Gulf and their basin, except the arable and residential sections. There remained unreserved the basins of James Bay and Hamilton River. In 1907 a large reserve on the northeastern shore of Ottawa River was planned. The minister also wanted to establish a nursery for the province's farmers, and other improvements. "The Forest Reserves of Quebec," *Canadian Forestry Journal* III, 2, June 1907, p. 69, describes the reserves as containing 165,474 square miles, referring to:

Laurentides National Park	3,271 1/3 sq. mi.
Gaspé Park	2,500
Rimouski Reserve	1,249 2/3
Saguenay and Labrador Reserve	109,360
Ottawa Reserve	27,652
St. Maurice Reserve	27,652
Chaudière Reserve	320

This article probably formed the basis of the conclusions of *Forest Leaves, supra*. See, however, *Canadian Forestry Journal* III, 2, p. 62, on the same point. In the *Annual Report of the Canadian Forestry Association*, 1910, pp. 74-79, W. C. J. Hall, Superintendent of the Bureau of Forestry of Quebec, said, "We have in Quebec 175,000 square miles of Forest Reserves."

established regulations requiring the limit holders to put rangers on their berths. Much more than half of the accessible forest areas were reserved. The far northern districts of Abitibi, Mistassini, and Ashuanipi, north of the Height of Land, were excluded as needing as yet no special attention. *Forestry Quarterly* in March 1908,[8] commented that the area reserved represented "probably a larger *timbered* area under reserve than there [was] in the United States national forests."

On February 20-21, 1907, the first Provincial Forestry Convention called together in Canada gathered at Fredericton, New Brunswick, to arouse the public to take measures to protect and administer twelve million acres of timberland still owned by the government.[9] New Brunswick crown lands in 1904 produced, it was said, from its mileage and stumpage a revenue of $257,016.68. Although since 1885 the province had had an excellent fire act, no fire ranger staff had been organized, and little more than $2,000 annually had been spent to enforce its provisions. In April 1904, in connection with surveys and the construction of transcontinental and other railways through forest lands, an act aimed toward protecting crown timberlands in the province had been passed. More, however, was needed. At the Provincial Forestry Convention of 1907 a forestry association was formed, and the government was asked to create a chair of forestry at the University of New Brunswick.

The crown timberlands in Nova Scotia in 1905 aggregated a little more than one and one-half million acres. Since 1883, after the Montreal meeting of the American Forestry Congress, Nova Scotia had had a fire prevention act on its statute books; but the law had remained practically dead until 1904 when an enforcement act authorized the appointment of rangers and subrangers in the different municipalities. At this time some attention was being given in the province to "reafforestation" and to setting apart of lands at the heads of navigable streams.

Forestry had been institutionalized in Canada since about 1882, but in 1905 Ontario, Quebec, New Brunswick, and Nova Scotia were the only provinces with phases of a forestry development. Forest protection had been neglected in Saskatchewan, Manitoba, British Columbia, and the other provinces and territories. The Dominion government had timber reserves in Manitoba, the Northwest Territories, and British Columbia. In 1907 the government boasted that a forest survey of the Riding Mountain reserve in Manitoba was being made.[10] In 1904 it was an-

[8] VI, 1, p. 108. See also G. C. Piché, "The Forest Situation in the Province of Quebec," *Report of the Ninth Annual Meeting of the Canadian Forestry Association*, Toronto, 1908, pp. 71ff.

[9] *Forestry and Irrigation* XIII, 4, April 1907, p. 174. The facts concerning New Brunswick and Nova Scotia forest conditions are based on Lotbinière's "Letter" (footnote 2 of this chapter) and an address of E. G. Lotbinière delivered at the 1906 meeting of the Association.

[10] *Forestry and Irrigation* XIII, 12, Dec. 1907, pp. 511f.

nounced that the Canadian Pacific Railway had completed preliminary surveys of between five and six million acres of land east of Calgary with a view to reclamation. It was estimated that one and a half million acres might be put under irrigation.[11] But the provinces themselves had done almost nothing. During its early years the Canadian Forestry Association occupied itself principally with perfecting its organization, increasing its membership, launching a forestry journal, corresponding with agencies in matters of fire protection, tree planting, and now and then giving publicity to reports of forestry commissions. For example in its report of 1904-1905 the Association told of recommendations recently presented by commissions in Quebec and Prince Edward Island. In 1903 the Association's report gave some attention to proposed forestry education at Queen's University and the University of Toronto. The reports evinced a pronounced interest in the fire protective service and afforestation activities of the Dominion government in the West, in the larger forestry projects in Ontario and Quebec, and in the general growth of forestry interest nationally. But they were compelled to admit that forest management was "a new study in Canada," and as late as 1905 to say of forestry in British Columbia that this province "with its unparalleled forest wealth [had] so far done very little towards protecting its forests. . . ." A "Bush Fire Act" there was almost impossible to enforce because of the sparseness of population. In 1902 there was imposed an export duty on logs cut from government lands. Privately-owned or crown-granted, lands, however, were not affected by the regulation. The lumber interests were in need of employees.[12] The fire problem was serious even in the vicinities of railways, settlements, and lumbering operations. Sir Henri Joly de Lotbinière as lieutenant-governor of the province initiated an interest in further afforestation and timber conservation. Only one bright hope, however, lit the forestry scene of western Canada. A fire patrol system on the Dominion lands within the provinces, inaugurated in 1901, was characterized by Stewart as "very effective, particularly in the railway belt of British Columbia."[13] The forest reservation policy was established to benefit agriculture and protect water supply. The thought of perpetuating the nation's timber resources was beginning to receive substantial recognition when timber reservations were contemplated. In 1905 it was prophesied that "further legislation may be shortly expected to facilitate the creation of reservations for the protection of timber, as well as fish and game."[14]

[11] *ibid.* X, 3, March 1904, p. 102.

[12] L. Edwin Dudley (Consul of Vancouver), "Conditions in British Columbia," *Oregon Timberman*, Nov. 1902, manuscript among the papers of Sir Henri Joly de Lotbinière.

[13] *Forestry Quarterly* IV, 3, Sept. 1906, p. 231.

[14] Lotbinière's "Letter" (footnote 2 of this chapter).

In Ontario the crown lands department had managed the province's crown timberlands for timber sales. A clerk of forestry had been added to the department, and his principal duty had been to prepare an annual report on forestry matters. A prophecy similar to that made for the Dominion government was made for Ontario in 1905. At least twenty-five million acres of forest land in the province would be "set aside to form a magnificent, permanent Crown forest."

The office of forestry was concerned with colonization. A director of the bureau of colonization and forestry was appointed, and a very able man, Thomas Southworth, was appointed. In 1904 he persuaded Judson F. Clark to leave the United States and accept the position of provincial forester of Ontario.

Fernow's analysis of the forestry situation in Canada had been presented to Canadians. In January 1903 he had delivered a series of forestry lectures at the school of mining in Kingston, Ontario. This event in the forestry of Canada surpassed in many ways the importance of the American Forestry Congress of 1882. Fernow squarely placed before educators of the province the real forestry issues confronting the nation and the provinces. In December of the previous year he had discussed forest problems from an agricultural viewpoint at the Ontario Agricultural and Experimental Union at Guelph. Moreover on January 21, 1901, he had lectured at a conference called "to consider the best means for the preservation and renewal of forests, for using them to advantage, and for providing proper education to these ends."[15] So cordially had the board of governors responded that plans were authorized "to proceed with the establishment of a Department of Forestry in connection with the School. . . ." Fernow during these years was still director of the New York State College of Forestry. That the premier and the minister of education reacted favorably to the proposal to extend forestry education to Canada signified the uncommon interest aroused in the subject. Fernow's lectures, regarded as "the first course on forestry given in Canada," were said to mark "the beginning of a new outlook upon one of our greatest industries." His subjects were organized as: I. The Forest as a Resource, and Forest Industries; II. What is Forestry?; III. How Trees Grow; IV. The Evolution of a Forest Growth; V. Silviculture, or Methods of Forest Crop Production; VI. Lumberman and Forester; VII. Forest Economy or Business Methods; VIII. Wood and Its Characteristics; IX. Forestry

[15] *Forest Leaves* VIII, 12, Dec. 1902, p. 187: Introduction to "Lectures on Forestry," see footnote 16; Reports of 2nd and 3rd ann. meetings of Canadian Forestry Association held at Ottawa, March 1901 and 1902, at pp. 7 and 22 respectively. In the report of the second annual meeting appears a reference to the forestry meeting held in Toronto in January 1901, under the joint auspices of the Association and the Canadian Institute. In the report of the third annual meeting an illustrated lecture by Dr. Fernow was announced, thus indicating Fernow's presence at the 1902 meeting of the Association.

Policy; X. The Forester, an Engineer. A few concise paragraphs about Canadian problems should be quoted:[16]

Before an annual sustained yield management will appear profitable in Canada, many changes in economic conditions will have to take place, among which we may single out reduction of danger from fire; opportunity for utilizing inferior material; increase in wood prices by reduction of the natural supplies on which no cost of production need be charged; the development of desire for permanent investments instead of speculative ones; an extension of government functions, leading to the practice of forestry by governments on a large scale.

Meanwhile, all that can be expected from private forest owners is that they may practice more conservative and careful logging of the natural woods, avoiding unnecessary waste, and as far as possible paying attention to silviculture, the reproduction of the crop, leaving to the future the attempt to organize a sustained yield management. Only governments and perpetual corporations or large capitalists can afford to make the sacrifices which are necessary to prepare now for such a management.

In order to secure the data upon which the felling budget may be regulated, a *forest survey* is necessary, which will embrace not only an area and topographic (geometric) survey, serving for purposes of subdivision, description and orderly management, but also an ascertainment of the stock on hand in the various parts of the property, and of the rate of accretion at which the different stands are growing.

After having determined upon the general policy of management, with due consideration of the owner's interests and of market conditions, general and local; and after having decided upon the silvicultural policy, including choice of leading species in the crop for which the forest is to be maintained, and silvicultural method of treatment, as coppice or timber forest, under clearing system or gradual removal or selection system—the most important and difficult question to be solved is that of the rotation, the time which is to elapse between reproduction and harvest, or the normal felling age, that is, the age, or, so far as age is in relation to size, the diameter, to which it is desirable to let the trees grow before harvesting them.

Studies in soil and water conservation, paleobotany, mycology, entomology, ecology, and other branches of learning were so skillfully advocated that the lectures constitute in eighty-five pages a prescription for forestry research which has been used for decades. Financial forestry, Fernow said, "means *foregoing present revenues or incurring present expenditure for the sake of future revenue*." Fernow pleaded for forestry education, saying that next to the schools or departments of instruction aided by the state, "no more efficient means of education in practical arts which, like forestry and agriculture, rely still largely on empirics, can be devised than the establishment of *experiment stations*." These lectures were delivered when controversy on silvicultural policy at the Cornell Forest was at its height.

16 "Lectures on Forestry," delivered at the School of Mining, Kingston, Ontario, Jan. 26-30, paper-bound pamphlet printed by the *British Whig*, Kingston, Ontario, 1903, see pp. 61f., 70.

At the close of the lectures[17] a committee of lumbermen and friends of the forestry movement was chosen to assist in promulgating the school of forestry, at that time evidently planned to be in conjunction with the school of mining at Kingston. "Substantial aid was promised" to this college of applied science and Queen's University, "to be given as soon as the buildings under construction afforded space for the new department." But the project, though "cherished for several years," did not materialize. September 21, 1907, when Director W. L. Goodwin of the school of mining congratulated Fernow on his appointment as dean and director of a faculty of forestry being established at the University of Toronto, he confided that he wished to express more than mere congratulations. "As you know," he wrote, "at one time I had the hope that you would begin that good work here at Kingston, but circumstances [prevented]." Early in 1904, forestry education in Canada again being considered, President Loudon of the University of Toronto addressed a letter on February 3 to Director Thomas Southworth of the department of colonization and forestry of Ontario, saying:

I note that you are under the impression that the subject of Forestry would be too delicate for public discussion by the University authorities, on account of their relations to the Government. Let me say that there is nothing in the situation to prevent such discussion on my part. The University has formulated its policy as regards teaching in forestry, and nothing but good in my opinion could come from bringing the details of the scheme fully before the public.

Director Southworth had begun late in 1903 to correspond with lumbermen on the matter of the proposed forestry school. The question was not which school should be selected, but whether a school should be established at all. The responses were many and various. Most of them favored the establishment of a school of forestry in Canada, but at least one believed that forestry education was a function for the Dominion government, not for the provinces. A few pointed out there were schools of forestry available in the United States. One urged that "forestry in Canada and forestry in the United States are entirely distinct and separate propositions. The southern pine, as you are aware, reforests much more rapidly than spruce in our country. So far as white pine is concerned it is entirely another proposition and much more difficult to carry out. . . ."

Nearly all saw the advantage to lumbering operations of combined scientific schooling and practical work in the woods. Lumber concerns could well afford to give the graduates employment. Several realized, as one said, that "the cutting in Canada [had] been very haphazard [and]

[17] The degree LL.D. was presented to Fernow three times, by the University of Wisconsin in 1896, by Queen's University in 1903, and by the University of Toronto in 1920. See *Journal of Forestry* XXI, 4, April 1923, p. 315.

the young timber [had] not been properly cared for." Another wrote, "All our old woodsmen tell us that more timber has been burned than ever was cut by the lumbermen in this section. . . ." A. E. Dyment of the House of Commons told Southworth that the high value of pine timber and the "rapidity with which it is being cut during the last 4 or 5 years" had turned the minds of lumbermen to "reforestry." Indiscriminate cutting was encouraged by the "extraordinary prices" of standing timber, the increase in crown dues, and the time exactions during which the timber limit remained "at the disposal of the purchaser for the removal of timber." Another complained of the uncertainty of tenure under the crown licenses, "an uncertainty which prompted their destruction rather than their conservation." This lumberman approved "the new departure of the Ontario government as to the treatment of a large portion of the timber territory of the Province not yet under license." This procedure was "eminently in the right direction in view of the extent to which already the crown domain [had] become denuded of timber." Should the government next decide to extend the policy to the licensed territory, a "careful examination" should be made to determine "what portions of it [were] suitable for bona fide agriculture and what portions of it [were] entirely valueless except for forestry purposes, and having done that, withdraw the portions unfit for agriculture absolutely from location and settlement, upon the understanding that the holder of the license should cut the timber in such a way as to promote the young growth, with a view to its becoming ultimately not only of value to the licensee, but also a source of revenue to the Government. . . . Take for example the territory on the C[anadian] P[acific] Railway between Perth and Peterboro. It was allowed to be taken up by settlers who have removed almost every green tree, leaving the land, which is absolutely unfit for agricultural purposes, practically a desert, in which condition it will probably always remain unless the Government later on undertakes to reforest it, whereas under different treatment it would still be of value for forestry purposes. . . . I fully understand that the interest of legitimate settlement must go hand in hand with the development of our forests; but by classifying the public lands in the way in which I have indicated, the best could be gotten out of both departments of industry without interfering in the slightest with the interests of either."

Fernow was to find that in Canada, no less than in the United States, "political considerations [were] as much in the foreground in shaping policies." But what of the enlightened views of lumbermen expressed in some letters to Director Southworth. Certainly they showed a cooperative spirit, but the needs of forest management and forest conservation were only lightly and indirectly touched upon. Nevertheless these tasks were visualized as work for foresters and reasons for the need of forestry education, and most intelligent lumbermen saw that sound technical management was the only salvation for the future of the Canadian forests.

On August 21, 1905, Prime Minister of the Dominion Sir Wilfred Laurier summoned "a public convention to meet in the City of Ottawa" on January 10-12, 1906, under the auspices of the Canadian Forestry Association. To this convention were invited members of the senate and the house of commons, lieutenant-governors of the provinces, members of the legislative councils and legislative assemblies of the provinces, Dominion and provincial forest officials, members of the Canadian Forestry Association, and representatives of lumbermen's associations, boards of trade, universities, agricultural colleges, farmers' institutes, railway companies, the Canadian Mining Institute, the Canadian Society of Civil Engineers, the Association of Land Surveyors, fish and game associations, and all others who took an interest in forestry.[18]

At the great American Forestry Congress held at Washington, D.C., in 1905, Elihu Stewart and R. H. Campbell, secretary of the Canadian Forestry Association, had invited certain United States foresters to attend the Quebec meeting of the Association that year. These included Fernow, Pinchot, Schenck (who by now was temporarily removing the Biltmore school into the North Carolina mountains), and Austin Cary and R. F. Willams, both of whom were employed by large paper and pulp companies in Maine. Cary, during the past summer, had examined spruce lands in New Brunswick for his firm, which had purchased timber limits there. It was believed that Roth also would attend the congress.The Quebec Limit Holders Association was meeting with the Canadian Forestry Association. The Quebec meeting heard that the Association's financial condition was good and the membership increasing. The board meeting was described by Campbell as "fairly representative." The main event of the year was, however, the publication of the *Canadian Forestry Journal* under the editorship of Campbell with an advisory committee of William Saunders, John Macoun, and Stewart. By letter of April 29, 1905, Campbell informed Joly of another development of importance:

> The Premier is prepared to ask for an appropriation from Parliament for the expenses of the Convention, including the publication of a report of the proceedings. The Board outlined the form which they thought the Conference should take, being somewhat on the lines of the American Forest Congress, that is, we thought it advisable to have the different sessions devoted to special sides of forestry subjects, such as lumbering, pulp manufacture, irrigation, agriculture, etc. We think that we can improve somewhat on the arrangements that were made at the Washington Congress.

[18] *Canadian Forestry Journal* II, 1, Feb. 1906.

Before the Canadian convention was assembled, however, two important matters came up for consideration. On September 27, 1905, Campbell wrote to E. G. Joly de Lotbinière, the son of Sir Henri:

The establishment of a Forestry School is certainly a matter that should be taken up soon, but in the project as suggested by you there is one difficulty which it seems to me will be a serious one. As intimated by Dr. Clark, and as undoubtedly would have to be the case, such a school, if established, would have to be affiliated or connected in some way with some College or University already established, as it would be necessary to have the services of Professors who are specialists in the allied sciences and who could hardly be provided for in a Forestry School, at least at the beginning. The question therefore arises as to the college with which the school should be affiliated, and if a request is to be made for Dominion aid we are likely to have the old educational controversy raised again. This would hardly be welcomed by the Premier. . . . The difficulty of course is a political one.

Moreover, Elihu Stewart wrote on November 16:

As you are aware, a Bill was prepared last session respecting the Dominion forest and game reservations. This bill gave the Governor General in Council power by Order in Council upon the recommendation of the Minister of the Interior based upon the report of the Superintendent of Forestry to set aside reservations for the protection of timber and of all animals, fishes and birds therein. These were to be known as Dominion forest and game reservations, and the Order in Council was to have all the effect of an Act of Parliament. Unfortunately, owing to the resignation of the late Minister of the Interior it was found impossible to have this bill introduced into the House during the last session, but it is hoped and expected that it may be presented and passed at the next session.

Stewart concluded his letter by saying, "I think the success of the Convention is assured. I find a very general interest in it all over the country. I am glad to know that there will be a good representation from the United States. Mr. Pinchot, as you are aware, intends to be present, and I am looking forward to his visit and the advice that he will be able to give us as being productive of very great assistance to our work here in Canada."

On Wednesday, January 10, 1906, the meeting was called to order by Sir Wilfred Laurier, who invited the governor-general formally to open the convention. The premier warned against committing the folly of New York, which had once let certain of its titles to watershed areas pass into private hands and was put to the necessity of repurchasing them. He affirmed a belief that the nation's immediate business lay in further watershed protection of the public domain, repurchasing lands wherever necessary. Urgently needed also was protection against fires, insects, and other agencies of destruction. Nor did he hold that the principal responsibility of fire protection reposed with the lumbermen. The premier praised the Dominion for encouraging such widespread tree planting on farmlands and prairies as he had seen on inspection trips. He probably read or listened to Director William Saunders' address, "Forestry on the Experimental Farms,"[19] in which was explained the agricultural research program in tree planting. On the east this embraced the work at the central farm at Ottawa under W. T. Macoun; it extended as far west as the station located at Agassiz, British Columbia, where mountain slopes and belts of timber in valleys were being planted. Eastern hardwoods were among the species used. Only at the station located at Nappan, Nova Scotia, was tree planting not extensively developed, and there was no need for it there.

When the premier finished his address, he introduced R. L. Borden, leader of the opposition in the house of commons, and it became evident that the belief in the need of forestry reform in Canada was practically unanimous. In the course of the convention's deliberations, Fernow's *Economics of Forestry* was several times quoted. Borden quoted Fernow to the effect that of the eight hundred million acres of forest area in Canada, only four hundred million acres were available.

The premier had taken a strong stand in favor of forest replacement. The government leadership seemed united on its policy. Judicious forest management and the repurchasing of watershed lands for reservations within the Dominion and the provinces were endorsed.

Fernow got down to fundamentals in forest management and forest and water conservancy. He said that he represented "nothing and nobody but myself," but that he "might claim to represent that small body of early reformers who laid the cornerstone and began building the foundation walls of that great structure that you are going to erect into the forestry system of the Americas." He expressed satisfaction at evidences in the addresses of His Excellency Lord Earl Grey and Premier Laurier "of a change of attitude on the part of the government. . . . The whole responsibility of the mismanagement of your timber wealth is chargeable to your government alone . . . government alone can remedy it. . . ." Pleased that the Dominion had begun to "mend" its policy, unafraid to say that while the provinces had "not done very much," Ontario had "made a good beginning at reform, [but] much [remained] to be done even by her," Fernow argued that governments must not only own but manage timberlands. He called for "a statesmanlike vision into the future." Intelligent revision of the timber-limit policies, rehabilitation of cut-over, burned, and barren areas, reinvestment of an adequate portion of present revenues from the forests for the sake of future forests, and the advancement of forestry, public and private, through education and forest management practice were some of the directions to which Fernow pointed.

19 This and the following addresses delivered at the Convention were published in *Report of the Canadian Forestry Convention*, bound with the Can. For. Ass. report for 1906, Gov't Printing Bureau, Ottawa, 1906.

Chief Forester Pinchot brought messages of greeting from President Roosevelt and Secretary of Agriculture Wilson. Other notables who spoke were Minister of the Interior Frank Oliver, President E. G. Joly de Lotbinière and Honorary President Aubrey White of the Canadian Forestry Association, as well as Stewart, Southworth, Schenck, and Rothrock. Representatives of the transcontinental railroads and of the water power interests of Canada presented their opinions. E. J. Zavitz, lecturer on forestry at the Ontario Agricultural College and a master in forestry science from Michigan and Yale, spoke on "Agricultural College Problems." Provincial Forester Judson F. Clark discussed "A Canadian Forest Policy," an argument later reenforced by another address, "Forestry in Canada," presented at the Vancouver meeting of the Association that year.[20] Clark attacked the prevailing systems of timber disposal and, of course, confined his program for the most part to forests in which the government was directly concerned.

The address of Thomas Southworth, director of forestry for Ontario, "Forest Reserves and their Management," was delivered to the convention at the same session as Fernow's address, the afternoon of the first day. By this time the delegates had heard Forestry Superintendent Elihu Stewart tell of the government's work on the Dominion lands, including explanations of the workings of the fire and theft protective service. Within the year examination of Dominion forest reserves had been started with a view to obtaining knowledge of the timber of the reservations—their quantity, quality, and varieties, their rate of growth, how to remove the dead and down timber, harvest the full grown crop, and foster permanent reproduction. Some reference was made to the prairie tree planting work in the department of the interior. The complete explanation, however, was left to the next day, when Norman Ross, presenting a paper on the subject, added that considerable planting on many of the western forest reserves would probably be inaugurated. He said, "Experiments on a very small scale were started in 1904 and continued last spring, in planting Scotch pine on the very sandy soil of the Spruce Woods reserve, east of Brandon."

Director Southworth's address was almost entirely concerned with Ontario. Reviewing the history of the reservations in that province, he pointed out that under the Forest Reserve Act of 1898, since 1901 the great Timagami forest reserve of 2,200 square miles in the Nipissing district including Lake Temagami had been added to, west and northwest, by what was known as the western Timagami Reserve of 3,700 square miles. Moreover, in 1903 three thousand square miles lying between the main line of the Canadian Pacific Railway and its Sault Sainte Marie branch had been placed under reservation and was known as the

[20] *Forestry and Irrigation* XII, 11, Nov. 1906, pp. 499ff.

Mississaga Reserve. Two years later another reservation had been constituted, 7,300 square miles around Lake Nipigon. "Aside altogether from Algonquin Park, the forest reserves of Ontario, that is the territory withdrawn from settlement under the provisions of the Forest Reserve Act, amounts to 16,395 square miles, or 10,493,000 acres." Then he appended:

> In the reserves already created the only step yet taken towards systematic forestry management consists in a system of fire control that has proved very effective. . . . It is assumed that the permanent forest estate of the province will be placed under systematic forest management, and no country was ever in better condition than the province of Ontario to institute such a system.
>
> In the timber territory outside the reserves which is under license, vested interests are in the way of introducing new methods, but in the reserves proper no licenses are in existence except in the case of part of the Temagami reserve where a concession to cut pulpwood was given to a pulp and paper company previous to the creation of the reserve, which agreement unfortunately did not provide for proper cutting regulations. Aside from this, however, the reserves already created and those likely to be created in the territory referred to are free from any entanglements of this sort.
>
> To achieve this result something more than harvesting the most valuable sorts of trees in the most economical way, as is the present practice of forest exploitation, will be required. That system is converting Algonquin park from a mixed pine and hardwood forest to a hardwood one. Working plans must be laid down covering a hundred years and more, plans that will provide for harvesting the present crop of various sorts of trees in such a manner as to secure the aftergrowth of the right kind of trees and to regulate the cutting so as to secure evenness of supplies and revenues.
>
> To do this the very highest technical skill will be required, not alone the skill acquired in the lumber camp and the mill, but the knowledge of silviculture, of botany, of forest engineering, &c., only acquired by a scientific training that according to the Ontario Minister of Education is soon to be provided in a Canadian School of Forestry.

Clark's address similarly endorsed a "Canadian School of Forestry for the training of [Canada's] coming forest service." Fernow, in his address, had recommended the reading of a discussion by Clark proposing revision of the prevailing system of timber disposal. Clark's address on a "Canadian Forest Policy" was heard on the last day and urged a policy similar to that which Fernow had advanced: (1) forest protection, including debris disposal to prevent fires, (2) forest taxation revisions, (3) classification of public lands, (4) municipal forest reserves, and (5) the adoption of rules and regulations in timber sales which would so limit logging operations as to insure forest reproduction and the future safety of the forest. "Fair stumpage rates gauged from time to time to market changes" was a key to the solution, as Fernow saw the problem. Both men realized that the change would have to proceed on a scientific basis, with the large ends of sound economy kept in view. Lumber supplies, present and potential, would have to be analyzed. Water and streamflow conservation was upheld. An adequate public revenue, fair and commensurate with a reasonable return on the forest estate's value, was to be safeguarded. There would of course have to be a thorough stock taking of resources,[21] not confined to the forest reserves but including the crown lands also. The central feature of the policy, as Clark defined it, would be a "system of practical forest management, having for its aim the perpetuation and improvement of the forest by judicious lumbering." Clark, occupying an official position, evolved a system depending on cooperation between lumbermen and the state in devising a system of crown timber sales which would at once supply present lumber needs and yet provide adequate forest renewal for the future. Clark's views were regarded as extreme. At the conclusion of the Canadian Forestry Convention, however, there was cause to be encouraged about the future of Canadian forestry. A resolution, enthusiastically supported, urged that a forest policy throughout Canada be adopted by the Dominion government.

The real question of the hour was forestry education. At the January 12 session of the convention, Monsignor J. U. K. Laflamme of Laval University at Quebec read a paper on "Forestry Education." He informed the delegates that two young men, G. C. Piché and Avila Bedard, had been sent to Yale Forest School with the understanding that they would finish their studies in Europe. They then would return to Laval University and form the nucleus of a Forest School.[22]

If the schools were to be organized on a basis of provinces, a Quebec institution would not be sufficient for Ontario. As a member of the Ontario University Commission, B. E. Walker, general manager of the Bank of Commerce and consistently a bulwark of strength for forestry at the University of Toronto, announced that he favored providing a chair of forestry at the university at Toronto.

The *Canadian Forestry Journal* took up the discussion, filled with echoes from the Association's meetings of that year, one at Ottawa in March and another at Vancouver in September.[23]

[21] J. F. Sharpe and J. A. Brodie in *The Forest Resources of Ontario, 1930* (Dept. of Lands and Forests, Ontario Forestry Branch, Toronto, 1931, p. 23) say, "The first general exploratory survey of the provincial resources was conducted in 1900, under the supervision of the Department of Crown Lands. Its purpose was to gather information concerning the region north of the Canadian Pacific railway, an area of some 60 million acres. The territory was divided into ten districts and one party detailed to examine each district. The main information sought was the general conditions as regards timber resources, agricultural possibilities and mineral chances. . . ."

[22] A. H. D. Ross, "Canadian Forestry Education," *Canadian Forestry Journal* II, 2, May 1906, p. 69.

[23] *ibid.* p. 61. Also *Forestry and Irrigation* XII, 10, Oct. 1906, p. 442. The Vancouver meeting was honored by the attendance of His Excellency Lord Earl Grey, Governor-General of Canada.

The Ontario University Commission had been created in October 1905 to study the university's needs. Established with a chairman, J. W. Flavelle, and secretary, A. H. U. Colquhoun, and five members, Goldwin Smith, W. R. Meredith, H. J. Cody, D. Bruce Macdonald, and B. E. Walker, its work had been performed so satisfactorily and was of such value that all of its recommendations except one had been incorporated in a University Bill and presented immediately to parliament. Parliament immediately enacted the legislation. The recommendations as to forestry were particularly noteworthy. The commission consulted with Fernow and Pinchot and recommended against the creation of a chair and in favor of a school of forestry.[24] Presented to the province as the *Report of the Royal Commission on the University of Toronto*,[25] the provisional commitments read, in part:

> We are strongly of the view that the people of Ontario will endorse the action of the Government in creating a School of Forestry, by means of which the scientific treatment of our forests can be effectively carried out. . . . The possession by the Crown of timber lands where practical instruction and experiments could be carried on simplifies the situation, and we recommend that the closest cooperation compatible with the end sought should exist between the University authorities and the Department of Lands. It should likewise be kept in view that the private owners of timber lands have a direct interest in the supply of trained men produced by such a school, and in the results of the experiments made.

Cognizance was taken of the large endowment being afforded Yale Forest School by the National Lumbermen's Association for courses of instruction. "Similar action in Canada should be encouraged," the *Report* said.

The year 1906, therefore, augured well for the realization of an institution such as Fernow had envisioned in his forestry lectures of 1903, and his still earlier lecture of 1902. The next question was, who was to head the school? In 1903, when Fernow had lectured in Canada, he was director of the New York State College of Forestry; but by 1906 he was out of forestry education altogether. It was assumed generally that Judson F. Clark would head the Toronto forestry school, but "a serious loss to the development of the new school of forestry at the University of Toronto" was occasioned by Clark's acceptance of a position with a private lumber concern in British Columbia. Although some of Clark's forest management principles were being adopted in recent Ontario timber sales, Clark had been severely criticized.[26] He resigned his position as provincial forester. No one was appointed to his

[24] *Canadian Forestry Journal* II, 3, Aug. 1906, pp. 104, 150.

[25] Printed by order of the Legislative Assembly of Ontario, L. K. Cameron, printer, 1906, p. 35.

[26] *Canadian Forestry Journal* II, 4, Dec. 1906, p. 175.

place. The real cause of Clark's resignation was revealed later by Fernow, who said:

> Dr. Clark is a very aggressive man, with decided opinions and views, and was bound to do something of a practical nature in forest work. But his efforts failed to bear fruit, perhaps because too advanced for the situation. Soon after, the entire bureau [of Colonization and Forestry] was transferred to the Department of Agriculture, and out of touch with the public domain.
>
> In consequence, Dr. Clark resigned his position, because he saw that there was nothing expected of him except to talk.

In 1906 Clifton Durand Howe was serving as acting director and acting forester of the Biltmore school and estate. Dr. Schenck had returned to his home in Darmstadt, Germany. Howe had been born and brought up on a New England farm near Newfane, Vermont. Five brothers aided their father, whose varied interests were not confined to farming; he knew birds, animals, and plants, and gave his sons an elementary knowledge of the outdoors. As a young man he had contracted tuberculosis. The doctors said that all that would save him was an outdoor life.

Clifton and Carlton Howe, twin brothers, went to the University of Vermont and there came in contact with one of North America's great plant pathologists, Lewis Ralph Jones.[27] Jones was much interested in forestry. In 1908 he wrote an article for *Forestry Quarterly*,[28] "Forestry in Vermont," in which he pointed out that sixty per cent of the state's acreage was either forest or wild land. In Vermont during the early 1900's there was little interest in forestry, but by 1908 it was an absorbing topic of discussion at farmers' institutes. While Jones' real leadership emerged from researches in the nature and control of plant diseases, as professor of botany and botanist of the Vermont Agricultural Experiment Station, he arranged experimental nursery and demonstration work to include forestry. Instrumental as an organizer of the Vermont Botanical Club, Jones also was an organizer and president of the Vermont Forestry Association. Among the many improvements secured, good state forest fire laws were outstanding. Vermont's long industrious reforestation activities by individuals were given scholarly sanction, especially by the work of Howe.[29] The northern New England states were slow to adopt official forest reservation policies. About 1907-1908, however, real beginnings were made. Maine's township reservation, Indian township, was not a formal reserve, but in a sense

[27] For a biographical sketch of Jones, see G. W. Keitt, *Science*, new series, 101, 2635, June 29, 1945, pp. 658-660.

[28] VI, 3, Sept. 1908, p. 234.

[29] C. D. Howe, "The Reforestation of Sand Plains in Vermont," *Botanical Gazette* XLIX, Jan.-June 1910, p. 126; and a review in *Forestry Quarterly* VIII, 2, June 1910, p. 241.

it was tantamount to one.[80] Massachusetts in 1908 made provision for a state system of reserves.[81] New Hampshire in about 1907 created from a gift to the state a reserve of six hundred acres on Mount Monadnock.[82] A tribute made during his lifetime, the L. R. Jones State Forest of Vermont, commemorates the contributions of this great student of the plant sciences.

After graduating from the University of Vermont, Clifton Howe taught school for a year at Woodstock, and then returned to the university to do graduate work. Howe's undergraduate study had been classical during the first two years, and the last years were spent specializing in botany and zoology. In the graduate school he continued his scientific studies. His master's thesis was on the flora of Burlington, Vermont, a taxonomic preparation which emphasized the concept of succession. He had read Henry Chandler Cowles's published studies. Interested in ecologic examinations of sand dune regions, he selected an old glacial area of Lake Champlain on the Vermont side, terrace and sand plains adjacent to mountains. The succession concept explained many matters which had puzzled him. Dr. Jones told him to apply for a fellowship at the University of Chicago. That year Jones made a trip to Madison, Wisconsin, where he later created one of the earliest and first ranking departments of plant pathology in the country. En route he stopped at the University of Chicago and interviewed John Merle Coulter, head of the department of botany. Howe obtained the fellowship and specialized at Chicago in ecology and physiology. He obtained the degree of Ph.D. in 1904.

An application came to the University of Chicago to send a botanist to the Biltmore Forest School. The Biltmore school was then in the Lower Gate House. A twelve-month curriculum was being given. Mornings were spent in the classroom, afternoons on horseback in the field doing practical work. Howe took the course in dendrology while teaching. Botany, of course, was his principal teaching course, emphasizing tree physiology. His predecessor had been Ernest Bruncken.

Raphael Zon of the United States forest service came to the school to lecture. Zon and Howe became warm friends as years went by. After Zon had lectured, Schenck asked Howe to take Zon to the railroad station. The train was late. Howe and Zon went to an organ recital. The recital over and finding the train already gone, they went to Howe's room, and Howe explained that he was dissatisfied with his situation at Biltmore. Zon said, "Dr. Fernow is going to establish a School of For-

[80] *Forestry Quarterly* V, 1, March 1907, p. 77; see *Forest Leaves* XI, 10, Aug. 1908, pp. 152f., to the effect that the township was of some 20,000 acres, and while not a "definite forest reserve," it was state-owned and the forest commissioner had sought to have it established as a state reserve.

[81] *Forestry Quarterly* VI, 3, Sept. 1908, p. 330.

[82] *ibid.* VI, 1, March 1908, p. 63.

estry at State College, Pennsylvania. He is looking for an assistant." Howe wrote to Fernow.

Zon was not Howe's only informant. John Foley also told Howe of the opportunity. On January 7, 1907, Fernow answered Howe from Ithaca:

Mr. Foley's information was slightly premature as I have not yet accepted the position in the Pennsylvania State College which would necessitate my looking for a man to fill an instructorship and eventual professorship.

I am nevertheless glad to hear of your desire to get into college work and shall, in case I come to conclusions, correspond with you, giving you an idea of the opportunities offered. Whatever results would not come before next fall, so there is plenty of time to consider the matter.

Again, on January 15, Fernow wrote in reply to an answer from Howe:

Mr. Foley did not betray any confidence or did anything wrong in mentioning to you the Pennsylvania matter as I had freely spoken before him without any caution. Merely at the time the matter had not come to a conclusion, and I was only inquiring. Now I have accepted the position, and am to organize a first class undergraduate department at the State College of Pennsylvania. This includes, beginning next fall, an instructorship at $1500, and the following year an assistant professorship, and I shall have to look out for men to fill these positions. . . . The whole organization is based upon the assumption that the necessary funds will be appropriated. This is a start *de novo*, but with the promise of making it an important institution.

Cornell Countryman,[33] the official publication of the New York State College of Agriculture, announced that the new Pennsylvania school was to be patterned after the former New York State College of Forestry.

Rossiter W. Raymond, who had remained Fernow's close friend and aide, wrote to Fernow on February 14, 1907:

I accept, with sincere gratitude and pleasure, the proposed dedication of your book [The History of Forestry]. . . . I congratulate you on your new work at State College; and after I get back I shall ask for the opportunity, and the necessary information to give it an appreciative and useful notice in the Engineering & Mining Journal or elsewhere.

Fernow responded three days later. Concerning the *History of Forestry in Europe*, which Dr. Graves regarded as "a valuable contribution to American literature," Fernow explained:

A few copies were printed and bound for the purpose of serving as a textbook in the Yale Forest School, which, of course, is a card for me. I wish I could get out of the need of writing up the United States.

Who knows but that by the time you return from your trip your opportunity for advertising me as at work in State College will be gone, for I

[33] IV, 6, March 1907, p. 189. The announcement said that the new forestry department would be modeled after the one at Cornell. *Forestry Quarterly* V, 1, March 1907, p. 119, announced the organization and beginning of instruction.

found a letter from another University asking to submit credentials with a view of getting a call. I do not give you the name, but it is out of the country, not very far, and certainly a more inviting place to reside in.

That year Fernow prepared for Pennsylvania State College a prospectus of "A Department of Forestry, professional in character. . . . The first registrations [have] been made for the spring session of 1907. The department is organically arranged in the School of Agriculture, the studies of the first year being in common. A *Four Year Course* is offered leading to the degree of Bachelor of Science, a fifth year of post graduate work leading to the Master's degree. . . . The State of Pennsylvania has set aside state forest reservations to the extent of nearly one million acres, and adds annually more.[34] It is only fair to assume that graduates of the Pennsylvania State College must ultimately find a field of usefulness in their management." Within the confines of this assumption there may have been echoes of a conference between Rothrock and Fernow. Rothrock, it is said, warned Fernow that if he accepted the chair at Pennsylvania State College he would be denied access to the Pennsylvania forest reservations. Rothrock's allegiance was pledged to Mont Alto Forest Academy. The issue may have involved no more than whether the state college work should be confined to farm forestry instruction. Certainly Fernow had never subscribed to such a limitation. His prospectus announced, "A course in *Farm Forestry* is also contemplated." Perhaps the president of the college, Dr. Atherton, believed that an agricultural college should confine itself to farm forestry. The prospectus, nevertheless, read:

> The last two years are occupied principally with forestry subjects, in which twelve separate courses are offered, comprising not less than 70 hours, one-half of which time is devoted to practical work. These courses are in *Dendrology* (9 hours), *Timber Physics and Wood Technology* (15 hours), *Silviculture* (12 hours), *Forest Mensuration and Estimating* (15 hours), *Forest Utilization, including Lumbering* (5 hours), *Forest Protection* (3 hours), *Forest Management and Finance* (16 hours), *Forest Administration and History* (5 hours), besides a *Synoptical or Introductory* Course (3 hours) designed for students of agriculture and other branches.

The "need of foresters," the prospectus said, "has grown more rapidly than the several schools which followed the first have been able to provide. At present the largest demand is made by the Federal Forest Service, but the various States, and especially the State of Pennsylvania, as well as private owners and corporations are bound to call for the services of fully equipped foresters in larger numbers." Howe was asked if he "would be prepared to undertake the course in mensuration and one or two other courses of minor importance."

[34] In recent years Fernow had not shown special interest in forestry in Pennsylvania; his appointment to head the work at Pennsylvania State College was doubtless based on his reputation rather than on special knowledge of the state.

Neither Fernow nor *Forestry Quarterly* had ever apologized for the "collapse" of the New York school. Rather, in the publication's June 1907 issue,[35] it was noticed "with satisfaction that a reform at Baden [Germany, had] copied almost precisely the plan, which was originally adopted in the New York State College of Forestry at Cornell University."

Fernow began to teach at Pennsylvania State College. The prospectus was issued before March 1907, as noted in *Forestry Quarterly* that month. That spring Fernow gave an introductory course attended by about forty students. There were, however, less than a dozen regular forestry students.[36] Fernow purchased a forestry library costing three hundred dollars,[37] similar to that purchased at Cornell and presumably similar in part to that arranged for at the United States department of agriculture.

Dean Buckhout had seen to it that some forestry instruction was given students of Pennsylvania State College. In fact it was announced in 1905 that Professor Buckhout had been placed in charge of an organized department there.[38] Joseph A. Ferguson, later professor of forestry at the college, however, wrote to Fernow on October 3, 1922:

> Although you were at Penn State but a short time, the impetus which you gave to the work here has kept the Forestry School going strong. . . . From a little bunch of 9 students with which you started, there are now 101 boys studying Forestry in The Pennsylvania State College. . . . We have your photograph on our walls labeled, "The First Forester to be in charge of the Forestry Department at The Pennsylvania State College." . . . Penn State is proud of her Forestry School and proud of the man who started it.

Mont Alto Academy naturally did not want another professional forestry school in Pennsylvania. Today the two institutions have been merged to build one great forestry institution for the state.[39] Fernow and Rothrock must have discussed Mont Alto Academy in relation to Pennsylvania forest work, for on December 16, 1907, after Fernow had resigned his position at Pennsylvania State College, he wrote to Hugh Potter Baker,[40] who resigned his position at Iowa State College to accept the position which Fernow had held:

> The trouble with the Mont Alto Academy is that they have departed from their original intention of making it a ranger school. I argued with Rothrock that that was a mistake, but his colleagues evidently have high aspira-

[35] *Forestry Quarterly* V, 2, p. 247. [36] *ibid.* V, 1, p. 119.

[37] *ibid.* V, 4, Dec. 1907, p. 452. When Hugh Potter Baker told Fernow that he was to fill the vacancy left by his resignation, he said, "I appreciate the start which you gave the work last spring."

[38] *Forestry Quarterly* III, 4, Nov. 1905, p. 415.

[39] *Forest Leaves* XXI, 7, Feb. 1928, p. 97; XXII, 4, Aug. 1929, p. 51; X, 10, Aug. 1906, p. 153; VIII, 1, Feb. 1901, p. 6; VIII, 9, June 1902, p. 135; XXVII, 1, Jan. 1937, pp. 5f.

[40] Baker's position at Iowa was taken by C. A. Scott.

tions, and unfortunately for you, have cash to carry out their high aspirations. This is one reason why I did not care to stay.[41]

The department at Pennsylvania State was not long denied access to the state forest reservations. A letter from Baker to Fernow, dated November 10, 1908, said:

> When I came here in September 1907, there were nine men who had had more or less work with you. During the past school year this number was increased to thirty-one and this fall we have seventy-four men classified in four year work in forestry. This, I believe, makes us the largest undergraduate school east of Michigan. Within the past month the State Forest Commission has granted us annual privilege of going onto their 7,000 acre reserve in this county at any time for study and demonstration. As this reserve is less than four miles away, I do not believe there is another forest school in the country with so large a tract of wild land so easily accessible for practical work.

If Fernow may be regarded as the founder of Pennsylvania Forest School, and there seems no doubt he was the first to introduce professional forestry instruction, the conclusion follows also that Hugh Potter Baker and Ferguson were the builders of the institution which in 1929 was merged with Mont Alto Forest Academy or Pennsylvania Forest Academy, as it became known. Under Baker the school grew so rapidly that soon practically one-third of the total number of four-year students in the college of agriculture were in forestry.

Fernow never moved his residence from Ithaca to State College. During the one spring he taught at Pennsylvania State College he commuted between the two places. The invitation to submit credentials to the University of Toronto was addressed to his home in Ithaca. When Fernow went to Toronto to conclude the new arrangements, he secured Walter Mulford to teach his classes during his absence of two weeks.[42]

The board of governors of the University of Toronto decided to establish a faculty of forestry on March 28, 1907. On that same day Fernow was selected as dean. In April a preliminary announcement of the school was drafted. Fernow prepared an educational prospectus on May 15, 1907.

The new school was a definite advance in forestry education. Founded at a Canadian institution as one of five major faculties, the school enjoyed the distinction of being the first forestry school of the entire Dominion, a school supported by a province of vast forest wealth. *Forestry Quarterly*[43] announced:

[41] Concerning accomplishments of Mont Alto forest school, see *Forestry Quarterly* XIV, 2, June 1916, p. 365; *Forest Leaves*, April 1916.

[42] See *Forest Leaves* XI, 5, Oct. 1907, p. 76, concerning Baker's appointment to Pennsylvania State College and the use of the two-story building for forestry instruction. Fernow probably recommended Baker for the position. On several occasions Fernow tried to further Mulford's opportunities.

[43] V, 2, June 1907, p. 248.

The course will be an undergraduate one, with a curriculum similar to the one originally adopted at the New York State College of Forestry, but the entrance requirements have been raised above those accepted by the other faculties of the University. The four years course leads to the degree of Bachelor of the Science of Forestry, and after three years' practical employment and presentation of a thesis the degree Forest Engineer is conferred. A three years course leading to a diploma as Forester will also be instituted. The sessions begin on October 1. It is expected that the government will set aside a large reservation for practice and demonstration ground, where the juniors and seniors will spend a six to eight weeks' term at the end of the academic work, besides visiting lumber camps during the Christmas vacations.

Obviously, Fernow saw a larger field of service offered in Canada. Ontario alone had 45,000 square miles of timberlands in its possession and no specific forestry instruction except that which was given at the province's agricultural college. E. J. Zavitz, a well-trained forester, lectured on forestry there. Fernow told Acting President M. Hutton of Toronto University that "a good beginning [had] been made, in advancing farm forestry." Fernow set about to achieve in Canada what he had accomplished in the United States. On May 21, 1908, he sent Ernest Bruncken a letter thanking him for a submitted manuscript. He said, "I take pleasure in sending you a calendar of our faculty, which will remind you much of the prospectus for Cornell University. I have seen no reason for changing our ways."

On March 14-15, 1907, the eighth annual meeting of the Canadian Forestry Association was held at Ottawa. Fernow was invited to lecture on "The Aims of the Forester." The members were gratified at the recent passage of the Dominion Forest Reserve Act, by which twenty-one forest reserves, with a total area of 3,420,200 acres, were set aside —six in Manitoba, three in Alberta, four in Saskatchewan, and eight within the "railway belt" in British Columbia.[44]

Fernow focussed attention on the Ontario situation. Ontario's reserved forest areas were withdrawn from all use and settlement on them was excluded. Some of the Lake states were more advanced. In Michigan progress in fire protection and trespass prevention, in reforestation and forest improvement, in land classification and surveying, had been made. In Wisconsin approximately 300,000 acres were in forest reservations. Indeed, the report of state forester Griffiths for 1907-1908 was reviewed in *Forestry Quarterly*[45] by Dean Graves, who

[44] *Canadian Forestry Journal* II, 3, Aug. 1906, p. 121; III, 2, June 1907, pp. 55-66; *Forest Leaves* XI, 5, Oct. 1907, p. 78. For Fernow's address see *Canadian Forestry Journal* III, pp. 62f. Fernow said that in studies of growth, volume and quality were the two important factors; figures of height or diameter alone were not sufficient. A great drawback to planting in America was the very high prices of trees. He had found it cheaper to import trees than to raise them here. Norway spruce and Scotch pine were the cheapest trees he knew.

[45] VII, 1, March 1909, p. 48.

pointed out that while 250,000 acres of forest land were being administered, less than $10,000 annually were being provided for forestry and the reservations were more to protect watershed and water power than to preserve and renew the forests. Encouragement was taken in the favorable attitude of lumbermen and railroads toward forestry. Many of the agricultural states, however, had been slow to inaugurate forest policies. In a sense, Ohio had cradled the forestry movement of the United States. Yet after the early educational efforts had come to naught, Ohio[46] had waited practically two decades before a state forestry department under the state agricultural experiment station at Wooster was established. In 1908, $8,000 annually for two years were placed at the disposal of the department. Under Dr. Green some of the most extensive tree plantations made at any state experiment station were set out at Wooster.

Connecticut's legislation (1901-1903) authorizing reforestation, land reclamation, and land purchases had resulted by 1908 in an accumulation of about 1,400 acres of forest reserves.[47] New York's state forest preserve now amounted to about five per cent of the state's land area. Since 1905 New Jersey had appropriated money for forest reserves, but the state still had only about 10,000 acres in reservation, mostly in the Kittatinny Mountains, although acquisition of more was contemplated.[48] Maryland, with a comparatively young forestry movement, had a state forester and a small amount of land in reservation. The work for several years stressed woodlot demonstration and practice. Considered as a whole, the forestry situation in the United States was not discouraging, and definite progress could be seen; but from the utilization standpoint, progress was slow. Massachusetts, wealthy and with large forest resources, could point only to the Mount Tom and Greylock reserves, established more for aesthetic and recreational than economic reasons. Michigan in 1904 occupied an almost unique place that year by virtue of a large addition to its reserved forest lands.[49] Still, despite demonstrations of forestry's value, the entire reserved area had not reached 100,000 acres, and Roth at Minneapolis in 1903 had pointed out that ". . . the State of Michigan has 16 counties in the Southern Peninsula which average but 6 per cent of improved land. . . . Census reports show that the older States, too, have their waste lands;

[46] E. C. Hirst, "Forestry in Ohio," *Forestry Quarterly* VIII, 4, Dec. 1910, p. 439. See also *First Report on Forest Conditions in Ohio* and *Forestry Suggestions*, bulletins of the Ohio Agric. Exp. Station, reviewed in *Forestry Quarterly* VI, 2, June 1908, p. 165. For the organization of the Ohio Forestry Association, see *Forestry and Irrigation* X, 1, Jan. 1904, p. 4; and *Forestry Quarterly* II, 2, Feb. 1904, p. 134.

[47] For data on state and national forest reservations, see John Birkinbine, *Forest Leaves* XI, 10, Aug. 1908, pp. 152f.

[48] *Forest Leaves* X, 7, Feb. 1906, p. 100; *Forestry Quarterly* IV, 1, March 1906, p. 76.

[49] *Forestry and Irrigation* XI, 1, Jan. 1905, p. 26e.

that Maine has still 88 per cent of her lands not tilled, Pennsylvania 55 per cent, Virginia 61 per cent, and even Massachusetts 77 per cent...."[50] He named Wisconsin along with Pennsylvania and New York as states which had abandoned "the policy of getting rid of tax title and other State lands, and [were taking] the poor lands of the State and [improving] them along forestry lines." Minnesota was among the ranks of states which had forest reservation policies. Yet as late as 1908 the reserved lands were said to aggregate only about 31,000 acres. Of course this did not include the national reservations. Furthermore, the state university rejoiced that year that a demonstration forest in Itasca State Park was permitted for its forestry work.[51] Looking to the South and West, state forestry development in many quarters was only embryonic. Alabama had just created a state forestry commission.[52] At the University of Georgia Alfred Akerman had organized a forestry association and begun to publish a forestry journal, *Southern Woodlands.*[53] Forestry development, like the expansion of scientific agriculture, was retarded for many years, and every advancement, large or small, meant much. Nor could one especially criticize the South. The southern states had been among the first to progress along forestry lines. Many factors explained why advancements, except in private forestry, were slow. Even Rhode Island waited until 1906 before it received a first annual report on forestry from a duly constituted government agency.[54] In the West the report of the state forester of California[55] revealed little progress in technical forestry. New York still led with its more than a million and a half acres in reservation. Pennsylvania, with an aggregate reserved area of almost 800,000 acres, and 100,000 acres more being acquired, was the hopeful second.

In 1908[56] the federal agricultural appropriation act allowed one-half a million dollars for permanent improvements on the national forests. During this year the number of national forests was increased from 169 to 182, and Secretary Wilson reported the only one not under administration to be the Luquillo in Puerto Rico, a reserve of almost 70,000 acres. At least four of these reserves were in Alaska, and by 1906

[50] "Forestry," *Recreation*, 1903.

[51] *Forestry Quarterly* VI, 2, June 1908, p. 171.

[52] *ibid.* VI, 1, March 1908, p. 107. Although establishment of this commission was directed by the legislature, it did not become the permanent commission. Establishment of permanent state forestry agencies in the South characterized the 1920's, although Virginia and Texas had such by 1914-1915. See, Recknagel and Spring, *op. cit.*, pp. 203-204.

[53] *Forestry Quarterly* V, 2, June 1907, p. 190.

[54] *ibid.* V, 1, March 1907, p. 82.

[55] *ibid.* V, 1, March 1907, p. 78.

[56] As to Pennsylvania and New York, see John Birkinbine, *Forest Leaves* XI, 10, pp. 151f. As to Philippines and Alaska, *ibid.* As to national forests, *Yearbook of U.S.D.A. for 1908*, pp. 71, 75, 79. As to Hawaii, *Forestry Quarterly* V, 1, March 1907, p. 75.

seven reserves of 68,901 acres in Hawaii were created, and more being planned. All the forests of the Philippine Islands, officially estimated at 38,000,000 acres, were under government control and being managed in a manner similar to the national forests. The volume of business on the national forests had so increased that during the past year seventy-eight per cent of the time of the administrative and protective force had had to be given to timber-sales, grazing, and other business. Grazing privileges alone had netted to the government nearly a million dollars. The government's attention was turning toward the Middle West. Samuel J. Record in September 1907 wrote an article on "The Forests of Arkansas,"[57] in which he commented:

> So far the policy has been wholly destructive, and little thought has been given to the perpetuation of so valuable a resource. The National Government has lent assistance by withdrawing from public entry nearly a million acres of vacant land in the Ozark region as a proposed national forest. It marks a good beginning, but since most of the lands are private property it remains for the State to demonstrate to the owners the practicability of forestry and to direct and encourage their efforts.

Samuel J. Record[58] had been born in Crawfordsville, Indiana, on March 10, 1881. He attended Wabash College and studied botany under M. B. Thomas, who gave one of the first courses in forestry in the middle western states. Graduating in 1903, Record continued his interest in trees and forests. He went to Yale and obtained the degree of Master of Forestry in 1905. In 1906, after a brief period of teaching botany at his alma mater, he was granted a Master of Arts degree from Wabash College. During these years Record spent some time with the United States forest service to gain a practical understanding of forestry problems. In March 1905 *Forestry and Irrigation*[59] had published his article on "Forestry in Indiana." He examined many woodlots and forests in Indiana, Ohio, and Michigan. Record became the first supervisor of the Arkansas and Ozark national forests, a region which contained a wide diversity of tree species. During 1910 he was called to join the faculty of Yale Forest School, and taught courses in classification and structure of wood, mechanical properties of wood, and wood preservation. Soon an assistant professor, in 1917 he became professor of forest products, in 1923 professor of tropical forestry, and in 1939 Pinchot professor of forestry and dean of the school. An authority on forest products and tropical forestry, he greatly increased the collection

[57] *Forestry Quarterly* V, 3, Sept. 1907, p. 296.

[58] See a biographical account of Dean Record by P. C. Standley, *Science*, new series, 101, 2621, pp. 293-295; also *Tropical Woods*, No. 82, June 1, 1945, including tributes by H. S. Graves, Standley, and a bibliography of Record's writings. See also *Yale Forest School News* XXVII, 2, April 1930, p. 23; XVII, 1, Jan. 1929, pp. 6f., and "The First Thirty Years of Yale School of Forestry," *op. cit.*, pp. 40-43.

[59] XI, 3, March 1905, p. 107.

of wood specimens at the Yale Forest School and was the founder of the magazine, *Tropical Woods*. Before joining the Yale faculty permanently, he had had practical as well as scholarly experience. Prior to teaching forest products, he had taught Professor Toumey's courses in wood technology, assisted in field work and in the summer school, and spent a summer in study at the forest products laboratory at Madison. While a student at Yale, the forest service laboratory under H. D. Tiemann was still functioning; and later, when this was discontinued, research was continued in the study of wood characteristics, variations under differing conditions, and the fundamental explanations. Structure, weight, grain, intrinsic strength, durability, color, and other qualities were investigated. Record's work was not confined to indoor laboratory research. In 1907, while chief of reconnaissance of the forest service as well as while supervising the Arkansas national forests, he acquainted himself with the work of forest administration; and investigations which he directed extended his knowledge of forest conditions of southwestern and northwestern United States.

In the United States during this period the West was a lively center of forestry activity. On April 17, 1907, a new plan of organization in the United States forest service had gone into effect to promote work in the growing problems of development of the national reserves.[60] In 1912 a new organization for investigative work, a central committee, with Raphael Zon, as chairman, was announced. Schools in the West were enlarged, and their graduates, trained in ecology and forestry, were prepared to deal with problems of forest and range management, grazing, forest products, and many other special phases. In the matter of grazing research, the leadership of James Tertius Jardine attained prominence.[61] From 1907 until 1910 Jardine was a special agent of the forest service in range and livestock management. For ten years he was an inspector of grazing, in charge of range investigations and surveys, and in 1920 became director of the Oregon agricultural experiment station at Corvallis. Samuel James Record had been raised in a rural home, a farm home of Indiana of pronounced intellectual and cultural interests. Jardine had been born at Cherry Creek, Idaho, and his youth, too, had been spent on a farm. A brother of the distinguished agronomist, dean and president of Kansas Agricultural College, and later secretary of agriculture, William Marian Jardine, he had been an instructor of English at Utah Agricultural College before devoting himself to forestry, and during 1905-1906 did graduate work at the University of Chicago. His knowledge of western farming, of the range problem in relation to forests and irrigation, together with his schooling in the

[60] *Forestry Quarterly* V, 2, June 1907, p. 249; V, 3, p. 308.
[61] *ibid.* X, 1, March 1912, p. 115.

fundamental sciences, equipped him for a career in forestry; and during 1915-1917 he was a special lecturer at Yale Forest School.

In 1907 Francis G. Miller left the University of Nebraska to go to the University of Washington, his place at Nebraska being taken over by Frank J. Phillips. That same year, the state agricultural college at Pullman, Washington, began forestry instruction supplementary to its agricultural work. This was under E. O. Siecke, also formerly with the forest service.[62] The institution at Seattle attained first rank under the leadership of Hugo August Winkenwerder, a Yale graduate. Winkenwerder had been in the office of publications of the forest service at Washington, and he had spent from January 1908 until September 1909 at Colorado College under Dean W. G. Sturgis. With new or enlarged schools of forestry established in Ontario, Toronto, Quebec, and New Brunswick in Canada and at many places in western United States, forestry education was coming closer to the great forest regions.

At a meeting of the Society of American Foresters held November 19, 1908, Samuel Trask Dana read a paper on "Experiment Stations in Connection with the National Forests."[63] In 1907, when the forest service had been reorganized, a reconnaissance section had been created in the office of management. Now, with the establishment of experiment stations, the office of silvics was to direct a program of scientific investigations to be added to the already efficient work of the service in organization and administration. Dana, the forest assistant chosen to present this new work to the society, described the plans, the proposed locations of the stations, and the investigations to be attempted on whole forest areas and sample plots. He announced that the first of these stations had been "established on the Coconino National Forest, and headquarters were also selected for a second station on the Pike Forest, although this station has not yet been organized. . . . In the United States, the general plan is to have at least one main station in each of the silvicultural regions of the West, and eventually also in the East in the white pine region, the Appalachian hardwood region, and the southern pine region. . . . [The stations are to be] located on the forest most typical of the region."

In May of that year Raphael Zon had written to Fernow that he had "just submitted to Mr. Pinchot a plan for establishing forest experiment stations in connection with the National Forests." On July 16 Zon sent another letter saying, "I take the liberty of sending you our plan for creating forest experiment stations, which has been approved by the Forester with some slight changes, namely, making the director of the experiment station entirely independent of the supervisor, and eliminating the Tahoe National Forest as a place for an experiment station."

[62] *ibid.* V, 3, Sept. 1907, p. 361, concerning both Phillips and Siecke.
[63] *Proc. Soc. Am. For.* IV, 1, 1909, pp. 22-29.

Fernow read the plan "with interest," and promised to give it space in *Forestry Quarterly*. On September 10 Zon wrote again, saying:

> I am going to Europe within 10 or 15 days chiefly for the purpose of making a study of the work done by the forest experiment stations. . . . I would like to have some letters of introduction from you as you are so well known abroad, to men like Schwappach, Cieslar, Henry Mayr, Buhler and so on. The places which I intend to visit in Germany are the Forest Academy at Eberswalde, where the Prussian Experiment Station is located, the University of Munich in Bavaria, the Forest Academy at Tharandt in Saxony, the University at Tübingen in Württemberg, the Polytechnicum at Carlsruhe in Baden, the School of Forestry at Eisenach in Thuringia, and the University at Giessen in Hesse.

He mentioned the "scheme of establishing six forest districts, giving each District Forester full executive control in his district as to timber sales, grazing, all other matters." Furthermore, Zon had told Fernow on July 2 of other plans he had in mind.

> I was just planning to organize a volunteer service for phenological observations, and it occurred to me that you had something of this character done before leaving the Forestry Division. I dug up some correspondence containing phenological observations, but could not find a single outline which you apparently sent out to your correspondents.

Fernow replied almost immediately, pleased that "the very first thing" he had started when becoming chief of the division had been recommenced. Spalding, now much interested in ecological research, must also have been pleased, since he used the outlines for many years.

Chief Forester Pinchot and Frederic Edward Clements, then professor of botany at the University of Minnesota, had previously chatted at a forestry banquet in St. Paul. Clements told Pinchot that it was time to organize forestry experiment stations in connection with national forests. Clements suggested, "I wish you would send Zon out to meet me in Colorado Springs, and we will go up to the Alpine Laboratory and select a site on the nearby Pike Forest." Clements, whose book on ecologic methods had received world recognition, whose studies of grasses and grasslands of the plains since 1893 under Bessey and independently had contributed to grazing and soils conservation research, and who since 1900 had conducted as his own experimental institution the Alpine Laboratory within the vegetational region of Pike's Peak, enlisted Pinchot's interest. In 1907 Zon was promoted from assistant to chief of the office of silvics in the forest service. Clements with others that year began a study of the life history of lodgepole pine;[64] and by the

[64] F. E. Clements, "The Life History of Lodgepole Burn Forests," *United States Forest Service Bulletin 79*, (1910), a study made with Dr. Edith Clements, his wife, and Professor Albert T. Bell during summers of 1907 and 1908 and with Dr. Raymond J. Pool during the summer of 1907. Dr. Pool had recently graduated from the University of Nebraska, was to obtain his master of arts degree there in 1908, his doctorate of philosophy in 1913, and since 1916 has been head of the department of botany of the

following May, Zon was informing Fernow that Clements was a collaborator of the office of silvics and "very much interested in our present studies."

Forestry research men had wanted experiment stations established on the national forests. Pinchot, in his volume *Breaking New Ground*, says that they, led by Zon, placed before him the plan later put into effect by Zon and Dana.

Dean Graves on March 5, 1908, before the Society of American Foresters, had called for agreement on "the underlying principles of American silviculture" and formulation of clear policies and definite aims in regard thereto. "Most of us," he told the members, "have been engaged in laying the foundations for forestry and have not done much in the way of practicing it. . . . We are handicapped by a lack of knowledge of the life history and requirements of our forest trees under different conditions and by a lack of empirical knowledge of the best methods of handling our woodlands to accomplish the objects of silviculture. The practice of forestry has only just begun in this country, so that there are almost no results of actual forest management which can be used as a guide. We have only the results of European practice to draw upon. . . ." To *Forestry Quarterly*, in June of that year, Graves also contributed an article, which strongly urged "The Study of Natural Reproduction of Forests."

The first special forest reconnaissance field party connected with the new experiment station movement in the United States started work on the Coconino National Forest in April of 1908. At that time working plans were devised which became standardized over the United States. The methods were explained in October by A. B. Recknagel before the Society of American Foresters. Reconnaissance estimates in the national forests were extended to each of the western districts. In 1910 an article by Recknagel on "The Progress of Reconnaissance" appeared in *Forestry Quarterly*.[65]

If priority is a claim to greatness, probably no forester has more rightful claim to recognition than Gustaf Adolph Pearson. Pearson had been born on a farm near Holdrege, Nebraska. Educated in the coun-

---

University of Nebraska. This study was important in that it elaborated silvicultural methods and artificial treatment of lodgepole burn forests and led to other valuable studies. See a discussion of the conclusions of this study presented in an address given before the Society of American Foresters at Berkeley, California, August 1921, by R. H. Weidman, "Forest Succession as a Basis of the Silviculture of Western Yellow Pine," *Journal of Forestry* XIX, 8, Dec. 1921, pp. 877-885, at 881-882. In this address reference was also made to J. V. Hofmann's studies of Douglas fir forest life history, "Natural Reproduction from Seed Stored in the Forest Floor," *Journal of Agricultural Research* V, 11, Nov. 1917, and "The Establishment of a Douglas Fir Forest," *Ecology* I, 1, 1920.

[65] VIII, 4, Dec. 1910, p. 415. Rechnagel's address and article of 1908 was entitled "The New Reconnaissance—Working Plans that Work," *Proc. Soc. Am. For.* IV, 1909, pp. 1-21.

try school and the high school of the community, he went to the University of Nebraska where he earned three degrees, Bachelor of Arts, Bachelor of Science, and Master of Science. On the plains there were few forests; and Pearson's father had become much interested in the tree planting movement. The forestry idea appealed to the younger Pearson, and at the university he took as many forestry courses as possible. When he entered, the forestry department was just being organized. He studied botany under Bessey and Clements and became familiar also with methods of ecological investigation. He studied forestry under Miller, who went later to the University of Washington and, until the arrival of Winkenwerder, maintained as dean a "one man school." Still later, Miller became connected with other forestry schools in the West, notably the University of Idaho at Moscow, where, as dean and professor of forestry, he was to further the development of a school which has been a leading teaching and research institution in forest and range matters. His place as dean of the school was to be taken in 1935 by Dwight Smithson Jeffers, graduate of Illinois Wesleyan University and Yale Forest School, who, after a decade with the forest service and years of teaching forestry at Iowa State College and the University of Washington, went to Idaho as an outstanding authority in forest policy and economics.

Pearson entered the United States forest service in 1907. He was sent to the Wallowa forest where during the first year he studied depleted ranges and grazing. To this forest came Arthur Sampson, another University of Nebraska student, to perform other first studies in range management.

Pearson was transferred by Zon in 1908 to the Coconino National Forest to study natural regeneration of ponderosa pine. When Pearson arrived in Arizona the land was heavily forested. It was regarded one of the most excellent timber stands in the United States. Zon and Pearson together selected the site for the Fort Valley Experiment Station, as it became known. An assistant, Willard M. Drake, accompanied them. Forest Supervisor Frank C. Pooler had recommended the location. Work began at the station in 1908, although officially the station was not established until January 1, 1909. At first Pearson followed the "seed tree" method to study regeneration.[66]

The next station site selected was that of the Frémont station, located on the Pike National Forest just across the ridge from the Alpine Laboratory of Dr. and Mrs. Clements, which was situated at Minnehaha-on-Ruxton at an elevation of 8,500 feet on the Cog Railway between

[66] Pearson immediately laid out sample plots to study the region's forest species. He harvested and sold timber, leaving seed trees for reproduction, but the presence of livestock and wild life complicated his use of the seed-tree method of regeneration.

Manitou and the summit of Pikes Peak.[67] The Fremont station, when organized, was placed under one of the ablest forestry research men in the United States, Carlos G. Bates, also a former student of Bessey and Clements.

Bates had graduated from the University of Nebraska in 1907 and that same year been appointed a forest assistant in the Rocky Mountain region. The Fremont station was established in 1909 at an elevation of approximately 8,850 feet and "almost at the middle of the forest range, timber line on [Pikes] Peak being at 11,500 feet, and the lower limit of forest growth at about 6,500."[68] Whereas the location of the Fort Valley Experiment Station on the Coconino National Forest was typical of western yellow-pine forests of the southwest, the site of the Fremont experiment station was selected "on account of the wide range of altitude which it covers and the versatility of physical conditions within its limits," the "forest types surrounding the station [being] those of western yellow-pine, Douglas fir, and Engelmann spruce."

During the following year, 1910, near the Fremont experiment station, but located on the Rio Grande National Forest near Wagon Wheel Gap, Colorado, and at the headwaters of the Rio Grande River, the forest service, to study the effect of forest cover upon streamflow, established the Wagon Wheel Gap experiment station, so-called, and watershed studies were commenced in conjunction with the federal weather bureau. In his report for the year 1911, the secretary of agriculture commented:[69] "At the three forest experiment stations which have been established in Colorado and Arizona, careful studies of forest influences, including the effects of forests upon streamflow, and of climatic requirements of different forest types have been conducted."

The next year, in his annual report,[70] the secretary announced: "Two new stations were established during the year. Though none of these stations has been established more than a few years, the results already secured have been of the greatest assistance in the actual work of forest management. Leading in the work of the past year were studies of the best silvicultural systems and degrees of cutting to secure natural reproduction; the effect of forest cover on streamflow, excessive wind movement, and evaporation; the damage caused by light surface fires; the deterioration of fire-killed timber; and the growth, yield, utilization, and life history of five important western trees."

[67] *Torreya* XIII, 3, March 1913, pp. 70-71, announced that during the summer a graduate school of ecology, directed by Dr. Clements, was to be held at the Alpine Laboratory. The teaching staff was to consist of Raymond J. Pool, assistant director, Mrs. Clements, instructor in botany, and Dr. Homer L. Shantz as special lecturer.

[68] "Review of Forest Service Investigations," *op. cit.*, I, pp. 29-30; John Ise, *op. cit.*, p. 308; Gifford Pinchot, *Breaking New Ground*, pp. 308-309; Jenks Cameron, *op. cit.*, pp. 256-257, 292-294, 367.

[69] *Yearbook of the U.S.D.A. for 1911*, p. 101.

[70] *ibid.*, for 1912, p. 70.

The two stations referred to by the secretary were the Priest River experiment station, organized in the autumn of 1911 and located on the Kaniksu National Forest near the town of Priest River, Idaho, and the Feather River experiment station, organized in the autumn of 1912 and located on the Plumas National Forest on the west side of the Sierras. The Priest River station's location in Idaho was regarded as "typical of the limited silvicultural region composed of western white pine and western larch," whereas the Feather River station's location at Quincy, California, was in "a region typical of the western slope of the Sierras where the most important species are western yellow-pine, sugar pine, and incense cedar, which occur in mixture with each other and with other species such as Douglas fir and white fir."

In the fall of 1912 also was organized the Utah experiment station at Ephraim. This, placed on the Manti National Forest, was established "chiefly for the purpose of carrying on intensive grazing studies, especially studies of the effect of grass cover and grazing upon floods, erosion, and purity of the water supply. Since this station [was] located in the Wasatch range of mountains in the midst of vast areas of aspen, opportunity [was] afforded also for carrying on silvicultural investigations in the management of aspen stands and their replacement by conifers."

In cooperation with the University of Minnesota, at Cloquet in the pine woods near Duluth, Minnesota, was created the Cloquet experiment station. These, together with the seed testing laboratory at the Arlington Farm and Willow Holt station of the office of silvics at Washington, the forest products, ground wood, and wood-testing laboratories, the dendrological laboratory at Washington, each of which has been referred to elsewhere, placed the forest service's scientific research facilities among the foremost of the world.

Before the important paper of Bates and others on "Climatic Characteristics of Forest Types in the Central Rocky Mountains,"[71] and before his announcement of "First Results in the Stream Flow Experiment,"[72] both studies made at the Fremont and Wagon Wheel Gap experiment stations, Bates published his noted bulletin 86 of the forest service, "Windbreaks, Their Influence and Value." This study, one of the first real attempts to apply modern ecologic methods to solve a large-scale forestry problem, was begun in 1908 and had for its main object the examination of the number, kind, and efficiency of windbreaks for use in a shelter belt area from Canada to Mexico.[73] By letter dated June 1, 1908, Zon told Fernow:

The study is to embrace the area from Minnesota and Montana to Texas

[71] *Proc. Soc. Am. For.* IX, 1, Jan. 1914, pp. 78-94.
[72] *Journal of Forestry* XIX, 4, April 1921, pp. 402-408.
[73] *Forestry Quarterly* VI, 3, Sept. 1908, p. 322.

and New Mexico, and will include the Prairie areas of California, Washington and Idaho. It is expected that the study will last two years. This year it is expected to cover the following states: Minnesota, Iowa, the Dakotas, Nebraska, and Colorado. The work is to be done in cooperation with the State Agricultural Experiment Stations, wherever possible. It is in charge of Mr. C. G. Bates, who is assisted by Professor Frank Phillips of the University of Nebraska, Cooper and Hamel [of the University of Minnesota?] and Morris and Morrison of the University of Michigan.

Zon forwarded a "statement" of the study prepared by Bates for use in *Forestry Quarterly.*

Other matters were being investigated in the light of new knowledge and improved techniques. While at Biltmore in April 1908, Zon had been shown by Director Howe an article written by Professor M. L. Fernald of the Gray Herbarium and published in the New England Botanical Club journal, *Rhodora.* Entitled "Soil Preferences of Certain Alpine and Subalpine Plants,"[74] this study discussed the relative importance of the chemical properties of soils as distinguished from their physical properties in their effects on plant distribution and their significances as applied to forest growth.

Modern research in the study of physical and biological factors of plant growth, including special problems in regeneration, growth, and mortality of forest species, each in relation to such fundamental factors as light, water, soil content, and climate, sometimes with carefully prepared data kept over many years and often with a vast amount of statistical information, began to characterize the work of a number of the stations. Since 1903 experiment stations for grazing study and research had been in existence, though not under the auspices of the forest service.[75] Beginning in 1912 and until 1922 when he became an associate professor and later professor of forestry at the University of California, Arthur William Sampson, plant ecologist and director of the Utah, or Great Basin, forest experiment station furthered valuable research in range and pasture management, the effect of domestic animal grazing on streamflow, and the most efficient methods of livestock husbandry on range and pasture. Range and grazing research was to take on such added importance, both economically and scientifically, that scarcely a few years would elapse before investigations in one direction or another would be found at each of the established forest experiment stations. Today all twelve of the forest service stations located on principal forest regions of the United States are called forest and range experiment stations.

In *Journal of Forestry*[76] Sampson had published "Suggestions for Instruction in Range Management," in which, urging that chairs of

[74] Reviewed by Zon in *Forestry Quarterly* VI, 2, June 1908, p. 177.
[75] Gifford Pinchot, *ibid.*, pp. 308-309.
[76] XVII, 1919, pp. 523-545. See also *ibid.* XXIII, 1925, pp. 476-486.

range management and grazing research be established in leading universities of the nation, two possibly in the east, one in the middle west, and two in the far west, he outlined a curriculum embracing range history and economics; the native, cultivated, and associated pasture plants; management of the range; management of range livestock; range reconnaissance and grazing working plans; and grazing and forest protection. In this he reminded his readers that "one highly important phase of forestry business, namely, range and live-stock management, [had,] up to [that] time, been all but overlooked." Some years later, at an annual meeting of the Society of American Foresters, Sampson presented a paper on "Range Management and Forestry," which, when published, was followed by comments of J. T. Jardine, who said: "The principles of 'deferred-and-rotation grazing' are sound. There is much yet to be accomplished for the best results in the application of these principles in grazing management on lands held in reservation primarily for production of timber. . . . The investigations prior to 1920 indicated . . . that much can be done to minimize grazing injury to tree growth and to range by timely use of the forage, by proper handling of the stock, and by discretion in deciding upon the class of stock for a given range. Unless conditions have changed since 1920 there is yet much opportunity for betterment through adjustments along these lines. . . ." He approved Sampson's suggestions for studies of grazing in relation to fire protection and reforestation on cut-over lands. From those years to the present, range management study and research has occupied an increasingly important part of forestry research, especially in the western states, and also in central, southern, and eastern sections of the nation.

At first the forest work overshadowed in importance the range research. From the high pine country emerging from the Arizona desert, on the Coconino plateau, and in part of the foothills of the San Francisco Mountains, forest experiment stations of the forest service had been extended northeast to the Colorado front range of the Rocky Mountains, then northwest into northern Idaho between the high northern Rockies and other mountain ranges of Idaho and Washington and not far from the Canadian boundary, thence west to the Sierra Nevada Mountains of northern California, and by the end of the year 1912 between the two great principal western mountain ranges into the Great Basin of Utah. As forest experimental work grew in importance, the Wind River forest experiment station was located in the Wind River Valley of Washington. In 1913, Julius Valentine Hofmann, who during 1912-1913 had been scientific assistant at the Priest River station, was made director, and almost immediately the scientific research staff, including E. J. Hanzlik and T. T. Munger, inaugurated a decade of special study into the characteristics and reproduction of Douglas fir. In 1924, about the time when Hofmann became assistant director of the Pennsylvania

State forest school, the United States department of agriculture published his important bulletin 1200, "Natural Regeneration of Douglas Fir in the Pacific Northwest" including a valuable bibliography of the subject. In 1921, assistant forester Earle H. Clapp, in an article on "Forest Experiment Stations,"[77] elaborating what the stations thus far created had accomplished, what the research programs and work of each station should be, where new stations were needed and why, and other interesting material, pointed to the accomplishments of a forest station in the northern Rocky Mountains. This, evidently the Wind River station, he found had "already demonstrated its value by working out reasonably successful methods of artificial reforestation for such important species as western white pine. Seed storage in the duff of western white pine stands," Clapp continued, "has been found somewhat similar to that described for the Douglas fir forests, and enough information as a basis for fire protection has been gathered to emphasize the need for continuing and greatly enlarging this class of work. There is work ahead in the determination of the best methods of cutting. Brush disposal, because of the large quantities left in logging operations, is as difficult and important as in the Pacific Northwest. The northern Rockies contain much larger private holdings than either the central or southern portions, and the results of forest investigations are therefore needed as a basis for private as well as National Forest practice."

About 1921 the Northern Rocky Mountain forest station was established at Missoula, Montana. Robert Harrison Weidman, who since his graduation from the University of Michigan in 1914 had spent all but a year or so with the forest service, was appointed silviculturist in charge, and in this capacity and as director of the station he was to serve there and in Montana until 1937, when he was made superintendent of the forest service's Institute of Forest Genetics at Placerville, California.

Assistant Forester Clapp in 1921 urged that five forest experiment stations be established in the East—in the southern pine belt, the Great Lake states, the northeast, the Allegheny Mountain states and Appalachian Mountain states. Concerning the work of the stations created for the northern, central, and southern Rocky Mountain areas, he advocated increased facilities and enlargement of the work. In 1920 the research personnel of the station established for the central Rocky Mountain regions had been reduced to one technical scientist, and other problems beside that of Nebraska sand-hill planting required investigation—for example, problems relating "mainly to the extensive lodgepole pine forests of the central Rockies and to the eastern outpost of the western yellow pine forests in the Black Hills of South Dakota."

[77] Department Circular 183, October 1921, U.S.D.A., 34 pages.

For the Pacific Coast forest region, Clapp wanted a station in California and one in the Pacific Northwest. For the latter he suggested a staff to "include a director, two men for work on fire problems, two men for Douglas fir, two for yellow pine, two for Alaskan forests, one man on tree planting, and two for all other problems including such forest types as the true firs and the coast forests of Washington and Oregon."

The wood deficit of the nation, then as today, was enormous. Achievements in scientific reforestation promised forest renewal in idle and unproductive lands. "It is now possible," he wrote, "to plant with reasonable success in the western yellow pine stands of the Southwest under conditions slightly, if any, less difficult" than in the Nebraska sand hills, which we will consider presently. "The delayed germination of western white pine seed interfered with and increased the cost of nursery and planting operations for a number of years in the northern Rockies. The problem involved has also been largely solved, and in general reasonably successful planting methods are now known for our most common western species." Accordingly, during the second decade of the century the Pacific Northwest forest experiment station of Oregon, located now at Portland, was established. It had been many years since Fernow and others had pointed to the tremendous economic importance of scientific study of the influence of forest cover on irrigation and water supply, especially for the maritime regions of California and for the growing metropolitan centers of the Pacific coast such as Los Angeles and San Francisco. California's national forests had long been known to be of immense potential value. So, also, a forest experiment station was established in central California, with Edward I. Kotok, holder of degrees from the University of California and who had spent many years of work in California national forests, as its director.

In 1915 the creation in the forest service of an office or branch of research controlling all forest investigations and studies except grazing, and the extension after 1921 of experiment stations to central, northeastern, southeastern, and southern timber-growing areas widened and intensified the research scope of the service. Pennsylvania and one or two other states established forest experiment stations. Many of the foresters placed in charge of the federal and state stations were graduated from schools where forestry and plant ecology were taught.

Forest research brought many able workers into prominence. In 1908 Thornton Taft Munger received his master of forestry degree from Yale, and soon became a forest service assistant, examiner, and silviculturist. In 1924 he became director of the Pacific Northwest forest experiment station, and its principal silviculturist in 1938. In 1907 Samuel Trask Dana, graduate in arts and science at Bowdoin College, obtained his M.F. degree from Yale and, after a few years as a forest assistant, became assistant chief of the office of silvics, forest investigations, and branch of research, and in 1923 director of the Northeast forest experiment stations. Many of the early directors of forest experiment stations, however, were not holders of forestry degrees, although each spent years with the forest service before being promoted to the office of director. Pearson, Bates, and Sampson were graduates of the University of Nebraska, Hofmann of the University of Minnesota as were also Donald Ross Brewster and W. H. Kenety, director of the Cloquet experiment station. Hofmann possessed three degrees: bachelor of science, master of forestry, and doctor of philosophy. At these two universities, these men studied plant ecology under Clements and forestry under members of the forestry faculty.

The scientific and economic programs of these stations is described in *Forestry Quarterly*[78] in an article which, while related to those of the Fort Valley station, presents the whole subject. Management methods of stations and foresters have varied, but the objectives have been the same—quality and quantity production of the forest harvest. In 1909 the Fort Valley or Coconino Ranger School, the first established on a national forest, was announced. It was heartily endorsed by the chief forester but was abandoned, evidently in favor of the new forestry school at the University of Montana.[79] Some of the most highly regarded studies of these stations have been Munger's work in Douglas fir; Bates' work in Douglas fir, lodgepole pine, and Engelmann spruce; at the Feather River station and elsewhere the work of Duncan Dunning, California forest authority, in ponderosa and sugar pine; Weidman's work in ponderosa and western white pine; and Hofmann's work at Wind River station. Many smaller stations have been located as a part of special work on the forests in the matters of streamflow, forest influences, grazing, and other specific phases. From the beginning the plan of the forest service was to locate main stations in each of the silvicultural regions of the West, in the eastern white pine region, in the Appalachian hardwood region, and in the southern pine region. This plan has been carried out, and much more than was first contemplated has been done. Today, in principal forest regions over the entire United States, experiment stations have embraced a nation-wide study of our timber and range resources. Planting stations and nurseries have been placed in various districts. Forest biology, ecology, soils,

[78] G. A. Pearson, "The Administration of a Forest Experiment Station," *Forestry Quarterly* XII, 2, June 1914, pp. 211ff.

[79] Theodore S. Woolsey, "The Coconino Ranger School," *Forestry Quarterly* VII, 3, Sept. 1909, p. 243. The Fort Valley station was especially notable for its development of forest sample plot study. A ranger station on the Coconino Forest was named the Fernow station. Concerning the founding of the Montana Forestry School, see *Forestry Quarterly* XII, 4, Dec. 1914, p. 653; see also *Journal of Forestry* XVI, 6, Oct. 1918, p. 671; XV, 6, Oct. 1917, p. 805.

mycology, pathology, planting, forest influences, and the entire gamut of business and economic research have enormously expanded the original field of silvicultural investigations. By 1922, Bates and Zon, in an elaborate study of "Research Methods in the Study of Forest Environment,"[80] defined the "investigations which come as a general rule distinctly under the work of forest experiment stations: (1) Forest meteorological observations; (2) distribution of species and types in relation to climate and soils; (3) studies of the growth, volume and yield of forest stands; (4) studies of the effect of the source of seed upon the resulting forest stand; (5) experiments with the introduction of exotic species; (6) experiments with different silvicultural methods of cutting for the purpose of securing natural reproduction; (7) methods of artificial reproduction; (8) the study of the effect of different methods of thinning upon the growth of the main stand; and (9) studies of the effect of site upon the technical properties of the wood produced." To this list were added studies which, without permanent forest experiment station facilities, were subjects of investigations such as microscopic and chemical studies of woods or studies of natural reproduction, distribution, and growth, and observations on climate in relation to forest vegetation.

Zon and Clements collaborated in research on the light requirements of forest species. Zon told Fernow on March 24, 1908:

> I have practically translated Zederbauer's article on "The Light Requirement of Forest Trees and Methods of Light Measurement," and should like to send it to you. . . . It is a most instructive paper and should cool off the enthusiasm of some of our "ecologists." I have also notes on durability and strength of wood from a silvicultural standpoint. I think it is worth while to bring out the bearing which different silvicultural measures may have upon the durability and strength of wood.

Fernow asked for the translation. He had already reviewed Zederbauer's article for the *Quarterly*, but he was still much interested in the subject.[81]

On May 14 Zon wrote Fernow again:

> I am at last able to send you the translation of Zederbauer which I promised some time ago. I am very anxious to see it in print. It is a subject which we are working on just now in the Office of Silvics and intend to bring out a circular on measuring light in the forest. I feel that we have reached a point where mere impressions or purely empiric knowledge is insufficient. We must actually measure the physical factors and know how to do this. I am sending another copy of the translation to Prof. Clements with the re-

[80] Contribution from the forest service, bulletin 1059, U.S.D.A., 209 pages, with 8 pages of bibliography, issued May 19, 1922. At this time Bates was silviculturist in charge of the Fremont forest experiment station and Zon held the title of forest economist. Such subtopics as forest air temperature, soil temperature, solar radiation, precipitation, soils, wind movement, and evaporation were discussed.

[81] Fernow's review of Zederbauer's article appeared in *Forestry Quarterly* V, 4, Dec. 1907, p. 414; see also *ibid.* VI, 3, Sept. 1908, p. 255.

quest that he should criticize and comment upon it. Prof. Clements' photometer is nothing but a modification of Wiesner's photometer, and he may want to say something in regard to Zederbauer's criticism of it.

The office of silvics was compiling brief bibliographies and preparing abstracts with indices of valuable articles. Fernow praised every effort to place departmental work on a permanent basis, but only occasionally did he yield any ground in criticizing Americans for lack of originality in scientific work. In each issue of *Forestry Quarterly* he reviewed foreign work. He warned Zon:

> You are not the first to think that more exact knowledge is desirable with reference to the physical factors, in order to practice silviculture. The German and Austrian Experiment Stations have long ago recognized it, and started it in a way, but it will be very many years before a sufficient experimental basis will be furnished upon which the practice can build.

On May 27 Clements wrote to Zon and forwarded a copy of his letter to Fernow:

> I find the [Zederbauer] paper unconvincing from the theoretical and the experimental standpoint, in spite of the fact that I have admitted all along that we must some day decide whether light has a qualitative effect in nature. I determined last summer that the time had come for taking up this matter and trying to settle it, and have arranged to carry out several series of experiments on the absorption of leaves and the spectrum analysis of forest light. These seem largely academic to me, however, in the light of practically all of my own work, and that of several students, especially that of Mrs. Clements in the quantitative study of leaf structure.

Clements criticized Zederbauer's conclusions on the ground that he seemed "to have little knowledge of the effect of the various parts of the spectrum on the various life processes of the plant. . . . It seems fairer to him and more in keeping with the ecological accuracy that I am urging, to withhold expression until his views have actually been put to the test this summer." Zon answered that it was entirely satisfactory to him to defer receiving Clements' opinion till later:

> I feel that the question involved is one which should be investigated before we proceed with our light measurements in the forest. I agree with you that some of Zederbauer's conclusions are questionable, and I do not think that his method has all the merits that he claims for it, yet I think that his arguments against the silver chloride method have a great deal of weight. What appears to me as one of Zederbauer's fundamental errors lies in his assumption that all of the light which is intercepted by the tree crowns is absorbed by the leaves, thus ignoring the reflected light which may be of considerable importance. The accuracy of all methods based upon the measurement of the chemical rays, it seems to me, depends upon whether or not the diffuse light of the forest is of normal composition. Wiesner's experiments on this question do not seem to be conclusive, and until more convincing experiments have been made, the measurements obtained by this method will naturally be open to attack.

Light and its related problems have remained central to forestry research. When Graves and Zon published their forest service bulletin, "Light in Relation to Tree Growth" (1911), Fernow reminded readers of *Forestry Quarterly*[82] that, while physical measurements served practical uses, the conclusions should be verified in the physiological laboratory. Fernow did not sympathize with attitudes which denied the hope that someday "a mathematical, practically useful, statement of light requirements" might be formed which would take into account not only light readings but also factors of tree growth—moisture, soil content, age and vigor of specimens, relative humidity, et cetera. In this review, Fernow added to the "very valuable" literary references of the article a reference to the pioneer American plant physiologist, Daniel Trembly MacDougal.

In 1906 Zon wrote a paper on the "Principles Involved in Determining Forest Types," published in the first volume of the *Proceedings of the Society of American Foresters.*[83] So pleased was Fernow with the article that he wrote to Zon that he had found the study "so highly suggestive [he] would like to reprint it in the Quarterly. . . . I would accompany it with a few remarks of my own, pointing out what I consider an omission on your part, namely, lack of consideration of the difference of ecological relations and economic desires." This criticism, nevertheless, did not seriously impair the value of Zon's study. In a letter dated December 21, 1908, to R. D. Craig, Fernow praised Zon's paper as "an admirable analysis of what a forest type is and how it should be described." Clements' study of "Plant Formations and Forest Types" was also welcomed, showing that the work of botany and forestry was being correlated. In 1911 Fernow reviewed Graves's *Principles of Handling Woodlands.* Commenting that this was the "first attempt in print to discuss systematically silviculture with special reference to American conditions," he said that "one [was] left with the impression that a number of the silvicultural methods described [were] in actual operation in this country."[84] All these advances delighted Fernow, who found the profession moving forward in science as well as economics.[85]

Some projects involved large outlays of time and expenditures. In 1911 *Forestry Quarterly*[86] reviewed Bates' Bulletin 86 of the United States forest service, "Windbreaks: Their Influence and Value." His experiments on large areas of forested watersheds and streams to study the forest's influences on soil preservation, streamflow regulation, and

[82] IX, 3, Sept. 1911, p. 455.

[83] No. 3; see also reprint in *Forestry Quarterly* VI, 3, Sept. 1908, p. 263.

[84] *Forestry Quarterly* IX, 3, Sept. 1911, pp. 454f.

[85] *ibid.* IX, 3, Sept. 1911, p. 526; IX, 1, March 1911, p. 134 (review presumably by Fernow). About 1908 the University of West Virginia established another "school" of forestry; see *ibid.* VI, 3, Sept. 1908, p. 329.

[86] *ibid.* IX, 4, Dec. 1911, p. 599.

climate, were studied from many angles, not the least of which were the disposition of rain and snow water, their run-off and storage, and erosion and silting of streams. Sixteen years went into this study.[87] Aside from experimental studies in seed testing and sand hill planting, important regional studies appeared, notably Bates' work on central Rocky Mountain forestry: silvicultural systems of management and climatic characteristics of forest types[88] there, as well as forest succession,[89] a subject investigated by many workers in various forest areas.

Bates' and Pierce's "Forestation of the Sand Hills of Nebraska and Kansas," bulletin 121 of the forest service, published February 3, 1913, increased scientific knowledge of a subject to which Bessey and Fernow had supplied foundations. Sand hill forest planting was reviewed, and the authors gave Dr. Bessey credit for suggesting the research to the division of forestry under Fernow. Establishment of national forest reserves in the sand hill regions of Nebraska and Kansas was reviewed as well as the location of forest nurseries at Halsey, Nebraska, near Middle Loup River, in 1902, and Garden City, Kansas, along the Arkansas River, in 1907, the first to produce primarily coniferous trees for Nebraska planting and the other mainly hardwood or broad-leaved trees for Kansas planting. In 1908, combining the Dismal River, the Niobrara, and North Platte reserves, the Nebraska national forest of 556,000 acres had been established. That year, also, the Garden City forest reserve had been constituted the Kansas national forest with an increase and total of 302,387 acres. Subsequent events with regard to at least one of these reserves is not as important today as the knowledge made available of the adaptability of various tree species to the arid climate.

Pierce was the deputy supervisor of the Nebraska national forest. Bates and he in their bulletin 121 described the nursery operations and field planting, the methods of planting, field sowing, the effect of climate on time of planting, ways to combat fire, insects, birds, and rodents, and, of course, discussed the important subject of growth. Their conclusions read in part:

"In summing up the sand-hill planting it may be said that the 85 or 90 per cent of success attained in 1911, as compared with 5 or 10 per cent in the first planting, is due largely to improve methods in the nursery. . . . The inauguration of transplanting has had as much to do with progress as anything else. Sturdier trees are now being grown as

[87] Jenks Cameron, *op. cit.*, pp. 268-278, 300, 367-369, John Ise, *op. cit.*, pp. 310-311; Bates, "Forests and Streamflow: An Experimental Study," *Proc. Soc. Am. For.* VI, 1, pp. 53-63; "First Results etc.," *Jour. of For.* XIX, 1921, pp. 402-408.

[88] Silvicultural management for Engelmann spruce, Douglas fir, yellow pine, lodgepole pine, etc., *Proc. Soc. Am. For.* VII, 1, 1912, pp. 106-116; climatic characteristics of Rocky Mountain forest types, *ibid.*, IX, 1, 1914, pp. 78-94. The latter study made with F. B. Notestein and P. Keplinger.

[89] *Jour. of For.* XV, 1917, pp. 587-592.

the result of the generous use of organic fertilizers and the application of plenty of water to the seedlings and transplant beds at the right time. Reduction in the amount of shading has also prepared the trees more fully for the sand-hill conditions."

They warned against taking seedlings from the forest to be grown in an arid climate, and called the most important single factor "earlier spring planting, which also makes possible earlier transplanting and earlier seed sowing. The conditions in the sand hills at the time when the frost leaves the ground are usually favorable." Fernow sustained a close interest in Nebraska sand hill planting until the last years of his life, especially the growth and development of the trees planted during his administration as chief of the division of forestry on the land of the Bruners in Holt County four miles west of Swan, Nebraska.

In 1913, answering a letter from H. B. Ayers, who maintained a Jack Pine Nursery at Kimberly, Minnesota, and had sent to Fernow some published articles concerning the Cuyuna Range, Fernow said: "I am interested to see the Jack Pine plantation in Nebraska, which you use in the letter-head. Can you give me any more details, such as size of the area that has remained in forest, and height and diameter of various trees? I have never seen the plantation, although I claim the credit of being its originator."

Forest sand hill planting was not without significance in Canada. Moreover, forest nurseries in the northwest and southwest began to flourish. By 1925 the forest service's Savenac nursery, located in Montana at the western end of the Lolo national forest in the Bitter Root mountain range at an elevation of 3,150 feet and covering about thirty acres devoted to raising seedling and transplant stock, had an authorized output of three million trees, mostly western white pine, western yellow pine, and Engelmann spruce, but also Douglas fir, western red cedar, western larch, and other species.[90] While the nursery had its own administrative and research personnel, foresters working at the experiment stations often gave part of their time to the nursery and other forest units of the service.

Throughout the first quarter of the century, silvicultural practice of the forest service[91] remained in considerable part that outlined by Zon and Clapp in an article entitled, "Cutting Timber on the National Forests," published in the *Yearbook of the U.S.D.A. for 1907*. Silvicultural practice on privately owned forest lands for many years would be found infrequent and scattered. But the government service was perfected

[90] G. Willard Jones, "Forest Nursery Working Practice at Savenac Nursery," *Jour. of For.* XXIII, 1925, pp. 635-644. The author also acknowledges help from Dr. Paul C. Kitchin, employed by the United States forest service 1917-1920, and now professor and secretary of the college of dentistry, Ohio State University.

[91] John F. Preston, "Silvicultural Practice in the United States During the Past Quarter Century," *Jour. of For.* XXIII, 1925, pp. 236-250, at 240.

more each year, scientific study continued, and judging by the number of times the service was consulted by private owners and the forest area extent on which its silvicultural advice was applied, the service to private agencies had grown with great effectiveness. Furthermore, silvicultural practice on the national forests was maintained for purposes of determining the most effective management system of the government forests and to enable the service to supply advice to owners of similar forests. Much valuable knowledge of silvicultural systems and their applications was, therefore, accumulated. That foresters, trained in ecology, contributed efficiently to the profession's advancement in this respect may be implied from Professor Ralph C. Hawley's answer to John F. Preston's criticisms of the prevailing silvicultural practice and his suggestions for improving both experimental knowledge and practice. Professor Hawley pointed out that illustrations of "all the more important systems" could be found in the United States and predicted these would "multiply as silvicultural practice increases." In proof, he cited articles written by forest service silviculturists engaged in work on the national forests in which flexible recommendations were made, varying with forest conditions and types: the selection and shelterwood systems,[92] and in one article by Weidman mention was made of a possible application of a clear cutting silvicultural system.[93] More to the point of the present discussion, however, Hawley commented with regard to recent scientific achievements by forest workers of the service:

". . . the sum total of acquired knowledge is impressive. Such reports as Pearson's 'Natural Reproduction of Western Yellow Pine in the Southwest,' Hofmann's 'The Natural Regeneration of Douglas Fir in the Pacific Northwest,' and Bates' 'Forest Types in the Central Rocky Mountains as Affected by Climate and Soil,' each representing years of investigation are scientific achievements of the first order."

While the work of each was done while working as a forester of the forest service, it is to be noticed that each had been schooled in ecology, and had made ecological investigation principal in their scientific research. Bates later became chief of the biological division of the forest products laboratory at Madison, and still later principal silviculturist of the Lake States forest experiment station. Hofmann is today director of the forestry school of North Carolina State College. Pearson is now director of the Southwestern Forest and Range experiment station, with its main offices at Tucson, Arizona. Each of these men had taken ecology under Clements, and their achievements are credits to themselves, the forest service, and their instruction. The other great American teacher of ecology was Henry Chandler Cowles of the department of

[92] Duncan Dunning, "Some Results of Cutting in the Sierra Forests of California," *U.S.D.A. bulletin 1176*, Nov. 24, 1923.

[93] "Forest Succession as a Basis of the Silviculture of Western Yellow Pine," *op. cit.*, see conclusions.

botany of the University of Chicago. While he did some ecological research in the west, ranging from Arizona on the south to Oregon (and Alaska) on the north, in the earliest years of formal ecological study on this continent Cowles was not a collaborator or official of the forest service and his studies were not preeminently on western national forests. Before eastern national forests were established, he and his students examined ecologically important regions in the southern, eastern, and central states—northern Michigan, the Tennessee mountains, the gulf coast states especially in Mississippi and the Florida Everglades and the *Torreya taxifolia* region near Apalachicola in the latter state, in Maine, and elsewhere.

In the next chapters Fernow's views on silvicultural practice will be further set forth when we consider his Canadian leadership in introducing and advancing forest management practice and scientific forestry there. Fernow, while attending forest schools in Germany, had studied ecology. "We had," he informed H. P. Baker on December 4, 1916, "a course on General Ecology, as well as in Entomology special, but no courses on Game and Fish, although in practice, hunting and fishing on forest properties is administered by foresters."

Among American foresters Fernow was first to urge that ecology be included in silvicultural investigations, and lived to see forest ecology become an established branch of science in North America. His student, Zon, not only helped to establish forestry experiment stations but also for fifteen years as chief directed forest investigations of the forest service; and in 1922 became director of the Lake States forest experiment station, professor of forestry at the University of Minnesota, and director of the university forest experiment station at Cloquet. Another principal in the United States forestry experiment station movement, Earle Hart Clapp, was a student of Fernow and Roth. In 1905 he obtained his degree from the University of Michigan, and he had been a student at the New York State College of Forestry at Cornell during 1902-1903. Clapp rose steadily in the forest service: in 1905 in charge of forest management, 1907-1908 associate district forester of the southwestern district, 1908-1911 forest inspector and specialist in silviculture, 1911-1915 assistant forester in charge of research, and since then has been both associate chief and acting chief forester. Before concluding this chapter, it should also be pointed out that, while the establishment of forestry experiment stations in connection with national forests began in the administration of chief forester Pinchot, the importance attached to scientific forestry investigations was both increased and strengthened during the administration of chief forester Graves. In fact, many if not most of the experiment stations were created during Graves' years in the highest office of federal forestry.

CHAPTER IX

Fernow and the Faculty of Forestry at Toronto

BEFORE Fernow went to Canada he had outlined his plan to develop "an educated class of foresters [which would secure] their employment and [be] an educational force." He wanted to "lay the foundation for an educational system which [would] bring to each class [of foresters] interested intelligence and information suited to its needs. University Extension work of the broadest kind is here called for," he said. Concerning the curriculum and facilities, he suggested:

> As far as I can judge from the Calendar of the University there are provided for the needs of forestry students satisfactory courses in Mathematics, Chemistry, Mineralogy and Petrography, Geology, Meteorology, also Political Economy and Law. In these departments apparently the only deficiencies are a course on Soil Physics, which would have to be provided for, and a desirable, if not necessary, course on Physiography. In the department of Biology, courses . . . cover well the zoological requirements, except that a needed course on economic entomology with special reference to forest insects seems absent. In Botany the department seems decidedly deficient from the standpoint of the needs of the forester, whose main business (silviculture) may be defined as applied botany (ecology). A somewhat wider elaboration of plant physiology and ecology, and an expansion in the direction of Dendrology, both systematic and biological, as well as a course in Timber Physics, would have to be made in the botanical department or supplied in the forestry department. A course on the Diseases of Timber would have to supplement [a course in botany]. Some of these botanical courses are perhaps best supplied in the forestry department itself. . . . It does not appear from the Calendar that courses in Civil Engineering are provided. The foresters need courses in plain and topographic surveying and in the principles of road and railroad building. . . . Forestry is a practical profession.[1]

E. J. Zavitz of Ontario Agricultural College was appointed by Fernow during the summer of 1907 as a class assistant. Fernow had proposed cooperative work with the agricultural college of the province. He was sure that soon "a number of young foresters of a government forest department would find employment" in farm forestry. Woodlot management and wasteland planting "would provide practical aids to the farmer." During the first year Zavitz gave part time from his duties at Guelph to the forest school at Toronto. Fernow needed another full-time instructor. He sought after a former student of the New York State College of Forestry, a graduate of Yale who had been since graduation with the United States forest service at Washington and later in the

[1] From an undated and unsigned memorandum addressed to Acting President Maurice M. Hutton of the University of Toronto, written by Fernow at Ithaca. A copy of this memorandum was found among Fernow's papers.

field, principally at Missoula, Montana. This was Karl W. Woodward, son of R. S. Woodward, Fernow's friend in years when Fernow was chief of the forestry division. Woodward did not wish to leave the United States. As yet he had not gone into teaching. He therefore refused Fernow's offer of a position with the faculty of forestry at Toronto.

In 1908, when inquiries came to Fernow to recommend persons to fill an instructorship at Colorado College and a directorship "of a newly founded Forest school on the Pacific coast with a large endowment" (it is not unlikely the latter position was offered to Fernow), on October 29 he wrote to the younger Woodward and asked him to recommend men. Fernow told Woodward that "a strong first class man [was] sought for," and the Pacific school was perhaps the University of Washington.

Someone to teach forest mensuration was needed. A. H. D. Ross[2] resigned from a position as inspector in the tree planting service of the Dominion forestry branch to become a member of the Toronto faculty to teach mensuration, forest utilization, and woodlands protection. Ross had been connected with the lumber industry and forestry since 1884. A year of special study of white pine reproduction had been spent with the United States bureau of forestry. In Zavitz and Ross, both holders of master's degrees, forestry instruction at the University of Michigan and at Yale were represented on Fernow's faculty at Toronto.

The student body consisted of James H. White, F. W. Mitchell, R. P. Wodehouse, L. M. Ellis, and T. W. Dwight.

The school began in various rooms in the university buildings, but in 1908 new quarters, a small brown brick residence fronted by the Queen's Plaza and the provincial parliament building, were made available to both forestry and the botany department. Fernow's office was in a front room of the second floor, through the windows of which one might look out on the exquisite gardens of the landscaped plaza. The classrooms and other instructors' offices were on the first floor.

An important addition was made to the faculty in 1908. At last Howe and Fernow made final arrangements for an association which was to continue uninterrupted for the balance of Fernow's life. Howe consistently asserted that he wished to teach dendrology and silviculture. He had explained, "I am much interested in certain silvicultural problems, particularly in the natural regeneration of forest trees. I am now carrying on experiments with natural regeneration of white pine and of yellow poplar. My purpose is to continue my research along these lines." Following Fernow's resignation at Pennsylvania State College to accept the "more remunerative position at the University of Toronto," P. O. Ray of the department of history and political science had urged Howe

[2] *Canadian Forestry Journal* III, 1907, pp. 154-156.

to apply for Fernow's position. By the time Ray's letter was received, however, Howe had promised to remain another year at Biltmore. Early in 1908 Fernow and Howe resumed correspondence. That year Hugh Potter Baker wrote to Fernow and expressed a willingness to take a position at Toronto "for a year" to teach silviculture before going to Europe to study this subject at schools and stations on the continent. At Montreal Fernow had told him that he was anxious to fill the position at Toronto open in silviculture. Baker had studied tree planting of the Middle West and Rocky Mountain regions. The United States forest service had published his circular on the planted timber of Iowa. He had spent a season locating rangers' nurseries in the southern Rocky Mountains, and he had placed the permanent nursery of the service near Las Vegas, New Mexico. The outcome was that Baker went, as planned, to Europe to study at the University of Munich, his departmental position at Pennsylvania State College being filled during his absence by Ferguson, graduate of Hamilton College and Yale. Howe received the appointment at Toronto, which Fernow wanted to be filled permanently. On July 11, 1908, Fernow told Baker that he expected that the school would have "just one student in silviculture, and a fine one, left over from the second year students (silviculture being with us a third year subject)," to which Baker replied that he was "sure [that] the wisest thing for [him] to do [was] to remain [at Pennsylvania State College] until next year and then take up the work abroad. . . . I still feel that a year with you would mean a good deal to me." Accordingly when Howe arrived at Toronto, he began to teach courses in both the department of botany and the forestry school—plant physiology and silvics, and part of silviculture. Not long before, the botany department had lost to Harvard University one of its most celebrated scholars, Edward C. Jeffrey, plant morphologist, physiologist, and anatomist.

On November 25, 1908, Fernow addressed a letter to R. H. Campbell, who was now superintendent of forestry at Ottawa. Elihu Stewart had resigned from the position and, like Judson F. Clark, had gone west to be employed by a large lumber concern. Fernow informed Campbell, "Last night the students organized their Club and propose, from time to time, to invite speakers to their monthly meetings." Campbell was invited to give the first address. Fernow added:

> We have now with us an excellent man as Lecturer on Dendrology and allied subjects, Dr. C. D. Howe, formerly Assistant Director of Biltmore Forest School. He is very anxious to do some useful work in the line of Ecology, a subject which I conceive of much importance for yours as for any other forest department in Canada, namely, to learn how natural reproduction over burned areas progresses, in order to come to a judgment as to what methods in recuperating such areas, by assistance of man, may lead to satisfactory results. I present this matter very early to you, in order to find

out what attitude you would take towards employing Dr. Howe, and perhaps as his assistant, who will be our first graduate, Mr. White, also an able man, for next summer. I sent you yesterday a circular letter which I have sent to the members of the Canadian Society of Forest Engineers, merely to make you acquainted with the movement.

Howe began his constructive work in Canada. Essentially his courses were based in forest biology. As a part of his course in biological dendrology, he developed soils study from the biological viewpoint, using lectures and laboratory experiments. Fernow, while at Cornell, had taught soils as a part of silviculture, principally because of the absence of a soils specialist there. He had not been satisfied. He wanted more than a "theoretical and superficial" instruction in this fundamental. Even now he desired more than theory and surveys in soils research; he wanted fundamental biological study supported by experimental research both at the school and within the forest.

In Canada the formation of the school was Fernow's first major triumph. The formation of the Canadian Society of Forest Engineers was the second.

Not until 1908 could Fernow write to Charles Sprague Sargent at Brookline, Massachusetts, and say:

Our school is thriving as much as we expect and want. I am not out for numbers but for quality especially since the forestry movement in Canada has not so far advanced as to call for many professional foresters. We started last year with five and have registered this fall twenty-six. Our university is growing rapidly in numbers as well as in facilities.

Roland D. Craig[3] had graduated from Cornell University as a forest engineer in 1903, studied natural production of forest trees in California for the United States bureau of forestry until 1904, and since April of that year had been inspecting tree planting and timber reservations in the West. Among the latter were Moose Mountain and Turtle Mountain, and reserves in the Northwest and British Columbia. On November 23 Fernow told Craig, "It will interest you to know that our Faculty is growing in and out of season, for I have just enrolled the 28th, [who is] coming from British Columbia." To W. R. Mattoon, at Albuquerque, New Mexico, Fernow wrote, "It will interest you to learn that our college has grown from five to twenty-eight, and that we have now satisfactory and sufficient quarters, and altogether we are on the boom." Adequate laboratory facilities had been provided. Dr. Hatt of Purdue University wrote, inquiring about structural conditions of wood in relation to preservative processes. Fernow replied that he had never done any experimenting in that direction but that he would "devise a

[3] *ibid.* III, 1, March 1907, p. 13. Dr. A. H. Unwin, an English forester preceded Craig in his employment by the forestry branch of the Canadian department of the interior.

few tests and [hoped] to be able by and by to give results for Canadian material." Fernow presented his library of about 2,500 books and pamphlets to the new school. He was officially thanked by the board of governors and President Falconer on January 9, 1908; this was the fourth North American library in forestry which Fernow had equipped, but it was the only one made up of his own collections.

During the spring he arranged with the railroads to take the school's students to Rondeau Park, the Algonquin Reserve, and the Timagami Reserve. The school did some planting of forest species at Rondeau Park, and Fernow photographed students engaged in planting. These pictures were shown at his lecture, "The Battle of the Forest." Fernow also sought to persuade the Timiskaming and Northern Ontario Railway and other lines to build tie-preserving plants. A correspondence school requested him to develop a home course of study in forestry.

The Canadian Society of Forest Engineers was organized at Montreal on March 14, 1908, at the annual meeting of the Canadian Forestry Association. Its membership was composed of a small but distinguished company:[4] Fernow; Zavitz; Ross; Reginald R. Bradley, forester of the Miramichi Lumber Company of Chatham, New Brunswick; G. C. Piché, forester of the Quebec provincial government; W. C. J. Hall, superintendent of the forest protective service of Quebec; Abraham Knechtel, inspector of the Dominion forest reserves, at Ottawa; E. Stewart; Thomas Southworth; Marshall C. Small, of the Laurentide Paper Company of Grand' Mère, Quebec; R. H. Campbell; and F. W. H. Jacombe, technical assistant of the forestry branch of the department of the interior, at Ottawa. Stewart, Southworth, Campbell, and Hall were not trained foresters, although they had served the forestry cause in Canada. Immediately the question arose whether or not they were entitled to full membership. When Fernow was asked, he said that the organization was intended to "keep the professional men together." Ellwood Wilson, forester of the Laurentide Paper Company, and another charter member, acknowledged to Fernow that the "plan of the Society was yours and I simply helped in the work." With respect to the first meeting, however, he commented:

I looked on in dismay at the trend of affairs and was powerless to prevent the Government men from getting control; not that I have any prejudices or any dislike to any of these men, but it seemed to me that what should be the most independent of organizations is really in the hands of men who from the very nature of their employment are bound. Then too, I do not think that the holding of a Government position entitles a man, ex-officio, so

[4] *Forestry Quarterly* VI, 1, March 1908, p. 114, says ten charter members were present. An organization committee had preceded formal organization of the society and Wilson, as a member of this committee, presided at the first meeting until the officers of the society were elected. The charter membership, as published in a four-page leaflet, consisted of more than ten members.

to speak, to election to office in our Society. For that reason I made the stand that I did in regard to Mr. Campbell's admission. . . . I insisted on you as President and I wanted the position on the executive committee. . . . At the earliest possible opportunity I shall move to amend the constitution so as to shut out entirely from the voting membership any man who is not actively engaged in the practice of Forestry and who has not some sound training. I think to gain active membership a man should have been in practice some time at least.

Fernow became the society's first president and held office for many years. It must be remembered that the Canadian Forestry Association existed for citizens of the Dominion interested in forestry. Campbell had long been a leading figure and officer. The Canadian Society of Forest Engineers was planned as an organization composed of men of the profession.[5] A forester, whether or not in government service, was entitled to membership. The matter of Campbell's admission presented a difficult question since no one had more zealously and admirably served forestry in Canada. Moreover, Campbell was a warm friend of Fernow and Wilson. Campbell became vice-president of the society, and Jacombe became secretary-treasurer. The executive committee for the years 1907-1908 was composed of these officers and Piché and Bradley. Fernow did not fear forest service officials as members. Speaking for the faculty of forestry members at Toronto and Wilson, however, he wrote to Jacombe on March 21 and insisted:

> The sole intention of our organization undoubtedly was to keep the *professional* men together. It was, therefore, a mistake to admit to active membership "officials" of the various forest services, because being official, especially since they may be, nay are apt to be, merely political appointees. I am sure the gentlemen present felt themselves that this was a mistake, and at least one of them so expressed himself to me. I am sure I need not go into lengthy arguments on this matter: it should be patent to any one who has a proper conception of the objects of a professional association.

Fernow carried this idea to such an extreme that he voted to exclude from membership Dr. Howe on the premise that he was a botanist, not a forester. He was forthright enough to tell Howe of his action, and to give his reasons. To Jacombe and others who wished to honor leaders of the Canadian forestry movement, the problem evidently was immediate but temporary. There were such men as Sir Henri, and his son, E. G. Joly de Lotbinière, "not trained foresters, and yet [they had] done far more for the cause of forestry in Canada than any trained forester among us." Fernow said, "As regards admission of Mr. Joly as [an] active member, I would favor it, but am not at all insistent. We have, I believe, an honorary membership which would perhaps, as well,

[5] J. D. B. Harrison, "President's Address," *Forestry Chronicle* XXI, 1, March 1945, p. 6, reported the Society's total membership at 452 persons. This address was delivered at the 37th annual meeting of the Society at Fort William, Ontario, Jan. 29, 1945.

take care of such cases. On second thought, I believe it will be well to admit the son at least to our active membership." Accordingly, on May 6 Secretary Jacombe announced that Wilson, seconded by Fernow, would move that the constitution be changed so that:

Active members shall consist of trained foresters resident in Canada, and the following named persons, in recognition of their eminent services in the interest of forestry previous to the advent of professional foresters, namely, E. Stewart, W. C. J. Hall, E. G. Joly de Lotbinière, R. H. Campbell, and Thomas Southworth. Only active members shall have the right of voting and holding office.

As officially constituted for the years 1907-1908, the membership embraced four classes: honorary, active, student, and associate. At the society's first informal meeting. Filibert Roth had lectured. That year, on June 25, Jacombe announced that Roth had been elected as an honorary member. On May 28 it was announced that Judson F. Clark and Roland D. Craig had been elected as active members, on June 11 H. R. MacMillan's election as an active member was announced, and on June 25 announcement was made of the election of Norman M. Ross, assistant superintendent of forestry for the Dominion. At the same time, ballots were circulated to make Charles A. Lyford an active member. Lyford's prominence was based on his completion, while a forest assistant of the United States bureau of forestry, of a forest survey of the state of New Hampshire. After leaving the bureau's employment he had become manager of a lumber company in West Virginia. A graduate of Yale in 1904, Lyford had also been a student of Fernow at the New York State College of Forestry during its last year. While in West Virginia, he and Fernow had had correspondence. Fernow was instrumental in bringing him to Canada in the capacity of forest manager of the Riordan Paper Mill Company, an employment in which he had been engaged since June 15. During these early months of the society, many ballots were circulated to elect individuals to one class of membership or another. A few may be mentioned who were elected to active membership: Professor R. B. Miller of the University of New Brunswick, Dr. Howe, G. H. Edgecombe, L. M. Ellis, J. D. Gilmour, and James R. Dickson.

Fernow's first year as dean of the faculty of forestry at Toronto was gratifying. The example in Ontario was quickly emulated in other provinces. On December 4, 1908, Fernow wrote Campbell:

I see by the papers that it is proposed to endow another forest school, at Quebec. Have you any hand in this? If so, I would suggest that what is now more necessary than another school for advanced foresters is one for logging bosses, forest rangers, etc. The only difficulty for such a school is to find capable instructors. I only want to suggest that [in view of] a multiplication of forest schools such as is going on in the United States it would be a pity to inaugurate in Canada [another] before any one is really properly on its feet and employment for their graduates assured.

On December 15, Campbell replied emphatically, "In regard to the new forest school in Quebec I may say that I am sufficiently loaded up with other business not to trouble about the school question. . . . I have not had anything to do with the starting of the school in any way whatever. . . ." Campbell regarded the new school as "superfluous." At the Canadian Forestry Convention of 1906 a forest school at Laval University had been promised. It was established as a department of the university in 1910. G. C. Piché, forester of the Quebec provincial government, became the director.

Piché had studied civil engineering at the École Polytechnique of Montreal. Between the years 1901-1903 he had worked in the woods department of a Belgian pulp company established at Shawinigan Falls, Quebec, and in 1904 chanced to read a review of the work of the school of forestry of Nancy, France. Finding the subject of much interest, he addressed a letter to Sir Lomer Gouin, then Prime Minister of Quebec, and suggested that the province provide forestry instruction by such a forest school. The Prime Minister took an alternative suggestion and, after consulting with Quebec's forest conservationist, Monsignor Laflamme, arranged that Avila Bédard from the Quebec district and Piché from the Montreal district be sent to Yale Forest School. Graduating there in 1907, both foresters were employed by the department of lands and forests of Quebec province. They were permitted to recruit a few assistants and with the aid of Monsignor Laflamme the plan of a forest school was evolved and by 1910 established as École Forestière. In 1919, one year after Piché had resigned as director to give all of his energies to the forest service of the province and during the incumbency of Bédard as director, the title of the school was to be changed to one of surveying and forest engineering, and today is known as the Faculty of Forestry of Laval University. A school for rangers would be organized in 1923 and a school of paper-making also created. Piché served for two years as president of the Canadian Society of Forest Engineers.

Ellwood Wilson,[6] born in 1872 at Philadelphia, had received a classical education at Lawrenceville Academy, New Jersey, and graduated in 1893 from the University of the South at Sewanee, Tennessee, where he specialized in botany and earned the degrees of bachelor of arts and science. For a doctorate in philosophy, Wilson had spent eighteen months in study at the University of Pennsylvania and then went to Germany where he studied with Karl Remigus Fresenius, the authority on chemical analysis. Four years were spent in England, during which Wilson established at London the Walker Gordon Laboratory Company of

[6] Material concerning Piché and Wilson obtained by the author in conferences with each, August 1948.

Boston, Massachusetts. From 1900-1905 he practiced civil engineering at Saranac Lake, New York, and then became affiliated with the Laurentide Company of Grand' Mère in Quebec province. Forestry had interested him since his youth. At fourteen years of age he had begun to read *Forest Leaves* and other sources of forestry information. The Laurentide Company sent him into their woods to survey their boundaries. He saw the conditions of their forest property and realized that some management was needed. He began to educate himself in the subject by studying the forestry literature.

European as well as American books on forestry were read. Roth's texts and published writings proved especially valuable. He studied Fernow's *Economics of Forestry*, and the works of Pinchot, Graves, Bryant, and others. Wilson was to be twice honored as president of the Canadian Society of Forest Engineers, once as president of the Canadian Forestry Association, and in 1920 he was chosen delegate from Canada to the first British Empire Forestry Conference.

He perhaps has done more for forestry in Canada than any individual connected with an industrial company. He has shared in the forestry contribution made by pulpwood companies in forest planting. He probably has planted or supervised the planting of more forests than any other individual. He has aided directly in shaping one of the best fire protective systems in Canada, devised a standardized system of mapping and estimating, inaugurated aerial mapping of forests, and demonstrated the practical application of aerial photography to land and forest classification. An acknowledged authority on silviculture, he taught the subject from 1932 to 1934 at the New York State College of Agriculture. Since then he has been a consulting forester with offices at Knowlton, Quebec province.

Fernow became acquainted with Wilson at the Saginaw, Michigan, forestry conference of November 1907. Their professional friendship and personal regard grew, and in 1908 Wilson supplied Fernow with "a short sketch of the work [the Laurentide Company was] trying to do and [Wilson's] ideas as to the conduct of large timber holdings for pulp mills" in Quebec province or where similar forest conditions prevailed. He answered Fernow's circular letter as to forest types and expressed a deep interest in forestry education. Fernow responded, and later when Wilson went to Europe and spent some time studying forestry matters, Fernow supplied him with cards of introduction. On February 24, 1911, Wilson thanked him: ". . . Messrs. Müller, Hessleman, Marchet, Schwappach, and Engler sent their best regards to you, also Phillip. . . . My trip was most successful, thanks to your cards, and I made a fairly careful study of administrative, silvicultural and lumbering conditions, besides visiting some of the schools and experiment stations. I met a good many private foresters in Norway and Sweden. . . ."

Fernow and Wilson were outspoken in their opposition to a division of energies in school and forestry association work. On April 2, 1909, Wilson wrote to Fernow, "I saw Bédard and Piché in Quebec. They are expecting a grant of $10,000 from the Quebec government for a School of Forest Rangers. . . . Piché is enthusiastic about his trip abroad." During this year the ranger school concept was advanced. This was clearly shown in a letter written by Piché to Fernow on May 6, 1909, which said:

> Things are not going smooth in Forestry affairs and our humble little school of Forest guards came almost to the point of being postponed till next year: this was the reason why I returned so abruptly from Europe. So with Monsignor Laflamme, we fought together and succeeded partly; partly as the matter is not finally decided, but I have been authorized to take in 3 more students, so that I am here [Berthierville] with six aspirants.

On February 11, 1910, Piché wrote again to Fernow, and explained that it was planned "seriously" to establish "a school of forestry . . . a government school, affiliated, however, for the degrees with one of your universities." He asked for a copy of the Toronto school's last annual report, "also with any information regarding the organization, cost of maintenance, etc." Fernow answered:

> Our school does not receive a subsidy directly from the Ontario Government, but you know, of course, that the whole university does, and to that extent, we, of course, are benefited. There is no such thing as [a grant of one million acres] in existence. There has been some talk about giving us a forest reserve,[7] but I have not pressed the matter, being satisfied for some time to shift from place to place for our practice work. . . . I am glad to hear that you propose establishing a school of forestry under the Government supervision which will, of course, commit the Government to use the men. Perhaps when this matter is more matured, or at the meeting of the Society of Forest Engineers we may talk it over.

Piché, for a while forester of the department of crown lands of the province, was to become chief forest engineer of a provincial forest service. A policy aimed at developing the forest domain, but not neglecting colonization, was promulgated. In 1911 Fernow said of Piché's work ". . . there is so far only one province which has been wise enough to introduce this technical branch into its department of lands. I refer to the province of Quebec, and it is my opinion that its progress in this respect has been really remarkable."[8]

The reservation of huge forest areas made available by a more northern transcontinental railroad, apart from the considerable private for-

[7] The Faculty of Forestry at Toronto has today a University Forest of 12,000 acres in Haliburton County. This includes areas of white pine, hemlock, and hardwood types representative of the forests of the region. It is well-suited to practice work in forestry—forest surveying and cruising, silvicultural studies, etc.

[8] *Report of the Canadian Forestry Association* held at Quebec on Jan. 18-20, 1911, p. 19.

ests on farmlands and seigniories and forests under lease or timber limits, led Piché to point out that no other country owned "such a reserve," an unleased forest area of 80,000,000 acres "free from any servitude."[9] The aggregate worth of Quebec forests was estimated at a minimum of $450,000,000. On September 15, 1910, the opening of a forest school[10] made it possible within the province to equip foresters and rangers to oversee conservative lumbering and extend the provincial forest protective branch. More or less coordinated with the forest service was a government hydraulic service, representing a movement which spread through a number of Canadian provinces to protect and develop water power. Staffed to do exploratory and survey work, classify soils, and eventually to administer an ambitious program of reforesting waste and cut-over farmlands, the forest service's growth spanned the years from 1907, when the forest nursery at Berthierville was established, to 1911-1912,[11] when Piché, confident of Quebec's forestry leader-

[9] "The Forest Service of Quebec," *ibid.*, pp. 81-91; also Piché's discussion of forest conditions and plans for Quebec forests in *13th Report of the Annual Convention of the Canadian Forestry Association*, 1912, pp. 100-102; Avila Bédard (Prof. of Silviculture at Laval Univ.), "Forestry Education in Quebec," *Report of Can. For. Convention*, 1911, pp. 100-103; Jules Allard (Minister of Lands and Forests), "Forestry Organization in Quebec," *ibid.* pp. 28-31, in which the Minister said that Quebec had established 111,400,900 acres of forest reserves.

[10] "The Forest Service of Quebec," *op. cit.* The creation of the forest school at Laval University was a distinct advance over the "humble little school of Forest guards." Piché wrote to Fernow, "I just returned from my trip in Europe, having visited somewhat hastily France, Germany (Eberswalde) and Sweden." *Forestry Quarterly* VIII, 3, Sept. 1910, p. 399, announced the establishment of the department at Laval, saying that it was to be "a high grade school instead of ranger school which [was] much more needed in Canada." On October 20, 1910, Piché answered Fernow's comment, "Our school is working its way ahead. I have appreciated your critic[ism] that 'it was another high school.' I believe like you that there are not enough low schools, but our position was such that we had to start higher than we wanted really. As you are perhaps aware Mr. Langelier had some 60 forest rangers under him who were appointed by influence, etc. To dismiss this staff was impossible, but to replace them gradually has been our scheme. In order to establish a good service and to compete with the old system, the would-be student has been obliged to begin as a forest ranger. . . . We will have a lower school at Berthierville, that will serve to train and educate the forest rangers. We expect to start it in 1912, that is when I will be able to leave the other school to work alone. . . ." Piché had been given "full charge over all the lumbering operations." On April 12, 1915, Piché explained to Fernow, "Our program of studies requires that the candidate must have a training equivalent to that of a BS and during the three years of studies—1200 lectures—we aim to develop a man having a fair knowledge of engineering, who will be able not only to build up a forest but to make the lumbering operations necessary for the harvest of the various crops, and to take advantage of the various possibilities to utilize his products to the best advantages. . . ." To this letter Piché appended a note saying, "I intend to withdraw from the management of the School, in favor of my friend Bédard, who will give more of his time to the School."

[11] The creation of township reserves was an especially interesting development in Quebec. Piché told the 13th Annual Convention of the Canadian Forestry Association in 1912 that there were then eleven such reserves in the province, aggregating some 120,000 acres. More were created later. Fernow's early influence in provincial forestry may be inferred from the fact that his lectures at the School of Mining at Kingston in 1903 were translated into French, probably by Monsignor Laflamme, and published under the title, *La Forêt*, by the Quebec department of lands and forests.

ship, promised that even more would be accomplished in the future. Ontario and Quebec early took the lead in forestry development in Canada. One other province soon shared leadership in forestry education, New Brunswick. Again a Yale graduate, R. B. Miller, took charge of this forestry department, fortunate in having its own forest near the university. Fernow maintained cordial relations with each institution, inviting contributions from each to *Forestry Quarterly*. Piché kept Fernow informed of what "little progresses [were being made] in our forestry organization." At least as soon as 1908 Piché responded to Fernow's offers of cooperation and collaboration. There was no rivalry. From its beginning the Quebec school developed foresters for its own province. Special emphasis was placed on forest engineering.

In October 1908 forestry instruction began at the University of New Brunswick at Fredericton, which was regarded at the time as "the second Forest School to be established in Canada."[12] At the provincial forestry convention held at Fredericton in February 1907, it was reported that funds to create a chair of forestry would be asked of the government, and $2,500 was granted when Chancellor C. C. Jones outlined a course of instruction. The department was created as part of a movement to improve the forest laws of the province.[13] Addressing the Canadian Forestry Association at Toronto in 1908 on "What We Want,"[14] Fernow welcomed the "similar step in the University of New Brunswick" to that taken at the University of Toronto "for the education of . . . technical men . . . although I am not an advocate of multiplication, but rather of increase in quality of educational institutions." Forestry progress in the United States had become a reality only after years of effort. Fernow said:

> It took 30 years of persistent propaganda to advance forestry interests in the United States so far as to secure for them at least a respectful hearing, and, if it had not been for the accident of a wealthy, independent idealist [Gifford Pinchot] and a fearless, independent, idealistic president [Theodore Roosevelt] coming together to Washington, the remarkably rapid progress made there during the last ten years in governmental forest administration would very likely not have occurred.

The New Brunswick school had had to give a principal share of its attention to the forest problems of its province. A very important feature of its work had been to train students in forest land surveying for work with large pulp and paper concerns.

In Canada Fernow proved to be no more adept at getting large ap-

[12] *Report of 10th Ann. Meeting of Can. For. Ass.*, March 11, 1909, p. 158.

[13] E. G. Joly de Lotbinière, *Report of Can. For. Convention*, 1906, pp. 17ff.; *Forestry and Irrigation* XIII, 4, April 1907, p. 174; R. B. Miller, "General Forestry Conditions and Forestry Education in New Brunswick," *Report of 10th Ann. Meeting of Can. For. Ass.*, pp. 69-74; W. B. Snowball, *ibid.* p. 41.

[14] *ibid.*, pp. 74-82.

propriations for forestry work. His thrifty German temperament sought to reduce expenditures to a minimum, but more than once, desiring to put across some worthwhile but expensive accomplishment, he was forced to complain of his institution's "chronic poverty." As late as 1910 he admitted to Piché, and repeatedly made similar reports to the president of the University of Toronto, "When I undertook to organize this Faculty, I made it a condition that, eventually, i.e. when we were in full running order, we should have not less than $12,000 to spend. As long as these classes have been so small, I have tried to get along with less and we have actually not spent more than around $8,000."

Fernow had retained his capacity as a consulting forester. Faithfully he had continued to perform his duties as editor-in-chief of *Forestry Quarterly*. His employment, however, made him also an advisor on matters of forest policy to the Ontario government. When investigating pulpwood forest lands on Cape Breton Island, Nova Scotia, he was consulted about "the pulpwood question" of the Dominion. He saw that there were certain regions, in some instances entire provinces, that needed special study. Nova Scotia was such a province. Ontario was another. Ecologists, notably the botanist George Elwood Nichols of Yale University, shared Fernow's enthusiasm for Cape Breton Island. In 1905 Nichols had "packed along the east shore [of] a section across the barrens from North River to Intervale," and again in 1909, before beginning his extensive ecological studies, he had "spent a month camping near Indian Brook." The region, therefore, was "not entirely unfamiliar country" to him, but, in 1914, planning "an ecological survey of the northern half of the western arm of Cape Breton Island," he consulted Fernow concerning literature on the geography and geology of this area.

From the start of his Canadian experience Fernow had recognized his duty to the Ontario government. He took the position that Ontario had first claim on the school's and students' services. But to his amazement, when he told the Ontario minister of lands, forests, and mines, F. W. Cochrane, that the province was without a proper forest policy, that what policy, except as to fire protection, the province had was destructive of the forests, and that someday the minister personally would be held accountable to the people, Fernow was shown to the door.

Fernow vigorously pursued his program in Canada. He spoke before a number of gatherings, among them the Canadian Manufacturers Association, to whom he spoke on "A Forest Policy for Canada, How to Perpetuate a Great National Resource,"[15] and to the Canadian Club of Montreal in January of 1908 he spoke on "Canada's Interest in Forestry." In the latter address he pointed out that only that week the On-

[15] *Industrial Canada* VIII, 3, Oct. 1907.

tario government had "committed itself to all the propositions which a forester could reasonably demand, namely, increase of the protective service, extension of the reservation policy, equitable arrangements with the present license holders, and disposal of timber henceforth under forestry rules." The announcement of this new, rational, conservative policy had so elated Fernow that he interpreted it as "a testimony of justification" for the existence of the faculty of forestry. But he was interested in the forest resources of all of Canada. His Montreal address continued:

> What then is needed in Canada everywhere above all other measures in dealing with the forest problems is (1) reduction of the causes of forest fires; (2) increase of the forces to prevent the origin of forest fires and to extinguish them; (3) such division in the use of soils as will open to settlement only bona fide farm soils; (4) such administration of the remaining timber wealth as recognizes the interests of the future. . . . That I may not appear as only criticizing and fault-finding, I shall add that beginnings in developing these ideas practically have been made by the Dominion Government in the West, and by the Province of Quebec.

To the Canadian Club of Toronto he spoke in February 26 on "The Forest Policy of Canada." He argued that the sawmill capacity of the United States could exhaust the U.S. timber resources and that that nation would have to look to Canada, that rises in timber prices were inevitable, that Canada's water power resources could be threatened by forest depletion, that the future of the wood-consuming industries depended on the policies of the eastern provinces and British Columbia, that there was need of technical advice and forest reserve management as well as regulation of logging and timber sales, and that there was need to segregate lands fit for colonization from that fit only for forest growth. Forest denudation and soil destruction already threatened civilized life on large areas in North America. He told the Canadian Club of Montreal: "If you want to study the effects of denudation in your own country, visit the Sudbury or the Muskoka districts and you will see how a rock desert is started. As yet, only here and there noticeable, soon the repetition of fires—and they repeat themselves easily on ground once burnt—will produce results such as are described by Prof. Roth from Wisconsin; a close neighbour in some respects not unsimilar to your conditions. A careful inspection from town to town made ten years ago brought out the information that of the eight million acres of cut over land one half is as nearly desert as it can become in the climate of Wisconsin. *A desert of four million acres made by man in less than fifty years.*" Soil deterioration invariably means deterioration of water conditions. Again quoting from Roth's report of "Forestry Conditions and Interests of Wisconsin," Fernow pointed out: "The flow of all rivers has changed during the last forty years; navigation has been abandoned on the Wisconsin, logging and rafting has become more difficult on all rivers, and the Fox River is failing to furnish the power which it formerly supplied in abundance."

"I repeat," warned Fernow, "now is the time for abandoning the politician's method, who works for the day and to please his party, and to substitute a statesman's broad view, who works for all time and to please the country now and forever."

Before the Orillia Canadian Club on March 19, 1909, Fernow spoke on "An Analysis of Canada's Forest Wealth," also the subject of his informative article which had appeared in 1908 in *Forestry Quarterly*[16] under the title, "An Analysis of Canada's Timber Wealth."

The Canadian Clubs of various cities of the Dominion were regarded by President Robert A. Falconer of the University of Toronto as a "movement... unique and distinctly Canadian. Nowhere else, so far as I know," he had told the Orillia Club, "are there such institutions. The gathering together of the young men, and all that is most virile in the community, to consider in a non-partisan way what is best for the country, cannot but have a great effect in promoting the good of Canada." To the members of the Canadian Club of Berlin, Ontario, Fernow presented on October 22, 1909, a discussion of "The Conservation of Canada's Forests."

Earlier in that year there had assembled in Washington a joint conference of representatives from Canada, the United States, and Mexico, which became known as the National Conservation Commission. In response to the historic conference of state governors in 1908, President Roosevelt had appointed a national committee to investigate natural resources and their conservation. State governments had established cooperating committees. The work of the subcommittee on forestry was notable. The United States forest service furnished data. Letters asking for suggestions were sent to the American Railway Association and other organizations. Early in December, after six months of work, a meeting of the commission was held in Washington to prepare the report requested by President Roosevelt.[17] A renowned document, its preliminary outline had been sent to Fernow during the summer, and it appeared the next year.

In Canada, by an act of parliament, a commission for the conservation of natural resources was established. Not until 1910 was its first annual meeting held. Fernow had been appointed a member of the Canadian conservation commission, and he addressed the first annual meeting. By 1909 a world conference on the subject was proposed, an International Commission like the North American Commission, and Fernow rejoiced

16 VI, 3, Sept. 1908, p. 334, and reprint. See also a preliminary study, *Canadian Engineer*, Dec. 4, 1908, pp. 858f.

17 *Torreya* VIII, 12, Dec. 1908, p. 302.

that formal government recognition had come to the cause to which he had given practically all of his years in America.

In 1909 the national forest movement in the United States crossed the Mississippi River and invaded the eastern states. President Roosevelt proclaimed the Ocala National Forest in Marion County, eastern Florida, and another North Dakota reservation, part of which was to be used for experimental forest planting.[18]

Fernow always took account of forestry progress in the United States. In his addresses, however, he accepted the doctrine which Roth laughingly criticized, "Canada for the Canadians." Most of Fernow's addresses were given as a part of university extension work. On March 31, 1909, he reported his season's audiences: the Nova Scotia Lumbermen's Association, the summer school at Toronto University, the Faculty of Education Literary Society of Toronto, the Canadian Club of Toronto, the Bathurst Methodist Church of Toronto, the Natural History Society of Hamilton, the Canadian Clubs of Stratford, Orillia, and Montreal, the Teachers' Association of Campbellford, and the high school at Cobourg.

The *Toronto Globe*,[19] had long supported the forestry cause. For it Fernow wrote "The Urgent Need of a Forward Forestry Policy," in which he said:

> The Dominion Government, as far as it could, may be said to have advanced the most. It has set aside, in its domain of over 2,500,000 square miles, some 10,000,000 acres or more as forest reservations, but it must not be overlooked that, while this is an important action for insuring local wood supplies and preserving satisfactory waterflow and cultural conditions, it has, with the exception of the small area reserved in British Columbia, nothing to do with the question of commercial timber supply, for the reservations are located in the region where practically commercial timber is absent and only domestic needs can be supplied. Similarly, while the Dominion Government's policy of encouraging tree planting on the prairies and plains is most commendable, and may lead to make life in the treeless country more pleasant, this has no bearing on the grave question of future timber supply, for such timber supply can only be produced in the natural forest country.

The organization of a forestry branch in the Dominion service, the adoption of a ranger system of patrol, the beginnings of investigating forest conditions in the reservations, and the regulation of exports were other elements which would in time make a real forest policy. But on January 20, 1909, Fernow told Consul General Franksen at Montreal, "The Forest Service in Canada is still in the most embryonic condition. . . . The only actually operating forest department in existence

[18] In this year also President Roosevelt signed a bill creating the Calaveras National Forest, containing 1,400 sequoias over six feet in diameter. See *Torreya* IX, 5, May 1909, p. 106 (referring to *Science*, March 19, 1909); also IX, p. 64.

[19] Feb. 29, 1908, p. 4.

is the Forestry Branch of the Dominion at Ottawa, R. H. Campbell, Superintendent." Not very much forestry advancement could actually be found in the provinces. He had told Robert B. Allen of the *Pacific Lumber Trade Journal* two days before:

> I have no definite statistics showing the acreage of stumpage conditions for Canada. They are not in existence. All that anyone can do is to study the geography and casual reports and estimate upon some reasonable premises. . . . Perhaps you do not realize that I am merely a teacher of young students at the University and not in charge of any Government work, hence my efforts are all of a private nature.
>
> You know, of course, that several of the eastern Provinces have a Forest Fire Service, which, on account of the political conditions surrounding it, work only indifferently. You may also know that the Province of Ontario last year started buying up waste lands in the agricultural sections for reforestation, and it is expected that this move of the administration will be translated into a law establishing municipal forests.

Nova Scotia, Fernow believed, had a "really good Forest Protective organization, mainly run by the Lumbermen's Association." After "the horse was practically stolen," the maritime provinces had introduced "a system of fire protection of the remaining fillies." A special agency was needed. In the December 10, 1908, issue of the *Farmers' Advocate* Fernow had discussed "The Farmers' Interest in Forestry." He had commended the Ontario government on its policy of reforesting waste land.[20] This should be done extensively on large tracts, and farmers could well do the same on limited areas.[21] He believed that four or five hundred square miles in areas of 3,000 acres or more could be located for such purposes. After all, four thousand dollars or less was not a very large amount of money to invest in such worthy work. Moreover, in Ontario, of fifty million acres of forest land which might be set aside, only ten million acres had been reserved, and as yet, except for fire protection,[22] no real forestry administration had been introduced. Almost no measures were being taken to "husband the actually grown crop of virgin timber," and wasteland areas were increasing. Fernow had explained that in a virgin forest there really was no substantive growth in volume. Increment was offset by decay and other destructive elements. Weed trees, after lumbering, often tended to crowd out more valuable species, unless provision was made for proper care of young growth and crop regeneration.

Fernow often spoke before the general public, but he was a specialist and as often as he could he presented his discussions to persons of special

20 "The Urgent Need of a Forward Forestry Policy," *op. cit.*

21 "Waste Land Planting at Home and in Foreign Countries," *Farm and Dairy and Rural Home* XXVIII, 44, Nov. 4, 1909.

22 "The History and Status of Forestry in Ontario," *Canadian Geographical Journal* XXV, 3, Sept. 1942, p. 135.

standing in the profession. In 1907 *Forestry and Irrigation*[23] published his study, "Financial Results of Forest Management."

In December 1908 Fernow received an invitation from the Canadian Mining Institute to "prepare a short paper . . . giving mining men some advice on the conservation of timber on their properties." Accordingly, at the institute's annual meeting at Montreal in March 1909, he spoke on "The Relation of Mining to Forestry." In preparation for this address Fernow sent out a circular letter to mine managers of the Dominion. Their answers and a mine canvass made some twenty years before furnished a basis of the address. Results showed that the mining interests were still vitally interested in timber supply and timber conservation. In the eastern provinces, although pine, tamarack, and hemlock were available, spruce was still the favorite timber used. Different species were used in various regions, especially where the mining companies owned their own limits. He pleaded for a forestry interest among mining companies. Forestry was more than tree planting. The forests were not mines. Forests are an exhaustible, but restorable, resource. "In other words," he admonished, "just as [mining companies] apply system and technical skill in exploiting their mines, they should manage their wood property; they should practice *forestry.*" Concerning another industry, he added:

> The first intelligent class of manufacturers, which has realized that provision for continuity of supplies of raw material is absolutely necessary, are the paper manufacturers, who have begun to practice forestry on their limits. Thus the Laurentide Paper Company employs a forester with a staff of 42 men to manage their land holdings. The Riordan Paper Company has commenced this work with a staff of a forester and 12 assistants to prepare for a regular management.[24]

Ellwood Wilson of the Laurentide Company had offered to make his company a "department" of the university, to afford the students an opportunity to learn fire ranging, estimating by the strip method and by sample acres, inspecting, valuation surveying, mapping, forest description, tree analysis, height measuring, camping, cooking, canoeing, and other activities. By a letter dated December 5, 1908, Wilson told Fernow, "In my humble opinion a forester is no forester unless he can find his way in the woods, handle the woods gear and understand practical conditions." Fernow described Wilson's propositions as "capital," so delighted was he to find "someone willing to take a real interest in the progress of our men." During the past summer three upperclassmen had been employed by the Turner Lumber Company as fire rangers and

[23] XIII, 2, pp. 81-86.

[24] Published by the Canadian Mining Institute, pp. 87-92. See also "Commercial Forest Planting," *Journal of Forestry* XVII, 1, Jan. 1919, pp. 95, 103; XVII, 3, March 1919, pp. 338, 349.

to make forest descriptions and surveys. "At the end of the summer," Fernow said, "they were complete woodsmen." Students had joined a rifle association. The school was trying to include in its curriculum a course on fish and fish culture. In the Foresters' Club arrangements were being made to study camp cooking. These activities were additional to the annual Christmas vacation visits to logging camps and the spring *practicums* at various forest locations. Roth also corresponded with Wilson about summer employment for some of his men. Experimental work supervised by Wilson was already in progress, and the results of some of it were offered for use in *Forestry Quarterly.*[25] A group went to Wilson that summer; among them was L. M. Ellis, who later became forester of the Canadian Pacific Railway.

During this period the Riordan Paper Company also engaged in work of special importance. On June 9, 1910, Fernow told Wilson, "I saw, on my way through Montreal, Mr. Carl Riordan who told me that they have finished their forest survey at the expense of some $50,000 and were now ready to make working plans." Lyford, it will be remembered, was in charge of forestry for this company.[26] A forest survey of 1750 square miles on the Rouge River was completed during his employment.

Eventually the work included large scale forest planting. Reforestation, age and vigor classification of tree species, growth and yield, and other special forest problems were studied experimentally. Site classification groupings were also included. Wilson reported to Fernow on November 18, 1909, that in addition to performing a fire ranging service along ninety miles of the transcontinental railroad for the province and timber limit holders, the Laurentide Company's "own fire ranging [had] also been successful. . . . We have mapped and located on our maps burns, black spruce swamps & pure types, nearly 400 square miles. We have measured nearly 1,000 trees as a nucleus for volume tables & last winter measured accurately at both ends over 3,000 balsam & about 2,500 spruce logs, in the woods, of nearly all diameters which we cut, & have worked up some tables from them." Educational and practical considerations were involved. Especially valuable at this time was the work in forest fire prevention. Early in 1910 the Canadian Forestry Association appointed a committee, with Fernow and Wilson as members, to recommend improved and uniform fire legislation among the provinces of the Dominion. A log rule committee, including Judson F. Clark, who worked out a cubic foot scale, was also at work. On April 19, 1910, Fernow told Wilson, "I have an indication that you may be-

[25] E. Wilson, "A Forester's Work in a Northern Forest," *Forestry Quarterly* VII, 1, March 1909, p. 2; "Survey Methods and Costs for a Large Area," *ibid.* VIII, 3, Sept. 1910, p. 287.

[26] See Fernow's "Saving the Tremendous Waste of Forest Fires," *Country Life in America* XII, Aug. 1907, pp. 414ff., on the costs and results of forest fire fighting in the United States and Canada, especially in New York.

come connected with the Commission of Conservation. If so, the report of the Forest Fire Committee and that of the Commission might become identical and be best in your hands."

James H. White, first graduate of the faculty of forestry at the University of Toronto, who became a lecturer and assistant in the school, was offered a place as assistant secretary of the commission. He refused, and the offer was made to Wilson, who chose to remain in industrial work.

Cooperative efforts of foresters and private industrial concerns have characterized forestry development in Canada. Students, foresters, and the private companies have found the work advantageous. The forestry principle and practical use of the permanent sample plot has been extended to basic forest research by government forest administrations. In this the pioneer work of Dr. Howe has been outstanding in Canada. Hundreds of forest acres have been dedicated to these purposes, in cooperation with government agencies and private pulpwood and lumber companies. The work has stimulated artificial reforestation and timberland management. Recognizing the need to put forestry more and more on a biological basis, research has been invigorated in laboratory and field study of the commercial uses of previously neglected forest species. Birch and poplar may be cited as examples. Fernow saw the use of sample plots by private companies reach into Newfoundland. On January 22, 1919, J. D. Gilmour, a graduate from Toronto employed by the Anglo-Newfoundland Development Company, wrote to Fernow, "We are going ahead with our sample plots and think that in time we will obtain something worth while." Private companies and governments established experimental cutting areas, and other areas for investigation in forest protection and management, notably forest entomology and forest pathology, and the introduction of ecological techniques has greatly aided in establishing answers to special forest problems. Older techniques—for example, clear cutting and replanting—have been converted to new uses.

Forestry Quarterly provided Fernow with opportunities to keep foresters of the United States informed of Canadian developments. Soon after his arrival in Canada, however, the existence of the *Quarterly* had been threatened. Although the publishing office remained at Ithaca, and Fernow indicated no intention to relinquish his citizenship in the United States, foresters of the United States assumed that the *Quarterly* would become a Canadian publication or the official organ of the faculty of forestry of the University of Toronto. On August 24, 1908, Dean Graves informed Fernow that the Society of American Foresters had approved a proposal to publish contributed articles in its *Proceedings.*

The status of science in forestry on the American continent was reflected in this correspondence. Graves had written on September 20, 1907:

> I have felt for a long time dissatisfied with the contributions that I have been able to make to the *Quarterly*. I have been interested in the paper and have desired to help build it up. I have been, however, in a sense, a long distance helper and the fact that we are still further separated emphasizes the difficulty. I cannot help feeling that we ought to have in the United States a technical paper which will be thoroughly representative of the whole country and be supported both financially and through contributions by the foresters throughout the West, as well as in the East. As I understand it, the *Quarterly* from now on will be really an official organ of the University of Toronto and, in a sense officially a Canadian periodical. Of course, the work of forestry in this country is now, and will continue to be, centered in Washington. It seems to me that there should be a technical periodical supported by the Society of American Foresters.

Fernow replied on October 9, 1907:

> I can of course understand the patriotic feeling which would not accept a publication whose editor and publisher lives three hours north of Buffalo instead of four hours east. There was and is no intention ever of making the *Quarterly* an "official" organ of Toronto University or official in any way, although the University offered to take over the burden of publishing it, having me entire arbiter of the editorial side. I did not accept the offer because I expected that the transfer would arouse the patriotic remonstrance alluded to, and hence I am still printing and distributing it from Ithaca. Now, I would like to ask two questions. 1. Would it be possible, desirable, and meet with approbation, to take over the *Quarterly* and continue it on similar lines as in the past? 2. Is it proposed to run the new journal on the same lines of the *Quarterly* i.e. the same department in the same manner? If I could have some light on these questions, I would readily come to a conclusion of what to do. Meanwhile, will you not allow your name and support to continue to the end of volume 5 which will occur with the end of the year?

Fernow told Graves that he thought that the society could properly publish a journal. But "someone with time to do the editing creditably" would have to be found. He awaited the pleasure of the society and told Zon, "I had long ago expected, and even hoped that the burden of the publication would be sooner or later taken from my shoulders. . . . I am ready at any time to abdicate, and I have suggested to [Graves] what I consider the decent thing, and which you seem to indicate as possible, namely, that the Society continue to publish [the *Quarterly*] on improved lines, and, in recognition of my services in having carried it on so long, allow me representation on the Board of Editors."

Fernow definitely had decided that if the society concluded to publish a journal other than *Forestry Quarterly* he would discontinue the *Quarterly*. He told this to Frederick Dunlap. He wrote and asked Zon how far the plan had "progressed, and whether the publication [would] be such as to exclude the *Quarterly* from the market, that is to say," he added, "whether it is to be of the same nature?" The question whether the Society's *Proceedings* would be transformed to a journal similar to the *Quarterly* and compete with the latter, or would merge *Forestry Quarterly* and publish more than strictly professional papers, was not settled for a number of years. Fernow always had lost financially on the *Quarterly*. Nothing now, he must have known, could dim his prestige. But his editorial leadership, and the forestry relations of Canada and the United States, might be affected.

On behalf of a committee of which Roth, Fisher, Schenck, and Zon were also members, Graves explained the motivation behind the proposal. It was, Graves said, "to make the Society of American Foresters what it ought to be, namely, an active influence in developing the science and upholding the standard of the profession. At the present time," Graves explained in a letter of November 14, 1907, "the activities of the Society are confined to the meetings in Washington. . . . The design is to stimulate scientific observation and research, to encourage the field men to write up their experiences and observations, to encourage public discussion of technical matters, and thus bring about an agreement on many points now in dispute." Fernow told Graves, "You understand, of course, that whenever the Society so decides, I shall be very glad to hand over the *Quarterly*, under reasonable arrangements."

Zon, too, understood that Fernow had decided to transfer the *Quarterly* with him to Canada. Believing that, it was to be expected that foresters of the United States would wish a technical journal published, and the *Proceedings* was the only other technical journal. But in a letter of November 19 Zon said more:

> *The Forestry Quarterly* cannot be devoted to pure abstract science as for instance a mathematical magazine would be, but must necessarily, if it is to be of interest to foresters, discuss problems close at home. . . . As far as I can make out from conversation with Professor Graves, there is not the least desire on the part of the committee to crowd out *The Forestry Quarterly*, and it would be exceedingly painful to some of the Cornellians who were more or less closely associated with it at first to see it go and then be forgotten. If you think, however, that the transformed *Proceedings*, which intend, I believe, to include a great deal of the features of a current magazine will compete with *The Forestry Quarterly*, could not some arrangement be made by which the two could be merged, and your efforts, together with the efforts of the Society of American Foresters, applied to produce a magazine of which we all would be proud? . . . The Society of American Foresters, as you can judge by the last *Proceedings*, has a goodly number of first-class articles and since the Society promises to be more active in the future, there will be no trouble in securing all the original articles that will be needed.

Graves's name was retained on the editorial board of the *Quarterly*. In January 1908 Zon informed Fernow that Graves was "not entirely prepared to recommend the publication of a regular periodical by the Society." Graves also wrote:

> The delay in the matter of the new publication of the Society of American Foresters is entirely my fault. My whole feeling about the matter is that something must be done to make the Society of American Foresters worth while, if it is to have any existence at all. . . . I cannot help feeling that our profession is losing a great deal because relatively few men are doing any writing and there is really no scientific activity on the part of any Association such as is possible by the Society of American Foresters.

Fernow replied:

> I am perfectly agreed with you, as I wrote you, that the Society of American Foresters should be able to publish a first-class journal, and that a monthly. But before that is done, much more interest in professional questions will be necessary than is exhibited in our subscription list, which contains many more subscribers of non-professional character than of young men who have graduated from the forest schools. I am still paying from $100.00 to $200.00 to the support of the *Quarterly*, besides my work.

To this, Graves answered:

> I am very much surprised to hear that your subscription list does not comprise a larger proportion of the graduates of the forest schools. For a number of years I have been struggling with the tendency on the part of some men to regard the executive and practical side of forestry of so much more importance than the scientific as to more or less lose their interest in the latter as soon as they leave the school. This is very well illustrated in the lack of interest and support of the Society of American Foresters. I believe that the failure of a good many men to subscribe is very easily explained and may be corrected. It is not due to any feeling that the *Quarterly* is not what it should be, for I have never heard anything but the highest praise for it. It is rather the tendency to regard the scientific side of forestry of comparatively little importance and this is why I am very anxious to see the Society of American Foresters amount to something in the scientific way.

Graves stirred up a revival of scientific interest. *Forestry Quarterly* went on "in the same unsatisfactory way," Fernow said, with Graves and E. A. Sterling his principal helpers. Fernow never questioned the "propriety" of the society's establishing a journal of its own. Graves concluded that while the society was not "ready for a regular periodical," the *Proceedings* might be extended to include contributed articles, with no news notes or book reviews, and "issued from time to time whenever enough material [could] be gotten together." An editorial board was to select and edit the papers. Fernow at Toronto found the same difficulty "as regards assistance with the briefing of material in foreign languages. Little "change of style" in *Forestry Quarterly* and little improvement along the lines Fernow desired was found possible. Fernow found some consolation in the belief that Graves had found it was not "so simple an affair to run a publication." Fernow believed that Graves "himself [was] fully enough occupied." The matter was left that at some future time the *Proceedings* might become a monthly publication, and the matter of a "combination with the *Quarterly*" could then again be taken up. Graves wrote in a letter to Fernow, "If we can ultimately bring about a forest society which will be representative of the whole continent, I think that it would be an admirable thing, and then its organ would also be representative of both Canada and the United States." Fernow agreed, and on February 21, 1908, he told Graves, "From my point of view [it would be] desirable and practicable, namely, to make common cause and publish either a Quarterly or a more frequent 'continental' periodical, under the auspices of the Society, with the University of Toronto represented on the Board of Editors."

Members of a university committee had suggested this course to Fernow. The final arrangement with the University of Toronto, so far as *Forestry Quarterly* was concerned, was to publish a certain number of copies with the university imprint for distribution in Canada. For the *Proceedings* an editorial board was organized consisting of the president ex-officio, Graves, Fernow, Roth, Zon, Schenck, Cary, Price, and Herbert A. Smith. Graves, as editor-in-chief, and Smith and Zon made up the executive committee charged with selecting and editing the papers. On April 23, 1908, Fernow acknowledged a letter from President Pinchot thus:

> I accept with pleasure the call to serve on the Editorial Board of the Society of American Foresters, with the objects of which I am in full sympathy, and I hope the relation will result in mutual benefit and co-operation among the professional men on both sides of the line.

Fernow, on going to Canada, followed for a number of years a practice of attending only those conferences in the United States which had a special bearing on forestry problems of Canada. In his first year he had attended the Saginaw Lake States conference,[27] called to secure uniformity of tax legislation, extension of uniform forest policies in the white pine belt, and better protection against fires. On November 15, 1907, he wrote R. H. Campbell of it, saying, "It was a rousing meeting, and I was gratified to see how much progress there has been in the last few years since I have dropped out of public life in those states. Wisconsin led the list with the most efficient service."

At the conference Fernow presented a paper, "Taxation of Woodlands." There was no doubt of a need for just taxation, as there was need for proper methods to estimate forest land values, whether for

[27] *Forestry Quarterly* V, 4, Dec. 1907, p. 455. At this time Fernow and Dr. William Saunders, Director of the Central Experimental Farms at Ottawa, were seeking to have a Dominion Arboretum established. On November 20, 1907, Saunders wrote to Fernow, "Sir Wm. Meredith expressed himself so strongly about the proposed arboretum that I think you will find him ready to assist in taking this matter up warmly. . . . The seed sown by you in past years is bound to bear good fruit sooner or later. . . ."

rent, sale, or tax purposes. Fernow questioned how far the taxing power could be used to enhance permanent forest revenue producing investments. He saw educational value in discussions of equitable taxation.

From October 6-9, 1908, Toronto was host to an International Conference on State and Local Taxation. Addresses were made by Fred Rogers Fairchild on "The Taxation of Timber Lands in the United States," by A. C. Shaw on "Taxation of Forest Lands," and by Fernow on "Forest Taxation and Conservation as Practiced in Canada." Fairchild was of Yale University; Shaw from the United States forest service. The conference was held under the auspices of the International Tax Association of Columbus, Ohio. Fernow had believed, and Fairchild seemed to substantiate the belief, that destruction due to "unconservative exploitation" had not been related to taxation. Tax law revisions, therefore, could promote conservation and sound forestry practice.

Forestry Quarterly[28] published both of Fernow's addresses, which were also published by the conferences. In Michigan Fernow created so favorable an impression that John H. Bissell, president of the Michigan Forestry Association, consulted Fernow concerning the wording of a proposed state-lands-and-forest provision to be incorporated in the state constitution. Fernow drafted a provision which required the state to reinvest proceeds from public land sales in state improvement, and unsold non-agricultural lands were to be reserved as state forests under management. Roth was not having an easy time in Michigan, but he had a rugged philosophy, he wrote to Fernow:

> The discord element is what I like. We have had mush enough to spare. I want discord. I have come to fight and am at it now, and shall not quit. Your critics would say that your criticisms did you and the cause harm; the Fact is they have done more to awaken the *right spirit* than ten times all your other labors combined. We have a jolly row on about Fire Protection and the fires are burning lustily this very day and are making propaganda against present political *shysterdom*. . . . We have enrolled 46 new ones. . . . I feel quite sure of 50 new men. Had a great *Campfire* on our farm last night, a jolly function. . . . Congratulations on last *Quarterly*; hope you keep it up. After a year or so I too hope to be able to help a little.

That year, on November 4, 1908, the Wisconsin board of forestry commissioners and Chairman Garfield of the Lake States forestry conference called a second meeting to be held at Madison. Michigan also had a meeting which Roth described to Fernow as "good." Fernow replied on December 9, "I am sorry that I missed both the meetings, yours and the Wisconsin one, but I was too full of work to leave here. I am continually called upon to deliver myself on Canada's Forest Con-

[28] V, 4, Dec. 1907, pp. 373ff.; VI, 1, March 1908, pp. 107ff., 4, Dec. 1908, pp. 387-392.

ditions and Policy."[29] Fernow particularly regretted that he could not accept the Wisconsin invitation, since he held a degree from that institution and "might have renewed [his] friendship."

On November 20, 1908, Fernow sent to members of the Canadian Society of Forest Engineers a letter which read:

> The first need, it appears to me, is better knowledge of our forest conditions from the economic, as well as silvicultural, point of view. The economic inquiry is, to be sure, too wide to be advanced much outside of government offices, but the silvicultural inquiry can most advantageously be forwarded by our members.
>
> For this purpose, allow me to ask you to describe in detail the local *forest types* which occur in the region in which you are working, or are best acquainted, with a view of securing simplification, as well as uniformity, of description and nomenclature.

At this time Fernow's own study of "the geographical and regional types of Canadian forests," later presented as "An Analysis of Canada's Timber Wealth," was being prepared.[30] He urged, however, that "what [was] now needed [was] a differentiation of local types." On November 17 Fernow had written Dr. C. Hart Merriam, chief of the biological survey of the United States department of agriculture, "It is with the greatest delight that I received your [Bulletin] Number 27 three days ago, just as I was finishing up my first paper on 'Forest Types in Canada,' and you may feel assured that I cut open the pages . . . with eagerness, possibly to catch a few new ideas."

The responses to Fernow's request for local forest type studies were neither numerous nor exact. Fernow's answer to Roland D. Craig of Vancouver, British Columbia, explained, "I shall look forward with great interest to your description of the various types which you have made in British Columbia, including of course the altitude types etc. . . . What I really wanted was a physical description of the types. In this connection I would call your attention to the article by Zon in the last *Forestry Quarterly*." Piché of Quebec approved the "suggestion of doing some cooperative work" and promised to send from time to time short descriptions "of the few types [he] had studied." H. R. MacMillan, a Yale graduate in forestry now connected with the forestry branch of the Canadian department of the interior, wrote offering to give all the information he could about the "forest types in that part of the Western country in which I have been working. . . . I should like very much to have the opportunity of interesting the Toronto men in

[29] A typical address was delivered in 1908 to the St. George Chapter of the Daughters of the Empire, in which Fernow urged that Canada could become "the wood producer of the world."

[30] In the period 1901-1908, though much occupied with propaganda, Fernow continued his technical work. In this period belong his studies for L. H. Bailey's *Cyclopedias* of American horticulture and agriculture, such as the articles on "Pine" and "The Farm Woodlot: Its Place in the Farm Economy."

the magnitude and the possibilities of the work in the West and to make them enthusiastic about the country." Norman M. Ross, chief of the tree planting division of the forestry branch's nursery at Indian Head, Saskatchewan, sketched in a general way types of "the country West of Winnipeg to the foothills of the Rockies, the Northern limits of the district being bounded by a line drawn from Winnipeg to Edmonton." On December 21, Fernow told Ellwood Wilson:

> I am much obliged to you for your scheme of forest types, but you cannot satisfy me so easily. It only stimulates my desire for more, that is to say, in order to satisfy my purpose for which I am trying to collect these various descriptions they will have to be somewhat fuller especially in the differentiation of physical conditions and references to the minor flora and regeneration so as to bring out more definitely not only the character but the cause of the type. In addition to this I would like very much to have an idea of the frequency of occurrence of these various types.

Fernow was somewhat disappointed. He told R. R. Bradley of the Miramichi Lumber Company of Boiestown, New Brunswick:

> I confess I am not much encouraged to secure the cooperation which I had in mind. . . . The object, of course, was to stir up interest in a systematic gathering of the information which shall be of use to all students of Foresty in Canada. Do you not think that just because you find some of the mixed types troublesome your problems might be solved by attempting a preliminary description when by comparison with the description of others you might come to a satisfactory conclusion more easily.

Study of forest types inevitably became associated with projects for forest surveys. In a letter of March 30, 1908, to Charles A. Lyford, Fernow had acknowledged receipt of "the report of [Lyford's] survey in Connecticut [New Hampshire][31]. . . . Can you tell me," Fernow asked, "approximately what the actual expense of this survey has been, how many men were employed and for how long a time, and if you can briefly do so, the methods you pursued. . . ." Lyford gave Fernow the information he wanted.

Little reliable and complete information of the timber resources of the United States and Canada was yet available. All data were estimates. Fernow presented estimates in an address delivered in 1908 before the Western Lumbermen's Association of Nova Scotia. On July 13, F. C. Whitman, president of the association, wrote him:

> If you could give me an outline of a proposition you talked about, of making a Forest survey of Nova Scotia, by bringing down a summer school of your students and with the assistance of the maps and help you could get here, take up the work next summer, I would put the matter before our Local Government and see if the matter can be arranged. Our government seems very reluctant to undertake this important work, claiming that the Crown Land interests are too indifferent to warrant the expense, but with an

[31] Albert E. Moss, "A Forest Survey of Connecticut," *Rpt. Conn. Exp. Sta.* XXXIX, 1916, New Haven, pp. 197-230; reviewed in *Torreya* XVIII, 5, May 1918, p. 94.

offer such as you suggested, I do not see how they could refuse to pay the expense if a little pressure is brought to bear upon them, by the Lumber people, and others in this province.

Again on July 17, Whitman wrote:

> I know that our meeting at Liverpool has made quite an impression, and people realize more than ever before, a proper survey of Nova Scotia forest land is absolutely necessary. I am endeavoring to get over the cost to the Province of making a complete survey by getting the Forestry Department of the Dominion Government to contribute a portion of the expense.

Five thousand dollars was suggested.

Fernow always had believed there was more need to reduce forest waste than to reforest areas, even though he knew reforestation in some regions was desperately needed. The fundamental procedure to reduce waste required a survey of resources, conditions, and needs. Fernow was selected by a province which knew almost nothing of its forests to "undertake a reconnaissance survey of the Province of Nova Scotia with H. B. Ayers as one of [his] attendants." Fernow had recommended Ayers, and would recommend him again in 1910 to examine timberlands of a coal company on the eastern Rocky Mountain slopes north of Calgary.

Fernow went into the Nova Scotia survey knowing full well that private forest owners were in such abundance in the province that the government could influence their forestry interest only slightly. But by February 1909 he announced that he was "informed that a beginning which [he had] suggested [had] been made in compiling existing map work for the purpose." On April 8 he informed Ayers at Aitkin, Minnesota, "I am in receipt of a letter this morning advising me the Government of Nova Scotia proposes to have [the] reconnaissance survey on an appropriation of $2,000,[32] and that they want me to superintend or plan the same. I have had during the winter all the possible map work attended to, that is to say, a map was compiled in the Land Office from the available data, to serve as a basis on which to place the information." Again on May 5 he wrote, "The forest survey of Nova Scotia is at last decided on but they have not been able to secure the Dominion grant, and the paltry $2,000 is all that can be devoted to it, which means that either only a small portion can be looked over, or else a very much more general reconnaissance can be made of the whole."

With a view to furnishing a basis for segregation of farm lands from

[32] The reconnaissance reported the composition or type of forest, the degree of culling, the extent of burnt areas, the condition of reproduction, the character of the barrens, the natural meadow lands, and the cleared lands. No precise separation of the woodlots in large farm areas was attempted. The total expenditure over the entire several years, including field, map, and report work, did not exceed $6,000 or "25 cents per square mile of country." Fernow regarded the work as "a first clearing of the decks." A more thorough survey was needed, but on the basis of this report a provincial forest policy might be adopted.

lands more suited to forest growth, Fernow addressed communications to authorities at the agricultural college at Truro concerning "lands and soils according to current usage in the Province."

The camp practicum work of the forestry school had to be postponed that spring because of the lateness of the season. But when the camp was made, a part of the work concerned the growth rates of pines and spruce in preparation for the Nova Scotia survey. Fernow had cherished the hope that the Ontario government would authorize a forest survey of one of its reservations and permit the school's students to take part. At least he had wanted to begin with forest surveys in Ontario. The Nova Scotia government, however, had seen the value of this phase of university extension work. By May 26, 1909, the Nova Scotia reconnaissance was in progress, and arrangements were made to meet at Middleton, Annapolis County, on June 25. The equipment was gathered together. It was decided to make "a rapid reconnaissance of the whole." Ayers was to be the experienced timber estimator during the first season. Three advanced students of the school aided during the second season. Provincial forest ranger, J. B. Whitman, assisted. Fernow, Howe, and White were the principals.

The Nova Scotia survey provided Fernow with a special opportunity to develop a pet theory that balsam fir was a superior timber for pulp wood. "Having been interested in Balsam Fir property of Cape Breton," he wrote on February 19, 1909, "I thoroughly investigated the availability of fir in the laboratory. I find that the fibre is of better dimensions and has better matting qualities than the spruce, and the trial by the well-known pulp chemists, Littel & Walker, confirmed my preconceived idea regarding its usefulness." This was in answer to an inquiry from John B. Gregory of Fredericton, New Brunswick, and by that time Fernow believed that at least two of the large paper companies were using balsam. In a letter of November 8, 1913, to A. G. McIntyre, editor of *Pulp and Paper Magazine of Canada*, he reiterated his belief that he "was responsible for the demonstration that balsam was as good or better material for pulp than spruce," and he added that "for best results" spruce and balsam should never be mixed. About 1903 he had observed fir and its natural regeneration after logging, "the difficulty with which forest fires progress in that kind of forest [an almost pure fir forest] and the readiness with which regeneration takes place." Later he had much correspondence with Gilmour on the subjects of logging costs, the strip system of regeneration, and the most effective methods by which to introduce forestry practices.

Years were required to complete the survey and publish the report. While preparing the report, to satisfy officials, wordings had to be changed. The truth, however, was finally told. In July 1912 Whitman was sent the page proof of the volume that was published that year by the commission of conservation. Whitman wrote to Fernow:

I appreciate very fully all you have done and hope other members are equally impressed with the splendid representation you have made of the Forestry conditions in this Province. I take it that it was probably the best Province to start this kind of work and hope it will lead to a more extended use of your very valuable knowledge in securing a better comprehension of what every Province should know of forest values.

The heart of the report, *Forest Conditions of Nova Scotia*,[33] emphasized the need to keep the forests productive by approved forestry. Fully two-thirds of the province area was found to consist "of non-agricultural land covered with forest growth or not fit for any other use than timber growing," and this forest resource which furnished "not less than four to five million dollars in value of product annually, [was] in danger of exhaustion within the next two decades." Eighty per cent of the non-barren lands of the Province was forest country and likely to remain so. Under proper management the resource was capable "of forever producing by annual increment, as interest, at least twice as much as [was then] being cut from capital stock," a resource which represented "a potential capital of at least $300,000,000." Efficient fire protection, improved logging methods, and employment of a technically educated provincial forester "whose business it should be to study the situation in the various localities and act as public advisor or instructor—a wandering teacher" were recommended. By this time there was a proven analogy in operation. The conservation boards of Sweden, doing effective work when the Nova Scotia report was presented to the public, were regarded as "most suggestive" in the light of the strong similarity between Nova Scotian and Swedish forest conditions. Futhermore the "presence of an intelligent, well-distributed population [could] aid enforcement of an adequate fire policy."

The conditions of forest growth were found to require extensive seeding, planting of seed trees, and thinning and pruning to foster natural regeneration. Natural reproduction could not altogether be relied on to reforest the extensive burned-over and cut-over areas. Repeated fires on lands of coarser soils, preemption of soil by shading, and other conditions had retarded natural regeneration. In some places natural reproduction was almost impossible. The report was illustrated by scenes of locations where no regeneration of economically valuable species was taking place. A quarter of the province's forest area was found "semi-barren of commercial trees." Stumpage values according

[33] Published by the Commission of Conservation, by permission of the Department of Crown Lands, Nova Scotia, Ottawa, Canada, 1912. Preface and "Forest Conditions of Nova Scotia," by Fernow; "Distribution and Reproduction of the Forest in Relation to the Underlying Rocks and Soils," by Howe. J. H. White also contributed. Quotations are taken from pp. 2, 7, 38f., 42, 80, 92.

to land parcels, growth rates in culled areas, extent of burned areas, the nature and value of natural meadowland, cleared, and barren lands, and much else were elucidated with force and clarity.[34] Government agencies, lumbermen, farmers, and numerous responsible sources cooperated in furnishing data.

Since his arrival in Canada, Dr. Howe had seen in Ontario and other provinces mile after mile of barren lands where immensely valuable pine forests had been. Ways to make these lands again productive had occupied his mind almost immediately. Howe's professional life, both in botany and forestry, had been spent largely with regenerative studies of plants, including forest species. The Nova Scotia survey gave him an opportunity to enter upon a new research. The reclamation of burned-over forest areas had evoked interest. When he presented a strong plea on behalf of this type of forest reconstruction to the commission of conservation, he won Fernow's unwavering support. Soils study was fundamental. Howe's studies of the "Distribution and Reproduction of the Forest in Relation to Underlying Rocks and Soils," treating conditions of the Atlantic slope and the Northumberland and Minas drainage basins, and especially his laboratory analyses of thirty soil samples which formed the basis of his article, "Forest Reproduction and Soil Conditions on Burned Areas," occupied more than half of the report. The latter were more valuable scientifically. Fernow praised the work. The Nova Scotia report was a pioneering analysis, it was the type of study that Fernow had advocated three decades earlier at the American Forestry Congress at Montreal.

In the course of the first summer's work in Nova Scotia, Fernow had remained with the surveying party until August. He had then returned to his summer home at Point Breeze, New York, to write on this and other matters, but especially on his revision of his *History of Forestry*. He found awaiting him a letter from authorities in the province of British Columbia.

Chief Commissioner of Lands Fred J. Fulton of British Columbia had written to Fernow on May 11, 1909:

> I understand it is likely you are coming West as far as Alberta in a short time to confer with the Government of that Province regarding forestry matters. As this question is now very much in evidence here and one on which we are very desirous of obtaining advice I write to know whether it would be possible for you to arrange to come through here as I should like very much to meet you, on behalf of the Province, in connection with forestry matters.

[34] The report recommended research into possible uses of barren lands and experiments to improve natural meadows and savannas; the investigations, including areas fit for forest planting, were to be conducted with the Agricultural College and Experiment Station at Truro. Thus Fernow made the survey valuable to agriculture as well as to forestry.

Fernow had answered that his trip west had had to be delayed, otherwise he would have been happy to discuss forestry topics with him. Already he had been interviewed regarding British Columbia "conditions and the possibilities of starting a proper forest policy."

During these years, Fernow was consulted by officials of other parts of the world. For example, the Victorian department of agriculture in Australia sought his advice in 1908. Alfred J. Ewart, government botanist and member of the forest board, wrote from the National Herbarium located at South Yarra:

> The Victorian Government intends to institute a course of instruction in forestry in this State and is appointing a Board to supervise and construct the course. I should be glad to receive a copy of the syllabus giving course of instruction followed in preparation for the Office of Forester in your department, and any information you are able to give which would be useful to us.

The invitation from officials of British Columbia was further recognition, and from it again may be inferred the early close relationship of forestry and mining. Fernow, in September 1908, in the company of members of the Canadian Mining Institute, had made a trip to British Columbia and gathered information of western timber resources. H. Mortimer-Lamb, secretary of the institute, was so impressed by Fernow's evaluation of the western timber situation that he requested that Fernow prepare a letter on the subject for the institute members. On November 11, 1908, Fernow wrote to Thomas Bamford, deputy commissioner of lands and works, with offices at Victoria, "I have, on the request of the Secretary of the Canadian Mining Institute, given vent to my impressions regarding the timber conditions in British Columbia, which to be sure are [products] in part of the conversation I had with you. That I may not be found in making a misstatement, will you be good enough to look over the enclosed statements and correct me in any particulars in which I may have failed to grasp the situation properly." Fernow believed there was "not to [his] knowledge, any printed information of value relative to the timber resources of British Columbia in existence, but presently," he told G. M. Hersey of Boston, Massachusetts on December 11, 1908, "there will be published in the *Forestry Quarterly* an article on the timber wealth of Canada in general which of course includes the conditions of British Columbia."

A week later, G. G. L. Lindsey, president of the Crow's Nest Pass Coal Company, with offices in Toronto, told Fernow, "I have had up with the British Columbia Government the question of the prevention of forest fires. Their system seems to me a lamentably weak one, and I have now a letter from the Provincial Secretary saying that he is fully alive to the necessity of having their fire protection system as efficient as possible." Lindsey asked Fernow to have lunch with him and discuss the matter. Early in the spring of 1909, British Columbia officials sought again after Fernow.

In answer to Commissioner Fulton's letter of May 11, 1909, Fernow said that he had "had an interview with Mr. Lindsey. . . . For the moment I am so busy that I cannot go into details [concerning] starting a proper forest policy. . . . Perhaps this cannot be satisfactorily discussed on paper, yet at some later occasion, if you desire I shall try to formulate at least an outline of what I think practicable." He suggested that the commission confer with Judson F. Clark, who was "well acquainted with the conditions in your province and with the successful methods of introducing forest policies of the various states of the Union." Since going to British Columbia, Clark had been managing director of the Continental Lumber Company, general manager of the Cedar Cove Lumber Company, secretary-treasurer of the British Columbia Timber and Forestry Chamber of Commerce, and consulting forester for the British Columbia Lumber, Logging and Forestry Association.

Fernow must have sent an outline of what he regarded "practicable." At any rate the province pursued the standard procedure; it created a commission of inquiry. Clark appeared before the commission and, informing Fernow of the details of his recommendations, elicited congratulations "on the very sane propositions regarding the change from the limited to the perpetual license. If," observed Fernow, "you can secure a proper professional supervision on the part of the Government I do not see why your scheme should not work. I have, myself, last week begun to attack the timber license system in Ontario. I am doing this in a very gradual and gentle way. . . . We have, today, Asa Williams, with us, who will address our students on 'Steam Logging'[35] tonight. He has met with considerable success in placing logging machinery in Ontario."

Clark was pleased with the commission, and he sent reports of their hearings to Fernow. He believed that the commission was "getting pretty well down to the bones of the matter." That year he told Fernow, "I would not be at all surprised if British Columbia should within a year or two have more advanced forest laws than any other Province."

In 1909 Roth made two western tours. On July 2 he wrote Fernow of his first trip:

> I was away to the Pacific, the first case of desertion of my post, and not a matter of my own motion. You have good cause for saying what you do about the *Quarterly* and the *little help* you have had. But most of us have

[35] See Asa S. Williams, "Logging by Steam," *Forestry Quarterly* VI, 1, March 1908, p. 1, a compilation of data secured by Fernow and Williams, who had just been appointed Forest Engineer to the Lidgerwood Manufacturing Company, builders of logging machinery.

been where we could just "hang on" and no more. By all means keep it up and I will promise to do better, even at risk of merely promising. . . . We, Mrs. Roth, Stella [their daughter], myself, with a niece are starting July 10 to make a trip to the Pacific via Canadian Pacific, along [the] coast to Los Angeles and [then to] Grand Canyon [on the] return. . . . Mulford will be here this summer, he is the same fine fellow and simply grows in goodness every day. At last we have in this state one little sign of progress; the legislature *fought over forestry*! Hurrah! And we now have a Commission with power over all State lands and with duty to round up at least 200,000 acres of land for Forest Reserve.

Again, after their tour to the coast, Roth sent Fernow more news:

We seem to have over 200 men here in forestry this year; the class in forest botany is starting out with over *70 men*, but we have not, as yet, adopted a separate register for foresters and thus the new men do not come to me at the start. . . . Our Forestry Club is so large that it can no longer meet in any room in West Hall. . . . I have a third man now. . . . In other directions too, things are working out well. We have about 1,200 acres of woods and bare lands turned over to us by a Water Power Company. We direct the work, use the ground for practice and they pay bills and hire the help. . . . Mr. Garfield of Grand Rapids is ailing and has had to give up active work, serious loss to [the] State. As I told you we have a new Commission, "Public Domain, with jurisdiction over all State lands." The law is good and all [that] is needed is: men.

Contrasting this situation with that of Fernow at Toronto, one quickly sees why Roth confined his attention to Michigan. Fernow was, however, in no sense dissatisfied with the progress at Toronto. "We are as successful as a new enterprise can be, having not so much increase in numbers as in quality, which means more to me than numbers. We have now a class of forty-two which will be sufficient for some time."

On July 27, 1909, Commissioner Fulton of British Columbia had written to Fernow and announced "that a Commission [had] been organized to inquire into Timber and Forestry matters." An itinerary of proposed sittings of the commission was enclosed. "I suppose," said Commissioner Fulton, "it will not be possible for you to be present at any of the meetings, but I should be very much obliged if you would send me a short statement of your ideas on the following subjects: the question of any and what rules should be adopted and enforced in regard to methods of logging, and the advisability of issuing hand logging licenses; the question of re-afforestation; the matter of forest fire protection, and any other point that may occur to you as having a special bearing on the subject." On August 9 the secretary of the timber and forestry commission of British Columbia expressed to Fernow his admiration for his address before the Canadian Club of Halifax and asked him "to indicate the most useful and authentic references" on forest preservation and renewal, and any "suggestions or memoranda" which Fernow thought valuable. Secretary Gosnell confessed himself not prepared with the thoroughness necessary to conduct the inquiries. He wanted "official sources of information."

When Fernow had planned the Nova Scotia survey, he had outlined the preliminary work of securing materials such as maps showing watercourses, lakes, roads, railroads, land ownership, and other data, the preliminary reconnaissance of soil and forest types to be studied, and finally the field work, which was conducted by inspection and inquiry, sometimes on foot and sometimes by bicycle, wagon, or railroad. Note-taking and mapping of ten to forty acre tracts was the basic system. As often as possible the data were written up in the field.

A much more elaborate plan of inquiry, however, was recommended to Commissioner Fulton for British Columbia:

> I find your invitation to assist your Commission of Inquiry on my return from Nova Scotia, where I had organized a forest survey reconnaissance of the extent and condition of the forest resources of the Province, with a view to shaping a forest policy for the government. I suppose your Commission is instituted for somewhat the same purposes, or at least its final step should be somewhat of the same character, namely, to secure as definite detail knowledge of actual conditions as possible before attempting to formulate legislation or rules. I regret that I shall not be able to appear personally at your meetings, and lack of definite detail knowledge of your provincial conditions debars me from answering your specific questions very definitely and categorically. I may only develop some general ideas and truths that probably are known to you, but the reformulation and reiteration of which may still not be amiss.

Before reforestation, even before logging restrictions, efficient fire protection was essential. Obviously, conditions in British Columbia, a heavily forested and thinly populated region, would require a more complex organization than Nova Scotia. A system much like the Ontario system was recommended: over all, a provincial chief ranger selected by the lumbermen who first organized the protective service; and chief rangers, sub-rangers, local fire wardens, and subordinates; the responsible persons vested with authority to enforce rules and regulations. Lumbermen had been "instrumental in securing this protection originally" and, "enthusiastic over its results," wanted an efficient service. Owners of five hundred or more acres, and benefited towns, were to be taxed to share maintenance costs, owners paying according to benefits and towns making up deficiencies. An efficient inspection service should enforce logging regulations, brush-burning, "downing tops," and so forth. Government and loggers' interests must both be kept in view, and wise determinations of stumpage values were required. Authority to collect fines and consider claims should be placed with the chief ranger.

Fernow approved no general rule for improvement, but discretion "in determining what is practicable, and inspection to insure its execution, will alone assure success." He opposed diameter limits for cutting, nor was leaving scattered seed trees everywhere the best way of securing new growth. He wrote:

> My principal advice is: institute in your department a forest service with technical advisors who will be able to gradually work out the details of your needs in forest utilization and evolutionize the final system. As to reforestation work I hold that as long as you have not learned or succeeded in keeping Nature's woods in reproductive condition, attempts at reforesting denuded areas may well be postponed at least for some years yet. Your Province, especially on the coast, has such favorable conditions for natural regeneration that no artificial planting should be necessary. In conclusion I should have liked to impress your Commission with this thought: it needs a radical change of attitude on the part of the people and their government to see that in the arrangements in timberland disposal and use, they have sadly neglected to consider the future, and to realize that their country is to live on, and it will take *radical* measures and courage to change these arrangements.

Fernow did not believe in "general prescription" in silvicultural solutions. He wished to submit each "proposition" to a "regular practitioner for specific diagnosis and prescription."[36]

On August 21, 1909, Commissioner Fulton thanked Fernow and told him that the Commission had commenced its sittings. A great accumulation of valuable information would be gathered together. The commissioner promised to consult Fernow further when more exact information about conditions was available. The commissioner asked that he might again "trespass upon your kindness [and] ask you for a further expression of opinion upon the various points which will have come up, giving you more exact information as to conditions on which you may base a conclusion."

That year when the British Columbia legislature convened, Premier McBride announced that the government might create a bureau of forestry with an expert at its head to look after timber matters of the province, including reforestation and other phases of a forest policy.[37] Within

[36] Silvicultural studies were in progress in the United States. See H. S. Graves, "The Study of Natural Reproduction of Forests," *Forestry Quarterly* VI, 2, June 1908, p. 115; R. C. Hawley, "Treatment of Hardwood Lands in Southwestern Connecticut," *ibid.* V, 3, Sept. 1907, p. 283; Max Rothkugel, "Management of Spruce and Hemlock Lands in West Virginia," *ibid.* VI, 1, March 1908, p. 40.

[37] *Forestry Quarterly* VII, 1, March 1909, p. 115. This announcement preceded Fernow's recommendation to create a forest service, but it must be remembered however that Fernow had corresponded with officials of the government and private citizens for more than a year before this. Very likely these officials and citizens conferred with the Premier. The Premier must have based his announcement on some plan, but apparently the plan was not communicated to the commissioners, or neither the secretary nor Commissioner Fulton would have needed to consult Fernow on the most effective course of procedure. Fernow became the leading advisor to the government of British Columbia until H. R. MacMillan was placed in charge. Even then, though he was familiar with Fernow's ideas through his work in the Dominion's forestry branch and association with R. H. Campbell, MacMillan consulted Fernow occasionally. See *Forestry Quarterly* X, 1, March 1912, p. 112, for forestry legislation in British Columbia.

a little more than a year's time Clark informed Fernow that the Vancouver School Board had organized a forestry course in connection with night school work, and that Clark was the instructor. The registration consisted "for the most part of teachers, timber cruisers, and surveyors, with a few scattering registrations from other lines." Fernow replied, "By all means, keep me advised of progress in forestry matters in your province."

Fernow gave silvicultural advice not only to Canadian provincial and private company officials but also to a private venture in Mexico. He wrote to Arthur Wood of Colima, Mexico, on November 26, 1909, "You will excuse me when I tell you that your inquiry regarding planting in the Sierra Madre made me smile. I take it that you will have your hands full to cut and mark the timber that you are cutting. If, however, you really have in mind some forestry practice, which in the first place should consist in not spoiling the chances of need, in attempt to reforest cut areas, instead of the more expensive planting, there is, of course, no reason why I should not encourage it. As to the selection of planting material, I believe that the native oak is not by any means a slow grower as you can find out easily by counting and measuring the rings in a cross section." It will be remembered that Fernow had done professional consulting work in Mexico and had examined oak forests there. He added, in his letter, that while as yet there were no experiments to show what the white pine would do in the Mexican climate, the native pine might serve the purpose. He cautioned, "Such an undertaking should not be made without an expert's investigation and advice."

During 1904 a forestry association in Mexico had been organized. Three years later the work had been recognized and aided by the government. French foresters had been imported to take charge of nurseries and plantations and possibly to manage a federal forest area. In 1909 there was a reorganization, and the work of the forest service was placed under the department of public works in the department of agriculture. Lands were reserved to protect water courses. Timber licenses were granted. The work, however, emphasized immediate practical monetary objectives. The horticultural and agricultural branches were placed in the foreground. Forestry was granted only a small annual budget.[38] There was little to show that Fernow, except in his capacity as an editor, exercised any influence on forestry development in Mexico.

In October 1909 Fernow wrote to procure a copy of the report of the joint committee of conservation, published as United States senate document 690 and which sought to link the reforms from Mexico to Canada. In September *Forestry Quarterly*[39] had published Fernow's review of the

[38] *Forestry Quarterly* X, 4, 1912, p. 715.
[39] *ibid.* VII, 3, p. 305.

proceedings of the meeting of the National Societies of Civil, Mechanical, Mining, and Electrical Engineers, which was held on March 24, 1909, and was devoted to conservation of natural resources. Five addresses, presented by engineers of such caliber as John Ripley Freeman, Lewis Buckley Stillwell, and Rossiter Worthington Raymond, portrayed the increasing adherence of these professions to the interests of this cause, including the forest, land, and water resources, and their realization of the need for more exact investigation and knowledge. Fernow, in his review, pointed to the special applications of forestry knowledge which might prove helpful in their endeavors.

Education obviously furthered the conservation cause. Gifford Pinchot invited all heads of universities, colleges, and schools in which technical forestry was taught to confer at Washington on December 30-31. He hoped to coordinate the work of different institutions with the needs of the forest service. Suggesting to Fernow that he discuss what the forest school should do in the community, Pinchot said, "Your own field in Canada is so largely along this line that I am sure no one could present so valuable a paper on this topic as yourself." Fernow accepted, although, he said, "the subject assigned to me has not yet occupied me in particular, neither is it particularly attractive to me. I shall endeavor to present some thoughts, heterodox though they may be, that may lead to a discussion by others." His title was "Public Responsibility of the Forest School."[40]

Fernow disapproved of any effort to popularize technical forestry. He clearly foresaw the abundant errors which emerge from superficial knowledge. He argued for a segregation of popular and technical education. There was a chance of educating more foresters than the demands would warrant. Professional schools were charged with no more than the plain duty to prepare well-trained foresters and good citizens. The public responsibility of the forest school began and ended with the student. Articles for the creation of an Association of American Forest Schools were adopted at the meeting.

Fernow sought always to stir interest in forestry education. When Hugh Potter Baker wrote on the subject, Fernow wrote to him on January 23, 1909, "I am very much obliged for the useful paper on 'Education' which I have read with interest, subscribing to nearly all your views and expect to print it in the next issue. It has recalled to me an article of my own on the 'Sciences underlying Forestry'[41] which might be coupled with your paper increasing the interest in this educational

[40] *ibid.* VIII, 1, March 1910, for papers by Graves, Fisher, Roth, and Fernow. See also "Standardization of Instruction in Forestry," *ibid.* X, 3, Sept. 1912, pp. 341ff.

[41] *ibid.* VII, 1, March 1909, p. 23; see also H. P. Baker's articles, "The Forest School and the Education of the Forester," *ibid.* VII, 1, p. 15, and "Value of Physics and Other Fundamental Subjects to Students in Forestry," *ibid.* XI, 3, Sept. 1913, p. 395.

question. I hope you will give me leave to either use or defer the use of your 'tree planting' paper.... There is one article on 'Coppice' by Mattoon which must go in and I may not have space for another silvicultural paper." The Conference of Forest Schools appointed a committee of five to consider and report to the conference on a plan for establishing a minimum standard curriculum in forestry. Pinchot was appointed chairman, but he objected, and he was requested to appoint a chairman. Graves was appointed. Other committeemen were Pinchot, Fernow, Roth, and Fisher.

Fernow reviewed[42] the three volume work of the *Report of the National Conservation Commission in the United States*, edited by Henry Gannett. Scant recognition given to Fernow, Roth, and others of the dozens of leaders who, through the American Forestry Association, founded professional forestry in America did not go unchallenged. The publication on this point did not typify the consensus of American foresters or officials of the conservation movement. July 23, 1908, Treadwell Cleveland, Jr., of the United States forest service, wrote Fernow, "I am planning a magazine article tracing the development of the conservation idea from the first movements to conserve the forests down to the latest developments of the National and State Conservation Commissions. In my work, I have always deeply appreciated the indebtedness of those who have worked in the movement to you and your work, and I shall particularly in this paper touch upon some of your earlier addresses in which, in my judgment, you outline in advance of others much of what is now receiving National prominence."

Many students of the American conservation movement have recognized Fernow's leadership. In 1913 Theodore S. Woolsey, Jr., prepared a book on French forestry. Wishing to dedicate this volume to Fernow, Pinchot, and Graves, he wrote to Fernow and closed his letter by saying, "Future foresters are going to recognize the great influence your teaching and writing have had upon American conservation." Since the American Forestry Congress in 1882, the forestry movement had been regarded as an international movement. *Forestry Quarterly*[43] observed:

> Utopia is surely coming earlier than we had expected, if, besides the North American Conservation Commission, the International Conservation Commission should become a fact before the display of Dreadnaughts may put a damper on the enthusiastic altruists who are engineering the movement.
>
> There is nothing in the declaration of principles issued by the North American Conservation Commission to which a forester will take exception, for, where forestry is practiced, these principles have already been recognized and acted upon long ago.
>
> The one new and apparently practical proposition, namely, the stocktaking of resources, if it is to be executed over the whole world, strikes us

[42] *ibid.* VII, 4, Dec. 1909, p. 415. [43] *ibid.* VII, 2, June 1909, p. 224.

as somewhat chimerical, and the difficulties still for a time, insuperable. Even in such highly civilized and organized countries as the United States and Canada, this would be a tremendous undertaking, while in South American Republics, Asia, and Africa, it is hopeless.

The true value of the movement was to arouse "popular interest to a realization of their duty." The declaration was recognized not to be in any sense a binding treaty. The interposing political differences between the various governments pointed to the size of the task. The Canadian commission to the Conference on the Conservation of Natural Resources of the Continent invited consideration of the "principles on which authorities having control over natural resources may act in their future treatment of their resources, either by legislation or by grants. While the Federal Government of Canada took part in this Conference, there is no thought or idea of any infringement or interference with the rights of the Provinces within the Dominion. The Declaration fully recognizes provincial, state and national authorities."

The Canadian government recognized in several ways the public interest involved in the work of the commission of conservation. For instance, free railroad transportation was given to foresters when on official investigations. As a member of the commission, Fernow informed Minister of Railways G. P. Graham that the forest survey of the province of Nova Scotia was in progress. "This work," said the letter, "while undertaken at the expense of the Province and primarily of importance to the Province, can claim to have general public interest for the Dominion, accomplishing part of the work for which the Commission of Conservation has been instituted, namely, taking stock of the natural resources."

Fernow early took the position that the commission of conservation should do cooperative but not competitive work with the established government forestry agencies. On October 4, 1911, he told R. H. Campbell of the Dominion forestry branch, "Incidentally, I may confide to you that I think the Conservation Commission should make common cause with you in doing its first business, not only utilizing but assisting you in securing the information that we should have regarding forest conditions in Canada." On April 13, 1910, he had told Kelly Evans of the game and fisheries commission, "I agree with you that the Conservation Commission should be active in propaganda and educational work." Fernow wanted active and efficient work. In a university lecture during 1911 he discussed "Conservation, What It Involves." Considering its history, he referred to the movement as composed of "fundamental philosophies . . . to a phase of which [he had] devoted the greater portion of [his] life, but which only within the last two years

[had] sprung into prominence." To Theodore Roosevelt[44] Fernow gave great credit for having called into conference the governors of all the states[45] and later the neighboring nations of Canada and Mexico. Earlier in the year Fernow had discussed the same subject when lecturing at Lehigh University on the history of forestry.

In other particulars there seemed evidence of a growing lack of co-ordination between Canadian and United States forestry work. December 2, 1910, Fernow told W. H. Jacombe of the forestry branch of the department of the interior:

> As to your proposition to enlarge the *Forestry Quarterly* on the professional side, I am favorably inclined especially as I have had lately correspondence from Washington with reference to an eventual transfer of the *Forestry Quarterly* to the American society which would indicate that they would not wish to make common cause with the Canadian society. I believe that the Canadian Association is of such character that a little professionalism will be rather welcome.

It was recognized that forestry in Canada was not as far advanced as in the United States. Canada was still laying its organizational foundations, still marshalling its forces to obtain fundamental knowledge on which to build and realize the most from its rich natural resources.

Conservation and forestry in Canada continued to progress. Fernow in 1908 addressed the forest, fish and game association on the subject, "Forest Conservation from the Standpoint of Sportsmen." He expressed the hope that Canadians would take a "wiser view" of the Canadian reserves and parks than the people of the state of New York had in creating a "luxury forest for the rich."

President Edward L. Nichols of the American Association for the Advancement of Science addressed the association's Baltimore meeting on "Science and the Practical Problems of the Future."[46] As retiring president, he said, "Forests may be renewed and the soil restored to its maximum fertility but the problem which is presently to confront the race is that of civilized existence without recourse to energy stored by the slow processes of nature. This problem must be definitely solved before the complete exhaustion of our inherited capital."

Soils study was the fundamental common to botany, horticulture, and forestry. Soil requirements of plants were being progressively investigated. Some research indicated that even for agricultural crops the soil mineral constituents were relatively unimportant. Certainly there was no widespread agreement on this subject. That plants feed on subsoil

44 See extracts of a message of President Roosevelt on conservation, *Torreya* IX, 2, Feb. 1909, pp. 42f.

45 *Forestry Quarterly* VI, 3, Sept. 1908, p. 334; VII, 2, 1909, p. 163; 3, p. 356; *10th Ann. Rpt. Canad. For. Ass'n, op. cit.*, pp. 74-82.

46 *Torreya* IX, 1, Jan. 1909, p. 16.

materials far below the roots was welcomed as a new principle.[47] Knowledge closely akin to this, however, had been available for years. Analysis of the surface soils seemed indicated for research purposes, but Cyril G. Hopkins had given an address in which he stated that because of proven "uncompensated loss by leaching of the upper soil in all normal humid sections, we dare not base our definite plans for systems of permanent agriculture upon a theory that by the rise of capillary water, plant food is brought from the lower subsoils sufficient to meet the needs of large crops and to maintain the fertility of the surface soils in all places and for all time. . . . It is certainly safe teaching and safe practice to return to the soil as much or more than we remove of such plant-food elements as are contained in the soil in limited amounts when measured by the actual requirements of large crops during one lifetime." These conclusions were applicable to agriculture, but what of forests? On July 24, 1908, Fernow wrote Milton Whitney, chief of the United States bureau of soils:

> The German Forest Experiment Stations have just elaborated a schedule of forest description with a view of covering the ground exhaustively and of securing uniformity. I have had this schedule translated but when it came to the soil description, the English nomenclature became doubtful, and I submit the matter to you.

Whitney replied on August 21:

> I have had the manuscript revised and the necessary changes in the English have been made in accordance with your request. In many cases the German nomenclature has not its counterpart in English and consequently roundabout ways of expression have had to be resorted to. The classification of German forest soils has been quite interesting and the classification of humus soils in particular is very detailed.

Whitney very soon was to issue a bulletin which sought to establish generally that long-cultivated soils of the leading nations are not only producing greater crops at earlier periods but are producing much more than the almost new soil of the United States.[48] In *Forestry Quarterly*[49] Dr. Howe reviewed Hopkins' book on *Soil Fertility and Permanent Agriculture*. Howe found it addressed to the agriculturist but of much interest and value to the silviculturist and forest ecologist. Exact studies of forest soil were yet to be made. In March 1910 Fernow invited Whitney to send one of his men to the faculty of forestry at the University of Toronto to give "a short practical course, say a week, on soil surveying." This was enlarged to include demonstration work. J. E. Lapham of the soils bureau was selected to give the lectures. The lectures, given that fall, proved to be so stimulating that Fernow wrote Whitney

[47] *ibid.* IX, 2, Feb. 1909, pp. 41f.
[48] *ibid.* IX, 11, Nov. 1909, p. 237.
[49] VIII, 4, Dec. 1910, p. 487.

that the school wanted to inaugurate a soils laboratory on a small scale. Combined with Howe's course in biological dendrology, soils research, including laboratory and field investigation, began to add to the American advances. Clinical soils analysis, coupled with field demonstrations, were favored by Fernow. The school's instruction, consisting of twenty-five lectures, one hundred laboratory hours, and thirty to forty experiments, was approved and recommended by him,[50] especially since under Howe fundamental biology joined to ecological and agricultural investigation was emphasized.

Forestry was being enriched in these years by numerous botanical publications. *The Silva of California*, by W. L. Jepson, supplied taxonomic and geographic knowledge of the state's timber trees. Many regional and state manuals of trees would be forthcoming. B. M. Duggar's *Fungous Diseases of Plants* and F. L. Stevens' and J. G. Hall's *Diseases of Economic Plants*, and the entire work begun by many workers in plant pathology and other research branches had significance for forestry. The causes of soil sterility and the methods of increasing soil fertility were important primarily to agriculture, but the methods devised opened the eyes of foresters to applications that might be made in forestry. All agricultural, horticultural, or botanical progress affected forestry.

Reforestation, the core of Fernow's early forestry plea, was no longer a discussion topic but was a recognized aspect of forestry research. Experimental techniques were being explored and verified to establish methods most effective under the variety of conditions presented by different forest regions.[51] When to employ broadcast seed sowing and of what species, when to make use of nursery grown stock, when and what should follow burning or cutting of areas, and so forth were the objects of study. The student was required to understand complex situations, climatic, meteorological, agronomic, hydrological. Bulletins of federal and state forest work accumulated a storehouse of knowledge. Bulletins of other bureaus also were of value, like number 53 of the bureau of

[50] In a letter to H. P. Baker, dated Feb. 24, 1916, Fernow explained his efforts to establish soils study at the Toronto school: "We first attempted to secure this Soils course from the Geological Department. It was a failure. Then we had a Soil Survey man from Washington for a week in the field. He was nothing but a Soil Survey man, who knew his business but not ours. Hence, we found it necessary to develop the right course for ourselves. . . . " Lapham's course (*Forestry Quarterly* VIII, 4, Dec. 1910, p. 573) gave the Toronto students a "practicum" in soil survey at the beginning of the academic year. Excursions were taken to the Don Valley to study glacial and lacustrine deposits, and to Lewiston, New York, to study soil types established in the course of a state survey there.

[51] *Forestry Quarterly* VIII, 3, Sept. 1910, p. 397; IX, 1, March 1911, p. 90 (a review of the Chief Forester's report for 1910); IX, 2, June 1911, pp. 350, 363. See also *Torreya* IX, Dec. 1909, p. 267; T. Cleveland, "The Status of Forestry in the United States," circ. 167, U.S.F.S., rev. by Graves in *For. Quar.* VII, 4, p. 424; *Yearbook U.S.D.A.* (1910), pp. 86-87; (1911), pp. 88-89, 95-98.

soils, "The Isolation of Harmful Organic Substances from Soils." This bulletin was believed capable of producing interesting results on heaths, moors, and barren lands. Moreover, bulletin 87, "Nitrogenous Soil Constituents and their Bearing on Soil Fertility,"[52] was recommended for study by silviculturists.

Reforestation, inaugurated experimentally at first in the Pacific Northwest, would not exceed ten thousand planted and seeded acres in the national forests during 1910. Nevertheless, the task of reforesting treeless areas was being recognized as an integral part of national forest administration, and with broadcast sowing over large areas it was extended over more acreage every year. The national forest programs included some of the largest forest planting projects ever undertaken. Fernow was in full sympathy with the objectives. Lack of definite knowledge as to what planting results might be obtained had retarded reforestation progress in America. Tests over sufficiently large experimental areas to ascertain local requirements were needed. Watershed areas, wastelands, chaparral lands, and many special regions became objects of field study. In 1909 reforestation on a large burned area, the scene of three severe fires, was being studied on the Olympic national forest in Washington, and for the seed-planting tests Douglas fir was foremost among the species selected. By 1911 Secretary of Agriculture Wilson reported that "permanent foundations" to develop constructively the national forest areas were established and among the many investigations and improvements being made artificial and natural reforestation on many thousands of acres of forest area was being forwarded to replenish the millions of acres of denuded land space.

George Wilcox Peavy had graduated at the University of Michigan as a student of Roth. After some experience with the forest service studying planted groves and growth rates of trees planted in eastern Nebraska under the homestead and timber culture laws, he had been assigned to California to do forest nursery and tree planting work in the federal forest reserves. Peavy told the forest service that a chaparral cover was best to prevent soil erosion and aid streamflow in the southern California regions. His belief, contrary to the general opinion that full forest cover was needed, was predicated on coppice management and the quick capacity of chaparral to spring from roots. Although his theory at first met opposition, he was made a district inspector for California and Nevada. Peavy remained in this position until a small group from Oregon State College at Corvallis requested forestry instruction. In 1910 the president of the university asked Peavy to come to Oregon State and establish the department of forestry which, because

[52] *ibid.* IX, 1, March 1911, p. 99; XI, 1, March 1913, p. 71, on these bulletins respectively.

Oregon is perhaps the most heavily timbered state in the United States, grew into a school of forestry by 1916. The department received a new building. Peavy himself became the president of the college before many years. Forestry remained a dominant interest and the school's equipment was increased to provide adequate demonstration material.

Soils study, entomological research, plant pathology, and forest mycology began to attack the devastating problems of the white pine blister rust, the chestnut blight, and other scourges which began to undo forestry progress. Again the commission form of inquiry, notably in Pennsylvania, where large sums of money were appropriated for the purpose, was summoned into action. Both the federal and state governments began to establish inspection or quarantine services to prevent the spread of diseases. In Canada, agricultural research at the Dominion experimental farms gave some attention to forest pathology. From the beginning of the faculty of forestry at Toronto, courses in cryptogamic botany, diseases of trees, and economic entomology were offered as part of the work in forest protection and forest biology. No professorship was maintained for this instruction, and the work was more lecture than laboratory study. At the turn of the decade North American phytopathologists began a desperate struggle of many years against the chestnut bark disease and white pine blister rust, and plant pathologists and foresters became much more interested in forest pathology. After going to Canada, Fernow's interest for some time was practical. No later than October 1908 he began calling the attention of government officials to the dangers of disease-introductions on foreign tree seedlings.

In this regard Fernow was dissatisfied with the instruction facilities at the faculty of forestry at Toronto. He told H. P. Baker on February 24, 1916:

> For Forest Pathology, we have a course in Entomology, a short course in Mycology, a week's work with Dr. von Schrenk, and what comes into the Forest Protection course. Our Zoology is somewhat neglected because we have not the right man, excepting what appears in the general course on Biology and a few talks before the Foresters' Club on Canadian animal life by some ornithologist or mammalogist. We had contemplated engaging Dr. Everman again, but he left for California before we could financially afford the arrangement.

Fernow contrasted the instruction in these subjects with that given two decades earlier in the New York State College of Forestry. At Cornell, Fernow explained to Baker,

> Zoology . . . which should be mainly field zoology, was from the start tolerably well taken care of by a special course for six or eight weeks, to juniors and seniors combined, at Axton, when Professor Everman, an excellent teacher and naturalist, gave a special course, the first of its kind, on Fish Culture and Game preservation, which, being conducted in the field, gave opportunity to branch out into all kinds of field knowledge. We had

also a particular class in Cornell under one of the enthusiastic instructors of the Zoological Department, who was not afraid to call his class together at 4 in the morning to learn to recognize the birds by their song. So, altogether, our men got a good knowledge of animal life. Forest Pathology was largely neglected except for a poor course in the Botanical Department on Mycology and whatever could be brought into the course of Forest Protection. We had, however, an excellent course on Entomology, given by Professor Comstock.

Fernow strongly believed that courses on soils, forest pathology, and forest zoology should form an important part of any curriculum in forestry.

The conservation movement took cognizance of the work in science, but its bulk of strength lay in economics. On December 4, 1909, Chief Forester Pinchot wrote for *Outlook* an article on "The A B C of Conservation." He was quoted in *Torreya*[53] and other periodicals of more professional character. Pinchot said, "Conservation holds that it is about as important to see that the people in general get the benefit of our national resources as to see that there shall be natural resources left." He further insisted that "Congress must decide at this session whether the great coal-fields still in public ownership shall remain so, in order that their use may be controlled with due regard to the interest of the consumer, or whether they shall pass into private ownership and be controlled in the monopolistic interest of a few. Congress must decide also whether immensely valuable rights to the use of water power shall be given away to special interests in perpetuity and without compensation, instead of being held and controlled by the public." William Howard Taft, earnest advocate of the conservation movement, was president-elect. Theodore Roosevelt, a still more ardent conservationist and the outgoing president, had indicated an intention to withhold water right titles "until Congress shall have had an opportunity to act."[54]

Forestry and Irrigation had changed its title to *Conservation*. Fernow had retained his honorary office as vice-president of the American Forestry Association. As such he was consulted by the board of directors of the association when it was proposed to change the magazine name to *Forestry*, "the main feature of all conservation, the keystone of the conservation arch. There is a great work to be done along this line," said the association's executive secretary, "and upon it the conservation work of the future will depend, especially in its most important branches of forests, soils, and waters." Fernow wrote on November 5, 1909,

Replying to your letter, *re* change of name of our journal *Conservation.* I have to say that I was much disappointed when the change to *Conservation* was made—as I believe, without warrant or proper authority. Yet, I

[53] *Torreya* X, 1, Jan. 1910, p. 24.

[54] *ibid.* IX, Dec. 1909, p. 268, quoting an editorial of the *New York Tribune* and the President.

am more opposed to change the name again after it has become familiar and established, especially when it is intimated that the conservation of all natural resources is after all to occupy the attention of the magazine. Especially, a change to such a weak title as *Forestry Magazine* would be most distasteful to me. *The Forester* was good enough, and *Forestry and Irrigation*, a change for the better and made for good reasons, but this further needless propagation of names appears to me—without meaning offense to those responsible for it—almost ludicrous. If it is felt that the Association suffers because the object of its main aim does not appear prominently in the title of its magazine, I would suggest printing the title—

CONSERVATION OF FORESTS, SOILS, AND WATERS

The contents, after all, are of more import than the name. A change of name, except to merit estate, as when irrigation became affianced to forestry, is invariably a loss. It shows fickleness, uncertainty of purpose, lack of continuity. I do not think the divorce proceedings should be especially advertised.

The question before the public was whether, without affirmative action by congress, the president should withhold from settlement, lands containing water power. The federal forest policy seemed firmly established. Soil conservation seemed more and more permanently entrenched. Protection of water power, especially falling water, whether on navigable or non-navigable streams, was a current issue. And with it went the protection of coal, gas, oil, and other exhaustible commodities. The legal status of this conservational work was not as definite as with improvable resources—forests, soils, and rivers. The issue ostensibly was private monopolistic or government control of those commodities vested with a certain public interest by virtue of their necessity. Of course the basic question was one of constitutional authority. Where the federal government owned, there was no question of the right of the president, subject to congressional directives, to withhold such lands from settlement.

When President Taft came into office there was pending before Congress a bill (at the time of his message[55] to congress already passed by the house of representatives) to appropriate federal forestry funds to reforest and improve the sources of certain navigable streams. These locations were to be selected by the United States geological survey. The president approved of this and of the extension of watersheds and the promotion of forest growth on denuded and waste areas.

Cooperative action of the states and the federal government was strongly endorsed to "conserve the new soils, improve the old soils, drain wet soils, ditch swamp soils, levee river overflow soils, grow trees on thin soils, pasture hillside soils, rotate crops on all soils, discover methods for cropping dry-land soils, find grasses and legumes for all soils,

[55] *ibid.* X, 5, May 1910, pp. 122-124, quoting important excerpts from President Taft's first message to Congress.

feed grains and mill feeds on the farms where they originate." The president viewed with pleasure the extension of "dry farming" by virtue of the act, which was applicable to "semi-arid parts of the public domain" and which enlarged the homestead privilege from 160 to 320 acres. The demonstration of the possibility of growing crops without the amount of water once believed necessary suggested agricultural advancement. President Taft called for more irrigation and reclamation projects in completely arid regions by means of water reservoir storage and intelligently planned distribution. Many engineering feats challenged the future. But of upwards of "400,000,000 acres of forest land in this country . . . in private ownership . . . only 3 per cent of it . . . being treated scientifically and with a view to the maintenance of the forests," control was regarded as "a matter for state and not national regulation because there [was] nothing in the Constitution that [authorized] the federal government to exercise any control over forests within a state, unless the forests [were] owned in a proprietary way by the federal government." If this was so of forest work, it was also so of regulation of other resources. Reputable periodicals and newspapers, therefore, asked whether the conservation movement could obtain the further federal and state legislation needed.

In January 1910 before the first annual meeting of the commission of conservation of Canada Fernow had presented a notable study, "Scientific Forestry in Europe: Its Value and Applicability in Canada."[56] The address condensed what Fernow had enlarged upon in two volumes, *The Economics of Forestry* (1902) and *A Brief History of Forestry in Europe, the United States and Other Countries*. At first written with reference to Europe, the latter book had been rewritten to include United States forest history, and published in 1907 by the Toronto University Press and The Price, Lee & Adkins Company of New Haven, Connecticut. Fernow in 1910-1911 revised and enlarged the work, and by 1913 the book had reached its third revised edition. Fernow, however, was criticized by some authorities on the ground that he had not sufficiently prepared himself for the French forestry account; some believed that Fernow was not entirely fair to the French forestry system. Other equally reputable authorities praised the *History* in its entirety. Perhaps the most interesting point was that European reviewers recognized that forestry in the United States had attained such a "remarkably rapid and healthy" development that its history and importance ranked beside its predecessors.

On April 29, 1910, Fernow wrote to Professor C. H. Guyot, Director of the Forest School at Nancy, France, saying:

I wish to thank you for the very interesting and illuminating review of

[56] *1st Ann. Rpt. of Comm. of Conserv. of Canada*, 1910, pp. 3-15, and reprint.

my *History* in the *Revue des Eaux et Forêts,* which is in excellent tone, and which I much appreciate for bringing me to a better realization of the position of forestry in France. You understand, of course, that not the slightest bias has guided my pen and that, where I seem to be deprecatory, it is due to impressions left on me from my reading. I think, on re-reading the chapter carefully, you will find that my judgments were, after all, not as harsh as you make them appear, being modified by the use of expressions of doubt which small adverbs permit. The brevity which I had to exercise accounts perhaps for sharpness of expression which, if space permitted, might have been modified.

Fernow confessed he had relied upon Martin's critical presentation of conditions. "Perhaps he has not done justice although his writings sound fair," said Fernow. "I know French forestry only from the literature and conversation with those familiar, except for what I saw during the French campaign," meaning, of course, his year in the German army during the Franco-Prussian War. Fernow had asked for corrections. He arranged with Professor Henry to help revise the references to France. This he told to Professor W. R. Fisher of Oxford, when thanking him for his review of the *History* in the *Quarterly Journal of Forestry.* In a letter of April 18, Fernow explained that this edition of only 500 copies was "in reality only a draft for a better book [and] a new revised edition [was] soon to follow. I am asking friends in all countries to be kind enough to correct all misstatements and misconceptions and if you would be good enough to give me further aid especially for Great Britain and India, I should be very much obliged."

Roth communicated to Fernow his congratulations on the *History,* "My hearty thanks for the copy of your history of forestry. Good lots of good stuff. Glad you included many countries; it lends much interest." Another interesting letter, among the many received, came from C. H. Shattuck, professor of forestry at the University of Idaho: "This supplies a great gap in our Forestry teaching and we have decided to introduce the work for the coming year." Although Fernow believed that, except on their own account, United States forest service officials were not being supplied with the book, he betrayed no bitterness. He financed publication of at least one edition of the book and did not use the *Quarterly* unduly to advertise it.

Other subjects discussed at the first annual Canadian conservation commission meeting were minerals, agriculture, water power, fish and game, fur-bearing animals, public health and water wealth. Forest tree diseases and destructive forest insects also were considered. Fernow pointed out that all "the nostrums which [were then] advocated in Canada, and more particularly in the United States, to relieve the situation," had been long ago "recommended and, in part, practised" in countries of Europe. The last of the countries of Europe to "fall in line—and they are still uncertain and undeveloped in their forest policies—were naturally the countries exporting forest products, Russia and Sweden; and now, the United States and Canada—the countries which erroneously suppose themselves to have a surplus of forest resources to dispose of—[are] joining the ranks."

Fernow believed that "every principle which [had] been found to work elsewhere [could] be put in practice in Canada." But a basis on which to decide where and when the applications were to be made had to be secured. The Nova Scotia survey, while not an "actual forest survey," furnished a model in that it eliminated guesswork and afforded an "authoritative collation of known facts" on which to decide future methods of forest treatment. Technical problems of each province would have to be solved individually. At the conservation commission's first annual meeting, Fernow took the rostrum for scientific forestry in Canada. He realized that his address should suggest lines of work for the commission to follow. "The country which most nearly resembles our own, both in physical character, forest conditions and methods of forest administration," he ventured, "is Sweden." Not failing to discuss points of value from German, French, and other forestry systems, he stressed the close resemblance of Swedish conditions to the Maritime provinces and sections of Quebec. But the commission's work was to embrace all Canada. Without minimizing the necessity of encouraging private forestry through assistance to experienced personnel, he believed that since the bulk of Canadian forest property was state owned, the change to improved methods, improved service, improved policies—the strengthening of a forest service in each province similar to that of the Dominion government—could be done with comparative ease. But first the commission must aid in securing a "radical change in the attitude of our people and Governments from that of exploiters to that of managers." They would then "astonish the practical men to find how much European methods and systems are really applicable, just as it lately surprised the Americans across the line." A reform in the timber license system was advocated. Reforestation conforming to best silvicultural practices, especially in view of the rise of white pine stumpage, would return compound interest yields. Now was the time for governments to invest in sound knowledge, sound practice, and sound research. Fernow regretted that more reviews of European periodical literature were not reaching the pages of *Forestry Quarterly*. In 1908 he told F. W. Beekman of New Haven, Connecticut, "I regret I am unable to read Swedish and that, therefore, the excellent work that is now being done at the Swedish Experiment Station remains unreported or comes in scraps through third hands."

During the summer of 1910 Dr. and Mrs. Fernow and two of their sons enjoyed a trip to Sweden and the Black Forest of Germany.

Fernow attended the meeting of the International Union of Forest Experiment Stations held at Brussels. He went under auspices of the conservation commission, but he paid his own expenses. He prepared a memorandum for the commission on his return and wrote an article on "The Swedish Forest Conservation Law."[57] Roth also went to Europe that year. On his way to the International Forestry Congress at Brussels he studied the forests and schools of Spain, Italy, and France. The French reclamation work to prevent soil erosion especially interested him. Some part of the summer was also spent in German forests.

Early in 1910 conservation and forestry circles were shocked by the resignation of Gifford Pinchot as chief forester of the United States forest service. On January 10, 1910, Fernow wrote to R. T. Fisher of Harvard University who had sent him a copy of the report of the conference on forestry education. Fernow informed Fisher that Professor Graves had written to him "that it had been discussed that the Government might publish a Bulletin on education and incorporate these papers. This morning I see in the papers Mr. Pinchot's dismissal . . . I consider the dismissal of Mr. Pinchot in the same light as my own misfortune at Cornell excepting that in his case the loss is more serious, and the desert more merited." On January 15 Roth wrote to Fernow, "Things have shaken up at Washington but it is merely in the look and not in fact; . . . evidently Taft is doing what he can to bring matters to a head and the crisis is not far off." The issue was one of conservation. Pinchot had taken a brave stand to conserve mineral lands, especially mineral lands of the public domain. An incident occurred in Alaska whereby coal lands of the public domain were leased. A controversy arose. Central figures of high responsibility became involved, and a scandal, the effects of which were heard for years in Washington and throughout the nation, emerged from an official senate and house investigation. No more is necessary here than to explain Fernow's reaction to Pinchot's resignation as chief forester. Secretary of Agriculture Wilson had issued an order that no employee of his department should confer with congressmen with a view to securing legislation other than through the appropriate channel of his office. Pinchot, sincere and honest believer in a cause, disregarded the secretary's order, and because of his letter to Senator Dolliver which contained criticism of the president, the able forester was forced to resign. Whether guilty of insubordination, or if from a worthy motive Pinchot gave the highest authorities adequate cause to request his resignation, he put in focus an economic issue still current today. Fernow saw the significance of Pinchot's removal in the light of forestry more than conservation. On January 8 he wrote to Ellwood Wilson, "This morning's paper brings the news that Mr. Pinchot has

[57] *Forestry Quarterly* IX, 1, 1911, pp. 59ff.

been dismissed for insubordination which I had anticipated. I believe it is a great loss although a deserved rebuke for improper behaviour. Who will be his successor?" The answer was soon forthcoming. Sixteen days later Fernow addressed a communication to Hugh Potter Baker who was studying at Munich, "Things are moving quite lively in the forestry world just at present as you will have learned from your other correspondents. Professionally, I do not think that any loss has come by Mr. Pinchot's dismissal since Professor Graves has been called into his place and everything will go on in the same way." Fernow must have believed that the essence of the analogy between his "own misfortune at Cornell" and Pinchot's dismissal was staunch heroism for a cause—or perhaps more realistically, politics.

January 30, 1910, the *Sunday Herald* of Boston carried an article concerning Fernow and entitled "The Man Who Made Pinchot and the Lately Deposed Chief Forester" with a subhead, "Fernow Made Forestry Issue." The *New York Times* of the same day likewise entitled its article " 'The Man Who Made Pinchot,' Dr. B. E. Fernow, 'Father of Forestry,' and His Pioneer Work in This Country and Canada." The article began, "The whole of the conservation movement in the United States started in one man, and he was neither Theodore Roosevelt, who made it a living issue, nor Gifford Pinchot, who pounded it across the nets at the famous tennis court at the White House." Then followed a review of the accomplishments of Fernow in the United States and Canada. Rossiter Raymond, secretary of the American Institute of Mining Engineers, wrote to Fernow, February 3, 1910, "Who wrote the article in last Sunday's *Times* on 'The Man Who Made Pinchot?' It is not perfectly accurate, but it is substantially so nearly true as to indicate a good deal of knowledge." Raymond on February 3 said that he was "burning with desire to 'pitch in,' " but, by February 7, promised Fernow that he was "not going to 'butt into' the Pinchot-Ballinger controversy at all." Raymond wished to be judicious, since he had already presented his professional views in his conservation address at the engineers' meeting of March 1909, and Fernow and Pinchot were members of the institute.

Fernow was completely astonished. There was no controversy in which, so far as he knew, he was involved. There was no side to be taken. The newspaper articles infuriated him. On February 2 Frank J. D. Barnjum wrote him that he "took a great deal of pleasure in reading a long article in our last Sunday's [Boston] *Herald* all about your good self. The only fault with it was it did not go far enough. . . . You should be head of the Forestry Department for the United States." Fernow replied immediately, "As to the article in the *Herald*, I am sorry that it has occurred especially with the heading given to it which is most distasteful to me and must necessarily roil Pinchot. There is just about as much fiction in the article as fact and the friend who wrote it, if I can find it out, will hear from me in no uncertain tones." On the morning of the article's appearances Ralph C. Bryant of Yale University wrote to Fernow, "Graves has left for Washington—I think he has jumped into a hornet's nest—but feel he is one of the very few men who could swing the job. He is strong minded and will not be swayed by politics." Fernow answered, "I was glad to hear from you, but I must tell I was by no means pleased with the article in the *Times* which put me in an entirely wrong position when there would have [been] enough told upon which to rescue my memory. An irresponsible newspaperman secured the little anecdote from Fritz and then invented all the rest. I believe with you that Professor Graves has not chosen an easy job just now, but he was probably the best man for the job. I am somewhat troubled by this change as it removes from activity one of my best contributors to the *Quarterly*. Professor Graves very conscientiously attended to his department." February 11, 1910, Fernow addressed a communication to Mr. Edwin Wildman of the Wildman Magazine and News Service of New York City:

> I am glad to find out the source of that article in the *Times*. You evidently think you have done me a service and that I should be pleased with the performance. But I can assure that the very opposite is true and I am disgusted and mortified, especially over the headline which is in absolutely bad taste. The little anecdotes which my son furnished are innocent enough, but your writer has added most inexcusable inventions, especially as to my relations with Mr. Pinchot. Any one who knows the history must recognize it as fiction and its connection with the intimate personal story will make it appear as if I had had a hand in its manufacture. I do not know what I can do to minimize the wrong impression your writer has produced. I can only warn you against employing such untrustworthy agents.

Fernow applied himself to the forestry problems of Canada. In 1910 a book which he had begun while living at Ithaca was published. It was first conceived as a pamphlet, and later enlarged as the need for it became more evident. This was *The Care of Trees in Lawn, Street, and Park*,[58] with a list of trees and shrubs for decorative use. Fernow dedicated the volume to his friend of many years in the forestry movement, William Saunders of Canada. The *Economics of Forestry* had been dedicated to Edward A. Bowers. The *History of Forestry* had been dedicated to Rossiter Raymond. On June 14 Charles Edwin Bessey wrote Fernow, "Yesterday I received my copy of your admirable little book on 'The Care of Trees'. . . . I am very greatly pleased with it, and I am going to say so in *Science* if I can reach it before some other admirer gives his opinion of the book. I congratulate you most heartily."

[58] Henry Holt and Co., New York, 1910; American Nature Series, Group IV. The book has two parts, one devoted to trees and the other on their diseases and pests.

In May Fernow had told Hugh P. Baker, "As you know, our forestry business in Canada is still almost entirely undeveloped and nobody can tell how rapidly it will develop, and whether positions for learned foresters are to be found. We want, of course, to reserve all the opportunities for our own Canadian men." Fernow was seeking to widen the scope of forestry activities in Canada. On January 3rd he had told the editor of the *Toronto Globe*:

> I am entirely of your opinion that Rondeau park should not be given up either for lumbering purposes or for commercial forestry purposes. But I differ as to the propriety of considering its management as a park necessarily involving an absolute let-alone policy. To be sure, as long as such matters are to be left to the ignorant, they had better be left alone. It is possible, however, that under intelligent management such a park can be made more effective, more accessible, more fit for its purpose, namely for exhibiting Nature's grandeur. This may be done, not by a landscape gardener's art, which as a rule is formal, but by what I would call esthetic forestry, which preserves the naturalness and merely removes the defective and inharmonious.

Graduates of the school were now filling positions with the Dominion forestry branch, the Canadian Pacific Railroad, and with private companies. T. W. Dwight and G. H. Edgecombe graduated with the class of 1910. Dwight spent a summer in the Rocky Mountain forest reserve, secured a master's degree from Yale University, and became assistant director of the Dominion forestry branch. During 1910 Edgecombe had charge of the boundary surveys on the east slope, and later became supervisor of Brazeau forest reserve of the Dominion service.

"Our Conservation Commission," Fernow wrote to Roth on January 22, 1910, "is now in process of consideration to be put into running order, but it is such a heavy machine that we have not been able in four days' session to put it really on the track. Political jealousies between the Provinces and Dominion Government have to be carefully guarded, yet I hope that eventually a really good piece of work will be done. We have divided up into committees on subjects and expect to meet again in June with definite plans for work, meanwhile, a few subjects are to be investigated; one of them I proposed was to bring out a report of the various methods of forest [fire] fighting. Together, this Commission considers itself merely an educative body without executive functions. There are some good men in it and and as usual some blowers."

During the spring the question of consolidating *Forestry Quarterly* and the *Proceedings of the Society of American Foresters* came up again. The *Forestry Quarterly* had met with an appreciative response among supervisors of the United States forest service. Clyde Leavitt in 1908 had been instrumental in getting the service to subscribe to the *Quarterly* for the supervisors' libraries. In March 1910 Fernow had notified Leavitt that Graves had written him "despairingly" regarding the issues of the *Proceedings* and expressed himself "as satisfied with the *Forestry Quarterly* as all that the profession needed at present." He had had about a year and a half as editor-in-chief of the *Proceedings* and was impressed with the difficulty of "getting the men, particularly those in the field, to make the kind of contributions which [he] would like." The matter of consolidating the two publications was placed by Graves with Zon.

Leavitt in 1909 had consulted Fernow concerning grazing privileges on the reserves and had elicited the advice that grazing rights, to help poor farmers, were justified, but to protect regeneration the contract should be personal and not attach as a right to the ownership of stock or farm land or farm holdings. In the following year Leavitt was transferred to Washington from Ogden, Utah, to become assistant forester in the branch of operations and replace C. S. Chapman, who thenceforth was at Portland, Oregon, and became manager of the Oregon Fire Protective Association. Although there were many matters related to conservation in which Fernow was interested, he traveled very little and refrained as much as possible from doing "propaganda and educational work" outside the classroom. But he had to respond to many calls. A great temptation to leave Canada and return to the United States came to Fernow in 1910, or perhaps during the last months of 1909.

On January 15, 1910, Roth wrote to Fernow, "By the way, what did you tell our New York friends? I have thought matters over and if they do the right thing I am willing to consider the offer and go down [at the] end of the month and look the ground over. Here all is going smoothly enough and, of course, I can stay as long as I like." Fernow replied, "I have, as I thought I had told you, refused the call to New York, although it was tempting. I did not feel justified in running away from here so soon. Am glad to hear that you are considering the matter favorably." What was meant by "New York"? In May 1909 *Torreya* announced, "Columbia University is contemplating establishing a course in forestry, with the degree of forest engineer." It is known that about this time Commissioner Whipple of New York State attempted to persuade Columbia University to found a school of forestry. Moreover, on July 22, 1909, Professor Carlton C. Curtis of the department of botany of Columbia wrote to Fernow and urged, "We very much desire to consult with you regarding the forestry work that is about to be established at Columbia. . . . It is desirable to have the matter considered at once, if possible." Unforeseen events, however, interfered with the conference, and not until the Washington forestry conference held December 30-31 of that year was another appointment set. Evidently this conference was held; and, Fernow refusing, the position was tendered to Roth. Columbia University was not the only New York institution during this period that sought to provide forestry education in its curriculum. *Torreya* also announced,[59] "Syracuse University will begin next fall courses in forestry and agriculture, leading to the establishment of a college of agriculture and forestry."

Judson F. Clark evidently received the same offer which Fernow and Roth had had. In a letter of June 9, 1910, to Clark, Fernow commented, "I know where the 'inquiry from a larger forestry school' came from since I had directed them to you having declined myself the offer." That there was more than one school seeking a dean or director was clearly indicated by Clark's answer of June 16th which said, "The inquiry from 'one of the large Forestry Schools' to which I referred was not the one which you had in mind. It is interesting and flattering to be remembered in this way by the professional schools even if it is not possible to return to the teaching profession." The conclusion is practically inescapable that the two universities planning to create a school of forestry were Columbia and Syracuse.

In answer to a letter dated May 8, from Dr. William L. Bray of Syracuse University, who informed Fernow that a bill was before the New York legislature to authorize the organization of "a State School of Forestry in connection with Syracuse University," Fernow disclosed, "You are aware, I suppose, that Columbia University has under contemplation a faculty of forestry of the highest type." Columbia University, in response to the widespread interest, wanted to establish a faculty of forestry in connection with its school of mines, so that two coordinated faculties would be available to students interested in the scientific study of natural resources. The most plausible argument against the school's founding was that it was situated in a great city and distant from agricultural and forest regions. In any event the school was not created.

During 1909 Dean Bailey of the New York State College of Agriculture had completed plans to re-establish forestry instruction at Cornell as a department of the college of agriculture. No new charter authority was needed. The old charter of the New York State College of Forestry had never been surrendered and its business matters were still being administered by a director and member of the University board. Cornell University and its board of trustees were still in the throes of the Brooklyn Cooperage Company lawsuit. President Schurman told Dean Bailey that he wished no more forestry instruction on the campus of Cornell University.

Dr. Bray's letter concerning a proposed new New York State College of Forestry in connection with Syracuse University originated the next year. He informed Fernow that the "bill has passed the Assembly and

[59] *Torreya,* May 1909, p. 107; Feb. 1910, p. 50; Gurth Whipple, *op. cit.,* p. 176.

is out of Committee in the Senate with apparently no opposition. It may pass and Governor Hughes *may* not veto it. . . . I may be altogether premature in my desire for counsel, but in any event I do not want to be found unprepared to advise Chancellor Day and the Trustees if called upon." Dr. Bray consulted Fernow concerning "what form this organization should take and what the school should undertake to do." He assumed that a four-year undergraduate course was contemplated.

For almost a decade Cornell University and Syracuse University had waged a struggle over whether Cornell was to be the center of agricultural education in the state, or whether several institutions were to be state-aided and authorized to give agricultural instruction. The struggle intensified over the matter of forestry instruction.

"If I recall correctly," said Dr. Bray later,[60] "as early as 1905 Chancellor Day sought to have a legislative act passed at Albany which would establish an agricultural college at Syracuse University. . . . At any rate the design was constantly in his mind for a period of years. As early as 1909 Chancellor Day began to link Forestry with Agriculture in his plans. The closing of the College of Forestry at Ithaca may have suggested this step to him. Possibly I myself may have had something to do with this. . . . Dr. Day wrote the copy for the announcement in the University catalogue of 1909-1910 announcing SPECIAL COURSES IN AGRICULTURE AND FORESTRY." The work was conceived as part of an agricultural college program, evidently planned to be financed either with state aid or by private endowment.

Governor Charles Evans Hughes vetoed the bill to create a New York State College of Forestry at Syracuse University. Abraham Knechtel told Fernow,[61] "Governor Hughes told me that he regretted that the College of Forestry in Cornell was closed."

On December 26, 1910, Roth wrote to Fernow, "As you probably saw from Papers, Cornell is starting up, and our old friend Mulford is to set things going. While I shall miss him, I could not put any obstacles in his way, but was rather glad or even anxious that he, rather than someone else, should take the place and thus assure a proper spirit and friendly helpfulness in place of the rivalry spirit so apparent elsewhere." To which Fernow replied on January 7, 1911, "Your news regarding Cornell and Mulford is entirely new to me; when is this to come off?" Fernow wrote to Mulford on January 30:

> I am very glad indeed to see you take up the instruction in forestry at Cornell. You must not for a moment think that I am looking with anything but satisfaction at the fact that one of my own boys was selected to take up the work again, and I wish you every kind of success. I think that the world has moved since I left there eight years ago, and you will have easier sailing.

[60] Read at a special convocation at the New York State College of Forestry, April 29, 1936; manuscript furnished by Dr. Bray.

[61] Letter dated Feb. 18, 1910.

To be sure, you will not have the glamour of a first enterprise, which put us on our mettle, but you will also not have the worry and trouble which goes with such fame.

During the summer of 1910 the board of trustees of Cornell University had authorized the creation of a department of forestry. Dean Bailey revealed the circumstances when later, presenting before the governors of the Cornell Club of Rochester a "Statement on the Forestry Situation" (1913), he sketched his efforts to reestablish forestry instruction since the discontinuance of the New York State College of Forestry at Cornell:

On November 7, 1910, the provisional plans for the forestry work [at the New York State College of Agriculture] were made in my office with Professor Mulford, and these plans very definitely included both professional and farm forestry. In fact, nothing else could have been expected in an institution of the grade of Cornell, in which post-graduate work is anticipated as a matter of course. Professor Mulford agreed to take up the work with that understanding, and the following month [Dec. 1910] the Board of Trustees elected him professor of forestry. Professor Mulford was on duty at Cornell from January 26 to February 23, 1911, and on June 15, 1911, he took up his residence in Ithaca.

But the unexpected happened. Governor Hughes was appointed to a place on the supreme court of the United States. His place as governor was taken by John A. Dix. It is said on excellent authority that strong political influence was brought to bear on Governor Dix. He was convinced that Cornell University did not propose to inaugurate a program of more than farm forestry. This was never the fact. In any event, chapter 851 of the laws of 1911 of New York State was signed in July by Governor Dix and the establishment of a state college of forestry at Syracuse University was authorized. The chancellor of the university made Bray acting dean of the new school. Bray was an outstanding authority in forest ecology. In 1910 he had been "drawn into conversations regarding plans for such a college and in a very minor way regarding a legislative act which might enable the plan to be consummated." In 1909 he had been "permitted to announce that Syracuse was offering a Forestry Preparatory course so that graduates going [from Syracuse] to Yale, Michigan, and Toronto could hope to take out a professional forestry degree in one year. In all this I had no thought of a College of Forestry at Syracuse." Bray had pioneered in forestry investigations in Texas. Since 1900, while at the University of Texas where he organized a botany department, he had been connected with the forestry crusade. In Washington he had met Chief Forester Pinchot, attended the latter's historic "baked apple" open-house evenings, become a United States forest collaborator for Texas, and made some notable ecologic and forestry studies. In the botany department he introduced a course in dendrology and another called forest ecology—introduction to silviculture. In 1907 he had come to Syracuse to take charge of its newly created department of botany.

"Naturally," said Bray, "the idea remained with me that Botany in college should have two aims: (1) those of a pure science; (2) the contribution of its teachings to practical courses of large significance, notably Forestry and Agriculture. Accordingly as early as the session 1908-9 I had announced in the botany curriculum (after conference with Chancellor Day, of course) three courses bearing on Forestry: namely, Introduction to Forestry; Dendrology; and Forest Ecology—Foundations of Silviculture." Dean Bray has told the author of this book that both Fernow and Roth were approached about the deanship of New York State College of Forestry at Syracuse University. Fernow had evidently rejected the offer of the deanship of the proposed faculty of forestry of Columbia University, and he could not accept the deanship of the New York State College of Forestry at Syracuse, even if he had wanted to leave Toronto and Canada.

Chancellor Day had invited Bray to become permanent dean of the new New York forestry institution, but when Bray did not accept, he was chosen by the chancellor to select the permanent dean. In October 1911 Edward F. McCarthy was brought to Syracuse. McCarthy had graduated from the normal school at Cortland, New York. He had gotten a forestry degree and a master of forestry degree *in absentia* from the University of Michigan. A brief period had been spent with the United States forest service, to which in later years he was to return for a while to found the Central States Forest Experiment Station at Columbus, Ohio. Bray arranged with McCarthy to teach the forestry courses of the new school. The combined courses under Bray and McCarthy constituted the first and the fundamental curriculum, consisting primarily of mensuration, silvics, and dendrology. Bray and McCarthy often discussed who should be asked to be permanent dean. Leading foresters were consulted with reference to the choice.

At the start of Mulford's negotiations with Dean Bailey concerning forestry teaching at the New York State College of Agriculture at Cornell, Mulford had wanted Roth also on the Cornell faculty. As early as 1909 Bailey had authorized Mulford to obtain Roth's services. The plans of that year called also for obtaining, if possible, Herman Haupt Chapman for the new department. During 1909 President Schurman had opposed the re-establishment of forestry instruction on the Cornell campus. In 1910, however, he had initiated proceedings to create a department of forestry within the New York State College of Agriculture. He wrote to Mulford; Mulford wrote to Bailey, and Bailey concluded the arrangements. Mulford arrived at Ithaca, and soon Syracuse University was authorized by the state of New York to create a new college of forestry. Mulford was young; he requested that Roth be brought on from Michigan to head the department at Cornell.

On January 6, 1912, Dean Bailey wired Roth at Ann Arbor that he had been appointed professor of forestry in the New York State College of Agriculture at Ithaca. On January 30 President Schurman addressed a letter to Roth. "I want to congratulate you on your appointment as head of the department of Forestry in our State College of Agriculture, and at the same time to congratulate the University and the State on your coming. . . . I look forward with the utmost confidence to great results for scientific forestry in New York State." A farewell banquet was tendered Roth at Michigan. He prepared to go to Cornell, but Junius E. Beal of the Michigan board of regents persuaded the board to improve the facilities for forestry instruction at the University of Michigan. Cornell University saw that with a separate school and department of forestry instruction furnished by the state, the New York State College of Agriculture would have to seek a private endowment in addition to the state's allowances. The New York State College of Forestry at Syracuse University began with the largest appropriations ever granted a forestry institution in North America. It was plain common sense for Cornell University to solicit endowment funds. Roth was requested to interview a donor. Roth was a teacher. He did not wish to assume the additional responsibility of securing endowment funds. Coupled with the University of Michigan's offer of improved facilities, Roth decided to stay at Michigan. Mulford was offered the permanent deanship of the New York State College of Forestry at Syracuse, but he refused the offer. Herman Haupt Chapman also was considered for the Syracuse position.

Hugh Potter Baker became the dean. By March 1911 the enrollment of the department of forestry of Pennsylvania State College had increased to more than one hundred and ninety. "While numbers do not, of course, make a school," wrote Baker to Fernow, "it does increase our appropriations and makes it possible for us to raise the standards considerably." In July of 1911 Thomas J. Burrill informed Fernow that, after numerous attempts to get bills through the legislature, at last an appropriation for forestry had been slipped into the general appropriation bill. He asked Fernow to recommend a man for the position.

On January 29, 1912, James B. Berry of Pennsylvania State College wrote Fernow, "Dr. Baker has accepted a 'call' to Syracuse and has accepted that in place of the Illinois position. Mr. Bray, Acting Dean at Syracuse, was at the Forestry Conference."[62] Fernow responded, "It is

[62] There were many rearrangements in forestry education during 1912. Baker resigned at Pennsylvania State College in April (*Forestry Quarterly* X, 1, March 1912, p. 123; *Forest Leaves* XIII, April 1912, p. 114). Berry went later to the University of Georgia (*Forestry Quarterly* XII, 4, Dec. 1914, p. 653). W. D. Clark took Baker's place, but went to Massachusetts Agricultural College at about the time when Frank-

interesting to hear that Dr. Baker has undertaken to organize a forest school at Syracuse. Professor Roth is going back to Cornell to start the college there again. Evidently, my pessimistic outlook as to a superabundance of foresters does not frighten anybody." On March 9 Roth communicated to Fernow:

Pardon delay in thanking you for your good wishes to my return to Cornell. It is not all joy, for we are very much attached here and our school, the College, and all, is in splendid condition and there is no lack of support. The State work here is in the dumps and only a change in Government will get it back on the track. The lands which we had are fooled away and so the interest, for the present, is gone.

Was in Ithaca, had the first glimpse of the new buildings and new order of things. We hope to start out in full force and develop:

1) Full 5 year professional course.
2) Teach courses to Agricultural students.
3) Teach Ranger course.
4) Do Extension work with the farm people.

Was down at Harrisburg; saw Rothrock, had a good meeting. Also met Baker who is to be our rival at Syracuse.

Fernow replied:

I am glad to have your letter and to see your programme, which appeals to me as ideal, especially the lengthening of the term to five years. We here with only 7 months teaching time have been discussing such lengthening of the course which, however, would arouse considerable discussion. This year for the first time our Forestry Branch is going to be organized on proper administrative lines. We had, last night, Mr. MacMillan before our Forestry Club, detailing the organization, and everybody is more hopeful than we have been for some time as to the likelihood of development. This summer I have before me a reconnaissance of from 1,000 to 1,500 square miles of cutover and waste lands in the province of Ontario, as a sample of what may be found on many thousands of square miles in our eastern provinces. This is done for the Conservation Commission with a view to devising propositions as to how such country might be managed.

---

lin F. Moon, who had been Associate Professor of Forestry in the Division of Horticulture there, was appointed among others to the new faculty of the New York State College of Forestry (*ibid.* X, 2, June 1912, p. 322). On August 24, 1912, Berry wrote to Fernow that Clark had gone to Massachusetts and that A. B. Recknagel would be at Pennsylvania State College "about September 20 and the expectation [was] that he [would] head the department. . . ." Recknagel, while with the U.S. Forest Service at Albuquerque had written to Fernow on June 7, 1911, asking for advice concerning postgraduate instruction at the Forstakademie at Eberswalde, and travel in Austria and possibly Russia, since he wished to "familiarize [himself] with European forestry method." When Recknagel returned from Germany he went to the New York State College of Agriculture at Cornell (*ibid.* X, 1, March 1912, p. 122; X, 2, June 1912, p. 323; X, 4, Dec. 1912, p. 780). For a while John A. Ferguson was at the University of Missouri. He returned to Pennsylvania State College and for many years headed the department (*ibid.*, p. 782). Fernow recommended Frederick Dunlap, then with the Forest Products Laboratory at Madison, Wisconsin, for the vacancy at Missouri. His recommendation was sent on Dec. 5, 1912, to Dean F. B. Mumford of the College of Agriculture, and Dunlap was appointed.

In a letter dated April 3, 1912, Fernow told Roth that the reconnaissance would cover about a thousand square miles of cut-over watersheds, "a sample area, representing the conditions of thousands of square miles of the two provinces of Ontario and Quebec, to be surveyed with a view of developing a co-operative plan of management. We have already advanced a few steps towards such an end by one of the counties having decided to acquire their watersheds and put them under management, and by the formation of an association of water power users on this same watershed," the now famous Trent Watershed.

In the fall of 1911 John H. Burnham had invited Fernow to look over the watershed with the canal superintendent. The Dominion government had spent millions of dollars on the watershed, building dams at some forty lakes to regulate waterflow without controlling the watersheds which furnished the waters. Fernow accepted the task of forming a new control program.

At this time there was developing "a movement to secure not only a wood laboratory but a general technological laboratory for the Dominion." Fernow was trying to secure a wood products laboratory modeled after the forest products laboratory at the University of Wisconsin and also to have it placed at the University of Toronto in connection with the faculty of forestry. He told[63] Robert Woodward of the Carnegie Institution of Washington, "I am trying to wake public opinion for the establishment of a Technological Laboratory and Bureau of Standards for the Dominion, if possible to be located here in some relation to the University. I understand that you have published an account of physical laboratories which might furnish suggestions, and perhaps you can also refer me to literature on technological laboratories, literature which details methods of administration more especially. The idea originated in the desire for a Wood Technology Laboratory somewhat like the one which the Forest Service has in Madison. An extension of such a laboratory to include other technical branches suggests itself naturally." This letter was written on March 26, 1912. That Fernow did not make the matter of the new laboratory his first business was shown in a letter written the following April 30th to E. B. Biggar of the *Pulp and Paper Magazine of Canada*, "I have been so busy in other directions that I have not been able to secure more information regarding our contemplated technological laboratory, but hope presently, with the closing of academic work, to accomplish more and then let you have data."

The laboratory, when created, went to McGill University at Montreal

[63] On March 25, 1912, Fernow wrote to E. Russell Burdon of the University of Cambridge, England, concerning "a movement to secure not only a wood laboratory but a general technological laboratory for the Dominion, which I am trying to bring into connection with the University here. . . ."

and not to the campus of the University of Toronto.[64] Several strong influences led to the laboratory's establishment, not the least of which was an address which was read at the thirteenth annual convention of the Canadian Forestry Association held at Ottawa in February. This address was given by Director of Forestry Campbell and prepared by H. R. MacMillan of the forestry branch of the Dominion department of the interior. The convention was opened by the new prime minister, R. L. Borden. MacMillan's address was entitled, "A Progressive Forest Policy Requires an Investment of Capital."[65] Among many suggestions for a program of Dominion forestry expansion were restocking and management of the Riding Mountain and Rocky Mountains forest reserves, methods by which to make the forests more "fire-proof," and the founding of a forest products laboratory and an experimental paper and pulp laboratory. Fernow's principal contribution at this convention was his presentation of the report of the committee on forest fire legislation. Sometime late in 1911 or early in 1912 he had discussed with "the Director of the Forestry Branch . . . his plans for an efficient organization of the forest service of his Branch, in which [University of Toronto] graduates might be employed." In March 1911 Fernow and one of his classes had discussed the matter of how a forest service in the Dominion's forestry branch should be organized, and forwarded their suggestions to MacMillan. Gifford Pinchot had been a principal speaker at the recent Ottawa meeting, and his address had impressed Fernow. The latter wrote to Campbell on February 10, 1912, "I am . . . concerned in promoting harmony, avoiding discontent, and keeping alive that loyal spirit among the crew which Pinchot so admirably pointed out as the keystone of success in [forest] administration."

In 1912 the Dominion forestry branch received "for the first time . . .

[64] *Pulp and Paper Magazine of Canada* X, 8, Aug. 1912, p. 233, previously published by Biggar-Wilson, Ltd., announced that it had been sold to a new organization, the Industrial and Educational Press, Ltd., of Toronto and Montreal. In April this publication (X, 4, pp. 115-119) took the position that "already the nucleus of a small experimental pulp and paper laboratory at McGill University" argued in favor of Montreal as the permanent location for the proposed government laboratory, though it admitted that "some might consider Ottawa or Toronto University as having equally good claims. But," said the editorial, "this is a question which may well be left open for the time being. The main point just now is to interest the Dominion Government." H. R. MacMillan and R. H. Campbell contributed to the magazine. During these years the Canadian Pulp and Paper Association became a powerful influence (XI, 3, Feb. 1, 1913, p. 63), and it combined with other agencies to persuade government officials to establish a forest products laboratory. The argument for establishment at Montreal was presented in *Pulp and Paper Magazine of Canada* XI, Feb. 15, 1913, p. 122. ". . . the unanimous choice seems to fall on Montreal on account of its central location and the many pulp and paper interests located there. A further argument has been that McGill University has done more along this line than any other institution in Canada." See also *ibid.* XII, Jan. 1, 1914, p. 3.

[65] *13th Report of the Annual Convention of the Canadian Forestry Association*, Ottawa, Feb. 7-8, 1912, pp. 12ff.

tolerably adequate appropriations," and the first large graduating class in forestry at Toronto all found employment in the federal service.[66] Director Campbell by letter of January 30, 1912, told Fernow:

> There is a good deal of construction work to be done and very little forestry work. This year's efforts are to be directed mainly towards fire protection, and the forestry students might act as clerks to the supervisors, as general assistants and messengers in districts where the supervisor has not good means of communication and cannot be everywhere at once, as lookout men, or as assistants in constructing telephone lines, trails or cabins. In other words, they would be put on as forest guards at the disposal of the supervisor. The supervisor will be instructed to give them as much experience as possible. I believe they would gain very much in this experience, and I am sure that they would have a very good effect on the morale of the forest force.

Nevertheless, forestry in the Dominion government had made noticeable progress. Since the Dominion forestry convention of 1906 the federal forest reservations had been divested entirely of their temporary status. Attaining an aggregate area of 17,000,000 acres,[67] the reservations had been gradually expanded and had come to be regarded as essential and permanent elements of the nation's economy. The perpetuation of an adequate timber supply was as much within their purview now, as water and streamflow protection had originally been. With the passage on June 6, 1913, of the Forest Reserves and Parks Act, the Dominion reservations assumed a total of more than 35,800 square miles of forest land in the western provinces, over two-thirds of the total area being in Alberta, owing to the fact "that practically all the eastern slope of the Rockies [had] been set apart as a forest reserve."[68] In 1911 the commission of conservation had helped to secure the establishment of the Rocky Mountains forest reserve. The commission justly claimed that it had aided materially in increasing the area of the Dominion forest reserves from less than 3,000 to about 25,000 square miles. Moreover, fire patrols had been extended to the Athabasca, Peace, Churchill, and Nelson valleys in the northern districts, and the number of rangers had been practically tripled. Forest surveys had been so extended that in 1910 seven parties were in the field as compared to one in 1906. The technical staff was enlarged from nine to seventeen men.

Forestry Quarterly,[69] on the page which concluded a discussion of the effects of the Dominion's Forest Reserves and Parks Act, also announced that the forestry branch of the Dominion government had decided to follow the example of the United States forest service in establishing a wood products laboratory. This was to be done in co-

66 *Forestry Quarterly* X, 2, June 1912, p. 326.
67 *Report of the Canadian Forestry Convention*, Quebec, Jan. 18-20, 1911, p. 35.
68 *Forestry Quarterly* XI, 3, Sept. 1913, pp. 451f.
69 *ibid.* XI, 3, Sept. 1913, p. 452.

operation with McGill University. During the spring of 1912, when the matter of a forest products laboratory in Canada was being considered, Fernow's attention had been preoccupied with employment of the school's graduates of that year. When "expected appointments [were] held up" temporarily and the students on that account had become "greatly disturbed," Fernow feared that the very existence of the faculty of forestry at Toronto was threatened. He told President Falconer by letter of May 6 that if this meant "that the attempt of the federal government to employ technically-educated foresters to look after the timber interests [was] to be given up, this Faculty has lost its right to existence, since the federal government is, as yet, alone developed enough to employ the graduates, the provinces not yet being developed on forestry lines, and private employ needing only [a] few . . . could be supplied from the United States." Obviously his concern was more with the forest work than a wood products laboratory. Fernow had welcomed Campbell's offer to arrange "to allow Mr. [Theodore W.] Dwight to prepare two or three lectures for the students at the Forest School." In the forestry branch Dwight had recently studied timber sale regulations tried out on the national forests in Montana. Morever he had "spent considerable time in studying the sylvicultural characteristics of the merchantable spruce of the Rocky Mountain Forest Reserve." Also, he was "devoting considerable attention [to] the present method of handling timber sales, cutting under timber licenses and cutting under permits on Dominion Forest Reserves."[70] MacMillan's lectures on fire protection and other subjects also met with instant favor in the school.

The laboratory had been operating nearly a year when formally dedicated; ceremonies did not occur until December 3, 1915.[71] McGill University, like the University of Wisconsin, offered quarters—the residence of the Molsons, a distinguished Montreal family—and a group of prominent Montreal citizens, notably Carl Riordan and others, persuaded Director of Forestry R. H. Campbell and Minister of the Interior W. J. Roche that the laboratory should be established in connection with McGill University, which had not developed an elaborate forestry school or department and did not contemplate so doing. From a list of candidates A. G. McIntyre, a graduate in chemistry at McGill, a born promoter and able organizer, editor of *The Pulp and Paper Magazine of Canada*, was chosen as the laboratory's superintendent.

[70] Letter from Campbell to Fernow, Feb. 17, 1912.

[71] *Forestry Quarterly* XIV, 1, March 1916, p. 168. See also the report of the secretary-treasurer of the Canadian Society of Forest Engineers, Jan. 13, 1916, particularly the report of the annual meeting held at the Laurentian Club at Ottawa, Jan. 18. This meeting was presided over by Clyde Leavitt, the newly elected president of the Society, first to hold the position after Fernow. In 1915 *Forestry Quarterly* XIII, 1915, pp. 127, 412, referred to several articles on the work of the Forest Products Laboratories of Canada: *Pulp and Paper Magazine of Canada* XIII, 1915, pp. 9-11, 241-247; *Canadian Forestry Journal* XI, 1915, pp. 115-117, 135f.

The magazine's principal office was transferred to Montreal so that McIntyre might, at the same time, develop the laboratory. Perhaps more than any one individual McIntyre had been responsible for enlisting the paper industry's interest in the laboratory's creation. While it cannot be denied that Fernow advised and guided Director Campbell in matters of forestry policy, nothing definite has been found which shows that Fernow shared in making the decision which placed the laboratory at a university where no forestry school existed. Fernow was pleased that cordial relations between the University of Toronto and McGill University had been preserved. No discord between the two institutions was engendered. When officials of the University of Toronto including Fernow were first interviewed, a proposal to establish the laboratory on the Toronto campus received no encouragement. Fernow actively supported the movement to create forest products laboratories in Canada. The most that he sought was to bring the laboratory into "some relation" or connection with the faculty of forestry or the university itself. He regarded his faculty as primarily a teaching and not a research organization. If for no other reason than the limited amounts of money with which the school had to be financed, his policy was wise and necessary. Fernow never neglected opportunities to advance the laboratory's interests, once it was established at Montreal. Indeed, one of his students, William Kynoch, was to be sent to the laboratory at the request of Superintendent John S. Bates to supply a graduate forester for forest products research.

The wood products laboratory of Canada in considerable part was modelled after the forest products laboratory at Madison, Wisconsin. McIntyre spent a month in study before taking up his duties as superintendent. Russel W. Sterns also took a leading part in the organization of the Canadian laboratory, and he had worked at Madison. The *Pulp and Paper Magazine of Canada* shows, furthermore, that the forest service's laboratory at Wausau, Wisconsin, also influenced the Canadian laboratory. Paper and pulp manufacture and forest products research constituted the main aims of investigation. Timber testing was conducted in McGill University laboratories. A museum was started. Many years later the forest products work was dissociated from the paper and pulp laboratory and research institute, and was transferred to Ottawa. This separation, however, did not occur until substantial growth in each sphere had captured the interest and support of segregated industries, and the industries themselves sponsored the separate laboratories.

McIntyre did not remain permanently as superintendent of the Canadian wood products laboratory. In his capacity as editor he published in the January 15, 1914, issue of *The Pulp and Paper Magazine of Canada* a dissertation, "Chemical Utilization of Southern Waste," prepared by John S. Bates in the research laboratories of Arthur D. Little, Inc., of

Boston, Massachusetts. This study, which covered two years of research in the manufacture of pulp and paper from resinous woods, enthused McIntyre with the belief that it, combined with investigations conducted by McGarvey Cline in the United States, would "certainly revolutionize the use of southern pine in the manufacture of paper." Immediately he sought after Bates to accept a position at the wood products laboratory at Montreal. Soon McIntyre informed Bates that he had been elected superintendent. In 1914 he took office. W. Boyd Campbell was named as his assistant.

Bates had received his early education at Amherst, Nova Scotia, and Acadia University, and had obtained the degrees of chemical engineer and doctor of philosophy from Columbia University. As a wood chemist and "one of the foremost authorities on wood pulp manufacture in America,"[72] he remained in his position through the crucial developmental research period before the years of World War I, when, under the pressure of war service, expansion of the forest industries achieved notable advancements, many of which contributed to peacetime prosperity and progress. Bates's active administration lasted only through most of the year 1916. At this time he was lent to the Imperial government for munitions manufacture, and W. Boyd Campbell became acting superintendent.[73] From the start of his administration, either on his own initiative or at R. H. Campbell's suggestion, Bates consulted Fernow. From Sackville, New Brunswick, on April 15, 1914, Bates wrote to Fernow:

> As Superintendent-elect of the Forest Products Laboratories of Canada, I am commissioned to make a trip to Europe this year to visit such points of interest as may prove helpful in the study of forest products. Realizing the necessity of carefully planning such a trip, I am taking the liberty of asking you for suggestions. In discussing this matter with Mr. R. H. Campbell in Ottawa, he felt that I would be fortunate in having your advice on the subject. No doubt Mr. Campbell has already written you in this connection. [Campbell had written to Fernow.]
>
> My interests will lie primarily in such matters as the manufacture and testing of pulp and paper, the testing, seasoning and technology of wood, and the study of wood preservation. Undoubtedly I should also visit the important 'forestry' centres. I have already on my list the Manchester [England] and Grenoble [France] Schools of Papermaking and the technical institutes of Darmstadt, Charlottenburg and Berlin. If opportunity offers, I shall visit paper mills, etc., in England, Germany, Norway, Sweden and Italy.
>
> I shall greatly appreciate any suggestions you may offer regarding important institutions and manufacturing establishments which should be visited, as well as the names of any investigators whom I would do well to

[72] *Forestry Quarterly* XII, 1914, p. 309.

[73] Bates was the official superintendent until 1919. R. W. Sterns, as well as Campbell, filled the position during his absence. See *Canada Lumberman*, April 1, 1944, p. 37.

consult. Perhaps you can also direct me to literature bearing on foreign institutions. . . .

For some years I have been interested in your work and writings on forestry, and have also heard my cousin, Herbert Christie, speak of you many times.

Fernow replied:

I have so long been out of touch with the particular line in which you are interested that my information as to where you should go on your trip can not be very full.

As I suggested to Mr. Campbell, your first trip in Germany should be to Charlottenburg, and to Eberswalde (which is close by), where you should consult with Dr. Schwappach, or whoever is now in charge of the utilization subjects. You will then be readily informed by these gentlemen how to proceed further. You will probably go to Mariabrunn near Vienna, where Professor Janka is located, and possibly to Munich and Zurich.

Altogether, you will probably find that there is only a limited development in this matter. I would also advise you first to make a visit to Madison, where they ought to have fuller information as to what is being done elsewhere.

Fernow's letter to Campbell, in reply to the latter's request for the same information, was more intimate, and added:

Mr. Bates will find that timber testing is pretty nearly all that is being done at [the Technological Institute at Charlottenburg, at Eberswalde, and the Bodenschule at Mariabrunn]. I would, however, advise him to study our early timber physics work, of which Mr. McIntyre seemed to have no knowledge whatsoever, for we developed at least in the timber testing line methods which I consider superior to the German ones. I had already heard that you were going to Europe, and I envy you the trip, being probably cut out, for the second time, from the journey that I had planned last year and this year. I shall be glad to talk over the trip with you when you come.

Bates's journey never took place. Campbell's, however, did. At first he planned to call on Fernow at Toronto, before sailing, to gain information "on some special things that [he had] in mind that affect our administration rather closely," and also to get from Fernow the "best points to visit in the short time [he] would have at [his] disposal. . . ." On June 9, Fernow wrote to Campbell:

As I can just as well satisfy your needs by letter . . . my advice as regards travel in Germany would be first to get hold of someone who speaks English and has broad enough views to direct you. I would suggest therefore, if you go by way of Hamburg, to go Eberswalde (two hours from Berlin) and call upon Dr. Moeller, Director of the Forest Academy, who used to know English at least and would be most capable of directing you, if you can say what exactly you wish to see. In order to have some additional advice, I would then run over to Dresden and from there to Tharandt (two or three hours' run), and call upon Dr. Jentsch, who has been in the United States and probably still knows some English, and who is a first-class man to direct you. If you can go to the Black Forest you should not miss calling upon

Oberforster Phillip, who is a good English scholar, has instructed English students for many years, and is a delightful companion. . . . If you go to Sweden, I would make a point to call on Jaegmaestare Neilson at Karlstadt. He is a good English scholar, and is in charge of the administration of the forest law for Jaemtland. Here you can see good private forest management.

The forest products research program, which Bates outlined in his letter to Fernow in April 1914, was put into effect at Montreal, and more was added. Engineering properties of Canadian woods became a major subject of investigation. Such valuable contributions as the so-called Canadian freeness tester for groundwood pulp, utilization research on such products as waste sulphite liquor, and the explanatory bulletin issued by the laboratory brought the Canadian institution into prominence. In 1915 Bates wrote to Fernow concerning a proposed "museum collection of timber specimens to include eventually all Canadian species of commercial importance." Potentially commercial species also were to be represented, and every species was to be illustrated by a trunk-bark specimen, a wheel specimen, small boards sawed in various ways to show surface sides and edges, hard specimens, and other points of special interest. In 1917 Bates forwarded to Fernow copies of a "Diagram of Forest Products from Canadian Tree Species," a chart prepared in connection with a paper on "Present and Possible Products from Canadian Woods" for the Canadian Society of Forest Engineers. This diagram was hung in the lounging room of the faculty of forestry building at Toronto.

So great have been the extensions of research techniques in forest products investigations, both in Canada and the United States, that today we are said to be "on the threshold of a New Age of Wood." This expansion expresses itself in thousands of commodities, many of them new discoveries or forms, many valuable improvements of older products. Wood products have been converted into so many and such widely used new forms that an even stronger emphasis on a continuous need of commercially valuable forest supplies, appropriate wood utilization, waste elimination, and sound forest economy has had to be written. By new and refined processing, by the application of discoveries in chemistry and physics, by various modifications of wood properties, and in a host of ways too numerous to be described here, woods in their natural state have been improved and entirely new forms have been devised. Today the forest products laboratories are among the great laboratories of the world. Advanced study of the subject now requires an elaborate library and extensive special laboratory equipment. Forestry has had two principal courses of development—first the development of the forest products laboratory and the extension of trade and marketing of forest products and by-products, and second the improvement of the forest's conditions of growth. Fernow continuously aimed to develop and coordinate both. The forestry organization on the North American continent and throughout the world became enormous. Specialization developed. Fernow, the school man, the policy maker, chose the work in the forest—silviculture. None may say, however, that he was not prepared for new research achievements in cellulose, lignin, etc. Not alone for lumber and pulp have wood supplies become necessary in our daily lives, but also in textiles, fibers, plastics, chemicals, and scores of other materials. The forest was recognized by Fernow and Roth as necessary as agriculture to human existence. Some of the most brilliant writings ever done on this continent on the interrelationships of agriculture and forestry were contributed by Fernow, Roth, and other foresters of their generation. To cite a few other products dependent on wood and wood supplies, and part and parcel of our economy today, one might point to the manufacture of rayon, cellophane, fiber board, wood sugars, alcohols, resins, glues, fertilizers, oils, and the plastic and laminated woods.

During the second decade of the twentieth century Fernow's services to the advancement of Canadian forestry continued to be numerous. Fire protection and the rehabilitation of burnt-over and cut-over lands were primary. He secured Clyde Leavitt's employment as expert forester for the conservation commission and chief fire inspector for the railway commission to organize and conduct a fire control system which Fernow had formulated.[74] Fernow disclaimed any credit for having selected Leavitt. He told Leavitt in a letter of March 30, 1912, that he had "pointed out [his] existence." On March 12 he had explained, "Your position would be mainly of an advisory character and, if you have ideas of what work should be done, almost independent. I take it that for the Railway Commission it would be to elaborate regulations in detail, for which I laid down the principles, and to see to their enforcement in co-operation with the Forestry Branch and the provincial fire control services." Fernow asked Leavitt to "have a hand" in the proposed forest reconnaissance of the Trent Canal watershed. After Leavitt's work as chief of organization of the United States forest service and his year and a half as district forester of Region 4 with offices at Ogden, Utah, he had spent a year in Washington as assistant forester. In March 1911 he had been made a forest inspector and assigned to work with William Logan Hall, who was in charge of national forest land acquisitions under the Weeks law, which extended the national forest reservation policy to the Appalachian and White Mountain ranges. Leavitt spent a year in obtaining lands for the national forests in eastern United States.

[74] *Forestry Quarterly* X, 2, June 1912, p. 326, announcing Leavitt's appointment, said that since the railway commission possessed extensive powers over all railroads operating under Dominion charter, the elaborate set of regulations which had been prepared would become effective under Leavitt's inspection. It was believed that the regulations foreshadowed the time when oil burning would become obligatory.

He was at work in the southern Appalachians, in the Blue Ridge Mountains of Georgia, when in 1912 he resigned to go to Canada to do the work which Fernow had suggested.

Fernow received with interest Roth's letter of April 18, 1912, saying, "I am *not* going to Cornell. Though properly appointed and all and though we had a good meet and all seemed just the best, there came up certain things which made me feel uncertain and anxious and I asked them to relieve me. It was not a personal matter but rather a matter subjective: I felt that a couple of *young* men were needed, men who would conquer the State work situation, and so I withdrew. What is going to be done at Cornell is not clear, but I have an idea they will go right ahead with Mulford as Chief. Yes, I too was glad to see Leavitt go into Canada work, and hope that the envy of 'Canada for the Canadians' may not affect him." On May 1, 1912, Fernow wrote Dean Bailey, "Sorry to hear that Roth could not be secured to revive the College of Forestry, but under the circumstances, with the competition in Syracuse, perhaps he acted wisely from his point of view." To which Bailey replied, having cause to correspond with Fernow on the revision of Fernow's articles on conifers, forestry, and the pines for the *Cyclopedia of American Horticulture*, "I am interested in your comment in the forestry situation here. Of course, Mulford will go on with it and we shall grow slowly as the occasion demands. The situation here is now very interesting. I wish that you might come back and see it sometime."

The prospect of an efficient forestry administration in British Columbia was high-lighted at the thirteenth annual convention of the Canadian Forestry Association as one of the real achievements of foresters in Canada. In May 1911 Fernow had revealed that he had discussed with Minister of Crown Lands W. R. Ross of British Columbia the matter of cooperation between agencies of Canada and the United States in fire protection. At the time he had been impressed by "the statements of the Minister that the Government of British Columbia [proposed] to vigorously pursue a protective policy and to organize to that effect." One year later Fernow wrote that "in general" he believed that "British Columbia is a desirable field for the future. It is bound to boom, and especially in our own line. It is the first province to establish a really efficient Forest Service this year." On June 11, 1912, Director of Forestry R. H. Campbell of the Dominion forestry branch at Ottawa informed Fernow, "I am sorry that MacMillan is leaving us but he got such a good offer from the British Columbia Government that I did not feel like trying to stand in his way. . . . It will mean however the opening of a good many additional positions for graduates of the Forest School, having the Forest Service of the British Columbia Government open up the way it is."

For a while MacMillan was acting chief forester, but before the year was completed the appointment was permanent and MacMillan, although he modified his policy in certain phases of work, began to put into application his belief that "throughout this Province forestry means fire protection . . . especially as a good fire record would be of great assistance to us in the further development of our work."

At Victoria, British Columbia, during 1910, the *Final Report of the Royal Commission of Inquiry on Timber and Forestry* had been published. In *Forestry Quarterly*[75] this report, which presented an analysis of timber resources and a brief history of legislation with respect to grants, leases, and licenses, was reviewed. The report confirmed Fernow's previous estimates. Adequate fire protection was more important on this account. British Columbia possessed slightly less than half of the entire estimated forest stand in Canada and had a merchantable forest area of twenty-six millon acres, with an existing timber stand of two hundred and forty billion feet. The public was warned that as yet the means to make a sound estimate of the timber resources of Canada were not available. Lack of reliable statistical information presented a serious impediment to future forestry progress. It was believed, however, that there were nine million acres of forest land under license. A million acres were estimated to be under lease. More than a million and a quarter acres were in private hands. Millions of acres had been granted to the railroads. British Columbia, more than ever, was revealed to be a fertile field for forestry development. Indeed, the entire forest area of Canada loomed as a great forestry challenge, in some ways more urgent than forestry development in the United States.

Forestry in the United States had attained mammoth proportions. The national forests including Alaska and Puerto Rico comprised about one hundred and ninety million acres; the national parks, about twelve million acres; the military reservations, several hundred thousand acres of forest land; the Indian forests, some ten million acres; state-owned forest lands, more than ten million acres, about three millions of which were reserved, and two-thirds of these reserved lands were in New York and Pennsylvania; and there were additional unreserved public forest areas with undetermined boundaries aggregating from ten to twenty million acres. All in all, the publicly owned forests in the United States amounted to approximately thirty per cent of the country's total forest area. How did this situation compare with Canadian conditions? Considered in the light of what Fernow regarded as real forestry progress, forest reproduction, perhaps the report that by 1910 reforestation, including planting and seeding, was vigorously under way on 106 national forests, with plans to enlarge operations to reforest annually as much as

[75] *Forestry Quarterly* IX, 1, March 1911, p. 75. In *ibid.* XI, 3, Sept. 1913, p. 452, the British Columbia forest resources were estimated at over 300 billion feet of timber, half of the total standing in the Dominion at that time.

one hundred and fifty to two hundred thousand acres after experimentation had demonstrated what areas would be most benefited, told more of the advanced state of United States forestry than the huge amount of forest land under reservation. Not only were the national forests being utilized profitably, by timber cutting, grazing, and so forth, but working plans were being drawn with regard for posterity's interests.[76]

Forestry in Canada was attaining an unprecedented geographical expansion. Little scientific work aside from protection against fires existed until any locality was made reasonably safe from devastation by fire. By 1913 the Dominion was very proud of its 35,800 square miles of reservations. Yet the aggregate area of the United States national forests was "over seven times as great."[77] It must always be kept in mind that in Canada the provinces, principally Quebec and Ontario, reserved the immense forests of the East; and the Dominion policy applied principally in the West. At the thirteenth annual convention of the Canadian Forestry Association, Director Campbell informed the delegates and members that appropriations for the coming year had been very considerably increased. Indeed, these had been more than tripled within less than half a decade.[78] The report of a year's work was revealing.

In March 1910 White had reviewed[79] Campbell's report for the year 1908-1909 as superintendent of forestry and irrigation. The total forest area of Canada had been estimated at between five and six hundred million acres, with a stand of as many billion feet. Systematic forest surveys conducted by both federal and local governments had been urged. Definite knowledge of the Dominion lands between Hudson Bay and the Rocky Mountains—some 400,000 square miles, part in reserves and parks—was urgently needed. Detailed surveys had covered about a million and a quarter acres of land within the reserves. Tree distribution, nevertheless, still constituted the principal forestry work of the Dominion government. Two and a half million trees, mostly hardwoods, had been distributed in a year to two thousand applicants. It was expected that in 1911 the general distribution of conifers, mainly white spruce, and Scotch, jack, and lodgepole pines, would begin. While hydrographic survey work had been separately organized, during the past season the activities had been more or less principally confined to inspection and stream gauging. White said in his review, "The work of the past year was conducted with a staff of 40 on an appropriation of $100,000. This is certainly very scant when one considers that the

[76] H. S. Graves, "The Present Situation in Forestry," *Forest Leaves* XIII, 6, Dec. 1911, pp. 91f.; also *Forestry Quarterly* IX, 1911, pp. 90, 350, 363.

[77] *Forestry Quarterly* XI, 3, Sept. 1913, pp. 451f.

[78] *ibid.* X, 2, June 1912, p. 326, where the appropriations were said to be $360,000, and plans called for effective fire control by watch towers, trails, telephone lines, etc.

[79] *ibid.* VIII, 1, March 1910, p. 75; also White's review of the "Report of the Superintendent of Forestry and Irrigation" for 1909-1910, *ibid.* IX, 1, March 1911, p. 78.

United States has a staff fifty times as large and an appropriation of half a million. . . . All through [the report] runs the cry of lack of information and a call for more generous appropriations. The Forestry Branch sees what is coming in the next decade and is anxious to be equipped when the time comes."

Moreover, in the United States the passage of the Weeks law marked the inauguration of another epoch in forestry history. The federal forest reservation policy went in full force to the Appalachian and White Mountains of the eastern states. H.R. 11798 passed the senate on February 15, 1911. *Forestry Quarterly*[80] joyfully announced that a new stage in the development of the nation's forest policy had arrived. Fernow regarded the new law as a favorable departure in principle. A one million dollar appropriation for 1910 had lapsed, and now two million dollars would be available before July 1, 1911. In all, a total of ten million dollars would be used for purposes not merely of reserving lands already owned but to acquire lands by purchase to fulfill the objects of the law. We will again consider the import of this law in the enlargement of state forest policies.

In Canada the fundamental consideration of fire prevention still dominated. In 1910, when Fernow found that because too much time would be required from his school duties to attend the eleventh meeting of the Canadian Forestry Association, he sent a letter to the assemblage which recommended measures relative to burning brush or requiring the downing of tops of trees while logging operations were in process.[81] Procedures applicable in "real pineries" and "mixed woods" were part of his outline. The method of downing the tops—"lopping the branches so that the branches and tops fall to the ground and may decay in a short time"—was recommended, especially if the pulpwood was utilized. "This method was first suggested by the writer in 1890, and last year, for the first time, the State of New York compelled lumbermen on their private holdings in the Adirondacks to adopt it." The faculty of forestry at Toronto during the 1909-1910 session enrolled forty students, "an increase," Fernow reported to President Falconer on April 18, 1910, "of fifty percent over the previous year." In the "academic year 1910-11 just an even 50 students were registered," and Ontario, New Brunswick, Nova Scotia, Alberta, British Columbia, and even the United States were represented. Fernow told the 1910 gathering of the Canadian Forestry Association that he hoped the committee on forests of the commission of conservation would soon have its first task ready, its report on fire fighting and fire prevention. On January 7, 1911, he addressed a letter to Roth and concluded by saying that he was preparing for "the

[80] *ibid.* IX, 1, March 1911, p. 169. See also John Ise, *op. cit.*, pp. 220f.; Jenks Cameron, *op. cit.*, pp. 275-276, 308.

[81] *11th Annual Report of the Canadian Forestry Association*, 1910, p. 10.

great forestry convention to be held at Quebec, as well as the meeting of the Conservation Commission." *Forestry Quarterly*[82] reported that this, the second great forestry convention called while Sir Wilfred Laurier was prime minister, stirred the "forestry world of Canada," being attended by "many prominent men from all parts of the Dominion, and a number of men, mostly professional foresters, from the States, the Forest Service being represented by Mr. Peters." Many lumbermen were present. Fernow wrote to Roth and told him that it had been a "great forestry convention at Quebec. You would have smiled at the manner in which that was conducted. It was, however, a very useful educational institution." Educational and useful, the *Quarterly* explained, because the "fire question naturally came in for the lion's share in the discussion, and it appeared that the downing of tops at least, if not the burning of brush, was admitted to be not an altogether impractical proposition. The Commission of Conservation held its annual meeting in Quebec on January 17. It was a short business session, at which the Chairman, Honorable Clifton Sifton, reported on the work done by the permanent force at Ottawa, which will form the subject matter of a forthcoming report. Amendments to be recommended for . . . the law defining the responsibility of railroads with regard to forest fires were discussed and adopted. A bill to regulate the use of water powers was endorsed."

The year 1911 saw the publication of the association committee's report on forest fire legislation.[83] Fernow was chairman, and Southworth, Clark, Piché, Wilson, W. C. J. Hall, and Frank Davison were members. On January 11, 1911, Fernow forwarded to Judson F. Clark in Vancouver a copy of the report, and when acknowledging Clark's approval, explained that it should be regarded as an "educational document." In its final printing the report was "somewhat improved and added to," but owing to the incapacity of Senator Edwards, it was not brought before the meeting. It was published in the thirteenth report of the Canadian Forestry Association's annual convention, held at Ottawa, February 7-8, 1912.[84] During 1911-1912 the commission of conservation and the Dominion railway commission published "Instruction for fire control by railroads." Since early in 1910 a committee had sought to improve and make uniform the fire laws applicable to forests throughout the Dominion. The report had a special significance to western regions. Adopting the principle that conditions and needs of areas should determine the treatment, the thinly settled West, obviously, would receive a different prescription than the more populated regions of Nova Scotia. Reference had been made to legislation in the United States and Canada. Rules prescribed the conduct of fire users—settlers, rail-

[82] *Forestry Quarterly* IX, 1, March 1911, pp. 183, 186.
[83] *ibid.* IX, 1911, pp. 577-588. [84] pp. 34-42.

roads, and others who came into the forest. A system of organization incorporating regulatory, directive, and advisory authorities, with a protective patrol to enforce the rules and regulations, was outlined by Fernow and his committees. The country was ready for the "supreme effort" to be rid of the fire evil and to "make the beginnings of forestry, a rational management of forest lands, possible." Fernow had persuaded Clyde Leavitt to forego "the delights of academic leisure" (Leavitt at the time considered accepting a teaching position offered at the University of Michigan) and spend his administrative energies in solving the enormous forest fire problem of Canada.

At the Quebec forestry convention of 1911 Fernow discussed the increasingly vital subject of "Forestry Education."[85] The subject was appropriately chosen, not by Fernow but by those who arranged the program. A committee appointed to draw up requirements for professional forestry education consisted of Fernow, Roth, Fisher, Pinchot, and Graves. Roth had written Fernow to ask how the Toronto school was "getting on with the plan of a 4-year and a 5-year course mixed, as it were." The committee on standardization did not meet until December; a statement in the interim was circulated among the committeemen for criticism and comment. Fernow wrote Roth:

> Your one query regarding our six-year course, I can answer readily to the effect that we have now four students in that course. It is the regular four-year course with Arts subjects of a general character added and duly distributed over the six years. The men in it seem to be enthusiastic at the idea of securing a liberal education besides the professional one.

"I am myself," he said in his address, "in education an aristocrat—the best and most varied is none too good." He hoped that "the not too distant future [would] require men of broader knowledge." But he approved a practical outlook and proposed a course of a type "entirely neglected and yet perhaps the most important . . . of a semi-technical, semi-popular nature for those who have the fate of the woodlands directly in their hands—the woodlands owners, timber limit holders and their woodsmen, logging bosses, rangers, etc." He characterized as "good work" the preparation of technical bulletins of usefulness to lumbermen, of cooperative working plans of management, the practice of sending out advisers to interview persons in need of services, and the maintenance of ranger schools in connection with western universities in the United States. Dr. Clark's venture of night school instruction in Vancouver was an early, if not the first, formal course of ranger instruction in Canada, certainly the first in western Canada, which badly needed it. Fernow told Clark in February 1911, "I am, indeed, very much interested in your first attempt at the kind of instruction which is now most necessary, namely to the woodsmen. I have added a note of that fact to my

[85] *Report of the Canadian Forestry Convention*, Quebec, 1911, pp. 103-107.

paper on 'Forestry Education.' The fact, therefore, will appear in the forthcoming report [of] the forestry convention." In 1911 Clark's class of about fifteen students included teachers, timber cruisers, and surveyors.

Fernow told Clyde Leavitt on March 12, 1912, when discussing whether he should accept the proffered teaching appointment at Ann Arbor:

> I still believe forestry education is being overdone in the States, and this in a few years will avenge itself. If you should find, however, the Ottawa position not congenial and want then to go into teaching, the opportunity will be right here. I consider that for an active man, who has interest in practical life, the teaching period should not begin until he is 40 or more, when he would be most effective through his practical experience.

Leavitt went to Canada as the chief fire inspector of the board of railway commissioners without salary, it being understood that his salary from the conservation commission was to cover his two positions. On May 21, 1912, he was notified that the board was "putting through the Regulations governing fire preventive provisions, which [they had] had under consideration for some time, and [he was] expected to use [his] best judgment in seeing that these regulations [were] enforced."

Within a year *Forestry Quarterly*[86] was heralding the program to protect the forests of Canada from fire. Energetic work was being pursued in the same direction in the United States. Private effort, expressed in the formation of a Western Protective Association, was imitated in Quebec by an organization of timber limit holders of the St. Maurice River valley who organized the St. Maurice Forest Protective Association. Even more important, however, was the work done under government authority. In his capacity as chief fire inspector of the railway commission, Leavitt had organized forest fire protection throughout the Dominion on about twenty-five thousand miles of railroad. This work, which became one of the most effective systems of its type in the world, brought into cooperation all official agencies. That same year *Forestry Quarterly*[87] reviewed Leavitt's first annual report as chief forester of the commission of conservation, *Forest Protection in Canada*. These volumes, published during the first years of this work,[88] were devoted to the railway fire protection phase, and the principles developed found application, more than the titles implied, to the whole subject of forest protection in Canada and to an extent in the United States. The work proved of value to all Canadian forestry agencies, and not the least of Leavitt's services was supervising the preparation and editing of many of the commission's most important publications. The

[86] *Forestry Quarterly* XI, 2, June 1913, pp. 295f.

[87] *ibid.* XI, 4, Dec. 1913, p. 564.

[88] See also Clyde Leavitt, "Railway Fire Protection in Canada," *Journal of Forestry* XXVI, 1928, pp. 871-877.

Canadian Society of Forest Engineers chose Leavitt to be the second president and follower of Fernow in the highest office of honor among Canadian foresters. Later he returned to the United States and became assistant dean of the New York State College of Forestry at Syracuse.

Early in 1912 the province of British Columbia enacted comprehensive legislation concerned with preserving, using, and improving its standing timber, and with regulating its commerce in timber and forest products.[89] For several years preparation, in which Fernow had had a part, had been in the making. Furthermore, the thirteenth annual convention of the Canadian Forestry Association officially recognized that British Columbia was about to enact into law recommendations advanced at previous meetings of organizations interested in forestry and conservation. The act was divided into fourteen parts, the first of which dealt with the establishment of a forest branch within the province's department of lands and a provincial forest board to control and administer matters pertaining to forestry. Matters of trespass prevention and protection of crown timberlands, methods of holding and disposing of crown timber, timber leases, timber licenses, rights of way, royalties, taxes, and charges, and fire protection were provided for. Authority to create forest reserves was provided.[90]

Fernow's advisory status persisted through these years. On April 22, 1911, he had written to Clyde Leavitt, who had not yet left the United States to take up his Canadian employment:

> I have been charged to find a man fit to organize a forestry department for British Columbia. He does not need necessarily to be a technical man, provided he is appreciative of technicalities which can be supplied by younger men. But he must be a man of judgment, an organizer capable of making an impression upon western people, and should not be younger, say, than between 30 and 35 years. They are liberal in their views of nationality, and would take an American as readily as a Canadian. Do you know of any such man, the idea being that he would first organize a fire protective service, technical work to come in after years.

Fernow sent out several inquiries and on May 18, 1911, addressed a letter to Minister of Crown Lands W. R. Ross:

> At last I have replies to my inquiries regarding various men, one of which looks very promising. My correspondent writes, "I think R. E. Benedict should be an ideal man for the work you mentioned in British Columbia. He has been in the Forest Service about eleven years, is about 35 years of age, has had long experience in the Washington office, as well as in the field as a General Inspector, Chief Inspector and Forest Supervisor. He is now Supervisor of the Olympic National Forest with headquarters at Olympia,

[89] *ibid.* X, 1, March 1912, p. 112.

[90] *Forestry Quarterly* (*ibid.*, p. 113) announced, "It is understood that Mr. Overton Price will organize the provincial service." On February 12, 1913, MacMillan wrote to Fernow, saying that Price was "largely responsible for the organization of the Forest Branch. . . ."

Washington. Last summer he made, for the Service, a detail study of fire protection in Oregon and Washington. His present salary is $2,400.00. I feel sure Allen would recommend him highly. He is not a forest school man, but has studied forestry carefully in connection with his work. He is unmarried, likes change and you might be able to get him. He is a man of strong and engaging personality, and there could be no question about his making a good impression on the western people."

I may add my correspondent is himself one of the strong men in the Forest Service, a former student of mine. In addition I may give you the two lacking addresses, E. T. Allen, the head man of the Western Forestry and Conservation Association, Portland, Oregon, to whom the Fire Protective Association movement is indebted, and Max Rothkugel, care of Forest Service, Portland, Oregon, the Austrian whom I mentioned to you as a possible man for your work, but whom I could hardly recommend as strongly as Benedict is recommended.

Fortunately for British Columbia, much of the province's best forest land was still in possession of the government. A great bulk was held for various periods of time under licenses and leases. Small areas of the province were devoted to fruit growing and other endeavors not under the control of the government. Except for a belt extending twenty miles on each side of the Canadian Pacific Railway, and except for the "Peace River Block," both owned by the Dominion government, the forest lands, subject to the act of 1912, belonged to the province. The task of building a forest branch within such a valuable forest resource would be a position of influence in the forestry sphere of Canada. H. R. MacMillan was finally chosen, because of his previous forestry experience in Canada. Contemporaneous with the announcement of Leavitt's appointments, it was announced that R. E. Benedict had been chosen to be chief of operations within the newly created forest branch of the provincial lands department, located at Victoria.[91] Immediately the new branch took over "all the forest work of the province including all business incidental to handling leases, collecting royalty and rent, scaling, etc. and fire protection. We are now in the field for seventeen foresters to begin work at once, permanent employment," MacMillan informed Fernow. Plans for that year included a reconnaissance of the province, on which to base policy; preemptions were to be examined; mill studies made; and silvicultural studies started.

That summer Acting Chief Forester MacMillan notified Fernow that "several first-class foresters" would be needed next year, since the work was "piling up . . . in tremendous quantities."[92] Fernow responded

[91] *ibid.* X, 2, June 1912, p. 326.

[92] The forest branch of British Columbia grew rapidly. Within four and a half months, according to MacMillan, "over one-half of the working foresters in Canada" were located at the branch. On June 3, 1912, MacMillan wrote Fernow that he had accepted the position of Chief Forester of British Columbia. Four "chiefs of office" were named: R. E. Benedict, chief of operations; H. K. Robinson, chief of surveys; H. Lafon, chief of management; and M. A. Grainger, chief of office. Benedict, two years before, had given a course in national forest management at the Yale Forestry School.

cordially, but cautioned against "driving too hard and undertaking too much at once," and suggested that he employ temporary assistants during "the next six months with the understanding that they will be supplanted as Canadians develop." MacMillan urged that it was extremely important to secure "valuable men this fall. Just at present the Government is inclined to push the forest policy here strongly, to agree to the appointment of a large number of new men, to give them a free hand in administrative work, to give them great responsibility, and, so far as I can see, a salary commensurate with that responsibility. We are the only Forest Branch in Canada having actual control of all timber business of one province, or jurisdiction. For this reason we shall require a large number of foresters of administrative ability, and I think will be able to pay a large number of men more highly than any other organization." A district organization similar to that of the United States forest service was begun; it was to "have charge of all the fire protection on about 200,000,000 acres of land, all of the timber administration [old licenses and leases], everything in connection with cutting on crown-granted and non-crown-granted timber, control of logging and sawing and agricultural settlement on forest lands, together with survey and creation of forest reserves. In order to retain complete control over the staff, I have made it a condition that all administrative men, in charge of our forest districts, must be graduate foresters, or have a similar training. At present I have not enough foresters to take charge of all the work. Each of our present districts is as large as the whole forest reserve area of the Dominion Government. We are now preparing a Code, or use book, and this system of administration, which has the full support of the Government is to be put into effect inside of about three months. The Minister has agreed that all ranger appointments shall be taken out of politics, and that only those men shall be appointed as rangers who have passed a civil service examination set by the Forest Board."

MacMillan explained the organization and its problems, and held to his position that he would wish three or four men that fall and would need "between 20 and 30 foresters next year, and could use more, if they were available." Fernow's only objection was that he did not wish to send out from the faculty of forestry "half-baked men . . . when six months [would] make such a great difference in them. By taking this attitude, I believe that I am acting in the best interests of all concerned, yours included." MacMillan was sincere in his belief that "no other place

---

In September 1912 Fernow permitted Roy L. Campbell to withdraw from the University of Toronto to go to British Columbia to write forest conservation propaganda. In the following year Campbell returned to Toronto and graduated, and afterward went to Montreal where he became editor of the *Pulp and Paper Magazine of Canada*, secretary-treasurer of the Canadian Pulp and Paper Association, and later attained other prominent positions.

in Canada at present [offered] such an excellent opportunity for administrative men as British Columbia." When in October it appeared that the forest branch of the province would not secure any men from the Toronto school that fall, the chief forester nevertheless was "very glad that [he] brought the proposition to [Fernow's] attention, as [he thought it would] help to establish a better acquaintance between the Toronto Forest School and the British Columbia forest branch. There is no doubt in my mind, but that the Toronto Forest School will continue to be the best Forest School in Canada, with the best class of students." Not until Ontario created a forest branch would "the same opportunities for work" be offered. He would be satisfied, he wrote, if two or three men from the school could be gotten the following spring.

A "great deal of organization work in connection with [the] programme of fire protection" was done during the winter. The last half of 1912 involved much work on "timber sales . . . cruising, mapping, determining of stumpage values and other work, upon timber." January 20, 1913, British Columbia's chief forester informed Fernow that twenty foresters[93] were employed, that the plan was now "to assimilate and train the men whom [they] already [had], before taking on any more," and to "strengthen our staff by employing such men as expert lumbermen, timber cruisers and first class forest rangers." He happily exclaimed:

> I am delighted with the progress we are making and absolutely nothing has occurred which indicates we need fear great troubles. Mr. [Overton W.] Price[94] has just been here and spent two weeks; drafted up an immense programme of work and has also made a very favorable impression upon the members of the Government. Our success here at present depends upon the manner in which we handle our administrative work. We should therefore, so far as possible, seek to strengthen our staff by the employment of men of executive ability. This being the case I have made an offer to Mr. Christie.

On graduating from the University of Toronto, H. R. Christie, highly recommended by Fernow, became connected with the British Columbia forest branch. About a half-dozen years later, when the University of British Columbia established forestry instruction as a part of an enlarged engineering department, Christie was named to occupy the new chair of forestry. By this time a forest products laboratory, a branch of the elder Dominion laboratory, was located on the campus and in a building of the university.

Early in 1913 a conference of Canadian forestry agencies was held, but MacMillan was unable to attend. Fernow wrote on February 4 and

[93] On October 19, 1912, MacMillan told Fernow, "I have not taken all the men from the Forestry Branch, but only about a dozen. Naturally they have quite a few left." Therefore most of the number came from the department of the interior.

[94] For a biographical account of Price, Associate Forester of the U.S. Forest Service and an officer of the National Conservation Commission, see R. S. Hosmer, *Journal of Forestry*, Nov. 1940.

told him that the conference had "made [the participants] better acquainted with the needs of the different Branches, there being now 10 agencies concerned in the questions which [they] discussed." MacMillan replied with an offer "to work out a scheme of cooperation between the Conservation Commission and this Forest Branch, whereby [the Branch] could secure a report on the forest resources of British Columbia similar to that which was published by [Fernow] on the forest resources of Nova Scotia." The commission was to take charge of this. Information collected by the branch in connection with other work was to be made available. Howe and White were to perform the work. Such firms as Clark and Lyford, and lumber companies from various territories, would supply data. Clark and MacMillan had worked harmoniously. Indeed, when MacMillan organized the Society of British Columbia Foresters, later called the British Columbia Forest Club, Clark was unanimously elected president.

Fernow wrote to R. C. Bryant of the Yale Forest School on January 17, 1913, "There is such a boom on here for foresters as we have never seen even in the United States; the British Columbia Government being a strong competitor to the Dominion Branch, and the Canadian Pacific Railway Company also calling for men." With a heavy demand for foresters in both the United States and Canada, forestry institutions prospered.

On May 9, 1912, Mulford at Cornell wrote Fernow, "I have had a hearty laugh over your remark. 'It would be rather interesting to learn to understand the situation.' The fact is that the old New York State College of Forestry at Cornell University has never been abolished. But we are not the College of Forestry—we are a new organization, a department of the State College of Agriculture. There are three forestry institutions in the state, two colleges of forestry and one department. One of the colleges exists only on paper. The legislature gave us $100,000 for a forestry building only seven months after it placed the College of Forestry at Syracuse because it recognized the justice of having a large Forestry Department in connection with its College of Agriculture. A somewhat similar situation exists in the Agricultural Schools, as the State already has three or four State Schools of Agriculture and the State College of Agriculture. It also has two State Agricultural Experiment Stations, one at Geneva, and one here." The new department was not a revival of the old New York State College of Forestry, as Fernow had hoped that it would be regarded and as Dean Bailey had planned it might be. Mulford was an authority on farm forestry. He and Bailey together, however, had sought to retain professional forestry instruction on a full scale at Cornell. The directive of the New York legislature at least implied that the New York State

College of Agriculture was to teach forestry as it was related to agriculture. Authorities at Cornell had never consented to any such limitation. The charter authority to teach professional forestry had never been surrendered. Nor had the charter lapsed by virtue of non-user. The Brooklyn Cooperage Company lawsuit was terminated as far as the New York courts were concerned on March 19, 1912; but this did not finish the lawsuit, or wind up the business matters of the college.

In 1913 Dean Bailey resigned his position as Dean of the New York State College of Agriculture and Director of the Experiment Station at Cornell University. He did not resign because of the forestry situation alone, although this was one reason why he surrendered the ten-year tenure of office which he had agreed to assume. Not in a spirit of controversy but that the public might know the truth of his viewpoint, Bailey presented on December 22, 1913, his already mentioned "Statement on the Forestry Situation," a copy of which Fernow kept among his valuable papers. Bailey said:

> When the staff of the old College of Forestry was disbanded, it had a faculty of three professors and an enrollment of 70 students. The Department of Forestry in the State College of Agriculture now has five professors of forestry and various assistants, and an enrollment in classes of some 260 students. More than 125 students are pursuing the professional forestry course. . . . It has been asked why the forestry work at Cornell was not resumed by securing another appropriation and re-officering the [old New York State] College for Forestry. The reason is that in the meantime a State College of Agriculture was established, and a separate College of Forestry was not necessary, nor was the resumption of that institution the best way of reaching the forestry situation there. Of course, the forestry work at Cornell can be accomplished much more effectively and also with less outlay by developing it in the State College of Agriculture than by maintaining two independent establishments. With two establishments it would have been very difficult to have prevented duplication.

A month before he delivered the address, Bailey wrote to Fernow, saying, "I do not want to draw anybody into any controversy nor to be engaged in one myself; but if I am asked what is the opinion of leading men concerning . . . the wisdom of the forestry development in this state . . . of course I shall express it. I am wondering whether you have any statement that you would care to have me make as coming from you if it is brought up." Fernow replied on December 1, 1913, "I consider, to say the least, that the State is in a foolish condition, in attempting to support two educational institutions in that subject." A few days afterward, Walter Mulford at Cornell notified Fernow, "The early part of this week I received notice of my official appointment at Berkeley. I shall not move to California until next summer." To which Fernow answered, "I consider that your position at Berkeley will be ever so much superior to that at Cornell. [I wish] you all sorts of happiness in the new field." During the month of August, Mulford had been invited to confer with officials at the University of California with reference to inaugurating a department or school of forestry there. Fernow had always liked Mulford. In fact, not only had Mulford taken Fernow's classes at Pennsylvania State College while Fernow arranged to establish the faculty of forestry at Toronto, but Fernow had urged Mulford to take his place at State College permanently. Mulford had also been asked to establish a school of forestry at the University of Washington.

By the summer of 1914 Mulford was in California. On September 7, 1914, he wrote Fernow, "I have written Hosmer that the University of Toronto forestry club should be asked to join the Association[95] which the boys formed at Ithaca last May. Things are starting off nicely here. Already my travels for the University have taken me from Los Angeles to Vancouver. So you see I am not stagnating just yet." Mulford's professorship at California was to be less stormy; the school enjoyed a steady progressive growth. Within three years the division of forestry of the university would move into new quarters in Hilgard Hall, occupy twenty-two rooms, and include laboratories for wood utilization, wood technology, logging engineering, and other phases of forestry research.[96]

Thus, out of seeming turmoil were created two great forestry institutions on the North American continent—the New York State College of Forestry at Syracuse under Hugh Potter Baker, and the school of forestry at the University of California under Walter Mulford—two of the four full-scale, "class A" institutions of forestry in America. In 1914 Ralph Sheldon Hosmer became professor of forestry at the New York State College of Agriculture.

Dean Baker on October 22, 1912, invited Fernow to address the students under the auspices of the forestry club of the New York State College of Forestry at Syracuse. He said, "Our work is opening up very nicely and I believe there is a good future for the College. We were swamped for a time with students, as many more than expected entered, and yet things are just now running very nicely. We have over one hundred Freshmen and forty-seven men from the second year on. These fellows represent sixteen states and two foreign countries. We held the men very closely to entrance requirements."

Fernow replied:

On my return to the office I find your kind invitation to let myself be seen and heard by your Forestry Club. I am very, very busy, so that I can hardly

[95] A conference of Forest School Clubs was held at Ithaca and an Association was organized. *Forestry Quarterly* XIII, 1, March 1915, p. 148.

[96] *ibid.* XIV, 1, March 1916, p. 172, to the effect that 354 students were enrolled in Mulford's "Elements of Forestry" course. Concerning the new quarters at the University, see *Journal of Forestry* XVI, 1, Jan. 1918, p. 140.

foresee any spare time for leaving my work here; but if you can leave my participation until towards the end of the season, that is February or March, I may feel more at leisure, and would like very much to satisfy you. I can do what you desire, namely give an informal talk on Canadian forestry problems, which would take somewhat the shape of the article which is presently to come out in the *Proceedings of the* [*Society of*] *American Foresters,*[97] and talk about "The early work of our Government in forestry,"[98] which also requires little or no preparation, in the evening. My time for illustrated lectures is passed; they require more leisure than I usually possess. You have undoubtedly an overplus of students, while we are not up to our present necessities. After having placed my 12 graduates this spring, a call for a dozen more was sent out from British Columbia, that we could not supply. Nevertheless, we are not going to allow our standards to drop, expecting that gradually the market and supply will come to equalize. I see that your entrance requirements are not very different from ours.

Fernow believed that forestry instruction in North America was being overdone. When G. B. MacDonald of Iowa State College wrote him on April 11, 1912, concerning the type of instruction to be maintained at that institution, Fernow replied:

I have not much hope for the near future in the development of high grade forestry by private owners; and even if the largest owners should come to employ foresters, one high grade man could do the work for half a million acres. In other words, a small number can supervise a large area. Hence, I hold that a differentiation of schools into various grades should be kept in view. I doubt whether there is need of any more schools attempting the education of full-sized, high-grade foresters. But there are needed, besides ranger schools, schools of various grades and partial forestry education, and the wise man would run only such a school as his opportunities specially fit him to run well. For instance, to become specific, if you are confining yourself merely to fit men for work such as is needed in your State you will not want to imitate Yale School or Harvard School, but develop a course which will best fit for woodlot work, that is the silvicultural side, which the farmer should know. If every school would specialize in some way according to its opportunities and as the nearest needs of the State require, and do what it does WELL, up to the handle, the future will be good to all foresters that may be turned out.

Fernow still viewed forestry in its widest applications. Other institutions turned to him for advice. Percy B. Barker of the college of agriculture at the University of Nebraska wrote early in 1911, saying that he was developing a course "confined to forest soils," and asked for outlines or suggestions. F. E. Kirkwood of the University of Montana at Missoula consulted Fernow about certain proposed summer forest

97 "Forest Resources and Problems of Canada," *Proc. Soc. Am. For.* VII, 2, Nov. 1912, pp. 133-144. This was said to be a revision of Fernow's "An Analysis of Canada's Timber Wealth."

98 This topic had been developed in other addresses and was to culminate in Fernow's great address, "The Birth of a Forest Policy," delivered at the New York State College of Forestry at Syracuse in 1916. This address or part of it was also presented at Mont Alto Forest Academy.

cruises. He was told that explanations of "local conditions, aims and results" were preferable to formal lectures. Christian H. Goetz of Ohio State University told Fernow in 1912 that "we have this year over 100 students [and] are going to give some forestry courses in the various agricultural courses as we think that the time has come when we should not only prepare men for the work in the U.S. Forest [Service] but also for private work, woodlot forestry and for the use of the lumbermen, paper-pulp men, etc." A class of ten men were using Fernow's *Economics of Forestry* and a class in arboriculture his *Care of Trees in lawn, street, and park.*

All such information was heartening. But what were to be the fields of opportunity? How was real forestry progress to be realized? On March 4, 1911, Fernow had addressed a letter to Karl Woodward's father, President Robert S. Woodward of the Carnegie Institution "to interest your institution in the study of tropical forest conditions and forest ecology, with a view of their eventual use to civilization as regards wood supplies."

> Our ignorance regarding this subject is, indeed, dense, for even the English and Dutch foresters, who have to deal with these questions on a limited area, have been remiss in securing any scientific data for their practices. We have now a man in the Philippine Forest Service, who, from all I know of him and his publications, would be an eminently fit man to enter upon such investigations—Dr. Whitford, a hard worker, with enough imagination to make a good investigator—and there are several young men like Curran who would make him good assistants. You are, of course, aware that forest resources of the temperate zone are everywhere rapidly dwindling, and so far the belief is that the hard tropical woods are not fit to supply our needs. But we do know that in the tropics there are soft-wooded species and medium hard species in relatively small quantities which would answer. Whether and how these can be made to supplant the less useful would depend upon biological knowledge. So far, the peculiar distribution of species in the tropics is unexplained and altogether biological and especially ecological knowledge is even less developed than that of desert plants, for which your Desert Laboratory has paved the way. While I realize that primarily your institution is to confine itself to purely scientific research, I believe the fact that it is for ultimately utilitarian purposes may not weigh against the undertaking. The tropics, on account of the rapid growth of vegetation there, may eventually become the producers of the forest products of the world, if biological knowledge is developed by which change of composition can be secured. There is now a proposition before me to start in without such knowledge with a demonstration forest along the Panama Canal, which is, of course, premature. . . . When Mr. Curran calls . . . you will be prepared to meet him.

Dr. Woodward rejected Fernow's proposition, not because of lack of sympathy with the proposal, but because his institution could not further commit itself financially.

Later, in 1913, Whitford, an authority on the plant family *Dip-*

terocarpaceae, at the suggestion of Dr. Howe, his former roommate at the University of Chicago, wrote to Fernow offering to deliver at Toronto a course of illustrated lectures on Philippine forestry he was preparing as the basis for a book on the same subject. At first the lectures were refused because of the school's inadequate finances. But that spring Whitford gave "a very interesting talk" which stimulated Fernow's interest in forestry work of the Philippines Bureau. The latter received an official invitation from Major Ahern to visit the Islands to see their "fine practical school for rangers [with] a reserve of 15,000 acres adjoining the school—a mountain 3,500 feet elevation—three railroads around its base—and a growing thriving community needing forest products." Located two hours from Manila, this school had students "from every one of the thirty-nine provinces" and was using Fernow's *History*. Fernow replied that he might be able sometime to accept a temporary appointment for half a year, but that year the International Geological Congress might occupy four weeks of excursions, and other work prevented his taking advantage of the opportunity to study tropical forestry. Howe and the Toronto dean wanted to bring Whitford to Canada. Howe wrote to Whitford and explained that employment might become possible in the proposed forest survey of British Columbia with the Canadian commission of conservation.

Fernow had forwarded MacMillan's proposal for such a survey to Secretary White of the commission, and, in turn, sent White's answer to MacMillan on February 25, 1913. This approved the project "if the right men [could] be secured." Fernow added, "Of course, I am in sympathy with the proposition. This year, I am afraid the right men could not be secured. We will, however, have our Mr. White travel over the Province for the Commission to become generally acquainted with the flora and conditions, and to take such notes as will enable us in cooperation with you to lay out a practicable plan, with a view of next season starting in on this great undertaking."

MacMillan had suggested that Howe and White be sent, but it was arranged that, following up the general survey of the Trent Watershed in Ontario, Howe was to go alone "into the field this summer to study the question of reproduction pure and simple." On March 6 MacMillan expressed pleasure that White was to be in the province for the summer to start the work with men from the provincial Forest Branch. "I believe," wrote MacMillan, "the Commission could do a great work in Western Canada by such a survey which would accentuate the importance of fire protection and prepare the way for the wisest administration of the forest." From timber inspection work, exploration parties, and special examinations of large tracts, the Branch was gathering together "a great deal of information," and White, a botanist and forestry instructor, was to study "the forest types, trees, flora, etc., of the Province."

Graduate foresters during these years were being employed for two dominant purposes—administrative work, and to pursue special programs of silvicultural research. All or most of the graduates of 1913, Fernow informed MacMillan, were "booked" for the Dominion forestry branch. Fernow was particularly eager to develop scientific study. On January 17 he proudly told Director Campbell that "Lately some of our students have made a study of the relation of climatic conditions to the distribution of species, which brings out very strikingly the fact that temperature conditions alone are responsible for the differentiation in the types, that means in species distribution."

On December 12, Campbell had written:

> Among the questions asked by the Dominion's Royal Commission of which I wrote you in October, is one relating to forestry schools. The question reads, "What encouragement is given to scientific forestry by the Government and what sums are expended from public funds in forestry schools, forest conservation, fire patrols &c." Could you give me an idea as to how much money is expended on the Forest School at Toronto from public funds and any other details of the encouragement given to the school by the Government?

Fernow answered that "during the five years of its existence the expenditure [had] averaged less than $10,000 a year, $2,200 of this being furnished by students' fees." Much of Fernow's time was consumed in getting employment for his graduates and students, and, whether the danger was real or imaginary, in fighting off political involvements and unfair attacks on what was being accomplished. On May 12, 1913, he renewed with President Falconer his plea for an associate professor. Every forestry teaching staff of the forestry schools in the United States much outnumbered the teaching force at Toronto. Indeed, two of the four on the faculty of forestry at Toronto gave part of their time and instruction to the botany department.

Late in December 1912, some time after he had reconnoitered forest conditions along what is now the Canadian National Railways east and west from Cochrane, northern Ontario, in the Clay Belt region, he followed up an interest in the problem of peat bogs and muck soils. He wrote for information as to what really had been done "in the way of examining these various conditions with reference to the use of the soil for agricultural purposes." Early the next year he wrote to Dr. Charles E. Saunders, Dominion cerealist and son of his friend, Dr. William Saunders, director of the Central Experimental Farms at Ottawa. These two were becoming world famous for their origination of Marquis and other prolific wheats, which almost alone revolutionized Canadian agriculture, especially on the prairies, because of their early-ripening and cold-enduring qualities. In fact, Charles Saunders was knighted for the accomplishment. Fernow told him that he hoped "that the whole clay belt [could] be turned into a big wheat field." Saunders first replied that he was glad that there was "someone in the country who [was] not afraid to get into trouble when necessary. Most of us are rather too timid for the good of the world." And on February 22, 1913, he further explained, "As a rule wheat grown in land which has been occupied by trees is soft though I think that after the land has been cultivated for some years on an ordinary farming rotation the wheat usually grows harder. This is probably a question of soil physics, the tree roots keeping the soil rather too open for the production of the best quality in wheat."

Saunders had received copies of the newspaper *New Liskeard Speaker*, which had discussed the subject. He was sure that Fernow's comments, contained in his report on "Conditions in the Clay Belt of New Ontario," a commission of conservation publication, would "help those interested to form a more correct view of the agricultural situation in Northern Ontario."

Fernow never had needed anyone to convince him of the value of scientific work. Certainly his close association with Dr. Howe on the faculty of forestry contributed to his desire to further ecological research in Canadian forests. Whitford was a thoroughly able ecologist. During the spring of 1913 Fernow wrote to Dean Thomas F. Hunt of the college of agriculture at Berkeley, California, where Whitford was a candidate to become a professor of forestry. While waiting, Whitford, at the department of botany of the University of Chicago, gathered materials for a book to be entitled *Forestry in the Phililippines*, and arranged to contribute to *Forestry Quarterly*. On April 23, 1913, Fernow forwarded to him a letter from Secretary White of the Canadian commission of conservation. During March, Minister of Lands William R. Ross of British Columbia had told White that he regarded the proposed "survey of the forest resources of British Columbia . . . one of the most important steps which could be taken towards the wise management of the forest resources of Western Canada," since it would "serve to show to what extent the people of the Prairie Provinces of Western Canada may depend in the future upon a timber supply from British Columbia," and promote forest land utilization "to the utmost in producing revenue and supporting industries" within the province. After receiving a reply from Whitford, Fernow wrote again on May 16, "I take it that you have come to conclusions with the Commission of Conservation regarding employment after September 1."

There began a cordial correspondence between the two men. Whitford, employed to examine some timberland near Colima, Mexico, sought to arrange a meeting with Fernow before taking up his work in

British Columbia. Whitford sought Fernow's advice frequently at the start of the work. On September 24, 1913, MacMillan thanked Fernow, "Dr. Whitford arrived a week or ten days ago and is now making one or two trips over the Island with District Forester Robinson in order to get acquainted with coast types. We are under great obligations to you for taking up so energetically the cooperation between the Conservation Commission and the Forest Branch. Dr. Whitford is of course taking up with you direct the plans for his work."

As late as 1914 reproduction and growth-rate studies in cut-over areas had received scant attention in Canada. Forest fire protection and timber inventories, both urgently needed, had appealed to economic and practical sense and had enlisted the first energies of the new agency, the Commission of Conservation. It is said that at one time the commission decided to give foremost attention to demonstration work. Fernow sought to coordinate the work of this useful institution with that of established agencies. The commission had been created to do work for which there was no established agency, or work which established agencies had not done. Fernow wrote on February 14, 1914, "The Commission of Conservation has as yet not published much regarding the stand of timber in Canada. A beginning has been made, but nothing definite published except my report on Nova Scotia Forest Conditions."

Following a recommendation of the Nova Scotia report, that province in 1913 enacted legislation to appoint a provincial forester.[99] Moreover, New Brunswick also took steps to have a similar survey, examination, and classification of the crown lands of the province. In 1916 it was announced that the outstanding feature of forestry in Canada during the past year was the forest survey and classification of the crown lands, for which the New Brunswick legislature had taken action early in 1913. P. Z. Caverhill had been appointed provincial forester to take charge of the work.[100] In 1914 the forest committee of the commission, of which Fernow was the leading member, recommended that forestry branches be organized in New Brunswick and Nova Scotia. Futhermore, Ontario and Quebec were urged to pursue timber inventories similar to that in British Columbia. Other recommendations were advanced, notably a requirement that all applicants for appointments in the forest service of the Dominion and provincial governments pass civil service examinations. Other special types of inquiry and rehabilitation—in the Trent Watershed and the Clay Belt areas in Ontario—were cited also as projects worthy of cooperative action of the commission and governments concerned.[101]

[99] *Forestry Quarterly* XI, 4, Dec. 1913, p. 612.
[100] *ibid.* XIV, 1, March 1916, p. 163.
[101] *5th Annual Report, Commission of Conservation,* 1914, pp. 37-42.

The plan of cooperation between the board of railway commissioners, the commission of conservation, and the Dominion and provincial governments in the matter of forest fire protection was commented on approvingly by the forest committee in its report to the fourth annual meeting of the commission at Ottawa, held January 21-22, 1913. The next forest investigation was in timber inventories. Study of the forest conditions and forest resources of British Columbia was announced as a cooperative arrangement.[102] Every available line of investigation was to be followed through, limited only by the time and financial allowances. Fernow wrote to Roland D. Craig on October 10, 1913:

> I am very sorry that you did not know earlier the changes of plans which put you into the market. We could have used you excellently in the undertaking which has now been begun by Dr. Whitford, namely, to secure an idea of the timber standing in British Columbia. . . . Nevertheless, I am writing to Mr. White of the Conservation Commission, suggesting that you might perhaps be used to assist Dr. Whitford, if the Commission still has funds left. . . . There is to be an examination made for the purpose of ascertaining how much it would cost to get out a forest survey such as they want for New Brunswick. Leavitt and Rothery are starting this week to make the first inquiries.

In the British Columbia study there was first a preliminary reconnaissance. After that, years of more thorough gathering of materials were required. Fernow told the January 1914 meeting of the commission of conservation:

> The Commission has been lucky in finding such a man [as] Dr. Whitford, who in less than four months accomplished the survey and plotted in more or less detail the gathered information of 20,000 square miles, classifying the land into five classes, namely, agricultural land with and without merchantable timber, absolute forest land with and without merchantable timber, and non-productive land or waste.
>
> Mr. Whitford writes that he is satisfied with the result of his labor and, if *he* is, you may rest assured, it is satisfactory. At this rate, in less than two years, if properly assisted, we may know with sufficient accuracy the extent of timber supplies and the forest conditions of our most prominent forest province, and have a very different basis, than now, for our position.

Fernow fought for this work. When its discontinuance was threatened he raised a strong voice in protest. Whitford communicated with him throughout the entire course of the survey. Moreover, Whitford and Craig were good as a team, and each performed his tasks creditably. Just as the Nova Scotia survey provided a model for a survey in British Columbia, the British Columbia plan was followed in Saskatchewan under J. C. Blumer and later in Ontario under Craig.

In Saskatchewan forestry, during Fernow's active years, seems to have been confined principally to the Dominion timber reservations.

[102] *Forestry Quarterly* IX, 1, March 1913, p. 128.

Except for its work in agriculture, that province gave little attention to forestry instruction or practice. In January 1909 President Walter C. Murray of the provincial university had visited the forestry school at Toronto and sent "best wishes for what promises to be one of the foremost Schools of Forestry on the Continent."

Progress in British Columbia went forward immediately, once a forest branch organization with trained personnel was acquired, and the work to be done confronted and understood. On March 10, 1914, MacMillan told Fernow:

> We found . . . that we had all the legislative authority necessary, and what we need is not more law but more public sentiment and more experience on the part of the Forest Branch staff including myself. Just as soon as we know what we should do we are going to do it; at the present we are trying to bring about cleaner logging and a slash disposal that will facilitate the best natural reproduction. Forest management of British Columbia is, I think, merely a question of the success or failure of these men whom we now have in the Forest Branch. I myself am extremely optimistic and think that there will be Province wide forest management here before any place else in Canada. I have been surprised at the attitude of the lumbermen; it is not antagonistic, but on the other hand seems very helpful.

British Columbia, like other provinces, was reaping millions of dollars in revenue from its forest resources and reinvesting comparatively insignificant sums. While its policy of trade extension was being furthered, silvicultural work also was coming into the foreground. This year Dr. Howe's forest reproduction and growth rate studies in cut over and burned areas reached this province.[103]

By 1915 the Dominion forest reserves were estimated to be almost twenty-eight million acres of forest lands, and although agricultural lands were being segregated, the federal forest reservation area was being annually increased. The pioneer forest service, the forestry branch of the department of the interior, maintained a larger personnel than it had had, but its chief duties still were fire protection, administration of grazing, including what MacMillan described that year as a "fine summer range," the supervision of small cuttings, and the introduction of valuable species. Very little timber was taken from the reserves for the good reason that, excepting that held under licenses and therefore not administered by the Dominion forestry branch, the reservations were principally burned over lands with little timber available. Re-

[103] H. R. MacMillan, "Present Conditions of Applied Forestry in Canada," *Proc. Soc. Am. For.* X, 2, April 1915, pp. 115-129. World War I was a great setback to forestry in British Columbia. Enlistments and resignations of such valuable men as Caverhill and Prince, and MacMillan's assignment to South Australia as Timber Trade Commissioner, reduced the forestry branch to "hardly a skeleton" of what it was in 1914. MacMillan wrote Fernow from Australia that about all he expected to find of the forestry branch on his return would be "footprints hard to fill." This difficult situation was characteristic of all forestry in Canada, including the school at Toronto.

production on the forest reserves was regarded by him "as a general rule, good, chiefly lodgepole pine, aspen, and jack pine." Until this time, nevertheless, the administration had consisted mainly in fire protection and trespass prevention. Agricultural areas within the reserves were not yet opened for settlement, as in the United States.

Moreover, in British Columbia, while grazing on public lands was being studied with a view to systematic administration, and while reproduction studies, volume tables, and investigations in the requirements of the most important species had been started, the chief accomplishments of the provincial forest organization had been improvements in organizational efficiency and the commencement of the forest survey.

The Dominion railway commission, under Leavitt, was vested with definite administrative authority. Of almost 30,000 miles of railway lines in Canada, a conservative estimate indicated that fully one-third of the area traversed was forest land. Effective regulations requiring railroads to protect adjacent areas from sources of fire were in force; the field work was principally done by the provinces. Also chief forester of the commission of conservation, at one time with eight technically trained foresters as subordinates, Leavitt divided his time between this responsibility and his duties with the commission of conservation.

CHAPTER X

New Honors for Fernow

ALTHOUGH Fernow did not realize it, his career reached its zenith during the years 1912-1915. Each year his honorary position as vice-president of the American Forestry Association had been renewed. Each year he had accepted, always half-apologetically insisting that the honor came as a tribute to his past and not present worth to the organization. In correspondence concerned with standardizing the curricula of North American forestry schools again he apologized for accepting "the honorable position on the editorial board of the Society of American Foresters because I know that I have been of no use in the past, and I do not see my way clear to be of much use in the future. I am one of those members, of whom I complain on the board of editors for the *Forestry Quarterly*."

Fernow little realized that before another year would go by his name would be presented for the presidency of the Society of American Foresters. On December 23, 1913, he wrote to Dr. Karl W. Woodward at Washington, "I find my name on the nominations for the Society of American Foresters. If it is not too late, I would like to have my name for the Presidency withdrawn for the reason that being out of the country I am not entitled to such consideration, and I am afraid my presidency would not be of value to the Society. If this can still be made known to the voters I shall be very much obliged." But Fernow was elected.

At the same time Fernow was president of the two most influential professional forestry organizations in America, the Society of American Foresters and the Canadian Society of Forest Engineers. On February 10, 1914, Roth congratulated him. "Delighted to see the boys come to their senses and elect you President. Congratulate the *Society*."

Fernow replied, informing Roth that he wished to consider during his administration the subject of forest terminology.

F. F. Moon, professor of forest engineering and later dean of the New York State College of Forestry at Syracuse, extended congratulations and affirmed that he was "also glad to see that the adjective American will be properly used now that our Canadian brothers have been admitted."

Eight years earlier Fernow had reviewed Forest Service Bulletin 61, "Terms Used in Forestry and Logging," and he had written an article on "Forest Terminology." *Forestry Quarterly*[1] in 1914 published

[1] *Forestry Quarterly* XII, 1, March 1914, pp. 1ff. The earlier article was titled "For-

an article, "A Suggestion for Securing Better Professional Terminology," by P. S. Lovejoy. Fernow prepared an editorial note in which he endorsed the "movement" to have appointed a permanent committee of the society on forest terminology, making whatever revisions were necessary.

During recent years Fernow had not attended many meetings in the United States. In November 1913, as a delegate of the American Institute of Mining Engineers, he attended the Fifth National Conservation Congress in Washington, D.C. When Philip W. Ayres of the Society for the Protection of New Hampshire Forests invited him to attend the society's meeting at Bretton Woods held on July 18-19, 1912, together with a preliminary day at North Woodstock to visit the Lost River tract recently purchased by the society, Fernow replied:

> I have for a number of years avoided attending meetings in the United States, having enough of this kind in Canadian centres, but I think it is time for me to renew old friendships and also to show that I am still in existence and in sympathy with the work of American foresters.

Fernow had been happy in Canada. He told Liberty Hyde Bailey on April 12, 1911:

> I see that you have refused to become the commissioner of Agriculture in New York, and I should say you would [best] stick to your policy in this respect for I am sure you could not improve your position by going among the politicians at Albany. I am well pleased with my surroundings here [Toronto], and find that I am thoroughly appreciated among my colleagues, as well as by the public. I hardly regret my recollapse at Cornell.

He was referring of course to the loss of the Brooklyn Cooperage lawsuit. Fernow had believed that the cause would be decided against the state's claim.

He accepted the invitation to the Bretton Woods meeting. Moreover he addressed the Society for the Protection of New Hampshire Forests at its meeting at Lake Sunapee on July 23, 1913. His subject was "A Plan Adequate to Meet Our Needs for Wood Timber," published in *American Forestry* and *Forestry Quarterly*.[2] The elements of his plan were:

1. Each State to ascertain its quota of planting area, classified for systematic procedure in its recovery.
2. A cooperative financial arrangement, by which municipalities may secure the credit of the State and States the credit of the

---

est Terminology," *ibid.* III, 3, Aug. 1905, pp. 255, 360. Fernow had been concerned about terminology when he was chief of the division of forestry of the U.S.D.A. Some authority accredits Dr. John Gifford with inventing the term "silvics" as a contraction for "silvicultural characteristics," *For. Quar.* XII, 3, 1914, p. 431.

[2] *ibid.* XI, 3, Sept. 1913, p. 307; *American Forestry*, Aug. 1913.

Federal Government for the purpose of acquiring and recovering their quota.

3. State planting to be done on a large scale.

The entire plan cannot be set forth here. These essentially new phases in forestry work were new in New Hampshire, which had not emphasized forest planting. Fernow said, "I wish then to go on record as holding the opinion, that our needs of the future will not be satisfactorily and adequately provided for until we take recourse to planting operations on a large scale. This conclusion, based on observation of biological conditions, is also borne out by statistical inquiry."

He did not favor "the desultory distribution of a few thousand plants to private planters, or the haphazard planting of a few acres." He said it required "systematic procedure on a large scale." Climatic and other conditions in many sections were not favorable to natural regeneration. Many other considerations militated against relying solely on it or the selection system or any other natural method to restock the forest. Some artificial reforestation on a large scale was imperative.

Fernow had come a long way since the years when as chief of the forestry division of the department of agriculture he had opposed the clear cutting and replanting method on the ground that it was "contrary to nature and the best interests of the forest, not being a product of the observance of natural laws, but a child of seeming financial necessity." He confessed he was then "imbued with Gayer's doctrines."

Ontario again had a provincial forester. Since Judson F. Clark had left the office the province's forestry program largely had centered about the waste land problem. In 1908-1909 a forest station, comprising more than a thousand acres, had been established in the Lake Erie district in Norfolk County. Demonstration forest stations were to be established at strategic places in the province. Municipalities and counties were becoming interested in forests and reforestation. The movement grew. Later a forest station was established in Prince Edward County in the Lake Ontario district, and in 1922 the important nurseries and stations in Durham County at Orono and in Simcoe County at Midhurst and Angus were organized. By 1942 the Norfolk station would cover an area of "3,800 acres with over 100 acres in nurseries and the remainder made up of demonstration forest plantations. . . . The Midhurst Station [would contain] about 2,500 acres and the Orono Station 300 acres. The combined output of nursery stock for the three stations [would run] from fifteen to twenty million trees a year."[3]

[3] N. O. Hipel, "The History and Status of Forestry in Ontario," *op. cit.*, pp. 138-140; J. F. Sharpe and J. A. Brodie, "The Forest Resources of Ontario," Dept. of Lands and Forests, Ontario Forestry Branch, 1931; E. J. Zavitz, "Reforestation in Ontario," *Journal of Forestry* XX, 1, Jan. 1922, pp. 1-66; A. H. Richardson, *A Report on the Ganaraska Watershed*, 1944, Toronto, p. 234.

In 1912 E. J. Zavitz was selected to become forester of the province's department of lands, forests, and mines. In December of that year *Forestry Quarterly*,[4] announcing his appointment, surmised that his initial activities probably would deal with lumber slash disposal, fire protection organization, and general reconnaissance. Zavitz's energies, while at Guelph, had been given to waste lands and their utilization by forest planting. He began to develop the work endeavoring to improve woodlots and waste areas, mostly abandoned farm lands, in southern Ontario, and to reforest the cut-over crown lands of the Laurentian plateau. He believed that the work of the forest stations had demonstrated that reforestation was a matter beyond academic discussion. For years Zavitz had charge of the province's Norfolk forest station. Ontario had a tremendous pulpwood resource, and it was one of the most important forest provinces of Canada. But like other provinces, it flourished in the luxury of the present at the expense of the future. Ontario reaped millions of dollars in revenues from the forests and, in return, spent only a few hundred thousand dollars to defray the expenses of administering and maintaining a forest department. Furthermore, the reinvestment for the sake of future forests and supplies was only a fraction of the administrative expenditures.

On June 14, 1912, before the Central Ontario Water Conservation Association, Fernow discussed the water conservation problem as it was related to the Trent watershed survey. "In two directions, the interests of the Central Ontario Water Conservation Association and of the foresters of the Conservation Commission touch. In the first place water conservation can never be quite as successfully accomplished as by keeping watersheds forested, and in the second place water power development is justifiable only where a perpetual supply of work for the power to do is assured."

No one, Fernow maintained, should be allowed to continue "skinning the country of its timber or wood pulp supply without provision for its reproduction." Either ruthless exploitation or neglect consumed capital and interest. In this instance, the main purpose was to conserve the water supplies of the Trent Canal, but the forest resource presented a tremendous potential interest. Moreover, the survey widened the scope of scientific forest investigation. Dr. Howe made an intensive study of white pine reproduction in the watershed area.

At the Canadian Forestry Convention early in 1912[5] the Trent watershed project was announced as definitely authorized. J. H. Burnham had interviewed Chairman Clifford Sifton of the commission of con-

[4] X, 4, Dec. 1912, p. 777.

[5] Quotations are taken from a letter from Burnham to the editor of the *Bobcaygeon (Ontario) Independent*, Feb. 9, 1912. See also comment on a speech by Fernow to the Canadian Institute at Toronto in the issue of March 29, 1912.

servation. They agreed that Dr. Fernow was "the big man of the meetings," which included delegates from the United States and elsewhere, and Sifton told Burnham that Fernow was to be placed in charge "with all the money he needed" for the projected survey. Western Peterborough County was "to receive some attention." From the standpoint of the work of the forest committee of the commission of conservation, this inquiry was defined as an effort to ascertain "conditions of limited areas which have been misused or are liable to misuse as samples for studying in given cases the practical measures which may be taken, in order to return them to usefulness or assure their rational development, e.g., the Clay Belt and the Trent Watershed inquiries."

The Trent Canal project was located principally in Haliburton and Peterborough counties—a thousand square miles of waste land in Ontario. During the first summer the survey had covered approximately two thousand square miles in the section of old Ontario north of the Kawartha Lakes, "a sample area." Fernow, who mapped out the policy and plan, said it was "representative of many thousands of square miles of Laurentian rock country, both in Quebec and Ontario." One phase of the work was to systematize timber cutting on farms wherever possible. Many farm lands were found already abandoned, and there were many more that should have been abandoned. Some lands were not suited to agricultural cultivation. These were often not even producing a tax revenue for the state. Fernow and his co-workers, Howe and White, suggested that lands salable for non-payment of taxes could be reserved and made to produce a timber industry worth millions, besides supplying pulpwood, posts, railroad ties, and other forest products. Timber fit for lumbering was gone in many places. Large areas had been converted into little better than rocky deserts. Fire had seriously damaged the timber crop that still stood. What did the government do with the revenues from lumber-bearing forest lands? The income from timber licenses was treated as current revenue, not capital investment, as Fernow maintained it should be regarded—at least in part. The situation was complicated even more by the fact that timber licenses were being sold on the market by speculators.[6]

Published by the commission of conservation in 1913 under the authorship of Howe and White and with an introductory discussion by Fernow, *The Trent Watershed Survey* was regarded by H. R. MacMillan as "the most valuable publication on forestry which [had] yet appeared in Canada."[7] In a later study[8] MacMillan estimated the Ontario forest reserves at about twenty-one thousand square miles.

[6] *5th Annual Report of the Commission of Conservation*, Jan. 1914.
[7] *Forestry Quarterly* XII, 3, Sept. 1914, p. 435.
[8] "Present Condition of Applied Forestry in Canada," *op. cit.*

These vast areas, which received little more forest administration than policing and fire protection, have since been admirably developed. A good illustration is the program for the Ganaraska watershed in southern Ontario. With the widening of the doctrines of multiple use in forestry in North America, further adaptations of uses to sites have been extended. In the western national forests, and to a lesser extent in the Dominion reservations, grazing and range management have been so perfected as to cause these interests to compete with the forest for primacy. In Ontario, Quebec, New York, certain of the New England states, and in certain of the western states and provinces, the interests of recreational forestry and wild life management have taken positions of growing importance beside timber production and watershed protection. Today in Ontario the Haliburton highlands and Trent waterways, although a wild and rugged country filled with little-known lakes and streams, deep valleys and high hills, is a favorite retreat for campers.

Although the watershed area had not been set apart as a reserve, MacMillan found special value in the *Survey* report because the study showed "how a great forest reserve will quickly pay for itself by the protection of valuable young [timber] stands from fire, by the encouragement of new industries in now barren districts, by the protection of the public timber from trespass and the collection of the full public revenue." MacMillan pointed out that the "area described [was] typical of the greatest forest region of Canada, the Archean formation characteristic of the permanent timberlands throughout Canada east of Lake Winnipeg, and even west of Lake Winnipeg, north of the prairies. What [was] true of the 2,100 square miles of the Trent valley in Old Ontario [was] true of hundreds of thousands of square miles in New Ontario, Quebec, New Brunswick, and Nova Scotia, where the forest, the only possible crop, [had] been left to manage itself."

In January 1914 Fernow told the commission of conservation that he regretted that the newspapers had "made one phase much more prominent than it [was] made in the report, namely the human phase. There is, however, no denying the fact, that quite a number of farmers farming rocks within the territory surveyed are in an unfortunate condition and should be assisted to improve their condition."

He believed that the interest of the Dominion in protecting the watershed was superior even to that of the Province. The Dominion government was urged to cooperate. While the report was being printed, a fire causing an estimated loss of more than three million dollars swept over approximately 190,000 acres. Previous fires on 600,000 acres of pinery had already caused an estimated loss of about eight million dollars. In these estimates, the prospective as well as actual losses were figured. Fire protection was a matter of cooperation between the Dominion and provincial governments. Ontario had an especially large interest in this situation:[9]

The Province still owns about 725 square miles, mostly in a compact body, 450 square miles still under license but soon to be abandoned, the balance with the licenses lapsed. Since the merchantable timber is mostly cut, the interest of the Province in the cut-over lands does not seem to be strong; at least protection against fires appears to be inadequate. Of the 16 separate fires, ten started on lands not patrolled by fire rangers. Of the five fires which were responsible for the largest loss (85%), three started on crownlands without patrol, and two where one ranger looks after about 100 square miles."

The serious consequence of recurrent fires was not only in the destruction of the timber stand but even more in the reduction of the chances of natural regeneration of pine. Actual count in the watershed area showed that with each succeeding fire, on sample acreage, the regenerative average showed thirty young pines after the first fire, six after the second fire, and still less or only inferior aspen and scrub growth after the third fire. The large cut-over areas of the watershed had been burned from one to nine times during the preceding forty years. Nature, with the aid of aspen and birch, had tried to reclothe the surface with a valuable growth. But where the seeds and seed trees were destroyed, there was no chance for reproduction.

Conservation to Fernow was a "business proposition pure and simple." On December 28, 1912, Fernow had rendered another report to Chairman Sifton of the commission of conservation. This was published by the commission under the title, "Conditions in the Clay Belt of New Ontario." As the name implies, the Clay Belt area which Fernow examined was a representative cross-section of an enormous total expanse. He reported on a region of about two hundred miles around the town of Cochrane along the right of way of the Canadian National (Grand Trunk Pacific) Railways in the newly-settled section of northern Ontario. To get there Fernow probably had to go to North Bay on the Canadian Pacific Railway, thence via the Timiskaming and Northern Ontario Railway to Cochrane, from which point he travelled by power speeder east and west along the Grand Trunk Pacific right of way.

To arrive at his conclusions Fernow analyzed briefly the economic and sociological situation from forestry, agricultural, and financial points of view. He discussed the physical and chemical[10] factors of the soil and recommended further laboratory study. He reiterated his stand with reference to soil analysis as related to timber physics research in

[9] Address to the Commission in 1914; on Dec. 12, 1914, Fernow had addressed the Canadian Club of Kingston, Ontario, on "Mortgaging the Future."

[10] Fernow's principal objections to chemical analysis in soils investigations were the cost and the time required.

1886-1887. Fernow supported the government's general policy of discouraging settlement on unclassified land. Within the Trent watershed area government officials had warned a roving population against impoverished lands. The same was true in the Clay Belt. In neither region, however, had there been any systematic procedure aimed toward constructive development. Through the years the problem of the "timber farmer" has not been a happy one. Fernow regarded the Clay Belt as a region of diverse conditions which needed to be classified.[11] His fundamental recommendations were (1) land classification, and that settlers be kept out of undesirable portions; (2) that forest reserves be set apart to provide fuel; (3) that cooperative systems of drainage be installed; (4) that an experimental farm be established to find to what uses various soils should be placed; (5) that a few small and inexpensive experiments be made to study the effects on tree growth of the lowering of the water table; and (6) that dense spruce stands be thinned to find whether better wood production could be achieved. Fernow approved the contract of the Ontario Colonization Company which provided that two of the better townships were to be colonized after or during logging operations. Out of the study issued the report of the committee on forests to the fourth annual meeting of the Canadian conservation commission. It was urged that the Clay Belt lands should be classified in advance of settlement, that settlers should be properly directed, and that non-agricultural lands be reserved from entry by settlers. A soils expert *in the field* should study and classify the lands.

Fernow remained active in the Canadian conservation movement, but he gave most of his time to the school and *Forestry Quarterly*. Experimental study of forest influences and the larger academic fields of research was still lacking. In the United States, through the work of the central investigating committee of the United States forest service, and other agencies in the states, real progress was being made in dendrological, grazing, forest products, and silvicultural research. Hundreds of thousands of dollars were being invested in research alone, mostly in forest products research. Next in importance were silvicultural investigations. The first business of the forest school, nevertheless, was to produce foresters who might also become research specialists.[12] Fernow's wisdom proved to be sound. The next administration of the faculty of forestry of the University of Toronto expanded the forestry research inaugurated during Fernow's regime. Fernow was "laying pipes" for future work. He was dealing with what he called the "squeezed lemons," the forests which were cut over and in need of new growth. Academic

[11] See an address by Fernow to the Canadian Club of Timiskaming, New Liskeard, Ontario, Nov. 29, 1913.

[12] *Forestry Quarterly* XII, 4, 1914, p. 596; 3, p. 397; 2, p. 296; H. S. Graves, "Some Problems in Forest Education," *Proc. Soc. Am. For.* II, 1, pp. 48-62.

forestry progress was clearly shown in the *Report of the Committee of the Conference of Forest Schools on Standardization of Instruction in Forestry,*[13] prepared by Graves, revised by Fernow, and read by Fisher.

Why did not the lumbermen apply forestry? Many of the most capable graduates of forest schools were employed by private interests. Fernow said[14] that a very small fraction of the number of private concerns used conservative methods in their forest work. Very few held acreage for future supplies; indeed, few protected their holdings against fires. Almost no attention was accorded protection against insect and other ravages. Private ownership, moreover, still represented about three-fourths of the total timber supply and forest area of the country. The "cold-blooded reasoner from facts" could find little justification to congratulate the profession on the spread of forestry practice and principles, but Fernow adhered to his faith that the schools should educate foresters, but not in such abundance that the supply would exceed the demand. He told Dr. Bailey:[15]

> There is a great deal of difference between "needed" and "wanted" [foresters]. I think the United States needs all the foresters that are preparing for this class of work, but unfortunately they are not wanted, except in a limited number, because private forestry, and as for that State forestry, is as yet undeveloped. I have always taken great care not to over-advertise, or to advertise at all, believing that it is better to let these matters develop naturally. Here in Canada, we were for two years, short of men, and had to import them from the States. Nevertheless, we did not lower our entrance requirements, or allow any half-baked men to graduate.

Fernow with the aid of Howe and White had steadily promoted scientific forestry in *Forestry Quarterly.* In the same issue in which the report on standardized forestry instruction appeared was also published a study by Karl W. Woodward on "The Application of Scientific Management to Forestry."[16] Much review space had been given to ecological studies and scientific forestry bulletins. Some treated forest regions with which Fernow was presently concerned. Cooper's study of "The Climax Forest of Isle Royale, Lake Superior, and its Development"[17] treated such subjects as the propagation of valuable species, including balsam, paper-birch, white spruce type, and others, together with methods for soil improvement according to forest types. Natural regeneration, nurse-planting, and underplanting were also considered with regard to large forest regions. Cooper's work was coming into prominence, especially his work in the mountains of Colorado. *Forestry Quarterly* reviewed this and other studies in the Rocky Mountain regions, as well as studies

[13] Also in *Forestry Quarterly* X, 3, Sept. 1912, p. 341.

[14] "Why Do Not Lumbermen Apply Forestry?" *American Forestry* XVIII, 10, Oct. 1912, pp. 613ff.

[15] Letter dated April 23, 1914.

[16] *Forestry Quarterly* X, 3, Sept. 1912, p. 407.

[17] *ibid.* XI, 1, March 1913, p. 90.

which issued from the Desert Botanical Laboratory, notable among which was Spalding's "Distribution and Movement of Desert Plants."[18] I. W. Bailey reviewed Cowles's study, "The Causes of Vegetative Cycles."[19] Ecological studies of forests and forest types accumulated. Such an article as Arthur W. Sampson's "The Relation of Soil Acidity to Plant Societies," published in the seventh volume of the *Proceedings of the Society of American Foresters*, was valuable to both ecologists and foresters. Forestry was not without its own scientific studies. Raphael Zon produced in 1911 "New Points of View in Silviculture," from Mayr's *Waldbau auf naturgesetzlicher Grundlage*, and in 1913 "The Relation of Forests in the Atlantic Plain to the Humidity of the Central States and Prairie Region."[20] B. E. Hoffman wrote on "Alaska Woods, Their Present and Prospective Uses."[21] In 1911 Burt P. Kirkland presented in *Forestry Quarterly* a strong article on "The Need of a Vigorous Policy of Encouraging Cutting on National Forests of the Pacific Coast."[22] W. B. Greeley's "A Rough System of Management for Reserve Lands in the Western Sierras," presented in the second volume of the society's *Proceedings*, was characterized by Barrington Moore as "the beginning of the true American Silviculture,"[23] and Greeley's study of "National Forest Sales on the Pacific Coast" was regarded as showing clearly the underlying economic principles which guided the United States Forest Service in its administration of timber sales. Especially worthy of notice were treatises on seed production by Dana, Bristow Adams, and Zon, and the bulletins on the proper locations of tree species. Forestry in the United States was growing to rival agriculture in governmental administration.

In Canada the Dominion experimental farms had been perfecting agricultural techniques for a quarter of a century. The Dominion government always had supplied agricultural research with ample funds, while forestry research had neither funds nor personnel with which to rival agricultural progress. Ecologists from the United States had supplied more exact knowledge of Canadian forest conditions than Canadians themselves. In ecology and silviculture, research methodology was available. Canadian progress, however, was years behind that of the United States. In June 1913 *Forestry Quarterly* published A. B. Connell's investigation, "Ecological Studies on a Northern Ontario Sand Plain."[24] It was prepared as a part of field practice work of the senior class in the autumn of 1912 at the school's practice camp at Frank's Bay, Lake Nipissing, Ontario. The presence of Howe, Whitford and White in Canada provided stimulus to research. Particularly

[18] *ibid.* IX, 1, March 1911, p. 100. [19] *ibid.* IX, 2, June 1911, p. 303.
[20] *ibid.* IX, 2, June 1911, p. 205; XI, 3, Sept. 1913, p. 421 (review).
[21] *ibid.* XI, 2, June 1913, p. 185. [22] *ibid.* IX, 3, Sept. 1911, p. 375.
[23] *ibid.* XII, 1, March 1914, pp. 47ff.; XIV, 3, Sept. 1916, pp. 375ff.
[24] *ibid.* XI, 2, June 1913, p. 149.

was this true of Howe's work for the commission of conservation in methods to regenerate forest growth in cut-over and burned-over areas. As the United States had once had to lay sound economic foundations on which to develop scientific forestry, Canada also had to pass through similar years. At first ecology and forestry went on divergent paths. Indeed, at one time in the United States there was discussed and officially approved a project to prepare a book on "Research Methods in Forestry." Fernow certainly gave no encouragement to this move.

We have traced beginnings of wood technology in America in laboratories of the two federal governments of the continent. We have traced beginnings at universities—Yale, the Universities of California and Washington, Purdue, and other institutions noted in forest products research. The work at the University of Michigan, with Roth present, was surely to develop. The work at the New York State College of Forestry at Syracuse and Harvard University also became notable. *Forestry Quarterly's* leading article of March 1913 was Contribution I from the Laboratory of Wood Technology of the Harvard School of Forestry, "The Preservative Treatment of Wood," by Irving W. Bailey. Bailey was regarded by Fernow as America's leading wood expert. Fernow told H. B. Ayers on January 20, 1913, "As regards an expert . . . the best man I know is Professor I. W. Bailey . . . who is our best wood expert now and a thoroughly reliable man, I believe. I know that he has given particular attention to the question of distinguishing pine and spruce. . . ." Bailey presented a scholarly coordination of forestry and botanical research.

Leading among plant morphologists was Edward C. Jeffrey, once a professor of botany at the University of Toronto, who had been called to Harvard largely as a result of his celebrated extension of phylogenetic research to plant anatomy. Study of plants from the standpoint of objective physiology had originated in Europe. A botanist, G. Klebs, had written one of the first treatises on the subject.[25] Many botanists, among them American research students, had elaborated the thesis. This led to the truly great discovery by Ezra Jacob Kraus and Henry Reist Kraybill of the carbohydrate-nitrogen relation present at the flowering and fruiting of the tomato.[26]

A botanist, David Pearce Penhallow of McGill University, interested in tracing relations between paleobotanical and modern floras, also from a standpoint of phylogeny, had given new interest to interior plant structural development, particularly in certain forest groups. Penhallow was prominent at the Canadian Forestry Convention of 1906, and in the

[25] B. E. Livingston, *Botanical Gazette* XXXVI, July-Dec. 1903, p. 311, a review of Klebs's work.

[26] These points are treated in more detail in the present author's *John Merle Coulter and Liberty Hyde Bailey*, Princeton Univ. Press.

next year he attempted to classify North American gymnosperms, exclusive of the Cycadales, on the basis of the mature wood's anatomy. Jeffrey had brought into studies of evolutionary sequence the woody system of plants. In 1910 Bailey's study of "Anatomical characters in the evolution of *Pinus*" was published in the *American Naturalist* and reviewed in the *Botanical Gazette*. His further researches also engaged Fernow's interest.

Fernow doubtless saw that forestry was furthered by biological studies. These were not atlas studies of geographic forest species distribution, such as George B. Sudworth of the forest service had begun in 1912. Taxonomic literature was being published each year by Sargent, Nathaniel Lord Britton, Benjamin Lincoln Robinson, and others, but physiological investigation was fundamental. No one had questioned that since the years of Goodale, Gray, and the leaders of a transitional period on botany. Since 1898 Clements in the West and Cowles in the Middle West studied American vegetation ecologically.[27] The work in phytogeography traced back many years before 1898. Since then, rigid experimental analysis under a corps of faithful energetic research students had been pursued in forests, deserts, prairies, swamps, and in every special type of land area where plants and forests grow. Light, climate, evaporation, moisture, temperature, soil composition, even root systems, were examined quantitatively in relation to plant growth and plant association. A study[28] in 1923 by Carlos G. Bates on the "Physiological Requirements of Rocky Mountain Trees," performed at the Frémont Experiment Station, was a culmination of this work.

Ecology was one phase of biological research of growing importance to forestry. Wood technology and forest products research represented a modernized timber physics study. From his first years in American professional work Fernow had sponsored both. The new progress, however, was almost tantamount to new beginnings. But Fernow had two indisputable points of leadership. He had spread the vision of each in forestry. His early writings were the pioneering outlines. Since those years a real plant physiology and plant anatomy had become partners in a new cytology which was pure research, though of immense practical

[27] See Cowles's review of Clements's "Development and Structure of Vegetation," *Botanical Gazette* XXXVIII, July-Dec. 1904, p. 303. See also Clements's "Plant Formations and Forest Types," *Proc. Soc. Am. For.* IV, 1. Each year the *Quarterly* reviewed the works of W. W. Robbins, William Cooper, L. H. Harvey, B. E. Livingston, Weaver, and other ecologists who contributed to forestry. For examples see *Forestry Quarterly* VI, 4, Dec. 1908, p. 398; VII, 1, March 1909, p. 66; VIII, 3, Sept. 1910, p. 365.

[28] C. G. Bates, "Physiological Requirements of Rocky Mountain Trees," *Journal of Agricultural Research*, 1923, was reviewed in *Botanical Gazette* LXVIII, Sept.-Dec. 1924, p. 126. See also "Forests and Streamflow, an Experimental Study," *Proc. Soc. Am. For.* VI, 1; and Hall and Maxwell, "Relation of Surface Conditions to Streamflow," *ibid.* VI, 2. Moore discussed Cleveland's paper on the forests' influence in increasing the nitrogen content of soils in *ibid.* V, 1.

value. Some indication of practical worth may be gathered from the fact that from eleven wood preservative plants in the United States in 1900, the number had increased to one hundred and one plants in 1911. By 1913 the United States had 110 hardwood distillation plants.[29]

Irving W. Bailey's scholarly study, "The Preservative Treatment of Wood," was pure and applied research combined. It considered theories concerning the penetration of gases and preservatives into seasoned woods, and their validity. It analyzed the distribution of "slits" in air-dry wood, the annual ring, and the layers of the cell wall, and the penetration of air through green wood and re-soaked dry wood, and other matters. The second branch of the inquiry minutely and exhaustively dealt with "The structure of the pit membranes in the tracheids of conifers and their relation to the penetration of gases, liquids, and finely divided solids into green and seasoned wood." The subdivisions of the subject were styled, "Detailed structure of the pit membrane," a summary and conclusions, and a bibliography. In this type of research it may be readily seen that chemistry, physics, engineering science, botany, and forestry knowledge were united.

When in November of 1916 Bailey was asked to present a paper on the subject before the Society of American Foresters, he wrote to Fernow, "I am asking Dr. Roth and yourself to [write a brief discussion of the subject] because I believe that you have a more fundamental appreciation of many of these problems than most of the foresters who are working directly in this field."

Fernow replied, thanking him for the honor of thinking that he was capable of discussing it to any advantage. He said, however, "My occupation with this subject dates back at least 18 years, and I shall, of course, not be able to discuss any details, but perhaps I may be able to add interest by raising a few practical questions in connection with the attempt to bring a scientific basis for our practice in general, and especially with reference to utilization."

Such valuable contributions as Samuel J. Record's "The Forest Conditions of the Ozark Region of Missouri," his *Identification of Economic Woods of the United States*, his *Mechanical Properties of Wood*, Ralph C. Hawley and Austin Hawes's *Forestry in New England*, "the first general treatise on practical forestry to be published in this country"[30] applied specifically to New England, Bailey *et al.*'s "Graded Volume Tables for Vermont Hardwoods," John F. Preston and Frank J. Phillips's "Seasonal Variation in the Food Reserves of Trees," Lyman J. Briggs and Homer L. Shantz's "The Wilting Coefficient for Different Plants and Its Indirect Determination," Ralph C. Bryant's

[29] *Forestry Quarterly* X, 2, June, 1912, p. 318; "Review of Forest Service Investigations," *op. cit.*, II, pp. 33-48.
[30] *Forestry Quarterly* X, 2, June 1912, p. 250.

Logging, The Principles and General Methods of Operation in the United States, George B. Sudworth's *Forest Atlas, Geographic Distribution of North American Trees*, H. W. Maxwell's *Uses of Commercial Woods of the United States*, A. B. Recknagel's *The Theory and Practice of Working Plans*, Filibert Roth's *Forest Regulation, or the Preparation and Development of Working Plans*, F. F. Moon and N. C. Brown's *Elements of Forestry*, Herman Haupt Chapman's *Forest Valuation*, as well as Roth's book on the same subject, not to omit the publication of the classes of 1913 and 1914 of the Toronto faculty of forestry, *Silvical Characteristics of Canadian Trees*,[31] a discussion of fifty-six species, and many other works published during these years, demonstrated the progress in forestry on the American continent.

In 1916 Barrington Moore in *Forestry Quarterly*[32] said that despite the fact that forestry had been closely connected with the nation's economic development and by necessity compelled to maintain a practical point of view, "most of the work which [was] building the foundations of forestry, such as the work of Shantz, of Livingston, and of Cowles, [was] being done by men who [were] not foresters." Forestry was destined to become "more than empiricism." In the September 1916 issue of *Forestry Quarterly* appeared the first part of R. H. Boerker's doctoral thesis, "A Historical Study of Forest Ecology: Its Development in the Fields of Botany and Forestry," in which the author said:

> In America, Clements, Livingston, Cowles, Transeau, Fuller, Shantz, Shreve, Pool, and others, have contributed to this field. . . . As has been said before, modern plant ecology is *dynamic*. More recently it has shown a tendency to become *applied* in character. . . . There is an ever increasing number of workers, especially on distributional problems. Among those in this field in our own country we find Shantz in the Great Plains, Fuller in the Chicago region, Pool on the Nebraska prairies, Transeau at Cold Spring Harbor, New York, Weaver in Washington, Clements in the Rocky Mountains, and Shreve in Southern Arizona. Among some of the workers on the comparative physiology of associated plants, we find Cannon upon the optimum growth temperature of roots, Livingston and Shreve upon the transpiring power of plants, Harris on the osmotic strength of the saps of plants, and Richards and MacDougal on several physiological aspects of the cacti. In this category is also included the author's recent work upon the effect of habitat factors upon the germination of forest seed trees. Some of these investigations deserve further mention. The recent work of Briggs and Shantz on the wilting coefficient of soils and the water requirements of plants is certainly an important contribution. . . .Only the future can tell what the value of this work will be to the forester.

That same year *Forestry Quarterly* published I. W. Bailey's article, "The Significance of Certain Variations in the Anatomical Structure

[31] *ibid.* XII, 3, Sept. 1914, p. 439.
[32] "The Relation of Forestry to Science," *ibid.* XIV, 3, p. 375.

of Wood."[33] Reviewers considered the significance of such studies as Toumey's *Seeding and Planting in the Practice of Forestry, A Manual,*[34] William H. Chandler's "The Killing of Plant Tissues by Low Temperatures,"[35] and E. P. Meinecke's "Forest Pathology in Forest Regulation."[36]

At last Fernow's "labor of love," *Forestry Quarterly*, had more articles submitted than it could publish. The task of discrimination grew increasingly difficult. Space was found for the best and worthiest. Fernow gladly accepted Barrington Moore's historical study, "Forestry in America as Reflected in the Proceedings of the Society of American Foresters,"[37] which collected and organized most valuable material under divisions of historical, general, description, silvics, ecology, forest influences, silviculture, forestation, mensuration, engineering, management, utilization, protection, pathology, grazing, economics, legislation, education, botany, soils, wood technology, translations, and auxiliary subjects. "The strength of Silvics and Silviculture," Moore said, "stand out particularly since these are subjects about which Americans must secure their own data and build up their own practice." Graves had pleaded for a knowledge of principles and fundamental conditions. Fernow also always had regarded forest situations as problems requiring diagnosis and remedies. Silviculture was still the subject of the hour in both the United States and Canada. In 1916 Fernow was asked by a publisher to criticize an outline of a proposed book on forest management. He replied that such a book would have to duplicate Graves's *Forest Mensuration*, Chapman's *Forest Valuation,* and Recknagel's *Forest Organization*, and include more. The need of forestry was not more or better books, certainly not encyclopedic books in an era of specialization. The need, Fernow seems to have believed, was experimental research in all branches of forest and forest products investigation.[38]

In 1911 or 1912 Fernow had written on "History of Forests and Forestry in Canada" for a volume partly devoted to "Canada and its Provinces" and published by the Publishers' Association of Canada. A few years later he contributed an article on "Forestry and Timber" to

[33] *ibid.* XIV, 4, Dec. 1916, p. 662.

[34] *ibid.* XIV, 3, Sept. 1916, p. 474.

[35] *ibid.* XIV 3, Sept. 1916, p. 483.

[36] *ibid.* XIV, 4, Dec. 1916, p. 719 (a review). See also J. R. Weir, "Some Factors Governing the Trend and Practice of Forest Sanitation," *ibid.* XIII, 4, Dec. 1915, p. 481; and a review of Hermann von Schrenk and Perley Spaulding's "Diseases of Deciduous Forest Trees," a bulletin of the U.S. Bureau of Plant Industry, *ibid.* VII, 4, p. 419.

[37] *ibid.* XII, 1, March 1914, p. 47.

[38] For other special studies in the *Forestry Quarterly* see Record's "Grain and Texture in Wood," IX, 1, March 1911, p. 22; "Pith Flecks or Medullary Spots in Wood," IX, 2, June 1911, p. 244; H. H. Chapman, "Method of Investigating Yields Per Acre in Many Aged Stands," X, 3, Sept. 1912, p. 458; and studies by Woolsey, Roth, and Lovejoy in XIV, 2, June 1916, pp. 188, 238, 255.

A. G. Brown, P. H. Morris, and H. J. Boam's *Twentieth Century Impressions of Canada*, published at Montreal in 1914. In 1912 for the University of Toronto Studies, volume sixteen, he reviewed twenty-seven bulletins including the very early issues of the forestry branch of the Dominion department of the interior, and styled his article "Canadian Timberlands." His initial comments pointed out:

> The growing interest in the future of Canadian timberlands finds for the first time expression in this publication. . . . Twelve of the [Forestry Branch] Bulletins are devoted to statistical matter regarding forest products marketed during given years; five contain descriptions of certain forest regions; three are discussing silvicultural matters, and four elaborate argumentatively on that worst enemy of Canadian forests, and at the same time, national disgrace, the forest fires. . . . Altogether this series promises to become an important contribution to the economic history of Canada with regard to her timber resources, which in the Eastern Provinces and British Columbia are destined under forest management to become more prominent as time goes on.

The silvicultural bulletins consisted principally of matters pertaining to farm woodlot planting in the prairies, a part of the government's program to distribute free plant material from its large nurseries. The bulletins on forest products collated statistical data of "consumption by provinces and species" and discussed "price changes and methods of increasing the usefulness of the material, as by preservatives." The very few bulletins offered concerning the Dominion forest reserves—a general one written by Abraham Knechtel; one by J. R. Dickson which discussed the Riding Mountain Reserve and the work there; and one containing the report of the boundary survey parties of the Rocky Mountains Forest Reserve to be established, by G. H. Edgecombe and P. Z. Caverhill—drew from Fernow no special comment, except that he noticed that of the territory investigated a very small per cent had "real timber" and that eighty per cent had been burned over during the past fifty years and forty-eight per cent during the past twenty-five years.

Addressing the Canadian Forestry Association at Victoria, British Columbia, September 4-6, 1912, Fernow vigorously insisted that forest reproduction was the forester's main business.[39] "The protection of forests against fire," he said, "is no more forestry than the preventing of the burning of your house is architecture. Forestry is very much like architecture, the building up of a new forest." The securing of conservative lumbering practices did not fulfill the forester's obligations. Weed trees could follow in the path of mere conservative lumbering. A logging engineer did not necessarily make a forester, although the forester had to know logging engineering. In 1913 Fernow wrote in the *Toronto*

[39] See the 14th Annual Report of the Association, Feb. 5, 1913, pp. 119-122.

Weekly Star, after a great flood of the Ohio River had accentuated forestry interest:

> Conservative forest management and reforestation, not only at the headwaters but along the streams to prevent the washing of soil into the rivers, seems to me most urgently needed. This does not exclude engineering schemes for water storage when necessary. But on the whole, soil management promises more lasting results than engineering work. The farmers can also help matters by better cultivation, so as to use water to improve crop production and at the same time reduce the surface drainage. But, I repeat, there is no use recommending generalities. Governments should send out experts, real ones, to investigate causes and prescribe remedies.

It was a matter of great pride to Fernow that his student, Ralph C. Bryant at Yale, was the occupant of the first chair of logging engineering and lumbering in the United States and Canada. In 1914 a new department of forestry was located at the University of Montana at Missoula, and Dorr Skeels, expert logging engineer of the United States forest service and a product of the University of Michigan, was named Dean. Fernow foresaw that available lumber supplies for the future were by no means inexhaustible. Authenticated reports showed serious diminutions and, what was more, poorer resources than conservative estimates had predicted. Indeed, the report on "Timber Conditions, etc., along the Proposed Route of the Hudson Bay Railway,"[40] prepared by Dickson in 1911 and published by the Canadian forestry branch, described them as "extremely poor, 'a mere fraction of one per cent of the area surveyed now carries merchantable timber'. . . . 'The fires of the past 100 years have destroyed nearly all the old stand.' Swamps and muskegs and almost pure rock outcrops (outside of 2,000 square miles of Clay Belt) form the largest portion of the territory."

The Canadian Society of Forest Engineers by 1914 numbered many more than fifty members, spread through forestry work in British Columbia, the prairie provinces, Ontario, Quebec, and the maritime provinces. The Toronto school had grown gradually—in 1910 only two B.Sc.F. degrees had been granted; in 1911, five; in 1912, twelve; and in 1913, seven. The advent of World War I devastated the Canadian foresters' ranks, many going into the armed forces. Fernow's own sons enlisted. Moreover, Fernow told his students that it was their duty to enlist. He himself remained a pacifist. But he addressed the students and urged that "as a sacred duty [they should] join the O.T.C. and prepare for the eventuality of joining a contingent." Fernow grieved over the war with the fatherland. He told State Forester A. F. Hawes of Vermont, "I think the war is a terrible piece of history. My sympathies naturally are divided, since I have some relatives in the old country who

[40] Bulletin 17, Dominion Forestry Branch, 27 pp. Quotation from Fernow's "Canadian Timberlands," *op. cit.* Quotations from *Toronto Weekly Star* article and address to Canad. For. Ass'n likewise taken from Fernow's mss, found among his valuable papers.

are bound to suffer." The war did much to shatter Fernow's health. Forestry progress was retarded. So intense became the war spirit that a movement was set in motion to require Mrs. Fernow to desist from teaching the German language to students of the Toronto forestry school. Mrs. Fernow, an American-born citizen, had performed this service gratuitously for eight years. For some time the study of French had been optional for certain students after the first year. Since forestry journals now presented translations of foreign literature, and that students might take more forestry courses, Fernow on June 26, 1918, agreed that German also might be made an optional course. Meanwhile, innuendoes and formal attacks on his patriotism had to be answered. He said that it was always a citizen's duty to fight for his country. In a newspaper interview, he replied to a reporter's questioning concerning his youthful service in the Franco-Prussian war, "Yes, I did fight for my country, just as you should fight for your country now." Dr. Schenck of the Biltmore Forest School announced in 1914 the discontinuance of the school and his appointment to a position in the government forest service in Germany. Vanderbilt, some time earlier, had terminated his employment of Schenck, and Schenck had endeavored to carry on the school. The struggling venture failed. Schenck returned to Germany and, when World War I broke out, enlisted with the German army. Foresters in America did not understand the "imbroglio" at Biltmore. Beginning about 1909 Schenck's influence steadily declined. Overton W. Price wrote Fernow on March 25, 1914, that he regarded Schenck's "work in America [had been] the very antithesis of yours."

On February 25, 1914, Fernow addressed a graduating class of Yale Forest School. He expressed pleasure that an old accusation born of rivalry, a distinction between a German or "theoretical" forestry taught at Cornell and the need of an American or "practical" forestry to be taught at Yale, had worn away.[41] Forestry was then regarded as an "applied science or art," knowing no "patriotic boundaries. At that time forestry was nowhere practiced on this continent." Therefore there could have been no valid distinction between theory and practice, because no forestry practice existed. Not so now, however. Theory and practice had so combined that promise of a real American forestry was everywhere in evidence. He told the graduates, "When you shall have devised, as eventually no doubt you will, successful methods of application of principles, which fit our special conditions, then, indeed, we may be permitted to speak of *American forestry* as describing these special methods." Fernow attacked the belief, current for many years, that the

[41] *Yale Forest School News* II, 2, pp. 15-18; reviewed by A. B. Recknagel in *Forestry Quarterly* XII, 3, Sept. 1914, p. 493. These quotations are taken from Fernow's original manuscript.

theoretical man was impractical. He believed that too often the "practical" man was impractical, for too often for the sake of progress, the practical "meant the maintenance of the *status quo*." To confine one's knowledge to formulas, artificial classification, or any closed system, was both impractical and stifling to progress. "As editor of *Forestry Quarterly*," he observed, "I am enabled to gauge the literary activity of the American forestry world, and while there is annually a healthy growth in that direction, yet it is questionable whether the advantages for keeping abreast with the professional development are fully utilized. Do not capitulate to the practical activities," he pleaded. "Keep up your intellectual advancement through contact with your academic past in the school of life."

The period of "adaptability and willingness" within the profession had been translated by the profession's pioneers—the majority of whom, Fernow said, had come from Yale—into a period where competition, selection, the survival of the fittest would weed out the less skillful and advance the more skilled members. The organizational aspects in the business of forestry would now yield to the more objective and scientific study of "silviculture, the growing of the crop." Attention had previously been fixed on the economic side, but he invited the graduates to give the closest attention to developing silviculture.

Fernow championed science as a practical way to realize a righteous life. He was not a churchman in the sense of being a subscriber to theological dogma, but he never attacked the church, and his closest friend, Rossiter Raymond, was an ardent churchman. Evolutionary doctrine during these years, however, was presumed to be at strife with the essentials of religion, and Fernow was on the side of evolution. An unsigned document was found among his papers, entitled "My Creed," written in his handwriting. One or two excerpts are revealing:

> Religion as well as theology is as much subject to the laws of evolution, as man himself in all his faculties; hence religion can never remain the same through the ages and its basis must vary; ideals always widen with broader knowledge and broader conceptions. . . . Religion is a necessity of the aggregate or social life of man, and the reason for its existence—whatever the history of its evolution—must be found in present necessities. . . . The moral conduct of man toward man is not actuated only by a desire for justice, which is mainly based on reason, but is tempered by the clemency of love, which is based on [the] heart. . . .

In a qualified sense, Fernow believed that each person was the architect of his own fortune. He told the Yale graduating class:

> Most of the time, most of us can succeed only by taking care of chances and accidents; and so I advise you to adopt the interpretation of accident which Schiller lays into the mouth of Marquis Posa: Was this but accident? —Perhaps " 'twas something more." What else is accident but the rough

stone which assumes life under the sculptor's hand? It is Providence that provides the accident for Man to mould it to his own designs and purposes!

On February 22, 1918, Fernow told Dr. Charles C. Adams of the New York State College of Forestry at Syracuse:

The best man anywhere is the man with scientific training if he combines with it practical insight and experience. If he lacks the latter, the so-called practical man with only vocational training may do better for a time. But he is only an emergency substitute, and eventually the better man will take his place, as the United States Forest Service has amply demonstrated. There is no question but that the scientifically educated man is the type of man most valuable in scientific or permanent field work. The world has progressed not through the efforts of the so-called practical man with a number of unsubstantiated theories, but by the theoretical man who holds few theories and requires that they be substantiated.

A few months after his graduation address at Yale, there came to Fernow an even more gratifying honor, an opportunity to preside as president at the first meeting held away from Washington, D.C., of the Society of American Foresters. The society's meeting was held as a part of informal dedicatory ceremonies of the new Forestry Building of the New York State College of Agriculture at Cornell University. The festivities lasted a full day, with morning, afternoon, and evening sessions. Eminent notables in agricultural and forestry ranks, such as W. B. Greeley, C. R. Pettis, James W. Toumey, F. L. Moore, H. S. Drinker, J. S. Whipple, L. H. Bailey, and Gifford Pinchot, addressed the sessions.

On Saturday morning, May 16, 1914, Fernow presided as chairman of an open meeting of the Society of American Foresters. State Forester Alfred Gaskill of New Jersey spoke on eastern states' forestry during the next decade; Roth on state forestry in the middle west; and Fernow on the work of the society. The outlook of state forestry was encouraging, though much work remained. Gaskill asked if every state would not have to choose "definitely and soon, whether it will advocate chiefly state forestry, as New York and Pennsylvania do, or private forestry, as is done in New Jersey and Connecticut. [For] if state forestry is strongly supported it necessarily weakens the effort to induce private owners to invest money in timberlands." Both policies were fundamental, and time might show one or the other to be right. But had the magnitude of New York's forest preserve policy so blinded the state that "other and more valuable forests, her woodlots," were overlooked? Roth said that Minnesota and Wisconsin had made fair beginnings in state forestry. But in Michigan, after eleven years of effort, state forestry had gotten little beyond a forest administration of about 50,000 acres—in all, a forest reserve area in scattered parcels of about 230,000 acres—although during 1901-1910 more than a million and a half acres had been deeded to the state for non-payment of taxes, and the state, by sales, had let go at proven losses more than a million and a half acres. Roth said that in Michigan 600,000 acres[42] then could be reserved if the state really wanted to reserve the forest acreage, and little opposition would be encountered. "State forestry is our only important question in forestry in Michigan," said Roth, "and state forestry we shall have."

Fernow attached "a special significance to [his] election [as president of the society], namely, the desire to free the society from the strong influence of officialdom which had quite naturally grown up." More than half of the society's membership, forty-nine per cent of the active membership, was outside of the United States forest service, either in state forestry, academic life, or private employment. He had promised to "make no reference to the situation of forestry education in New York State, but confine [himself] entirely to generalities and to the discussion of the functions of the Society." To prepare for the address, Fernow had written to Rossiter Raymond and asked for written discussions of professional ethics and ways to advance the interests of professional societies. Fernow wanted to establish standards, both technical and ethical. He wanted the society "to be the standard bearer of professional honor" and to promote brotherhood, not "solitariness." The American Medical Association, the Boston Society of Architects, and the Canadian Society of Civil Engineers had attempted to codify their professional codes of ethics. Fernow, noticing that a prepared code of ethics had been recently abandoned by the Medical Society of the State of New York, expressed the belief that at least in part a code of ethics should not be written. But he said that over and above the "spirit of the golden rule and the decalogue," which in most doubtful situations sufficed, there occasionally arose points of question about which the best men might honestly differ, and in these cases the society should set standards of conduct. Fernow suggested that a committee of the older, more experienced members, in whom the younger members had confidence, and whose wisdom and maturity would assure a fair and impartial hearing, could bring such matters before the Society.

The address of the Cornell forestry building's dedication ceremonies which attracted widest interest was Dean Bailey's address on "The Forest." Dr. Bailey recently had resigned as dean of the New York

[42] *Journal of Forestry* XV, 6, Oct. 1917, p. 1075, to the effect that by 1917 Michigan owned 540,000 acres which were to be planted and treated systematically over a long stretch of time by the Public Domain Commission. Roth pointed out (*ibid.* XVI, 2, Feb. 1918, pp. 145f.), "In 1903 a Michigan legislature and the State authorities could not even be induced to listen to forestry. Last winter the commission in charge received its appropriation without dissenting votes, and it received $130,000 simply for reforestation, in spite of the fact that it was made clear that this was merely the beginning of a sixty-year investment program. . . ."

State College of Agriculture and director of its agricultural experiment station. President Roosevelt had appointed him chairman of a Commission on Country Life, a commission which Roosevelt said was exceeded in importance by only one other, the Commission for the Conservation of Natural Resources. Bailey planned to give over the balance of his life to country life development and to study in the plant sciences.

At the same session Gifford Pinchot delivered an address on "The National Movement for Conservation" in which he said:

> Today the essential of conservation is to further prevent destruction, as this makes the article that is destroyed high in price to the average buyer. It must also take measures to prevent the monopoly of natural resources. Third, and that is the part that still remains to the future, it must provide for the handling of the concentrations that have already taken place. . . . There are in the hands of one group of Western lumbermen thousands of acres of public timber, passed into private hands partly because of the bad administration and partly because the laws were bad. For less than a tenth of what that timber was worth it has passed into the hands of a small group of men from the people of the United States—a property worth, in round numbers, nine hundred million dollars. It is the same with water power. Sixty-five per cent of the developed water power is in ten companies or ten groups of companies, and they also control undeveloped water power; so that there is not only an enormous increase in the power developed, but still more rapid increase in the water power held for development in the future. The ground work is laid for a giant monopoly, a greater control than in any other country. Eighty per cent of the anthracite coal is in the hands of one group or company, so that about forty men have in their power the domination over the use and price of this public necessity over a large part of the United States. Sixteen hundred and forty-one men, owners or group owners, own one out of every twenty acres in the United States, and there is a concentration of oil, lead, and all other natural resources. . . .

Pinchot believed that the conservation movement grew directly from the forest policy and "was, so to speak, put on the map by what [had] seemed to [him] to be one of the most important things in history, when there were gathered in Washington in 1908 all the governors of the States." There had followed "the first inventory ever made of the natural resources of any country in the world. The resources of the Federal Government were laid open for that purpose, and the work was completed in six months. Then came a most significant meeting; a group of ten men chosen from the United States, Mexico, and Canada in 1909 came together in Washington, making it evident that conservation of resources was not bounded by natural lines within the United States and that it was to the interest of all North Americans to join together and decide how the resources might be used for the best interests of all. They in turn invited the President of the United States to lay before the nations of the world a plan for a world-wide conference." Owing to the change of administration at Washington, however, the proposal for the world conference had been dropped.

Pinchot, president of the National Conservation Association, said, "It is perfectly clear to me—at least in the nature of certain natural resources, possibly very limited in number but very important in character—that the solution will be public ownership, or such public control as will amount to giving the people of the country and the State the benefit of public ownership." Pinchot had not left forestry. Later he again became interested in forestry—in the state of Pennsylvania, of which he eventually became Governor.

Forestry Quarterly[43] reviewed the ceremonies which dedicated the forestry building of the New York State College of Agriculture. It commended as a "most notable contribution" the address on "National Forestry" by W. B. Greeley, who since 1911 had been assistant forester of the forest service in charge of timber sales, reforestation, etc. and in 1920 was to become chief forester. He said:

> We conceive it to be the first and foremost function of the timber retained in public ownership to maintain competitive conditions in the lumber industry whenever there shall be any tendency toward closely controlled production; and to prevent as far as is possible, through the sale of public stumpage, monopolistic increases in the price of forest products or increases unwarranted by rational adjustments of the trade to changed conditions of supply and demand. That is, as far as the public reserves can influence the market, it is their business to give the country the lumber it requires, at the lowest price justified by the supply available for present and future needs.

This policy would provide, it was believed, an effective check on any unwarranted growth of monopolies in the lumber industry. Greeley added:

> At the same time we conceive it our duty to promote effective utilization of timber and to prevent serious waste of a resource the supply of which is all too limited. In other words, there is a definite point in competitive conditions below which the Government will not go in disposing of the public timber. That point is determined solely by consideration of the public welfare, but requires stable conditions in a manufacturing industry, rightly adjusted to its available supply of raw material. . . . It requires also close utilization of the raw materials produced in the woods. . . . Our chief concern is to develop the sales of national forest timber, not only by methods of sound silviculture, however simple they may be, but also by methods of sound business and sound public policy in relation to the local and general benefits that the national forests should serve.

Under the Weeks law, fourteen areas aggregating 188,904 acres had been acquired as nationally owned forest tracts at the headwaters of navigable streams in the Appalachian ranges. Additional areas of almost a million acres had been approved for purchase, and by 1914 the total was well past a million acres.

[43] *Forestry Quarterly* XII, 2, June 1914, p. 299.

Forest service surveys in the eastern states were being planned in 1914 with a view to inaugurating conservative timberland management. Fire protection cooperative agreements operated over millions of acres in numerous states and afforded protection against fire to vast areas of forest lands at the headwaters of navigable streams.

During the years 1911, 1912, and 1913 the national forest areas had remained practically the same, amounting to approximately 187,500,000 acres at the end of the fiscal year of 1912. Excluding Puerto Rico and Alaska, the national forests at the end of 1912 totalled about 160,600,000 acres distributed in approximately 160 national forests. Excluding acquisitions under the Weeks bill, national forests were found in twenty states. Within California there were twenty-eight million acres of national forest land. Within Montana and Idaho each there were almost twenty million acres. Nine forest experiment stations had been established. By 1912 the work of classifying agricultural as distinguished from forestry lands, and making available home lands for cultivation purposes, was highly developed. Reforestation was the most active research being pursued; investigations included methods of seed extraction, direct seeding, nursery work, field planting, studies in breeding, seed-tree fertility, mensuration, thinning, and forest influences. Roads, fire and telephone lines, bridges, fences, and buildings were being constructed or improved. Water power development would soon become of immense practical value. Range use and control had been and was being further systematized. Range management was gradually being transformed from an economic interest into a systematic science. Protective phases extended to prevention of stream pollution, unnecessary wild life depredations, and inimical diseases. Especially interesting was the recognition that 7,500,000 acres of the national reservations would have to be reforested by artificial means; and this amount was additional to natural regeneration in the large cut-over areas, the results of annual harvests of hundreds of millions of board feet. During 1913 approximately 30,000 acres were reforested artificially.[44] In 1911 Secretary Wilson disclosed that "over 250,000 acres are being reforested annually by creating conditions favorable to natural reproduction."

Greeley, in his "National Forestry" address, reviewed the history and hopes of the forest service:

> It [was] no slight task to transform one hundred and sixty-five millions of acres of virgin wilderness in the most rugged and inaccessible sections of a new country into developed forest properties. . . . Working plans [would] be attempted in the course of the next years on all but a very few national forests, where the demand of local industries [was] making rapid inroads on the timber and there [was] danger of early depletion. In such cases,

[44] A. J. Jaenicke, "Progress of the United States Forest Service as Reflected in the Forester's Reports for 1911, 1912, and 1913," *ibid.* XII, 3, Sept. 1914, p. 397.

rough plans for regulating the cut [would] be worked out with a view to gradually restricting it to the current production of the forest. Elsewhere, with enormous areas of mature virgin stands in need of cutting, the immediate thing [was] to work out and apply simple methods of silviculture which are practicable under existing methods of logging and which will accomplish the fundamental requirements of utilizing mature stumpage and leaving the stand in improved condition. The great bulk of our pine forests lend themselves readily to partial cutting, conforming with the natural grouping of the timber by age and size, under which we retain a quarter or a third of the merchantable timber with usually a fair stocking of young growth, sufficient to afford a second cut in thirty to fifty years. In the heavy, even-aged stands of Douglas fir and western white pine in the Northwest, we have found the most practicable plan to be clean cutting with the reservation of a small percentage of the stand for reseeding, to be supplemented in some cases by artificial planting. These simple provisions, with the cleaning-out of insects and disease as far as practicable and the burning of slashings, represent about all that should be attempted for the present in the way of technical forestry. In the meantime, however, a chain of experiment stations has been established covering all the more important forest regions in the West, at which intensive studies of silvicultural methods on small areas are being conducted together with observations on the influences of the forest on water storage and meteorological conditions. Another important function of the experiment stations is in developing the technique of reforestation. This chain of stations furnishes the Service with a series of miniature forests, on which the problems of technical administration as they arise can be solved on a laboratory scale, and methods developed that can be applied with certainty on the big forest areas surrounding them. At our experiment stations, manned with a corps of trained investigators, we are thus seeking to develop the science of Western American silviculture and meet the technical requirements of administration as they develop. From a practical standpoint, probably our greatest present concern on the investigation side is the effective utilization of the three or four billion feet of wood which by the end of the next decade will be cut annually from the national forests; and restoring to usefulness the five or six million acres of burned-off timberlands whose idleness represents an annual loss of at least half a million dollars. On these two problems our efforts in technical investigation will be largely concentrated.

Forest products laboratory research supplied another fundamental potential. "I am convinced," Greeley urged, "that progress toward the fundamental economic basis of forestry, which must be gradually approached as the supply of mature-grown timber is exhausted—that the value of a grown tree must equal the cost of growing it—will depend during the next ten years largely on better ways of utilizing the raw products of the forest. The value of a long-leaf pine tree when cut into the grades of lumber commonly salable may be trebled if its turpentine and resin are extracted, its top and limb wood manufactured into kraft paper, and the parts of the trunk that would make but low-grade lumber put into paper or fiber-board. This sort of thing, to my thinking, will largely measure the progress in forestry within the period immediately confronting us. That is why better utilization—through pulp and paper manufacture, the manufacture of ethyl alcohol from wood (which chemists tell us is the future industrial fuel of the United States), and the production of other distillates and by-products—is one of the foremost lines of investigation conducted by the Forest Service."

Significant also would be the extension of reforestation on the national forests, work which had previously consisted "chiefly of experiments applicable to an enormous range of climate and soil conditions." The reforestation of western Nebraska sand hills, especially results of investigation performed at the plant station at Halsey, Nebraska, Greeley believed, had "direct and practical bearing on American forestry, in all national forest regions. . . . On the national forests as a whole, the reforestation work has reached the point where it can now be extended on a much larger scale with reasonable certainty of the results. We have developed an equipment of seventeen good-sized nurseries and twenty-one small nurseries, having an annual capacity all told of around twenty million seedlings. With this nursery stock and with a limited amount of direct seeding in a few localities such as the Black Hills, where this method has proved successful, the next ten years should witness very definite progress in reforesting our denuded lands at the rate of not less than twenty thousand acres annually, increasing to that extent the permanent resources and value of the national forests."[45]

The United States and Canada each had a national forestry interlinked with forestry work in the states or provinces. Curiously, federal forestry in the United States has been steadily strengthened, while in Canada the provinces more and more have become the forestry strongholds. In Canada today, even the Dominion timber reservations have been turned over to the provinces. Uniformity of practice, of course, comes with centralization of authority. On the other hand, the Canadian system allows regional government of regional resources. During Fernow's years in both the United States and Canada the states and federal governments, and similarly the provinces and the Dominion, began to relate and integrate forestry work—a new step which pleased Fernow much. In Canada the Dominion forest service, with adequate office and field facilities, still directs an important program of forest research and administration.

At the Cornell meeting of the Society of American Foresters, Associate Forester Greeley introduced the resolution that the society should "investigate scientific problems through its own membership and resources, or in collaboration with other agencies," that the results of the investigations should be published in the *Proceedings* or otherwise, but

[45] Greeley also discussed "constructive regulation of the exploitation of privately owned forests. . . ."

that the society should not "officially endorse conclusions as to scientific facts; but may, with the concurrence of two-thirds of the members balloting, take an official position upon matters of policy."[46] Greeley became president of the Society of American Foresters for 1915. After Greeley's period of office, Fernow again was elected to the highest honor which forestry in North America could confer.

The society's meeting of October 18, 1915,[47] was held in the Lumbermen's Building of the Panama-Pacific International Exposition at San Francisco, at a time when the Western Forestry and Conservation Association, the American Forestry Association, and the Pacific Logging Congress were also meeting. As a part of an elaborate forestry week planned for the Exposition, Fernow sent his address on "Professional Ethics."[48] The program committee asked him to enlarge upon this theme, which he had introduced at the society's Ithaca meeting. A trip to the Canadian prairie and Rocky Mountain forest regions prevented Fernow from delivering his address at the Exposition, but he wrote, "This summer on an inspection trip through the Canadian forest reserves, I was struck more than ever with the fact that knowledge and even intellect are of less moment in the personnel that administers these properties than the moral qualities, zeal, devotion to duty, fidelity, reliability, loyalty. The forester in the woods being removed from the stabilizing influences of contact with the pillars of society must rely on his own moral stamina to keep him straight." Fernow pleaded for friendship between institutions, for open dealings, for forthright honesty in every forester. Fernow wanted no formal, rigid, and binding code of ethics. The society could serve as a forum to discuss ethical practices.

Fernow told that he had testified in a law suit brought by the state of Georgia against the Tennessee Copper Company on the question of the extent of certain damages. He mentioned another case "where the expert made a written report, bringing favorable argument for his client, but accompanying the report by a letter affirming his disbelief in his own argument." In 1918 Fernow was invited by the American Publishers' Association to testify as an expert in a case before the Federal Trade Commission; the question related to financial considerations in paper manufacture. Fernow candidly told the association's special representative, A. G. McIntyre, that his qualifications as an expert witness would be based "on [his] general reputation and general knowledge." He outlined his opinion that "the pulpwood supplies ready for use in the Northeastern States and Canada [were] quite limited." Because of methods employed "there [was] practically no hope of re-

[46] *Forestry Quarterly* XII, 2, June 1914, p. 299.

[47] *ibid.* XIII, 3, Sept. 1915, p. 415. Quotations from Fernow are taken from a typewritten copy found among his papers.

[48] *Proc. Soc. Am. For.* XI, 1916, pp. 52-58.

turn for even a second cut, and reproduction [was] almost nil." He doubted if the association would want his testimony that woodpulp prices were bound to rise "unless substitutes and economies in manufacture [produced] a counterbalancing. . . . The rate of growth of the most prominent woodpulp species, spruce, is so low that it takes 100 years to grow to suitable size."

Fernow, in his address, related he had once had a hard time "to escape from endorsing a California Eucalyptus venture. The case becomes worse," he said, "when the professional man has accepted stock, or other advantage, and especially a contingent fee for his work based on the success of the enterprise."

On January 11, 1915, Fernow addressed a business meeting of the society in New York "There are six directions in which we can improve our Society to fulfill its mission:

1. Broadening its membership through classification of members.
2. Incorporation of the Society to assure its members special standing in the community.
3. Amalgamation of the *Proceedings* with the *Forestry Quarterly*.
4. Return to the original membership fee of $5.00.
5. A paid permanent Secretary.
6. Organization of Sections with increased membership beyond that of the Society itself."

Almost all of these objectives of 1915 have since been realized. Fernow wanted the society "to work out standardized methods of procedure in various lines of investigation." Cooperative experimentation was being ably handled by the Forest Service but it was "conceivable that some problems would be better solved by committee work of the Society."

During 1915 Fernow also addressed the Milwaukee City Club. Wisconsin was starting a conservation commission which included forestry. Fernow opposed the change.[49] A bill which consolidated in one department under commissioners—fish and game, the state forestry board, the state park board, and the state conservation commission—had passed the assembly. Authority to appoint the commissioners was to be vested in the governor. State Forester E. M. Griffith welcomed Fernow to Wisconsin to address a distinguished and influential audience.

Forest conditions on the upper Missouri, Ohio, and Mississippi rivers,

[49] Fernow wrote to Griffith, "To my mind [the proposed consolidation legislation] is a worse break than you seem to think—a return to a political commission, which should have been avoided." Griffith had explained the bill as "practically . . . adopted by the Assembly . . . by a vote of 67-5. . . . One commissioner must have a practical knowledge of the propagation and care of fish and game, one must be a technically trained forester, and one a man with a thorough business training. (I hope the bill will be amended so that the third man will be a good lawyer with practical business training). . . ."

Fernow argued, were "responsible for the huge expenditures in the lower reaches—dredging to keep navigation open, diking to keep the corn and cotton fields of Mississippi and Louisiana from being drowned." Wisconsin needed forests as well as farms to promote its own agriculture by sound methods of soil utilization and conservation. It seemed almost superfluous to discuss the necessity of future timber supplies. Fernow opposed the state's new legislation tactfully. He was concerned whether under the new system trained forestry personnel and administration were assured. If appointees would continue to be men of ability and training, the new legislation merely changed the structure and form of conservation work, not the substance. Within two years, however, State Forester Griffith had "abdicated." Forestry work became a division of the conservation commission. The Wisconsin conservation commission began "to develop a much more statewide scheme of forestry than was carried on by Mr. Griffith, and [we] are succeeding admirably I believe," wrote F. B. Moody, one of the commissioners, in 1917. From 1906-1912 Moody had been assistant state forester under Griffith. He next taught forestry at New York State College of Agriculture but returned to Wisconsin when this commission was created. He continued: "All of the state parks totalling some 7,000 acres are under our full control," in addition to the "approximately 20,000 acres of land that was granted to the state for forestry purposes, together with some 600 islands in inland lakes." Forest nursery practice, education in matters of forest planting, woodlot planting, the planting of 1,000 acres, fire protection, and a few other features of a program had displaced the earlier system. The State Supreme Court had not helped the cause by declaring certain laws unconstitutional.[50] Fernow told the Pennsylvania Forestry Association in June, 1917, "In Wisconsin, which was on the road of equaling you in a sane forest policy, unsuspected provisions of the State constitution have under the construction of the State Supreme Court made illegal the acquiring and devoting to forestry purposes and spending money for reforestation of waste lands." Moreover, Commissioner Moody told Fernow on April 16 of that year, "All lands purchased by the former Forestry Board totalling 159,000 acres, have been declared to have the cast of Normal School lands, and in a measure come to the Public Land Commissioners for administration, at least, so far as sales are concerned and investment of funds arising from said

[50] Griffith recounted the famous Wisconsin "forestry case" in detail in a note to Fernow. See Griffith's "History of Forestry in Wisconsin," *op. cit.*, and "The Acquisition and Use in Wisconsin of State Forest Reserves," *Proc. Soc. Am. For.* VIII, 1913, pp. 202-210, in which Griffith set forth that, while thirteen million acres of land in the state awaited development, the result of the court's decision was to leave to the legislature the "question whether 374,452 acres of forest reserves will be allowed to continue as such," that is, managed as reserves, income to be paid into the school fund, or, if the entire forest reserve area (which had taken ten years to build up) was to be placed on the market and sold.

lands. . . . The land laws as revised and now pending, give us full authority to administer all public lands with the exception of the sale and the proceeds thereof."

To transfer control of this 159,000 acres to a more efficient board or commission would require an amendment of the constitution. The public land commissioners were the secretary of state, the attorney-general, and the state treasurer, but jealousies had arisen between them and the conservation commission. Moody informed Fernow, "In the past [the public land commissioners] sold approximately three and one-half million acres of school lands for a paltry sum. They never had any real knowledge of the lands, never took any real interest in their proper management, never provided any funds for their administration, and never will. . . . This commission . . . is very jealous of the work we are attempting to do in the way of providing adequate fire and trespass protection and other features of field management. . . . We, however, are maintaining our organization, as well as the forest nursery work." Moody forwarded to Fernow a copy of the state forester's report for 1911-1912 which outlined "the policy of the Forestry Board relative to reserving 1,000,000 acres or more in solid block [in Vilas, Oneida, Forest, and Price counties] for forestry purposes. . . . The report [showed] the map of the Wisconsin Forest Reserve and it was planned to purchase approximately 1,200,000 acres within this area. Had this been done, it would have meant that at least ¾ of the area would have been set aside for forestry purposes. . . . There are, undoubtedly, two or three million acres of non-agricultural lands in northern Wisconsin which should be used in growing trees, and to my mind, the only way of working out a policy that will stand in the State, is to secure such areas as should be used for this purpose throughout the various counties. In other words, follow out the Pennsylvania plan!" This was told to Fernow on May 7, 1917, before Fernow delivered his lecture to the Pennsylvania Forestry Association on June 23 of that year. Moody, furthermore, observed "I am not ready as yet to put my stamp of approval on the consolidation idea. Under present conditions it has worked out well in Wisconsin. I fully realize that the general consensus of opinion is that the consolidation idea is not a good one."

Wisconsin was not the only state which presented an involved or discouraging situation. After half a year of advising the state authorities of California as to principles which should determine forestry laws, on March 12, 1915, Fernow felt impelled to write State Forester G. M. Homans, "I have looked over the two bills now before the Legislature regarding forestry work in your State. I naturally favor Senate Bill 460 because it gives broader scope and powers to the State Forester, while Bill 348 seems to confine his entire activity to forest fire prevention, which should be only one of his duties. It is rather sad to contemplate that in your State, which in 1887 had taken the lead in the forestry movement of all the States, it has collapsed to such an extent as not to have arrived at a leading position by now." Fernow had given almost as careful study and advice concerning the forest situation and forestry needs of California as he had given to British Columbia. On May 14, 1915, Acting Forester W. B. Greeley wrote W. N. Millar of the faculty of forestry at Toronto, "You are right in describing state forestry affairs in California as considerably mixed. . . . The essential situation appears to be that the State Forester has requested rather more drastic legislation than the lumber interests, the railroads, and others are willing to see passed. . . . The fact of the matter is that neither the State nor its lumbermen have developed as yet any definite policy in the protection of timbered lands analogous to the policy followed by Oregon and Idaho." Walter Mulford and the new forestry instruction at the University of California were needed.

Other states had been struggling. Announcing in 1914 that a fifty thousand dollar bond issue was to be floated by the American Forestry Association, Secretary P. S. Ridsdale and President H. S. Drinker of the association had written Fernow, "Fifteen states still lack forestry laws, seventeen states have deficient forest laws, and four others lack appropriations for forestry work." The bond issue proceeds were to be used to improve the association's magazine, *American Forestry.*

On June 29, 1914, Harris A. Reynolds, secretary of the Massachusetts Forestry Association, told Fernow that his state had obtained a forest taxation bill, "one of the best measures of its kind in this country," a slash bill, and a state forest bill which was described as making "a good beginning [toward committing] the state to a real conservation policy." Reynolds said, "I only wish that we could interest more states in taking up the idea of forestry associations."

Fernow helped to make the American Forestry Association meeting at Chautauqua, New York, a success. That year the association took over the business direction of *Forestry Quarterly.* It was advocated by Fernow, and expected, that the publication would become a monthly journal. In 1908 Dr. Graves had helped the American Forestry Association to reorganize. He told Fernow, "I have been a good deal disturbed about how things were going in that association and I believe that we are on the road, now, to make something out of it." The respective spheres of the American Forestry Association and the Society of American Foresters were slowly being defined. The former was retaining its earlier status, more and more appealing to a great popular interest in the forestry movement. The Society of American Foresters was striving to remain strictly professional. That *Forestry Quarterly*'s business direction was turned over to the association did not change its strictly professional character. Fernow remained as its principal editor, and its policies were not changed. Fernow was hoping for unity of purpose and action within the forestry ranks. Wide expansion of effort and action had led a period of readjustment to new conditions. Fernow relied on the fundamental stability of the profession and its work. New sectional organizations were developing, and Fernow evidently regarded these as a natural result of expansion. After the Chautauqua meeting, Fernow wrote H. P. Baker:

I found your letter of July 14 on my return from the New Hampshire meeting. . . . It was an unquestionable success, both the meeting of the [Association of] Eastern Foresters and of the Society for the Protection of New Hampshire Forests. I met Pettis at the Chautauqua meeting and he told me that he was laying pipe for the organization of a section of the Society of American Foresters in New York. So I hope you will all get together in a friendly spirit in spite of the little friction which naturally exists in your state. As regards the propagandist work done by technical schools, my opinion is not absolutely settled. I discussed the matter in an article which was assigned to me at the first meeting of the Standardizing Committee. You, to be sure, have the funds, and therefore the men, who can devote themselves to propagandist work, and hence my objection to it should vanish.

Texas had a new forestry organization, effected by a law which gave the state a complete forest policy.[51] A state board of forestry was not created, but the new law's administration was centered in the board of directors of the Agricultural and Mechanical College, who were authorized to select a state forester. A promising development was the new cooperation between the federal government and the states, made possible by extending the Weeks law.[52] Forester Philip W. Ayres of the Society for the Protection of New Hampshire Forests wrote to Fernow, "We are all very happy over the passage through the House on last Friday of the bill to re-appropriate the $3,000,000 that could not be used when the Weeks Act first passed in 1911. It had previously passed the Senate and has now become a part of the regular agricultural appropriation bill, so we feel quite secure. I will ask Karl Woodward also, who is now Professor of Forestry at our New Hampshire State College, to write you and send you appropriations under the Smith Lever Act to foster woodlot demonstration. He has an appropriation [a college appropriation, the work performed exactly like Smith-Lever projects]

[51] *Forestry Quarterly* XIII, 2, June 1915, p. 299; *ibid.* XIII, 3, Sept. 1915, p. 435, correction based on a letter written to Fernow on June 12 by Chief of State Cooperation Peters of the U.S. Forest Service.

[52] See A. J. Jaenicke, *op. cit.*, pp. 397ff., concerning mangement plans, including grazing privileges, special permits, timber sales, reforestation, etc., on the fourteen originally acquired areas and more than a million acres subsequently approved for purchase in the Appalachian and White Mountains. Also, W. B. Greeley, "National Forestry," *op. cit.* Ayres letter dated August 7, 1916.

and is making some valuable experiments in New Hampshire this summer." Five days previously, Ayres, informing Fernow that "National Parks, National Forests and the Administration of State Forests" were to comprise the general themes of the New England Forestry Conference to be held that year, September 5-7, at Crawford House, Crawford Notch, New Hampshire, had asked Fernow:

Would you like to consider the topic: "The State as a Leader in Woodlot Management"? I mention this because Vermont, Connecticut, New Hampshire and Massachusetts have all been acquiring as demonstration tracts small areas in different parts of the states under the charge of the state foresters, where planting and thinning are done under their direction. Hawes has done some very good work in Vermont. . . .

New Hampshire now owns seventeen tracts of land, one of which, the Crawford Notch, was acquired primarily for scenic reasons. Two or three gifts have been made to preserve the beautiful woods and to protect the scenery. Of late the State has been making a small appropriation of $5,000 a year for the purpose of small tracts of land, and it has appropriated $5,000 more annually of late to replant these and otherwise take care of them.

Connecticut began a demonstration forest policy, rather experimental planting, under Mulford as State Forester and has continued it ever since, and under the excellent management of Mr. Filley has acquired lately several new tracts in different parts of the state with a special view toward demonstration thinning and logging.

Massachusetts for a number of years has been acquiring waste land and planting it up usually at strategic points for demonstration; but of late, under the new Forestry Commission, a purchasing board, it is buying to demonstrate thinning also.

Both Massachusetts and New Hampshire have legislation under which private owners may donate their land to the state, and it will be planted up by the state at cost, plus interest. Five such areas at strategic points were planted by the state this year in New Hampshire.

Ayres urged Fernow, if he attended the conference at Crawford Notch, to "say again some of the things that [he had] said two years [before in 1914] in urging state organization that is adequate to the needs of the nation. In all our states," said Ayres, "we are just puttering, losing valuable time which ought to be improved against the future needs of the people who will live upon the North American continent. The problem is a continental one, and not a local or even a Federal one."

Austin Hawes, state forester of Vermont, told Fernow by letter of August 9, 1916:

There is not as yet as much interest in handling of the woodlot as there is in forest planting, and it is one of the difficult things to explain why the landowners should take more interest in planting, the results of which are most distant, than in the case of the proper handling of the woodlot. The county agents, working under the Smith-Lever Bill, are cooperating with us and we have held a series of woodlot conferences. . . . It may be also of interest to know that through the Experiment Station here we are carrying on some technical investigations in the reproduction of our important species. We have a number of permanent sample plots established on our various state forests where we are keeping very close tally of the reproduction and the way it responds to different conditions of light and moisture etc.

In New Hampshire the forest department contemplated continuing to acquire tracts "until there [were] three or four in each county well-located for demonstration purposes and the timber markets."[53] Nineteen state forests, five of which were state parks where forestry practice was a secondary consideration, plus demonstration planting tracts, and a number of town forests, presented quite a contrast to the humble beginnings of three decades earlier when a forestry commission was created but could do little more than investigate the state's forest conditions.

State Forester Frank William Rane of Massachusetts reported to Fernow on August 12, 1916, that "the Massachusetts woodlot demonstration work [was] somewhat more complicated than in other states as [they had] not only the general work of advising the farmers as to the handling of their woodlot according to forestry methods, but [they had] in addition, the serious menace caused by the gypsy and brown-tail moths. As a matter of fact, the desperate condition of our forests where they have been defoliated by moths has brought about the necessity of our carrying on some practical demonstrations for the utilization of the products, dead and dying, and at the same time given us an opportunity to emphasize the importance of retaining those species that are more or less immune from those insects. My last two annual reports touched more or less upon the thinning work that is primarily done for moth suppression." State Forester Filley of Connecticut told Fernow, "We have made no attempt to establish small demonstration woodlots in cooperation with private owners, as has been done in New York and Massachusetts. Neither have we purchased any areas which were not sufficiently near to one of the State Forests to be handled as a part of it. We have at the present time four woodland tracts owned by the State and managed by [the department of forestry of the Connecticut Agricultural Experiment Station] as State Forests. Their acreage is as follows: Portland, 1140 acres; Cornwall, 1100 acres; Union, 287 acres; Simsbury, 130 acres." New Hampshire was in the leading position. Forester Woodward of the New Hampshire Agricultural Experiment Station wrote Fernow that after finding suitable woodlots through the county agent, they went to the ground, mapped and estimated the timber, and logged and marketed the product in the fall. White pine species were given the most attention.[54]

[53] State Forester E. C. Hirst to Fernow, August 10, 1916.

[54] Woodward wrote Fernow, "We have two projects, one the marketing of mature white pine stands, and the other the thinning of mature white pine stands. You will see that we have tackled the forestry problem at the financial end of the game, and also

Walter Mulford asked Fernow what degrees in forestry the University of California should confer. Mulford also wrote to Fernow on May 29, 1915, and sought to obtain information on publications which dealt with European methods of mountain torrent control, to be used by the board of engineers in charge of flood control for Los Angeles.

F. H. Newell, who after twenty-six years of continuous service in the United States geological survey and reclamation service had accepted a position as head of a department of civil engineering at the University of Illinois, also wrote to Fernow and requested information about publications on the subject of forest influences, particularly the influence of the forest on the rainfall and water run-off, and the new features of engineering in forestry.

In 1915 the New York State College of Forestry at Syracuse invited Fernow to be the speaker at their annual banquet. Fernow had to decline the honor, but the following year he gave the school an example of his best efforts, an address on "The Birth of a Forest Policy in the United States."

On April 10, 1915, Fernow, exercising his right of "citizenship in New York," addressed a letter to Senator Elihu Root, chairman of the forthcoming New York constitutional convention, and urged the selection of Charles M. Dow as chairman of the committee on forestry and conservation. Fernow urged Dow because of "his excellent work on the Niagara reservation and in other directions in the conservation of natural resources [which gave] promise that he [would] take the right attitude towards [their] efforts to secure a saner, more rational forest policy than the present Constitution [permitted]." Dow, like another leader in forest conservation ranks, Charles W. Garfield of Michigan, was a banker, "a successful business man and not a mere sentimentalist on this subject," Fernow said. As the director of Letchworth Park and Arboretum, he had spoken at the dedication exercises when the Forestry Building at Cornell University was opened. His subject had been "Forestry as an Investment." Forestry was a sound business investment which should be guarded safely and yield a monetary return. He found good sense in the Canadian "timber limit" system, which, while open to certain criticism, was wise in that timber wealth was effectively safeguarded. Private forestry would develop "if American foresters [would] devote more attention to laying before private forest owners the essential facts regarding the money returns to be expected from forestry. . . . In the last analysis, the question of how rapidly private forestry [would be] applied to private forest lands in the United States [was] not a question of silviculture primarily, nor a question of general welfare

---

with the species which is most important." In August 1916 they had nine tracts totalling 1,110 acres.

primarily: but it [was] primarily a question of the actual financial returns that the individual forest owner [might] expect from forestry. [He] earnestly [commended to the audience's] attention the need of a practical textbook on the finance of forestry, expressed in terms so plain and so direct that the layman [could] clearly comprehend it."

Dow warned Fernow that during the constitutional convention there would be "some sharp divisions regarding the conservation of our natural resources during the next constitutional period" in New York. And New York was not alone. In California, for instance, State Forester Homans told Fernow in his letter of March 3, 1915, that his proposed legislation, prepared after receiving Fernow's "suggestions and those from other progressive forest schools and state forestry departments," together with amendments to be offered "providing for the cooperation of the State with private agencies, for the payment of persons employed to fight fire, and a compulsory fire fighting clause . . . [would] meet with the usual opposition—in [their] case represented by the California Forest Protective Association, composed of lumbermen of the state, and the California Conservation Commission, which [had] no administrative or executive power in forestry matters of the state." On November 5, 1914, Homans by telegram had sought Fernow's indorsement of legislation providing a "state protective system adequately financed" and maintained on forestry principles. Fears had arisen that, if the state acquired "proper control over the fire situation as was done in 1905," the grant of power to the state board of forestry would "result eventually in some control of privately owned timber lands, particularly watersheds from which municipalities [derived] their supply." Fernow answered that the State should "interfere with such practices on the part of forest owners (lumbermen) as increase the fire danger, and [might], for instance, legislate on brush disposal, forcing the owner to keep his premises without a public nuisance. . . . The State [might] do what the individual [could] not do or [could] not do as well as the State, especially if thereby broader interests of the State [were] served. If the destruction of forest cover would unfavorably influence the water-stages of a river, the stability of the soil of the denuded area, or cause other damage, the State should exercise its authority." Foremost, however, Fernow considered "that the State should set aside forest reservations and manage them with a view to the future interests of the commonwealth." Machinery should be provided to make legislation effective. "A sane board of forestry should be given power to inaugurate measures in detail under the legislated principles," Fernow wrote Homans on November 6, 1914, and his recommendations typified his present policy of no involvement in state or provincial political situations. Homans, in October 1914, asked Fernow to submit "what, in [his] opinion are the essential principles that should be embodied in a strong forest law." Adhering closely to the request, Fernow's opinion was given in an advisory capacity as an authority on forestry and forest legislation. He did not refer to earlier proposed legislation which Governor Hiram Johnson had not signed because, Homans explained, "under its provisions no effective work could be accomplished."

Fernow reminded Chairman Root of the New York constitutional convention that, although "at present [he was] in Canadian service as Dean of the Faculty of Forestry at Toronto University and a member of the Commission of Conservation of Canada," he had retained his interest "as regards the development of [New York's] forest policy," and been author of the state legislation of 1885 "which instituted the first Forest Commission and Forest Reserve." Moreover, he had "organized and for 12 years conducted the federal forestry bureau in Washington." When the convention was assembled, Fernow wrote a strong argument,[55] reviewing the situation which surrounded enactment of the legislation on which New York's original forest policy had been based. He reviewed the circumstances which prompted inclusion of Article VII, Section 7, in the constitution. Fernow reasoned that, owing to great forestry progress since those years, the forestry policy of the state should be rewritten. Trained forestry personnel now were available, and an efficient state forest service could be maintained. In other words, Fernow urged that the constitutional clause be so modified as to permit conservative rational management on state-owned lands. Certainly any question of constitutional authority with reference to the state's elaborately developed planting and reforestation activities should be settled in their favor. He pointed out that New York had recently invested large sums of money in forestry instruction at the state college at Syracuse University and in a forestry department of the New York State College of Agriculture at Cornell.

The convention had before it the examples of forest management on the national and other publicly owned forests. The convention knew, also, of the state and national parks and their administration. But neither Fernow's letter nor the need of forest management carried enough weight with the framers of the proposed constitution. A provision authorizing the creation of a nine-member conservation commission proved objectionable to many organizations and a majority of the voters. The constitution failed of adoption, despite the argument and belief of its proponents that by such a commission political influences would be removed from work connected with conservation of the state's natural resources. *Forestry Quarterly*[56] unhesitatingly assured its readers

[55] *Forestry Quarterly* XIII, 4, Dec. 1915, p. 584.
[56] *Forestry Quarterly* XIII, 4, Dec. 1915, p. 584; XIV, 1, March 1916, p. 181.

that general education about forestry—the intention of Colonel Fox two decades earlier—was still much needed. Therefore Fernow continued to tell schools that propaganda as well as research was a legitimate function, together with the regular teaching.

In 1917 Fernow addressed the Pennsylvania Forestry Association, warning that the basis of this state's forest reservation policy, the claimed influence of the forest cover on water flow and the once imperative necessity to reforest the headwaters of streams to protect against floods, might be found by some future administration no longer to exist, and the state's reservation and planting policy might be either discontinued or seriously disturbed. Fernow based his argument on an article, "The Present and Future of Pennsylvania Forests" by S. B. Elliott, member of the state's forestry reservation commission. Fernow wanted a new law based on "practical common-sense reasons . . . why the State should engage in forest work—and that more extensively than it has so far." Two reasons were prominent: "Under the careless exploitation of the native forest by the private owners, large areas of waste land have been and will continue to be created. These waste lands are fit only for timber growing" and should not become, or remain, worthless brushland. "The other only slightly less cogent reason for the State forestry," said Fernow, "is to secure wood materials for the industry."[57]

During 1915 Fernow joined with other members of the Society of American Foresters to make Rothrock, "the father of Pennsylvania forestry," an honorary member. Fernow wrote Raphael Zon on December 8, 1915, that there was "hardly any other person deserving this honor as much as he." In the tribute which Fernow wrote of Rothrock, he said, "To those who know Dr. Rothrock intimately his persistency and singleness of purpose in pursuing the task he had set himself has called for the greatest admiration. He had the gift of impressing audiences, especially in rural communities, by the simplicity of his diction, the clearness of his argument, the wealth of illustration. It is this gift that enabled him to bring his State into line for a forest policy. He was and is a born propagandist, and as such his work was invaluable in the discouraging pioneering days of forestry. He, however, never sank his professional attitude or lost sight of the practical and technical aspects of the problems, and deserves full recognition by the profession."

Fernow could not accept Secretary Ridsdale's invitation to attend the Boston meeting of the American Forestry Association because at the same time he had to attend a meeting of the Canadian commission of conservation in Ottawa. "I expect, however, to be in Washington on

[57] See J. S. Illick, "The Subdivision of Forests," *ibid.* XIII, 2, June 1915, p. 183; "Forest Tree Planting Camps," *Journal of Forestry* XV, 4, April 1917, p. 394; to the effect that Pennsylvania had more than a million acres in forest reserves divided into forty-nine state forests in 1915, and 5,492,020 trees were planted in these forests in 1916.

Saturday of the same week," explained Fernow, "at the meeting of the Society of American Foresters, when, perhaps, it may become possible to take a further step toward the amalgamation of the two publications." On December 15, 1915, Walter Mulford, telling of the San Francisco meeting of the society, commented to Fernow, "If you could have been a mouse in the corner at the evening dinner when only members of the Society were present (35 of them), when the possibility of combining the two periodicals was discussed, you would have realized the respect with which the simple mention of your name is met in a gathering of foresters. The attitude toward you by everyone present was one of the greatest respect. Perhaps you will not object to my having told you this." With the December 1916 issue of *Forestry Quarterly* the publication completed its fourteenth and final volume.[58] It was merged with the *Proceedings of the Society of American Foresters* under the title of *Journal of Forestry,* with Fernow as its editor-in-chief and Raphael Zon as its managing editor. Members of the editorial board were R. C. Bryant, B. P. Kirkland, Barrington Moore, A. B. Recknagel, H. D. Tiemann, J. W. Toumey, and T. S. Woolsey, Jr.

At the Washington and Ottawa meetings, Fernow delivered two of the most important addresses of his entire career. Before the commission of conservation of Canada he spoke on "Silvicultural Problems of Forest Reserves,"[59] and before the Society of American Foresters on January 22, 1916, he addressed an open meeting on "Possibilities of Silviculture in America."[60] Both addresses were of continental significance, although the former was primarily concerned with the Canadian reservations. Because of their importance, we must trace their history briefly.

In 1915 at the sixth annual meeting of the commission of conservation, Fernow, as chairman of the committee on forests, had made a brief but pointed address on the need of "Cooperation in Forestry."[61] He reasoned that the three separate and independently organized government branches which divided the forestry work of the Dominion should be reorganized—the timber branch in charge of licensed timber limits, the forestry branch in charge of the forest reservations where timber limits had not already been licensed before the reservations were constituted, and the parks branch in charge of the park areas. "A rational arrangement which can be effected without much upheaval," Fernow said, "would be to place the administration of these timber limits, within the reservations at least, wholly under the Forestry Branch. There will

[58] The magazine had risen from a student publication of 176 pages a year to more than 700 pages annually.

[59] 7th Annual Meeting of the Commission of Conservation of Canada, Jan. 18-19, 1916, *7th Ann. Rpt.*, pp. 66-74; *Forestry Quarterly* XIV, 1, March 1916, pp. 14-23.

[60] *Proc. Soc. Am. For.* XI, 1916, pp. 171-176.

[61] *6th Ann. Rpt.* of the Commission of Conservation of Canada, 1915, pp. 120-126.

then be a territorial subdivision of authority which will obviate the antagonisms between different policies." As to the parks branch, it was admitted that although other than economic objectives were served, it was conceivable that a management to serve both park and economic interests could be devised. Fernow was interested in the extension and organization of the forestry branch to permit systematic study and investigation of silvicultural problems. "We are still lacking in Canada the most fundamental knowledge of the biology of our tree species upon which their silviculture is based. We are lacking volume tables as aids to timber estimating, and yield tables as a basis for calculating the results of our silviculture; all of which the Forestry Branch will then be equipped to furnish. It will then also be in a position to do necessary experimental work and to establish demonstrations as to proper procedure in the field, by organizing systematic management of the forest areas." The Trent watershed survey had pointed out the way.

Since 1913 the report of this survey had been available. Fernow continued:

> One of these demonstrations, an object lesson of wide usefulness to the people of the Eastern provinces, could be made in the Trent watershed, to show how a mismanaged tract may be recuperated and become productive again. I shall not repeat the arguments advanced in the report on the "Trent Watershed Survey" as to why the Dominion Government should undertake the management of this tract. In the report, it is suggested that the Dominion either purchase the necessary area, or else secure it free of immediate charge, under some financial arrangement with the province of Ontario. Under present circumstances the latter method will recommend itself, the *quid pro quo* to the province to consist of financial returns when the property begins to bring a revenue.

Land reclamation and forest improvement as principles had demonstrated their worth in other countries. Production of second growth white pine in New England already had exceeded expectations, as shown by a comparison of present statistics and bulletin 13 of the United States division of forestry. That a blister rust subsequently affected white pine production did not alter the fundamental truth that New England again might have a rich harvest of pine and spruce.

On November 2, 1916, Fernow wrote to Secretary Harris A. Reynolds of the Massachusetts Forestry Association, "Allow me to express satisfaction at the spirit which your circular on the white pine blister rust breathes. So far the blister rust is still localized, so that it should be tolerably easy to combat it. I do not belong to the pessimists who believe in the possibility of the utter destruction and extinction of our best timber tree species by nature, unless aided by man. Although we are still ignorant as to the complete life history of the rust, I consider we know enough to encourage us in the belief that it can be controlled, though not eradicated, provided an energetic and persistent effort is made to do so."[62] The rust had also been found in the Dominion; enough had been found in the province of Ontario to cause alarm. Fernow recommended removal of infected young stock of white pine. Sometimes removal of parts of the tree affected was sufficient. Evidently, the older trees were believed not susceptible to the disease. Mixed planting of red and white pine was both good silviculture and sound as a method of disease control. Fernow said:

> The experience this summer in the investigations which the Dominion and the Province of Ontario governments have carried on show the presence of the rust in the Province in a number of localities, but also quite an erratic or sporadic infection on the currant, unaccountable immunity of currant patches within infected pine areas having been observed, so that the radical remedy of destroying all currant and gooseberry bushes may eventually not even be necessary. . . . [Red and white pines], particularly on many sites, form a desirable mixture. As regards the immunity of Red pine, however, we do not know, of course, what may develop if it is widely used in plantation. It is an unfortunate experience that pests develop under the practices of man by increasing host plants.

Massachusetts State Forester Rane wrote a paper on the blister rust and presumably expressed to Fernow the fear that he might be exaggerating the facts concerning the scourge. Fernow replied on December 21, 1916, that he considered the paper "perfectly sound. The only reason for exaggerating is that in our democratic constituency it seems impossible to make an impression or force action unless you overstate the case. We have had this experience in all directions; but for overstating the case of the influence of forests on water-flow, we could not have committed the federal government to purchase lands for National Forests, and any number of other cases might be cited." So alarming became the condition that the Dominion government took up the problem. Fernow wrote to Dr. H. T. Güssow, botanist of the Central Experimental Farm at Ottawa, on March 20, 1917, "Let me congratulate you on the exceedingly clear memorandum *re* white pine blister rust problem, and on the very commonsense propositions of combating the evil. I am perfectly agreed with every point you have made, including the proposition to develop forest pathological work in general." Fernow suggested that the authorities cooperate with the state of New York in its plan of procedure. He regretted in January 1917, in response to an invitation from President Charles Lathrop Pack, that he could not attend the twenty-seventh annual meeting of the American Forestry Association, particularly since some of the addresses and discussions were to consider

[62] The white pine blister rust is now effectively controlled. One method is the removal of plants of the genus *Ribes*, especially the black currant, which serve as another host of the rust. A modern counterpart of this struggle is the fight against the spruce budworm which has taken a toll of hundreds of millions of cords of spruce and balsam timber over many thousands of square miles in Canada. On the spruce budworm see *Save Ontario Forests*, I, 6, Dec. 1945-Jan. 1946, p. 8.

"methods to cope with the White pine blister disease, in which we here in Canada are seriously interested."

Since 1913 official interest had been stirred by the forestry faculty's recommendations outlined in their report of the Trent Valley watershed survey. During 1914 trade and professional journals, newspapers, and current periodicals had given the project favorable notice. Located in central and northwestern Ontario between the heavy forest regions of the north and the agricultural lands of the province in the south, this area, once a very valuable pinery, could be restored to pine production. During the 1860's and 1870's the Trent Valley had supported a lumber industry of first magnitude. "Despite the deterioration during the last forty years in the character of the forested area of the Trent watershed," argued one trade journal,[63] "this region still possesses much forest wealth—one worthy of conservation by progressive methods of treatment." The pine-cut for the season 1911-1912, moreover, was shown to be less than one-tenth of what it had been thirty-one years ago. Now the beginnings of "man-made deserts" and bare rock conditions were evident: in three townships as much as "nearly 150,000 acres of such desert" already existed. The Dominion government was interested in the area by virtue of the canal and protection of water rights. Industries dependent on utilization of water-power in the watershed still existed. Municipalities wanted to expand established industries and attract new ones. Landowners would benefit if wastelands were reforested, fire risks reduced, and forests, soils, and streams effectively managed and improved. The province still controlled about one-third of the area, some of it under timber licenses and some abandoned or cancelled lots. The Commission of Conservation saw in the Trent watershed development sound work to be performed. *Forestry Quarterly*[64] said a movement was on foot to place the non-agricultural crown lands of the Trent Canal watershed under the Dominion forestry branch. Within the area it was proposed to establish an experiment station and to create national forests similar to those being created under the Weeks law in the eastern United States. Lands of the watershed were similar to depleted lands of other white pine belts. A demonstration forest to be of value to both Ontario and Quebec was planned. It could be shown that the areas could be restored to commercially valuable timberlands. No easy problem had been presented by Howe's and White's preliminary report, of which the introductory discussion was written by Fernow. It was no small concern to reckon with six interests, the Dominion government, the provincial government, the territory's municipalities, the private owners of property, the timber licensees, and the public. Fernow said, nevertheless, "Nobody who has studied the conditions presented

[63] *Canada Lumberman and Woodworker,* April 1914, pp. 32f. at 33.
[64] XIII, 1, March 1915, p. 138.

in this report will hesitate a moment in agreeing that the bulk of the country involved should be placed in, and managed as, a permanent forest reserve for the growing timber." Today this watershed is part of a permanent forest reserve, as recommended; but years were required to bring the recommendation to consummation. The movement was spurred by simple obvious necessity. For instance, in 1916 forestry in Ontario was bolstered by a tragedy, the consequence of inertia and lack of adequate policy. In that year there occurred a "horrible holocaust" of fire with a dreadful loss of life, due, Fernow pointed out, "to the absolute inefficiency of organization and absence of preventive measures" in the province. "On the other hand," argued Fernow, "the entire absence of any serious fire losses in Canada from a once most potent cause—railroads—can be directly traced to the efficient organization of the protective service inaugurated by the Railway Commission in cooperation with the Commission of Conservation."[65]

On March 16, 1914, Fernow had written to R. H. Campbell, "Your interesting inquiry regarding cost of production and net returns from forest management came to hand just as I was laying aside the latest bulletin on that subject from the United States Forest Service, namely on White Pine planting as an investment, and I laid it aside with the conviction that it was unreliable and that someday I would take it up critically." Fernow pointed out to Campbell that calculations on the basis of then existing stumpage prices were fallacious. Were prices to retain that level, "it would certainly only rarely pay to plant," he said. "The history of price movement shows, however, that wood prices have steadily risen for the last century, and especially during the last quarter of the century. . . . You are perfectly right in assuming that as long as virgin supplies come to market—as they are also coming in Germany, from Russia, Sweden, Austria, Canada and the United States—stumpage prices are going to remain unprofitable for the planter, but, since your plantings made now will not come into market until 80-100 years, there is little doubt that they will be profitable: it is future prices that you must figure with, of course. This financial question is an important and complicated problem, and it must be handled with very considerable circumspection. What you should do is to employ me for, say, 6 weeks this summer to look over your reserves as a basis for a discussion of the financial aspects of the forest reservation policy." Fernow argued that "the statistical data of the German State forest administrations (some quite small)" furnished "ample proof, that forestry pays well in the long run, when it is considered that it is mostly carried on on soils which are not fit for anything else and would be mere waste. Whatever the at-

[65] "A National Forest Policy," an address given by Fernow at Crawford Notch, N.H., Sept. 5-7, 1916, quotations taken from his typewritten manuscript.

titude of private owners of such lands, the State is justified in carrying on the business, even if it did not furnish a profit."

Campbell went to Europe that summer. Before leaving he doubtless carried out his plan of calling on Fernow at Toronto to decide on what places in Great Britain and on the continent he should visit. He returned from his tour of the European forests determined that the Dominion forestry branch should emphasize Canadian forest investigations.[66] Field exploration and forest products laboratory research at Montreal had previously occupied the principal attentions of the branch. Fernow that summer published in *Forestry Quarterly*[67] an article. "The Forestry Situation in Great Britain." In February 1914 he had urged R. Gilman Brown, consulting engineer of London, England, who after twenty-five years still remembered the chess games in which Rossiter Raymond and Fernow engaged on the train to Colorado, that the British firm, although it represented a Russian company, might learn much to its advantage in logging were the company's chief forester sent to Canada. Great Britain up to this point, except in India and a few other possessions, had never perceptibly influenced the world of forestry. There had been foresters of ability in England, and there had been forestry instruction and some forestry practice; but although Americans had been slightly influenced, contrasted with the influences of the German, French, and Swedish schools, the forestry influence of Great Britain was negligible.

Late in March of 1915 Fernow received a letter from R. H. Campbell, who said:

> There are a good many questions in connection with the development of the forest reserves in the prairie districts which your experience would enable you to give us very helpful advice on, and there is the whole question of the determination of what should be permanently reserve land in those districts in regard to which I confess to a good deal of uncertainty. Your knowledge of European development should be of great value to us in reaching a conclusion on this question. You will see that I am looking at the question rather from the advantage that we would gain than from any advantage that you might gain by the investigation, but of course the both objects can be served at the same time.

Fernow replied:

> I am also in receipt of your letter regarding my own possible job with you. I hope that it is not so circumscribed that it would not also take me into the mountains, which, of course, is the more attractive portion of your domain. I can see very well that inspection of the prairie states can yield considerable information of value, but would like to cover the whole field in one trip.

Campbell reported on the same day, March 23:

> I submitted formally a proposal to have you visit some of our work in the West with the object of giving you an opportunity of seeing what is being

[66] *Forestry Quarterly* XIII, 1, March 1915, p. 141.
[67] *ibid.* XIII, 2, June 1915, pp. 149-153.

done and what the men graduating from the Forest School are being trained for, and also with the object of having the advantage of your advice in regard to some matters affecting the development of the forestry policy. The Minister has approved the suggestion and has agreed to allow your living and traveling expenses while engaged in the investigation.

On April 15 Campbell suggested an itinerary of their proposed journey:

Beginning with July would be . . . most satisfactory for me for going to the West. It would be my suggestion if the arrangement should be carried out that we should visit either the Riding or Duck Mountain Forest Reserve in the province of Manitoba so that you could get an idea of the character of the territory that we have to handle in that province. I would like you to see the character of the land and of the forest and some of the improvement work that we are carrying on there, and also meet some of them that we have employed, particularly the students from Toronto. From there I would like to go by way of the Prince Albert line of the Canadian Northern Railway to the Porcupine-Pasquia reserve where Mr. A. B. Connell is at present located and where one of the most important and extensive timber tracts that we have to administer is located. From there going on to Prince Albert we would visit the headquarters of the administration of the province of Saskatchewan and at least see the Nisbet Forest Reserve which is a tract of sand land fairly well covered with jack pine, lying immediately north of the Saskatchewan River from Prince Albert. The forests to the north and west of Prince Albert would be interesting to see but as they are a good deal of the same character as those in eastern Saskatchewan on the Porcupine Forest Reserve it will hardly be necessary to visit them unless there is plenty of time. From there I would like to go down to the prairie part of Saskatchewan and show you one or two of the sandy areas which we have reserved for forestry purposes. We would go south from Prince Albert to Saskatoon and possibly reach the Elbow Forest Reserve from there for a day, besides seeing the new nursery that we are establishing at Saskatoon for the distribution of trees to the farmers, and from there would take the Great Trunk Pacific stopping off to see the Manitou Reserve which is a tract of sand lands just at the western boundary of Saskatchewan. From there we would go right on to Edmonton and the rest of the time could be spent in the Rocky Mountains in Alberta and in the Railway Belt in British Columbia. The visit to Manitoba and Saskatchewan could easily be covered in the first month, leaving the rest of the time for Alberta and British Columbia. We would probably have to separate in Alberta. . . . I am writing out to Mr. [E. H.] Finlayson and Mr. [D. R.] Cameron in regard to the matter. . . . I am sending you separately a map of the western provinces on which the reserves are marked, from which you can see the proposed itinerary in Manitoba and Saskatchewan.

Fernow was "satisfied and gratified at the plan [Campbell was] making for [their] prairie trip together. . . . I shall await with patience," wrote Fernow, "the final arrangements for our mountain trip. Meanwhile, I have a letter from Nordegg, giving details of a trip that can be made from Nordegg to Laggan, by way of the Siffleur River, as one of the possible trips. Another that I am particularly desirous of making, is to go out to one of the Clearwater Stations and spend a week or 10 days looking around for details; this, preferably, preceding the long general trip."

In regard to the trip to the Rocky Mountains, Campbell suggested:

> I do not know that you could get a much better idea of the mountains than by taking the trip of the Clearwater Division of the Rocky Mountains Forest Reserve, and going from there through to Laggan and down to Banff. I have no doubt that all of the men from the Forest School who are in the Rocky Mountains would like to have you visit them, and they are scattered from McFayden up on the Grand Trunk Railway at Entrance on the north to S. H. Clark at Mountain House on the Brazeau, Manning at Nordegg on the Clearwater; Greenwood at Calgary or Morley; and R. M. Brown at Pincher Creek on the Crowsnest. I do not suppose you can get to see all of them, but perhaps it would be possible to get into the Brazeau and if you liked to keep in the mountains it would be possible to get over from the Brazeau to the Clearwater, and then take the trip over to Laggan. . . . There will be no difficulty about arranging for the trip to the Clearwater and through from Nordegg to Laggan as part of the arrangement.

On July 17 Fernow telegraphed Campbell that he was leaving his summer home at Point Breeze, New York.[68] He had arranged that his dufflebag be shipped from Toronto to Calgary, Alberta. An auto trip was taken from Oak Orchard, New York, to Albion, and from there he went by railroad through Chicago direct to Winnipeg, Manitoba. He arrived at Winnipeg on the morning of July 19, and the day and night were spent there. The next day an excursion was taken to Douglas, Manitoba, and on the night of July 20 the real journey was begun by an overnight trip to Dauphin. The journey was carried out much as Campbell and Fernow had planned. At Douglas the party must have begun their forest inspection. Two days and nights were spent en route to Garland where the Canadian National Railway was again taken for the trip to Swan River. Remaining the night of the 24th at Swan River, the party journeyed to Kamsack and again returned to Dauphin, from which an overnight train trip on the night of the 30th brought them to Hudson Bay Junction in the Province of Saskatchewan. They had been in the regions of Riding Mountain and Duck Mountain in Manitoba and the Porcupine Mountains in Saskatchewan. Next they proceeded to the Pasquia Hills and boarded the train again at Tisdale, from where by a day trip in the parlor car they arrived on August 3 at Prince Albert, a forest and lake region interspersed with numerous streams. A side trip was made from Prince Albert to McDowall, where forest reserves on prairie lands had been set aside. On August 5 another day of train travel brought them to Saskatoon, where it was planned to inspect the new nursery and the Elbow forest reserve. From August 6-9 an excursion was made from Saskatoon to Regina and Indian Head.

[68] These facts are based upon Fernow's expense account.

By coincidence Fernow and David Fairchild almost met again at Indian Head. Fairchild called the famous nursery "Ross' wonderful place"; he was greatly interested in the Dominion government's large nursery-planting tests of Scotch pine, tamarack, ash, white spruce, and other trees, species which would grow on the prairies and make "low forests and shelter belts on these treeless wastes." Fernow's state of health was none too secure. He had vigor of mind and body but he realized that the years of retirement from active duty in the school were approaching. He and Mrs. Fernow planned perhaps to return to live in Washington. A meeting with Fairchild, therefore, would have been a welcome renewal of an old friendship.

On August 10-11 the party journeyed by railroad from Saskatoon to Edmonton and en route inspected the Manitou forest service. Next they passed through Chauvin, Evesham, and Unity, and stopped for two days at Edmonton. By night they travelled by railroad to Calgary. On August 16 the group proceeded to Morley and the Rocky Mountain regions, where they stayed for more than three weeks.

E. H. Finlayson, district inspector of forest reserves, had written to Fernow after the journey had begun. The letter, which reached Fernow at Winnipeg, said:

> In your previous letter you suggest going in from Olds to the Red Deer Ranger Station and spending a few days in the Red Deer River District for the purpose of seeing the country in that valley and also for the purpose of getting hardened up to foot-hill travel. After that you propose to come out to the railway and go in by Red Deer and Rocky Mountain House to Nordegg. From this latter point you propose to take horses and go through the mountains to Laggan.

Finlayson offered objections to this plan, principally based on the lack of horses and the road and stream conditions. We cannot be certain of what happened, but apparently the party, perhaps Fernow and Finlayson alone, left Morley and went to Red Deer Ranger Station. Finlayson wrote:

> From the Red Deer Ranger Station you and I could ride over to the James River country merely taking saddle horses so that you would see the valley drained by that River. We could also come south a day's trip at some time and see the character of the country to the south. After having spent several days at the Red Deer Ranger Station we could pack our outfit up the Red Deer to the mouth of the Panther or possibly to Brewster's Ranch. From either one of these points we could take saddle horses and travel very light through to Laggan. . . . From Laggan we might work over toward Banff or at least might return by somewhat different trail to the Brewster camp. . . . Returning to the Panther by the Brewster Camp we could then work north to the Pipestone Pass from which point we could either go down the Siffleur River to the Saskatchewan or we could turn east to the Head of the Clearwater River and go up a tributary of the latter to the headwaters of the White Rabbit down which stream we would go to the Wilson Ranger Station on the

Saskatchewan. From the Wilson Ranger Station we could reach Nordegg quite easily. . . . Nordegg would then be the winding up point of the pack trip.

Another suggested tour commenced at Morley, proceeded to Ghost River, then to the Fallen Timber, and Red Deer, one which was certain to give Fernow "a fair idea as to the conditions in the foot hill section of the Bow River reserve." All of these points might have been reached by Fernow. On September 7 he was at Nordegg; on that same day the party went by railroad from Nordegg to Sylvan Lake. The night of September 8 was spent at Rocky Mountain House, and the party then motored from Sylvan Lake to Red Deer, where the train was taken to Calgary. On September 9 Fernow took a Pullman at Calgary and reached Toronto four days later, having spent almost two full months in forest exploration and inspection.

Fernow's western trip was important both because of its direct results, which were incorporated in an address which exerted wide influence and because of the added stimulus to a new project which came up during the spring. On May 4, 1915, Campbell had written to Fernow:

> I have felt for some time that it would be advisable to bring together the organizations that are interested in forest research in Canada with the object of systematizing and developing it so as to obtain the necessary information as soon as possible to place forestry work in Canada on a scientific and efficient basis. With this object in view it has been suggested that there might be formed in connection with this Branch an advisory committee which would include most of the leading men directly interested in forest research in this country, to cooperate with this Branch and with other forestry organizations. . . . The work of the Committee will be to suggest problems for investigation and methods of carrying out such projects; to pass upon all projects of scientific investigation planned; and to revise for publication the results of such investigations. Of the advisory committee it is proposed to have an executive committee consisting of Mr. Clyde Leavitt, Forester of the Conservation Commission; Mr. W. N. Millar, Assistant Professor of Forestry, University of Toronto; and yourself.

A special officer of the branch was to take charge of the work. A chairman of the executive committee was to be selected. The executive committee was to meet once or twice a year at Ottawa. Fernow, named to represent forest management and silvicultural aspects of forest research, was later made chairman. The matter of his chairmanship, however, was not at that time mentioned. Fernow replied on May 8, "In the first place, let me congratulate you on the happy thought of creating an Advisory Board to plan and supervise research work to be developed in the Forestry Branch! I believe a large amount of investigation, under local conditions, is necessary, in order to furnish a basis for rational management of the Forest Reserves, and this should be systematically and carefully planned." Fernow and Campbell saw that all forestry services would benefit from accurate information of the forests of Canada and their conditions of growth. By July 1915 Fernow, Leavitt, Millar, R. B. Miller (Dean of the University of New Brunswick Forest School), Ellwood Wilson, G. C. Piché, E. J. Zavitz (Forester of Ontario), H. R. MacMillan, L. M. Ellis (Forester of the Canadian Pacific Railway), Judson F. Clark (of Clark and Lyford, consulting foresters), F. W. Broderick (Professor of Horticulture and Forestry at Manitoba Agricultural College), and Howe and White had agreed to serve.

Willis N. Millar had graduated from the University of Pennsylvania and taken a master of forestry degree at Yale Forest School. He had entered the United States forest service and become supervisor of the Kaniksu National Forest in Idaho. Acquiring a reputation as an organizer and administrator, especially in forest fire service, he had entered the Canadian forest service in 1912 and in 1914 became a member of the Faculty of Forestry at the University of Toronto. On February 20, 1914, MacMillan had written Fernow, "I am delighted to know that you have secured Mr. Millar, he is the best man I know of for your work and will, I know, become a most competent assistant to you." Piché also recommended Millar. In February of that year A. H. D. Ross left the school and Millar received the appointment. Fernow and Millar[69] at once sought to persuade Campbell to have the Forest Products Laboratories perform cooperative investigations, for example, to investigate whether the manufacture of potash from fallen timber and rotted aspen could be made profitable. Fernow wanted to make use of forest waste as well as mill waste. As late as November 26, 1915, no progress had been made toward organizing the work under the Advisory Board. No man able to direct the details of the work of investigation had been found. Fernow wrote to Judson F. Clark and asked about Craig and his qualifications. Clark replied, "I think it is safe to say that Craig is as likely a person to grow into the work you have in mind as anyone who is available." In December the executive committee unanimously recommended immediate appointment of a chief of investigations. Fernow reported that H. R. Christie could "be expected to have the ability to handle this position."

[69] W. N. Millar, "Forest Investigations in Canada," *Forestry Quarterly* XIII, 4, Dec. 1915, pp. 504ff.

CHAPTER XI

Fernow, First Forester of North America

THE first meeting of the executive committee of the forest investigation advisory board was held in Toronto on November 12, 1915. Plans for general organization were discussed and a tentative program of work for the next field season was prepared for Campbell's consideration. It was decided to try out men in the forestry branch's service and eventually select the one who showed the greatest promise to take charge of the work. The work was divided into two main classes, that which could be handled by a single investigator and that which required the employment of small crews under the direction of a forester. The war had taken a heavy toll from the ranks of foresters left in the Dominion and the provinces and had greatly reduced the number of forestry students. It was decided, therefore, to undertake no projects of the type requiring a special investigator. Many important projects, most of which were in the nature of compilations, had to be deferred as a consequence. The committee decided that it would be necessary to train an efficient staff both for investigation and administration. The committee recommended first that detailed silvical reports be prepared for each forest reserve, those reserves being first studied where the greatest amount of business was handled. The committee had prepared outlines for such reports and it was urged that the forest assistants on the reserves fill out the reports. Forestry practice on the reserves was still absent; indeed, many reserves were under the supervision of men who were not technically trained. Most of the reserves were located where as yet no or only a limited market prevailed. Therefore the immediate program provided only for present care, such as the reduction of waste or guarding against destructive fires.

"But what of the future?" Fernow asked in his address given in January 1916 on "Silvicultural Problems of Forest Reserves." The Trent watershed survey report showed how present expenditures and investments would realize future profits and supply. The same principles, in part, were applicable to the reserves.

> There are some Reserves, located near well populated districts, whose natural supplies are already being heavily drawn upon, as e.g. the Cypress Hills Reserves in Alberta and Saskatchewan, the Pines and Nisbet Reserves in Saskatchewan, the Turtle Mountain Reserve in Manitoba. Here there should be immediately inaugurated a well considered felling plan and a judicious reforestation program. . . . Next, we have Reserves which as yet are but lightly drawn upon, but which within the next decade promise to come into market more fully, as the settlements come up to their boundaries

and the settlers' wood supplies are giving out. Such are the Duck and Riding Mountain Reserves in Manitoba. Here, every opportunity for more careful study of the silvicultural problems should be embraced, and a thorough preparation for technical management should be begun now, in anticipation of their coming fully into market soon. Then there are a number of Reserves that were not set aside on account of their timber, which was either used up, burned up, or naturally absent, but on account of the unsuitability of the soil for farm purposes and the possibility of using it for timber crops. Such Reserves are the Spruce woods Reserve in Manitoba, partly wooded, and the Manitou Reserve in Saskatchewan, largely without natural growth and several other sand hill territories. Here, planting operations should be begun at once, first trial plantations with various species and methods, and, after experience has been gained, on a larger scale, with or without assistance by natural regeneration as the case may be. Lastly, there are extensive Reserves in the northern prairie regions and in the Rocky Mountains which are as yet so far removed from market as to place them last from the standpoint of technical management. Here the problems are still mainly of administrative character: to prevent further deterioration of the properties, especially by fire; to regulate the use of whatever resources may be available like, e.g. pasturage; to improve these resources; to make them accessible and as far as technical interest is concerned, to study the silvicultural problems against the day when they must be solved. All reserves, however, once set aside for permanency, should be administered under systematic working plans, more or less elaborate, especially with reference to their utilization.

There were many special considerations in preparing working plans. In some western reserves growth rates were more rapid than in the eastern provinces. Some valuable crops, notably the white spruce, matured earlier. Mapping, subdividing for close management, stock-taking of resources, preparation of felling budgets and felling areas, and special studies of growth conditions, marketing facilities and other reserve problems called for technically trained men. Fernow indicated many particular problems, such as the aspen problem of the Riding and Duck Mountain Reserves and its relation to white spruce production; the utilization of aspen, "chunky" and "punky" wood timbers, by establishment of industrial plants in or near the reserves; the underbrush problems; the planting problems (Fernow seems to have been impressed that on some forested as well as forestless reserves planting operations would be necessary to supplement natural regeneration, and even provide the most important reproduction); the jack pine problem, thinning to permit improved development; thinning of black spruce stands on peaty muskeg areas which occupied large portions of the reserves; investigation of effect of lowered water-tables; research in proper use of the peat bogs; the utilization of rotted materials; methods of removal and use of waste materials; the fallen timber problem and others. Fundamental, however, were stock-taking and mapping, marketing including "a stimulation of the market for the minor materials," the study of growth conditions correlated to "effects and results in regard to regeneration and increment," and the allocation of felling areas and preparation of felling budgets. Cooperation of all agencies was necessary to accomplish maximum results with minimum expense.

The second recommendation of the executive committee of the advisory investigating board made to Campbell was to prepare volume tables for all the commercial species on all the forest reserves where there was any timber disposal whatever. In securing the data for these tables it should be possible to make volume and growth studies at the same time, Fernow said. It was also recommended that permanent sample plots should be established to study growth and yield and to determine the results of different methods of timber land treatment on the reserves. Howe was recommended to take charge of the work. A. B. Connell was to be first assistant.[1]

On January 4, 1916, William L. Hall, chairman of an approaching meeting of the Society of American Foresters, wrote Fernow and asked him to address the society on the "Possibilities of Silviculture in America." Fernow replied, "I regret that you have 'spotted' me as one of your victims to perform at the meeting. I will, however, follow your invitation and talk for 20 minutes on the 'Possibilities of Silviculture in America,' which happens, in a way, to be the subject I am to discuss before the commission of conservation in Ottawa the coming week."

In the Washington address Fernow found three sources militating against silvicultural practice: (1) natural conditions, (2) economic conditions, and (3) financial considerations. Nature set no bar to silvicultural development. "Plantings of forestless sandhills and arid territory with or without irrigation" attested to man's superiority over nature. Limitations as to *methods* could be encountered. But it was not known "whether, for instance, natural regeneration would be applicable to the dry soils and dry atmosphere of the West, or to the undergrowth-pestered mismanaged woods of the East, or whether under these conditions artificial reforestation [promised] better success." Much more pertinent were the economic and financial considerations. In the midst of a harvest of plenty with small or no production costs, of course, the matter of providing timber supplies for the future—most certainly where costs of silvicultural research were superimposed and where the persistent danger of crop destruction by fire loomed—seemed to argue against silviculture on all but limited classes of forest land. The farmer on his woodlot could profit more surely and readily than the large owner of several classes of forests. Practice, however, was proof, and the large

[1] Facts of Nov. 12, 1915, meeting of forest investigation advisory board are taken from a letter of Fernow to Campbell Dec. 9, 1915. Concerning silvical studies of Canadian Commission of Conservation and Dominion forestry branch, a few years later; see Roland D. Craig, "Silvicultural Research in Canada," *Illustrated Canadian Forestry Magazine*, March 1923, pp. 158f.

paper owners were finding it profitable to "insure continuity of wood supplies." In the final analysis the financial test was the factor to be met. Fernow deplored that because of the forest's time requirements forest-finance calculations were speculative. Long range investments discouraged private enterprise, and private forestry in Canada was a potential forestry stronghold. What was the forester to do to attract and improve investments? Two methods of calculation, too often confused, were fallaciously applied: (1) compound interest was computed somewhat like soil rent theoretically when, owing to conditions, forest rent would be more apt. It was wrong "to apply present prices and current interest rates to figure returns in the distant future," in view of the believed certainty that wood values would rise. "The only question [then was] how fast and to what height [would] they rise. . . . I think we are safe in assuming they will exceed highest present European prices." Fernow ventured a few estimates and cautioned in favor of low interest rates. Volumes have been written on forest finance; the course was required of every graduate of the Toronto forestry school. Fernow had faith that an improved silviculture would be realized under the "providential function" of governments. As American economic and demographic conditions approached more closely those of Europe, the reasons for government practice of silviculture would become more plain. Fernow argued:

> All energies ought to be bent on making silvicultural studies, on securing by field work and experiment the biological and ecological knowledge which should underlie silvicultural practice. I suppose the Forest Experiment Stations are doing this. I would, however, accentuate that only the best men, best as to knowledge, imagination and judgment, can be expected to secure trustworthy results. Indeed, specialists who are thoroughly competent to apply modern methods of ecological research are needed for this work. Beware of doctrinaires is my parting advice! They have kept silviculture back for a century even in Germany. . . . The government at least, which has a providential function to fulfill, and whose finances are based on the long run, can have no excuse whatsoever of a financial character for not applying silviculture and that of a high grade on its properties, just as I consider a management for the eventual sustained yield the only justifiable one for a government, and this is possible only by the application of silviculture.

On February 28, 1916, Fernow forwarded to R. H. Campbell "brief suggestions" to enable the latter to prepare "technical management at once" for Dominion reserves which had a ready market for their materials. He presented a working plan which included (1) a survey and map which located stands according to age and description, and topographic data subdividing the property into working units; (2) a descriptive area table characterizing stands as to maturity and nearness of markets; (3) mature timber estimates with volume tables and increment data; (4) felling areas. "The most important need," Fernow advised, "is the development of silvicultural knowledge, which can only be done by experiment and careful field study by very competent men. For this purpose, in each of the reserves first the biological conditions must be examined to come to a conclusion as to what special problems are to be solved, and a series of experimental areas or plots must be laid out on which to secure the best solution.

Fernow was president of the Society of American Foresters during 1916. He was followed in the position by Roth, who held the office during the next two years. Until 1916 Fernow retained the presidency of the Canadian Society of Forest Engineers, when he was succeeded by Clyde Leavitt.

In his numerous addresses in this period, Fernow made almost no reference to forest products laboratory research. The reason was contained in a letter dated October 10, 1915, to R. E. Benedict, assistant forester of the forest branch of British Columbia. Fernow told Benedict that he regarded the curriculum of a forestry school to lie in other directions than forest products research. "There will be always necessity of specialists to be developed and if one or the other school makes a specialty of one of the other lines of work which is not strictly forestry, but allied to it, it will be a satisfactory solution of the problem." Trade extension work, the marketing of the forest crops, had long been recognized by Fernow as important, but he believed that courses along this line should not be added to the forest school curricula. He wrote to Benedict, "The very fact that this work is being developed by your office without any such specialists proves the case. There are always some men that take special interest and have special ability in developing such lines. There will be always only a few of this kind needed; the great crowd must walk the common way."

Early in 1917 the need of establishing a forest products laboratory in British Columbia was brought to a head by the problem of whether the laboratory should be founded by the province as part of a departmental forestry program at the University of British Columbia, or should be created and conducted like the program of the Dominion's main laboratory at McGill University and the United States forest products laboratory at the University of Wisconsin. The decision was made to follow the latter plan. Fernow must have been consulted, or he could not have acquired such a large file of papers on the subject. The teaching and research functions in forestry were being differentiated in recognition of the fact that teaching and research called for different qualifications. The forestry schools were training students to do basic field research, to learn the fundamentals of forestry, and to lay the foundations for specialization, one branch of which was the highly technical and more specialized work among forests products. On January 13, 1917, as chairman of the advisory board[2] of the Dominion forestry branch, Fernow presented to R. H. Campbell at the request of the recently appointed government council a memorandum on forest research. One of the four main directions of investigation was "the possibility of closer and more economic utilization of [forest] products, including problems of mill, factory and logging operations." Said the board:

> The investigations into the use of forest products are essentially a matter of laboratory research and have already been inaugurated in the Forest Products Laboratories at Montreal with a program of investigation, partly undertaken, partly merely suggested, and capable of indefinite extension. We would only accentuate in this connection the urgency of investigating how the enormous waste in logging and milling which amounts in the average to possibly 65 percent of the volume of the tree as it stands in the woods, may be avoided or economically utilized.

"A List of Research Problems Under Way in the United States Forest Service" was furnished. Similar systematic field work, both statistical and experimental, among valuable forest species indigenous to Canada still seemed an apparent necessity. Direct attention was focussed on the pulpwood situation. Moreover, there were no complete surveys of forest resources and conditions in New Brunswick, Quebec, Ontario, and the prairie provinces. The conservation commission was praised for its work thus far in Nova Scotia and British Columbia.

Concerted efforts had been productive of results. In September 1916 *Forestry Quarterly*[3] announced that a Canadian research bureau had been established to investigate, organize, and systematize Canadian resources in minerals, metals, hydroelectric power, chemical wealth, and so forth. Utilization of waste in forests, factories, mines, and mills, was contemplated.

On December 4, 1916, Fernow told H. P. Baker what he thought the extent of forest school research should be. Wide differences of opinion could exist, he said, "especially as regards research in accessory lines that do not strictly belong to forestry. There is enough scope for investigation in truly silvicultural lines having to deal with tree growth in all its manifold aspects to justify leaving the accessory lines to a time when the silvicultural field is taken care of, or to specialists in these other lines. . . . There is no reason why all our educational institutions[4] should

[2] On Jan. 24, 1917, T. W. Dwight of the Forestry Branch forwarded to Director Campbell the "memorandum prepared, for the information of the Honorary Advisory Council for Scientific and Industrial Research, by the members of the advisory committee"—Fernow, chairman, Millar, Howe, White, Leavitt, Ellwood Wilson, and Piché.

[3] *Forestry Quarterly* XIV, 3, Sept. 1916, p. 551.

[4] *ibid.* XIV, 3, Sept. 1916, p. 552. The U.S. Forest Service listed the institutions at which forestry instruction was available. There were 52 institutions, 23 of which gave courses leading to a degree. The largest proportion presented short courses in forestry and a number of the degree-conferring places gave ranger instruction. Georgia, Colo-

follow one pattern, and no reason why not one institution may lay accent on research, having the funds to do it; nay, a research investigation without educational function is thinkable and defensible. Only if the educational functions are to be attached to it, they should be made of university order, that is to say, post-graduate courses not curriculum, but for personal choice, with a view of educating a class of specialists." The only phase that Fernow frowned on was the use of research to advertise an institution and its work. He followed no pattern in research or study, although he always systematically organized what he did.

During the last months of 1916 he furnished a revision of his article on pines for Bailey's *Cyclopedia*. Complying with a request of K. A. Ryerson, editor of the University of California *Journal of Agriculture*,[5] he prepared an article on the "Relation of Forests to Our Civilization, Past, Present, and Future." New Hampshire State Forester Philip W. Ayres was delighted with Fernow's address, "A National Forest Policy," prepared for the New England conference and delivered in September of that year at Crawford House, New Hampshire. Fernow, whether ailing or in the best of health, never allowed his forestry journal editorship, the school, or research interests to be neglected. But not even the honor of being advisor on matters of forest research to the Dominion government's Honorary Advisory Council for Scientific and Industrial Research was preferred to being dean of the faculty of forestry of the University of Toronto. Nor were the Canadian Forestry Association, the Canadian Society of Forest Engineers, and their honors preferred. The school and the *Journal of Forestry* were Fernow's two great responsibilities. Because of his health he had to refrain from assuming numerous other duties and opportunities he would have enjoyed. Some of the work went to younger men.

In 1917[6] the commission of conservation began sponsoring forest regeneration surveys and growth studies of cut over pulpwood lands; especially in the great forest regions of eastern Canada. Studies of the effect of fire on species-reproduction, of the extent to which cut over pulpwoods were reproducing, and other research phases were begun. Within a year Fernow informed Millar, who had joined the armed forces, "We are planning for the Commission of Conservation quite a large enterprise under Dr. Howe's direction, continuing the investigation of pulpwood reproduction, and if we can get the men will have three, four, or five parties in the field. Also, sample plots are to be estab-

---

rado, Michigan, Washington, Pennsylvania, and New York had two degree-conferring institutions each.

[5] *Journal of Agriculture,* Forestry Number, IV, 3. Nov. 1916, pp. 75f.

[6] *Journal of Forestry* XV, 6, Oct. 1917, p. 820, on Howe's work with Wilson for the Commission.

lished, with the cooperation of Wilson and Piché."[7] Fernow trusted that two points would be established: "the number of young trees per acre to be expected from natural regeneration and the rate at which these are growing." From these, yield calculations could be made. Each year the methods were changed and improved. Dr. Howe explained to H. H. Chapman in 1920:

> For the past four summers the Commission of Conservation has been carrying on a forest regeneration survey and growth study on cut-over pulpwood lands. We usually conduct an ordinary 5 per cent cruise to determine the amount of small material of pulpwood species left after logging. I do not say young material because most of it is not young, but simply small. The object of the work is a survey to determine the average stand per acre on cut-over lands within a given type, then to determine the rate of growth of the trees in this average stand. We have changed our method of growth study nearly every year and have not yet found one that is entirely satisfactory. During the first summer's work we made complete stem analyses of all the trees on model acres or fractions of such acres. We did in all about 5 acres in this manner. We tried to select a plot that most nearly represented average conditions. This is really difficult to do; I mean to find a plot that approaches the average of the strip survey tallies within a given type and given degree of culling. The second and third summers we made stem analyses of all trees on each tenth chain in the strip survey. Thus we obtained a series of tenth acre plots taken as they happened to fall at the end of each tenth chain. During these two summers we made about 50 of such plots, again making 5 acres. This season we are making a growth study survey by means of the Pressler borer, following out the methods in Graves's *Forest Mensuration*, sections 159, 196, 197 and 198. We will have by the end of the season Pressler borer records of close to 10,000 trees. The data are not yet worked up, but I feel that this method is going to prove most satisfactory.

The commission had its own corps of foresters and employed or authorized studies using its own selected experts. The areas which Howe studied were almost exact counterparts of Adirondack forest regions. As late as 1920, however, he confessed that he believed that there were then no "satisfactory methods for determining increment on large tracts."

About 1918 Dominion government investigations in cooperation with the Laurentide Company of Grand' Mère, Quebec, were instituted to study pulpwood production on cut-over lands and on abandoned farms. By that time the Laurentide Company had the largest private forest nursery in Canada. Studies of most effective planting methods and growth-rates were begun. The Riordan Pulp and Paper Company also had extended its operations to include large-scale reforestation. The two companies cooperated in buying huge quantities of planting material.[8]

[7] *ibid.* XVII, 3, March 1919, p. 338.

[8] *ibid.* XVII, 1, Jan. 1919, pp. 95, 103; XVII, 3, March 1919, pp. 338, 349; also G. A. Mulloy, "Experiments in Planting Timber Trees," *Illustrated Canadian Forestry Magazine*, March 1923, pp. 179ff. Foresters Lyon and Cosens are now again working to-

The Riordan Company failed in the financial depression which followed World War I. The Laurentide Company carried on until 1932 when, under new management, its reforestation program was abandoned. But the Spruce Falls Power and Paper Company of Kapuskasing, Ontario, established similar experimental work. The chief forester of the old company, Robert W. Lyon, became forester of the new company, and he took with him as his assistant Gordon G. Cosens, graduate of the class of 1923 at Toronto and later dean of the faculty of forestry of the University of Toronto following the administration of Dean Howe.

In "A National Forest Policy," delivered at the 1916 New England Forest Conference, Fernow presented the aims, results, direction and progress of the subject.

> Pennsylvania, I believe, is the only state which has a forest department with broadest administrative functions based on business aspects and managing its state forests in a business-like manner for wood-production. Unfortunately, temporary financial embarrassment has stopped the further acquisition of State forests. In all the other States we are, as a friend puts it, "just puttering, losing valuable time which ought to be improved against the future needs of the people who will live upon the North American continent. The problem is a continental one and not a local or even a federal one."[9] It can be solved only by cooperation of State and Federal agencies. . . . We may as well now as later face the fact that to satisfy only a reasonable demand for wood materials of a nation of say two hundred million, and at the same time secure it from the absolute forest land, will require from four hundred to five hundred million acres of managed forest, and we should begin now to prepare for it. We need to take a broad national view of the problem and realize that, if left to private effort, it is not likely to be solved; if left to State initiative, its solution will lag due to financial difficulties. Another Weeks law is needed, to bring about cooperation between the State and Federal governments in order to extend the reservation policy and to begin the work of recovery on a large scale. Our problem is that of the Sybilline books. Every year it becomes more complicated, more difficult, more urgent.

Fernow did not go uncriticized. R. D. Forbes, superintendent of forestry in the Louisiana department of conservation, questioned whether a jury of twenty-nine of the thirty state foresters of the United States would support the assertion of Fernow, which, in fact, was a quotation, that the states were not occupied with the forester's main business, "continuous forest production on true forest soils, publicly owned" and that alone Pennsylvania had "a really businesslike forest policy." In an article

---

gether. The reforestation program of Hollingsworth and Whitney Company, with offices at Neenah, Wisconsin, is one of the most elaborate in the history of forestry in North America with an investment aggregating $7,000,000 and a nursery which produces annually ten million trees.

[9] Unsigned letter, heretofore quoted, from the forester of the Society for the Protection of New Hampshire Forests. Philip W. Ayres was the Society's forester. The "puttering" charge was repeated by Fernow in an address, "The Situation," hereafter considered. Quotations are taken from Fernow's original manuscripts.

in the *Journal of Forestry*[10] Superintendent Forbes explained why state forest work was preoccupied with dendrological manuals, shade-tree work, illustrated lectures, supplying market data to lumbermen and woodlot owners, forest nurseries for planting stock to reforest limited acreages, and demonstration forests of more extensive acreage. The war, of course, aggravated conditions in government forest administration. Especially was this so of the state and provincial administrations, and of the lesser county and municipal administrations. The period of reconstruction impeded progress at some points; at others it accelerated advancement. Fernow's reviews of department reports must have been bracing. Some were congratulated; others rebuked. In 1919[11] Fernow besought British Columbia to reestablish more than "merely a timberland administration." California was flayed for failing to provide a forestry administration adequate to the state's needs. On the other hand Minnesota was congratulated for its businesslike administration. Some states had placed their forestry interests with their geological work. New York's state forest preserve was still managed as a forest park.

To appraise the growing national forest policy called forth Fernow's highest capacities. In his address before the New England Forest Conference he expressed gratification that the profession could dispassionately discuss the claimed influences of the forest on climate and water flow and point to proof, however "specific, localized, [or] limited" the illustrations might be. Abstractions were being shaped into concrete realities. Governments now, more than reserving their own forest lands, were purchasing large forest areas in recognition of proven beneficial influences of the forests—flood control, assured water supply, soil conservation, and so forth. "Altogether," said Fernow "in the earlier years we were long on sentiment and short on economic thought." Furthermore, foresters had their own "particular domain." At least seventy per cent of Canada's land area, and perhaps one-half of the land areas of the United States were "absolute forest lands," fitted only for the growing of woods and forests.

The Society of American Foresters became affiliated with the American Association for the Advancement of Science. On December 29, 1916, Fernow presented his second presidential address to the society, this time selecting as his subject, "The Situation."[12] He saw, notwithstanding the still many unsolved problems, much to be proud of, especially when contrasting the progress of the British in India, who began their forestry work there twenty years before the United States and Canada began theirs. "There are five directions in which the progress should be

[10] *Journal of Forestry* XVII, 5, May 1919, p. 503.

[11] *ibid.* XVII, on British Columbia, p. 571, on California p. 570, on Minnesota p. 567, on Virginia p. 566.

[12] *ibid.* XV, 1917, pp. 3-14.

traced," said Fernow, "namely in the development of forest policies, federal, state and municipal; in the development of private forestry; in the professional and public educational development; the development in scientific direction; and finally in forestry practice, the actual application of knowledge in the management of forests." He centered his attack on those phases which were most in need of attention. Only four states owned extensive state forest areas—New York, Pennsylvania, Wisconsin, and Michigan—the last two were said to have at that time 400,000 acres and 277,000 acres respectively. Thirteen states had recognized the principle[13] and owned much less extensive forest areas, but the appropriation for forestry work in all but Pennsylvania was inadequate, even in those twenty-six other states where forestry administrations were maintained "in one form or other." Pennsylvania was not free of financial problems. Those states which had financed their forestry work best had employed sound business management. Substantial enough progress on the whole, however, warranted a conclusion that state forestry in the United States was firmly established.

Dangers could beset either national or state forestry. Only recently efforts to abolish the Alaska National Forests and to open parts of other public forest regions to private and municipal acquisition were defeated because the president vetoed the proposals. New York still led in state-owned forest lands. Yet the "park idea, without economic conception, [was] still uppermost."

The great forests about which Fernow was now concerned were the privately-owned forests which were not being managed for continuity. The introduction of the cooperative principle between the states and federal government embodied in the Weeks law provided a new source for encouragement. "Perhaps we do not realize that the Eastern forests and forest lands—the absolute forest soils in the East," he said, "represent three to four fifths of the total forest area of the country; they serve the largest contingent of the population, and their proper management for continuity is almost more important than that of the Western forests, for which the federal government has made such good beginning. The fact that these Eastern forests are practically altogether in the hands of private owners and can, therefore, become State forests only by purchase for hard cash, is sufficient explanation of the slow, almost negligible progress in this direction." While not unmindful of gains in conservative lumbering, utilization economics, fire protection, private forest plantations, and other phases of private forestry, Fernow insisted

[13] R. H. D. Boerker, *op. cit.*, Chap. XV, pp. 206-225. In contrast to Fernow's figures, we see that in 1944-45 thirty-nine states owned approximately 13,400,000 acres of state forests in 732 units. The high ranking states are given as: Minnesota, 5,338,238 acres; New York, 2,674,473; Pennsylvania, 1,650,937; Michigan, 1,000,000; Montana, 520,000; Idaho, 448,000; Washington, 355,000; New Mexico, 258,000; Massachusetts, 171,360; Wisconsin, 170,190; the Southern States, 143,833 acres.

still, "If we think of forestry as a management of forest properties under a sustained yield management, i.e. for continuity under a purposeful method of reproduction," then "we may claim that private forestry does not as yet exist." Municipal forestry was begun with ten cities owning some one hundred and fifty thousand acres. Privately-owned woodlot forests, said to have contained ten per cent of the nation's timber stand, were still not under consistent programs of management. No one of these phases of forestry development promised to "solve the problem of rehabilitation of the vast areas outside the farms." Fernow wanted to enlarge the principle of mutuality of interest between the state and federal governments to recognize that "there are *nation-wide* economic interests in this forest problem which call for national action. . . . We have learned as a general political principle that the State should undertake only such work for the welfare of the community as the individual cannot undertake better or as well, and similarly we may extend this principle and call upon the nation at large when the single States by themselves cannot solve as well or better such economic problems; where the nation as a whole is concerned, federal action, or at least cooperation of federal and State governments, is called for. If continuity of a lumber supply and the recuperation of the waste acres is a national concern, as I believe it is, then such a cooperation should be called in." Financial assistance of the federal government to the states was advocated—perhaps "lending the federal government's credit to a bonding scheme of the State for the acquisition of forest lands and their management" and cooperatively to give to the federal and state governments joint control of "the expenditure of funds, the selection of purchases, the making of working plans and their execution. Finally, State legislation would be desirable, by which private forest lands could come under State control not by purchase, but by contract under an annual rental, participating in the returns of the larger and hence safer State forest management—cooperation between State and private forest owners—by which the latter profit in pooling their smaller interests with the larger." On points of silviculture[14] and finance he cited suggestions by Professor B. P. Kirkland, Professor of Forest Finance at the University of Washington. "While Mr. Kirkland proposes the organization of a big trust outside of, and merely supervised by, the government, I propose a trust in which the government plays the large part and allows private owners to participate in a sustained yield management of the pooled properties."

Fernow summarized the progress made in forestry education. "Altogether some 52 institutions offer forestry courses, 23 of them with two to five year curricula leading to a degree, while some 40 run ele-

[14] "Possibilities of Silviculture in America," *op. cit.*

mentary or short courses. There must be now well-nigh 5,000 students occupying themselves with the subject in one way or another. In 21 of the degree-conferring institutions alone over 3,500 students are enrolled for longer or shorter courses, and not less than 1,200 may be found working for a degree under the guidance of over 100 instructors."

He ended his address with the problem closest to his mind and heart at the time. "Forestry practice, especially silviculture, is still largely undeveloped, even in the administration of the National Forests. In this respect, again the State of Pennsylvania seems to have taken the lead. Forestry practice is largely built on empiricisms, and the accumulation of experience takes time. Meanwhile, the modern more scientific spirit of attacking problems upon the basis of experiment and systematic investigation has made praiseworthy progress." Although the United States Forest Service had so systematized its investigations in the past three years as to rival the research of the German and Austrian experiment stations, out of "162 listed problems, nearly half [were] occupied with forest products, and less than 30 with real forestry problems."[15] Fernow's address expressed little faith that much change could be expected in private forestry. Forestry "in the main [was regarded as] a business for the State,[16] and only under very special conditions for private enterprise." This view was held despite the inadequate forestry of the southern states, whose pine regions furnished a resource valued "at over $300,000,000 [and] half the lumber cut in the United States."

At this meeting of the society in New York, ecologists, geographers, and foresters gathered to hear scientific papers. The role of light in forest growth[17] and in natural and artificial reforestation[18] were among the subjects discussed. Notable in the ecological connection was E. H. Frothingham's study, "Ecology and Silviculture in the Southern Appalachians; Old Cuttings as a Guide to Future Practice."[19] He wrote to Fernow February 7, 1917:

With reference to the study of cut-over areas in the Southern Appalachians, I am enclosing a copy of my working plan, a brief report on the aims and progress of the work, a brief summary for each of the first 26 plots studied . . . and samples of the various forms used in assembling the data. This study is properly a "silvicultural reconnaissance," aimed to secure general rather than specific, detailed information, to meet the immediate needs of a management just being begun. . . . The present plan, which was not developed until well toward the close of the first season's work, aims to

[15] See also E. H. Clapp, "The Correlation of American Forest Research," *Journal of Forestry* XV, 2, Feb. 1917, p. 165.

[16] See also *ibid.* XVI, 3, March 1918, p. 335; *Forest Leaves*, Aug. 1917, an abstract of Fernow's "State Forestry."

[17] Raphael Zon, "Some Problems in Light as a Factor of Forest Growth," *Journal of Forestry* XV, p. 225.

[18] C. G. Bates, "The Role of Light in Natural and Artificial Reforestation," *ibid.* XV, p. 233.

[19] *ibid.* XV, 3, March 1917, p. 343.

make each separate cutting tell its own story, and to make such general deductions and inferences as are warranted by similarities between different plots in apparent cause and effect.

Similar studies were being made in other districts.

Fernow found[20] in Clements' *Plant Succession An Analysis of the Development of Vegetation* a volume "of such size and importance" in analyzing facts, principles, and methods by which to investigate phenomena that he left to "competent hands and time" the task of evaluating its "special interest" to foresters. He considered it a "most complete summary of present ecological knowledge."

In the April issue of *Journal of Forestry* was printed Bates's answer to certain constructive criticisms made recently by Fernow with regard to forest research. In an article on "The Biology of Lodgepole Pine as Revealed by the Behavior of Its Seed,"[21] Bates entered upon a discussion of American forestry research and methods by which to improve its usefulness:

Some friendly critics of the Forest Service have recently, consciously or unconsciously, conveyed the idea that forest investigations at present are not producing a proper quota of fundamental data, usable as the foundation of scientific silvicultural practice. Notable among recent articles in this tenor are Dr. Fernow's "Suggestions as to Possibilities of Silviculture in America" and Barrington Moore's "Relation of Forestry to Science." I must confess to feelings, at times, entirely in keeping with the ideas expressed by them. It has struck me that our experimentation has been of too limited a scope, representing, as it so often does, a purely local test of the "best method" of performing some silvicultural operation. This is true of nearly all of our work in reforestation, natural regeneration, and thinnings. Yet, I think it is erroneous to assume that because the working plans for these investigations carefully avoid any mention of the broader principles at stake, the results will fail to bring out the fundamental data that truly scientific foresters want and must certainly have. I think you will agree with me that, in general, scientific principles and specific biological characters are to be established not by assuming an hypothesis and searching for proof of it, but by free-minded analysis of all the data bearing on the point, from all possible sources, each of which must reflect a certain local character. I feel, then, that our present need is for more analytical treatment of the enormous collection of data which are available from numerous, and in many cases, very simple experiments.

At this time probably no one excelled Bates in scientific forestry research. Fernow never presumed to be an exact scientist in forestry, although he was North America's earliest and most ardent advocate of forestry as both a science and an art.

Forestry research in Canada before World War I was largely of a practical and applied nature; the post war research proceeded along the lines of more exact, pure, and experimental science. Methodology has

[20] *ibid.* XV, 4, April 1917, p. 479.

[21] *ibid.* XV, 4, April 1917, p. 410.

been refined and the research scope enlarged. In 1917 the memorandum outlined for the Dominion Advisory Council on Industrial and Scientific Research set forth four principal types of investigation: (1) complete the stock-taking of timber standing in the eastern provinces, paying particular attention to pulpwood supplies; (2) make a rapid reconnaissance, partly in connection with the stock-taking, of the condition of cut-over land and commercial timber reproduction; (3) begin the study of possibilities of methods to secure reproduction of the most important timber trees, notably the white pine and spruce; (4) make the necessary measurements to determine rates of growth in volume of Canada's most important timber trees, individually and in forest stands, to calculate possible quantity production. The first problem was in the hands of the commission of conservation. The second could be combined with the first. A larger personnel was needed to further the work, which also included forest products laboratory research to reduce waste and promote utilization of all the resources of the forest. Had not the war interrupted forestry progress in Canada, Fernow and other Canadian foresters—Howe, White, Leavitt, Wilson, Piché, and others—might have gotten the work largely under way years sooner.

Silviculture was bound to win new victories. The *Journal of Forestry* of October 1917[22] announced that, following recommendations of the Canadian advisory council, 100 square miles of the Petawawa Military Reservation in Renfrew County, Ontario, about 125 miles northwest of Ottawa, had been set apart by the military department for a forest experiment station to be maintained cooperatively with the Dominion forestry branch. A forest survey of the reservation was in progress. The University of Toronto considered placing a practice camp there, and possibly a school for rangers. By 1918 the university staff was actively engaged in field research over Canada, at points including the Petawawa reservation, the Cypress Hills forest reserve, and other localities. Sample plots to study forest regeneration and growth of various species, pine and spruce especially, under different conditions were located.[23]

Canada had a history of nursery and planting stations before the establishment of the Petawawa station. This earlier station work had been founded by the provinces; the Dominion experimental farms, especially the nursery at Indian Head, had also included forestry work. In these, however, experimental work was incidental to the main purpose, the growing and distributing of nursery stock. The Petawawa experiment station was the Dominion government's first forest ex-

[22] *ibid.* XV, 6, p. 817.

[23] *ibid.* XVI, 5, May 1918, pp. 594-596, a review by Fernow of the Report of the Director of Forestry for 1917, *Annual Report of the Department of the Interior*, Part IV.

periment station comparable to those stations which were set up almost a decade earlier by the United States forest service.

By 1940 the Dominion forestry service maintained, in addition to the Petawawa station located in Renfrew County, Ontario, two forest experiment stations in the Maritime District—the Acadia station located near Fredericton, New Brunswick, and the Valcartier station seventeen miles northwest of Quebec City. There was a station in the Manitoba-Saskatchewan district, the Riding Mountain research station, located in the Riding Mountain National Park 175 miles northwest of Winnipeg, and a station in the Alberta District, the Kananaskis forest experiment station, situated near the confluence of the Kananaskis and Bow rivers between Calgary and Banff, and located to investigate the growth and development of the subalpine forest region there, particularly the Rocky Mountain eastern slope foothills types. The Valcartier station administers the Lake Edward experimental area in Champlain County. Research projects in botany, particularly phenology and genetics, in ecology, silviculture, mensuration, forest influences, forest protection including forest pathology, forest administration, forest economics, and wood technology, have been maintained. It is significant that ecological investigations share rank with silvicultural research.

By 1917 Dominion forestry work was committed to a research program similar to that of the United States forest service. The latter's 100-page report on its work during 1916 had been studied by the Dominion's advisory board. There were 162 problems, "of which 70 referred to forest products and 25 to purely forest studies, grazing, protection, [while] mensuration and lumbering [divided] the balance." At the fourth annual dinner of the Foresters' Club of the University of Toronto, on January 22, 1915, Director Toumey of the Yale Forest School had assured his audience that "progress toward a normal forest" was being made in the United States, more in national and state forestry than in private forestry. Knowledge of normal stands, sustained yields, improvement thinnings, and appropriate silvicultural methods could not hope to transfer wildernesses into arranged woodlands until forest areas on which to apply that knowledge had been offered. During recent years in the United States notable advances had been achieved. Builders of fences and fire lanes, of trails and roads, and of cabins and mills were joining with professional foresters in their scientific work.[24] The forest situation of North America had not reached a crisis, but a crucial scarcity of valuable timber species was clearly in the offing. Paper consumption was increasing. Timber demands were growing. Higher prices drove home the lesson that the legend of inexhaustible forest resources was false. Research in forest life histories, in the life histories of individual

[24] "The Point of View," *Forestry Quarterly* XIII, 1, March 1915, pp. 1ff.

forest species, and in forest biology generally went forward along with management studies in growth and regeneration on permanent sample plots.

Forest products research enjoyed a steady growth. On June 26, 1917, Fernow wrote to Earle H. Clapp, assistant forester of the United States forest service, thanking him for the "appreciative tone" of a letter received "and the recognition of the fact that the Forest Products work was originated by me. As regards making a suggestion for work of the laboratory, I would consider it presumptuous on my part since I have not occupied myself with this line of work to any extent since I left Washington. From our only line of work which we had intended to take up and which might still perhaps be suggested—perhaps it is on the way as I am not informed of the detail of your proposition—namely, to study in detail the effects of various defects, so that a judgment may be framed as regards the influence of various standardized defects on the strength of timber as derived from laboratory specimens; also the testing of columns in the manner in which we had started it. I might add that I was most excellently treated on my brief visit to the laboratory." Clapp answered saying, "Upon the [former] a considerable amount of work has already been done. The results of our tests have been adopted by the American Society for Testing Materials and by the Southern Pine Association for their best grade of structural timber. Considerable progress has been made in securing the adoption of somewhat similar rules for Douglas fir by the West Coast Lumbermen, and considerable preliminary work has also been done which I hope will result eventually in rules for hemlock. On the testing of columns I am not able to report as much progress. Its importance, however, is fully appreciated, and it is probable that some work will be undertaken in the near future. I am delighted that you had a pleasant visit at the Laboratory."[25]

World War I and the development of the airplane industry tremendously expanded forest products research. In August 1917 Irving W. Bailey of the Bussey Institution for Research in Applied Biology of Harvard University consulted Fernow concerning a subcommittee on forestry for the National Research Council of the United States. Bailey wrote to Fernow as "Canada's leading Forester" and said he expected to call on him for further suggestions and cooperation when matters had progressed further. The substance of Fernow's reply was that foresters with a knowledge of biology should be selected. Indeed by 1918 the university was establishing closer contact with the Dominion Forest Products Laboratories. On May 20, 1918, Fernow informed President Falconer of the University of Toronto, "For the first time a candidate

[25] *Journal of Forestry* XVII, 8, Dec. 1919, p. 1013, commenting on an article in the July issue of the *Yale Forest School News*. See also *ibid.* XVII, 5, May 1919, p. 619, telling of the reorganization of personnel in the U.S. Forest Service.

for the degree of Forest Engineer (F.E.) has made his appearance and the degree has been conferred on him. Mr. W. Kynoch, having secured the B.Sc.F. degree in 1914, and having been employed four years in the Dominion Forest Products Laboratories, where he attained the position of Chief of the Division of Timber Physics, secured this honor upon the basis of a thesis on 'The Adaptability of Jack Pine and Eastern Hemlock to Preservative Treatment with Creosote Oil.' " On January 12, 1919, Kynoch offered himself to the University of Toronto Faculty of Forestry as an instructor in wood technology.[26]

Fernow believed that "the first or pioneering stage of the Faculty [was] coming to an end," and reorganization with increased personnel was imminent. But he was suffering from an ailment for which diagnosticians could suggest neither adequate cause nor remedy. Nothing toward school reorganization could be done immediately. Fernow suffered more each year, but there were intermittent moments of pleasure. During the summer of 1917 he was twice invited to visit the Cornell University forestry camp, located at Madawaska, New York, near St. Regis Falls. Early in August Professor Spring of Cornell arranged that his students would visit the mills at Tupper Lake under Professor Bryant's direction, and Fernow was asked to guide the students over the old Cornell forest tract, explaining the plantations and policy. Fernow replied that he "would be delighted . . . to explain to them the policy which we proposed to follow and then return with you to your own camp for a day or so."

On July 17 Fernow, resting at his summer home, had written Piché and said:

> I was very sorry circumstances did not shape themselves so that we could meet you as was planned by Mr. Leavitt, to talk over Dr. Howe's investigation and secure your cooperation more specifically. As you know, Dr. Howe's investigation is concerned with what becomes of the cut over pulpwood lands in the Eastern Provinces, and as he has started the investigation in your province, due to the offer of cooperation of the Laurentide Company, he should have earlier made an effort to see you and talk things over.
>
> We need especially your knowledge as to the extent of the forest type in which the investigation is made, and it would also be a good thing if you could put in an independent party, working under the same scheme and comparing results before generalizing. I found that the type in which Dr. Howe is working is almost an exact counterpart of the Western Adirondacks, and, hence, the experiences of that region shall repeat themselves.
>
> I hope you will be able to arrange a meeting with Dr. Howe soon, preferably at his camp, so that you can see the character of his work and talk things over in the field.

Because of the similarity of western Adirondack forest conditions to forest areas being studied in Quebec, Canadian foresters late in July had

[26] Kynoch eventually became director of the Forest Products Laboratories of Canada and is now a professor at the Michigan School of Forestry and Conservation.

arranged to confer with Fernow at Axton. Ellwood Wilson and Leavitt planned to call for Fernow by automobile sometime toward the end of August or the first part of September. In accordance with Fernow's suggestion, Howe and Piché conferred and "agreed," Piché wrote Fernow, "to cooperate together and discuss the report that [Howe was] going to make." It was agreed that neither was bound by their conclusions and each reserved the right to report his own investigation. A. B. Recknagel, forester of the Empire State Forest Products Association, revised his plans so as to meet with the Canadian foresters at Tupper Lake on August 31. August 30 was arranged as the day for the mill inspection, and August 31 would be used to inspect the Axton plantations.

Fernow believed confidently that, although the Cornell forest tract had received almost no management since the year 1903, part of the forest having been burned or cut over, the remnants which had survived through fifteen years would attest the wisdom of the silvicultural policy instituted by him. An eminent group—Fernow, Howe, Leavitt, Craig, Wilson, Recknagel, F. A. Gaylord (forester at Ne-Ha-Sa-Ne Park), R. Stubbs (Gaylord's assistant), Spring, Professor John Bentley Jr. of Cornell, Bryant, and six students—gathered at the appointed time and place, examined the plantations, and then at an evening session engaged in general discussion. Spring and Recknagel had prepared an outline of silvicultural management on which the discussion in part was based. The results were presented to foresters in articles written by Bryant and Fernow,[27] both of whom were highly pleased.

Discussion persisted for years. On August 20, 1920, Austin Cary, stopping at the Hotel Altamont at Tupper Lake, wrote to Howe:

> Today I have been over Fernow's work here, not, I am sorry to say, with most competent guidance. We all know what cost and row was involved here. How does it stand today, 18 years after?
>
> The land cut over by the Brooklyn Cooperage Co. when unburnt, as I saw it, is now thick in hardwood—lots of hard maple, yellow birch, ash, etc. Good, isn't it? I thought it so—good enough to be accepted. Lots of it is 30 feet high. Mr. Craig of Grand Mere told me spruce was planted on that land and had grown but I didn't see it and can't believe it. On the other hand, looks to me as if it would take a lot of cost to keep any coniferous tree away from the hardwoods on this thin [cover] territory. So the operation, as I see it, (I mean the cutting) would have been good forestry just as it is if only it had been made at a time when the timber netted something and also when the fine quality material could have been put to good uses. The trouble was we didn't wait till the time was ripe. Am I not right?
>
> Another thing—the last year the company operated a heavy fire swept over ⅔ of their cut area. On that area poplar and some other stuff has come

[27] R. C. Bryant, "Silviculture at Axton and in the Adirondacks Generally," *Journal of Forestry* XV, 7, Nov. 1917, p. 891; B. E. Fernow, "Axton Plantations," *ibid.* XV, 8, Dec. 1917, pp. 988-990.

up, . . . short lived; under it the state has made successful spruce plantations. This opportunity to do what was planned to do at the start came in spite of us.

Howe answered, arguing against a policy of letting nature take its course unrestrainedly. To follow such a course would admit the failure of tending woodlands, "the application of brain power to the forest. . . . I fear you did not see some of the finest plantations at Axton," wrote Howe, and proceeded to recall his impressions of the 1917 conference. "I cannot locate them for you very well, but I recall that about three years ago, we came out through Tupper Lake village, went down a long hill to a flat sandy place. On the right of the highway, where the Scotch pine and spruce were planted, was a place called Cross Clearing. Then we got on the road again and went I think about half a mile, getting into some hard woods, when we turned I think to our left and found where Dr. Fernow planted after clean cutting, and saw Norway spruce 18 or 20 feet high and 4 or 5 inches in diameter. Then I remember approaching the old headquarters at Axton, we crossed a little creek, perhaps Ampersand, then went up onto a sandy plateau where the old headquarters buildings were located and went beyond them I think to the East, and there we found some of the Scotch pine, White pine, Norway spruce, and European larch, the latter making particularly good growth. As I remember it some of the trees were 40 feet high, 35 anyway, and 6 or 7 inches in diameter."

In 1917, after the inspection, Fernow believed that "the various plantations [had] proved themselves entirely successful after 15 years." But this was not the only bright spot to illumine the last years of a valiant struggle against encroaching illness. Research by the members of the faculty at Toronto steadily had gone forward—in the West on the Dominion forest reserves and in the East at the Petawawa military reservation through the Dominion forestry branch, as well as through the commission of conservation in connection with private companies, such as the Laurentide and the Riordan Companies in Quebec, the Abitibi Power and Paper Company, and the Spanish River Pulp and Paper Mills in Ontario. Forest surveys of pulpwood limits were being done for these. The basis for future regeneration and growth and other studies related to the more valuable forest species was well under way. Most important was the establishment of the system of permanent sample plots in the St. Maurice valley in cooperation with the Laurentide Company and in the Rouge River valley in cooperation with the Riordan Company "to determine by actual measurement what happens in terms of growth and reproduction of balsam and spruce on virgin and semi-virgin areas, on areas lightly culled, moderately culled and severely culled, on areas cut clean and on areas burned with different degrees of severity. From the plots also will be determined," a report dated 1918(?)

read, "what percentage of the death rate in passing from infancy to maturity may be ascribed to fungous diseases and what to insect diseases. Studies will be made upon the rate of growth of the young trees in relation to climatic conditions, also the amount of seed production per tree and per acre and the distances to which seed will be carried from the mother tree in quantities to establish seedlings in potential commercial quantities. A detailed investigation is being carried on to find out what constitutes a successful germinating bed for the seed of spruce and balsam." As many as twenty-five one-acre samples and several hundred subsidiary plots were placed and others were planned to be studied over a twenty-five year period. Dr. Howe, working with the commission of conservation, made two experimental cutting areas of 160 acres and 500 acres, one with the Laurentide Company in Quebec and the other with the Bathurst Lumber Company in New Brunswick, both designed "to find some method of logging profitable to the limit owner and yet insuring another crop of spruce or balsam on the same ground." Fernow was glad to read reports of this progress.[28]

In May 1918 Fernow received an interesting invitation from the department of forestry of the New York State College of Agriculture at Cornell. Samuel N. Spring wrote, offering another trip into the Adirondacks, and said:

> Dr. Howe has told you of the plans of the New York Section of the Society of American Foresters concerning sample plots to study growth. Some of these plots are now being laid out and the data recorded on land in the Eastern Adirondacks, belonging to Finch, Pruyn Company. The Sample Plot Committee are going to look these over the latter part of this month and it would be a very great pleasure to all of us if you could make this trip with us. The ones we will look over will be within reaching distance of Newcomb and I think trips from this point will not be unduly arduous.

Fernow appreciated the "extra effort to get [him] out into the woods," but he had to decline the invitation both because of his health and because of a contemplated visit to one of his sons in Milwaukee.

When in 1919 Cornell University, through Ralph Sheldon Hosmer, invited Fernow to attend its fiftieth anniversary celebration, Fernow could not accept. No specialist had been able to help his failing health, and he was prevented from appearing in public. In 1915 the department of forestry had taken over from the forest service the periodic remeasurement every five years of the sample plots at Axton. To secure from Fernow all the information possible, it was arranged that the second remeasurement would be advanced a year, to take place while

[28] In a letter dated Oct. 6, 1919, Howe told Fernow that "the Bathurst Lumber Company [would] try some experimental cuttings in the semi-barren spruce type on an area of 500 acres. The cuttings [would] be by strip methods and circular patches and thinning to various diameter limits. . . . Similar arrangements [had] also been made with the Laurentide Company, who [would] carry on experimental cutting on 320 acres."

Fernow was at his summer residence in New York. Fernow rejoiced that the Axton plantations were being restudied. Arrangements for the restudying of the "Bruner plantations" in the Nebraska sand hills had been requested and placed in the hands of Forest Examiner C. G. Bates in 1917. In October 1919, although in the Hahnemann Hospital at Rochester, Fernow, sustaining the same determined spirit to serve forestry everywhere, received reports and conducted his duties as editor-in-chief of the *Journal of Forestry*. Despite a condition which manifested itself in a lack of control over his muscles, he continued to perform his daily duties. A dinner, arranged at the University of Toronto in his honor, was refused. He knew it would be too much of a strain for him.

In 1918 he had seen another forest products laboratory erected in the Dominion. At Vancouver during 1919 the new wood-testing laboratory, established to test airplane spruce at the point of production, Douglas fir, and other timbers of use in World War I, was established in a new building. The vistas opened and widened by forest products research survived far beyond the period of the war. Swift development of the airplane industry prompted the realization that wood and forest research had tremendous new fields to conquer. In turn, the airplane was to be utilized by forestry in patrolling forests, to locate fires and help rid widespread insect and fungous infestations, and for other purposes. Since the new laboratory was located in one of the important forest areas of the world, with great industrial possibilities, a permanent program was shaped. Before Fernow's death the superintendence of this useful institution in the West, as well as the professorship of the department of forestry of the University of British Columbia,[29] would be held by men who had been students of forestry at the University of Toronto. Forest products research in a province was not without precedent. In 1917 three states of the United States, as well as a number of private companies, supported such laboratories.

In 1918 Fernow saw another cherished proposal which he had advocated from Nova Scotia to British Columbia made a reality—an extension of the work of the Canadian commission of conservation to inform the Dominion of the forest resources of each province. *Forests of British Columbia*, Whitford and Craig's report published that year, became the best and only analysis of its kind for many years. As late as 1917 Craig, and doubtless Whitford also, sought and received criticisms from Fernow while the work was being written.

In the previous year Whitford again had been honored by foresters, this time being chosen for the task of developing the study of tropical

[29] On March 21, 1918, R. H. Campbell wrote to Fernow, "We are sympathetic to the proposal and are assisting with a scheme which is apparently going to work out successfully for the establishment of . . . a ranger school in Vancouver." For other developments see *Journal of Forestry* XVII, 6, Oct. 1919, p. 763; XVII, 4, April 1919, p. 461; XVII, 1, Jan. 1919, p. 106.

forestry at the Yale Forest School. In 1916 a department of tropical forestry, made possible by an endowment of $100,000 presented to the school by Gifford Pinchot, had been established. On May 5 of that year Director Toumey had written to Whitford in care of the commission of conservation at Victoria, British Columbia, concerning "proposed work of Yale in tropical forestry."

> The work as planned is to be of permanent character and is backed by a permanent endowment of $100,000. Until this endowment becomes available, the enterprise will be supported by a contribution from the University of $5,000 per year for the period of two years. . . . The work offers permanency and, I believe, great opportunities for the man selected as the expert, as he is expected to devote his entire time to tropical work, which is relatively a new field. . . . I understand that Professor Bryant has written you at length regarding our proposed work. . . . It is expected that later the title will be changed [from assistant professor] to professor of tropical forestry. There would probably be but a small amount of teaching at present, but great opportunity would be afforded for field work, research and publication.[30]

From May 29 until September 27, 1917, Whitford visited Colombia and Venezuela, and on December 12 plans for tropical forestry in South America were reported. First an understanding of what forestry practice meant and what might be accomplished was to be promoted by propaganda. For a period of eight years Whitford was to train foresters for work in the Latin American countries. Courses in tropical dendrology, silviculture, and forest management were elaborated, but the task became so great that more abundant resources were required, and when the work was taken over by Samuel J. Record, it became more or less confined to studies of tropical woods and their technology. The tropics were known to contain the only remaining large stands of virgin timber. To explore these regions, collect and arrange authentic information concerning the extent and location of forest areas, of the woods, including the new species and their availability, and of other forest products there, presented an immense challenge worthy of a share of a great forest school's efforts. Again, in this field, the botanists had preceded the foresters in exploration. Whitford and Record, able both as botanists and foresters, were chosen to outline and forward the work.[31]

Fernow, years before, had discussed the subject of tropical wood supplies before a section of the American Association for the Advancement of Science. Both by letters and in his editorial capacity he encouraged students and correspondents who went to South America as foresters. H. M. Curran, who later joined with Whitford to develop tropical forestry at Yale, had written to Fernow on September 6, 1913:

[30] In a bound volume titled *Tropical Forestry at Yale*, Papers 1916-1941, by Record and Whitford, in the library of the Yale Forest School.

[31] See Record's lecture, "The Role of Yale in the Tropics," *Yale Forest School News* XVII, 1, Jan. 1929, p. 6. Concerning *Tropical Woods*, a quarterly journal originated by Record, see S. F. Blake, *Torreya* XXVI, 5, 1926, pp. 99f.

> Forestry takes men far. What a debt the future owes to Germany for her care of the world's forests. Brandis in the East and your work in the West, that now takes a new scope. I hope, if health and opportunity are mine, to do here in the South what you did in the North, and always remember it is your work. I came from a short term of service in the Bureau of Forestry with practically no idea of what forestry is or means. I left Cornell, after an all too short stay with you. . . . You will be glad to hear that the Philippine Island work grows steadily. The little school we started a few years ago turns out its grist of men each year.

Curran and Max Rothkugel had gone to South America and become engaged in forest work under Dr. Holmberg at Buenos Aires. As the letter indicates, Curran had had preliminary experience in forestry of the Philippine Islands, and he explained much to Fernow about the organization of the Argentine service. In a letter of October 31, 1914, he summarized by saying, "The work of the North American foresters is mainly exploration and investigation, with in the case of Mr. Rothkugel, the preliminary organization of grazing control and fire protection work in Patagonia." Curran regarded as his own the " forest region of the Chaco" which was part of "the principal forest wealth of Argentina," where "extensive logging operations" were carried on. Especially useful were the soft woods which were found in quantity and other valuable species in large number, "as yet unknown to the home and foreign markets," and some of it suitable for pulp making. Evaluation of the development of tropical forestry in America must be left to another book, but Fernow saw this trend extended into forestry education during his lifetime.

The Yale school's program was a valuable extension of forestry research. In 1916-1917 plans were announced to place an experiment station and research laboratory in South America in order to study tropical diseases, colonization and educational systems suitable for tropical lands, crops of the tropics, the mineral wealth, water power, and other resources to be found there. This movement was evidently conceived as an enlargement and necessary corollary of the already flourishing introduction of scientific agriculture in the South American countries, especially Brazil. In 1918 Whitford visited the southern part of Brazil and investigated two forest tracts—one, a hardwood forest on the coast north of Rio de Janeiro; the other, a large coniferous area in the celebrated Paraná forests.[32] In the following year Whitford went to Central America, where he served on a commission of the state department to investigate the economic resources of a boundary region in dispute between Guatemala and Honduras.[33] A few more years would pass and a hemispheric plant science research program would be pro-

[32] *Journal of Forestry* XV, 1, Jan. 1917, p. 137; *ibid.* XVII, 1, Jan. 1919, p. 105, concerning Whitford's work in Colombia, Venezuela, and Brazil.

[33] *Torreya*, July 1919, p. 142.

posed to accentuate further agricultural and forestry development and to include comprehensive botanical investigations—crop introductions, crop improvements, disease and insect surveys, taxonomic collecting and systemization of the wild and economically valuable agricultural, horticultural, and forest species, including wood sets and herbaria, ecological and physiological examinations, the relations of vegetation to soils and climates under the wide diversity of growth conditions, and full scale research to coordinate forest study and utilization, management, products and by-products, and lumbering.[34] The plant science study of the Central and South American countries originated with the early botanical explorers. Forestry, however, received its real impetus, so far as the work of North Americans was concerned, when specialists trained principally in the Philippine Islands extended their interests to the Latin American countries. Nine years of forestry work in the Philippines as an associate professor of botany had made Whitford an acknowledged authority in tropical forestry. In the spring of 1913 he had studied a Mexican timberland area near Colima, the same locality where Fernow had investigated an "oak property of the Sierra Madre." Immediately afterward he went to British Columbia.

After three years of close study—begun in the coastal regions of British Columbia, extended to the Cranbrook Forest District, the Upper Kootenay and Upper Columbia valleys, the East Kootenay District, the Nelson District, the Railroad Belt, and in time covering practically the entire province, Whitford and Craig's model forest survey publication, *Forests of British Columbia*, was presented. It was at once regarded as "an encyclopedia of information on forest conditions and forest resources of British Columbia and an excellent basis for developing a permanent forest policy for the Province."[35] Fernow was partly responsible for the quality of the work. Whitford consulted him. MacMillan consulted him and allowed Whitford and Fernow to shape the plan and purposes of the investigations. The three men agreed that the survey should record British Columbia's forest types and values, furnish an authentic timber estimate, and portray the provincial agricultural situation. Fernow was sorry to see MacMillan leave the province's forest work to serve the Dominion in official capacities during World War I. He believed that MacMillan's "presence at the head of affairs in British Columbia [was] of more value to the country at large" than any other service for the country, special or otherwise. He considered it a mistake to take away men needed for the efficient conduct of local governments. A national

[34] W. A. Orton, "Botanical Problems of American Tropical Agriculture," *Bulletin of the Torrey Botanical Club* 53, 2, Feb. 1926, pp. 67-75.

[35] *Journal of Forestry* XVII, 7, Nov. 1919, p. 865, a review of *Forests of British Columbia.*

emergency in no wise diminished the importance of continuing sound government in the provinces.

Between 1913 and 1918, the first and last years of the survey, it seemed that Canada would at last become efficiently and accurately informed of its forest resources, problems, and indicated solutions. The hope was not confined to British Columbia. Stock-taking of forest resources, especially of pulpwood supplies in Ontario, Quebec, New Brunswick, and Saskatchewan, with results already obtained in Nova Scotia, seemed to promise that good forest crops on all appropriate lands in Canada could be provided.

Craig and his staff became employed in a forest survey conducted cooperatively by the province of Ontario and the commission of conservation, a project similar to that in British Columbia. Craig organized the work, but unfortunately for the forest surveys of Ontario, New Brunswick, and Saskatchewan, the commission of conservation was abolished in the spring of 1921. The Ontario survey had done little, if any, field work. Beginning in the summer of 1919 systematic forest surveys were begun by the Ontario forestry branch to determine the province's forest conditions and take an inventory of its forest resources. In November 1919 *Journal of Forestry*[36] announced that the survey under Craig was in progress in order to secure reliable estimates of the standing timber and pulpwood, the location and distribution of species, and other data. Areas covered by forests were to be mapped, as well as waste lands and areas suitable for agriculture. Those areas which should be devoted to forest production were to be specially noted. Among other methods of obtaining correct estimates, forest inventories of pulp and paper companies were to be secured. The value of this knowledge to future governmental forestry service was so definitely established that, despite the inability of the commission of conservation to continue its work, the provincial forest branch about 1920 continued the Ontario survey over about seventy-three million acres of land. The results were published in 1931 by the department of lands and forests in "The Forest Resources of Ontario 1930," a sixty-page pamphlet with charts and maps which described the province's forest area under eight regions.

The Faculty of Forestry at the University of Toronto had engaged in some valuable work for the province. In a "Description of Research Work being carried on by the Members of the Staff," it was reported in 1918(?):

> Dr. J. H. White has been employed with the Provincial Forestry Branch during the summer months. The project of conducting a detailed mapping of the forest conditions of the Province and the collection of the data required as a preliminary to putting the forest area under technical management has been going on for several summers under his superintendence. Last summer

[36] *ibid.* XVII, 7, Nov. 1919, p. 893.

a special investigation was made into the present conditions of the much burned old pineries of the Province, especially with reference to the regeneration of white pine. What percentage of the old burns is restocking to pine in potentially commerical quantities is being determined by careful surveys and what may be expected in the future from such areas in terms of pine sawlogs is being disclosed by detailed studies upon the rate of growth of the young trees. This investigation has already covered some 75,000 acres in central Ontario and it will be continued on representative areas throughout the Province.

This investigation, together with enlarged research activities of the commission of conservation under Dr. Howe and an increased demand for technically educated foresters by private concerns, added new opportunities for professional employment. Forest regeneration and growth rate study surveys, especially of balsam fir and spruce, were being conducted in New Brunswick, Ontario, and Quebec. The principle of the permanent sample plot was being established, as well as that of experimental cutting areas. Despite the war and post war reconstruction, the work pursued in Ontario as part of the Trent watershed survey was having far-reaching effects. In 1918 Fernow reported to the university that, while White would remain in lecture work at the school, he had accepted a position with the provincial forest service. May 23, 1919, he informed again that while White had continued his courses, he was working for the Ontario forestry branch on leave of absence.

Forest type studies continued in the United States and Canada. In Canada forest type investigations were much needed because of the wide diversity in types and the intermingling of species. Each type had to be studied to find the most effective method of management. In eastern Canada it was estimated that three-fourths of the commercial timberlands had been logged over at least once and much of it several times. Fernow said this repeatedly and warned that the future supply of sawlogs evidently would have to come from cut-over lands. Reforestation or planting alone could not solve the problems. Forest ecology had become a prominent course in college curricula, but ecology was not sufficient. The industries and their needs had to be examined. Lumber and milling cost surveys, begun by Fernow, had to be broadened and verified. The work of improving forests in the United States[37] and Canada had been well-started. Progress in regulating the grazing industry was proceeding effectively. Stock grazing on the national forests of the United States had increased enormously in the decade. Fernow did not neglect grazing, but there was much of more immediate importance to forestry development in Canada.

Fernow's position in North American forestry was unique. Filibert Roth in 1912 had called Fernow America's "*first* National Forester." In

[37] For example see C. A. Gillet, "Forests and Forestry in North Dakota," *ibid.* XXV, 1927, pp. 38-43.

February 1918 the members of the Society of American Foresters voted to elevate six members to the rank of Fellow. The six selected, in the order of choice, were Pinchot, Graves, Fernow, Roth, Zon, and Greeley.[38] Fernow had retained his residence in New York State, but he was living in Canada and was the only forester who was closely familiar with the history and conditions in forestry over the whole continent.

On June 26, 1917, Fernow wrote Philip W. Ayres:

> I have just returned from a meeting of the Pennsylvania Forestry Association at Pittsburgh, where I continued in the discussion of your idea that we should cease "puttering" and take up persistent working plans for just such developments as the State of Pennsylvania has entered upon, working out the need of a bond issue of One Million Dollars for the first unit of one million acres.

That year Fernow was unable to be present at the meeting of the Society of American Foresters. On January 7, 1918, he wrote to editor-in-chief P. S. Ridsdale of *American Forestry*, who had requested an advance copy or excerpts of the address he was to give:

> Your letter of 21 December found me out of town and hence I could not comply with your desire for an advance copy of my proposed address at Pittsburgh. As it was, I was under the weather to such an extent that I [had] finally to abandon the side trip and, therefore, did not deliver my address. Nor was it really elaborated to the extent to which it was entitled. For your purposes, however, I suppose it will be sufficient to make an abstract and I sent you the article as it stands at present, there being only one idea of value in it, namely, to utilize the present socialistic attitude of the government for extension of State forestry.

The first address was delivered on June 23, 1917, and was published in August by *Forest Leaves* under the title of "State Forestry." The second address was titled "Forestry and the War," and was published in 1918 in the *Journal of Forestry*.[39] In the latter address Fernow emphasized that "forestry is and must become State business." According to his view, the bulk of the forest resources inevitably would be owned and managed publicly: preferably by the larger, long-lived, permanent units. Federal and state governments were to cooperate, and the local and community units were subdivisions within the rights of ownership and management. Fernow was not arguing for a program of confiscation, and the principle of government ownership did not extend in its application beyond the forests. He did include forests then in private ownership, but his reasons for this presented no radical departure either in practice or political philosophy. It was a belief predicated solely on the inherent nature of the forest resource and the necessity of preserving it for posterity. If he found new hope for developmental forest policies in the new

[38] *ibid.* XVI, 2, March 1918, p. 376.

[39] *ibid.* XVI, pp. 149-154; pp. 141-143, accounts of 1917 meetings of Society of American Foresters, one a joint meeting with Ecological Society of America; *ibid.* XVII, 1919, pp. 220-224, accounts of 1918 meetings and resolutions.

post-war "socialistic tendencies," it was as a means to an end and not an end in itself. He argued:

> We have tried persuasive and promotive methods to induce private enterprise to engage in forestry, but the inherent troubles which surround this business have rendered the result negligible. We might apply methods of control and supervision over the use of private property, which might insure continuity of supplies. Experience in the old countries has shown, that in spite of much more perfect machinery for enforcing laws, and in spite of much more ready disposition to submit to laws, the attempts to control private management have been largely without the desired result.

Cooperation between federal and state governments was again called for. Reforestation was receiving attention now from nearly all governments, especially at the headwaters of streams, and on cut-over, barren, waste, and burnt-over lands.

The following year at the Baltimore meeting, the Society of American Foresters passed a resolution that the society "urge the immediate initiation of a permanent policy of national and state or other public acquisition of forest land until the acreage of publicly owned land capable of producing timber is sufficient eventually to supply the bulk of the raw materials required by the nation." Only thirty per cent of the present forest area and but little more than twenty per cent of the existing timber stand was said to be in public forests in the United States, and this was regarded as "a wholly insufficient basis for the future timber supply of the country." Fernow was not able to be present at either the Pittsburgh or Baltimore meetings. J. A. Ferguson, who presided as chairman of the meeting which passed the resolution, addressed a letter to Fernow in which he told that all forty foresters present regretted the absences of three of their most important professional leaders: Fernow, Roth, and Colonel Graves. To the eldest of the three, he said, "We have so long looked to you for leadership in Forestry that your absence was much regretted at this time when important points came up for discussion." Members considered "whether private enterprises can afford to carry on Forestry. This led to the resolution favoring [federal], state or other public ownership of forest lands. The question whether government ownership or regulation would be the proper thing was discussed." Fernow replied that he was glad that "apparently the consensus of opinion [had] come back to my attitude with regard to the Profitableness of forestry. I have long taught that financially forestry is defined as 'making present expenditures or foregoing present revenues for the sake of future returns,' and that future a distant one. Hence, I have never believed much in the expectations of private enterprise. Only long-lived persons can engage in forest management under sustained yield."

Silvicultural research in the United States and Canada had never received financial appropriations comparable to the amounts for scientific agricultural investigations. In the *Illustrated Canadian Forestry Magazine* of March, 1923, this circumstance was pleaded in two articles. Dean Toumey[40] argued that "Canada and the United States, both with vast areas of potential forest land, should spend as freely in research that leads toward keeping this land in continuous production as they do in research that leads toward keeping agricultural lands in continuous production. Stations for research in enduring timber production are needed in every timber producing province in Canada and in every timber producing state in the Union. . . . Silviculture is the weakest link in American forestry today and it ought to be the strongest." Roland D. Craig[41] pointed out that the "Dominion Government devoted $1,315,000 this year to the Experimental Farms for the maintenance of 21 experimental farms, 5 sub-stations, 8 biological laboratories and about 100 illustration farms, which with the exception of the latter, were practically engaged in agriculture research. . . . This year, the Forestry Branch secured $35,000 for [study of the silvical problems of Canada] and, though considerable work was accomplished, the field is so large and the need for knowledge so great, that it has been possible to undertake the study of only a very small portion of the problems confronting foresters."

The forestry world, more than ever, was being awakened to the facts of Canadian forest wealth and the prospects for its intelligent utilization and conservation. During his last years Fernow by a number of articles sought to direct more attention to this vast field for forestry development.[42] In the issue which honored Fernow with a commemorative appreciation of his life and work was the following observation:[43] ". . . No other forest region in the world contains such a large number of commercial species and so widely adapted to various uses, or has so large contiguous areas so well provided with transportation facilities and so easily accessible to great and growing markets as that of Eastern Canada. This vast area properly stocked and under intelligent use for forest purposes could supply the markets of the world." One of Fernow's great enthusiasms was to present to American foresters the challenge of the eastern Canadian forests. Preparation by him of a paper on "Silvicultural Problems in Eastern Pulpwood Forests," to be read in December 1918 at a joint meeting of the Society of American Foresters

[40] J. W. Toumey, "Research as Aid to Forest Production," *Illustrated Canadian Forestry Magazine*, March 1923, pp. 176-190. See also I. W. Bailey and H. A. Spoehr, *The Role of Research in the Development of Forestry in North America*, 1929, The Macmillan Company.

[41] "Silvicultural Research in Canada," *op. cit.*

[42] "The Significance of our Eastern Forests," *Canadian Forestry Journal*, April 1919, p. 178; "Forestry in Eastern Canada," a series of articles in the *Montreal Daily Star*, March-April 1919.

[43] *Illustrated Canadian Forestry Magazine*, March 1923, p. 191.

and the American Association for the Advancement of Science, was announced,[44] but evidently the paper was not read.

The period of Fernow's usefulness was passing. Fernow wrote a number of articles[45] of lesser importance, on "The Aspen," the utilization of which he regarded a national problem; on the old question "Do Forests Increase Rainfall?" in which he concluded that, "All we can safely claim is that the forest condition, due to its lower temperature and greater relative humidity, is favorable to precipitation as against the open field with its higher temperature and drier air, which furnish less favorable conditions for precipitation. Extensive forest areas are as a rule favored by large rainfall, but it is an open question whether the forest is the cause or the result. We must doubt, however, whether the small woodlot is a rainmaker." On February 24, 1919, he wrote an article titled "Timber's Horn of Plenty" as answer to an article which a popular magazine had briefed and which appeared in *Hardwood Record* arguing against the efforts for conservation of timber resources.

There were a few important addresses made by Fernow during his last years. On February 15, 1917, he appeared before the hydroelectric convention of Ontario at Toronto and spoke on "Trimming Trees in Transmission Lines," an address published in the commission's first bulletin[46] of that year. An impressive New England Forestry Congress held in Boston, February 24 and 25, 1919, a meeting organized by the Boston chamber of commerce and the Massachusetts Forestry Association, heard Fernow's paper, "Forest Policies of European Countries," in which he considered the policies of Germany, Russia, France, and every country except Great Britain, on which he had already written. In 1919 Fernow was made an honorary member of the Swedish Forestry Association. At the beginning of the autumn session in 1919 he retired as dean of the faculty of forestry of the University of Toronto.[47] Dr. Howe was immediately made acting dean and was accorded the full appointment the following year. At a convocation on June 3, 1920, the University of Toronto conferred on Fernow another honorary degree, the Doctorate of Laws.[48]

On July 30, 1919, Fernow spoke at the ranger school of the New York State College of Forestry at Syracuse, located at Wanakena, New York, which had been for a number of years under Professor McCarthy. The address was delivered before the New York section of the Society

[44] *Journal of Forestry* XVI, 7, Nov. 1918, p. 845.

[45] "The Aspen," *Canadian Forestry Journal* XIII, 7, July 1917, p. 1185; and "Do Forests Increase Rainfall," *ibid.* XIII, 11, Dec. 1918, p. 1965.

[46] pp. 20-22. See also the comments of Fernow, M. A. Ewer, and H. E. Stockbridge on an article by C. F. Korstian, "A Decimal Classification for Forestry Literature," *Journal of Forestry* XV, 1917, pp. 449-462, in *ibid.* XVI, 1918, pp. 203-209.

[47] *ibid.* XVII, 6, Oct. 1919, p. 766.

[48] *ibid.* XVIII, 4, April 1920, p. 440; *Canadian Forestry Journal* XVI, 7, July 1920, p. 344.

of American Foresters. Fernow formulated twelve "fundamental commonplace" points of national forestry, by which he arrived at his conclusions, first, as to the future of state forestry and, second, the right of the state of regulate forests in private ownership:[49]

All points considered, forestry as a business can be successfully applied only or mainly by the community, municipality, or state.

The problem here involves the prevention of nuisance on private lands, or the conversion of timberland into waste land, through improper handling by the private operator. The private individual can not be expected to engage in business which will show results only in a lifetime of a man, and he will not figure on returns for his children, or his children's children. The state, however, must take charge and prevent nuisance, such as destructive fires arising from improper care of this private land. I hold that the states should take the initiative and only have the assistance of the Federal Government either under some such plan as the Weeks law, or the Carnegie method of sharing costs, by which the Federal Government loans to the state its greater credit, so that the state can expropriate the land of a private owner who makes a nuisance of himself.

As to methods, the private owner can not be forced to a given method for we do not yet know them ourselves. If land is not used, the state should expropriate it. The private owner must protect the public property contiguous to him.

Large areas of thirty thousand acres or more, and where home markets were undeveloped, were favored as sources of business and profit in private forestry. When in 1917 Allen Chamberlain of the Massachusetts Forestry Association consulted Fernow with reference to a proposal to give that state's legislature "the power to exert control over logging operations," he cited a New York top-lopping law requiring preserve private forest owners "to take care" of logging debris, and Supreme Court decisions of both Maine and Louisiana which asserted "the right of the State to impose any restrictions on forest use, which the welfare of the State requires." He concluded by saying:

As to my own opinion regarding the introduction of forest control in the constitution, I am a democrat and believe that in the organic law of the constitution, only broad principles should be asserted and definite details of procedure left as much as possible to the legislature. The only principle I can see that may be properly asserted is that upon which the New York State Top-lopping Act rests, namely, the Roman law principle, *Utere Tuo ne Alterum Noceas*, preventing anyone from using his property so as to endanger the neighboring property. For the rest I believe in promotive legislation and above all, state forestry, for the long time element and forest production makes it undesirable for private enterprise.

Fernow did not say that governmental control of private forest management was undesirable in principle or impossible of attainment. Because of the difficulties of enforcing regulatory measures, however, he

[49] *Journal of Forestry* XVII, 6, Oct. 1919, p. 768; bulletin 20, *News Print Service Bureau*, pp. 8ff.

preferred cooperative to compulsory tactics. The Canadian forestry situation was complicated first by its crown lands ownership, and second by its timberlands held under licenses. The Dominion's timberland areas were principally in Manitoba, Saskatchewan, and Alberta, where its forest reservations were mainly situated. A "few insignificant parcels in the other provinces, and a portion of the so-called railway belt in British Columbia" were also owned. The areas were districted under inspectors and supervisors in each reserve. Rangers supervised fire protection and enforced such cultural requirements as the Dominion forestry branch imposed when timber was sold, and such regulations as had to do with conservative lumbering and brush burning.

In other provinces the bulk of the commerical timberlands was crown-owned and managed by the local province. During the period immediately following World War I, New Brunswick's forestry system was much improved by a new forest act and the institution of a forest service within the crown lands department.[50] Ontario, with a large forest area, still lacked a good system of timber limits control. When in May 1918 Fernow reviewed in *Forestry Quarterly*[51] the province's *Report of the Minister of Lands, Forests, and Mines* for 1917, he still complained that Ontario was "cashing her wood capital without any adequate attempt at reforestation, or even conservative lumbering or preparation for either." The one bright spot was effective fire protection, wherein about eleven hundred men were engaged. A few years later, Forester Zavitz with the aid of Professor White would organize the province in districts, each under trained foresters, and the province's fire protective service and its detailed forestry work would be much improved.

The Dominion's forestry service also would be improved. In 1920 its forestry branch, administering a forest area approximating the whole of Ontario's licensed and reserved areas and pulpwood concessions, employed twenty-one technically trained foresters. British Columbia had fifteen trained foresters in its forest service. Quebec province had twenty-five; and Ontario was spending about $360,000 annually in forest fire protection. In British Columbia, Quebec, and New Brunswick—the former two of which, Fernow believed, led in forest policy reform and organization—trained foresters, all university graduates, carried out the provisions imposed by timber regulations. These facts, culled from writings of Fernow and Howe, point to great progress in forestry education and practice in Canada during less than a decade and a half. At least nineteen foresters in Canada earned salaries ranging from $3,000

[50] G. H. Prince, "Forestry Administration in New Brunswick," *Journal of Forestry* XX, 1, 1922, p. 54, describing the forest act of 1918. See also *ibid.* XV, 6, Oct. 1917, p. 814, on the forest survey of New Brunswick.

[51] XVI, 5, May 1918, p. 580.

to $10,000 annually. Of course there was a different cleavage between public and private forestry in Canada than in the United States, where private interests owned large forest areas, especially in the eastern states, free of all regulation except that which applied to all owners of private property. The cooperative principle in Canada, however, was so well established in fire protection and forest research that the commission of conservation was appropriating annually $10,000 for forest investigations alone. In the United States also public forestry was firmly and soundly progressing, and in the matter of regulating private forest owners and their property the question was: Could and would cooperation be sufficient? An intelligently conceived conservative national forest policy was promulgated by Chief Forester Graves.[52]

Fernow always maintained that from the standpoint of a national forest policy there must be regulation and control "of the exploitation of private timber lands." But at some points he was in disagreement with Chief Forester Graves, who had presented the subject to the nation in addresses before the National Lumber Manufacturers' Association and other groups. Fernow wrote, "While we would employ every method that promises results ever so little, we take the position that the control of private forest management is surrounded with such difficulties that no early and satisfactory results may be expected from that quarter, if for no other reason than the naturally inimical attitude of the forest owners. We say naturally, because of the inherent unsuitableness of the forestry business to private enterprise," and he postulated the twelve "simple, fundamental, commonplace truths" which led to his conclusion. These had been contained in the statement made by Fernow at the New York Section of the Society of American Foresters meeting at Wanakena on July 30, 1919.[53]

Fernow watched the war reconstruction programs of other nations, Great Britain especially.[54]

The appearance in 1919 of such books as A. B. Recknagel and S. Bentley's *Forest Management*, of J. A. Ferguson's *Farm Forestry*, of Nelson C. Brown's *Forest Products, Their Manufacture and Use*, and in earlier years regional books on forests and forestry such as F. W. Besley's *Forests of Maryland*, R. C. Hall and O. D. Ingall's *Forest Conditions in Illinois*, and R. H. D. Boerker's *Our National Forests* absorbed

52 H. S. Graves, "A Policy of Forestry for the Nation," *Journal of Forestry* XVII, 8, Dec. 1919, pp. 901ff.

53 President F. E. Olmsted of the Society of American Foresters had criticized the lumber industry so severely in an address and article, "The Work Ahead," that several groups of foresters felt it necessary to resolve that the address expressed Olmsted's own views and not those of the profession. Fernow said that Olmsted had used such "forceful language" in order to point out "that a national forest policy must include regulation or control of private timber lands." See *Journal of Forestry* XVII, 7, Nov. 1919, p. 880; XVII, March 1919, p. 227.

54 "Forestry and the War," *ibid.* XVI, 2, Feb. 1918, p. 149.

Fernow's interest as editor and critic. Several of these he himself reviewed. The years of retirement from education arrived, but Fernow carried on in his editorial capacity to his last year.

Filibert Roth, for the April 1920 issue of *American Forestry*, wrote an appreciation of the work of Fernow in an article entitled, "Great Teacher of Forestry Retires," saying:

Fernow, as few men have ever done, blazed trails in the wilderness; he did his work well, the trails are now traveled by many, the wilderness is opening up. New conditions of supply and demand, of industry and transportation; conditions long foreseen and foretold by the master, are now extending the trails, and expanding them into broad highways, where travel is comfortable and work does not require the self-sacrifice and special abilities of the pioneer; he led the way in forest education of our people and our foresters; he laid plans and began the great task of gathering the information on which forestry in North America must base its work; he secured the first important forest legislation for the nation and directed most of the pioneer legislation in our states; he gave us a forestry journal ranking with the best; he planted in the New World the right ideals without which forestry will never succeed in any country.

To know Fernow, the man, one must have had the privilege of seeing him in his home, on trips in the woods, on water, on the ice, with his family and friends; must have walked with him in the forest; or climbed Mt. Lafayette; have seen him in a company of scientific men, whether mining engineers or entomologists; have heard him among the foresters and economists of the world gathered at the international congress at Brussels; have heard him discuss philosophy with Dr. Ward; and more than all, have seen him seated at his piano, playing, enraptured, far away in another, gentler world.

At the second national conference on forestry education, held at New Haven on December 17-18, 1920, representatives of thirty forest schools united to send Fernow "an expression of appreciation for [his] great services to the profession and to the country as founder and dean of forestry education in America." The following December 21 the Society of American Foresters at its annual meeting sent greetings to Fernow as its "oldest and most distinguished member. . . . We take this occasion to express to you what is in the mind of every member, the high esteem and appreciation of the great work that you have done and are still doing on behalf of forestry. We hope that you will continue for many years to come to be the inspiration and leading spirit, as you have been in the past, for the profession of forestry in America."[55] Tributes from students, friends and co-workers arrived by scores, testimonials acknowledging that in the minds of many the name Fernow was synonymous with forestry in America. Foresters' abilities were so definitely linked with Fernow's teaching and example that it seemed that forestry in America, with Fernow absent from meetings, was being deprived of its founder and father. Fernow replied, "In returning grateful thanks for

[55] *ibid.* XIX, 2, Feb. 1921, p. 217.

the kind words and thoughts of the Society meeting in New York, I realize that I am a happy man in having friends who do not wait till I am dead to say nice things about me. I have been unusually lucky, too, in living to see the results of my work. I have been a plowman who hardly expected to see the crop greening, yet fate has been good to me in letting me catch at least a glimpse of the ripening harvest. We are standing at the beginning of a new era, largely brought about by the good work of the members of the Society. When a national forest policy is being discussed in commercial bodies like the Paper and Pulp and Lumbermen's Associations, we may well hope for a realization of our aims."

In 1921 the annual meeting of the Society of American Foresters was held with the Canadian Society of Forest Engineers at Toronto. The attendance, including members and guests, totalled one hundred persons. Fernow made the opening address on "The Forest Situation in Canada."[56] This meeting was in strong contrast to the American Forestry Congress of 1882 at Montreal, when Fernow brought to the American continent a prospectus for scientific forestry. His address there, "Conditions of Forest Growth," was the beginning of organized forestry of America. The Toronto address of 1921 was the climax of his active speaking career. A scientist at the old American Forestry Congress had been a rarity; now scientists filled the ranks. The members of the old congress were lay protagonists of a cause; now forestry was an accepted profession.

Of the Toronto students who graduated under Dr. Fernow as well as those who spent three years under his tutelage, four have become university professors; three of the five who have served as chief foresters of the Dominion were Fernow's students; one has been a provincial forester, and one an assistant provincial forester; ten have held positions corresponding to that of district foresters in the United States; two have had charge of large reforestation stations; two have been directors of Dominion forest products laboratories; two have been in charge of research in Dominion or provincial forestry branches; six have occupied positions as wood managers, four of pulp and paper companies; one became vice-president of a large pulp and paper company; two have been engaged in lumber sales promotion; two have been secretary-managers of a lumbermen's association; one has been an assistant manager of the Canadian Forestry Association; one became the secretary of the Canadian Society of Forest Engineers; one has been occupied in forestry extension work in the Dominion forest service; one has been in a commercial tree seed company. Of the forty-eight foresters who had all or most of their forestry school work under Dr. Fernow, seventy per cent have remained in the profession.

[56] *ibid.* XX, 1, Jan. 1922, p. 1.

Not many months later, on January 19, 1923, at Hart House, the University of Toronto, Dr. Graves addressed a banquet in honor of Fernow and extolled him as the "creator of Modern Forestry in the United States."[57] Fernow was able to attend this banquet and was able to speak a few words of cheer and encouragement to the foresters, but he was not able to attend the ceremonies which conferred on him his most lasting honor.

Over the entrance to the Forestry Building of the New York State College of Agriculture at Cornell University, there was unveiled on October 5, 1922, a tablet bearing the words "Fernow Hall." Fernow wrote a letter to the ceremonies and said, "Had I been present I would have pointed out that my deserts are more than duly recognized by the handsome compliment of naming the building after me, and that it was only the accident of my being the first in the field and my persistence therein that gave me the proud position in which my friends have insisted on placing me. I would also have elaborated the fact that a teacher lives in his students and that the honor heaped on the former is earned by the doings of the latter, and would have enumerated the graduates of the earlier years now occupying prominent positions. My pride is centered in them. To your students I would have recommended the adoption of my motto, borrowed from Horace, *carpe diem*, 'doing the duty of the day,' with confidence in the due development of the future." Dr. Livingston Farrand, President of Cornell University, addressed the gathering after Fernow's letter had been read, and replied, "It is no accident that brings about a career such as Dr. Fernow's. To be the first in the field in point of time, and to continue to be the first in the field in point of quality, is one of the rarest things in this world. . . . It must be said that in naming a building for such a man Cornell honors herself more than she honors him. We cannot, by such an act, add to Dr. Fernow's stature."

On February 6, 1923, Fernow slept quietly. On the previous Saturday night he had discussed forestry matters with a student, on Sunday and Monday he became weaker than usual, and the next morning his life gradually and peacefully ebbed away. His death was mourned by all the forestry world. Fernow's body was cremated, and in accordance with his expressed wish his ashes were cast to the brilliant gentle waters of Lake Ontario, symbolic of his belief that man returns to energy in a state of nature. He had been content to rest from his toil and labor, although the final years had not been spent as he and Mrs. Fernow had planned. The funeral ceremony was held at Point Breeze, New York, adjacent to the lake which washed the shores of the province of Ontario and the State of New York, where Dr. Fernow had begun and ended his school work in forestry and bound together professional enterprise

[57] *University of Toronto Monthly*, 1923, p. 300.

in the United States and Canada. A memorial service was held in the Knox College Chapel of the University of Toronto.

The April issue of the *Journal of Forestry* was given over to the work of Dr. Fernow. In 1934 in Connecticut, a camp and bridge of the Civilian Conservation Corps were named in honor of his memory. Spanning the Natchaug River and connecting Natchaug State Forest with route 91, the bridge was built by the men at Camp Fernow of the CCC. A forestry window to honor Bernhard Eduard and Olivia Reynolds Fernow was placed in Sage Chapel of Cornell University. On the window, below the pictorial representation of forest trees on either side of a path leading to the hills, was inscribed, "Their Children Shall Arise and Call Them Blessed." Only a few years after Fernow's death, the Faculty of Forestry at the University of Toronto was given a new building for its use, which, while it was built during Dean Howe's administration, was of itself another memorial to Fernow's work in Canada.

Acknowledgments

Much of the material of this book has been quoted direct—or obtained from unpublished correspondence which has never before been generally available. For information that has been previously published the most authoritative sources have been used and references to these have been incorporated in the text or as footnotes. For valuable assistance in securing this material and for helpful criticism afforded the author in writing this book, he wishes to express his indebtedness to the following persons and institutions.

To Clyde Leavitt, now of Pascagoula, Mississippi, to Dean Emeritus Henry Solon Graves of Yale School of Forestry, and to Karl Wilson Woodward, Professor Emeritus of Forestry, University of New Hampshire, who have read the manuscript at various stages of progress, given much helpful aid and advice, suggested corrections, and other forms of improvements, I express sincere appreciation. The chapters concerning the New York State College of Forestry at Cornell University have been examined by Ralph S. Hosmer, Professor Emeritus of Forestry of the New York State College of Agriculture at Cornell University. In many ways Professor Hosmer has aided the author and given him valuable advice and suggestions. Mrs. O. W. Boston and Professor Dow Baxter of the School of Forestry and Conservation of the University of Michigan have read the material concerning Filibert Roth and given the author criticisms, suggestions, and access to materials. Ellwood Wilson, consulting forester of Knowlton, Quebec, Canada, and Alain Joly de Lotbinière of Point Platon, Quebec, Canada, have examined the manuscript, especially those portions concerning Canadian forestry; the author acknowledges great indebtedness for access to the family archives of Sir Henri de Lotbinière and the loan of valuable letters and documents. Professor Karl Fernow of the department of plant pathology of the New York State College of Agriculture has both read the manuscript when submitted for publication and lent the author valuable letters and papers formerly possessed by Mrs. Bernhard Eduard Fernow. Materials concerning the establishment of the faculty of forestry of Laval University have been examined by Professor Emeritus of Forestry G. C. Piché and Professor and Dean Avila Bédard. The author acknowledges especial indebtedness to the members of the faculty of forestry of the University of Toronto for their loan of books, documents, correspondence files, and all of the valuable papers saved by Dr. Fernow during his administration as dean of the school, and also some from the period of deanship of Clifton Durand Howe. Dean Emeritus Howe, as also Dean Samuel J. Record of the Yale School of Forestry, were most helpful by loans of books and materials and conferences.

Indebtedness is acknowledged also to many persons who have been interviewed by the author, and in numerous instances have furnished documentary material and data, among them, the aforementioned, officials of the Society of American Foresters, the American and Canadian Forestry Associations, Pennsylvania Forestry Association, and other forestry organizations, and the following North American foresters: Hugh Potter Baker, H. S. Betts, R. M. Brown, R. L. Campbell, H. H. Chapman, H. R. Christie, H. Clepper, J. Foley, C. A. and P. L. Lyford, E. F. McCarthy, W. Mulford, G. A. Pearson, G. W. Peavy, G. Pinchot, A. B. Recknagel, H. A. Smith, S. N. Spring, H. A. Wickenwerder, G. H. Wirt, and R. Zon. Others associated with important forestry work and interviewed were J. S. Bates, W. B. Campbell, H. von Schrenk, and ecologists W. L. Bray, F. E. (and Mrs.) Clements, and E. N. Transeau. It may be added that the author has not hesitated to take materials from his other books, studies in the history of botany. Valuable points of information were furnished by many others: C. G. Bates, E. H. Clapp, P. C. Kitchin, C. MacFayden, J. J. Harpell, J. Reynolds, Mrs. R. T. Fisher, and Miss Alice E. Andrews.

Indebtedness to libraries, too many to list, is acknowledged, especially the libraries of the forestry schools of Toronto and Yale universities, and the botanical and zoological library of the Ohio State University.

The author again acknowledges his debt to his father, now deceased, and mother, Mr. and Mrs. Andrew Denny Rodgers, for encouragement and interest.

Index